The **Rough Guide** to

written and researched by

Mike Parker and Paul Whitfield

ROUGH GUIDES

NEW YORK · LONDON · DELHI

www.roughguides.com

Contents

Great Welsh outdoors
insert following p.216

Festivals and events
insert following p.408

◄◄ Capel Curig, Snowdonia ◄ Conwy Castle

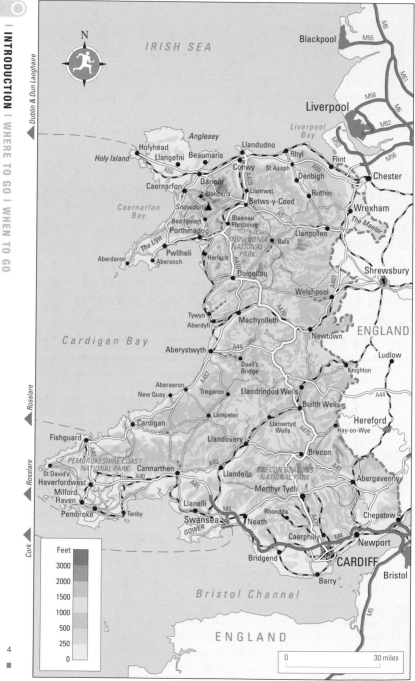

4

Introduction to
Wales

Perched on the rocky fringe of western Europe, Wales often gets short shrift in comparison to its Celtic cousins of Ireland and Scotland. Neither so internationally renowned nor so romantically perceived, the country is usually defined – if it is known at all – by its male voice choirs and tightly packed pit villages. But there's far more to the place than the hackneyed stereotypes, and at its best, Wales is the most beguiling part of the British Isles. Even its comparative anonymity serves it well: where the tourist dollar has swept away some of the more gritty aspects of local life in parts of Ireland and Scotland, reducing ancient cultures to misty Celtic pastiche, Wales remains brittle and brutal enough to be real, and diverse enough to remain endlessly interesting.

Within its small mass of land, Wales boasts some stunning physical attributes. Its **mountain ranges**, **ragged coastline**, **lush valleys** and old-fashioned **market towns** all invite long and repeated visits. The culture, too, is compelling, whether in its Welsh- or English-language manifestations, its Celtic or its industrial traditions, its ancient cornerstones of belief or its contemporary chutzpah. Recent years have seen a huge and dizzying upsurge in Welsh self-confidence, a commodity no longer so dependent upon comparison with its big and powerful neighbour of England. Popular culture – especially music and film – has contributed much to this revival, as has the arrival of a **National Assembly** in 1999, the first all-Wales tier of government for six hundred years. After centuries of enforced subjugation, the national spirit is undergoing a remarkable renaissance. The ancient symbol of the country, *y ddraig goch* or the **red dragon**, seen fluttering on flags everywhere in Wales, is waking up from what seems like a very long slumber.

Once you've crossed the border from England into Wales, the differences in appearance, attitude and culture between the two countries are

Fact file

• Wales is the smallest of the three countries of mainland Britain, with an **area** of approximately 8000 square miles (20,800 square km). Constitutionally, it is part of the United Kingdom of Great Britain and Northern Ireland and a member state of the European Union. While it elects members of parliament to the UK government in Westminster (London), Wales also has its own devolved **National Assembly**, responsible for certain local affairs.

• The total **population** of Wales is around 3 million, sixty percent of whom live in the southeastern corner of the country. One quarter of the population of Wales was born out of the country, the vast majority being in-migrants from England. Cardiff, the capital city, has a population of 300,000, the second city of Swansea has 190,000.

• Historically, Wales has been largely an **Anglican** nation, although the British establishment church (here named the Church in Wales) has never had such deep roots as in neighbouring England. Nonconformism swept Wales between the seventeenth and nineteenth centuries, spawning many different divisions of Methodists, Baptists and Calvinists, as can be seen in the legacy of chapels everywhere in the country.

• Wales is officially a **bilingual** nation. Around one quarter of the population speak Welsh, the strongest survivor of the Celtic languages. The vast majority of Welsh speakers are concentrated in the north and west of the country. Everyone also speaks English.

▲ Sheep

immediately obvious. Wales shares many physical and emotional similarities with the other Celtic lands – Scotland, Ireland, Cornwall, Brittany and even Asturias and Galicia in northwest Spain. A rocky and mountainous landscape, whose colours are predominantly grey and green, a thinly scattered, largely rural population, a culture rooted deeply in folklore and legend and the survival of a distinct, ancient language are all hallmarks of Wales and its sister countries. To the visitor, it is perhaps the **Welsh language**, the strongest survivor of the Celtic tongues, that most obviously marks out the country. Tongue-twisting village names

Prehistoric and legendary Wales

Whether trudging through a dew-soaked field to some mysteriously inscribed standing stone, or catching the afternoon sun as it illumines the entrance to a cliff-top burial chamber, exploring Wales' prehistoric sites is thoroughly rewarding. At all but a few of the most popular sites, the bleating of sheep will be the only sound to break the contemplative silence of these spiritual places.

Prehistoric sites litter Wales. Hut circles defensively set atop wind-swept hills attest to a rugged hand-to-mouth pre-Celtic existence dating back four or five thousand years, while stone circles, intricately carved monoliths and finely balanced capstones set at crucial points on ancient pathways suggest the more spiritual life led by the priestly druids. Britain's greatest druidic centre was Anglesey, and the island is still home to many of Wales' best prehistoric sites, including the splendid chambers of Barclodiad y Gawres (see p.489) and Bryn Celli Ddu (see p.487). Elsewhere, numerous standing stones and circles can be found on the mysterious slopes of the Mynydd Preseli in Pembrokeshire (see p.222) and throughout Ardudwy in Gwynedd (see p.338). Many sites take their names from great figures in Celtic history and folklore, such as Arthur and Merlin (Myrddin in Welsh); legends abound to connect much of the landscape with ancient tales – details are scattered throughout the Guide and in boxes on p.96 and p.173.

and vast bilingual signposts point to a glorious tale of endurance against the odds, slap next to the heartland of English language and culture, the most expansionist in history. Everyone in Wales speaks English, but a quarter of the population also speak Welsh: TV and radio stations broadcast in it, all children learn it at school and visitors too are encouraged to try speaking at least a fragment of the rich, earthy tones of one of Europe's oldest living languages.

Land of song

"Praise the Lord! We are a musical nation," intones the Rev Eli Jenkins in Dylan Thomas' masterpiece *Under Milk Wood*. It's a reputation of which the Welsh feel deservedly proud, and it is squarely based in some considerable truth. Although plucky miners singing their way to the pithead was the dewy-eyed fabrication of Hollywood (*How Green Was My Valley*), Wales does make a great deal more noise, and make it a great deal more tunefully, than most other small countries.

The country's male voice choirs, many struggling to survive in the aftermath of the decimation of the coal industry that spawned them, are the best-known exemplars of Welsh singing, but traditions go much further back, to the bards and minstrels of the Celtic age. And although the choirs may be a shadow of their former selves, Wales continues to nurture big voices and big talent, from the hip-swivelling Sir Tom Jones to young divas like Charlotte Church and Katherine Jenkins. It should, however, be remembered, that for every Shirley Bassey, there's also likely to be a Shakin' Stevens.

Although it's often the older aspects of Welsh and Celtic culture, from **stone circles** to **crumbling castles**, that bring visitors here in the first place, contemporary Wales is also a draw. The cities and university towns throughout the country are buzzing with an understated youthful confidence and sense of cultural optimism, while a generation or two of so-called "New Age" migrants have brought a curious **cosmopolitanism** to the small market towns of mid-Wales and the west. Although conservative and traditional forces still sporadically clash with these more liberal and anarchic strands of thought, there's an unquestionable feeling that Wales is big enough, both physically and emotionally, to embrace such diverse influences. Perhaps most importantly of all, Welsh culture is underpinned by an iconoclastic democracy that contrasts starkly with the establishment-obsessed divisions of England, or even, to some extent, of Scotland or Ireland. Wales is not – and never has been – so absorbed by matters of class and status as its near neighbours. Instead, the Welsh character is famously endowed with a **musicality**, lyricism, introspection and sentimentality that produces far better bards and singers than it does lords and masters. And Welsh culture is undeniably popular, arising from an inherently democratic impulse. Anything from a sing-song in the pub to the grandiose theatricality of an Eisteddfod involves everyone – including any visitor eager to learn and join in.

Where to go

O nly 160 miles from north to south and 50 miles from east to west, Wales is smaller than Massachusetts and only half the size of the Netherlands. Most of its inhabitants are packed into the southern quarter of the country, a fact which will largely dictate where you travel and what you do.

Like all capital cities, **Cardiff** is atypical of the rest of the country, but as the first major stop on both rail and road routes from England into south Wales, it's a good place to start. Most national institutions are based here, not least the infant National Assembly, housed in brand-new splendour amidst the massive regeneration projects of Cardiff Bay. The city is also home to the National Museum and St Fagans National History Museum – both are excellent introductions to the character of the rest of Wales – and the superb Millennium Stadium, the home of huge sporting events and blockbuster gigs. The only other centres of appreciable size are loud-and-lairy **Newport** and breezy, resurgent **Swansea**, lying respectively to the east and west of the capital. All three cities grew as ports, mainly exporting millions of tons of coal and iron from the **Valleys**, where fiercely proud industrial communities were built up in the thin strips of land between the mountains.

Much of Wales' appeal lies outside the towns, where there is ample evidence of the warmongering which has shaped the country's development. Castles are everywhere, from the hard little stone keeps of the early Welsh princes

9
■

Wales and England

Like most countries that border each other, there's a distinct air of mutual suspicion that hovers between Wales and its bigger, better-known neighbour, England. It's not really a battle of equals: Wales occupies a small, rocky part of the island of Britain and is home to just short of three million people. England, with fifty million inhabitants and far greater wealth, is used to having the upper hand, having welded its smaller sibling to it by force over seven hundred years ago. Memories are long hereabouts though, and those seven centuries sound like mere seconds when you listen to some of the more passionate Welsh nationalists calling for, if not outright divorce from England, at least a trial separation.

The mutual antipathy is almost all good-natured and perhaps best seen on the sporting field. But it shouldn't be underestimated. Wales and England are two different countries, and they look, sound and feel like it. Often the greatest offence to Welsh people is when those very obvious differences are blatantly disregarded or patronized. And like calling a Kiwi an Aussie or a Canadian an American, the worst thing you can possibly do is to call a Welsh person English. You have been warned.

to Edward I's incomparable series of thirteenth-century fortresses at **Flint**, **Conwy**, **Beaumaris**, **Caernarfon**, **Harlech** and **Rhuddlan**, and grandiose Victorian piles where grouse were the only enemy. Fortified residences served as the foundation for a number of the stately homes that dot the country, but many castles were deserted and remain dramatically isolated on rocky knolls, most likely on spots previously occupied by prehistoric communities. Passage graves and stone circles offer a more tangible link to the pre-Roman era when the priestly order of Druids ruled over early Celtic peoples, and later religious monuments such as the great ruined abbeys of **Valle Crucis**, **Tintern** and **Strata Florida** lend a gaunt grandeur to their surroundings.

Whether you're admiring castles, megaliths or Dylan Thomas's home at **Laugharne**, almost everything in Wales is enhanced by the beauty of the countryside, from the lowland greenery of meadows and river valleys to the inhospitable heights of the moors and mountains. The rigid backbone of the **Cambrian Mountains** terminates in the soaring peaks of **Snowdonia** and the angular ridges of the **Brecon Beacons**, both superb walking country and both national parks. A third national park follows the **Pembrokeshire Coast**, where golden strands are separated by rocky bluffs overlooking offshore bird colonies. Much of the rest of the coast remains unspoilt, though seldom visited, with long sweeps of sand often backed by traditional British seaside resorts: the **north Wales coast**, the **Cambrian coast** and the **Gower peninsula** have a notable abundance.

When to go

The English preoccupation with the weather holds equally for the Welsh. The **climate** here is temperate, with Welsh summers rarely getting hot and nowhere but the tops of mountain ranges ever getting very cold, even in midwinter. Temperatures vary little from Cardiff in the south to Llandudno in the north, but proximity to the mountains is a different matter: Llanberis, at the foot of Snowdon, gets doused with more than twice as much rainfall as Caernarfon, seven miles away, and is always a few degrees cooler. With rain never too far from the mind of any resident or visitor, it is easy to forget that throughout much of the summer, Wales – particularly the coast – can be bathed in sun. Between June and September, the Pembrokeshire coast, washed by the Gulf Stream, can be as warm as anywhere in Britain.

The bottom line is that it's impossible to say with any degree of certainty that the weather will be pleasant in any given month. May might be wet

▲ Welsh rugby fans

and grey one year and gloriously sunny the next, and the same goes for the autumnal months – November stands an equal chance of being crisp and clear or foggy and grim. Obviously, if you're planning to lie on a beach, or camp in the dry, you'll want to go between June and September – a period when you should book your accommodation as far in advance as possible. Otherwise, if you're balancing the likely fairness of the weather against the density of the **crowds**, the best time to get into the countryside or the towns is between April and May, or September and October. If **outdoor pursuits** are your objective, these are the best months for walking, June to October are warmest and driest for climbing, and December to March the only times you'll find enough water for kayaking.

Wales' climate

Average daily temperatures and monthly rainfall.

	Jan	Feb	Mar	Apr	May	Jun	Jul	Aug	Sep	Oct	Nov	Dec
Aberystwyth												
max (°C)	8.0	7.9	9.8	12.2	15.7	17.7	19.8	19.5	17.5	14.2	10.6	8.9
max (°F)	46	46	50	54	60	64	68	67	64	58	51	48
min (°C)	2.0	2.0	2.8	3.4	6.2	8.5	11.4	11.0	9.2	7.1	4.2	2.9
min (°F)	36	36	37	38	43	47	53	52	49	45	40	37
rainfall (mm)	126	92	99	71	66	79	72	91	104	134	140	140
rainfall (in)	5.0	3.6	3.9	2.8	2.6	3.1	2.8	3.6	4.1	5.3	5.5	5.5
Cardiff												
max (°C)	7.9	8.2	10.6	13.1	16.7	19.2	21.5	21.3	18.4	14.6	10.9	8.9
max (°F)	46	47	51	56	62	67	71	70	65	58	52	48
min (°C)	2.1	2.1	3.7	4.8	7.8	10.5	12.8	12.5	10.0	7.5	4.3	3.2
min (°F)	36	36	39	41	46	51	55	55	50	46	40	38
rainfall (mm)	119	91	89	65	65	66	61	90	104	117	117	128
rainfall (in)	4.7	3.6	3.5	2.6	2.6	2.6	2.4	3.5	4.1	4.6	4.6	5.0
Llandudno												
max (°C)	8.2	8.2	9.9	11.5	14.8	17.0	19.3	19.2	17.0	14.1	10.8	9.1
max (°F)	47	47	50	53	59	63	67	67	63	57	51	48
min (°C)	2.8	2.6	3.9	5.0	7.3	10.0	12.1	12.1	10.2	7.9	5.3	3.7
min (°F)	37	37	39	41	45	50	54	54	50	46	42	39
rainfall (mm)	77	48	58	47	54	59	44	63	67	91	89	92
rainfall (in)	3.0	1.9	2.3	1.9	2.1	2.3	1.7	2.5	2.6	3.6	3.5	3.6
Tenby												
max (°C)	8.5	8.0	9.7	11.7	14.8	17.3	19.5	19.3	17.1	14.2	11.2	9.5
max (°F)	47	46	49	53	59	63	67	67	63	58	52	49
min (°C)	3.1	2.8	3.8	4.7	7.4	9.9	12.0	11.8	10.3	8.3	5.3	4.0
min (°F)	38	37	39	40	45	50	54	53	51	47	42	39
rainfall (mm)	115	90	87	61	52	67	53	93	102	131	130	126
rainfall (in)	4.5	3.5	3.4	2.4	2.0	2.6	2.1	3.7	4.0	5.2	5.1	5.0

30
things not to miss

It's not possible to see everything that Wales has to offer in one trip – and we don't suggest you try. What follows is a selective taste of the country's highlights: outstanding buildings and natural wonders, plus the best festivals and outdoor activities. They're arranged in five colour-coded categories, which you can browse through to find the very best things to see and experience. All highlights have a page reference to take you straight into the guide, where you can find out more.

01 **The Valleys** Page **98** • Colourful terraces of housing, hunkered down under the hills, are the hallmark of Wales' world-famous Valleys, the old mining area in the south.

02 **Pistyll Rhaeadr** Page **284** ● Narrow lanes thread their way through the border country of mid-Wales to what, at 240ft, is the country's highest waterfall.

03 **Transporter Bridge** Page **94** • "A giant with the might of Hercules and the grace of Apollo" was how Newport's Transporter Bridge was described when it opened in 1906.

04 **National Waterfront Museum in Swansea** Page **151**
• The newest addition to the National Museums stable, offering the latest in technical wizardry to understand the mysteries of the past.

05 **Soar-y-Mynydd chapel** Page **262**
• Drive into the wild country of Mynydd Eppynt, for spartan simplicity and the reminder that Duw Cariad Yw (God Loves You) at Wales' most remote chapel.

06 Portmeirion Page **425** • The grandest folly of them all, Portmeirion is a gorgeous visual poem that will melt the hardest heart.

07 Aberglasney Page **176** • Rescued from near-terminal decay, these formal gardens in the Tywi Valley are a perfect counterpoint to the nearby National Botanic Garden of Wales.

08 **Castell Carreg Cennen** Page **178** • The most romantic ruin in Wales, Castell Carreg Cennen sits in glorious isolation amidst the velvet green of Carmarthenshire.

10 **Laverbread** Page **52** • Seaweed for breakfast? Yes, and very tasty it is too, if it's Welsh laverbread, rolled with oats and fried with bacon.

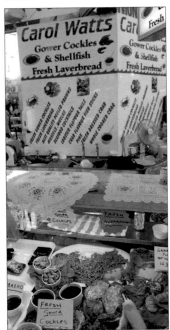

09 **A Welsh oak wood** Page **529** • Once the sacred place of the druids, the twisty oak woods of Wales, often with lively streams burbling through, clear the mind and soul.

11 **Rugby** Page **67** • Although Wales' standing in international rugby has plummeted, the game is still near religion here, never more so than when the national team are playing at Cardiff's awesome Millennium Stadium.

13 **Conwy** Page **465** • One of north Wales' finest walled medieval towns, Conwy contains over two hundred listed buildings within its tight grid.

12 **Ffestiniog Railway** Page **424** • Of Wales' many "great little trains", the Ffestiniog Railway, winding down through the Snowdonia mountains, is by far the best.

14 Pem-brokeshire coast Page **192** • The Green Bridge of Wales is one of the most popular photo opportunities on the 187-mile Pembrokeshire Coast Path.

15 Tryfan Page **396** • Jumping the gap between the Adam and Eve rocks, on the top of Tryfan mountain in Snowdonia, is the traditional encore for any climber who's made it to the summit.

16 Aberystwyth Page **308** • The capital of sparsely populated mid-Wales, Aberystwyth is a breezy and bright university and seaside town surrounded by luscious countryside.

17 Cadair Idris Page **320** • The dominant mountain of southern Snowdonia, Cadair Idris is a magnificent beast chock-full of classic glacial features.

18 Brains beer Page **54** • "It's Brains you want" say the ads, and they could be right. Cardiff's famous pint can be supped in any number of traditional pubs.

19 National Museum and Gallery, Cardiff Page **125** • One of Britain's finest collections, with archeological treasures, stunning Impressionist paintings and some fabulous sculptures.

20 **St Fagans National History Museum** Page **137** • An unmissable chronicle of Welsh life, featuring period buildings from all over the country.

21 **Llandudno** Page **459** • North Wales' most genteel seaside resort, Llandudno spreads languidly around the bay beneath the ancient rock plug of the Great Orme.

22 **Dyffryn Arms (aka Bessie's)** Page **225** • Head for a pint and a chinwag at perhaps Wales' finest old-fashioned pub. There's no food and only middling beer but places like this surely won't be around for much longer.

23 **Llechwedd Slate Caverns** Page **414** • What coal mining was to south Wales, slate quarrying was to the north. Visitors get a taste of the industry at Blaenau Ffestiniog's Llechwedd Slate Caverns.

24 **Mawddach Bridge** Page **336** • Wales' finest estuary, the Mawddach, is best seen from the 2253-foot rail and foot bridge into Barmouth.

25 **Cardiff Bay architecture** Page **128** • The wonderful National Assembly Building is one of many striking modern structures around the rejuvenated Cardiff Bay.

26 **A night out in Swansea** Page **152** • For sheer boisterous, boozy fun it is hard to beat Swansea's Wind Street.

27 **Harlech Castle**
Page **342** • Of all of Edward I's mighty fortresses, Harlech Castle is the finest, its setting as impressive as the medieval building itself.

23

29 Machynlleth market Page **321** • Old boys in flat caps mingle with rosy-cheeked hippies in the lively weekly market of Machynlleth, good for everything from fresh produce to second-hand tat.

28 Male voice choirs Page **111** • Burly miners singing their hearts out at eisteddfodau may be a thing of the past, but Welsh male voice choirs still survive and thrive.

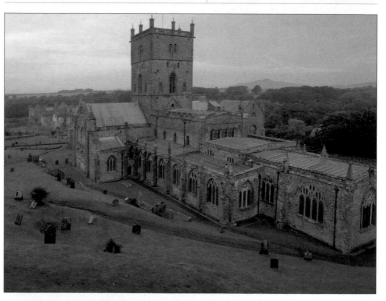

30 St David's Cathedral Page **213** • The heart of Welsh spirituality, St David's Cathedral is at Wales' westerly extremity and has drawn pilgrims for a millennium and a half.

Basics

Basics

Getting there

The only regular scheduled intercontinental flights into Wales are Zoom Airlines' weekly services into Cardiff Airport from Toronto and Vancouver, though through connections do operate to Cardiff from Atlanta, Orlando and other US cities via Amsterdam or Paris. Otherwise, you're best off flying into an English airport and continuing overland. The range of options will always be greatest – and the fares usually lowest – flying into London, Britain's busiest gateway city. Two of London's airports – Heathrow and Gatwick – handle long-haul flights, and in terms of convenience for onward travel they're about equal. For quicker access to mid- or north Wales, you might consider one of the limited number of direct flights into Manchester or Birmingham airports, both of which are directly linked to the rail network. If you want to avoid England altogether, it is possible to arrive at Cardiff International Airport (ⓦwww.cwlfly.com) on flights from Belfast, Cork, Dublin, Edinburgh, Glasgow, Paris and several other European cities. See p.28 for full details on flights to Cardiff.

Airfares always depend on the **season**, with the highest being around May to August, when the weather is best; fares drop during the "shoulder" seasons – September and Aprll – and you'll get the best prices during the low season, October to March (excluding Christmas and New Year when prices are hiked up and seats are at a premium). Note also that flying on weekends ordinarily adds five or ten percent to the round-trip fare; price ranges quoted below assume midweek travel.

You can often cut costs by going through a **specialist flight agent** – either a consolidator, who buys up blocks of tickets from the airlines and sells them at a discount, or a **discount agent**, who in addition to dealing with discounted flights may also offer special student and youth fares and a range of other travel-related services such as travel insurance, rail passes, car rentals, tours and the like. Some agents specialize in charter flights, which may be cheaper than anything available on a scheduled flight, but again departure dates are fixed and withdrawal penalties are high.

Booking flights online

Many airlines and discount travel websites offer you the opportunity to book your tickets online, cutting out the costs of agents and middlemen. Good deals can often be found through discount or auction sites, as well as through the airlines' own websites.

Online booking agents and general travel sites

ⓦ **travel.yahoo.com** Incorporates a lot of Rough Guide material in its coverage of destination countries and cities across the world, with information about places to eat, sleep, etc.

ⓦ **www.cheapflights.com** Good links to travel agents and other travel sites.

ⓦ **www.cheaptickets.com** Discount flight specialist.

ⓦ **www.etn.nl/discount.htm** A hub of consolidator and discount agent Web links, maintained by the non-profit European Travel Network.

ⓦ **www.expedia.com** Discount airfares, all-airline search engine and daily deals.

ⓦ **www.flyaow.com** Online air travel info and reservations site.

ⓦ **www.gaytravel.com** Gay online travel agent, concentrating mostly on accommodation.

ⓦ **www.hotwire.com** Bookings from the US only. Last-minute savings of up to forty percent on regular published fares. Travellers must be at least 18 and there are no refunds, transfers or changes allowed. Log-in required.

ⓦ **www.lastminute.com** Offers good last-minute holiday package and flight-only deals.

ⓦ **www.skyauction.com** Bookings from the US only. Auctions tickets and travel packages using a "second bid" scheme. The best strategy is to bid the maximum you're willing to pay, since if you win you'll pay just enough to beat the runner-up regardless of your maximum bid.

@ **www.travelocity.com** Destination guides, hot web fares and best deals for car rental, accommodation and lodging as well as fares. Provides access to the travel agent system SABRE, the most comprehensive central reservations system in the US.
@ **www.travelshop.com.au** Australian website offering discounted flights, packages, insurance, online bookings.

Getting there from the UK and Europe

Crossing the border from England into Wales is straightforward, with train and bus services forming part of the British national network. Minimal time savings mean that flights within Britain are of little use, with the exception of those from Scotland. If you're driving from England, you'll probably be using one of the half-dozen or so roads which all run east to west through Wales. The two providing the quickest access into the heart of the country run along opposite coasts: the M4 motorway in the south, and the A55 expressway in the north. These are both fast and busy roads, but minor routes are more appealing if you aren't in too much of a hurry.

If you're travelling from Ireland, **ferries** are by far the cheapest and easiest way of getting to Wales. From the rest of Europe, there's the choice of using either the traditional cross-Channel ferry services or the Channel Tunnel to England and making your way onwards from there.

By plane

From Europe, the quickest way to Wales is to fly. The only airport of any size in Wales is Cardiff International Airport (@ www.cwlfly .com), ten miles southwest of the capital, which has scheduled flights from Canada, selected European cities and a few British and Irish destinations. The main international carrier is KLM (UK information on ☎ 0870/507 4074, @ www.klm.com), which flies into Cardiff from Amsterdam. The other main carriers flying into Cardiff are Ryanair (☎ 0871/246 0000, @ www.ryanair.com) for flights from Dublin; bmibaby (☎ 0870/264 2229, @ www .bmibaby.com) for services from Alicante, Edinburgh, Faro, Geneva, Malaga, Palma

and Prague; and Air Wales (☎ 0870/777 3131, @ www.airwales.com) from Aberdeen, Belfast, Cork, Dublin, Glasgow, Jersey, Liverpool, Newcastle, Paris and Plymouth. Many of the most useful routes run mostly business flights, timed and priced accordingly, and often not operating at weekends.

Plans are afoot to start scheduled flights within Wales, possibly using Swansea Airport and Valley airfield on Anglesey, though nothing is firm yet on this.

By train

Britain's **rail network** is split between different companies, although through-ticketing is always available: the **national rail enquiries** line (☎ 08457/484950, minicom ☎ 0845/605 0600, enquiries in Welsh ☎ 0845/604 0500; @ www.nationalrail.co.uk) should be your first port of call for all queries regarding train travel. For sales, @ www.thetrainline.com offers some good deals on all services. For more details on ticket types and booking, see the box opposite.

From France and Belgium

You can travel from Calais in northern France to Folkestone in southeast England by train through the twenty-mile-long **Channel Tunnel** with **Eurostar** (☎ 0870/160 6600, @ www.eurostar.com), which runs hourly **passenger trains** between London Waterloo, Paris and Brussels. The least expensive return fares to London (which must be booked three days in advance and span a Saturday night) are €90 from Paris or Lille and €80 from Brussels. Full fares with no restrictions are €415 from Paris, €345 from Brussels and €320 from Lille. Youth tickets (for under-26s) have no restrictions attached and cost €90–150 from Paris or Brussels and €70–130 from Lille. Eurostar also offers frequent promotional fares. In 2007, Eurostar is scheduled to move to its new terminus at London St Pancras, with intermediate stops to the Continent at Stratford (east London) and Ebbsfleet (Dartford, near the M25).

A 35-minute bus, motorbike and **carrying train service** through the Channel tunnel known as "Le Shuttle" is operated by **Eurotunnel** (☎ 08705/353535, @ www .eurotunnel.com). You can just turn up on

Train fares and savings

Ordinary standard-class fares on UK trains are high, and first-class costs an extra 33 percent, but there are six types of reduced-fare ticket.

Savers are return tickets that can be used on all trains on Saturdays, Sundays and bank holidays, on most weekday trains outside the morning rush hour for the outward journey, and all trains for the return leg. If you buy a return ticket at any station outside the morning rush hour, you'll routinely be issued with a Saver ticket. **SuperSavers** are cheaper, but cannot be used on Fridays nor on half a dozen other specified days of the year, normally Saturdays during July and August. A **Super-Advance** ticket costs much the same as a SuperSaver and must be bought before 6pm the day before you travel, but guarantees a seat in both directions. Saver and SuperSaver tickets are valid for one month (outward travel has to be within two days of the date on the ticket), and allow a break in the return (but not outward) leg of the journey.

Like the SuperAdvance tickets, the even cheaper **Apex** tickets are issued in limited numbers on certain journeys of 150 miles or more, but these have to be bought at least seven days before travelling and you must specify your outward and return departure times. They include a seat reservation in the price.

In practice, you can buy Saver and SuperSaver tickets to just about anywhere, but other tickets are only available in limited numbers on long, popular journeys. For Wales, that means journeys between London and the main stations on the north and south coast lines.

Children under 5 travel free, while those aged 5–15 inclusive pay half the adult fare on most journeys – though there are no discounts on Apex tickets. In an apparent effort to dissuade people from using their services, awkward pieces of luggage – skis, large musical instruments, etc – now incur a fee, and there are restrictions on **bicycles**, which incur a £3 reservation fee on longer routes.

As a guide to **prices**, a standard-class return ticket on the London–Cardiff route can cost anything between £24 (Apex) and £123 (open ticket), with Savers (£51), SuperSavers (£43) and SuperAdvance tickets (£36) in between.

---

the day you want to travel, but booking is advised, especially at weekends. Prices are lower for short stays, but assuming you're staying in Britain longer than five days a car and four passengers costs £190 to £235.

Despite the tunnel, **car ferries** remain well and truly in business, often undercutting the tunnel prices and, in the case of the Calais–Dover service, not taking much longer (see p.32 for contacts).

From England and Scotland

While services in Wales and the Borders are operated by Arriva Trains Wales (see "Getting Around", p.41), those into Wales are operated by other groups. Fast, frequent services for the **south coast** from London Paddington to Newport, Cardiff and Swansea are operated by First Great Western (ⓦwww.firstgreatwestern.co.uk; sales ☏0845/700 0125). Very few direct trains from England go

beyond Swansea, although connections at either Cardiff or Swansea link up with services to Carmarthen and stations in Pembrokeshire. The **north coast** service, from London Euston to Chester, Llandudno Junction, Bangor and Holyhead is operated by Virgin Trains (ⓦ www.virgintrains.co.uk; sales ☏0845/722 2333). **From other cities in England and Scotland**, you'll probably need to change en route – at Bristol or Bath for the south coast line, at Crewe for the north coast.

Mid-Wales is best reached via Birmingham and Shrewsbury, with two lines plunging deep into the heart of the country. The faster route heads through Welshpool, Newtown and Machynlleth, beyond which it divides at Dyfi Junction. The southern spur goes a few miles to Borth and Aberystwyth, the northern one crawls up the coast through Tywyn, Barmouth, Harlech and Porthmadog to Pwllheli. Even slower (but very picturesque) is the second route from Shrewsbury, the Heart of Wales line, which limps four times daily into Wales, through Knighton, Llandrindod Wells, Llanwrtyd Wells, Llandovery, Llandeilo and a host of tiny halts on the way to Llanelli and Swansea.

Journey times between main centres are remarkably short: London–Cardiff takes around two hours and London–Swansea around three hours. Heading for the north coast, expect the London–Holyhead service to take just over four hours.

By bus

Inter-town **bus** services duplicate a few of the major rail routes, often at half the price of the train or less, but at considerably less speed. Buses are reasonably comfortable and often have drinks and sandwiches available on board on longer routes. By far the biggest national operator is **National Express** (℡08705/808080, @www .nationalexpress.com) whose network covers England and sends half a dozen tendrils into Wales. The chief routes are from London to Cardiff, Swansea and on to Pembroke and Milford Haven; London to Wrexham; London to Aberystwyth; London along the north Welsh coast to Holyhead and Pwllheli, both via Birmingham; Birmingham to Cardiff and Swansea; Birmingham to Haverfordwest; Chester along the north coast to Llandudno, Bangor and Holyhead; and Cardiff to both Glasgow and Edinburgh. National Express services are so popular that for busy routes and services during weekends and holidays, it's a good idea to buy a reserved journey ticket, which guarantees a seat.

One-way tickets are usually little cheaper than an **economy return** ticket, which is good for travel on any day except Friday and is valid for three months. If you travel on Friday, expect to pay around twenty percent more. Typical economy return **journey costs** to Cardiff are £31 from London; £57 from Edinburgh, Glasgow or Newcastle; £34 from Manchester; and £19 from Birmingham. On some popular routes a further saving of around ten percent can be made by buying an Apex Economy return at least a week before you travel.

If you're planning to travel extensively throughout Britain by bus, the various

National Express **discount passes** may save you a lot of money. UK residents under 26, in full-time education or over fifty can buy a National Express **NX2** discount card (£10), which is valid for one year and entitles the holder to up to thirty percent off many fares. All foreign passengers are entitled to buy a **Brit Xplorer pass**, which offers unlimited travel on the National Express network. Choose between seven days (£79), fourteen days (£139) or 28 days (£219). You can buy these passes direct by phone, or in Britain from major travel agents and at major National Express offices. In North America, these passes should be available through any travel agent or direct from British Travel International (see p.33 for address).

For more on bus passes that can be used within Wales and the rest of Britain, see "Getting around", pp.41–47.

By road: driving

Travelling to Wales by car from England, the main roads into **the north** are the upgraded coastal **A55** route, an expressway all the way from Chester to the Irish ferries at Holyhead. The major road into north Wales from the Midlands and the south of England is the **A5** through Llangollen, best approached from the **M6** just north of Wolverhampton, via the fast **M54** and Shrewsbury bypass. Much of the A5 has been improved in recent decades, although there are still bottlenecks at Llangollen and Betws-y-Coed.

The Shrewsbury route is also the best for access into **mid-Wales** as far south as Newtown and Aberystwyth, using the **A458** to Welshpool from the Shrewsbury bypass. Further south, the **A456** from Birmingham, via Kidderminster and Leominster, is occasionally slow when passing through towns, but generally easier than the route through Worcester and Hereford to reach the A44 in Radnorshire and, to the south, the A438/470 to Brecon. This road connects with the swift westbound A40 at the Brecon bypass, best for routes from the Midlands and north of England to southern Cardiganshire and northern Carmarthenshire. An alternative route from the Midlands is via the **M50** "Ross Spur", a quiet motorway off the M5 south of Worcester, meeting the A449 dual carriageway at Ross-on-Wye. The road continues south, dividing at Raglan into the quick A40 for Brecon and the A449 down to Newport, the M4 and all destinations west.

The **M4 from London** makes the most dramatic entry into Wales, across the twin River Severn Bridges. Stay on the M4 and you'll be ushered into Wales across the **Second Severn Crossing** (£4.80 toll), a graceful bridge a few miles south of the M48 and the original **Severn Bridge** (same toll), rising high over the mud flats as it descends towards Chepstow. Both motorways reconnect just west of Caldicot. The M4 coasts quickly westwards, although tailbacks are frequent around Cardiff and Newport. At Pont Abraham, a few miles north, the M4 mutates into the A48 dual carriageway, connecting with the excellent A40 at Carmarthen and coursing west to Haverfordwest for connections to Pembrokeshire and southern Ceredigion.

Hitching and lift-sharing

The extensive motorway network and the density of traffic makes long-distance hitching through England and Scotland to the Welsh border and along the M4 to Cardiff and Swansea relatively easy. Key junctions on the edge of metropolitan areas and motorway service stations are the favoured hitching spots, and standing with a sign at the exit produces the best results.

However, **hitching is not generally advised**, especially if you are a woman travelling alone. A way around this impasse is offered by **lift-sharing** whereby you share the travel costs (typically 5p per mile) with someone already going in your direction. One of the best ways is through web-based agencies such as Liftshare (ⓦwww.liftshare .org) and Freewheelers (ⓦwww.freewheelers .co.uk) where you register (free) and enter your desired route so that the database can come up with suitable matches. You then contact the resulting matches by email and make contact arrangements. It's also worth checking notice boards in health food shops and other "alternative" establishments to see if there's anyone going your way.

By ferry

Wales has three main ferry ports all serving boats **from Ireland** (see box on p.32). Ferries

and high-speed catamarans from Dublin, and catamarans from Dun Laoghaire (six miles south of Dublin), arrive at Holyhead on the northwest tip of Wales, while Rosslare, just outside Wexford, is the departure point for ferries and catamarans to Fishguard, and ferries to Pembroke Dock, both in southwest Wales.

Stena Line operates ferries from Dublin to Holyhead, fast cats from Dun Laoghaire to Holyhead, and both ferries and cats between Rosslare and Fishguard; Irish Ferries runs ferries and cats from Dublin to Holyhead, and ferries between Rosslare and Pembroke Dock. **Ferry prices** for the two companies are almost identical, whichever ports you travel between, though for cars, winter fares tend to be a little cheaper from Rosslare, as are high-summer fares to Holyhead. One-way foot passenger fares range from £24 in winter to £28 on summer ferry sailings and around £32 for peak cat sailings.

The one-way fare for a car and driver starts at £114 but typical winter fares are £159 for ferry and £189 for a cat. Summer ferry fares are around £160–200 with Friday and Saturday fares £10 higher and fast cat fares a further £30 higher. Huge savings are available by booking round-trip tickets, and by maximizing various midweek and advance purchase offers you can get a return ticket in summer for around £200.

There is also a ferry from Cork to Swansea, operated by Swansea–Cork Ferries. Most are ten-hour night sailings costing £22–32 for foot passengers and £95–169 for a car and driver, plus up to three passengers, with special offers for returns also available.

There's a much greater choice of **ferries from Europe** to ports in England. Competitive pricing, especially since the Channel Tunnel opened, means that unless you are in a hurry lower prices may lure you onto a boat rather than into the tunnel. There are regular crossings with SeaFrance and P&O from Calais to Dover, the shortest route, for which the lowest fare for a small car and driver is around £95, though there are frequent specials. For full details of ferry routes and prices, contact the ferry companies direct. The Seaview ferry **website** (ⓦwww.seaview.co.uk/ferries.html) is a particularly handy resource with links to all the following companies:

Ferry connections from Ireland to Wales

	Company	Frequency	Duration
Cork–Swansea	Swansea–Cork	mid–March to Dec Ferries	4–6 weekly 10hr
Dublin–Holyhead	Stena/Irish Ferries	2–6 daily	1hr 40min/3hr 15min
Dublin–Liverpool	P&O Irish Sea	Jan–Sept 1–2 daily	6–8hr
Dublin–Mostyn	P&O Irish Sea	2 daily	6hr–7hr 30min
Dun Laoghaire–Holyhead	Stena (Catamaran)	4 daily	1hr 40min
Rosslare–Fishguard	Stena/Stena Sea Lynx	2–6 daily	1hr 35min–3hr 30min
Rosslare–Pembroke	Irish Ferries	2 daily	3hr 45min

Brittany Ferries UK ☏ 08703/665 333, ⓦ www.brittanyferries.co.uk, Republic of Ireland ☏ 021/4277 801.
Condor Ferries ☏ 0870/1243 5140, ⓦ www.condorferries.co.uk.
Irish Ferries ☏ 08705/171717, ⓦ www.irishferries.com.
P&O Ferries ☏ 08705/980333, ⓦ www.poferries.com.
Sea France ☏ 08705/711711, ⓦ www.seafrance.com.
Stena Line ☏ 08705/707070, ⓦ www.stenaline.com.
Swansea–Cork Ferries ☏ 01792/456116, ⓦ www.swanseacorkferries.com.
Transmanche Ferries ☏ 0800/917 1201, ⓦ www.transmancheferries.com.

Flights from North America

The enormous volume of air traffic crossing the Atlantic keeps prices relatively low and virtually guarantees you'll find a seat at all but the busiest times. Currently the only scheduled services direct to Wales are with Zoom Airlines, which flies Toronto–Cardiff once a week charging fares as low as CAN$200 each way.

Dozens of other airlines fly from the eastern seaboard and the Midwest to London, the principal British gateway for visitors to Wales. You'll also come across direct flights to regional airports with good links to Wales, such as Manchester and Birmingham. Fares are usually higher than those to London, but deals can be found.

Low-season fares from New York, Boston and Washington start at around US$300, though US$450 is more normal, and through the summer you can expect to pay US$500–800. Add US$50–150 from other eastern cities.

Several airlines – American, British Airways, United, Virgin and others – fly nonstop from Los Angeles and there are easy connections to London from San Francisco and Seattle. Low-season West Coast fares start at a little over US$500, though these step up markedly in summer and around Christmas.

In **Canada**, you'll get the best deal flying to London from the big gateway cities of Toronto and Montreal, where low-season fares start at around CAN$700 round-trip, and high-season round-trips cost just over CAN$1000. Flights from almost all other eastern Canadian cities route through these two hubs, with those from Ottawa costing about the same and those from elsewhere CAN$100–200 more. From the west, flights from Vancouver are cheapest, starting around CAN$850 in the low season (high CAN$1100); those from Edmonton and Calgary start around CAN$950 (high season CAN$1150).

Airlines

Aer Lingus ☏ 1-800/IRISH-AIR, ⓦ www.aerlingus.com.
Air Canada ☏ 1-888/247-2262, ⓦ www.aircanada.com.
American Airlines ☏ 1-800/433-7300, ⓦ www.aa.com.
British Airways ☏ 1-800/AIRWAYS, ⓦ www.ba.com.
British Midland ☏ 1-800/788-0555, ⓦ www.flybmi.com.

Continental Airlines ☎1-800/231-0856, ⓦwww.continental.com.
Delta Air Lines ☎1-800/241-4141, ⓦwww.delta.com.
Lufthansa US ☎1-800/645-3880; Canada ☎1-800/563-5954, ⓦwww.lufthansa.com.
Northwest/KLM Airlines ☎1-800/447-4747, ⓦwww.nwa.com, ⓦwww.klm.com.
United Airlines ☎1-800/538-2929, ⓦwww.united.com.
Virgin Atlantic ☎1-800/862-8621, ⓦwww.virgin-atlantic.com.
Zoom Airlines ☎1-866/359-9666 ⓦwww.flyzoom.com.

Discount travel companies

Air Brokers International ☎1-800/883-3273, ⓦwww.airbrokers.com. Consolidator and specialist in round-the-world tickets.
Airtech ☎212/219-7000, ⓦwww.airtech.com. Standby seat broker; also deals in consolidator fares and courier flights.
Educational Travel Center ☎1-800/747-5551 or 608/256-5551, ⓦwww.edtrav.com. Student/youth discount agent.
STA Travel ☎1-800/781-4040, ⓦwww.statravel.com. Worldwide specialist in independent travel; also student IDs, travel insurance, car rental, rail passes, etc.
TFI Tours ☎1-800/745-8000 or 212/736-1140, ⓦwww.tfitours.com. Consolidator.
The Travel Site ⓦwww.thetravelsite.com. Consolidator and charter broker.
Travelers Advantage ☎1-800/835-8747, ⓦwww.travelersadvantage.com. Discount travel club; annual membership fee required (currently US$1 for 3 months' trial).
Travel Cuts US ☎1-800/592-2887, Canada ☎1-866/246-9762, ⓦwww.travelcuts.com. Canadian student-travel organization.
Worldtek Travel ☎1-800/243-1723, ⓦwww.worldtek.com. Discount travel agency for worldwide travel.

Packages and organized tours

Although you may want to see Wales at your own speed, you shouldn't dismiss the idea of a package deal. Many agents and airlines put together very flexible deals, sometimes amounting to nothing more restrictive than a flight plus accommodation and car or rail pass, and these can actually work out cheaper than making the same arrangements yourself on arrival – this is particularly true for car rental, which is expensive in Britain. A package can also be great for your peace of mind, if only to ensure a worry-free first week while you're finding your feet for a longer tour.

There are hundreds of tour operators specializing in travel to the British Isles. Most can do packages of the standard highlights, but of greater interest are the outfits that help you explore Britain's unique points: many organize walking or cycling trips through the countryside, boat trips along canals, and any number of theme tours based around Britain's literary heritage, history, pubs, gardens, theatre, golf – you name it. A few of the possibilities are listed below, and a travel agent will be able to point out others. For a full listing, contact the Wales representative at the British Tourist Authority or the Wales Tourist Board directly (see p.36).

Be sure to examine the fine print of any deal, and bear in mind that everything in brochures always sounds great. Choose only an operator that is a member of the United States Tour Operator Association (USTOA) or has been approved by the American Society of Travel Agents (ASTA).

British Travel International ☎1-800/327-6097, ⓦwww.britishtravel.com. Agent for independent arrangements: rail and bus passes, and hotels, with a comprehensive cottage rental and B&B reservation service; also apartment rentals in London.
CIE Tours International ☎1-800/243-8687, ⓦwww.cietours.co.uk. All-inclusive coach tours, independent travel arrangements, accommodation and car-rental deals.
Contiki Tours ⓦwww.contiki.com. Organized tours with a party-like atmosphere geared toward 18–35-year-olds. Book through a travel agent.
English Experience Travels Limited ☎1-800/892-9317, ⓦwww.english-experience.com. Small group tours focusing on British life; some homestay options.
Home at First ☎1-800/523-5842, ⓦwww.homeatfirst.com. Independent travel packages including airfare, ground transportation and cottage, house or apartment rental.
Insight Vacations ⓦwww.insightvacations.com. Fully escorted coach tours.
Le Boat ☎1-800/922-0291, ⓦwww.leboat.com. Inland waterway travel on hotel boats, self-crewed boats and yacht charters; also golf cruises.
Select Travel Service ☎1-800/752-6787, ⓦwww.selecttravel.com. Customized history, literature, theatre, horticulture and other specialized tours.

All these tours can be booked through a travel agent at no extra cost.

Flights from Australia and New Zealand

To get to Wales from Australia or New Zealand you'll need to route through London, though there are also a few direct flights from Australia or New Zealand to Manchester in northern England. For all onward details, see "Getting there from the UK and Europe", pp.28–32. The route from Australasia to London is a highly competitive one, with flights via Southeast Asia generally being the cheapest option.

Fares from Australia's **eastern cities** are generally common rated while flights from Perth via Asia and Africa are around A$200 less, and via the Americas about A$400 more. The cheapest **scheduled flights** are around A$1600 with Garuda, Gulf Air, Korean Air, Japan Airlines (JAL) and Royal Brunei, usually involving a transfer (and perhaps an overnight stay) in the carrier's hub city. For a little more, Virgin Atlantic, Malaysian Airlines or Qantas can get you to London via Kuala Lumpur from A$1800, though in high season rates start at closer to A$2200.

From New Zealand low-season fares start as low as NZ$1900 with Air New Zealand and Lufthansa via LA and Frankfurt though flights with Asian carriers are also very competitive. High-season fares start at around NZ$2400.

If you're planning to visit Wales as part of a long trip, a **round-the-world ticket (RTW)**, typically stopping in London, can be very good value. All sorts of deals are available, usually involving a combination of airlines affiliated through either the One World or Star Alliance. Some just offer a couple of stops on the main routes to and from your destination and start around A$2000 (NZ$2300), while others' more complex combinations are likely to be in the vicinity of A$2900/NZ$3300.

Airlines

Air New Zealand Australia ☎ 13 24 76, ⓦ www.airnz.com.au, NZ ☎ 0800/737 000, ⓦ www.airnz.co.nz.
British Airways Australia ☎ 1300/767 177, NZ ☎ 0800/274 847, ⓦ www.britishairways.com.

Cathay Pacific Australia ☎ 13 17 47, NZ ☎ 0508/800 454, ⓦ www.cathaypacific.com.
China Airlines Australia ☎ 02/9244 2121, NZ ☎ 09/308 3371, ⓦ www.china-airlines.com.
Delta Australia ☎ 02/9251 3211, NZ ☎ 09/379 3370, ⓦ www.delta.com.
Emirates Australia ☎ 1300/303 777, NZ ☎ 09/968 2200, ⓦ www.emirates.com.
Garuda Indonesia Australia ☎ 1300/365 330 or 02/9334 9944, NZ ☎ 09/366 1862, ⓦ www.garuda-indonesia.com.
JAL (Japan Airlines) Australia ☎ 02/9272 1111, NZ ☎ 09/379 9906, ⓦ www.jal.com.
KLM Australia ☎ 1300/303 747, NZ ☎ 09/309 1782, ⓦ www.klm.com.
Korean Air Australia ☎ 02/9262 6000, NZ ☎ 09/914 2000, ⓦ www.koreanair.com.au.
Lufthansa Australia ☎ 1300/655 727, NZ ☎ 0800/945 220, ⓦ www.lufthansa.com.
Malaysia Airlines Australia ☎ 13 26 27, NZ ☎ 0800/777 747, ⓦ www.malaysia-airlines.com.
Philippine Airlines Australia ☎ 02/9279 2020, NZ ☎ 09/379 8522, ⓦ www.philippineairlines.com.
Qantas Australia ☎ 13 13 13, NZ ☎ 0800/808 767 or 09/357 8900, ⓦ www.qantas.com.
Singapore Airlines Australia ☎ 13 10 11, NZ ☎ 0800/808 909, ⓦ www.singaporeair.com.
Thai Airways Australia ☎ 1300/651 960, NZ ☎ 09/377 3886, ⓦ www.thaiair.com.
United Airlines Australia ☎ 13 17 77, ⓦ www.united.com.

Discount and specialist travel agents

Adventure World Australia ☎ 02/8913 0755, ⓦ www.adventureworld.com.au, NZ ☎ 09/524 5118, ⓦ www.adventureworld.co.nz. Various tours around Wales and the rest of Britain.
Explore Holidays Australia ⓦ www.exploreholidays.com.au. Organized tours of Britain plus bus and coach passes and accommodation vouchers. Book through travel agents.
Flight Centre Australia ☎ 133 133, ⓦ www.flightcentre.com.au; NZ ☎ 0800/243 544, ⓦ www.flightcentre.co.nz. Discount flights.
Holiday Shoppe NZ ☎ 0800/80 84 80, ⓦ www.holidayshoppe.co.nz. Discount flights.
STA Travel Australia ☎ 1300/733 035, ⓦ www.statravel.com.au; NZ ☎ 0508/782 872, ⓦ www.statravel.co.nz. General travel agent specializing in student and youth fares.
Trailfinders Australia ☎ 1300/780 212, ⓦ www.trailfinders.com.au. One of the best-informed and most efficient agents for independent travellers.
travel.com.au Australia ☎ 1300/130 483. Comprehensive online travel company.

Visas and red tape

Citizens of all European countries – other than Albania, Romania, Bulgaria, some Balkan states and most republics of the former Soviet Union – can enter Britain with just a passport, generally for up to three months. US, Canadian, Australian and New Zealand citizens can travel in Britain for up to six months with just a passport. All other nationalities require a visa, available from the British Consular office in the country of application.

For stays longer than six months, **US, Canadian, Australian and New Zealand citizens** should apply to the British Embassy or High Commission (see below). If you want to extend your stay, you should contact The Under Secretary of State, Home Office, Immigration and Nationality Directorate, Lunar House, 40 Wellesley Rd, Croydon CR9 2BY (☎0870/606 7766, ⊛www.ind.homeoffice.gov.uk), before the expiry date given on the endorsement in your passport.

Embassy contact details are listed on the website of the Foreign and Commonwealth Office (⊛www.fco.gov.uk): look for links to "UK Embassies Overseas" and "Foreign Embassies in the UK".

Overseas representation in Britain

Except for the Irish consulate in Cardiff, foreign embassies are all found in London.
Australia ☎020/7379 4334, ⊛www.australia.org.uk
Canada ☎020/7258, ⊛www.canada.org.uk.
Ireland ☎020/7235 2171, ⊛www.irlgov.ie;
Consulate, Brunel House, 2 Fitzalan Rd, Cardiff CF24 0EB ☎029/2066 2000.
Netherlands ☎020/7590 3200, ⊛www.netherlands-embassy.org.uk.
New Zealand ☎020/7930 8422, ⊛www.nzembassy.com.
USA ☎020/7499 9000; ⊛www.usembassy.org.uk.

Customs

Since the inauguration of the EU Single Market, travellers coming into Britain directly from another EU country do not have to make a declaration to **customs** at their place of entry, and can effectively bring almost as much wine or beer across the Channel as they like. The guidance levels are 90 litres of wine and 110 of beer, which should be enough for anyone – any more than this, and you're supposed to have proof that it's for personal use only, though even that is seldom checked. If you're travelling to or from a non-EU country, you can still buy duty-free goods, but within the EU, this perk no longer exists. The duty-free allowances are as follows:

Tobacco: 200 cigarettes; or 100 cigarillos; or 50 cigars; or 250g of loose tobacco.

Alcohol: Two litres of still wine, **plus** one litre of drink over 22 percent alcohol, or two litres of alcoholic drink not over 22 percent, or another two litres of still wine.

Perfumes: 60ml of perfume plus 250ml of toilet water.

You're also allowed **other goods** to the value of £145.

There are **import restrictions** on a variety of articles and substances, from firearms to furs derived from endangered species, none of which should bother the normal tourist. However, if you need any clarification on British import regulations, contact HM Revenue & Customs, Dorset House, Stamford St, London SE1 9PY (☎0845/010 9000, international ☎44 208 929 0152, ⊛www.hmrc.gov.uk).

Biosecurity is also an issue, especially after the disastrous 2001 outbreak of Foot and Mouth disease, and it is now illegal to import meat, milk and other animal products from outside the EU: see ⊛www.defra.gov.uk for more details. For similar reasons you are not allowed to bring **pets** into Britain without subjecting them to prohibitively long periods of quarantine.

VAT

Most goods in Britain, with the chief exceptions of books and groceries, are subject to

Value Added Tax (VAT), which increases the cost of an item by 17.5 percent and is usually included in the quoted price. Visitors from non-EU countries can save money through the **Retail Export Scheme**, which allows a refund of VAT on goods to be taken out of the country. Shops participating in this scheme will have a sign in their window and can provide you with the documentation necessary to claim your refund when leaving the country. Note that you cannot reclaim VAT charged on hotel bills or other services.

ℹ Information and maps

Wales promotes itself enthusiastically, broadly through the British Tourist Authority (BTA) and more specifically through the Wales Tourist Board – addresses for both agencies are listed below. Both have extensive websites offering a wealth of free literature, some of it just rose-tinted advertising copy, but much of it extremely useful – especially the maps, city guides and event calendars. Glossy brochures can be ordered online or downloaded directly.

The Wales Tourist Board and tourist offices

The Wales Tourist Board operates a central information service that's good for pre-trip planning, with a detailed website and plenty of free brochures which can either be downloaded or sent by mail. Contact the Visitwales Centre (☎08701/211 251, ⓦ www.visitwales.com). There is also representation at the Britain Visitor Centre, 1 Regent St, London SW1Y 4XT (☎020/8846 9000, ⓦ www.visitbritain.com).

Tourist offices (usually called Tourist Information Centres) exist in virtually every Welsh town – you'll find their contact details and opening hours in the relevant sections of the Guide. The average opening hours are much the same as standard shop hours, with the difference that in summer they'll often be open on a Sunday and for a couple of hours after the shops have closed on weekdays; opening hours are generally shorter in winter, and in more remote areas the office may well be closed altogether. All centres offer information on accommodation (which they can often book – see p.49), local public transport, attractions and restaurants, as well as town and regional maps. In many cases all of this is free, though some offices make a small charge for their accommodation list or the town guide with accompanying street plan.

Areas designated as national parks (the Brecon Beacons, Pembrokeshire Coast and Snowdonia) also have a fair sprinkling of **National Park Information Centres**, which are generally more expert in giving guidance on local walks and outdoor pursuits.

Wales online

Weaving your way in and out of the numerous websites before leaving for Wales is a good way to familiarize yourself with the place, book up accommodation and arm yourself with tips and information. We've included numerous websites throughout this book, but listed here are some useful general sites.

Castles of Wales ⓦ www.castlewales.com/home .html. Essential site covering over 400 Welsh castles with photos, history, ground plans and direct links to Ordnance Survey location maps.

Countryside Council for Wales ⓦ www .ccw.gov.uk. Rural campaigning organization with listings of National Nature Reserves, National Trails, useful publications as well as discussion of marine, landscape and habitat issues affecting Wales.

Data Wales ⓦ www.data-wales.co.uk. A fascinating miscellany of all things Welsh including ancient Christmas customs, Welsh surnames, and tracing an American family's roots with the aid of a Welsh bible.

ICWales @ icwales.co.uk. First stop for the latest in Welsh news and extensive links.

North Wales Index @ www.northwalesindex .co.uk. Excellent set of North Wales links, many relevant to Wales in general.

Royal Society for the Protection of Birds @ www.rspb.org.uk. UK-wide site with masses of detail on birding along with avian conservation issues.

A Welsh Course @ www.cs.brown.edu/fun /welsh. Learn to speak Welsh online with a basic course which includes good cultural links.

Welsh Unlimited/Popeth Cymraeg @ www .popethcymraeg.com. Bilingual Welsh learners' site with news, articles, links and details of low-cost classes throughout Wales.

Welsh Witchcraft @ tylwythteg.com. Welsh witchcraft homepage with links to druidism, benign witchcraft and festival listings.

General British sites

British Travel International @ www.britishtravel .com. Details hotel accommodation, cottage rental, bus and rail information.

Knowhere @ www.knowhere.co.uk. Self-styled user's guide to Britain, with up-to-date information and readers' comments.

MultiMap @ www.multimap.com. Detailed online scalable maps to the whole of Britain and beyond.

Ordnance Survey @ www.ordnancesurvey.co.uk. Details the full range of Ordnance Survey maps, plus online scalable map with search facility.

Seaview ferries @ www.seaview.co.uk/ferries .html. Comprehensive ferry information on services from and to Britain.

UK Online @ www.ukonline.co.uk. A guide to events throughout Britain, sport, up-to-the-minute news and access to telephone books.

Maps

Most bookshops will have a good selection of **maps of Wales** and Britain, though the best can be found in specialist travel bookshops. Virtually every petrol station in Britain stocks one or more of the large-format **road atlases** produced by the AA, RAC, Collins, Ordnance Survey (OS) and others, which cover all of Britain at a scale of around three miles to one inch and include larger-scale plans of major towns. The best of these is the Ordnance Survey road atlas, which handily uses the same grid reference system as their accurate and detailed folding maps.

If you want more detail, the most comprehensive maps are again produced by the **Ordnance Survey** (@ www.ordnancesurvey .co.uk), a series renowned for its accuracy and clarity. The 204 maps in its 1:50,000 (a little over one inch: one mile) Landranger series (£6.50 each) cover the whole of Britain in enough detail to be useful for most walkers. The 1:25,000 Explorer series (£7.50 each) is more detailed, but most serious hikers favour the same-scale Explorer OL maps which cover only the most frequently walked areas. Each is sensibly designed to take in a specific area, and even shows fencelines and field boundaries to aid navigation. There are eight Explorer OL maps for Wales, three covering Snowdonia from the north coast down to Cadair Idris, three large double-sided ones spanning the Brecon Beacons, Black Mountains and Wye Valley, and another two charting Pembrokeshire. OS maps are widely available in bookshops, but in any walking district of Wales you can be sure to find the relevant maps on sale locally.

Insurance and health

Wherever you're travelling from, it's a good idea to have some kind of travel insurance to cover you for loss of possessions and money, as well as the cost of any medical and dental treatment. Before paying for a new policy, however, it's worth checking whether you are already covered: some all-risks home insurance policies may cover your possessions when overseas, and many private medical schemes include cover when abroad. In Canada, provincial health plans usually provide partial cover for medical mishaps overseas, while holders of official student/teacher/youth cards in Canada and the US are entitled to meagre accident coverage and hospital in-patient benefits. Students will often find that their student health coverage extends during the vacations and for one term beyond the date of last enrolment.

After exhausting the possibilities above, you might want to contact a specialist travel insurance company, or consider the travel insurance deal we offer (see box). A typical travel insurance policy usually provides cover for the loss of baggage, tickets and – up to a certain limit – cash or cheques, as well as cancellation or curtailment of your journey. Most of them exclude so-called dangerous sports unless an extra premium is paid: in Wales this can mean whitewater rafting, windsurfing and coasteering, though probably not ordinary hiking. Many policies can be chopped and changed to exclude coverage you don't need – for example, sickness and accident benefits can often be excluded or included at will. If you do take medical coverage, ascertain whether benefits will

be paid as treatment proceeds or only after return home, and whether there is a 24-hour medical emergency number. When securing baggage cover, make sure that the per-article limit – typically under £500 – will cover your most valuable possession. If you need to make a claim, you should keep receipts for medicines and medical treatment, and in the event you have anything stolen, you must obtain an official statement from the police.

Health

No vaccinations are required for entry into Britain. Citizens of all EU countries are entitled to free medical **treatment** at National Health Service hospitals; citizens of other countries are charged for all medical services except those administered by accident

---

Rough Guides travel insurance

Rough Guides has teamed up with Columbus Direct to offer you travel insurance that can be tailored to suit your needs.

Readers can choose from many different travel insurance products, including a low-cost backpacker option for long stays; a short break option for city getaways; a typical holiday package option; and many others. There are also annual multi-trip policies for those who travel regularly, with variable levels of cover available. Different sports and activities (trekking, skiing, etc) can be covered if required on most policies.

Rough Guides travel insurance is available to the residents of 36 different countries, with different language options to choose from via our website – ⓦwww .roughguidesinsurance.com – where you can also purchase the insurance.

Alternatively, UK residents should call ☎0800 083 9507; US citizens should call ☎1-800 749-4922; Australians should call ☎1 300 669 999. All other nationalities should call ☎+44 870 890 2843.

and emergency units at National Health Service hospitals. Thus a US citizen who has been hit by a car would not be charged if the injuries simply required stitching and setting in the emergency unit, but would be if admission to a hospital ward were necessary. Health insurance is therefore strongly advised for all non-EU nationals.

Pharmacists (known generally as chemists in Britain) can dispense only a limited range of drugs without a doctor's prescription. Most pharmacies are open during standard shop hours, though in large towns some may stay open as late as 10pm – local newspapers carry lists of late-opening pharmacies. Doctors' surgeries tend to be open from about 9am until early evening; outside surgery hours, you can turn up at the casualty department of the local hospital for complaints that require immediate attention – unless it's an **emergency**, in which case ring for an ambulance on ☎999.

Costs, money and banks

With the current strength of the pound, Wales has become a relatively expensive place to visit, though if you're coming from England, particularly London, prices will seem reasonable in comparison.

The British **pound sterling** (£; *punt* in Welsh, and widely referred to as a "quid") is divided into 100 pence (p; in Welsh, c for *ceiniogau*). Coins come in denominations of 1p, 2p, 5p, 10p, 20p, 50p, £1 and £2. Notes come in denominations of £5, £10, £20 and £50. Shopkeepers will carefully scrutinize any £20 and £50 notes tendered, as forgeries are widespread, and you'd be well advised to do the same (though few people do). The quickest test is to hold the note up to the light to make sure there is a thin wire filament running through the note from top to bottom; this is by no means foolproof, but will catch most fakes.

You may also come across Scottish bank notes which are legal tender in England and Wales, though often refused by traders. They come in the same denominations and have the same value as the British notes but are issued by three different banks; the Bank of Scotland, the Royal Bank of Scotland and the Clydesdale Bank.

Average costs

The **minimum expenditure**, if you're camping and preparing most of your own food, would be in the region of £20 per day, rising to around £25–30 per day if you're using the hostelling network, some public transport and grabbing the odd takeaway or meal out. Couples staying at budget B&Bs, eating at unpretentious restaurants and visiting a fair number of tourist attractions are looking at around £40 each per day – if you're renting a car, staying in comfortable B&Bs or hotels and eating well, you should reckon on at least £60 a day. Single travellers should budget on spending around sixty percent of what a couple would spend, mainly because single rooms tend to cost more than half the price of a double. For more detail on the cost of accommodation, transport and eating, see the relevant sections.

Youth and student discounts

Once obtained, various official and quasi-official youth/student ID cards should soon pay for themselves in savings; if you already have one then bring it, if you don't it is barely worth making a special effort. Full-time students are eligible for the International Student ID Card (ISIC, ⊛ www.isiccard.com), which entitles the bearer to special air, rail and bus fares and discounts at museums, theatres and other attractions. For Americans there's also a health benefit, providing up to US$5000 in emergency medical coverage and US$100 a day for sixty days in hospital, plus a 24-hour helpline to call in the event of a medical, legal or financial emergency. The card costs US$22 for Americans; CAN$16 for Canadians; A$18 for Australians; NZ$22 for New Zealanders; and £7 in the UK.

The only requirement for the International Youth Travel Card, which carries the same benefits (and costs the same), is that you are 26 or younger. Teachers qualify for the International Teacher Identity Card, offering similar discounts and again costing virtually the same. All these cards are available from: Council Travel, STA and Travel CUTS In the US; Travel CUTS in Canada; and STA in the UK, Australia and New Zealand.

Several other travel organizations and accommodation groups also sell their own cards, good for various discounts. A university photo ID might open some doors, but is not as easily recognizable as the ISIC cards.

Credit cards and traveller's cheques

Most hotels, shops and restaurants in Wales are happy to accept the major **credit and charge cards** – Access/MasterCard, Visa/Barclaycard, American Express and Diners' Club – and **debit cards**, although they're less useful in the most rural areas, and smaller establishments all over the country, such as B&B accommodation, will often accept cash only. Some places that do accept cards require a £10 minimum purchase. With a suitable personal identification number (PIN; ask at your bank before leaving home) your card will also enable you to get cash advances from most ATMs, though there may be a standard fee which makes it more cost effective to withdraw one large sum rather than several small amounts. In addition, you may be able to make withdrawals from your home bank account using your ATM cash card via the international Cirrus and Plus networks – check before leaving home.

The safest, if not the most convenient, way to carry your money is in **traveller's cheques** (in sterling), available for a small commission (normally one percent) from any major bank. The most widely accepted traveller's cheques are American Express (Amex), followed by Visa and Thomas Cook – most cheques issued by banks will be one of these three brands. You'll usually pay commission again when you cash each cheque, normally another one percent or so, or a flat rate – though no commission is payable on Amex cheques exchanged at Amex branches. Traveller's cheques – even those issued in sterling – are not usually accepted as currency and will need to be converted to cash at a bank or through the issuing agency. Keep a record of the cheques as you cash them, and you can get the value of all uncashed cheques refunded immediately if you lose them.

There are no exchange controls in Britain, so you can bring in as much cash as you like and change traveller's cheques up to any amount.

A compromise between traveller's cheques and plastic is **Visa TravelMoney**, a disposable pre-paid debit card with a PIN which works in all ATMs that take Visa cards. You load up your account with funds before leaving home, and when they run out, you simply throw the card away. A transaction fee is charged per withdrawal. You can buy up to nine cards to access the same funds – useful for couples or families travelling together – and it's a good idea to buy at least one extra as a back-up in case of loss or theft. There is also a 24-hour toll-free customer assistance number (☏0800/891725). The card is available in most countries through Travelex. For more information, check the Visa Travel-Money website at ⊛http://international.visa.com/ps/products/vtravelmoney.

Banks, exchange and wiring money

Banks are almost always the best places to **change money and cheques**, and in every sizeable town in Wales you'll find a branch of at least one of the big five: NatWest, Halifax, HSBC, Barclays and LloydsTSB. As a general rule, **opening hours** are Monday to Friday 9am or 9.30am to 4.30pm or 5pm, and branches in larger towns are often open on Saturday mornings. In the larger towns you may be able to find a **bureau de change** (often the post office), which will be open longer hours but may charge high commission. Hotels are expensive places to change money.

Having money wired from home is expensive and should be considered a last resort.

If it comes to this, MoneyGram International (Ⓦ www.moneygram.com) and Western Union (Ⓦ www.westerunion.com) both allow the sender to transfer limited funds online using a credit card.

Getting around

The large cities and densely populated valleys of south Wales support comprehensive train and bus networks, but the more thinly populated areas of mid- and north Wales have to make do with skeletal services. That said, it is rare to find somewhere that isn't reached by an occasional bus, even if it also picks up the local mail. Getting about by car is easy, and unless you are planning to spend all your time in Cardiff and Swansea, sheep and agricultural equipment are likely to be a more persistent problem than other road users. Take the more scenic backroads unless you're in a real hurry. Cyclists should skip to the outdoor pursuits section, p.64.

Trains

Following the confusion of rail privatization in the 1990s, things are getting slowly better on Britain's train network. In Wales, all but the major inter-city services from England (see "Getting There", p.28) are run by one company: **Arriva Trains Wales** (Ⓦ www .arrivatrainswales.co.uk; train information on ☎ 0845/748 4950, bookings ☎ 0870/900 0773). For very efficient **public transport** information for trains and buses alike, contact **Traveline Cymru** (☎ 0970/608 2608, Ⓦ www.pticymru.com): its website is particularly useful for planning integrated journeys. You can also pick up the very useful **Wales Bus, Rail & Tourist Map & Guide** for free from tourist offices.

For all its complications, the train is nonetheless one of the best ways to get around Wales: the views are superb and the

---

Rail information and booking

All **rail timetable enquiries** are directed through a central agency reached on ☎ 08457/48 49 50. Calls are charged at the local-call rates – at peak times you may have to wait ten minutes or more for a reply. They'll tell you the operator's credit card booking number (or see overleaf) and advise you of the cheapest of the many tickets usually on offer. Once you've decided which service you need, you can make debit or **credit card bookings** (Amex, Visa, MasterCard, Diners' Club and Switch) with one of the many train-operating companies: tickets can be mailed to a UK address (allow 5 days) or you can pick them up at the station. For more information on UK train services, including online booking, go to Ⓦ www.nationalrail.co.uk, Ⓦ www.thetrainline.com or Ⓦ www.qjump.co.uk.

Tourist offices have free copies of the handy *Wales Bus, Rail & Tourist Map & Guide*.

engineering often impressive. In addition to the mainline network, there are over a dozen volunteer-run train lines (see pp.43–44). All run steam trains, most on narrow-gauge tracks and predominantly as tourist attractions.

Services in Wales cover all the main cities and a seemingly random selection of rural towns and wayside halts. The two **major lines** run along the **north** (Chester–Llandudno Junction–Bangor–Holyhead) and **south** (Newport–Cardiff–Swansea) coasts, although there is plenty of stopping local traffic along each line too. Services on the remainder of Wales' train lines are infrequent, and are occasionally replaced by buses on

Sunday: quieter lines include the Heart of Wales from Swansea to Shrewsbury, and the mid-Wales line from Shrewsbury and Aberystwyth and Pwllheli.

You can buy **tickets** for trains at stations or from major travel agents and online through operators' websites – details of the **different types of fare** available are given on p.29. At many smaller stations, the ticket offices are closed at weekends, and in a lot of minor towns they've shut for good. In these instances, there's sometimes a vending machine on the platform. If there isn't a machine, you can buy your ticket on board – but if you've boarded at a station with a machine or ticket office and haven't bought

Train and bus passes and discounts

In addition to the passes listed below, savings can be made by obtaining a discount Railcard (Ⓦ www.railcard.co.uk): available to full-time students and those aged 16–25, the Young Persons Railcard costs £18, is valid for a year and gives 33 percent reductions on most rail fares. A Seniors Railcard, also £18 and offering 33 percent reductions, is available to those aged 60 or over. The Family Railcard costs £20, and gives discounts of between 33 percent for up to four adults travelling with up to four children (aged 5–15), who get sixty percent off. Kids under 5 travel free.

Britain and Wales

All-Line Rail Rover Ⓦ www.nationalrail.co.uk. Unlimited travel on the entire network throughout England, Scotland and Wales for seven (£355) or fourteen consecutive days (£540). Available within Britain.

BritRail Pass If Wales is only a part of your wider British travels, foreign visitors might find a BritRail Pass, which must be bought before you enter the country, a wise investment. The BritRail Classic Pass gives unlimited travel in England, Scotland and Wales for four consecutive days (US$209, CAN$269), eight days (US$299, CAN$379), fifteen days (US$449, CAN$575), 22 days (US$575, CAN$729) or a month (US$679, CAN$859). The BritRail Flexipass is good for travel on four days in a two-month period (US$265, CAN$339), eight days in two months (US$385, CAN$489) or fifteen days in two months (US$585, CAN$739). Note that both these passes allow further Youth (under 26), and Senior (over 60) discounts of 20–40 percent, and that one child can travel free on each adult pass (other children aged 5–15 travel at half price).

All these tickets can be booked online at Ⓦ www.britrail.com. Alternatively, **North Americans** can visit the British Travel Shop in New York City (details on Ⓦ www.visitbritain.com), or go to Ⓦ www.raileurope.com or Ⓦ www.europrail.net. **Australians and New Zealanders** can buy BritRail passes from most travel agents at equivalent prices and get information at Ⓦ www.railplus.com.au or Ⓦ www.railplus.co.nz.

Freedom of Wales Flexi Pass Ⓣ 0845/606 1660, Ⓦ www.walesflexipass.co.uk. Comprehensive ticket allowing both bus and train travel throughout Wales – and the connecting services through England. The eight-day pass (late May to late Sept £55, late Sept to late May £45) gives the full eight days' bus travel and four days' rail travel within that period; the fifteen-day pass (late May to late Sept £92; late Sept to late May £75) is similar, allowing eight days of train travel. Additional benefits are a ticket, you're liable for an on-the-spot fine of £10.

Steam railways

With the rising demand for quarried stone in the nineteenth century, quarry and mine owners had to find more economical ways than packhorses to get their products to market, but in the steep, tortuous valleys of Snowdonia, standard-gauge train tracks proved too unwieldy. The solution was rails, sometimes less than a foot apart, plied by steam engines and dinky rolling stock. The charm of these railways was recognized by train enthusiasts, and long after the decline of the quarries, they banded together to restore abandoned lines and locos. Most lines are still largely run by volunteers, who have also started up new services along unused sections of standard-gauge bed.

Although run primarily as tourist attractions, several of the **steam railways** operate as public transport and are detailed as such in the text. Note, though, that most are seasonal in their operation, with few, if any, winter services. Tickets are generally sold separately, but eight railways – under the umbrella name of The Great Little Trains of Wales (designated by "GLT" in the list overleaf) – offer a Passport ticket (£55), allowing one full return journey on each during one season. For more

free travel on the Ffestiniog and Welsh Highland (Caernarfon) railways, twenty-percent discounts on most other narrow-gauge railways, and reduced entry to CADW and National Trust properties. Flexi Pass and Flexi Rover tickets (see below) can be bought at most staffed train stations, major tourist offices and travel agents, the larger YHAs, online and by phone.

North and mid-Wales
Arriva Explorer and Wanderer ☎01492/580587, ⓦwww.arriva.co.uk. Bus passes valid on the north and mid-Wales Arriva network except the #701 TrawsCambria bus. One day costs £5, three days £10 and five days £15.

North and Mid-Wales Flexi Rover Bus and train travel in the northern half of Wales; either three days in seven (£29) or seven consecutive days (£43).

North and Mid-Wales Day Ranger One day's regional train and bus travel after 9.15am (and all weekend) for £20.

Red Rover All-day bus travel throughout northwest Wales for £4.95. Buy on the bus.

Snowdon Sherpa Day Ticket All-day travel on the routes immediately surrounding Snowdon for £3. Buy on the bus.

West and mid-Wales
Cambrian Coaster Day Ranger One day's train travel between Aberystwyth and Pwllheli (£7), valid after 9.15am and all weekend. There's also a bargain Evening Ranger (£3.70; valid after 4.30pm).

Mid-Wales Day Ranger One day's regional train travel after 8.30am Mon–Fri and all weekend, but not valid Sat in July & Aug (£18.50).

West Wales Rover Ticket All-day bus travel in West Wales south of Aberysytwyth for £4.95. Buy on the bus.

South Wales
Freedom of South Wales Flexi Rover Seven days' bus travel and three days' train travel within that week in south Wales (June–Sept £35; Oct–May £30).

Valley Lines Day Explorer One day's Cardiff and Valleys bus and train travel (£7); valid daily except during major sporting events.

Swansea Bay Day Out All-day bus travel in the Swansea Bay area for £2.50. Buy on the bus.

information, check the GLT website ⓦwww
.greatlittletrainsofwales.co.uk.

The steam railways below are listed north
to south:

**Rheilffordd Eryri (Welsh Highland Railway:
Caernarfon)** ☎01766/516000, ⓦwww.festrail
.co.uk. Caernarfon to Rhyd-Ddu, gradually being
extended to Beddgelert and ultimately to the WHR in
Porthmadog, Will be 25 miles in all. 24-inch gauge.
GLT. See p.442.

Llanberis Lake Railway Llanberis ☎01286
/870549, ⓦwww.lake-railway.co.uk. 24-inch
gauge. GLT. See p.403.

Snowdon Mountain Railway Llanberis
☎0870/458 0033, ⓦwww.snowdonrailway.co.uk.
Climbs Wales' highest peak. 31.5-inch gauge. See
p.401.

Ffestiniog Railway Porthmadog ☎01766/516073,
ⓦwww.festrail.co.uk. The best of all: Porthmadog to
Blaenau Ffestiniog. Links two standard gauge lines. 13
miles. 23.5-inch gauge. GLT. See p.424.

Welsh Highland Railway Porthmadog
☎0870/321 2402, ⓦwww.whr.co.uk. Tiny line.
24-inch gauge. GLT. See p.424.

Llangollen Railway Llangollen ☎01978/860951,
ⓦwww.llangollen-railway.co.uk. Llangollen to
Carrog. Standard 56.5-inch gauge. See p.359.

Bala Lake Railway Bala ☎01678/540666,
ⓦwww.bala-lake-railway.co.uk. Four-mile lakeside
run. 24-inch gauge. GLT. See p.418.

Talyllyn Railway Tywyn ☎01654/710472,
ⓦwww.talyllyn.co.uk. Lovely seven-mile run to
Abergynolwyn. 27-inch gauge. GLT. See p.327.

Welshpool and Llanfair Railway Llanfair
Caereinion ☎01938/810441, ⓦwww.wllr.org.uk.
An eight-mile shuttle to Welshpool. 30-inch gauge.
GLT. See p.283.

Corris Railway near Machynlleth
☎01654/761303, ⓦwww.corris.co.uk. Tiny line.
27-inch gauge. See p.326.

Fairbourne Railway Fairbourne ☎01341/250362,
ⓦwww.fairbourne-railway.co.uk. Short seafront
shuttle. 12-inch gauge. See p.331.

Vale of Rheidol Railway Aberystwyth
☎01970/625819, ⓦwww.rheidolrailway.co.uk.
Stunning twelve-mile run to Devil's Bridge. 13.5-inch
gauge. GLT. See p.315.

Gwili Steam Railway Carmarthen
☎01267/230666, ⓦwww.gwili-railway.co.uk. Short
but sweet valley journey. 56.5-inch gauge.

Brecon Mountain Railway Pant, near Merthyr
Tydfil ☎01685/722988, ⓦwww
.breconmountainrailway.co.uk. Two-mile lakeside
line. 24-inch gauge. GLT. See p.247.

Buses and coaches

With the skeletal nature of the train system
in Wales, you're going to find yourself relying on **buses**, which provide a much deeper
penetration into the countryside. There
are a limited number of inter-town buses
(known as **"coaches"** in Britain) run by
National Express (☎08705/808080, ⓦwww
.nationalexpress.com; see p.30), but for
travel within Wales you'll be using the **local**

Guided bus tours

If time is of the essence, consider one of the growing army of guided tour operators
to whisk you around Wales. Some of the best include:

Bus Wales ☎0800/328 0284, ⓦwww.buswalestours.com. Wide range of backpacker and smarter tours, from one-day beanos (£25) to a week's Wild Wales trip
(£135). Also runs weekly weekend tours to Wales from London (£65).

Dragon Backpacker Tours ☎01878/658124, ⓦwww.dragonbackpackertours
.co.uk. A good selection of tours from two-day mountain breaks (£110) to five-day
all-Wales trips (£175 plus hostel accommodation). A smarter range, using hotels, is
also available. Good links with ferries to Ireland for those who want to travel on.

Road Trip ☎0845/200 6791, ⓦwww.roadtrip.co.uk. London-based outfit running
all-inclusive minibus trips: the weekend Snowdonia and Wales tour (£143) spends
two full days around Snowdon, the South Wales activity weekend (£130) focuses on
the Brecon Beacons, while the five-day Northern Exposure trip (£259) visits Wales
for a day on the way back from Scotland.

Shaggy Sheep Tours ☎01267/281202, ⓦwww.shaggysheep.com. Great fun and
hugely enthusiastic, the booziest backpacker tours around leave twice-weekly from
London. Choose between a long weekend (£108) or a four-day (£138) trip – both
cheaper if you join at Cardiff.

bus services run by a bewildering array of companies. Integration is improving: check with **Traveline Cymru** (☎0970/608 2608, ⓦwww.pticymru.com) for all details. Though services are more expensive and less frequent in the rural areas, there are very few places without any service, even if it's only a private minibus on market day or one of the "**postbuses**" (see below) that also pick up mail.

For occasional bus journeys, just pay as you get on, but good savings can be made with one of the various bus passes and combined bus and rail passes (see box).

In the **northern** half of Wales, Llandudno-based Arriva Cymru (☎01248/750444, ⓦwww.arriva.co.uk) runs the majority of local services as well as the handy #X32/701 TrawsCambria run from Llandudno to Bristol via Aberystwyth and Cardiff.

In the **southern** section of the country, the system is far less unified, though most services west of Cardiff and south of Carmarthen are run by the Swansea-based First Cymru (☎01792/580580, ⓦwww.firstcymru.co.uk). Bws Caerdydd (☎0870/6082608), the major company serving Cardiff and the Vale of Glamorgan, offers a wide range of day, evening and weekly tickets; prices depend on the number of zones involved. For a short visit, you'll probably get better value from the **Cardiff Card**, which also gives access to the major sights. All regions have their own detailed local **timetable**, easily obtained from tourist offices, libraries and stations.

Postbuses

In parts of west and mid-Wales, bus services and mail delivery are combined in a network of **postbuses** which cover some of the most remote and beautiful Welsh regions. Few postbuses service destinations are of interest to most visitors, but as a way of seeing quiet countryside at low cost (comparable with other bus fares for similar distances), and gaining a small insight into life in rural Wales, they can't be beaten. There are currently fifteen postbus routes – the northernmost based at Aberystwyth and the most southerly running from Pembroke Dock – usually plied by a morning delivery and an afternoon collection run.

Driving

If you want to cover a lot of the countryside in a short time, or just want more flexibility, you'll need your own transport. England's busy but comprehensive motorway system means that getting to Wales is fairly straight-forward, but over the border, the only really fast roads are the A55 expressway along the north Wales coast to Holyhead and the M4 **motorway** in south Wales. The latter is the main westbound route from London, which enters Wales across the newer of the two Severn bridges and skirts Newport, Cardiff and Bridgend before petering out just beyond Swansea. You can also cross from England to Wales from the M48 via the older Severn Bridge; both bridges carry a £4.80 toll on the westbound journey only. An extensive network of dual carriageways and good-quality A roads link the major centres, but in rural areas you'll often find yourself on steep, winding, single-track (but usually asphalt) lanes with slightly broader sections where two vehicles can squeeze by – with this in mind, you might want to select a compact rental car. In very remote areas, you may still occasionally have to open gates designed to keep sheep from straying.

In order to **drive in Britain**, you must have a current **driving licence**; most foreign nationals will get by with their licence from home, but if you're in any doubt, you can supplement this with an **international driving permit**, available from national motoring organizations for a small fee. If you're bringing your own vehicle into the country, you should also carry vehicle registration or ownership documents at all times. Furthermore, you must be adequately **insured**, so be sure to check your existing policy.

As in the rest of the UK, you **drive on the left** in Wales, and this can lead to a few tense days of acclimatization. **Speed limits** are 30–40mph (50–65km/h) in built-up areas, 70mph (110km/h) on motorways (freeways) and dual carriageways, and 50mph (80km/h) on most other roads. As a rule, assume that in any area with street lighting, the speed limit is 30mph (50km/h) unless stated otherwise. Road signs are pretty much international ("Give Way" means "Yield"), and road rules are largely common sense: unlike in some American states, you are not permitted

Accommodation

Welsh tourist accommodation has changed for the better in recent decades. Gone are the fearsome guesthouses used by English holiday-makers in the postwar years, to be replaced by a variety of places offering considerably better standards – top-rank international hotels, farmhouse accommodation, hostels and ubiquitous bed and breakfast (B&B) establishments.

Wales has traditionally been a holiday centre for the millions of English who live within striking distance – particularly those in Birmingham and the Midlands or Manchester, Liverpool and the northwest. This is evident at some of the more faded, tackier seaside resorts in the shape of vast and ugly caravan parks. However, with the lower cost of the foreign package holiday, more English people are choosing to fly abroad for their fortnight of sun and sand, freeing up Wales – its spectacular countryside as much as its coastline – for an increasing number of international visitors.

A useful resource for anyone wanting to ensure that they go to places where Welsh is spoken is the website ⓦwww.gwyliaucymraeg.co.uk, covering accommodation and pubs/restaurants.

Hotels and B&Bs

The distinction between hotels, B&Bs and most other forms of serviced accommodation is blurring all the time. A bad, fully fledged hotel (so called because of its licensed status) can be vastly inferior to a similarly priced or even cheaper B&B or guesthouse. This is especially the case amongst the growing army of farmhouse B&Bs and country houses, which quite often outstrip any hotel for the sheer warmth of welcome, informal hospitality and quality of home cooking.

A **B&B** is likely to be a private house with a couple of bedrooms set aside for paying guests, and often has a more personal touch than the larger **guesthouse**, which is commonly a dedicated establishment with half a dozen rooms plus a guests' lounge. In both places you'll get a room with TV, tea- and coffee-making facilities and, usually, your own en-suite bathroom, for £20–30 per person, sometimes a little less out of season or in less popular areas. A few places still have rooms without a private bathroom (though usually with a sink in the room) for which you'll pay £2–5 less. You can assume that recommended establishments throughout the Guide have private facilities unless we've told you otherwise.

In the countryside you're more likely to find places described as a farm (essentially

Accommodation price codes

Throughout this guide, hotel and B&B accommodation is priced on a scale of ❶ to ❾, the number indicating the **lowest price** you could expect to pay per night in that establishment for a **double room in high season**. For backpacker **hostels** and camping barns we've listed the price of a dorm bed, and added a price code when double or twin rooms are also available. Campsite prices are either listed per person, or per pitch based on two people in one tent.

The prices indicated by the codes are as follows:

❶ under £40
❷ £41–50
❸ £51–60

❹ £61–70
❺ £71–90
❻ £91–110

❼ £111–150
❽ £151–200
❾ over £201

The accommodation grading system

The Wales Tourist Board (WTB) currently operates a grading system for hotels, country hotels, country houses, guesthouses, B&Bs, farms, cottages and hostels, assigning them a minimum of one star (seldom used) to a maximum of five stars. Rather than measuring the level of amenities, it is a subjective indication of the level of service and quality of a place within its particular category.

To achieve a star rating, an establishment must be "verified" by WTB inspectors, which ensures that you shouldn't be short-changed. For various reasons, some wonderful establishments choose to remain outside the official verification system, and where appropriate we've mentioned such places in the text.

Starting in 2006, the tourist boards of Wales, England and Scotland will finally have a common system for rating accommodation, one that will be in line with that used by the AA and RAC. Places will still be given a rating from one to five stars, though individual ratings may change. Rolling the system out will take some time and it will probably take until 2007 for things to settle down.

"Hotels" will be subdivided into the categories of Country House Hotel, Small Hotel, Town House Hotel and Metro Hotel. The term "Guest Accommodation" covers B&Bs, guesthouses, farmhouses, inns and restaurants with rooms.

a B&B on a working farm) or an inn (usually village pub with rooms above). As visitor expectations and the demand for weekend breaks increase, some places in all the above categories are ramping up the standards with sumptuous furnishings, better food and those little touches which make your stay special. Of course, you pay considerably more for such pampering. In all except the more expensive places you should expect to pay cash, though bottom-end B&Bs are increasingly accepting credit and debit cards.

In town centres, B&Bs and guesthouses are supplemented by **hotels**, often just rooms above a noisy bar, but also larger places that are often the grandest in town. Once the staple of travelling salespeople, these have now largely been supplanted by town-fringe business hotels with all the facilities but little character.

Wherever you stay, **breakfast** will almost certainly be included in the price. This may just be continental (orange juice, cereal, toast and tea or coffee) but more often will also include a full cooked breakfast of eggs (normally fried, but often poached or scrambled if you prefer), bacon, sausage, fried tomato and perhaps baked beans and hash browns. In fancier places there'll be a choice of juices, preserved fruit, yogurt, and the like.

The WTB produces a couple of free publications worth looking out for: the *Great Little*

Places booklet (available in its entirety at ⓦ www.little-places.co.uk) which lists around fifty of the best small hotels, country inns, and farmhouse B&Bs in Wales; and *Welsh Rarebits* (ⓦ www.welsh.rarebits.co.uk), a similarly select listing of more substantial hotels and country mansions. Both websites give full coverage of all listed establishments, and you can pick up the booklets at tourist offices. There is also the WTB's comprehensive *Farm Holidays* brochure which can be ordered through its website.

Reservations can be made directly by phone and sometimes over the Internet. Alternatively you can book though the local **tourist office**, which will only provide information on "verified" accommodation (see box), though can sometimes be reluctant to divulge details of places that don't advertise in the official local guide: if you don't see something suitable in the Guide, don't be afraid to ask if there is anywhere else that matches your requirements for price and location. When you book, you'll have to pay the tourist office ten percent of the cost on the spot, which will then be knocked off your bill at the hotel.

Hostels

The network of the **Youth Hostels Association** (see below for contact details) comprises almost forty properties in Wales, offering bunk-bed accommodation in single-sex dormitories or smaller rooms. A few of these

Coastal Cottages of Pembrokeshire
☎01437/767600, Ⓦwww.coastalcottages.co.uk.
Approaching 500 cottages, chalets, flats and houses
– some with impressive leisure and activity facilities
– around or near the Pembrokeshire coast.
North Wales Holiday Cottages & Farmhouses
☎0870/755 9888, Ⓦwww.northwalesholiday
cottages.co.uk. Nearly 200 cottages in the
Snowdonia National Park and throughout north Wales,
both coast and countryside.

Powell's Cottage Holidays ☎0800/378771,
Ⓦwww.powells.co.uk. About 250 properties, mainly
in south Wales and the Gower.
Quality Cottages ☎0800/169 2256, Ⓦwww
.qualitycottages.co.uk. Around 200 coastal cottages
throughout Wales.
Wales Cottage Holidays ☎01686/628200,
Ⓦwww.wales-holidays.co.uk. A varied selection of
500 properties all over Wales.

Food and drink

For many centuries, Welsh cuisine has been considered to be little more than
a poor relation of the English culinary art, itself hardly well regarded on the
international scene. Restaurants were on the whole uninteresting and the pubs
were strictly male-dominated and cheerless. Times have changed considerably, for traditional Welsh cuisine is now climbing a slope of resurgence, and
this, combined with improved British fare and an eclectic range of international
options, has turned eating and drinking into an interesting and enjoyable part of
any stay in Wales. That said, never underestimate the potential for sore gastronomic disappointments.

Eating

Indigenous British cuisine has taken an
upturn in recent years. The pies, cheeses,
puddings and meat from all of the regions
are being offered in increasing numbers
of establishments. Popular British dishes
– steak and kidney pies, the ubiquitous fish
and chips, cuts of meat with potatoes and
vegetables, and stews, for example – are
available everywhere in Wales.

Native **Welsh cuisine** is also making
something of a comeback. Not surprisingly,
such food is frequently rooted in economical ingredients, although this does not
mean that it is of a poor quality. Traditional
dishes, such as the delicious native lamb
(best served minted or with thyme or rosemary), fresh salmon, sewin (sea trout) and
other trout can be found on an increasing
number of menus, frequently combined with
the national vegetable, the leek. Specialities
include laverbread (*bara lawr*), a thoroughly

tasty seaweed and oatmeal cake often fried
with a traditional breakfast of pork sausages,
egg and bacon. Other dishes well worth
investigating include Glamorgan sausages (a
vegetarian combination of local cheese and
spices), cawl (a chunky mutton broth), and
cockles, trawled from the estuary north of
the Gower.

Dairy products, in a predominantly rural
country, feature highly, especially in the range
of Welsh **cheeses**. Best known is Caerphilly,
a soft, crumbly, white cheese that forms the
basis of a true Welsh Rarebit when mixed with
beer and toasted on bread. Creamy goat's
cheeses can be found all over the country. Also stemming from the cheapness of
their ingredients are some traditional **sweets
and cakes**: Welsh Cakes are flat pancakes
of sugared dough, and *bara brith*, a popular accompaniment to afternoon tea, literally
translates as "speckled (with dried fruit) bread".
Menus comprising Welsh dishes can be found
in numerous restaurants, hotels and pubs,

For advice on tipping and service charges see "Directory" on p.74.

many of which are part of the **Taste of Wales** (Blas ar Gymru) scheme to encourage local cuisine. Such establishments generally display a sticker in their windows, and many are listed in the free, annual *Dining Out in Wales* book, which is available at tourist offices. For further Information on Welsh food, go to ⓦwww .walesthetruetaste.com.

Where to eat

If you're staying in a hotel, guesthouse or B&B, a cooked breakfast (generally served 8–9am) will usually be offered as part of the deal. A hearty breakfast is usually enough to see most people through the day, with maybe a snack around lunchtime (noon– 2pm). Evening meals are served from 6pm to 10pm, though in rural areas, especially early in the week, you may find it difficult to get served after 9pm.

Cafés and **tearooms** (the terms used pretty much interchangeably) are found absolutely everywhere, and are generally the cheapest places to eat, providing hearty, if cholesterol-laden, breakfasts, a solid range of snacks and full meals for lunch and, in a few instances, evening meals as well. Wales' steady influx of hippies and New Agers over the past thirty years has seen the **wholefood café** become a standard feature of most mid- and west Welsh towns. Cheap and usually vegetarian, these rely extensively on fresh local produce. Throughout the land, cafés and restaurants are increasingly equipped with **espresso** machines, though cappuccino incompetence remains widespread outside the more cosmopolitan enclaves.

Food in **pubs** varies as much as the establishments themselves. In recent years, intense competition has required that they sharpen up their act, and many pubs now offer more imaginative dishes than the standard microwaved lasagne and chips. Most places serve food at lunchtime and in the evening (usually until 8.30 or 9pm), and in many towns, the local pub is the most economical place to grab a filling evening meal.

The growth in upmarket **restaurants** has mirrored Wales' increasing sophistication and attraction to the outside world. People of all nationalities have settled in Wales and few towns are without their Indian and Chinese restaurants, joined over recent years by Japanese, French, Thai, American, Mexican, Belgian and more. In the more cosmopolitan centres, **bistros** and **brasseries** have sprung up, many offering superb Welsh and international cuisine at thoroughly affordable prices.

Our restaurant listings include a mix of high-quality and good-value establishments, but if you're intent on a culinary pilgrimage, you'd do well to arm yourself with a copy of the annual *Good Food Guide* (Which? Books), which includes detailed recommendations. Throughout this book, we've supplied the phone number for all restaurants where you may need to book a table. Generally speaking, in pubs and cafés you can expect to pay under £10 per head; in most restaurants and bistros it should be between £10 and £30; only exceptionally will you pay over £30.

Drinking

Daytime cafés are not usually licensed to sell alcohol, and though restaurants invariably are, you'll find yourself doing much of your drinking in **pubs**. These are as much the centre of social activity as in others part of the British Isles, though they are gradually shedding their booze-only image, as more of them serve **tea** and **coffee**, as well as a heavily marked-up range of soft drinks.

The **legal drinking age** is 18, though those 16 and over can enter a pub unaccompanied. Some places offer special family rooms for people with children, and beer gardens where younger kids can run free.

Pubs

Pubs in Wales vary as much as the landscape, from opulent Edwardian palaces of smoked glass, gleaming brass and polished mahogany in the larger towns and cities, to thick-set stone barns in wild, remote countryside. Where the church has faltered as a community focal point, the pub still holds sway, with those in smaller towns and villages, in particular, functioning as

Useful phone numbers

National operator (freecall) ☎ 100
International operator (freecall) ☎ 155
National Directory Enquiry Several services are available including ☎ 118 500 (23p per minute plus 40p connection charge).
International Directory Enquiry ☎ 118 505 (£1.50 per minute; £1.50 minimum charge).

International dialling codes

To **call Wales** from outside the UK, dial the international access code (☎ 011 from the US and Canada, ☎ 0011 from Australia and ☎ 00 from New Zealand), followed in all cases by 44, then the area code minus its initial zero, and finally the number. To call **overseas from Wales** dial ☎ 00, then the appropriate country code, the area code (without the zero if there is one) and finally the number. If you have a problem getting through, call the international operator (see above).

Country codes

Australia 61
Canada 1
Ireland 353
New Zealand 64
USA 1

Mobile phones

If you want to use your **mobile phone**, you'll need to check with your phone provider whether it will work in Britain, and what the call charges are. The GSM system used in Britain is compatible with other European systems, Australian systems and some in New Zealand, though most North American phones don't work here.

A better bet might be to buy a pre-pay phone in the UK from one of the numerous high street outlets from as little as £50. With no contract you simply top up your account as you need to.

The media

The media that you will encounter in Wales is a predictable hybrid of Welsh and Britain-wide information. Although the London-based UK media attempts to cover life in the other corners of Britain, few people would agree that Wales, Scotland and the northern regions of England receive a fair share of coverage in any medium. Of all the solely Welsh media, newspapers are probably the weakest area, and periodicals and TV coverage the strongest and most interesting.

Newspapers and magazines

Of the **British daily newspapers**, all available in Wales, the majority are avowedly Londoncentric – news of Wales is not terribly well covered. In most ordinary weeks, for instance, you could count on the fingers of one hand the number of stories in the UK national papers that have emanated from, say, the Welsh Assembly in Cardiff, let alone any other area of Welsh life. As devolution bites, however, there is the likelihood that an increasing number of the English papers will produce targeted Welsh editions, although this may amount to little more than them displaying a special dragon or daffodil masthead and the odd football report on Wrexham or Swansea City. The London-based **tabloid newspapers** – known otherwise, and with good reason, as the "gutter press" – are the papers you are most likely to see read in any part of Britain. Specializing in prurient gossip and scandal, the two leaders in this field are Rupert Murdoch's boisterous *Sun* and the damply leftish *Daily Mirror*, which does at least manage some hard-hitting investigation and comment on occasion. Slightly more upmarket, adding in a bit more news but always filtered through a severely right-wing analysis, are the *Daily Mail* and *Daily Express*. Best of the quality broadsheet papers are the vaguely left-leaning *Guardian*, the right-wing *Daily Telegraph* and the generally robust *Independent*. Although there are hopes for new daily papers written in both English and Welsh, currently the only quality **Welsh daily** is the *Western Mail*, a sometimes uneasy mix of local, Welsh, British and a token smattering of international news coupled with an increasing amount of populist lifestyle pap and features on TV stars. The arrival of the National Assembly has at last given some purpose to the paper, though with a few honourable exceptions, the quality of writing and analysis veers too readily towards the lightweight. What the *Western Mail* is to south Wales, the *Daily Post* is to the north of the country, with an ever-expanding catchment area and a fairly decent spectrum of news and features that marks it out from other local dailies. Of these, the *Wrexham Evening Leader* is parochially newsworthy, as are the *South Wales Echo* in the Cardiff area, the evening *South Wales Argus* in Gwent, and, out in Swansea and the southwest, the *Swansea Evening Post*, Dylan Thomas' old sheet, a pale shadow of its former self. All areas have their own long standing **weekly papers**, generally an entertaining mix of local news, parish gossip and events listings. Wales' national **Sunday paper**, *Wales on Sunday*, from the same family as the *Western Mail*, has descended somewhat into tabloid trivia, but it's still worth buying for its bright, colourful take on Welsh life and occasional hard-hitting exposés and campaigning journalism. It's also very good on Welsh sport.

Go into any bookshop in Wales, and you'll be surprised by the profusion of Welsh **magazines**, in both English and Welsh. For a broad overview of the arts, history and politics, it is hard to beat *Planet*, an English-language bimonthly that takes a politically irreverent line, combining Welsh interest with a wider cultural and international outlook. The more serious English-language monthly *New Welsh Review* is steeped in Wales' political, literary and economic developments, while *Poetry Wales* is an excellent publication of new writing. The bimonthly glossy *Cambria* subtitles itself as the "national magazine of Wales", an epithet that it's doing its best to fulfil with sparky writing about all matters Cymric, together with superb photography. For a wider view of Welsh social issues, with insights into "alternative" culture and news untouched by the papers, together with creative writing and a hearty infusion of cynical humour, pick up the weekly *Big Issue Cymru*, sold by homeless vendors on the streets of major towns and cities. It's the little sibling of England's *Big Issue* magazine, launched to runaway success in 1991. If you're half-proficient in Welsh, the weekly news digest *Y Cymro* is an essential read, although younger, funkier features can be found in the weekly glossy *Golwg*, and more political topics are chewed over in the monthly *Barn*. If you're attempting to master the language, try *Lingo Newydd* magazine, aimed at learners at all levels.

For **listings** and news of arts events, pick up free copies of *Buzz* in Cardiff and Newport, *What's On* in and around Swansea, and the quarterly *This Week Wales* in the north.

Television and radio

It is in TV and radio that the Welsh media becomes most distinct from its London-based counterparts. Cardiff is the home of Britain's second-largest concentration of TV and radio stations, both Welsh arms of devolved broadcasting organizations like the mighty BBC and ITV and indigenous Welsh operators such as S4C. The whole-hearted way in which UK-wide TV and radio has moved out of southeast England is in marked contrast to the Londoncentric print media.

On terrestrial television, the state-funded British Broadcasting Corporation (BBC) operates two **TV** channels in Wales – the mainstream **BBC 1 Wales** and the more esoteric **BBC 2 Wales**. Although these official titles make the stations sound avowedly Welsh, the vast majority of programming is UK-wide, with Welsh programmes, principally news and sport but also features,

Admission to museums and monuments

Many of Wales' most treasured sites – from castles, abbeys and great houses to tracts of protected landscape – come under the control of the privately run UK-wide National Trust or the state-run CADW, Welsh Historic Monuments whose properties are denoted in the Guide by "NT" and "CADW". Both organizations charge an entry fee for most places, and these can be quite high, especially for the more grandiose NT estates. If you think you'll be visiting more than half a dozen NT places or a similar number of major CADW sites, it's worth buying an annual pass. Membership of the National Trust (℡0870 458 4000, ⓦwww.nationaltrust.org.uk; £38, under-26s £17.50) allows free entry to its properties throughout Britain. Sites operated by CADW (℡01443/336000, ⓦwww.cadw.wales.gov.uk; £28, seniors £20, those 16–20 £18, under-16 £14) are restricted to Wales, but membership also grants you half-price entry to sites owned by English Heritage and Historic Scotland. In addition, CADW offers the Explorer Pass, which allows free entry into all CADW sites for three consecutive days (adult £9.50, two adults £16.50, family £23), or seven days (£15.50/£26/£32) and, like the annual passes, are also available with a vast array of family, senior and youth concessions. CADW properties are also accessible using the Great British Heritage Pass (see below).

A few Welsh **stately homes** remain in the hands of the landed gentry, who tend to charge in the region of £5 for edited highlights of their domain. Many other old buildings, albeit rarely the most momentous, are owned by the local authorities, and admission is often cheaper. Municipal **art galleries** and **museums** are usually free, and as part of the Welsh Assembly's drive to popularize the nation's cultural heritage, so are sites run by the National Museums and Galleries of Wales (ⓦwww.nmgw.ac.uk), including the National Museum and Gallery and St Fagans National History Museum, both in Cardiff. Although a donation is usually requested, **cathedrals** tend to be free, except for perhaps the tower, crypt or other such highlight, for which a small charge is made. Increasingly, **churches** are kept locked except during services; when they are open, entry is free. (You'll normally be able to find a notice in the porch or on a board telling you where to get a key if the church is locked.) Wales also has a number of ventures exploiting the country's **industrial heritage**, mostly concerned with mining for coal, slate, copper or gold. A short tour supplemented by a video should cost a couple of pounds, while the full underground interactive "experience" can be up to £10. Keen birders might consider joining the **RSPB**, where membership (ⓦwww.rspb.org.uk; £30 a year, £7.50 for three months) gives you free entry to its reserves throughout Britain.

Entry charges given in the Guide are the full adult rates, but the majority of the fee-charging attractions located in Wales have 25–35 percent **reductions** for senior citizens, the unemployed and full-time students, and 50 percent reductions for children under 16 – under-fives are admitted free almost everywhere. Proof of eligibility is required in most cases. Family tickets are also common, usually priced just under the rate for two adults and a child and valid for up to three kids; those offered by CADW are particularly good value. Most attractions are **open** daily in summer and closed one or two days a week in winter, though major sites are open daily all year – full details of opening hours are given in the Guide.

Finally, foreign visitors planning on seeing more than a dozen stately homes, monuments, castles or gardens might find it worthwhile to buy a Great British Heritage Pass (@www .gbheritagepass.com) which gives free admission to almost six hundred sites throughout the UK. Over sixty of these are in Wales, including the Bishop's Palace in St David's, Tredegar House at Newport and Cardiff Castle, as well as all National Trust and CADW properties. The pass can be purchased for periods of four days (£28), seven days (£39), fifteen days (£52) or a month (£70) either online or from the main air and sea ports, and tourist offices in the largest cities.

Annual events

Although the scale and scope of Welsh festivals has increased immeasurably in the last few decades, there's an ancient pedigree here too. Most notable are the eisteddfodau – age-old competitions in poetry and music – that still form the backbone of national culture. The colour section goes into more detail on this and some of the country's other big annual jamborees.

Many towns and cities now have annual **arts festivals** of some kind, mentioned throughout the Guide and, in the case of the major events, in the list below. Aside from these, the old working traditions of Wales have spawned such occasions as the annual Cilgerran **coracle races** (see p.302). Some of Wales' events have a distinctly bizarre background and appearance; for instance the snorkelling competition in peat bogs and the pilgrimages for *Prisoner* fans to the surreal village of Portmeirion. There's also plenty of chance to get raucous: **rock festivals**, **DJ-led events** and New Age **fairs** and **festivals** are a common feature of summer throughout Wales; these are usually publicized by handbills, posters in wholefood shops and cafés, and by word of mouth.

Events calendar

The Wales Tourist Board maintains a fairly comprehensive events list on its website (@www.visitwales.com).

January 1 Mari Llwyd, Llangynwyd, near Maesteg. Most authentic survivor of the ancient Welsh custom of parading a horse's skull through the village streets. See p.113.

February–March Six Nations rugby championship. Last won by Wales, with a tremendous Grand Slam over everyone else, in 2005.

March 1 St David's Day. *Hwyrnos* and celebrations all over Wales.

Mid-April Bay Lit Festival, Cardiff Bay ☎029/2047 2266, @www.academi.org. Wide-ranging literary bash in the capital.

Mid-May Tredegar House Folk Festival @www .tredegarhousefolk.ik.com.

Late May–early June Hay-on-Wye Festival of Literature ☎0870/990 1299, @www.hayfestival .co.uk. London's literati flock to the borders for a week.

End of May–first week in June St David's Cathedral Festival ☎01437/721682, @www .stdavidscathedral.org.uk. Superb setting for classical concerts and recitals.

End of May–first week in June Eisteddfod Genedlaethol yr Urdd ☎01678/541012, @www .urdd.org. Vast and enjoyable youth eisteddfod – the largest youth festival in Europe – alternating between north and south Wales.

Mid-June Cardiff Singer of the World competition ☎029/2087 8444, @www.bbc.co.uk/cardiffsinger. Huge, televised week-long festival of music and song held in odd-numbered years, with a star-studded list of international competitors.

Mid-June Man Versus Horse Marathon, Llanwrtyd Wells, Powys @www.man-v-horse.org.uk. A 22-mile race between runners, cyclists and horses: a human won for the first time in 2004 and pocketed a cool £25,000.

Late June Gwyl Ifan (folk dance festival), various locations in and around Cardiff @www.gwylifan.org.

61

Safety in the Welsh hills

Welsh mountains are not high by world standards, but they should still be treated with respect. The fickle weather makes them more dangerous than you might expect, and you can easily find yourself disoriented in the low cloud and soaked by unexpected rain. If the weather looks like it is closing in, get down fast. It is essential that you are properly equipped – even for what appears to be an easy expedition in apparently settled weather – with proper warm and waterproof layered clothing, supportive footwear, adequate maps, a compass and food. Always tell someone your route and expected time of return – and call when you get back so they know you're safe.

Some less scrupulous owners have been known to block rights of way by destroying stiles – and with some walkers wilfully straying from official rights of way, some resentment is perhaps understandable. Disputes are still uncommon but your surest way of avoiding trouble is to meticulously follow the right of way on an up-to-date map.

Ordnance Survey maps also indicate routes with **concessionary path** or **courtesy path** status; though these are usually open for public use they can be closed at any time.

Rock climbing and scrambling

As well as being superb walking country, Snowdonia offers some of Britain's best **rock climbing** and several challenging **scrambles** – ascents that fall somewhere between walks and climbs, requiring the use of your hands. One or two of the tougher walks included in the text have sections of scrambling, but for the most part this is a specialist discipline, well covered in the walking books listed in "Contexts" (see pp.555–556). We've covered the subject in more detail in the colour insert.

The best general guide for experienced climbers, *Rock Climbing in Snowdonia* by Paul Williams (Frances Lincoln), is stocked in the region's numerous climbing shops.

Beginners should contact Plas y Brenin: The National Mountaineering Centre (see p.394), or the British Mountaineering Council, 177–179 Burton Rd, ManchesterM20 2BB (℡0870/010 4878, ⌘www.thebmc .co.uk), which can put you in touch with climbing guides and people running courses.

Cycling

In the last few years, Wales has positioned itself as one of Britain's premiere **cycling** destinations, with a complex web of traffic-free bike paths and low-traffic cycle routes, and some excellent mountain-bike parks (see colour insert). Backroad routes along river valleys and over mountain passes have a sufficient density of pubs and B&Bs to keep the days manageable, and while steep gradients can be a problem, ascents are never long, with Wales' highest pass barely reaching 1500ft. The picture isn't so rosy in most towns and cities, where cyclists are still treated with notorious disrespect by many motorized road users and by the people who plan the country's traffic systems. If you plan to ride in built-up areas, get a **helmet** and a secure **lock** – cycle theft is an organized racket.

Transporting your bike by **train** is a good way of getting to the interesting parts of Wales without a lot of stressful pedalling. What with the privatization of the rail network and the profusion of companies running services, it's hard to be specific about what you'll encounter, but in general, bikes are carried free on suburban trains outside the weekday rush hours of 7.30–9.30am and 4–6pm. On most routes in Wales, there is only space for two bikes (first-come-first-served) and reservations are not accepted – not much help if you're working to a schedule. On inter-city routes, say from England into Wales, space is still very limited but free reservations are accepted. The free *Cycling by Train* brochure published by Arriva Trains Wales, and the *National Rail Guide: Cycling by Train* are both useful resources: look for them on the Web, or at train stations and visitor centres.

Bike rental is available at bike shops in most large towns (outlined throughout the Guide) and many resorts, but the specimens are seldom top-quality machines – alright for a brief spin, but not for any serious touring.

Expect to pay in the region of £15 per day, more for specialist off-road machines with suspension.

Finding **spare parts** might be a problem in remoter areas, but most decent-sized towns now have well-stocked bike shops: the CTC (see below) lists places in its annual handbook.

Cycle touring routes

The best of Wales' narrow lanes, disused railway lines and forest paths have been linked together to form **cycle routes** as part of the National Cycle Network created by **Sustrans** (☎0845/113 0065, ⊕www.sustrans.org.uk). Set up in 1977, this charity promotes sustainable transport, principally by developing cycling routes – over 6500 miles have been created and there's more to come, half of it on traffic-free paths and trails, the rest on quiet roads. The entire network is covered in the official *Cycling in the UK* handbook (£15).

Three major cycling routes cross Wales. The main north-south **Lôn Las Cymru** (the Welsh National Route; Route 8) was opened in 1996 and covers three hundred hilly miles from Anglesey, through Snowdonia, the Brecon Beacons and the industrial valleys of the south, to the Severn Bridge. Sustrans publishes two maps of the route (£6 each), one covering Holyhead to Builth Wells and the other from Builth Wells to Chepstow and Cardiff. **Lôn Geltaidd** (the Celtic Trail; Route 4) traverses 186 miles across the south of the country (70 percent of it traffic-free) from Fishguard to the Severn Bridge: again two £6 maps cover the route. Along the north coast the busy roads are avoided on the **North Wales Coastal Route** (Route 5). In addition there are numerous other local routes, sometimes on dedicated traffic-free paths but often directed along quiet lanes: free leaflets available locally are easy to follow. Areas worth considering are the Gower peninsula, Pembrokeshire, Anglesey and the Llŷn.

Mountain biking

Mountain biking, featured in the colour insert, is a big deal in Wales, with dedicated **bike parks** throughout the managed forests. There's no charge for using them (though there may be a small parking fee), but bike-rental facilities are rare and you are usually better off bringing your own machine or renting one from a nearby town.

Elsewhere, off-road cycling is allowed along designated bridleways, including the Snowdon Ranger, Rhyd Ddu and Llanberis paths up Snowdon (detailed on pp.406–407), but conflict between hikers and bikers has led to the creation of the **Snowdon Voluntary Cycling Agreement**, which limits the hours riders can use them. Anytime in winter (Oct–April) is OK and you can ride before 10am and after 5pm throughout the summer. Footpaths, unless otherwise marked, are for pedestrian use only, and cyclists should always pass walkers at considerate speed and with a courteous warning of your presence.

For more **information** check out: ⊕www.mbwales.com, a Wales Tourist Board site concentrating on the main bike parks, or ⊕www.mtb-wales.com, which has excellent articles on routes and gear along with a forum and online shop. Local bookshops and bike stores stock relevant guides, but some of the best trails the country has to offer are covered by *Bikefax: The best mountain bike trails in Snowdonia* (Cordee: £17).

The CTC and holidays

Britain's biggest **cycling organization** is the Cyclists' Touring Club (CTC), Cottrell House, 69 Meadrow, Godalming, Surrey GU7 3HS (☎0870/873 0060, ⊕www.ctc.org.uk), which supplies members with touring and technical advice as well as insurance. Its free sheets for members cover dozens of routes through Wales. Those planning their own touring routes would do well to buy the OS 1:220,000 (3.5 miles to an inch) Wales Touring Map. These are detailed enough to show relief and almost all tarmacked roads – and you won't find yourself cycling across a whole map in one day. The Ordnance Survey's excellent series of regional *Cycle Tour* guides have now been extended to include Wales: one covers North Wales, the other the rest of the country.

If you want a guaranteed hassle free **cycling holiday**, various companies offer easy-going tours where you ride from hotel to hotel, and a van carries your bags. Some give you an arranged itinerary, while others guide you. The best of the latter is Bicycle Beano, Erwood, Builth Wells, tickets are allocated months before a match, and touts will often be found selling tickets for hundreds of pounds outside the gates on the day. Away from the international arena, a thriving rugby scene exists at club level, with upwards of a hundred clubs and 40,000 players taking to the field most Saturdays throughout the season (September to just after Easter). The upper tier is known as the Welsh Premiership though the top teams – the Cardiff Blues, Llanelli Scarlets, Newport Dragons and Swansea Ospreys – also play in the Celtic League against teams from Scotland and Ireland.

It's often worth going to a match purely for the light-hearted crowd banter – if you can understand the accents. Check with individual clubs for fixtures and ticket prices, which start at under £10.

Football

Compared to rugby, **Welsh football** (soccer) is seen as a minority sport, but in fact there are just as many Welsh footballers who prefer not to pick up the ball and run with it as those who do. The three top sides in the country are Cardiff City, Swansea City and Wrexham, which all play in the English Football League. Currently Cardiff City are mid-table in the second of the four divisions, Swansea are top of the third, while Wrexham are languishing mid-table in the fourth. The rest of the clubs play in the lacklustre (but improving) **League of Wales** (@www.lofw.tk).

It doesn't seem many years since Mark Hughes was a stalwart of the Wales side as a player, but in 2002 he took over as manager and immediately put his stamp on the national side. In his first eight games Wales remained unbeaten (including morale-boosting wins over Finland and Italy), but Wales narrowly missed out on reaching the finals of Euro 2004. That would have been their first major finals since the 1958 World Cup when they lost to eventual winners Brazil in the quarter finals.

Recent results haven't been great, with few wins in the team's unsuccessful campaign to reach the finals of the 2006 World Cup in Germany.

For more on the Welsh game, check the website of the Football Association of Wales (@www.faw.org.uk).

Emergencies and police

As in any other country, Wales' major towns have their dangerous spots, but these tend to be inner-city housing estates where you're unlikely to find yourself. The chief risk on the streets – though still minimal – is pickpocketing, so carry only as much money as you need, and keep all bags and pockets fastened. Should you have anything stolen or be involved in an incident that requires reporting, go to the local police station; the ☎999 number should only be used in emergencies.

Emergencies

Although the traditional image of the friendly British "Bobby" has become tarnished by stories of corruption and crooked dealings, the **police** continue to be approachable and helpful. If you're lost in a major town, asking a police officer is generally the quickest way to get help – alternatively, you could ask a **traffic warden**, a much-maligned species of law enforcer responsible for parking restrictions and other vehicle-related matters. They're distinguishable by their flat caps with a yellow band, and by the fact that they are generally armed with a book of parking-fine tickets; police officers on street duty usually wear a distinctive domed hat with a silver top, and are generally armed with just a truncheon.

Working and studying in Wales

Unless you're a resident of an EU country, you need a permit to work legally in Wales, which, in this regard, maintains the same laws as the rest of the UK. Without the backing of an established employer or company, such a permit can be very difficult to obtain. Commonwealth citizens aged between 17 and 30 may work in the UK under the Working Holidaymaker Scheme (search under Ⓦwww.ukvisas.gov. uk), which entitles you to a two-year stay in the UK during which it is permitted to undertake work of a casual nature (ie, not in a profession, or as a sportsperson or entertainer). The certificates are only available abroad, from British embassies and consulates, and when you apply you must be able to convince the officer you have a valid return or onward ticket, and the means to support yourself while you're in Britain without having to claim state benefits of any kind. Note, too, that the certificates are valid from the date of entry into Britain – you won't be able to recoup time spent elsewhere in the two-year period of validity.

In **North America**, full-time college students can get temporary work permits through BUNAC (℡203/264 0901, Ⓦwww.bunac.org). Permits are valid for up to six months and cost US$290; send an application form, college verification form and two passport photos to the above address; allow two to three weeks to process the application.

Other visitors entitled to work in Britain are **Commonwealth citizens** with a parent who was born in the UK. If you fall into this category, you can apply for a Certificate of Entitlement to the Right of Abode. If you're unsure about whether or not you may be eligible for one of these, contact your nearest British embassy or consulate, or the Foreign and Commonwealth Office, King Charles Street, London SW1A 2AH (℡020/7008 1500, Ⓦwww.fco.gov.uk).

The **kind of work** you can expect to find in Wales as a visitor is generally unskilled employment in hotels, restaurants, cleaning companies and on farms. Working conditions may not be up to much, and as a casual employee you can be fired at short notice. Pay is barely enough to survive on, being little more than the **minimum wage**

(£5.05 per hour if you are 22 or over, £4.25 for those aged 18–21). So unless you're desperate, try to save at home before travelling. With **voluntary work**, the choice of jobs improves considerably, ranging from farm camps to placements with service organizations. Timebank (Ⓦwww.timebank.org.uk) is a good resource for prospective volunteers. *Summer Jobs in Britain* by David Woodworth and Guy Hobbs (£10.99; Vacation Work Publications) gives comprehensive information on paid seasonal work in the UK.

If you're single, aged between 17 and 27, and don't have children, you might also consider working as an au pair. This enables you to live for a maximum of two years with an English-speaking family. In return for your accommodation, food and a small amount of pocket money (say £40 per week), you'll be expected to help around the house and to look after the children for a maximum of five hours each day. The easiest way to find au pair work is through a licensed agency. The Recruitment and Employment Confederation (REC), 36–38 Mortimer St, London W1W 7RG (℡020/7462 3260, Ⓦwww.rec.uk.com), handles reputable agents (ie, those that are

Lesbian and gay Wales

Homosexual acts between consenting males were legalized in Britain in 1967, but it wasn't until 2000 that the age of consent for gay men was made equal to that of straight men at sixteen. Lesbianism has never specifically been outlawed, apocryphally owing to the fact that Queen Victoria refused to believe it existed. In December 2005, civil partnerships between same sex couples were legalized – marriage in all but name.

With such a rural culture, it's perhaps not surprising that Wales is less used to the lesbian and gay lifestyle than its more cosmopolitan English neighbour. That said, there's little real hostility, with the traditional Welsh "live and let live" attitude applying as much in this area as any other. Several Welsh musicians, academics, TV stars and politicians have come out in recent years, and no-one's really batted an eyelid.

The organized gay scene in Wales, however, is fairly muted. The main centres of population – Cardiff, Newport and Swansea – have a number of pubs and clubs, with Cardiff especially beginning to see a worthy and confident gay scene – a Mardi Gras festival in early September included (see p.134) – more in keeping with the capital's size and status. Details are given in the text of the Guide. Out of the southern cities, however, gay life becomes distinctly discreet, although university towns such as Lampeter, Bangor and Wrexham manage support groups and the odd weekly night in a local bar, while Aberystwyth is a significantly homo-friendly milieu. Cardiff's lesbian and gay telephone lines (see p.134) are the most up-to-date source of information on places, events, accommodation and contacts throughout Wales. Alternatively, there are some informal but well-established networks, especially amongst the sometimes reclusive alternative lifestylers found in mid- and west Wales. **Border Women** (who should surely have called themselves Offa's Dykes; Ⓦwww.borderwomen.co.uk) is a well-organized lesbian network for mid-Wales and the Marches, with house meetings and monthly discos. For groups, events, pubs, clubs and **gay-friendly tourist accommodation** in all corners of Wales, by far the best resource is the excellent **Gay Wales website** (Ⓦwww.gaywales.co.uk).

Alternative, New Age and green Wales

Possibly more than any other part of Britain, Wales – the mid and west in particular – has become something of a haven for those searching for alternative lifestyles. This process dates back nearly a century, but it was the 1960s that saw mass migration west, something that has continued unabated since. Permanent testimonials to this include the Centre for Alternative Technology (CAT), near Machynlleth, now one of the area's most visited attractions, and Tipi Valley, near Talley, a permanent community in Native American tipis who run a regular public sweat lodge. Both institutions were founded in the idealistic mid-1970s and have prospered through less happy times. For the most part, it's been a fairly smooth process, although antagonism between New Agers and local, established families does break out on occasion, usually stoked by the sometimes liberal smugness of some incomers.

For visitors, the legacy of this "green" influx is evident throughout Wales. Even in some of the smallest rural towns, you'll often find a health-food shop, wholefood café, somewhere flogging esoteric ephemera or an alternative resource centre. Any of these will give you further ideas and contacts for local happenings, places, groups and individuals. We've tried to give details of such places throughout the Guide. Other manifestations of such prolific non-mainstream activity include a robust **free party scene** in the rural parts of north, mid- and west Wales. These are often held in spectacularly beautiful settings – by lakes, on beaches – and take place virtually every weekend throughout the summer. Keep your eyes and ears peeled for information and don't hesitate to ask people for guidance. To complement the free events, there's a plethora of good **festivals** from spring to autumn, ranging from big folk and blues bashes to smaller gatherings in remote fields, with little more than a couple of banging sound systems. Again, information for smaller events travels best by word of mouth, although for more organized and larger events, you'll see adverts and fliers months in advance. Especially in the wake of the vicious 1995 Criminal Justice Act, there are now far stronger laws against trespass and free parties, although their imposition is sketchy.

For ecologically minded tourists, there are now numerous package deals that include walking, cycling, dancing and healing holidays and retreats in remote centres, usually with vegetarian and vegan food as part of the deal. Some of these are static, many are in temporary sites, while others keep you on the move. Again, we have included many of these within the body of the Guide, and some further ones are listed below.

Retreats and holidays

Buckland Hall Bwlch, near Brecon, ☎01874/730276, ✆www.bucklandhall.co .uk. Beautiful hall and gardens hosting many holistic lifestyle courses and workshops.

Cae Mabon near Llanberis, Gwynedd ☎01286/871542, ✆www.caemabon.co.uk. Stunning Snowdonia setting for residential courses, storytelling and arts events, with accommodation in barns, bothies and benders.

Centre for Alternative Technology Llwyngwern, near Machynlleth, Powys ☎01654/705950, ✆www.cat.org.uk. Residential courses on green themes such as self-build homes and organic gardening.

Cwm Bedw Barns Abbeycwmhir, Llandrindod Wells, Powys ☎01597/851929. Monthly meditations and regular retreats.

Dance Camp Wales Pembrokeshire ✆www .dancecampwales.org. Ten-day dance festival held in August in a beautiful location, with about 500 participants.

Hatha Yoga Retreats Pembrokeshire ☎01994/448369, ✆www.hathayogaretreats.com. Classes and residential retreats in west Wales.

Guide

Southeast Wales

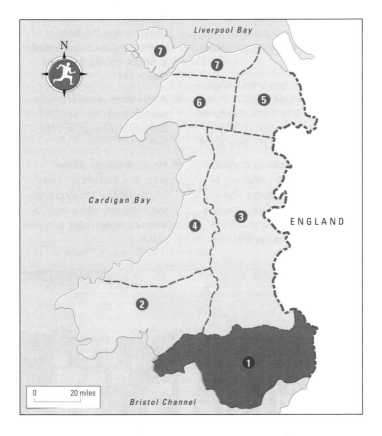

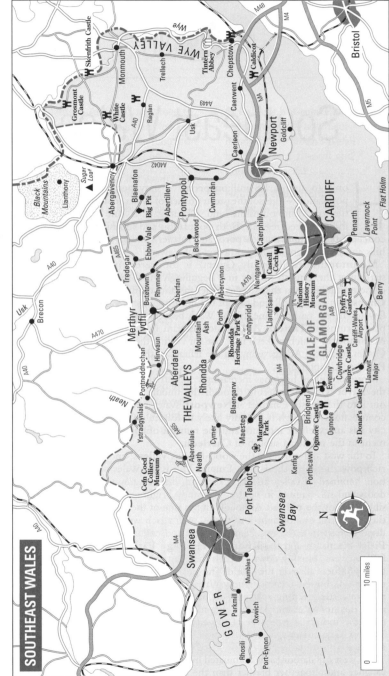

SOUTHEAST WALES

© Crown copyright

◀ Cork

0   10 miles

N

the shape of the new National Waterfront Museum. Like Cardiff, Swansea grew principally on the strength of its docks, and sits on an impressive arc of coast that shelves round from the belching steel works of **Port Talbot** in the east to **Mumbles** and **Oystermouth**, holiday towns of amusement arcades, pubs and chip shops, on the jaw of the delightful **Gower peninsula** in the west. Gower – one of the country's favourite playgrounds – juts out into the sea, a mini-Wales of grand beaches, rocky headlands, bracken heaths and ruined castles.

Getting around

Southeast Wales is by far the easiest part of the country to travel around. Swift new dual carriageways connect with the M4, bringing all corners of the region into close proximity. **Public transport** is similarly thorough: this is the only part of Wales with a half-decent train service, and most suburban and rural services interconnect with Cardiff, Newport or Swansea. Bus services fill in virtually all of the gaps, though often rather slowly.

The Wye Valley

Perhaps the most anglicized corner of Wales, the **Wye Valley** – along with the rest of Monmouthshire – was only finally recognized as part of Wales in the local government reorganization of 1974; before this, the county was officially included as part of neither England nor Wales, so that maps were frequently headlined "Wales and Monmouthshire". In this easterly corner, the two main towns are decidedly English in flavour: **Chepstow**, at the mouth of the Wye, with its massive castle radiating an awesome strength; and **Monmouth**, sixteen miles upstream, a spruce, old-fashioned town with the lingering air of an ancient seat of authority.

Six miles north of Chepstow lie the inspirational ruins of the Cistercian **Tintern Abbey**, worth seeing at odd hours when the crowds of coach-trippers have evaporated. Running parallel to the river, albeit on the English side of the border, the southern segments of the **Offa's Dyke** earthworks are closely followed by a long-distance footpath.

Chepstow

Of all the places that call themselves "the gateway to Wales", the old border town of **CHEPSTOW** (Cas-Gwent) has probably the greatest claim, being the first Welsh town on the main road into the country. Situated on the western bank of the River Wye, just over a mile from where its tidal waters flow out into the muddy Severn estuary, Chepstow is a sturdy, slightly soulless, place with little of the charm or quirkiness of many other Welsh market towns. However, the town's fantastic castle makes Chepstow well worth a stop.

Arrival, information and accommodation

Trains between Cardiff and Birmingham stop at Chepstow's **train station**, five minutes' walk south of the High Street. The town's **bus station** is on Thomas Street on the other side of the West Gate, and has frequent services to Newport but only one every couple of hours to Tintern and Monmouth. The **tourist office** is located in the castle car park, off Bridge Street (daily: Nov–Easter 10am–3.30pm; Easter–Oct 10am–5.30pm; ☎01291/623772, Ⓔ chepstow .tic@monmouthshire.gov.uk). **Accommodation** is not especially abundant, though a few good places do exist.

starts from the castle car park. A map – or a £1 leaflet available from the tourist office – is advisable, as the path tucks and meanders around and above the twisting Wye. You could return along the other side of the river on the Offa's Dyke Path (see p.273), which passes the dramatic viewpoint of Devil's Pulpit (just off the B4228) and reaches its southern end at Sedbury Cliffs, a mile or so east of town on the English side of the border. The Wye Valley Walk brushes past the old Picturesque estate of **Piercefield Park**, a mile north of town, centred on a crumbling Georgian mansion – good for an hour's poking around. Part of the Piercefield estate has metamorphosed into **Chepstow Racecourse** (☎01291/622260, ⓦwww.chepstow-racecourse.co.uk), one of the country's premier racing venues, with regular, year-round meets. The entrance is off the A466 north of town.

Eating and drinking

With a handful of decent **restaurants**, and a few good **pubs**, some by the river, you'll do fine for a night in Chepstow.

Boat Inn The Back. An enormously convivial waterside pub with a good, vegetarian-friendly menu.

Caramelle Patisserie & Chocolatier St Mary's St. First stop for clotted-cream fudge, yogurt-coated dates and the wonderful Sidoli's ice cream.

Castle View Hotel (see p.82). Highly rated hotel restaurant serving succulent meals such as pan-fried red snapper for under £10, and also offering lighter lunches.

Five Alls High St. Genuine local inn with a friendly atmosphere and one of the best pub signs around.

Pizza Express 29 High St ☎01291/630572. A particularly good branch of the ever-reliable chain.

Sitar Balti The Cellar, Beaufort Square ☎01291/627351. Excellent Indian restaurant, specializing in balti lamb and chicken dishes, in the basement of a townhouse. Open every night.

Wye Knot The Back ☎01291/622929. Chepstow's finest, albeit with patchy service. Pricey gourmet meals served on linen tablecloths adorned with fresh flowers. Good fish and vegetarian choices.

Tintern Abbey

Six miles north of Chepstow on one of the River Wye's most spectacular stretches, **Tintern Abbey** (June–Sept daily 9.30am–6pm; April, May & Oct daily 9.30am–5pm; Nov–March Mon–Sat 9.30am–4pm, Sun 11am–4pm; £3.25; CADW) has inspired writers and painters for over two hundred years, ever since the Reverend William Gilpin published a book in 1782 extolling the picturesque qualities of the abbey and its valley. On a quiet day, the sight of the soft, roofless ruins is hugely uplifting; the "tall rock/The mountain, and the deep and gloomy wood" written about by Wordsworth are still evident today. Such is the abbey's enormous popularity, however, that in the middle of a summer's day, the magic can all but evaporate: it is better to go out of season or at the beginning or end of the day when the crowds have thinned out.

The abbey lasted as a monastic settlement from its foundation by the Cistercian order in 1131 to its dissolution in 1536, and the original order of monks was brought wholesale from Normandy, its members establishing themselves as major local landholders and agriculturalists. This increased the power and wealth of the abbey, attracting more monks and necessitating a massive rebuilding and expansion plan in the fourteenth century, when Tintern was at its mightiest. Most of the remaining buildings date from this time, after which the influence of the abbey and its order began to wane. Upon dissolution, many of the buildings were plundered and stripped, leaving the abbey to crumble into advanced decay. Its survival is largely thanks to its remoteness, as there were no nearby villages ready to use the abbey stone for rebuilding. From the eighteenth century onwards, travellers searching for a picturesque rather than religious experience have been attracted to the romantically placed, ivy-clad ruins; and a trip to Tintern was essential for the Romantics – Wordsworth and Turner amongst them.

The centrepiece of the complex was the magnificent Gothic **church**, built at the turn of the fourteenth century to encase its more modest predecessor. The bulk of the building remains, with the remarkable tracery in the west window and intricate stonework of the capitals and columns firmly intact; amazingly, these details withstood both the elements and the efforts of plundering raiders over four hundred years.

Around the church are the less substantial ruins of the **monks' domestic quarters**, mostly reduced to one-storey rubble. Rooms are easily distinguishable, however, including an intact serving hatch in the kitchen and the square of the monks' **cloister**. The course of the abbey's waste disposal system can be seen in the **Great Drain**, an irregular channel that links kitchens, toilets and the infirmary with the nearby Wye. The **Novices' Hall** lies handily close to the Warming House, which, together with the kitchen and infirmary, would have been the only heated parts of the abbey, suggesting that novices might have gained a falsely favourable impression of monastic life before taking their final vows. In the dining hall, you can still see the **pulpit door** that would once have led to the wall-mounted pulpit, from which a monk would read the scriptures throughout each meal.

The best way to appreciate the scale and splendour of the abbey ruins is by taking a walk on the opposite bank of the Wye. Just upstream from the abbey, a bridge crosses the river, from where a path climbs a wooded hillside. Views along the way and from the top are magnificent.

Four miles northwest of the ruins, the sleepy hilltop settlement of **TREL-LECH** (literally "three stones") was one of the largest boroughs in the vicinity. Reminders of its ancient status abound: there's a thirteenth-century steepled church on a seventh-century site, and, nearby, the curious **Tump**, an ancient mound that, legend has it, cannot be disturbed without deadly reprisal. A few hundred yards further south, by the B4293 Llanishen road, are the three **stones** of the village's name. Also known as Harold Stones, the straining fingers of rock, around 3500 years old and thrusting up in the middle of a sheep-filled field, are thought to be aligned with The Skirrid mountain, Monmouthshire's holiest. Off the lane to Tintern, you'll find the **Virtuous Well**, long a place of pilgrimage, with reputed healing qualities that probably stem from the water's high iron content.

Practicalities

Now cluttered with teashops and overpriced hotels, the tiny village of **TINTERN** (Tyndyrn), immediately north of the abbey, is strung along a mile or so of the A466 around a loop of the river. The principal **visitor centre** (April–Oct daily 10.30am–5.30pm; ☎01291/689566) is located another few hundred yards towards Monmouth at the **Old Station** complex. Though you won't want to stay long, there's an interesting exhibition on the old Wye Valley railway and a good selection of leaflets on local walks, including sections of the Offa's Dyke path (see p.273) and cliff rambles above the meandering river. B&B **accommodation** is available locally at the excellent *Parva Farmhouse*, north of the abbey off the main road (☎01291/689411, ⓦwww.hoteltintern .co.uk; ❸) or slap opposite the abbey, in the sumptuously refurbished *Abbey Hotel* (☎01291/689777, ⓦwww.theabbey-hotel.co.uk; ❼). For by far the best pint locally, go to the charming *Cherry Tree*, half a mile up the road that forks off by the 🍴 *Royal George Hotel* in Tintern; as well as beer, it also does great

White Castle

Named for its coating of white rendering (a few patches remain on the exterior walls), **White Castle** (Castell Gwyn; Easter–Sept Wed-Sun 10am–5pm; £2; all other times free access, generally 10am-4pm) lies about eight miles west of Monmouth, just north of the village of Llantilio Crossenny. The most awesome of the three castles, it's situated in open, rolling countryside with some superb views over to The Skirrid mountain (see Chapter 3, p.253). From the grassy Outer Ward, a bridge leads over the moat into the dual-towered Inner Gatehouse, where the western tower, on the right, can be climbed for its vantage point. Here, you can appreciate the scale of the tall twelfth-century curtain walls in the Inner Ward. Of the domestic buildings within the walls, only the foundations and a few inches of wall remain. At the back of the ward, there are massive foundations of the Norman keep, demolished in about 1260 and unearthed in the early part of the twentieth century. The southern wall that took the place of the keep was once the main entrance to the castle, as can be seen in the postern gate in the centre, on the other side of which a bridge leads over to the Hornwork, one of the castle's three original enclosures, although now no more than a grassy mound.

Skenfrith Castle

Seven miles northeast of White Castle, alongside the River Monnow, the thirteenth-century **castle** (unrestricted access), in the centre of the tiny border village of **SKENFRITH** (Ynysgynwraidd), is dominated by the circular keep that replaced an earlier Norman incarnation. While not as impressive as White Castle, Skenfrith is in a pretty riverside setting on the main street of an attractive village.

The castle's walls are built of a sturdy red sandstone in an irregular rectangle. In the centre of the ward is the 21-foot-high round keep, raised slightly on an earth mound to give archers a greater firing range, and containing the vestiges of the private apartments of the castle's lord on the upper floors. The Hall Range of domestic buildings includes an intact thirteenth-century window, complete with its original iron bars.

Grosmont Castle

Five miles upstream of Skenfrith, right on the English border, the most dilapidated of the Three Castles, **Grosmont Castle** (Castell y Grysmwnt; unrestricted access) sits on a small hill above the village of **GROSMONT**. Entering over the wooden bridge above the dry moat, you first pass through the ruins of the two-stage gatehouse. This leads into the small central courtyard, dominated on the right-hand side by the ruins of a large Great Hall, dating from the first decade of the thirteenth century. The village **church** is also worth a look, with some impressive Norman features, most notably the nave arches and the font. A memorial in the nave is popularly believed to be of John Kent, a fifteenth-century bard and magician sometimes believed to have been Owain Glyndŵr in hiding.

Practicalities

Though you can drive around all three castles in a couple of hours, the nature of this peaceful countryside makes a more sedate mode of transport preferable. Bikes can be rented locally (see above and p.251 for Abergavenny) for a pleasant day-long outing, or you can hike the eighteen-mile circuit of paths detailed in a **booklet** (£3.50 from the tourist offices).

Accommodation in the area is sparse but good: half a mile north of White Castle, near the village of **LLANVETHERINE** (Llanwytherin), is the very friendly *Great Tre-Rhew Farm* (☎01873/821268, ⓔtrerhew@btopenworld .com; ❷), where you can also camp for £2 per person. In the nearby village of **LLANGATTOCK LINGOED**, there's a wonderful foodie pub, which also has great rooms, in the shape of the ☘ *Hunter's Moon Inn* (☎01873/821499, ⓦwww.hunters-moon-inn.co.uk; ❸). Yards away is a great B&B in the *Old Rectory* (☎01873/821326; ❷), though the plushest option hereabouts is the eminent gastropub *The Bell* at Skenfrith (☎01600/750235, ⓦwww.skenfrith .com; ❻). If you can't afford to stay there, the three-course dinner at £30 is a very worthwhile treat.

Mid-Monmouthshire

The disputed past of mid-Monmouthshire is obvious from yet more castles that dot the landscape with dependable regularity. Stretching up from the wide-skied marshland that falls gently into the Severn estuary, the land reaches the flat, ugly settlement of **Caldicot**, only notable for its over-restored castle. The A48 runs from the border into south Wales, passing **Caerwent**, a quiet village that was once a great Roman town.

To the north is an undulating land of forests and tiny villages, crisscrossed by winding lanes that offer unexpectedly delightful views – and quaint pubs – around each corner. The contours shelve down in the west to the valley of the **River Usk**, the former border of Wales as decreed in the sixteenth century by Henry VIII. Today, the A449 road roars through the valley, bypassing lanes, villages and the peaceful small town of **Usk**, home of an excellent museum, before joining the A40 near the spectacular ruins of **Raglan** castle.

Caldicot and the Gwent Levels

Sandwiched between the main motorway and rail links between south Wales and London, **CALDICOT** (Cil-y-coed) is a sprawling, overgrown village of modern housing. The only possible diversion is the heavily restored **castle** (March–Oct daily 11am–5pm; £3.50), on the eastern side of the village. Built in the twelfth century as one of the Norman Marcher castles, to keep a wary eye on the Welsh, it crumbled in the years leading up to the 1800s, before being rebuilt by a wealthy Victorian barrister, Joseph Cobb. The only original parts are a large fourteenth-century round tower and elaborate gatehouse, situated either side of a grassy courtyard, whose centrepiece is one of Nelson's battle cannons from his *Foudroyant* flagship. The castle buildings contain an impressive furniture collection from the seventeenth to the nineteenth centuries.

The Gwent Levels

Caldicot is the first sight of Wales for train travellers using the main line from London, and drivers using the second Severn bridge crossing (£4.80 toll westbound only) from Bristol on the English side of the estuary. Recently constructed access roads have, to some degree, eaten into one of Wales' most unexpected landscapes to the southwest of Caldicot: the pancake-flat lushness of the **Gwent Levels**, great for gentle cycling, walking and poking around the tiny villages and ancient churches that loom large on the landscape. The best place to appreciate the area's tranquillity is at **Goldcliff**, a straggle of houses petering out by the mudflats of the estuary. Here, you can walk along the sea walls and watch diving sea birds and fishermen competing for the same catch. A new **wildlife and wetland centre** (open access) can be found just to the west of the village

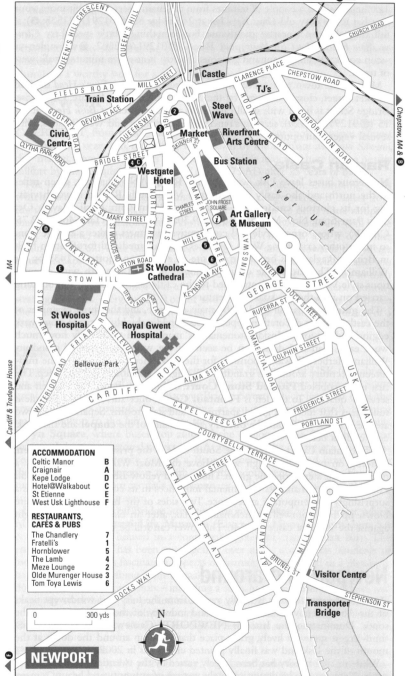

Caerleon & ❶ ▲

CHURCH ROAD

Chepstow, M4 & B ▶

Castle

TJ's

CLARENCE PLACE

CHEPSTOW ROAD

QUEEN'S HILL CRESCENT

QUEEN'S HILL

MILL STREET

FIELDS ROAD

Train Station

DEVON PLACE

GODFREY ROAD

Civic Centre

CLYTHA PARK ROAD

BRIDGE STREET

QUEENSWAY

HIGH ST

RODNEY ROAD

CORPORATION ROAD

Ⓐ

Steel Wave

❷

❸

Market

SKINNER ST

Riverfront Arts Centre

Westgate Hotel

❹ Ⓒ

CAERAU ROAD

BLEWITT STREET

ST MARY STREET

NORTH STREET

STOW HILL

COMMERCIAL STREET

Bus Station

River Usk

YORK PLACE

ST WOOLOS ROAD

CLIFTON ROAD

CHARLES STREET

JOHN FROST SQUARE

Ⓓ

M4 ◀

Ⓔ

STOW HILL

St Woolos' Cathedral

DEWSLAND PARK ROAD

KEYNSHAM AVE

HILL ST

Art Gallery & Museum

ⓘ

❺

❻

KINGSWAY

LOWER DOCK STREET

GEORGE STREET

❼

RUPERRA ST

St Woolos' Hospital

FRIARS ROAD

BELLEVUE LANE

Royal Gwent Hospital

Bellevue Park

ROAD

ALMA STREET

COMMERCIAL ROAD

DOLPHIN STREET

DOCK STREET

USK WAY

Cardiff & Tredegar House ◀

WATERLOO ROAD

STOW PARK AVE

CARDIFF

CAPEL CRESCENT

FREDERICK STREET

PORTLAND ST

COURTYBELLA TERRACE

MENDALGIEF ROAD

LIME STREET

ALEXANDRA ROAD

MILL PARADE

ACCOMMODATION
Celtic Manor   B
Craignair   A
Kepe Lodge   D
Hotel@Walkabout   C
St Etienne   E
West Usk Lighthouse   F

RESTAURANTS, CAFES & PUBS
The Chandler   7
Fratelli's   1
Hornblower   5
The Lamb   4
Meze Lounge   2
Olde Murenger House   3
Tom Toya Lewis   6

0   300 yds

N

DOCKS WAY

BRUNEL ST

Visitor Centre

STEPHENSON ST

Transporter Bridge

Ⓕ ◀

NEWPORT

© Crown copyright

particularly along the river by the monumental **Transporter Bridge**, the scant ruins of the riverside **castle** and, high on a hill above town, the **cathedral** of St Woolos. The superb municipal **museum** draws together the strings of the town's vibrant past, including a memorable and informative section on the nineteenth-century **Chartist movement**, formed to fight for universal franchise. The pearl of the district is **Caerleon** – the "old port" on the River Usk – now little more than a northern suburb of the town, although it predates Newport by at least a thousand years. Its well-preserved remains constitute one of the most important Roman military stations in Britain, though some venerate it more for its reputed association with King Arthur.

The City

Scything the city in two is the River Usk, dank and muddy as the tidal waters flow down to the Severn estuary, three miles away. Wedged in between the rail and main road bridges are the risible remains of the town's **castle**, first built in 1191, rebuilt in the fourteenth century, sacked by Owain Glyndŵr in 1402 and refortified later in the same century.

On the other side of the Newport Bridge, a walkway leads along the river bank past Peter Fink's giant red sculpture, **Steel Wave**, a nod to one of Newport's great industries. Nearby, building work in 2002 on the new Riverfront arts centre revealed the remains of a medieval ship, built in 1465 and currently being restored (see latest plans on ⓦ www.thenewportship.com). The primary route into the city centre proper is up the pedestrianized High Street, which soon meets the main crossroads at Westgate Square. Here stands the **Westgate Hotel**, an ornate Victorian successor to the hotel where soldiers sprayed a crowd of Chartist protesters (see box below) with gunfire in 1839, killing nearly two dozen – the hotel's original pillars still show bullet marks.

Commercial Street, leading south from Westgate Square, is Newport's chief shopping thoroughfare, lined with chain stores, but beautifully framing the famous Transporter Bridge (see below). One hundred yards along Commercial Street, the pedestrianized **John Frost Square** (named after a former mayor and one of the 1839 Chartist leaders) lies to the left. Though little more than an ugly 1960s precinct, it does contain the distinctly quirky **Newport clock**, built for the 1992 Garden Festival at Ebbw Vale, which on the hour shudders, shakes, spits, smokes and comes near to apparent collapse.

In front of the clock is the town's library, tourist office and imaginative, well-presented civic **museum** (Mon–Thurs 9.30am–5pm, Fri 9.30am–4.30pm, Sat

---

The Chartists

In an era when wealthy landowners bought votes from the enfranchised few, the struggles of the **Chartists** were a historical inevitability. Thousands gathered around the 1838 People's Charter that called for universal male franchise, a secret (and annual) ballot for Parliament and the abolition of property qualifications for the vote. Demonstrations in support of these principles were held all over the country, with some of the most vociferous and bloodiest taking place in the radical heartlands of industrial south Wales. On November 4, 1839, Chartists from all over Monmouthshire marched on Newport and descended Stow Hill, whereupon they were gunned at by soldiers hiding in the *Westgate Hotel*, killing around 22 protesters. The leaders of the rebellion were sentenced to death, which was commuted to transportation, by the self-righteous and wealthy leaders of the town. Queen Victoria even knighted the mayor who ordered the arbitrary shooting.

9.30am–4pm; free). Starting with the origins of Gwent, the displays examine the county's original occupants and their lifestyles, and include a section on mining with a roll call of those killed in local pit accidents – 3508 men between 1837 and 1927. Newport's spectacular growth from a small Uskside dock in 1801 with a population of 1000 to a grimy port town of 70,000 people by the early twentieth century is well charted through photographs, paintings and contemporary documents. The two most interesting sections deal with the Chartist uprising and the Roman mosaic remains excavated at Caerwent. The top-floor art gallery contains the **Wait Collection** of Edwardian kitsch, most noted for its three hundred-plus teapots in all shapes and sizes. Before leaving John Frost Square, wander across to the far side to see the impressive Chartist mural which outlines their main grievances on banners.

The other road heading south from Westgate Square is **Stow Hill**, one of Newport's few handsome rows of Victorian and Georgian townhouses. A ten-minute walk up the hill leads to **St Woolos Cathedral**, a curious jigsaw of architectural styles and periods. The tiny, whitewashed twelfth-century Lady Chapel leads through a superb Norman arched doorway – supported by columns reputedly of Roman origin from Caerleon – into the Norman nave, notable for its clerestory windows, bounded by two fifteenth-century aisles. Sporting a circular east window in a swirl of autumn colours locked in a marbled, round-headed arch that harks back to the Norman features, the modern east end of the cathedral harmonizes well with the rest of the building.

Dominating the Newport skyline is the 1906 **Transporter Bridge** (April–Sept Mon–Sat 8am–9.50pm, Sun 1–9pm; Oct–March Mon–Sat 8am–5.50pm, Sun 1–5pm; car toll 50p, free for cyclists and pedestrians), built to enable cars and people to cross the river without disturbing the shipping, by hoisting them high above the Usk on a pristine blue dangling platform. Its comical, spidery legs flare out to the ground, connecting Brunel Street on the west bank and Stephenson Street opposite. Eccentric it may be, but the ride is smooth and the two-minute crossing has successfully cut commuting times for some since the bridge was reopened in the mid-1990s. A small **visitor centre** (April–Sept Wed–Sat & bank holidays 10am–5pm, Sun 1–5pm; Oct–March Sat 10am–5pm, Sun 1–5pm) on the river's west bank elaborates on the bridge's history.

Tredegar House

Buses #15 and #30 go two miles out to the westerly suburbs of Newport and to **Tredegar House** (house Easter–Sept Wed–Sun 11.30am–4pm; park daily 9am–dusk; house tour & gardens £5.40), just off junction 28 of the M4. The home of wealthy local landowners, the Morgan family, from 1402 until 1951, Tredegar and its grounds have been transformed into a recreation park complete with boating and fishing lake and craft workshops. The house itself is an unassuming seventeenth-century pile in warm red brick, built to replace the Morgans' earlier home. Its interior is lavish, with some thirty rooms open. Most memorable is the first-floor Gilt Room: an explosion of glittering fruit bosses, an intricate gilded marble fireplace, mock-walnut panelling and an elaborately painted gold stucco ceiling. The formal walled gardens behind the housekeeper's shop are being relaid in patterns culled from eighteenth-century designs.

Practicalities

Newport's **tourist office** is in the museum complex on John Frost Square (Mon–Sat 9.30am–5pm; ☎01633/842962, ✆newport.tic@newport.gov.uk), a hundred yards from the **bus station** on Kingsway and a quarter-mile from the **train station** on Queensway.

The range of **accommodation** in Newport is limited, and you might prefer to stay in nearby Caerleon. If you want to be central, the *Hotel@Walkabout* (formerly the *Queen's Hotel*), 19 Bridge St (℡01633/235990, ⓦwww.walkabout .eu.com; ❸), is modern and reasonable, if pretty noisy at times. For B&B, there's the cheap and fairly cheerful *Craignair* at 44 Corporation Rd (℡01633/259903; ❷) and the genteel *St Etienne*, 162 Stow Hill (℡01633/262341; ❸). At the western end of Bridge Street, Caerau Road rises up sharply to the south, passing the relaxed, hospitable *Kepe Lodge* at no. 46a (℡01633/262351; ❸). Newport's ritziest hotel is the five-star *Celtic Manor* (℡01633/413000, ⓦwww .celtic-manor.com; ❸), high above junction 24 of the M4 at the eastern approach to the city. With its accompanying golf course, the hotel has been chosen as the venue for the Ryder Cup in 2010. For a more ethereal stay, the *West Usk Lighthouse* (℡01633/810126, ⓦwww.westusklighthouse.co.uk; ❻) offers strikingly unusual B&B, together with a floatation tank and all manner of holistic therapies. It's at the mouth of the Usk on the western bank, beyond the suburb of Duffryn. There's a **campsite** at Tredegar House (see above; ℡01633/815600; £10 per pitch).

There are lots of chain **food** outlets along Bridge and Commercial streets, but downtown is pretty much a culinary desert. *The Chandlery*, on the edge of the city centre at 77-79 Lower Dock St (℡01633/256622) is a smart new city restaurant that can be excellent, although it sometimes seems like a triumph of style over substance. ⚑ *Fratelli's*, at 173 Caerleon Rd (℡01633/264602; closed Sun & Mon), is easily the finest of the city's many Italian restaurants. For coffee and a light snack, try the *Oriel* café on the top floor of the museum, from where you can view the hourly antics of the Newport Clock. Stylish snacks are available throughout the day at the trendy *Meze Lounge* bar, 6 Market St, which becomes a venue for live music and DJs in the evening.

Despite the profusion of **pubs**, none is terribly special: the 1530 *Olde Murenger House*, on the High Street, is one of the best, with a beautiful Tudor frontage and a recently refurbished interior. Otherwise, try Wetherspoon's enormous *Tom Toya Lewis* at 108-112 Commercial St, the cosy *Lamb* at 6 Bridge St or the raucous bikers' bar, the *Hornblower*, at 127 Commercial St.

Newport is one of the centres of the buoyant Welsh **rock and dance music** scene – this is, after all, the city that produced gloriously daft hip-hop outfit Goldie Lookin' Chain. The legendary try-out pub venue, *TJ's*, over the river from the castle at 14 Clarence Place (℡01633/216608, ⓦwww.tjs-newport .demon.co.uk), has seen better days, but is still worth checking out. For late-night dancing try the youthful *Voodoo* on Bridge Street (℡01633/213138), the older *Zanzibar* (℡01633/250978) at 40 Stow Hill, the studenty *Cotton Club* (℡01633/252973) on Cambrian Road, or the more chilled-out *Meze Lounge* (see above).

Caerleon

Frequent buses wind their way along the three-mile journey north of Newport to **CAERLEON** (Caerllion), whose compact town centre is situated to the northwest of the town bridge over the River Usk. The remnants of the Roman town lie scattered throughout the present-day centre.

It was the Usk (Wysg) that gave Caerleon its old Roman name of Isca, a major administrative and legionary centre built by the Romans to provide ancillary and military services for smaller, outlying camps in the rest of south

Wales. Its only near equivalents in Roman Britain were Chester, servicing north Wales and northwest England, and York, dealing with the Roman outposts up towards Hadrian's Wall and beyond. Founded in 74 AD and lasting until its abandonment late in the fourth century, Isca was a garrison housing up to six thousand members of the Second Augustan Legion in a neat, rectangular walled town. Although the settlement fell gradually into decay after the Romans left, there were still some massive remains standing when itinerant churchman and chronicler Giraldus Cambrensis visited in 1188. In his effusive writing about the remains, he noted with evident relish the "immense palaces, which, with the gilded gables of their roofs, once rivalled the magnificence of ancient Rome". Although time has had an inevitably corrosive effect on the remains since Giraldus' time, the excavated bath house and preserved amphitheatre still retain a powerful sense of ancient history.

At the back of the *Bull Inn* car park are the Roman **fortress baths** (Easter–Oct daily 9.30am–5pm; Nov–Easter Mon–Sat 9.30am–5pm, Sun 11am–4pm; £2.50; CADW). The bathing houses, cold hall, drain (in which teeth, buttons and food remnants were found) and communal pool area are remarkably intact and beautifully presented, using audiovisual equipment, sound commentary and models. A few steps along the High Street, a Victorian Neoclassical portico is the sole survivor of the original **Legionary Museum** (Mon–Sat 10am–5pm, Sun 2–5pm; free), now housed in the modern building behind. There are hundreds of artefacts dug from the remains of Isca and a smaller fortress at nearby Burrium (Usk). These include intricately carved gemstones, lamps, tools, dental equipment, belt buckles, soldiers' amulets, dice, game counters and personal hygiene items such as tweezers and nail cleaners. The museum's new

King Arthur

King Arthur is a name frequently invoked in Wales, whether in books of history and folklore or in dozens of placenames on the map (only the Devil has more places named after him across Britain!). He has become one of the greatest Celtic allegories, a figure to be invoked for all manner of causes and one claimed by almost every part of the British Isles, but the earliest and strongest evidence for the reality of Arthur comes indisputably from Wales.

The first mention of King Arthur came around 800 AD in the *Historia Britonum* (History of the British), by the Welsh monk Nennius. Three centuries later, his compatriot Geoffrey of Monmouth used this work, amongst others, as the source material for his magisterial twelve-volume *Historia Regum Britanniae* (History of the Kings of Britain), in which he writes that Arthur was a sixth-century Celtic British king who defeated the invading Saxon army in the turbulent decades after the departure of the Romans. From sparse, semi-factual beginnings, epic stories developed. Arthur became an idealized medieval European knight, a totem of Celtic resistance and supernatural powers.

Arthur's court was known as **Camelot**, and many places have laid claim to it. One of the strongest contenders (mentioned by Geoffrey in the twelfth century and much augmented by later Romantic poets such as Tennyson) was Caerleon. Other claims have placed Camelot near Llangollen, and in England at Glastonbury, Winchester and in Cornwall.

Interest in Arthur is at an all-time high, and shows no sign of abating. There are dozens of areas of Wales with Arthurian associations, and books abound with further information. The best, with some great practical walks to get you to the remotest spots, is Laurence Main's *In the Footsteps of King Arthur* (Western Mail Publications, £7.95).

△ King Arthur

Capricorn Centre, although aimed squarely at school parties, is interesting for the re-created Roman barracks where you can try on a typical soldier's armour.

Opposite the Legionary Museum, Fosse Lane leads down to the hugely atmospheric Roman **amphitheatre** (unrestricted access), the only one of its kind preserved in Britain. Hidden under a grassy mound called King Arthur's Round Table until excavation work brought it to light in the 1920s, the amphitheatre was built around 80 AD, the same time as the Colosseum in Rome; legions of up to six thousand would take seats to watch the gory combat of gladiators, animal baiting or military exercises. The amphitheatre is backed by grassy stepped walls, on which the members of the legion would sit, tightly packed in, to watch activities in the middle. Over the road, alongside the school playing fields, are the scant foundations of the legion's **barracks**.

The belief that Caerleon was the seat of King Arthur's court is a long-standing one. Lord Tennyson came here to research the rumours, and today, you can do no better than wander around the sublime **Ffwrrwm Centre** (most shops daily 9.30am–5.30pm), off the High Street, and talk to the various traders there who subscribe passionately to the belief. Whatever, the Ffwrrwm is a very special place: stunning courtyard sculptures draw their inspiration from ancient Celtic and Arthurian lore, surrounded by some great craft and New Age shops and a wonderful café-cum-bistro. Near the entrance to the complex, you can even clasp the gold horns of a Welsh fertility bull, an act that is supposed to lend you untold powers of procreation.

Practicalities

Caerleon's **tourist office** (daily: April–Oct 10am–6pm, Nov–March 10am–4pm; ☎01633/422656, ✉caerleon.tic@newport.gov.uk) is beside the legionary museum on High Street. More esoteric information can be found in the various outlets in the Ffwrrwm Centre (see above), notably in the gateside antique shop and the Awen Celtic Spirit shop.

As a result of the formidable terrain, each valley was almost entirely isolated. Canals, roads and train lines competed for space along the valley floor, petering out as the contours became untameable at the upper end. Not until the 1920s were any connecting roads built, and even today, transport is frequently restricted to the valley bottoms, with roads and train lines radiating out through the south Wales coalfield like spokes on a giant wheel. For a good mix of urban and rural, the Valleys offer one of the best areas of Wales for an unforgettable **walking** holiday. Paths are best on the high ridges between valleys.

This section covers the Monmouthshire and Glamorgan valleys from Pontypool in the east to Cwm Afan and Port Talbot in the west. For the account of the Vale of Neath, see p.146.

Some history

The land beneath the inhospitable hills of the south Wales valleys had some of the most abundant and accessible natural seams of **coal** and **iron ore** in the world, readily milked in the boom years of the nineteenth and early twentieth centuries. In many instances, wealthy English capitalists came to Wales and ruthlessly stripped the land of its natural assets, while paying paltry amounts to those who risked life and limb in the mines. The **mine owners** were in a formidably strong position – thousands of Welsh peasants, bolstered by their Irish, Scottish and Italian peers, flocked to the Valleys in search of work and some sort of sustainable life. The Valleys – virtually unpopulated at the start of the nineteenth century – became blackened with soot and packed with people, pits and chapels by the beginning of the twentieth.

In 1920, there were 256,000 men working in the 620 mines of the south Wales coalfield, providing one-third of the world's coal resources. Vast **Miners' Institutes**, paid for by a wages' levy, jostled for position with the Nonconformist chapels, whose muscular brand of Christianity was matched by the zeal of the region's politics, trade-union-led and avowedly left-wing. Great socialist orators rose to national prominence, cementing the Valleys' reputation as a world apart from the rest of Wales, let alone Britain. Even Britain's pioneering National Health Service, founded by a radical Labour government in the years following World War II, was based on a Valleys community scheme by locally born **Aneurin Bevan**.

The Valleys' **decline** has taken place in rapid bursts, with over half of the original pits closing in the harsh economic climate of the 1930s. World War II saw a brief respite in the closure programme, which continued even more swiftly in the years immediately after. As coal seams have been exhausted and the political climate has shifted, the number of men employed in the industry has dipped down into four figures, precipitated by the aftermath of the **1984–85 miners' strike**. No coalfield was as solidly behind the strike as south Wales, whose workers and families responded wholeheartedly to the call to defend the industry which their trade union, the National Union of Mineworkers (NUM), claimed was on the brink of being decimated. The year-long war of attrition between the Thatcher government and Arthur Scargill's NUM was bitter, finally seeing the government victorious as the number of miners returning to work outnumbered those staying out on strike. Over twenty years on, and all but one of the south Wales pits have closed, the sole survivor having been reprieved in 1994 and run as a workers' co-operative ever since.

The Valleys without coal seemed unthinkable, but nonetheless, some of the larger, better-populated valleys have staged considerable recoveries: high-tech industries have moved into industrial estates hewn out of smoothed-out slag heaps, museums have been established at the old pit sites and civic amenities such as sports and arts centres are springing up all over the place. The Valleys' proximity to Wales' big cities has brought in new money, particularly in property in the ever-smarter towns. Well-heeled city commuters are thick on the ground these days, as can be seen in the flashy new pubs, restaurants and ubiquitous Tesco superstores emerging throughout the area.

Pontypool

The first identifiably Valleys town – although never a coal-mining centre – heading west is **PONTYPOOL** (Pontypŵl), on the Llwyd River that winds up from the Usk at Caerleon. A sprawling, hilly town, it's hardly likely to keep you busy for long, although it's worth finding time for a short stop at the **Pontypool Museum** (Mon–Fri 9.30am–4.30pm, Sat & Sun 2–5pm; £1.20, free Wed & Sun), housed in a Georgian stable block at the western entrance of Pontypool Park. The building was part of the estate of a mansion belonging to the Hanbury family, local landowners and industrial pioneers, and the museum casts a wide net over the town's history and trades, all of which seems to have sprung from this one family. Founding father Richard Hanbury (1538–1608), the exhibition dryly notes, was a true entrepreneur, "but on occasion his enterprise led to prison sentences for fraud". The Hanburys established Pontypool's staple tinplate-making industry, which led, in turn, to elaborate japanning (of which the museum has many examples) and thence to ironworking. The museum makes a good starting point for a stiff but short hike up through the park to a couple of products of Victorian whimsy (both May to early Sept Sat, Sun & bank holidays 2–5pm; free): the **Shell Grotto** (30min), with its interior completely plastered in molluscs; and the more traditional **Folly Tower** (20min further).

Pontypool's handsome town centre is a stone's throw from the museum: over the river and up onto the main shopping streets. The **market hall** here is great for fresh food and some oddball stalls.

The **train station** is inconveniently situated over a mile to the east of the town centre, making **buses**, which stop by the handsome Victorian town hall, a far better option. The hourly (Mon–Sat) #18 service will take you to **Griffithstown**, a mile south of the town centre, home of a superb **railway museum** (daily 10am–5pm; £1) on Station Road. Housed in an old goods shed, the museum is one man's life collection of memorabilia, mainly from the extensive local network, most of which has long gone. Together with his own model railway upstairs, it's fascinating stuff.

If you want to stay round these parts, there's a lovely farmhouse B&B in the village of **MAMHILAD**, a couple of miles north of Pontypool by the Monmouth & Brecon Canal. *Tŷ Cooke Farm* (☏01873/880382; ❸) is a great base, and handy for the village's wonderful *Star Inn*.

Blaenafon and around

Road and river continue six miles north from Pontypool to the iron and coal town of **BLAENAFON** (or Blaenavon), at the source of the Llwyd River. With a lofty hillside position making it feel far less claustrophobic, Blaenafon has a very different feel to many valley towns, but its decline is testified by a population of little more than 5000, a third of its nineteenth-century size. It's a spirited and evocative place, a fact recognized when it gained UNESCO World Heritage Site status in 2000. The town's Victorian boom can be seen in its architecture, most notably the impressively florid **Working Men's Hall** that dominates the town centre, and where miners would pay a halfpenny a week for the use of the library and other recreational and educational facilities. The parish **church of St Peter** is a good example of what became known as Enginehouse Churches – an enginehouse being the sole type of building familiar to local masons. If it's open, wander in to see the tomb covers, pillars and even the font, all fashioned out of iron.

On one day in June 2003, nine new bookshops opened in Blaenafon, part of a local drive to establish the place as Wales' newest **book town**. Although it's not a patch on the variety you'll find in Hay-on-Wye, Blaenafon is a great stop for bibliophiles, with the shops covering a wide range of specialisms. For more details, visit the website (Ⓦwww.booktownblaenafon.com) or, when in town, call in at Blaenafon Books, 71–72 Broad St (Mon–Sat 10am–5pm).

Blaenafon's **tourist office** just off the Brynmawr Road (Easter–Oct Mon–Fri 9.30am–4.30pm, Sat 10am–5pm, Sun 10am–4.30pm; ℡01495/792615, Ⓦwww.blaenavontic.com), shares a building with the town's **ironworks** (same hours and phone; £2; group tours all year, minimum £20; CADW). Though the works were founded in 1788, iron smelting in this area dates from the sixteenth century. Limestone, coal and iron ore – ingredients for successful iron smelting – were locally abundant, and during the early nineteenth century, the Blaenafon works grew to become one of the largest in Britain, finally closing in 1900. The remains of the site offer a thorough picture both of the process to produce iron and the workers' lifestyles that went with it. At the **museum**, housed in the Stack Square cottages (built for the foremen and craftsmen between 1789 and 1792), there are exhibitions on the history of iron- and steel-making in the Llwyd Valley.

Big Pit

Just as it is now possible to visit the scene of Blaenafon's iron industry, the town's defunct coal trade has also been smoothly transformed into a tourist attraction: the **Big Pit National Mining Museum** (mid-Feb–Nov daily 9.30am–5pm; last underground tour 3.30pm; free) lies three-quarters of a mile west of the town in wide, open countryside; a half-hourly shuttle bus runs from Blaenafon. The colliery closed exactly a century after its 1880 opening. Of all the mining museums in south Wales, Big Pit brings the visitor closest to the experience of a miner's work and life, as you descend 300ft, kitted out with lamp, helmet and very heavy battery pack, into the labyrinth of shafts and coal faces for a guided tour. The guides – most of whom are ex-miners – lead you through explanations and examples of the different types of coal mining, from the old stack-and-pillar operation, where miners would manually hack into the coal face before propping up the ceiling with a wooden beam, to more modern mechanically worked seams. Constant streams of rust-coloured water flow by, adding to the dank and chilly atmosphere that must have terrified the small children who were once paid twopence for a six-day week (of which one penny was subtracted for the cost of their candles) pulling the coal wagons along the tracks. Back on the surface, the old pithead baths, blacksmiths, miners' canteen and winding engine house have all been preserved and filled with some fascinating displays about the local and south Wales mining industries, including a series of characteristically feisty testimonies from the miners made redundant here in 1980.

Blaenafon makes a great base for exploring the area, with good B&B **accommodation** at the smart new extension to the *Rifleman's Arms* on Rifle Street (℡01495/792297; ➍), off the Abergavenny Road. On the main Broad Street, the effusive ⚔ *Red Rooster Café* at no. 23 (℡01495/791840; ➌) has three smart rooms and is also one of the best places for daytime **food.** In the evenings, you're best off eating in **pubs** such as the *Queen Victoria* on Prince Street (which also has regular live music) or the *Rifleman's Arms* (see above). A mile or so out of town are two great pubs, both serving food: the mining memorabilia-filled *Whistle Inn*, off the road to Brynmawr, and down the lane off the Abergavenny Road to the north (on the Blorenge mountain), the atmospheric *Lamb & Flag*, sole survivor of the demolished pit village of Pwll-du.

Ebbw Vale

West of Pontypool and Blaenafon, the settlements of the **Ebbw Vale** are hemmed in by some of the Valleys' best forest scenery. Particularly popular is the **Cwmcarn Forest Drive** (Easter–Aug daily 11am–7pm, 9pm July & Aug weekends; Sept daily 11am–6pm; March & Oct daily 11am–5pm; Nov Sat & Sun 11am–4pm; £3 per car), reached from the main A467 in **Cwmcarn** village, two miles north of Risca. The seven-mile route includes superb views, kids' play areas, a decent visitor centre, an Iron Age hillfort, mountain bike trails and a good, grassy **campsite** (℡01495/272001) where you can pitch a tent for £6 (£7.50 in July & Aug).

The Ebbw Valley divides in two just short of **ABERTILLERY** (Abertyleri), a classic Valleys town of scruffy, vertiginous streets rising up from the Ebbw Fach River. The town's **museum** (Mon–Thurs 10am–1pm & 2–4pm, Fri & Sat 10am–1pm; free), in an old theatre on Market Street, offers an eminently browsable ramble through local history, with an emphasis on the social conditions of the miners. You might consider continuing through to the sprawling upland settlement of **NANTYGLO**, four miles north. Signposted on the western edge of the town are two remarkable fortified **roundhouses**, now in a sorry state of disrepair. They were built in the nineteenth century by local ironmaster Joseph Bailey, an English Anglican renowned for his harsh treatment of workers. Bailey was fearful enough of insurrection to build these mini-castles in 1816, complete with four-feet-thick walls and iron plate doors with musket holes.

The other branch of the Ebbw Vale, including the eponymous town, **Ebbw Vale** (Glyn Ebwy), has little to detain you. The town in particular, is a forlorn place since the final closure of its massive steelworks in 2002. Even the site of the memorable 1992 Garden Festival, the last of a series designed to regenerate hard-hit parts of Britain, is now just a cheesy shopping mall. It's to be hoped that the imminent revival of the Ebbw Vale's passenger railway should help matters.

Caerphilly and the Rhymney Valley

Travelling west, the next major settlement is **CAERPHILLY** (Caerffili), seven miles north of Cardiff and at the foot of the **Rhymney Valley**. The town, now almost a Cardiff suburb, has smartened itself up in recent years, particularly the area around its staggering town-centre **castle** (Easter-May & Oct daily 9.30am–5pm; June–Sept daily 9.30am–6pm; Nov–March Mon–Sat 9.30am–4pm, Sun 11am–4pm; £3; CADW), looming out of its vast surrounding **moat**. The castle is striking for its sheer bulk and for being the first in Britain to be built concentrically. Occupying over thirty acres, the medieval fortress with its cock-eyed tower presents an awesome promise that's not, however, entirely fulfilled inside. Built on the site of a Roman fort and an earlier Norman fortification, the castle was begun in 1268 by Gilbert de Clare, who wanted to protect the vulnerable coastal plains around Cardiff from the warring of Llywelyn the Last. For the next few hundred years, Caerphilly was little more than a decaying toy, given at whim by kings to their favourites – most notably by Edward II to his minion, and some say lover, Hugh le Despenser, in 1317. The Civil War necessitated the building of an armoury within the castle, which prompted Cromwell to seize it, drain the moat and blow up the towers. By the early twentieth century, Caerphilly Castle was in a sorry state, sitting amidst a growing industrial town that saw fit to build in the moat and the castle precincts. Houses and shops were demolished to allow the moat to be reflooded in 1958.

You enter the castle through a great **gatehouse** that punctuates the barbican wall by a lake, much restored and now housing an exhibition about the castle's history. A platform behind the barbican wall exhibits medieval war and siege engines, pointing ominously across the lake. From here, a bridge crosses the moat, part of the wider lake, to the outer wall of the castle itself, behind which sits the hulking inner ward. On the left is the southeastern leaning tower, with a great cleft in its walls where Cromwell's men are said to have attempted to blow it sky high. It now seems that Cromwell had less to do with the tilt than common old subsidence, but the story is too good to pass up. With the exception of the ruined northeastern tower, the other corner turrets have been blandly restored since the Civil War, with the northwestern tower housing a reasonably interesting exhibition on Welsh castles, their methods of construction and some speculative facts and figures about the day-to-day life of their medieval inhabitants. More interesting is the massive eastern gatehouse, which includes an impressive upper hall and oratory and, to its left, the wholly restored and reroofed **Great Hall**, largely built around 1317 by Hugh le Despenser.

Caerphilly is also, of course, known for its crumbly white **cheese**, which is made the traditional way at several dairies around town and sold in the shop below the **tourist office**, opposite the castle entrance in Lower Twyn Square (daily: Jan–Easter 10am–5pm; Easter–Oct 10am–6pm; Nov & Dec 10am–5pm; ☎029/2088 0011, ✉tic@caerphilly.gov.uk). Both the castle and the tourist office are a five-minute stroll down Cardiff Road from the **bus** and **train stations**. You're unlikely to want to stay here: Caerphilly is best as a day-trip from Cardiff. There are plenty of **eating** options in town, none hugely special. The view of the castle alone makes a stop in the *Courthouse* inn on Cardiff Road, behind the NatWest bank, worthwhile, though you can also partake of its predictable menu of chain pub classics. For the best Caerphilly cheese Welsh Rarebit in town, go to *Glanmor's Tearooms*, facing the castle on the edge of the Castle Court shopping precinct.

The Rhymney Valley

North of Caerphilly, the Rhymney Valley becomes increasingly industrialized as it steers past a seamless succession of small towns. Ten miles up the valley from Caerphilly is **NEW TREDEGAR**, where the **Elliot Colliery Winding House** (Easter–Sept Wed–Fri 11am–4pm, Sat, Sun & bank holidays 2–5pm; free), with its gleaming steam engine that once powered the colliery's high-speed lifts, is worth a visit. It's on White Rose Way, a ten-minute walk from Tir-phil station.

At the head of the valley, a mile beyond Rhymney town and just short of the A465 Heads of the Valleys road, **BUTETOWN** (Drenewydd) is a tiny settlement unlike any other in the area. Built as a model workers' estate in 1802–03 by the Marquess of Bute, a member of Wales' richest land- and minerals-owning family, it was originally conceived as the beginning of a whole new, airy workers' community. His idealism was unusual amongst the ironmasters and coal owners of the day and, sadly, only the central grid of houses was built. Two ironworkers' cottages in the main street have been converted into **Drenewydd museum** (Easter–Sept Sat, Sun & bank holidays 2–5pm; £1; other times by appointment on $\textcircled{T}$029/2088 0011), a small local affair detailing life for nineteenth-century employees, which was still arduous despite the uplifting surroundings.

A mile east of Butetown, the **Bryn Bach Country Park**, on the northern edge of the close-knit little town of **TREDEGAR**, has an attractive **campsite** by a small lake, with showers and a visitor-centre-cum-café. There's also a great independent **hostel** in the middle of Tredegar – the *Hobo Backpackers* ($\textcircled{T}$01495/718422, $\textcircled{W}$www.hobo-backpackers.com; beds £12.50) on Morgan Street, just down from the town clock. On the same street is the parkland of **Bedwellty House**, a Georgian mansion built for the local ironmaster. In the grounds you'll find an arboretum, icehouse, long arcade and the world's largest lump of coal, a fifteen-ton block exhibited as part of the 1951 Festival of Britain.

The Taff and Cynon valleys

Like the River Rhymney, the River Taff also flows out into the Bristol Channel at Cardiff, after passing through a condensed 25 or so miles of industry and population that obscure the former **china works** at Nantgarw. The first town in the Taff Vale is **Pontypridd**, one of the most cheerful in the Valleys, and where the Rhondda River hives off west. Continuing north, the river splits again at **Abercynon**, where the Cynon River flows in from **Aberdare**, site of Wales' only remaining deep mine. Just outside Abercynon is the enjoyable sixteenth-century **Llancaiach Fawr** manor house, while to the north, the Taff is packed into one of the tightest of all the valleys, passing **Aberfan** five miles short of the imposing valley head town of **Merthyr Tydfil**.

Nantgarw

Barrelling north along the A470, you'd never suspect that the **China Works Museum** (Tues–Sun 10am–5pm; £1) lurks behind a copse of trees just by the junction for **NANTGARW**. For less than five years in the 1810s, the pottery here produced some of the finest porcelain in the world, the few florid examples on display only serving to whet your appetite for the extensive collection in the National Museum in Cardiff. Master porcelain painter William Billingsley set up the works with high ambition using Valleys coal and Cornish clay, but the extremely difficult "soft paste porcelain" process resulted in just a ten-percent firing success rate and the enterprise soon folded. One of the firing kilns has now been rebuilt and the main building contains small displays on the process and the history of the site.

Just up the road, on Heol Crochendy, is the **Collections Centre of the National Museum of Wales** ($\textcircled{T}$029/2057 3560), basically a huge store for all that isn't on show at any of the museum's seven sites. Visitors are welcome, but you must telephone for an appointment first.

Pontypridd

PONTYPRIDD's quirky arched **bridge** of 1775 was once the largest single-span stone bridge in Europe. It was built by local amateur stonemason William Edwards, whose previous attempts had crumbled into the river below. His final effort stands to this day, its three holes either side designed to lessen the bridge's overall weight and allow gusty winds through.

On the far side of the river from the town centre is **Ynysangharad Park**, where Sir W. Goscombe John's cloying double statue and tomb in honour of Pontypridd weaver Evan James and his son represents allegorical figures of music and poetry. In 1856, James composed the stirring *Hen Wlad Fy Nhadau* (*Land of My Fathers*) that became the Welsh national anthem.

Brychan, Prince of Brycheiniog, was captured as she rode through the area, and murdered for her Christian beliefs. She became St Tydfil the Martyr, and her name was bestowed on the scattered population of the area.

In the seventeenth century, the village became a focal point for Dissenters and Radicals, movements which, through poverty and oppression, gained momentum in the eighteenth century as the town's four massive ironworks were founded to exploit locally abundant seams of iron ore and limestone. Merthyr became the largest iron-producing town in the world, as well as by far the most populous town in Wales: in 1831, the town had a population of 60,000, more than Cardiff, Swansea and Newport combined. Workers flocked from all over Britain and beyond, finding themselves crammed into squalid housing whilst the ironmasters built themselves great houses and palaces on the better side of town. Merthyr's **radicalism** bubbled furiously, breaking out into occasional riots and prompting the election of Britain's first socialist MP, Keir Hardie, in 1900. It was here that the red flag was first raised, when rioters in 1831 gathered around a standard dipped in the blood of a killed calf.

However, the town's precipitous development saw it peak and trough earlier than anywhere else: of the four mighty ironworks, only one was still open at the end of World War I, and that closed in the 1930s. In 1939, a Royal Commission suggested that the town be abandoned and the inhabitants shifted to the coast. The plan was forgotten when war broke out.

The Town

The town centre is wedged in between the High Street and the River Taff, but the sights listed here are all around the Taff to the immediate northwest. The **Ynysfach Engine House** was once the powerhouse behind the mighty Cyfartha ironworks. It's now been opened up to the public – to arrange access, call the castle (see below); you'll pay £1 to enter – with costumed mannequins portraying scenes from Merthyr's past as a centre of iron and steel making, and an entertaining video about the town's industrial history.

Half a mile further up the River Taff, tucked amongst modern houses just off the A4102 (Bethesda Street), is **Chapel Row**, a line of skilled ironworkers' cottages built in the 1820s. One of these holds composer **Joseph Parry's Birthplace** (April–Sept Thurs–Sun 2–5pm; free), though this mini-museum is most interesting as a social record of slightly better-than-average workers' domestic conditions of the nineteenth century. Parry's music, including the national favourite *Myfanwy*, is piped between rooms, and the upstairs section of the house is given over to a display of his life and music.

Back across the other side of the river, just beyond the Brecon Road, is a home in absolute contrast to Parry's humble and cramped birthplace: **Cyfartha Castle** (April–Sept daily 10am–5.30pm; Oct–March Tues–Fri 10am–4pm, Sat & Sun noon–4pm; free). Built in 1825 as an ostentatious mock-Gothic castle for William Crawshay II, boss of the town's original ironworks, it's set within an attractive, 160-acre park that slopes down to the river and once afforded Crawshay a permanent view over his iron empire. Cyfartha's current incarnation, though, is as a museum, and a great one at that. You start in a well re-created Valleys Italian café on the ground floor; Italian emigrants flocked to south Wales in the nineteenth century, many shunning mining and opening quite grand, chrome-plated coffee houses that became legendary in the region. You then go downstairs into the old wine cellars for a gutsy history of the town. Starting with tales of the martyr Tydfil, the Penydarren Roman fort and ruined Morlais Castle, the narrative soon leads into Merthyr's industrial and political heritage. Merthyr's place in working-class history is well examined, with an interesting set of panels and pamphlets on the 1831 riot. Other exhibits examine Aberfan, the 1984–85 miners' strike, pubs and the temperance movement as well as the beleaguered 1980s Sinclair C5 car, constructed here at the Hoover plant – "built by Hoover, driven by suckers" as the local phrase memorably had it.

Upstairs, the castle's opulent main rooms, all chandeliers and acres of curtains, now house a superb collection of Welsh and international **art**. Welsh highlights include an uncharacteristically gentle study of *The Elf* by monumental sculptor Goscombe John, and works by local painters Penry Williams, Augustus John, Cedric Morris, Kyffin Williams and Alfred Jones, whose double portrait of Salome is quite mesmerizing.

The surrounding **park** contains landscaped walks, a plant nursery, café, bowling green, tennis courts, a pitch-and-putt course and a stage set next to the main lake.

Practicalities

The **train station** lies east of the town centre, a minute's walk from High Street. North from here is Glebeland Street and the **bus station**, where services depart for all parts of south and mid-Wales. The **tourist office**, 14a Glebeland St (April–Sept Mon–Sat 9.30am–5.30pm; Oct–March Mon–Sat 10am–5pm; ℡01685/379884, @tic@merthyr.gov.uk.), is behind the bus station. The nearest **bike rental** is from the Garwnant visitor centre, off the A470 five miles north of town (℡01685/723060).

Accommodation is varied, ranging from the plush *Tregenna Hotel* in Park Terrace, next to Penydarren Park (℡01685/723627, ⓌWwww.tregennahotel .co.uk; ❹), to the less fussy *Chaplin's*, 30-31 High St (℡01685/387272, Ⓦwww .chaplinshotel.co.uk; ❸), and, cheapest of all, the *Penylan* guesthouse, 12 Courtland Terrace (℡01685/723179; ❶). There's a **campsite** four miles north of town in the beautiful surroundings of *Grawen Farm*, Cwm Taf (℡01685/723740; £8–12 per pitch).

There are plenty of daytime **food** outlets in the main shopping area of the town centre, with a few cafés and Chinese and Indian restaurants open into the evening along the High Street. *Chaplin's* (see above) is pretty good for standard bistro fare, or there's reasonable beer and food at Wetherspoons' *Dic Penderyn* at nos. 102–3. At the bottom of the High Street, the friendly *Fountain Tearooms* does nice sandwiches and cappuccino. You could also try the historic *Three Horseshoes Inn* on Dynevor Street, where up to three hundred Chartists once crammed into the small bar. Either of these will also prove amenable for a night's **drinking**, as will the sporty *Rose & Crown* on Morgan Street, up towards Cyfartha Park.

The Rhondda

For many people, the twin valleys of the **Rhondda** – each sixteen miles long and never as much as a mile wide – are the essence of all that the region stands for. Others may disagree, but the Rhondda was certainly the heart of the massive south Wales coal industry, an industry that provided around one-third of the entire world's coal, and it's here that you'll find the region's quintessential heritage distilled into tight-knit hillside communities. Hollywood played its part in romanticizing the area, with the 1947 Oscar-winning weepie *How Green Was My Valley*, although the story was based on author Richard Llewellyn's early life in nearby Gilfach Goch, outside the valley.

In 1841, Rhondda was a rural backwater with a population of less than a thousand. Coal was found soon after, and by 1924, 167,000 people were miners, connecting Treherbert to the forests and lakes of Hirwaun Common en route to Brecon.

Spectacular **walks** abound in the Rhondda. A mildly difficult two-mile hike from Blaencwm, for instance, leads to the remarkable mound of **Penpych**, sitting sentinel over the Rhondda Fawr, while a diversion east at Ferndale in the Rhondda Fach passes the remains of a Roman marching camp, **Twyn-y-Briddallt**, and **Old Smokey** (aka the Tylorstown Tip), a huge pile of colliery spoil with excellent views, before winding up at the isolated little ridge-top village of **LLANWONNO**, with its remote glades, an ancient church and a cracking village pub, the ⚔ *Brynffynon Arms*.

Practicalities

A **train** line, punctuated with stops every mile or so, runs the entire length of the Rhondda Fawr, from Pontypridd to its terminus at Treherbert. **Buses** also cover the route, continuing up into the mountains and the Brecon Beacons. **Accommodation** in the twin valleys is sparse, but decent places include the business-oriented *Heritage Park Hotel*, beside the Rhondda Heritage Park at Trehafod (℡01443/687057; ⑥), which has its own pool; and *The Bertie* bar and B&B (℡01443/688204; ❸) at 1–3 Phillips Terrace, not far away. Nearer the top end of the Rhondda Fawr is the reasonable *Baglan Hotel* (℡01443/776111; ❷) on the main road in Treherbert. There's **hostel** accommodation at the *Glyncornel Environmental Centre* on Nant-y-Gwyddon Road, five minutes from Llwynypia station (℡01443/431727, ✉glyncornel@rhondda-cynon-taff.gov .uk; beds £13.20), for which pre-booking is essential. For the most part, **eating** options in the Rhondda towns consist of a dizzying range of chip shops and Chinese takeaways, though a few **pubs** offer good food – try the *Greenfield* at 13-14 William St in Ystrad, where the road from Penrhys and the Rhondda Fach joins the Rhondda Fawr, or the *Lion* at 102 Bute St in Treorchy, both on the main A4058 through the Rhondda Fawr.

The Ogwr, Garw and Llynfi valleys

Running west from the Rhondda, these three valleys are different to their big neighbour: the contours are slightly softer, the open spaces wider and the towns less bustling. The **Ogwr Valley** plunges south from the Rhondda Fawr's Treorchy village, through the moribund settlements of **Nant-y-moel** and **Ogmore Vale**, before the main road forks at **Pont-yr-awel** for the branch road over to the Garw Valley. High between the two is the one-horse hamlet of **LLANGEINOR**, little more than a fine medieval church, circular village green, good country pub and the starting point for numerous paths radiating out over the upland moors.

The Ogwr Valley descends through orderly little townships en route into **BRIDGEND** (Pen-y-bont ar Ogwr), an ancient settlement that guards the entrance to the three valleys. Consequently, it was deemed important enough to house two Norman castles, either side of the river. The "old castle" survives only in the name of the suburb on the town-centre side of the river, while opposite, the scant remains of the "new castle", high on a wooded hill above the A4063 Maesteg road, are notable mainly for the surviving late-Norman decorated gateway. That aside, there's not much to occupy you in Bridgend, although it's a useful transport interchange, with a good selection of shops and a few handsome buildings. Just over a mile northeast of the town are the more substantial remains of **Coity Castle** (free access; CADW), built around the end of the twelfth century by one of the earliest Norman knights in the area, who, it is said, married the daughter offered to him by the local Welsh chieftain. Bridgend is also very handy for Porthcawl, Ewenny Priory and beyond, detailed in the Vale of Glamorgan section (pp.137–146).

The **Garw Valley** is a world of its own; one of the dead-end valleys that consists of a road, river and the disused railway crammed in on the valley floor, before they all peter out into the wooded hillsides. Most of the scars of its mining past have now been levelled and landscaped, leaving the valley surprisingly pretty, and, as it's well off any tourist track, very rewarding for good walks and congenial company in the pubs and shops.

At the lower end of the valley, the **Bryngarw Country Park** (daily dawn–dusk; peak season parking £2) is a pleasant diversion. Landscaped gardens, exceptional flower collections and mature woodlands are gathered around the restored Bryngarw House, which now houses a bistro and conference centre. The head of the valley is at **BLAENGARW**, location for the 2001 film *Very Annie Mary*. The old **Workmen's Hall** (☎01656/871911) has been transformed into a bustling community space with cinema, workshops, Internet access and performance areas, all behind a frontage stunningly enhanced with murals and mosaics.

The **Llynfi Valley**, stretching up from Bridgend and Tondu along the A4063, is broad-bottomed and leafy, the main settlement being the downbeat town of **MAESTEG**, notable for its spacious main street, reputedly Wales' widest. This is because the original street ran parallel with a tram line, which was later tarmacked over as an extension of the road. A section of the original tram line from the early nineteenth century can be seen in a monument down near the iron bridge over the Afon Llynfi in the centre of town. On the hill above is a more contemporary memorial: the imposing bulk of the 1839 blast engine house from the Llynfi Ironworks, which has been cleverly incorporated as the entrance lobby of the new civic sports centre. Even so, you get the feeling that Maesteg is struggling to find replacements for its lost collieries, for it is in these more westerly corners of the Valleys that the economic pinch is felt most keenly. There is understandable resentment that the better-known valleys, particularly the Rhondda, Cynon and Taff, have soaked up so much of the area's publicity and available funds. Continuing through Maesteg, the main road links up with the A4107 at Cymer, for Cwm Afan (see below).

On top of the mountain to the south of Maesteg is the beautiful village of **LLANGYNWYD**. Birth- and burial-place of bard Wil Hopcyn, it has an ancient atmosphere in stark contrast to the ex-mining towns below. The splendid *Yr Hen Dŷ* pub is said to be the oldest inn in south Wales, where revellers traditionally congregate on New Year's Day for the hallowed Welsh custom of the **Mari Llwyd** (Grey Mare). A horse's skull is paraded through the village to ward off evil spirits during the forthcoming year.

The only **accommodation** in this area is at *Bryngarw House* (☎01656/729009; ❺ including dinner) in the country park, which usually caters for pre-booked conferences, wedding parties and the like. If you're exploring the area, or want to catch something at the Blaengarw Workmen's Hall, telephone the hall for suggestions as to someone local who might offer B&B. Otherwise, there are many fine wild sites to pitch a **tent**.

Cwm Afan, Port Talbot and Margam

Although not as idyllic as its optimistic "Little Switzerland" tourist-board tag would have it, **CWM AFAN**, winding its way between the top of the Llynfi Valley and the coast at Port Talbot, is nonetheless a bucolic spot that warrants

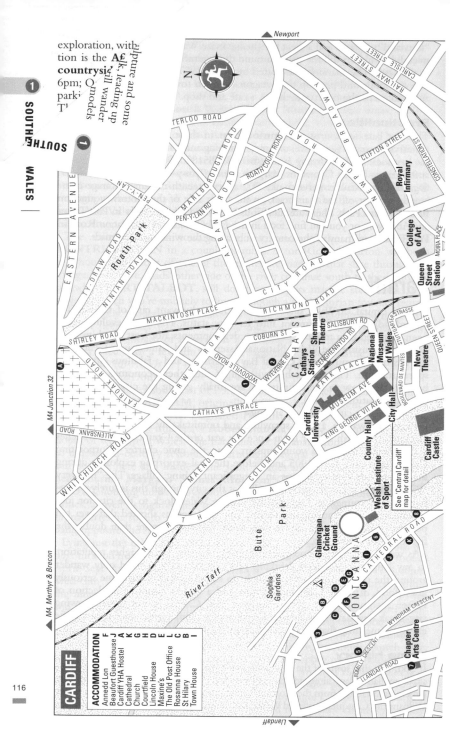

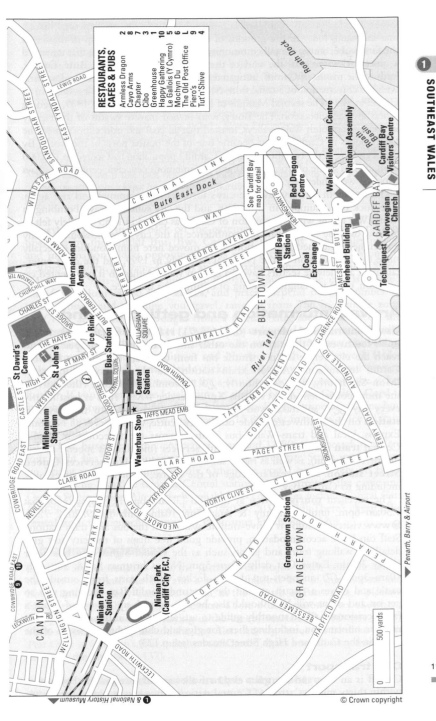

RESTAURANTS, CAFÉS & PUBS

Armless Dragon	2
Cayo Arms	8
Chapter	7
Cibo	3
Greenhouse	1
Happy Gathering	10
Le Gallois (Y Cymro)	5
Mochyn Du	6
The Old Post Office	L
Piero's	9
Tut'n'Shive	4

© Crown copyright

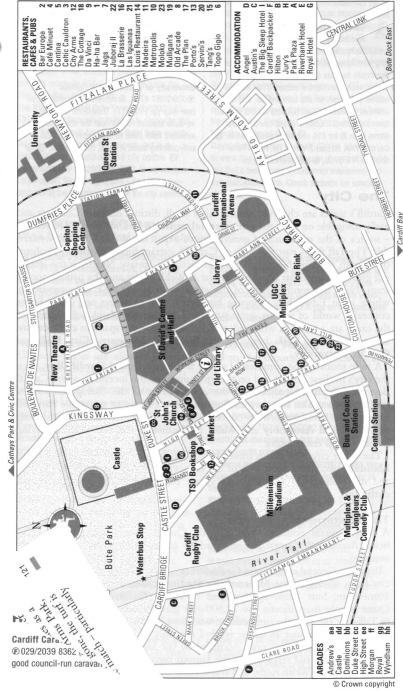

RESTAURANTS, CAFÉS & PUBS

Bar Europa	2
Café Minuet	4
Cantina	5
Celtic Cauldron	3
City Arms	12
The Cottage	18
Da Vinci	9
Ha-ha Bar	1
Jags	7
Juboraj II	22
La Brasserie	16
Las Iguanas	21
Louis Restaurant	14
Madeira	11
Metropolis	10
Moloko	23
Mulligan's	19
Old Arcade	8
The Plan	17
Porto's	13
Servini's	20
Tang's	15
Topo Gigio	6

ACCOMMODATION

Angel	D
Austin's	C
The Big Sleep Hotel	I
Cardiff Backpacker	F
Hilton	B
Jury's	H
Park Plaza	A
Riverbank Hotel	E
Royal Hotel	G

ARCADES

Andrew's	aa
Castle	dd
Dominions	bb
Duke Street	cc
High Street	ee
Morgan	ff
Royal	gg
Wyndham	hh

© Crown copyright

against old enemy England – the stadium and surrounding streets are charged with good-natured, beery fervour. These days, the stadium is also used for Wales' international football matches and for a host of huge rock gigs and other musical spectaculars. The stadium tours include walking the players' tunnel, visiting the dressing rooms, VIP areas and a rugby museum. They start from the stadium **shop** at Entrance Gate 3 on Westgate Street. The stadium's **ticket office** can be found at 98 St Mary St (℡08705/582582).

Running up from Central station to the castle walls is **St Mary Street**, one of the city's grandest boulevards of ornate Victorian and Edwardian shop frontages. St Mary Street leads north to become the **High Street**, where at no.18, you'll find the **TSO Bookshop** (Mon–Sat 9am–5.30pm), a good stockist of Welsh-interest publications, maps and travel paraphernalia. Off High Street is the elegant Victorian **indoor market**, great for fresh food and specialist bric-a-brac stalls. Along both streets, renovated Edwardian arcades, with some of the city centre's most interesting shops inside, lead off between the buildings. Of these, **High Street** and **Castle arcades**, at the top of High Street, are the most rewarding, packed with great club clothes shops, quirky gift places, fab little coffee houses and a range of esoteric emporia where you can pick up fliers for clubs and events. Further down the High Street towards Central station, the glorious Morgan Arcade and its near neighbour, the Royal Arcade, run east to the bottom of **The Hayes**, a pedestrianized street of disparate restaurants and some great pubs. A few yards to the south, The Hayes meets up at a junction of five streets by the old **Brains brewery**, opposite the **Wales National Ice Rink** (℡029/2039 7198), home to one of Britain's top ice hockey teams, the Cardiff Devils, but due to be demolished as part of the area's forthcoming redevelopment: an upgraded replacement is due in the projected International Sports Village in the Bay. At the junction, Bridge Street runs away to the east and into the elegant Regency part of the city centre around David and Charles streets. Slicing off south from The Hayes, opposite the *Marriott* hotel, is cheerful Mill Lane, Cardiff's self-proclaimed **café quarter**.

The Hayes leads north to the beautifully sandblasted and colonnaded frontage of the **Old Library**, home to the city's tourist office (see p.118). At the Old Library, The Hayes divides around the fifteenth-century grey limestone parish **church of St John**. The most notable feature – the slender tower – is difficult to appreciate with the cluster of buildings around it, although the light and graceful interior is worth seeing, especially for the floridly pompous altar in the south aisle by prolific Victorian sculptor, Goscombe John. The right turn at the Old Library is **Working Street**, a very busy shopping area, especially around the entrances to the gargantuan **St David's Centre** and the **St David's Hall** complex, which, between them, have succeeded in obliterating a huge section of the old city centre, although St David's Hall serves as a much-needed concert and entertainment venue.

Queen Street is Cardiff's most impressive shopping thoroughfare, now pedestrianized with many of the fine nineteenth-century buildings spruced up, only to be effaced by the frontages typical of a British shopping street. That said, Queen Street is usually dependable for the buskers, street theatre, hawkers and idlers that make it a very easy place to while away a few hours. At the western end of the street, a typically pugnacious statue of **Aneurin Bevan**, postwar Labour politician and classic Welsh firebrand, stands aloof from the bustle.

Cardiff Castle

The geographical and historical heart of the city is **Cardiff Castle** (daily: March–Oct 9.30am–6pm, tours every 20min; Nov–Feb 9.30am–5pm, 5 tours daily; full tour £6.50, grounds only £3.30), an intriguing hotchpotch of remnants of the city's past. The fortress hides inside a vast walled yard, each side measuring well over 200 yards long and corresponding roughly to the outline of the original fort built by the Romans. A few dozen yards of **Roman wall**, the sole reminder of their presence, has been unearthed to the immediate right of the entrance in the thirteenth-century Black Tower on Castle Street, and is now lit and labelled, along with some excellent three-dimensional murals depicting life in a Roman fort. Tucked into the southeastern corner wall beyond the Roman segment are the dry **regimental museums** of the Queen's Dragoon Guards and the Welsh Regiment, filled with a starchy collection of military memorabilia. From here, walkways lead along the **battlements**, for some excellent views over the city.

Occupying the northwestern corner of the castle grounds is a neat Norman motte crowned with the eleventh-century **keep**, with views down onto the turrets and towers of the **domestic buildings**, dating in part from the fourteenth and fifteenth centuries, but much extended in Tudor times, when residential needs began to overtake military safety in terms of priority. Ultimately, it was the third Marquis of Bute (1847–1900), one of the richest men on the globe, who lavished a fortune on upgrading his pile, commissioning architect and decorator William Burges (1827–81) to aid him. With their passion for the religious art and the symbolism of the Middle Ages, they systematically overhauled the buildings, adding a spire to the octagonal tower and erecting a clocktower; but it was inside that their imaginations ran free, and they radically transformed the crumbling interiors into palaces of vivid colour and intricate, high-camp design. These buildings can only be seen as part of the guided tour, making the extra fee well worthwhile.

The tour starts in the square-cornered **clocktower**, running through the **Winter Smoking Room** at the bottom, up to the **Bachelor's Bedroom** and bathroom and, above that, the **Summer Smoking Room**. All are decorated in rich patterns of gold, maroon and cobalt, with many of the images culled from medieval myths and beliefs. From here, the tour goes through the 1878 **Nursery**, with hand-painted tiles and silhouette lanterns depicting contemporary nursery rhymes, the 1881 **Arab Room**, decorated by imported craftsmen, and into the grand **Banqueting Hall**, which dates orginally from 1428, but was transformed by Bute and Burges with the installation of a riotously kitsch fireplace. In all the rooms, fantastically rich trimmings complement the gaudy style so beloved of two nineteenth-century eccentrics, and it's worth remembering that, as one of over sixty residences owned by the Butes in Britain alone, Cardiff was only lived in for six weeks of the year.

The last point of note in Cardiff Castle can only be seen from outside the precincts. The **Animal Wall**, where stone creatures are frozen in impudent poses, was another tongue-in-cheek nineteenth-century creation, running all along the route of Castle Street west to the river bridge.

Cathays Park and the civic centre

On the north side of the city centre, only a hundred yards from the northeastern wall of the castle precinct, is the area known most commonly as **Cathays Park**. The park itself is really the large rectangle of greenery that forms the centrepiece for the impressive Edwardian buildings of the **civic centre**, but the term Cathays Park is generally used for the whole complex. Dating from the first couple of decades of the twentieth century, the gleaming white buildings arranged with pompous Edwardian precision speak volumes about Cardiff's self-confidence, a full half-century before it was officially declared capital of

Wales. The busy **Boulevard de Nantes**, named after Cardiff's twin city in Brittany, fronts the complex on the city-centre side.

The centrepiece is the magnificent, domed, dragon-topped **City Hall** (1905), an exercise in ostentatious civic self-glory that is open to the public in normal office hours. Note the Peace Sculpture in the main entrance lobby as you go in: it depicts one of the women who marched from Cardiff in 1981 to establish the Greenham Common peace camp. In absolute contrast, the ornate interior is a riot of finery that reaches a peak in the particularly showy first-floor Marble Hall: all Sienese marble columns and statues of Welsh heroes. Amongst the figures are twelfth-century chronicler Giraldus Cambrensis, thirteenth-century native prince of Wales, Llywelyn ap Gruffydd, fifteenth-century national insurgent and perpetual hero, Owain Glyndŵr, Welsh king Henry Tudor and tenth-century architect of Wales' progressive codified laws, Hywel Dda (Howell the Good). Overseeing them all is the figure of Dewi Sant himself – the national patron saint, St David. Also in the Hall is a syrupy triple portrait of the late Diana, Princess of Wales, and there are numerous other works of art throughout the building.

The low-key **Law Courts** (1906) stand to the left of the City Hall, with the **National Museum and Gallery** (see below) balancing the view on the right-hand side. Behind them, two ruler-straight boulevards, evidently designed with ceremonial splendour in mind, run through the rest of the civic centre, arranged in symmetrical precision around **Alexandra Gardens** in the middle. At the very centre of the park is the colonnaded circular **National War Memorial** (1928), a popular and surprisingly quiet place to sit and contemplate the rush of civic and governmental duty all around. At the north end of the western boulevard, **King Edward VII Avenue**, is the **Temple of Peace** (1938), dedicated just before the outbreak of World War II to Welsh men and women the world over who were fighting for peace and relief of poverty. The eastern road, **Museum Avenue**, runs past an assortment of buildings belonging to Cardiff University. At the northern head of Cathays Park is the ugliest and most forbidding building of them all: the executive departments of the **National Assembly** and other assorted governmental offices.

National Museum and Gallery

The **National Museum and Gallery** (Tues–Sun & bank holidays 10am–5pm; free, headset tour £2.50) is one of Britain's finest. Housed in a massive domed Portland-stone building that was constructed in sections from 1912 through to 1992, it manages to carry off the illusion of a singular *grand projet*. As a national museum, it attempts both to tell the story of Wales and reflect the nation's place in the wider, international sphere.

The most obvious crowd-pleaser, starting on the ground floor, is the epic **Evolution of Wales** gallery, a natural history exhibition packed with high-tech gizmos and a staggering amount of information. It starts with a stirring large-screen video presentation, *Dyma Gymru* (This is Wales), full of stunning aerial footage taken over mountains, waterfalls and other natural Welsh wonders. It then goes on to explain, through fossils, rocks and footage of volcanoes, earthquakes and the galaxies, the slow beginnings of life on earth. Dinosaurs and the early mammals get a good look in, notably in a terrific Tyrannosaurus rex skull.

The environmental education continues in the adjacent **Natural History** galleries, with a magnificent collection of sparkling crystals, re-creations of assorted environments – mountain, wetland, seashore, dunes – and some great interactive technology and interpretive boards. It then heads upstairs with a display entitled "Man and the Environment", featuring numerous animals and their habitats, and culminates in the world's largest leatherback turtle, caught off Harlech in 1988. Displays looking at the effect of mankind on our changing environment complete the section.

The first floor also houses the excellent **archeology galleries**, whose treasures include intricate gold torques from the Bronze Age and the dazzling **Caergwrle Bowl**, a gold votive container in the shape of a boat that's more than 3000 years old. Leading off is an unusually interesting **coin** collection, with some good panels on the history of Welsh and British minting, and the **Tregwynt Treasure Trove**, found near Fishguard in 1996: an impressive cache of gold and silver coins dating back to the Civil War. At the back, there's an inspirational collection of 23 stones and 14 casts, spanning the earliest carved fragments (around the fifth century), through Celtic and early Christian standing stones to the more elaborate examples of the early medieval age.

The art collections

The Evolution of Wales and Natural History galleries occupy the entire western and central flank of the ground and first floors. The eastern side of the building is home to the **art galleries**. Galleries One to Ten examine Wales' artistic heritage, starting with a marble altar from the first century BC and taking in works from the medieval Renaissance, including some stunning pieces from the studios of Botticelli and El Greco. There's a strong collection from the **eighteenth-century** British and Italian schools, inevitably rich in the work of Wright, Gainsborough and Reynolds. This era was perhaps the heyday of Welsh art, and the three main protagonists – Richard Wilson, William E. Parry and Thomas Jones – are well represented. Wilson's skill in capturing Wales' unique light can be seen to lustrous effect in his studies of castles at Caernarfon, Dolbadarn and Pembroke, as well as more emotionally intense pieces such as the beautiful *Pistyll Cain*. One of Wilson's protégés, William Hodges, also makes an appearance, most notably in his gentle evocation of *Llanthony Priory*.

Scattered throughout the first ten rooms is an intriguing, eclectic ragbag of British art of the last 150 years: Frank Brangwyn's teeming canvases, a typically rich and detailed collection of Pre-Raphaelites, and an astonishingly gaudy gold, silver and enamel table centrepiece given by the people of Wales to the Duke and Duchess of York (later King George V and Queen Mary) for their wedding in 1893. Welsh painters are well highlighted: you'll find cool, blanched portraits by Gwen John, and her brother Augustus' measured, intensely poetic depictions of Dylan Thomas and Newport "supertramp" W.H. Davies. There's also a superb, and growing, collection of **ceramics**, one of Wales' most prolific areas of applied art.

But the most exciting artworks are contained in Galleries Eleven through Fifteen, kicking off with a fabulous **sculpture** collection, including many by the celebrated one-man Welsh Victorian statue industry, Goscombe John. Far better here than on the dreary municipal plinths they usually adorn, his male studies verge on the homoerotic and his female forms are exquisite.

Mesmerizing pieces by Rodin pepper the building, particularly in Gallery Twelve, where a copy of *The Kiss* and his original *Eve* share space with the watery landscapes of Boudin, Renoir's coquettish *The Parisienne*, and numerous works by Manet, including the intricately observed *Effect of Snow at Petit Montrouge*.

Gallery Thirteen houses what is arguably the museum's strongest suit, its collection of **Impressionists**, the bequest of two local wealthy sisters, Margaret and Gwendoline Davies. The sisters' favourite was Cézanne, whose work features alongside artists such as Sisley (including his view of Penarth), Carnière, Degas and Pissarro. Van Gogh's stunning *Rain at Anvers* – angry slashes of rain run right across the otherwise harmonious canvas – was painted just weeks before his suicide. Gallery Fourteen includes Postimpressionists, Futurists and Surrealists such as Magritte, Sickert, Sylvia Gosse, Harold Gilman's colourful London scenes and studies by Edward Morland Lewis, including a bold depiction of *The Strand, Laugharne*. Finally, Gallery Fifteen houses a hearty collection of British **abstractionism**, with a strong Welsh bent. Highlights include some stunning and wild pieces by Welsh supremo Ceri Richards, Evan Walters' piercing 1936 portrait of a *Welsh Miner*, Josef Herman's rousing *Miners Singing* and Kyffin Williams' brooding Welsh skies and jagged landscapes. Some sculpted pieces, including some fine works by Henry Moore, among them *Upright Motif*, and Barbara Hepworth's haunting *Oval Sculpture*, complete the room.

Cardiff Bay

Although you can get there by waterbus (every hour from Bute Park and Taff's Mead Embankment), train (every 20min from Queen Street station) or bus (#2, #7 or #35 from outside Central station), **Cardiff Bay** is just a half-hour stroll from the city centre, with a choice of routes. Both start from the huge new

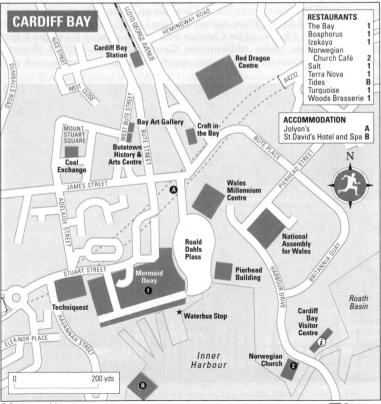

CARDIFF BAY

RESTAURANTS
The Bay	1
Bosphorus	1
Izakaya	1
Norwegian Church Café	2
Salt	1
Terra Nova	1
Tides	B
Turquoise	1
Woods Brasserie	1

ACCOMMODATION
Jolyon's	A
St David's Hotel and Spa	B

© Crown copyright   ▼ *Barrage*

The Mermaid Quay district

Continuing west along the waterfront from the Pierhead brings you straight into **Mermaid Quay**, an airy jumble of shops, bars and restaurants that on a warm day is a fine place to hang out and watch the world amble by. The city's waterbuses (see p.119) leave from here, and information boards carry details of a variety of boat-rental opportunities to get you out onto the water.

Further west around the waterfront, the metal-and-glass-crowned **Techniquest**, on Stuart Street (Mon–Fri 9.30am–4.30pm, Sat & Sun 10.30am–5pm; £6.90), is one of the largest and most impressive "hands-on" science museums in the UK, packed full of exhibits, experiments and numerous chances to play like a five-year-old. It also includes a planetarium (£1) and science theatre.

Jutting proudly over the water like an ocean-going liner, the five-star **St David's Hotel** (see p.120) acts as a stylish full stop to the sweep of the bay. From its car park, a path leads a couple of hundred yards to an eight-hectare **wetland reserve**, created partly to help offset the loss of wading-bird habitats when the barrage was built and the Bay flooded. It's a surreally peaceful spot in which to gather your breath or have a picnic.

Butetown

The area immediately inland from the Bay is the salty old district of **Butetown**, whose inner-city dereliction still peeps through the rampant gentrification that has taken place here over the past two decades. James Street, behind Techniquest, is the main commercial focus, while to its north are the cleaned-up old buildings around **Mount Stuart Square**. Many of these are trendy offices and bars now, but the most impressive is the mammoth **Coal Exchange Building** (℡029/2049 4917, ⓦwww.coalexchange.co.uk); built in the 1880s as Britain's central Coal Exchange, the building saw the world's first £1 million cheque signed in 1908 and is now used for conferences, exhibitions and concerts. Close by, on the corner of West Bute Street, the old church of St Stephen has been converted into **The Point**, a superb venue for music and, occasionally, drama (see p.135).

A block further east is Bute Street, where the community-based **Butetown History & Arts Centre** at 5 Dock Chambers (opening times vary; ℡029/2025 6757, ⓦwww.bhac.org) aims to record and celebrate the remarkable multicultural pedigree of a district that is home, for example, to one of the oldest black communities in Britain; to that end, the centre mounts exhibitions, offers guided tours and maintains a growing archive. A few paces up the street at no. 54b, the cool, contemporary **Bay Art** gallery (Tues–Sat 10am–5pm; free) has a varied programme of exhibitions. Even more impressive is **Craft in the Bay** (daily 10.30am–5.30pm; free), an old maritime warehouse now marooned rather stylishly in the middle of the new Lloyd George Avenue, one block further east. Craft practitioners from all over Wales exhibit here, and there's a cute café in which to mull over the talent. Across the way, the sweeping roofline and glass-brick curtain wall of the **Red Dragon Centre** (formerly Atlantic Wharf) make a striking front for what is essentially a big box filled with a twelve-screen multiplex, bowling alley, bars and restaurants. From here it's just a short hop across the road back to Cardiff Bay train station.

From Bute Park to Llandaff

Between Cardiff Castle and the River Taff lies **Bute Park**, once the private estate of the castle, and now containing an **arboretum**, superb flowerbeds, a gorsedd stone circle, the foundation remains of an old priory and some pleasant walks along the Taff banks. The main road crosses over the river at Cardiff Bridge, with a right turn leading up into the coolly formal **Sophia Gardens**. A quarter of a mile along the river is the multipurpose **Welsh Institute of Sport**, the national sports centre. Beyond this is the home of Wales' sole first-class cricket team, Glamorgan, and the less formal open spaces of **Pontcanna Fields**, which lead along the Taff for a couple of miles to the suburb of Llandaff.

A small, quiet ecclesiastical village, **Llandaff** is two miles northwest of the city centre along Cathedral Road. The church that has now grown up into the city's **cathedral** is believed to have been founded in the sixth century by St Teilo, but was rebuilt in Norman style from 1120 and well into the thirteenth century. From the late fourteenth century, the cathedral fell into an advanced state of disrepair, hurried along by the adverse attention of Cromwell's soldiers during the Civil War. In the early eighteenth century, one of the twin towers and the nave roof collapsed. Restoration only began in earnest in the early 1840s, and Pre-Raphaelite artists such as Edward Burne-Jones, Dante Gabriel Rossetti and the stained-glass firm of William Morris were commissioned for colourful new windows and decorative panels. Llandaff is evidently not a lucky cathedral, however, for in January 1941, a German landmine destroyed whole sections of it. Faithful and painstaking restoration was finally completed in 1960.

The fusion of different styles and ages is evident from outside, especially in the mismatched western towers. The northwest tower is by Jasper Tudor, a largely fifteenth-century work with modern embellishments, whilst the adjoining tower and spire were rebuilt from nineteenth-century designs. Inside, Jacob Epstein's overwhelming *Christ in Majesty* sculpture, a concrete parabola topped with a circular organ case on which sits a soaring Christ figure, was the only entirely new feature added in the postwar reconstruction, and dominates the nave today. At the west end of the north aisle, the **St Illtyd Chapel** features Rossetti's cloying triptych *The Seed of David*, whose figures – David the shepherd boy, David the King and the Virgin Mary – are modelled on Rossetti's Pre-Raphaelite friends. Along a little further, in the south presbytery, is the tenth-century Celtic cross that is the cathedral's only pre-Norman survivor.

At the far end of the cathedral is the elegantly vaulted and beautifully painted **Lady Chapel**, notable for its gaudy fifteenth-century reredos on the back wall that contains, surrounded by golden twigs and blackthorn in each niche, bronze panels with named flowers (in Welsh) in honour of Our Lady. Over two dozen flowers take their Welsh names from the Virgin Mary.

While you're here, it's worth having a quick look at the medieval **walled garden** (open access; free) of the Llandaff Bishops' Palace on the Cathedral Green. With herbaceous plants planted according to medieval patterns, it makes a pleasant – and fragrant – place to sit for a few minutes.

Eating

The city's long-standing internationalism, particularly its Italian influence, has paid handsome dividends in its range of **restaurants**. Most places are within easy walking distance of the city centre, with a particular concentration in the "Café Quarter" around Mill Lane. There are also good options in the cheaper corners of Cathays and Roath (particularly the curry houses along Crwys, Albany and City roads), a stone's throw from the centre beyond the university. Some of the action has now moved a mile west to suburban Canton, and to Cardiff Bay; the latter seeing more and more showpiece bars and restaurants opening all the time. Note that we've only listed telephone numbers for places where a reservation is recommended. Out of the city, don't miss the fabulous ⚑ *Old Post Office* at St Fagan's (see p.137).

For bargain-priced **takeaways** in the city centre, your best bet is Caroline Street, between St Mary Street and the bottom of The Hayes.

Chapter Market Rd, Canton. A trendy bar in the arts centre, with a good choice of real ale, imported lagers and whisky. Frequented by the Canton media and arts crowd.

Mochyn Du Sophia Close, off Cathedral Rd. Relaxed pub with tables spilling out into the greenery. Good bar menu, great beer and popular with Welsh speakers.

Tut'n'Shive 56 City Rd, Cathays. Loud and leery student hangout that has managed to survive refurbishment and remain as fun as before.

The lesbian and gay scene

Although the scene in the city is far from massive, it has grown in both size and confidence over the last few years. One unmissable event is the annual **Mardi Gras** festival (ⓦwww.cardiffmardigras.co.uk), which has become one of the most successful free Pride events in Britain. The best source for current information and advice is the Mardi Gras website or **South Wales Friend**, an information–line for lesbians, gay men and bisexuals (Tues–Thurs 7.30–9.30pm; ☎029/2034 0101). It doesn't take too much effort to discover what's going on, as practically all of the venues are on Charles Street, just off Queen Street in the city centre. All venues are for men and women.

Bar Icon 60 Charles St. Trendy new bar, with a muted, comfy decor and a tendency to get funky towards the weekend.

Club X 39 Charles St. Stylish and popular gay club that manages to span both cheesy and cutting edge. Also has a wonderful roof garden and a great atmosphere. Open Wed till 2am, Fri 3am, Sat 4am & Sun 1am.

Exit Bar 48 Charles St. Opposite *Club X*, this late-opening (2am) disco bar has definitely seen better days, but if you want your night out smothered in cheese, this could be for you.

Golden Cross 283 Hayes Bridge Rd. Laid-back restored Victorian pub, rich in atmosphere and with some beautiful tiled pictures of yesteryear Cardiff. Camp entertainment a speciality, as is the cheap food.

King's Cross Hayes Bridge Rd/Caroline St. Large and long-established gay pub, with few frills but a friendly atmosphere.

Nightlife and entertainment

There's plenty of choice when it comes to **nightlife** in Cardiff, whether your tastes run to sweaty rock gigs (in English or Welsh), pumping clubs or genteel classical affairs. **Theatre** in Cardiff encompasses everything from the radical and alternative at The Point and Chapter to big, blowzy productions at the New Theatre or West End spectaculars at the new Wales Millennium Centre, home of the Welsh National Opera (ⓦwww.wno.org.uk). Classical **music** is best heard at the WMC or St David's Hall. Cardiff is usually on big world rock tours, thanks to the Millennium Stadium. There's no shortage of multiplex **cinemas** for the latest blockbusters, though Chapter is best for arthouse movies.

Clubs

Clwb Ifor Bach 11 Womanby St ☎029/2023 2199, ⓦwww.clwb.net. Sweaty and massively fun live music and dance club on three floors with nightly gigs, sessions or DJs, including Seventies and funk nights. Widely known as the "Welsh club", due to the prevalence of Welsh-language acts and punters, most notably on Saturdays.

Evolution UCI Building, Atlantic Wharf☎029/2046 4444. Cardiff's biggest and flashiest club, stationed firmly in the mainstream.

Metros Bakers Row ☎029/2037 1549. Grungey, scruffy venue that hosts some of the best Indie/alternative dance nights in town, with lots of students drawn by the drink promotions.

Sam's Bar 63 St Mary St ☎029/2034 5189. Lively mixed bar-cum-club, with everything from live heavy metal, drag and comedy shows to pumping house DJs. Good for the happy hour (Mon–Thurs 5–7pm), when you can hang outside and check the pulse of the café quarter.

Toucan 95 St Mary St ☎029/2037 2212, ⓦwww.toucanclub.co.uk. Hip-hop, jazz, world music and funk are the main menu of this Cardiff institution, a place for serious music lovers.

The Union 3 Churchill Way ☎029/2064 1010. Big-name live bands and assorted dance nights in this impressive club complex, open to non-students.
Vision2K 43–45 Queen St ☎029/2022 7717. Humungous club, with a packed party atmosphere and a range of mainstream hard house, R&B and UK garage. Late licence, with one all-nighter at least most weekends.

Classical and rock music venues

Barfly Kingsway, ☎029/2066 7658, ⊛www .barflyclub.com. Dark and sweaty club, opposite the side of the castle, that hosts at least a couple of live bands every evening, including many on the verge of making it.
Cardiff Castle Castle St ☎029/2087 8100. Increasingly used for big gigs, from Proms-style flag-wavers to visiting rock gods.
Cardiff International Arena Mary Ann St ☎029/2023 4500 (enquiries), ☎029/2022 4488 (bookings). Large and imposing venue rising high over the city centre's southern streets and playing host to classical concerts, opera and major rock and pop gigs.
Coal Exchange Mount Stuart Square, Cardiff Bay ☎029/2049 4917. A lovely Victorian building that has been well converted for all manner of musical treats.
Millennium Stadium Westgate St ☎029/2082 2228. Home of mega-gigs as well as major sporting occasions.
Norwegian Church Harbour Drive, Cardiff Bay ☎029/2045 4899. Lovely venue for all kinds of musical and performance evenings.
Royal Oak 200 Broadway, Newport Rd, Roath ☎029/2047 3984. Odd live-music pub, with something of a fetish for boxing memorabilia – there's even an old boxing ring.
St David's Hall The Hayes ☎029/2087 8444, ⊛www.stdavidshallcardiff.co.uk. Part of the massive St David's shopping centre, this large venue is home to visiting orchestras and musicians from jazz to opera, and is frequently used by the excellent BBC National Orchestra of Wales.
University Concert Hall Corbett Rd, Cathays Park ☎029/2087 4816. Home of public concerts by university and local orchestras, jazz groups and easy-listening ensembles.

Wales Millennium Centre, Roald Dahls Plass, Cardiff Bay ☎029/2040 2000, ⊛www.wmc.org .uk. Permanent home of the Welsh National Opera, together with a collection of other music and dance companies. Also used for touring mega-productions.

Theatre and comedy

Chapter Arts Centre Market Rd, Canton ☎029/2030 4400, ⊛www.chapter.org. Multifunctional arts complex that's home to fine British and touring theatre and dance companies.
Glee Club Mermaid Quay, Cardiff Bay ☎0870/241 5093, ⊛www.glee.co.uk. Cardiff's best comedy club, with some of the biggest names of the British stand-up circuit.
Jongleurs Comedy Club Millennium Plaza, Wood St ☎0870/787 0707, ⊛www.jongleurs.com. More corporate than the *Glee*, but dependable for some decent comedy.
New Theatre Park Place ☎029/2087 8889, ⊛www.newtheatrecardiff.co.uk. Splendid Edwardian city-centre theatre that plays host to big shows, musicals and pantos.
The Point West Bute St, Cardiff Bay ☎029/2049 9979, ⊛www.thepointcardiffbay.com. This performance space converted from an old church is good for experimental theatre, music and dance, as well as more mainstream events.
Sherman Theatre Senghennydd Rd, Cathays ☎029/2064 6900, ⊛www.shermantheatre.co.uk. An excellent two-auditorium repertory theatre hosting a mixed bag of new and translated classic Welsh-language pieces, stand-up comedy, children's entertainment, drama, music and dance. Many plays on Welsh themes in both English and Welsh.

Cinema

Chapter Arts Centre Market Rd, Canton (see above). Cardiff's main arthouse and alternative film centre.
Odeon Red Dragon Centre, Cardiff Bay ☎0870/010 2030. Twelve-screen megaplex in swish new building.
Ster Century Cinemas Millennium Plaza, Wood St ☎0870/767 2676. Flashy multiscreen complex opposite Central station.
UGC Mary Ann Street ☎0870/907 0739. Nicest multiscreen complex in the city centre.

Listings

Airport Cardiff International, out at Rhoose, near Barry ☎01446/711111, ⊛www.cial.co.uk.
Banks and exchange All major banks have branches along High St or Queen St. In addition

there's American Express at 3 Queen St (Mon–Fri 9am–5.30pm, Sat 10am–1pm; ☎029/2066 5843), and Thomas Cook at 16 Queen St (Mon–Fri 9.30am–5pm, Sat 10am–1pm; ☎029/2022 on many visitors' itineraries, as most speed through from Cardiff to Swansea, Gower and the west. It's their loss, for the quiet and pretty towns, together with the sheer profusion of excellent beaches and tumbledown castles, warrant a good couple of days' exploration. Brash seaside resorts at **Porthcawl** in the west and **Barry** to the east contrast with the far more refined, breezy atmosphere of **Penarth**, a prim seaside town clinging to the coat-tails of Cardiff. In between lie yawning wide bays and spectacular ruins, linked by bracing coastal walks. At the western tip of the Vale coast is **Kenfig**, a vast, grass-spotted desert of coastal dunes and nature reserves.

Inland, the lower parts of the Vale are a curious mix of urban reminders such as Wales' major **airport** at Rhoose and occasional looming factories, set against rolling green pastureland sprinkled with charming, if scarcely thrilling, market towns like **Cowbridge**, **Llantrisant** and **Llantwit Major**.

Its proximity to Cardiff makes the Vale easy to explore using **public transport**. The main-line train route through the Vale has a stop at Bridgend, a useful interchange for bus services to the coast and some of the larger inland settlements, while the Vale of Glamorgan line, an alternative route from Cardiff to Bridgend has stops at Rhoose and Llantwit Major. Barry and Penarth, almost suburbs of Cardiff, are easily reached by bus and train.

Penarth and around

Considering itself a cut above the boisterous capital of Cardiff and the downbeat resort of Barry, **PENARTH** is a quietly enjoyable town wedged between the two. The Cardiff Bay developments over on the other side of the Ely estuary are changing the town, and new roads are drawing Penarth ever more inexorably into the big city's net, much to the worry of some locals. Penarth is an easy, enjoyable day out from Cardiff, and a reasonable place to stay, made all the more appealing by being able to walk across the Barrage to the Cardiff Bay area less than a mile away; access is from Penarth Marina. The Bay waterbus (see p.119) is an even better way to reach Cardiff city centre and the Bay.

The Town

Penarth is the end of the train line from Cardiff, receiving half-hourly shuttle trains that ply their way from here, through the capital, and out into the valleys. From the train station, a path on the right leads up to Stanwell Road, which continues into the clean-cut Edwardian shopping streets of the town centre.

Opposite the station, the red-brick **Turner House Art Gallery** (Tues–Sun 10am–5pm; free; ☎029/2070 8870) is on the Plymouth Road, and houses some top-notch exhibitions, particularly in photography.

The Dingle path runs down the left-hand side of the Turner House, leading into the showy **Alexandra Park**, the spirit of Penarth with its oceans of flowerbeds, bandstand and benches full of pensioners. This picture only intensifies on continuing down the hill onto the charmingly fusty **Esplanade**, with the amusement arcade in the green bubble of a hall on the pier, which also houses the seasonal tourist office and a few fish-and-chip stands. The overall effect is sedately pleasing.

It seems thoroughly in keeping with the spirit of Penarth that you can spend the day **cruising** the local coastline aboard the *Waverley*, a genuine seagoing paddle steamer that makes regular visits to Penarth Pier throughout the summer (though it's sometimes replaced by the more conventionally propelled but no less gracious *Balmoral*). A schedule is published well in advance, covering day-trips ranging from cruises around Flat Holm to longer journeys up the

Severn estuary or across the Bristol Channel to ports on the north Devon coast (£14–25; ☎0845/130 4647).

Flat Holm and Lavernock Point

Two miles due south of Penarth is **Lavernock Point**, jutting out into the Bristol Channel, a forlorn setting for campsites and pubs, but notable as the place in which conversation was first heard by means of radio waves. This – as a plaque on the wall of the dismal Victorian chapel notes – took place on May 11, 1897, when Guglielmo Marconi sent the immortal words "Are you ready?" over to his assistant George Kemp on the island of **Flat Holm** (Ynys Echni), three miles out in the Bristol Channel, and officially Wales' most southerly point.

Over the years, Flat Holm has been used as a Viking anchorage, a cholera hospital and a lookout point. Today it's an interesting and beautifully remote **nature reserve**, the nesting place of thousands of gulls and shelducks. **Boats** operated by the Flat Holm Project, Pier Head, Barry Docks (☎01446/747661, ⓦwww.cardiff.gov.uk/flatholm; £13.50) sail weekends in summer from Barry Harbour and should be booked well in advance. Most are day-trips giving three hours on the island (including a history, flora and fauna tour), though it's occasionally possible to stay overnight in a farmhouse **hostel** on the island.

Lavernock Point is a fifteen-minute walk from the bus stop on the B4267. Half-hourly bus #94 operates from Cardiff and Penarth, dropping just near the mildly diverting **Cosmeston Medieval Village** (daily: May–Sept 11am–5pm, Oct–April 11am–4pm; £3), which, if you can catch it when it isn't too busy, makes for an agreeable half-hour.

Practicalities

Penarth's **tourist office** kiosk (Easter–Sept daily 10am–5.30pm; ☎029/2070 8849, ⓔpenarthtic@valeofglamorgan.gov.uk) is at the head of the pier on the Esplanade. For those wishing to see Cardiff without the bustle of city life, staying in Penarth is an option, though **accommodation** here is surprisingly sparse and not terribly good. There's the functional *Trelawne* guesthouse at 4 Albert Crescent (☎029/2070 9184; ➋), the smarter *Hickman Lodge*, 17 Hickman Rd (☎029/2070 1044, ⓦwww.hickmanlodge.co.uk; ➌), or, on the Esplanade, the fairly characterless *Seacot Hotel* (☎029/2070 0333; ➌). For **camping**, there's only the downbeat *Lavernock Point Holiday Estate* on Fort Road (☎029/2070 7310; £10 per pitch), but at least the views are good.

Along Penarth Esplanade are a number of reasonable **restaurants**, though by far the best food is in town at the *Olive Tree*, 21 Glebe St (☎029/2070 7077; closed Mon), which does a wonderful three-course table d'hôte for £20. Just nearby, the newish *Corner House* at 46 Plassey St (☎029/2033 0829; closed Sun & Mon) is gaining a good reputation for its French cuisine. For **pubs**, there's good beer and food to be had at the *Clive Arms* on John Street, up towards the Barrage, and the *Windsor*, going down the hill from the town centre on Windsor Road.

Barry and around

Six miles southwest of Penarth, **Barry** (Barri) is the quintessential Welsh resort of old, whose speciality of loud, chip-swallowing, beer-swilling seaside fun is a million miles from the effete coastal charms of Penarth. However, although the funfair and fun pubs are still here, even Barry is getting slightly gentrified these days, and it can be a decent base. Until the 1880s, when it was developed as a rival port to the Bute family's Cardiff, Barry was a small fishing village, and line new gastropub that's winning rave reviews for its well-cooked local specialities. There's a stack of **pubs** in Llantwit: of them all, the *Old Swan Inn* on the Square is best for food, although the nearby *Tudor Tavern* is more of an earthy drinking hole. Four miles east of town, the gorgeous thatched *Blue Anchor* in East Aberthaw is well worth the trip, either for a cosy fireside pint or a brilliant meal.

Southerndown and Ogmore

West of Llantwit Major, the coast ducks and dives past remote cliffs and sandy beaches. **SOUTHERNDOWN** is a diffuse holiday village of touristy pubs and one excellent restaurant – the French-inspired *Frolics* on Beach Road (①01656/880127; booking advisable). However, the real reason for coming here is **Dunraven Bay**, a beautiful, wide beach backed by jagged cliffs of perfectly defined layers of limestone and shale. In the busy car park by Dunraven Beach is the **Heritage Coast Centre** (April–Sept daily 10am–5pm; Oct–March Sat & Sun 10am–5pm; ①01656/880157), a small information point about walks and drives along this splendid section of the south Wales coastline. Dunraven is at the western end of a magnificent five-mile **coastal walk**, dipping down into tiny, wooded valleys and up across wide stretches of cliff and sand.

The village of **OGMORE** (Ogwr) is a straggling, windswept sort of place, but lies close to the remains of **Ogmore Castle**, situated about a mile north along the coast from Southerndown. Stunningly situated at the very bottom of a flat valley, the castle dates from the Norman Conquest in around 1100, but its solid central stone keep, in which a few original windows are still intact, was added later in the twelfth century. Below the castle, the **stepping stones** across the river make a fun diversion.

Ewenny Priory

The village of **EWENNY**, two miles further up the B4524, is interesting mainly for the towering remains of Benedictine **Ewenny Priory** (private), tucked away down leafy lanes three-quarters of a mile to the east. Founded in 1141, the priory's formidable, fortress-like walls were strengthened continuously throughout the thirteenth century, and are still very much intact today, broken only by the two huge gateways in which the portcullis holes can still be seen.

You can get in to see the adjoining priory **church**, which is squat and powerful, brooding over the ecclesiastical remains scattered around it. It is divided into two sections by a plain early medieval rood screen. On the western side (nearest to the rest of the priory) is the nave, whose damp, cold interior includes some splendid Norman windows. This nave served as the parish church, as opposed to the eastern chancel, which housed the monastic chapel.

Merthyr Mawr

On the banks of the Ogmore River two miles west of Ewenny, the small village of **MERTHYR MAWR** seems like an outpost of chocolate-box Dorset in south Wales. A narrow lane steers around into the village of neat thatched and whitewashed cottages, continuing along a wooded glen to its end on the edge of the great dune desert of Merthyr Mawr, stretching over to the distant sea. By the car park is the gaunt ruin of **Candleston**, a fifteenth-century fortified manor house that was abandoned in the nineteenth century as the shifting sands came too close.

Porthcawl

With the usual selection of tatty bungalows and caravan parks, **PORTHCAWL** is one of Wales' most enduring family resorts. But after resting on its laurels for years, the town has finally pulled its socks up: the seafront has been spruced up with new paving and a liberal lick of paint and there are some fine new eateries around too. Once you've exhausted the fun of the fair, though, there's little to do other than striking out on enervating walks along the coast or **surfing** from the sandy beach – an activity which is massive here.

Half-hourly **buses** connect Bridgend with Porthcawl, depositing travellers at the top of the pedestrianized John Street in the town centre. A two-minute walk straight down John Street leads to the Old Police Station, housing the **tourist office** (Easter–Sept Mon–Sat 9am–5pm, also Sun in July & Aug; Oct–Easter Tues & Fri 10am–5pm, Sat 10am–4pm; ☎01656/786639) where you can pick up a fairly useful free town guide, as well as a local history **museum** (same hours; 50p). John Street continues down to the Esplanade, Porthcawl's extensive seafront promenade which stretches the full length of the town and changes its name throughout. The section known as the Espalande is a typical array of Victorian and Edwardian hotels along the rocky beach, where you'll find the domed **Grand Pavilion** (box office ☎01656/786996), home to assorted seaside entertainment shows, pantomimes and a cinema. East, the Esplanade runs to a lifeboat station at the harbour before veering north alongside the coast as Eastern Promenade, the home of Porthcawl's solid seaside attractions: the **Coney Beach amusement park** behind whelk stalls and candy floss shops that look out over the donkey rides on Sandy Bay, and two vast caravan parks perched over this cove and neighbouring Trecco Bay. On the northwest side of town, a twenty-minute walk from the centre, is the far quieter and more beautiful **Rest Bay**, noted locally as a swimming and, when conditions are right, **surfing beach**. The grandiosely named Simon Tucker Surfing Academy (☎07815/289761, ⓦwww.surfingexperience.com) operates from the old car park attendant's hut above the beach – as well as tuition, you can pick up information on the local scene. During the summer, several ageing passenger cruisers offer occasional day-trips (around £15) out into the Bristol Channel and across to the Devon coast: call the tourist office for details.

Accommodation in Porthcawl is plentiful, cheap and concentrated around Mary Street, Gordon Road and along the promenade in its various guises. The best option in town is the shoreline *Fairways Hotel* on West Drive (☎01656/782085, ⓦwww.thefairwayshotel.co.uk; ⑥), though the Art Deco elegance of the *Seabank Hotel* on the promenade (☎01656/782261, ⓦwww.seabankhotel.co.uk; ⑤) might appeal too. Cheaper options include the *Foam Edge* guesthouse, popular with surfers, at 9 West Drive (☎01656/782866; ③) and the no-frills *Val's* right in the centre at 13 Esplanade (☎01656/782813; ①). **Campers** can stay about fifteen minutes' walk north of town at *Brodawel* (☎01656/783231; £11.50 per pitch), a simple field site on Moor Lane.

There are dozens of places to **eat** in the town centre, the best being ⚒ *Coast* at 2-4 Dock St (☎01656/782025), with its minimalist decor and elegant twists on sturdy Welsh classics. Otherwise, *Enrico's*, 33 The Esplanade, turns out respectable pizza, pasta and an extensive range of main courses, while the *Peach Pit* café at Rest Bay is a surfers' hang-out. Of the many **pubs**, the *Royal Oak*, 128 John St, has decent beer and generous food, as does the cheerful *Lorelei* at 36-38 Esplanade Ave.

Kenfig

The cliffs and beaches north of Porthcawl stop at the one-time fishing port and medieval borough of **KENFIG** (Cynffig), two miles up the coast. Here, a thriving community founded in the Bronze Age was finally overwhelmed by shifting sand dunes in the sixteenth century which buried houses and the church in

If you've got some spare cash, Cowbridge will quickly absorb it. There's **accommodation** at the comfy *Bear Hotel* (℡01446/774814, Ⓦwww.bearhotel .co.uk; ➎) on the High Street, or, a mile west of town, in the grand old manor house of *Crossways* (℡01446/773171, Ⓦwww.crosswayshouse.co.uk; ➍). Cowbridge is chock-full of good **food** possibilities, especially the very reasonable *Farthings Wine Bar*, 54 High St (℡01446/772990), or the posher *Huddart's* restaurant at no. 69 (℡01446/774645; closed Mon). Of the many pubs along the High Street, the *Vale of Glamorgan* is the cosiest, while the atmospheric thatch-roofed *Bush Inn* in St Hilary serves delicious food.

The Vale of Neath

The **Vale of Neath** likes to think of itself as a world apart from the Valleys, looking more towards Cymric Swansea than anglicized Cardiff. **Neath**, focal point of the Vale, is a curious town with antiquities from the Roman, Norman and medieval periods, all set in post-industrial surroundings that somehow make them all the more remarkable. The River Neath flows in from the northeast, past **Aberdulais**, with its impressive, industrial waterfalls, harnessed to generate hydroelectric power. The falls are on the Dulais River, which heads north to the **Cefn Coed Colliery Museum**. The valleys to the east of the Vale of Neath are dealt with in the Valleys section (see pp.98–115).

Neath

The town of **NEATH** (Castell-Nedd) has overcome its past as a centre of copper smelting to become a spacious, pleasantly ordinary place that is much overshadowed by near-neighbour Swansea. The tumbledown **castle** ruins (closed to the public) sit unhappily in a corner of the Morrisons car park, and not far away in the Gwyn Hall on Orchard Street, you'll find the borough **museum** (Tues–Sat 10am–4pm; free), a mildly interesting ramble through Neath's history over the past six thousand years, housed in the splendid surroundings of the Old Mechanics' Institution. Just outside of town off the A465 are the remains of **Neath Abbey** (free access; CADW). The ghostly, dark silhouette of the abbey, founded in the early twelfth century, is wedged in amongst an industrial estate and oily canal. In the sixteenth century, a chunk of the building was converted into a mansion, which later metamorphosed into a copper-smelting works.

Aberdulais and Cefn Coed

Two miles further up the River Neath (accessible by hourly bus #154 from Station Square in Neath) is the village of **ABERDULAIS**, where the River Dulais tumbles over the scoops and platforms of the **Aberdulais Falls** (March & Nov–Christmas Fri–Sun 11am–4pm; April–Oct Mon–Fri 10am–5pm, Sat & Sun 11am–6pm; £3.20; NT). The natural power of the site was first harnessed in 1584 for a copper works that developed into a corn mill, ironworks and a tin-plating unit during the nineteenth century. One hundred and sixty million litres of deep-green water course over the rocks every day, gouging out bowls of rock and pouring over precarious lips jutting out over the spume below. Some of it is still harnessed, via a mini-hydro station installed during the site's restoration in 1991, and by Europe's largest generating water wheel, built in the original wheel pit. Nearby, in the old stable block, there are replicas of some of the many paintings of the falls, a venue beloved of eighteenth-century landscapists, including Turner.

The main A465 heads up the Vale from Aberdulais, with the A4109 off north towards Crynant and the **Cefn Coed Colliery Museum** (April–Oct daily 10.30am–5pm; free), three miles away. Although not as full of gimmicks as the Rhondda Heritage Park or Big Pit, Cefn Coed is an interesting stop, and includes a huge working winding engine and some well-presented exhibitions about the site – once the world's deepest anthracite mine. There are also some glorious signposted walks from the museum up into the surrounding wooded hills.

Swansea

Over fifty years ago, local boy Dylan Thomas called **SWANSEA** (Abertawe) an "ugly, lovely town"; more recently, poet Paul Durden updated the reference in his cult movie *Twin Town* to "pretty, shitty city". Both have a ring of truth to them. Large, sprawling and boisterous, Swansea may only be the second city of Wales, but it's the undoubted Welsh capital of attitude, coated in a layer of chunky bling.

Thomas' scathing but affectionate epithet is well deserved. A jumble of tower blocks and factory units dot the sloping horizons, gathered around the concrete city centre, massively rebuilt after devastating bomb attacks in World War II. But multifarious charms show themselves on closer inspection: some intact old corners of the city centre, the spacious and graceful suburb of Uplands, a wide seafront overlooking the huge sweep of Swansea Bay, and a bold marina development around the old docks. Spread throughout are some of the best-funded **museums** in Wales, including the stunning new **National Waterfront Museum** – itself reason enough to include Swansea on a tour of Wales. Another great bonus is the city's position on the fringe of the ever-popular Gower, with the seaside resorts of **Mumbles** and **Oystermouth**, now little more than salty suburbs, and some of Britain's best **surfing** opportunities on the doorstep.

Some history

The city's Welsh name, Abertawe, refers to the settlement at the mouth of the River Tawe, a grimy ditch that is slowly being teased back to life after centuries of use as a sewer for Swansea's metal trades. The English name is believed to derive from Viking sources, suggesting that a pre-Norman settlement existed in the area. The first reliable origins of Swansea came in 1099, when a Norman castle was built here as an outpost of William the Conqueror's empire. A small settlement grew near the coalfields and the sea, developing into a mining and shipbuilding centre that, by 1700, was the largest coal port in Wales.

Copper smelting became the area's dominant industry in the eighteenth century, soon attracting other metal trades to pack out the lower Tawe Valley. Drawn by the town's flourishing metal trades, a swiftly growing port and the arrival of the Swansea Canal, thousands of emigrants moved to the city from all over Ireland and Britain; by the nineteenth century, the town was one of the world's most prolific metal-bashing centres.

Smelting was already on the wane by the beginning of the twentieth century, although Swansea's port continued to flourish. Britain's first oil refinery was opened on the edge of the city in 1918, with dock developments growing

White House Hotel 4 Nyanza Terrace, Uplands ☎01792/473856, ⓦwww .thewhitehouse hotel.co.uk. Extremely well-kept guesthouse with excellent rates for its well-appointed rooms, all with satellite TV. Extensive breakfasts are included in the rates, and you can get a good three-course evening meal for £10. Internet access is available. ⑤

Windsor Lodge Hotel Mount Pleasant ☎01792/642158, ⓦwww.windsor-lodge .co.uk. Like a country hotel in the city, this two-century-old house has nicely decorated en-suite rooms, elegant but comfortable lounges and an evenings-only restaurant serving British and French cuisine. ④/⑤

The City

Swansea's train station faces out onto the **High Street**, which heads south into Castle Street and past the remains of the **castle**. The most obvious landmark of the ruins are the semicircular arcades, built into the wall between 1330 and 1332 by Bishop Gower to replace a Norman predecessor. The castle enjoys a new, improved setting against the recently overhauled **Castle Square**, a pleasant amphitheatre of steps surrounding a fountain. The ragbag of architecture around it, however, is still postwar Swansea at its most unadventurous – particularly the dull 1950s block entirely given over to McDonald's. Running south from the square, Wind Street (pronounced as in "whined") has been designated as the main drag of nocturnal Swansea, and it is now chock-full of theme and chain bars, pubs and restaurants, with a few more unusual establishments sprinkled into the mix.

A block behind the High Street, the retail park on the Strand includes the great pyramidal glasshouse of **Plantasia** (Tues–Sun & bank holiday 10am–5pm; £3.15), a sweaty world of wondrous tropical plants inhabited by a mini-zoo of tamarin monkeys, butterflies and numerous insects, an aquarium and a thirteen-foot Burmese python.

Alexandra Road forks right off the High Street immediately south of the station, leading down to the **Glynn Vivian Art Gallery** (Tues–Sun 10.30am–5.30pm; free), on the corner of Clifton Hill, a road so steep that the pavement gives way to steps every few yards. This delightful Edwardian gallery houses an inspiring collection of Welsh art including works by Gwen John, her brother Augustus, whose mesmerizing portrait of *Caitlin Thomas*, Dylan's wife, is a real highlight, and Kyffin Williams; the grimy mining portraits of Josef Herman; and a whole room of the huge, frantic canvases of Ceri Richards, Wales' most respected twentieth-century painter. In the early nineteenth century, Swansea was a noted centre of fine porcelain production, of which the gallery houses a large collection, together with pieces of contemporary works from Nantgarw, near Cardiff. Look out too for the frequently changing temporary exhibitions, which are of a consistently high standard.

Belle View Way, off Alexandra Road just south of the gallery, leads to the ugly traffic island, the Kingsway Circle, that acts as a focus for Swansea's shopping districts, with Orchard Street (a pedestrian link to the High Street), Kingsway and Princess Way all converging on the same spot. The main shopping streets lie to the southwest, bounded by Kingsway and Princess Way. Sheltering underneath the Quadrant Centre, the curving-roofed **market** makes a lively sight, with plenty of bustle, colourful stalls and the smells of flowers, fresh baking and food. On sale are local delicacies such as laver bread, a delicious savoury made from seaweed, as well as cockles trawled from the nearby Loughor estuary, typical Welsh cakes, fish and cheeses.

The Maritime Quarter

The spit of land between Oystermouth Road, the sea and the Tawe estuary has been christened the Maritime Quarter – tourist-board-speak for tarted-up old docks – with a centrepiece of a vast marina surrounded by legions of modern flats. To the north, a small grid of nineteenth-century streets is home to a couple of worthwhile sights.

Entering the area from the east, the main road bridge over the Tawe is guarded by a World War II ack-ack gun that stands as a memorial to the Luftwaffe decimation suffered by Swansea. The city's old South Dock, now cleaned and spruced up, features the **Swansea Museum** (Tues–Sun 10.30am–5.30pm; free), or more properly the Royal Institution of South Wales, on Victoria Road. Wales' oldest public museum was founded in 1835, and much of it is still enticingly old-fashioned, although recent revamping has glitzed up many of the displays. The biggest draw is a wizened Egyptian mummy, but there are lots of archeological finds, local porcelain and pottery in ancient glass cases, and a marble bust of Gower son, Edward Evans, who perished with Scott in Antarctica in 1912. A small grid of nineteenth-century streets around the museum has been thoughtfully gentrified, and now houses some enjoyable cafés, pubs and restaurants.

Tucked behind the museum in Somerset Place is the **Dylan Thomas Centre** (daily 10am-4.30pm; free; ℡01792/463980), the National Literature Centre for Wales. Opened in 1995, it houses a theatre space, two galleries, a restaurant, bookshops and craft shops. The building combines the heavily spruced-up nineteenth-century Guildhall with a honeyed modern extension. Inside, there's an extensive display on Dylan Thomas, including a mock-up of the shed in which he wrote at Laugharne, where a fascinating video on his life and work plays continuously.

A hundred yards or so west, behind the *Evening Post* building, the city's **Environment Centre** (daily 10am–4pm; free) is housed in the old telephone exchange on Pier Street. As well as a resource centre for all things green and peaceful, there are regularly changing exhibitions inside.

From here, Burrows Place leads down to the marina and the sublime new **National Waterfront Museum** (daily 10am–5pm; free), a £33 million project that opened in late 2005. Carved out of the shell of the old Industrial and Maritime Museum, the original building has been stunningly extended to accommodate a breathtakingly varied set of exhibitions dealing with Wales' history of innovation and industry. The museum is divided into fifteen zones, looking at topics such as energy, landscape, coal, genealogy, networks and money. Each section is bursting with interactive technology, some of which takes your breath away. You can, for instance, fly over Swansea, explore the people and places of the 1851 census, and go virtual shopping through history. The metals section includes three paternoster lifts whirring around to exhibit some of Wales' many contributions to the world. Within the complex, there are shops, a café and a lovely waterfront balcony. Without doubt, this is the most impressive museum in Wales, and should not be missed.

The museum faces out onto a flotilla of yachts bobbing in the marina. Close by stands John Doubleday's statue of Dylan Thomas, dubbed "A Portrait of the Artist as Someone Else", since it looks nothing like the poet. Just behind the statue, on Gloucester Place, is the mural-splattered warehouse that has now become the **Dylan Thomas Theatre**, which intersperses productions of his work with visiting and local companies' offerings.

West Swansea

West of the city centre, St Helen's Road dips down to the seafront near the tall white tower of the **Guildhall** and Walter Road, staying inland until the airy suburb of **Uplands**. The Guildhall, a typically soaring piece of 1930s civic architecture, contains **Brangwyn Hall** (℡01792/635489 for access), taking its

Listings

Bike rental Swansea Cycle Centre, Wyndham St, near the tourist office ☎01792/410710. From £15 a day.

Books Dylan's Bookstore, Salubrious House, 23 King Edward Rd; Uplands Bookshop, 27 Uplands Crescent; Waterstone's, Oxford St.

Bus enquiries Quadrant Centre bus station, Plymouth St (Mon–Fri 8.30am–5.30pm, Sat 8.30am–5pm); for telephone enquiries call ☎0870/608 2608.

Car rental Enterprise ☎01792/480484 has the best value rentals, will deliver and pick up, and often have excellent value weekend specials.

Ferries Swansea–Cork Ferries ☎01792/456116, ⓦwww.swanseacorkferries.com leave every day for Cork in Ireland from the dock about a mile east of the town centre. The crossing takes about 10hr and generally leaves at 9pm.

Festivals The annual Swansea Bay Summer Festival takes place from May to September, the highbrow Swansea Festival through October and the city's Dylan Thomas Festival in early November; details of all from the tourist office.

Football Swansea City FC play at the new Liberty Stadium, Landore (ⓦwww.swanseacity.net).

Hospital Singleton Hospital, Sketty Park Lane, Singleton, West Swansea ☎01792/205666.

Internet access Swansea Central Library, Alexandra Rd, opposite the Glynn Vivian Art Gallery (Mon–Sat 9.30am–5pm, 6pm Mon–Wed & 7pm Fri; free); XL Wales in the Family Technology Centre, on the corner of Princess May and St Mary St (☎01792/610000; £2.50/1hr).

Laundries Hafod Laundrette, 16 Neath Rd; Uplands Laundrette, 73 Uplands Crescent.

Pharmacies Kingsway Pharmacy, 39 Kingsway (Mon–Sat 10am–6pm).

Police The main station is near the train station on Orchard St (☎01792/456999).

Post office 35 Kingsway ☎01792/655759.

Rugby Ospreys Rugby Club, one of Wales' premier sides, play at the new Liberty Stadium, Landore (ⓦwww.ospreysrugby.com).

Surfing Information and equipment (including second-hand boards) from Big Drop Surf Shop, 1 St David's Square, St David's Centre (☎01792/480481, ⓦwww.big-drop.com).

Swimming The sparkling new Wales National Pool on Sketty Lane near the University is Wales' only 50m facility. ☎01792/513513, ⓦwww.walesnationalpoolswansea.co.uk.

Gower

A fifteen-mile peninsula of undulating limestone, **GOWER** (Gŵyr) is a world of its own, pointing down into the Bristol Channel to the west of Swansea. The area is fringed by sweeping yellow bays and precipitous cliffs, caves and blowholes to the south, and wide, flat marshes and cockle beds to the north. Brackened heaths with prehistoric remains and tiny villages lie between, with castle ruins and curious churches spread evenly around. Out of season, the winding Gower lanes afford opportunities for exploration; but at the height of the summer, they can be horribly congested.

Gower can be said to start in Swansea's western suburbs, along the coast of Swansea Bay that curves round to a point in the pleasantly old-fashioned resort of **Mumbles** and Mumbles Head, marking the boundary between the excesses of Swansea Bay and the rocky inlets that dip and tuck along coastline of southern Gower. This southern coast is punctuated ited for their defensive capacity, best seen in the eerie isolation **Pennard Castle**, high above **Three Cliffs Bay**. West, the Bay sit next to inland reedy marshes, beyond which is **Eynon**. West again, the coast becomes a wild, frilly pped by a five-mile path that stretches all the way to westernmost point, **Worms Head**. tacular four-mile yawn of sand backed by the village of e entire western end of Gower from Worms Head to the ms, and provides some of the best **surfing** opportunities in

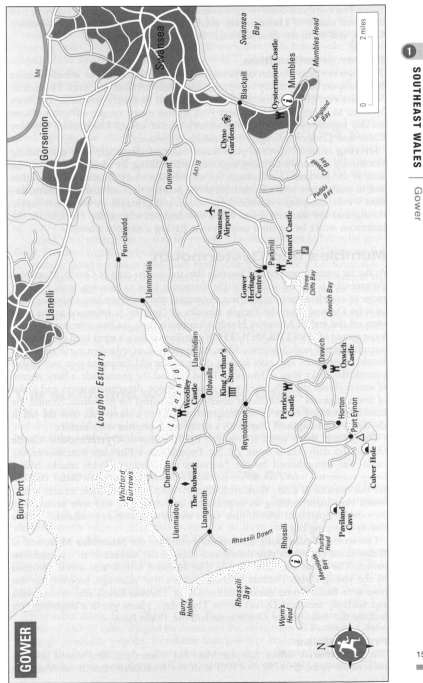

GOWER

Swansea

Gorseinon

Llanelli

Burry Port

M4

Swansea Bay

Mumbles Head

Mumbles

Langland Bay

Caswell Bay

Pwlldu Bay

Oxwich Bay

Three Cliffs Bay

Blackpill

Oystermouth Castle

Clyne Gardens

Dunvant

A4118

Pen-clawdd

Llanmorlais

Swansea Airport

Parkmill

Pennard Castle

Gower Heritage Centre

Oxwich

Oxwich Castle

Penrice Castle

Horton

Port Eynon

Culver Hole

Loughor Estuary

Llanrhidian

Llanrhidian

Llanhidian

Oldwalls

King Arthur's Stone

Weobley Castle

Reynoldston

Llanmadoc

Cheriton

Langennith

The Bulwark

Whitford Burrows

Rhossili Down

Rhossili

Burry Holms

Rhossili Bay

Worm's Head

Mewslade Bay

Thurba Head

Paviland Cave

N

0   2 miles

© Crown copyright

Cliffs Bay, where you turn inland and follow the boundary of the golf course to the castle. Otherwise, you can try one of the paths that fan out along the tufty valley of the Pennard Pill from **PARKMILL**, a tourist honeypot on the main A4118. Here, the **Gower Heritage Centre** (daily: April–Oct 10am–5.30pm; Nov–March 10am–4.30pm; £3.90) is only suited to folk needing to entertain bored kids.

A mile north of Parkmill (reachable via the lane that heads past the Heritage Centre) is the Neolithic (3000–1900 BC) burial chamber known, in honour of the thirteenth-century lords of Oystermouth Castle, as **Parc le Breos**. Although over-restored, the roofless chamber is impressive, if only because of its age and sheer size – seventy feet long and divided into four separate chambers. In 1869, the skeletons of two dozen people were found inside. Just beyond the chamber and to the right, a deep fissure in a limestone outcrop marks the position of the dank and musty **Cathole Rock Cave**, in which flint tools, dating back over 12,000 years have been found.

The best local **B&B** is almost a mile up a lane beside the Heritage Centre: one of the original Gower manor houses, the grand and welcoming *Parc-le-Breos House* (℡01792/371636, ⓦwww.parc-le-breos.co.uk; ❸) also rents bikes (£12 per day), and leads full-day horseback sightseeing trips for £25. **Campers** should make for the *Three Cliffs Caravan Park* at North Hills Farm (℡01792/371218; open April–Oct; £10 per pitch), overlooking Three Cliffs Bay between Parkmill and Penmaen.

Oxwich

One of the most curious landscapes in Gower is the reedy **nature reserve** around **Oxwich Burrows**, a flatland of salt and freshwater marshes reached via the lane that forks left off the A4118 at the ruined gatehouse of the privately owned **Penrice Castle**. Close by on the coast, the scattered village of **OXWICH** is grouped next to the gaping sands of Oxwich Bay. The sands and sea around here regularly receive awards – including the coveted EU blue flag – for their quality, and this is certainly one of Gower's most popular resorts. One way to sample the waters between May and mid-September is with Gower Windsurfing (℡01792/391686), who will take you out for about £10 an hour and offer tuition for beginners and experts. Also based here is Euphoria Sailing (℡01792/234502, ⓦwww.euphoriasailing.com), which offers tuition and rental for sailing, water-skiing and wakeboarding.

The squat church of St Illtud sits alone, away from the village, at the top of the beach. A quieter beach can be found just over a mile away at **Slade Sands**, reached along the lane that climbs from the Oxwich crossroads past the ruins of a Tudor manor, known as **Oxwich Castle** (Easter–Sept daily 10am–5pm; £2; CADW). It's a fine example of early sixteenth-century house gentrification, by Sir Rice Mansel (member of a powerful Welsh dynasty). His son Edward added the multiwindowed eastern range, a pile of rooms together with a highly fashionable long gallery that fell into ruin shortly afterwards.

The popularity of Oxwich is evident in its plentiful **accommodation**: B&Bs include *Little Haven* (℡01792/390940, ⓦwww.littlehavenoxwich.co.uk; ❷; closed Dec), complete with an outdoor pool; *Surfsound Guesthouse* (℡01792/390822, ⓔsurfsound@btinternet.com; ❸; closed Nov–Feb); and *Woodside* (℡01792/390791; ❷; closed Nov–Feb); all on the main street and with en-suite rooms. Nearby, the plain *Oxwich Bay Hotel* (℡01792/390329, ⓦwww.oxwichbayhotel.co.uk; ❹) enjoys its splendid isolation by the sands near the parish church. It's a good place to eat, too. The *Oxwich Camping Park* on the Penrice road over a mile back from the beach (April–Sept; ℡01792/390777; £8–12 per pitch) has a swimming pool and laundry on site.

Horton and Port Eynon

The rocky cliffs from Oxwich Point fade into wide stony bays towards the quiet village of **HORTON**, with a decent beach, and brasher **PORT EYNON**, busy and touristy by comparison, with a clutch of chip shops and the laid-back *Ship Inn*. The villages' sands and dunes are sheltered by a prominent headland, easily reached by a series of paths that wind their way along the shore from the car park, past the Victorian lifeboat station, now the youth hostel, and above the bleak ruins of the old shoreline salt house and oyster pools. The headland, owned by the National Trust, is a wild and windy spot, where tufted grass gives way to sharp limestone crags. A natural cave at the tip can be seen from above, a great dome-shaped chasm that plunges into the hillside. Around the headland to the west is the quite remarkable, but fairly hard to find, **Culver Hole**, built into the cliffs. A man-made cave, it may originally have been a stronghold for the long-gone Port Eynon castle, and has served its time subsequently as a smugglers' retreat, dovecote and armoury.

inly

, a spring
ined chapel
passes numer-
ged with a special
s and dots in hitherto

from the road, which provide clear views to both Gower coasts, but you might be best off stopping at the small car park about a mile east of Reynoldston; from here, a path across the boggy moor leads to **King Arthur's Stone**, a massive and isolated burial chamber capstone dating from at least 4000 BC and weighing over 25 tons.

From Llanrhidian to Llanmadoc

The small and unremarkable village of **LLANRHIDIAN** sits above the great marsh of the same name, a largely inaccessible goo of mud and water virtually indistinguishable from the sands of the Loughor estuary. Views from the former village pub, now the exquisite *Welcome to Town* bistro (℡01792/390015), are superb. Half a mile west, in the hamlet of **Oldwalls**, the *Greyhound Inn* is a cheaper food option, but very good nonetheless. A further mile west and you come to **Weobley Castle** (daily: April–Oct 9.30am–6pm; Nov–March 9.30am–5pm; £2; CADW). Gaunt against the backdrop of the marsh and the estuary, the castle was built as a fortified manor in the latter part of the thirteenth century.

The lane continues two miles west to the village of **Cheriton**, with its charming thirteenth-century church, and then on to **LLANMADOC**, where you can park and venture onto the land spit of **Whitford Burrows**, a soft patch of dunes now open as a nature reserve. Paths lead from Llanmadoc village up the steep hump of **Llanmadoc Hill** to the south. **The Bulwark**, a lonely and windy hillfort, can be seen at the eastern end of Llanmadoc Hill's summit ridge.

B&Bs along Llanmadoc's main road include the seventeenth-century *Britannia Inn* (℡01792/386624; ❹), where you can get a decent pint of real ale, and the *Tallizmand Guesthouse* (℡01792/386373; ❷), which has en-suite rooms and accepts dogs.

Travel details

Unless otherwise stated, frequencies for trains and buses are for Monday to Saturday services, Sunday averages 1–3 services though the main routes are more frequent and some routes have no Sunday service at all.

Trains

Cardiff to: Abergavenny (hourly; 40min); Barry Island (every 20–30min; 30min); Bridgend (every 30min; 20min); Bristol (every 30min; 50min); Caerphilly (every 30min; 20min); Carmarthen (6 daily; 1hr 45min); Chepstow (hourly; 40min); Crewe (mostly hourly; 2hr 40min); Haverfordwest (10 daily; 2hr 40min); Llanelli (17 daily; 1hr 10min); Llantwit Major (hourly; 45min); Llwyny-pia (every 30min; 50min); London (hourly; 2hr); Maesteg (hourly; 50min); Manchester (mostly hourly; 3hr 10min); Merthyr Tydfil (hourly; 1hr); Neath (hourly; 40min); Newport (every 15–30min; 10min); Penarth (every 20min; 10min); Pontypool (hourly; 30min); Pontypridd (every 15min; 30min); Swansea (every 30min; 50min); Tenby (7 daily;

2hr 30min); Trehafod (every 30min; 30min); Ystrad Rhondda (every 30min; 50min).

Newport to: Abergavenny (hourly; 30min); Bristol (every 30min; 40min); Caldicot (hourly; 10min); Cardiff (every 15–30min; 10min); Chepstow (hourly; 20min); Hereford (hourly; 50min); London (hourly; 1hr 50min); Pontypool (hourly; 20min); Swansea (hourly; 1hr 20min).

Swansea to: Cardiff (at least hourly; 50min); Carmarthen (hourly; 50min); Ferryside (10 daily; 40min); Haverfordwest (7 daily; 1hr 30min); Kidwelly (10 daily; 30min); Knighton (4 daily; 2hr 50min); Llandeilo (4 daily; 1hr); Llandovery (4 daily; 1hr 20min); Llandrindod Wells (4 daily; 2hr 20min); Llanelli (hourly; 20min); Llanwrtyd Wells (5 daily; 1hr 50min); London (2 daily; 3hr); Milford Haven (7 daily; 2hr); Narberth (7 daily; 1hr 20min); Newport (hourly; 1hr 20min); Pembroke (6 daily; 2hr); Tenby (7 daily; 1hr 40min); Whitland (hourly; 1hr 10min).

Buses

Bridgend to: Blaengarw (every 20min; 35min); Cardiff (hourly; 50min); Cowbridge (every 30min; 20min); Cymer (every 15min; 1hr); Kenfig (hourly; 45min); Llantrisant (3 daily; 1hr 20min); Llantwit Major (hourly; 40min); Margam Park (every 30min; 30min); Swansea (hourly; 50min).

Cardiff to: Abergavenny (hourly; 1hr 20min); Aberystwyth (2 daily; 4hr); Bangor (1 daily; 8hr); Barry Island (hourly; 50min); Birmingham (5 daily; 2hr 30min); Blaenafon (hourly, 1 change; 1hr 40min); Brecon (5 daily; 1hr 25min); Bristol (10 daily; 1hr 10min); Caernarfon (1 daily; 7hr 40min); Caerphilly (every 30min; 40min); Cardiff–Wales Airport (every 30min; 30min); Chepstow (hourly; 1hr 20min); Cowbridge (every 30min; 40min); Heathrow Airport (8 daily; 2hr 50min); Holyhead (1 daily; 8hr 50min); Lampeter (2 daily; 3hr); Llantwit Major (hourly; 1hr); London (6 daily; 3hr 10min); Machynlleth (1 daily; 5hr 30min); Merthyr Tydfil (every 30min; 45min); Nelson (hourly; 35min); Newport (every 30min; 30min); Penarth (every 30min; 30min); Pontypridd (every 15min; 30min); Senghenydd (hourly; 50min); Swansea (every 30min; 1hr).

Chepstow to: Bristol (hourly; 1hr); Caerwent (hourly; 15min); Cardiff (hourly; 1hr 20min); Monmouth (at least hourly; 50min); Newport (hourly; 50min); Penhow (hourly; 40min); Tintern (8 daily; 20min); Trellech (7 daily; 30min); Usk (6 daily; 45min).

Merthyr Tydfil to: Abergavenny (every 30min; 1hr 30min); Brecon (9 daily; 40min); Cardiff (every 30min; 45min); Swansea (hourly; 1hr).

Monmouth to: Abergavenny (6 daily; 40min); Chepstow (at least hourly; 50min); Newport (8 daily; 1hr); Raglan (hourly; 15min); Ross-on-Wye (6 daily; 40min); Tintern (7 daily; 30min); Trellech (8 daily; 20min); Usk (6 daily; 30min).

Neath to: Aberdulais (hourly; 15min); Cymer (hourly; 35min); Pontrhydyfen (hourly; 25min).

Newport to: Abergavenny (hourly; 1hr); Abertillery (every 30min; 1hr); Birmingham (5 daily; 2hr); Blaenafon (every 15min; 1hr); Brecon (every 2hr; 2hr 20min); Bristol (10 daily; 50min); Caerphilly (every 30min; 40min); Caerwent (hourly; 30min); Cardiff (every 30min; 40min); Chepstow (hourly; 50min); London (5 daily; 2hr 50min); Monmouth (8 daily; 1hr); Pontypool (every 15min; 25min); Raglan (8 daily; 45min); Usk (8 daily; 30min).

Swansea to: Aberdulais (hourly; 45min); Aberystwyth (2 daily; 3hr); Brecon (3 daily; 1hr 30min); Bristol (10 daily; 2hr 30min); Cardiff (every 30min; 1hr); Dan-yr-ogof (4 daily; 1hr); Llangennith (3 daily; 1hr 20min); Merthyr Tydfil (hourly; 1hr); Mumbles (every 10min; 15min); Neath (every 30min; 30min); Oxwich (8 daily; 1hr); Pennard (hourly; 30min); Port Eynon (8 daily; 50min); Rhossili (Mon–Sat 10 daily; 1hr).

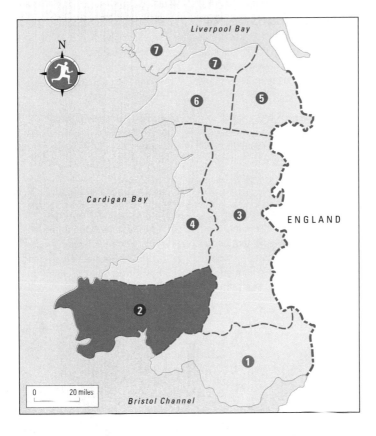

2

Southwest Wales

CHAPTER 2 # Highlights

* **The Tywi Valley** Castles, follies and the fledgling National Botanic Garden set amongst one of Wales' lushest and most atmospheric valleys. See p.175

* **Carreg Cennen Castle** The country's finest fortress, perched on a vertiginous plug of rock and framed by green hills and glowering mountains. See p.178

* **Laugharne** A must for all Dylan Thomas devotees, but much more than that. This quirky place is the quintessential small Welsh coastal town. See p.182

* **St Govan's chapel** A tiny grey chapel wedged into a fissure in the cliffs, just above the churning sea: a phenomenal statement of faith and an awesome sight. See p.195

* **Skomer, Skokholm and Grassholm** Rough and rugged islands, where squawking colonies of birds rule the roost. See p.209

* **St David's** The jewel of Pembrokesire, Britain's smallest city is surrounded by fabulous scenery and fosters a burgeoning surf scene with superb après-surf. See p.211

* **Carn Ingli** One of Wales' holiest mountains, with great views over the mysterious Mynydd Preseli and the charming little seaside town of Newport. See p.223

* **Dyffryn Arms, Pontfaen** A time-wraped pub in the front room of a house where publican, Bessie, serves beer drawn from barrels behind the bar. See p.225

△ St Govan's chapel

Southwest Wales

The most westerly outpost of Wales, the counties of Carmarthenshire and, in particular, Pembrokeshire attract thousands of visitors each year. The principal draw is the fabulous scenery: bucolic and magical inland, where Carmarthenshire follows the Tywi Valley into the heart of the country; rocky, indented and spectacular around the Pembrokeshire Coast National Park and its 186-mile path.

The last remnants of industrial south Wales peter out at **Llanelli**, before the undistinguished county town of **Carmarthen**. Of all the routes that converge on the town, the most glorious is the winding road along the Tywi Valley, past ruined hilltop forts and the **National Botanic Garden of Wales** on the way to **Llandeilo** and Wales' most impressively positioned castle at **Carreg Cennen**, high up on a dizzy plug of Black Mountain rock. Burrowing further inland, the sparsely populated countryside of remote hills and tiny valleys is broken only by endearing small market towns such as **Llandovery**, and the gloomy ruins of **Talley Abbey** and the Roman gold mines at **Dolaucothi**.

The wide sands of southern Carmarthenshire, just beyond Dylan Thomas' adopted hometown of **Laugharne**, merge into the popular south Pembrokeshire bucket-and-spade seaside resorts of **Tenby** and **Saundersfoot**. Tenby sits at the entrance to the south Pembrokeshire peninsula, divided from the rest of the county by the Milford Haven and Daugleddau estuary, which brings its tidal waters deep into the heart of the pastoral county. The peninsula's turbulent, rocky coast is ruptured by some remote historical sites, including the Norman baronial castle at **Manorbier** and **St Govan's chapel**, a minute place of worship wedged into the rocks of a sea cliff near Bosherston. At the top of the peninsula is the old county town of **Pembroke**, dominated by its fearsome castle, across the Milford Haven estuary from small seaside villages and tiny islands along the rugged curve of **St Bride's Bay**, inland of which is the market town and transport interchange of **Haverfordwest**, dull but seemingly difficult to avoid. St Bride's Bay's rutted coastline is one of the most glorious parts of the coastal walk, leading north to brush past the impeccable city of **St David's**, where the exquisite cathedral shelters from the town in its own protective hollow. St David's, founded by Wales' patron saint in the sixth century, is a magnet for visitors; aside from its own charms, there are opportunities locally for spectacular coast and hill walks, hair-raising dinghy crossings to local islands, surf galore and numerous other outdoor activities.

The coast turns towards the north at St David's, becoming the southern stretch of Cardigan Bay. Sixteen miles away by road, and well over thirty by rugged nips and tucks of the coastal walk, is the pretty port of **Fishguard**,

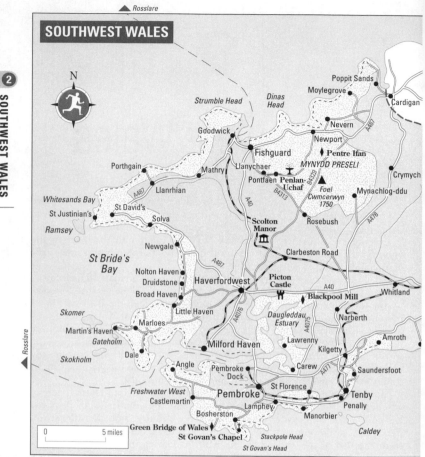

SOUTHWEST WALES

Rosslare

Poppit Sands
Moylegrove
Cardigan
Strumble Head
Dinas Head
Nevern
Goodwick
Newport
Fishguard
Pentre Ifan
MYNYDD PRESELI
Porthgain
Mathry
Llanychaer
Llanrhian
Pontfaen Penlan-Uchaf
Foel Cwmcerwyn 1750
Crymych
Mynachlog-ddu
Whitesands Bay
St David's
St Justinian's
Solva
Ramsey
Scolton Manor
Rosebush
Newgale
Clarbeston Road
St Bride's Bay
Nolton Haven
Druidstone
Haverfordwest
Picton Castle
Broad Haven
Blackpool Mill
Whitland
Skomer
Little Haven
Daugleddau Estuary
Narberth
Marloes
Martin's Haven
Gateholm
Milford Haven
Lawrenny
Kilgetty
Amroth
Skokholm
Dale
Angle
Pembroke Dock
Carew
Saundersfoot
Freshwater West
Pembroke
St Florence
Tenby
Castlemartin
Lamphey
Penally
Bosherston
Manorbier
Caldey
Green Bridge of Wales
St Govan's Chapel
Stackpole Head
St Govan's Head

Rosslare

0   5 miles

© Crown copyright

terminus for ferries to Rosslare in Ireland. The northernmost section of the Coast Path, from Fishguard to the outskirts of Cardigan and past the delightful little town of **Newport**, is the most dramatic and remote. To the south and southeast are the eerie **Mynydd Preseli**, relic-spattered mountains overlooking windswept plateaux of heathland and isolated villages – none more remote than along the leafy **Cwm Gwaun**, a lovely and much-bypassed valley cutting through the hills.

Getting around

Despite the remoteness of much of southwestern Wales, public transport is surprisingly efficient and comprehensive, though you'll have to plan carefully. Direct **train** services connect Cardiff and Swansea with Llanelli, Carmarthen, Tenby, Haverfordwest, Milford Haven and Fishguard, while the Heart of Wales line shuffles out of Swansea and Llanelli to Llandeilo and Llandovery before delving into Powys. Connecting bus services out to the smaller towns and villages are regular and dependable, especially to the more popular destina-

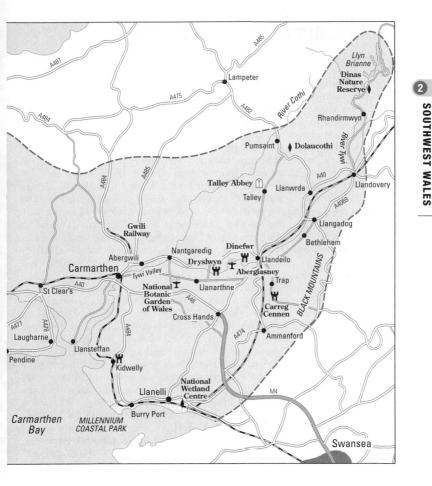

tions of Laugharne, Saundersfoot, Broad Haven and Dale on St Bride's Bay, and St David's.

Bus services are more thorough in peak tourist season, when most coastal villages have a fairly regular operation. Carmarthen and Haverfordwest are the principal bus terminuses, with some services radiating out from Tenby, Pembroke and Fishguard. The Pembrokeshire coast is particularly well catered for, with various winsomely titled services – the Coastal Cruiser, the Puffin Shuttle, the Poppit Rocket and more – operating under the banner of Pembrokeshire Coastal Bus Services. Only in the deserted lanes of northern and eastern Pembrokeshire does bus travel become difficult, although it's excellent walking and cycling country, and there are ample places to rent **bikes** throughout the area. Off the mainland, most of the islands are connected by regular (seasonal) **boat** services, although few of these allow for overnight stops.

Bus timetables are widely available locally, and online at ⓦ **www.pembroke shiregreenways.co.uk** where you'll find full details of all the local transport options.

From Llanelli to Carmarthen

LLANELLI marks the informal border between anglicized southeast Wales and the *bro*, Welsh Wales, where the native language is part of everyday conversation. Once known as Tinopolis after its major industry, Llanelli is now famed for the sprawling Felinfoel and Buckley breweries, and for the **Llanelli rugby club** (T 01554/783900, W www.scarlets.co.uk), known as the Scarlets, one of the most successful teams in Wales. In 1972, they managed to beat the New Zealand All Blacks, a slender victory over which there is still much crowing. The Scarlets play at Stradey Park, a mile out on the A484 to Burry Port, where the goalposts are topped with red tin saucepans as a reminder of the town's origins; the famous Welsh ditty *Sosban Fach* ("little saucepan") is the club's anthem.

If neither rugby nor beer appeals, there's little to keep you in Llanelli, though half a mile north of the centre, off the A476 Felinfoel Road, the graceful upland houses of the metal masters surround the pleasant glades of **Parc Howard**, with superb views down to the sea. The park centres on the Victorian home of Sir Stafford Howard, tinplate merchant and Llanelli's first mayor, which now serves as the town **museum** (Mon–Fri 11am–1pm & 2–4pm, Sat & Sun 2–4pm; free), a diverting enough collection of old photos, Llanelli pottery and a few surprises, such as a nightdress and chemise belonging to Queen Victoria.

There's more of interest a mile east of town on the muddy banks of the River Loughor (Afon Llwchwr) where the **National Wetlands Centre** (daily: Easter–Sept 9.30am–5pm; Oct–Easter 9.30am–4.30pm; £5.50; W www.wwt .org.uk) overlooks an extensive area of salt marsh dotted with bird hides and landscaped walkways. Uneconomic farmland has been adapted to the needs of wildfowl, with "natural" ponds created around existing mature hedgerows, and even owl nesting sites fashioned from old sewer pipes. Important populations of lapwing, redshank, and over-wintering pintail, widgeon and teal are already drawing legions of bird-watchers, but the centre caters just as well to kids and the curious, mainly through the imaginative Discovery Centre – it's easy to lose most of a day here. **Bikes** can be rented from just beside the Wetlands Centre (May–Sept Sat & Sun, plus daily during summer school holidays; £3 per hour) for exploring the fourteen-mile **Millennium Coastal Park** (free access), a traffic-free cycle path along the Loughor estuary, which is dotted with viewpoints, modern sculpture, lakes and a new golf course. It forms part of the 220-mile Celtic Trail (see p.65).

The pick of Llanelli's **accommodation** is *Llwyn Hall*, Llwynhendy (T 01554/777754, W www.llwynhall.com; ⑤), a comfortable, relaxed and tasteful antique-filled house almost two miles east on the B4297. Otherwise, there are a few fairly ordinary B&Bs, such as *Awel y Môr*, 86 Queen Victoria Rd (T & F 01554/755357; ②). For **food**, there are cheap Indian and Chinese restaurants on Station Road and elsewhere in the town centre, and several good, boozy **pubs**: try Murray Street for a variety, including the cheery *Queen Victoria*. Half a mile east of the Stradey Park rugby ground on the main A484 is the rugby lover's shrine of the *Tafarn y Sospan*, well worth a visit.

Burry Port and Kidwelly

Both the coastal cycle path and train line run four miles west from Llanelli along the sands of the Loughor estuary to the humdrum town of **BURRY PORT** (Porth Tywyn). Five minutes' walk south of the train station, the harbour is a pleasant surprise, as the town itself shows no sign of any nautical inclination. It was here that Amelia Earhart, the first woman to fly the Atlantic, landed after a journey of nearly 21 hours in June 1928 – there's a memorial stone by the harbour.

A further ten miles along the train line from Llanelli is **KIDWELLY** (Cydweli; request stop only), a sleepy little town dominated by an imposing **castle** (June–Sept daily 9.30am–6pm; April, May & Oct daily 9.30am–5pm; Nov–March Mon–Sat 9.30am–4pm, Sun 11am–4pm; £2.50; CADW), strategically sited overlooking the River Gwendraeth and a vast tract of coast. The castle was established around 1106 by the Bishop of Salisbury as a satellite of Sherborne Abbey in Dorset. On entering through the massive fourteenth-century gatehouse, you can still see portcullis slats and murder holes, through which noxious substances could be tipped onto intruders. The **gatehouse** forms the centrepiece of the impressively intact semicircular outer ward walls, which can be climbed for some great views over the grassy courtyard and rectangular inner ward above the river. This is the oldest surviving part of the castle, dating from around 1275, with the upper storeys added in the fourteenth century by Edward I's nephew. Views from the musty solar and hall, packed into the easternmost wall of the inner ward, show the castle's defensive position at its best, with the river directly below. Although the whole castle is long since roofless, the remains are some of the most intact of any medieval Welsh castle that has not been extensively restored. A fourteenth-century town **gate** shields the castle approach from Castle Street, which is the main road through Kidwelly.

Two miles out of town up Priory Street, a former tinplate works now houses the small-scale and entertaining **Industrial Museum** (May–Sept Mon–Fri 10am–5pm, Sat & Sun noon–5pm; free). Many of the works' old features have been preserved, including the rolling mills where long lines of tin were rolled and spun into wafer-thin slices.

On the other side of the train station from town is the old **quay**, cleaned up and restored into an appealingly remote and forlorn picnic area and nature reserve. From here, there are views of wading birds skimming over the nearby mud flats and old salt pans of the Gwendraeth estuary, once an important port for the medieval town.

In Kidwelly, there's superb farmhouse **accommodation** at *Penlan Isaf* (☎01554/890084, ⓦwww.penlanisaf.com; ❷), a dairy farm overlooking town. For something grander, try *Gwenllian Court*, Mynydd-y-Garreg (☎01554/890217, ⓦwww.gwenllian.net; ❸), a country hotel with plenty of amenities. You can **camp** at the caravan-oriented *Carmarthen Bay Touring & Camp Site*, Tanylan Farm (☎01267/267306, ⓔtanylanfarm@aol.com; closed Oct–Easter; £12 per pitch), which perches alongside the estuary between Kidwelly and Ferryside. Good **food** and **drink** are available at the cosy *Boot and Shoe*, 2 Castle St; *Time For Tea*, 7 Bridge St, is great for daytime snacks.

St Ishmael and Ferryside

As the train leaves Kidwelly and hugs the side of the River Tywi's estuary, the views out across the water are magnificent. You'll pass by a tiny chapel at **ST ISHMAEL**, built to serve a medieval village that was completely destroyed in a storm three hundred years ago, and is now buried deep beneath the flats; a huge storm in 2000 briefly revealed some remains. A mile further on, **FERRYSIDE** (Glanyfferi) is a tiny village that grew as a day-trip destination for Valley miners. Although the train station still remains (request stop only), Ferryside is tranquil today, its narrow streets facing Llansteffan Castle across the calm waters and circling sea birds. The *White Lion Hotel* on the main square is the best place for **food** and **drink**, as is the inexpensive, daytime-only *Ferry Cabin* restaurant, which does wonderfully fresh sea trout – known around these parts as *sewin*.

② Carmarthen and around

The ancient and unquestioned capital of its region, **CARMARTHEN** (Caerfyrddin) does not entirely live up to the promise of its status. Although it's a useful transport interchange and lively market town, with some excellent shops and sixty pubs for 15,000 inhabitants, there's an undeniably cheerless atmosphere which doesn't encourage you to stay for long – fortunately, with so many beautiful and interesting places nearby, there's little need to. It's the first major town in west Wales, where the native language is heard at all times, and was once – in the early eighteenth century – the largest town in all of Wales on the strength of its position at the tidal limit of the River Tywi.

Founded as a Roman fort, Carmarthen's most popular moment of mythological history dates from the Dark Ages and the supposed birth of the wizard **Merlin** just outside the town (see box) – Myrddin, in Welsh, gives Carmarthen its name. In the late eleventh century, the Normans began a castle near the remains of a Roman fort, extending its walls to encompass a growing village. In 1313, Carmarthen was granted its first charter by Edward I, helping the town to flourish as an important wool centre, and the town was taken by Owain Glyndŵr in the early years of the fifteenth century. An eisteddfod was inaugurated in the mid-fifteenth century, and is still used as the basis for today's National Eisteddfod. The importance of the town grew, attracting trade and new commerce, industrial works, a key port and a position as a seat of local government, a status it still holds as the county town of Carmarthenshire.

A mile out of town, **Abergwili** is primarily of interest for the quality Carmarthen County Museum, and its role as Merlin's resting place.

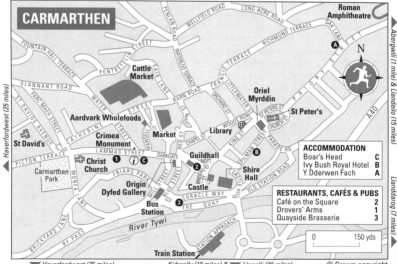

Merlin

Merlin (Myrddin) is a difficult character to pin down. A mythic figure throughout Europe's Celtic fringe, he is variously described as wizard and prophet, though half-demon, antichrist and creator of Stonehenge have also had currency over the centuries. His most common association, of course, is with King Arthur (see box, p.96) to whom he was tutor, wizard and advisor. It was Merlin who arranged Arthur's ascendancy to the throne through the sword-in-the-stone contest, Merlin who founded the Round Table, and Merlin who accompanied Arthur to the Isle of Avalon at the end of his life.

This interpretation dates back to the twelfth-century writings of Geoffrey of Monmouth who, in his 1134 work *Historia Regum Britanniae*, drew on all sorts of tales and folklore (plus a fair bit of fabrication) to create the Merlin we know today. He is even credited with inventing the Latinized "Merlin" form to avoid his character being associated with "merde", the French for excrement.

According to Monmouth, Merlin was born in Carmarthen, a conjecture supported half a century later by Giraldus Cambrensis (see box, p.428) who reported the same on his travels around Wales.

Monmouth built on earlier stories of very different Merlins under different names – Myrddin Wyllt (Merlin the wild), Merlin Caledonensis (Scottish Merlin), and the most Welsh, Myrddin Emrys (Merlin Ambrosius). These may have been separate people whose stories have blended, or the same person whose stories have diverged in the centuries of telling.

Local legend has it that Merlin lives on under Merlin's Hill, where he will remain until King Arthur and his men rise up when the country is in great danger. Another story tells of Merlin predicting that "when Merlin's tree shall tumble down, then shall fall Carmarthen town". The oak, which once stood in the centre of Carmarthen, died a few years back, but Carmarthen remains. A piece of the tree can be seen in the Carmarthen County Museum.

Today Carmarthen celebrates its legendary connection with the Gŵyl Myrddyn (Merlin Festival; ☎01554/747542, ⊛www.carmarthenshire.gov.uk) which takes place in Carmarthen Park in mid-June with a funfair, coracle racing, medieval village, fortune tellers and, of course, magicians.

The Town

Approaching from the train station, the stern facade of the early twentieth-century **Shire Hall** shields the rambling streets of the town centre, and largely swallows up the uninspiring remains of the **castle**, Edward I's reworking of an earlier Norman fortress, off **Nott Square**. The most picturesque eighteenth- and nineteenth-century part of town lies spread out at the base of the castle, around King Street and Nott Square, the town's main shopping hub.

From Nott Square, the broad, sloping Darkgate leads down to Lammas Street, a wide Georgian thoroughfare flanked by coaching inns. To the north is the indoor **market**, a great centre for local produce, second-hand books, antiques and endearingly useless tat, with several cheap cafés. On the main market days – Wednesday and Saturday – stalls spill outside into a slate-grey modern square. Off Darkgate is Blue Street and the excellent **Origin Dyfed Gallery** (Mon–Sat 10am–5pm; free), the public face of a local art and craft co-operative.

From the other side of Nott Square, King Street heads northeast towards the sturdy tower of **St Peter's church**, architecturally undistinguished but well placed amongst the trees and surrounding townhouses. Inside, Carmarthen's status as one of the most important Roman towns in Wales is evident from the altar in the (often closed) western porch. Opposite is the Victorian School of Art that has now metamorphosed into the excellent **Oriel Myrddin** (Mon–Sat 10am–5pm; free), a craft centre and art gallery that shows the work of local artists.

Half a mile further east, just off Priory Street, are the insubstantial remains of a **Roman amphitheatre**, excavated in the late 1960s. In contrast with the atmospheric bowl at Caerleon, Carmarthen's remnants, surrounded by modern housing, are no more than a few grass humps.

Abergwili

The severe grey Bishop's Palace at **ABERGWILI**, a mile east of Carmarthen, was the seat of the Bishop of St David's between 1542 and 1974, and now houses the **Carmarthen County Museum** (Mon–Sat 10am–4.30pm; free), a spirited amble through the history of the area. This surprisingly interesting exhibition covers the history of Welsh translations of the New Testament and Book of Common Prayer – both translated for the first time here in 1567. Local pottery, archeological finds, wooden dressers and a lively history of local castles are presented in well-annotated displays, along with material on crime and policing, geology, education, the local coracle industry and the origins of Wales' first eisteddfod in Carmarthen in 1450.

A mile east of Abergwili, the main A40 road passes the sharp slopes of **Merlin's Hill** (Bryn Myrddin), reputedly the sleeping place of the great wizard. Alltyfyrddin Farm, on whose land this lies, has cashed in with the cheesy **Merlin's Hill Centre** (daily: April–Oct 10am–7pm; Nov–March 10am–5pm; £2), full of sub-Harry Potter exhibits aimed mainly at kids, but which at least gives access to the hill.

Practicalities

Trains between Swansea and Pembrokeshire stop at the **train station**, which lies over the Carmarthen bridge on the south side of the River Tywi. All **buses** terminate at the bus station on Blue Street, north of the river, and many connect with the arrival and departure of trains. The **tourist office** is at 113 Lammas St, near the Crimea Monument (daily 9.30am–5.30pm; ☎01267/231557, ⊛www .carmarthenshire.gov.uk), while information on the alternative scene can be found at Aardvark Wholefoods in Mansel Street or, for Welsh-language events, Siop y Pentan in the market square. For free **Internet access** visit the library on King Street near St Peter's church.

The range of **accommodation** and eating in Carmarthen is limited and few places are truly notable, so the following listings include a selection of places in the adjoining Tywi Valley.

Accommodation

Boar's Head 120 Lammas St ☎01267/222789, ⊛www.boarsheadhotel.com. One of the town's grandest old coaching inns with modest but comfortable rooms and a good bar and restaurant. Breakfast is £5 extra per person. ④

Ivy Bush Royal Hotel Spilman St ☎01267/235111, ⊛www.ivybushroyal.co.uk. Recently refurbished town-centre hotel with its own gym, sauna and a decent restaurant where you're served breakfast (included). ⑥

Tresi Aur Llanddarog, off the A48, 7 miles east of Carmarthen ☎01267/275741. Luxurious and good-value guesthouse that's handy for the National Botanic Garden. ③

Tŷ Castell B&B Station Rd, Nantgaredig ☎01267/290034, ⊛www.ty-castell.co.uk. Wonderful outdoors-oriented farmhouse B&B on the banks of the Towy, 6 miles east of Carmarthen along the A40, with a licensed restaurant on site. ②

Y Dderwen Fach 98 Priory St ☎01267/234193. The best of the central B&Bs. ①

Eating, drinking and entertainment

Boar's Head 120 Lammas St. Old coaching inn with a good bar and frequent live music.

Café on the Square Nott Square. Arguably the pick of the town's coffee and lunch spots.

Drovers' Arms 106 Lammas St. Unpretentious spot that's more sedate than some of the town's other pubs, with some superb beers.

Quayside Brasserie Coracle Way ☎01267/223000. Superb restaurant that's great for fresh local meat, fish and seafood (mains £9–15), and especially popular at lunchtime.

White Hart Llanddarog, off the A48, 7 miles east of Carmarthen. Thatched pub serving fine food and its own brewed beer.

Whitemill Inn Whitemill, just off the A40, 5 miles east of Carmarthen. Very good-value pub food in a quiet roadside hamlet.

The Tywi Valley

The **River Tywi** curves and darts its way east from Carmarthen through some of the most spellbinding scenery in south Wales. It's not hard to see why the Merlin legend has taken such a hold in these parts – the landscape does seem infused with a kind of eerie magic. The thirty-mile trip from Carmarthen to **Llandovery** is punctuated by gentle, impossibly green hills topped with ruined castles, notably the wonderful **Carreg Cennen** near Llandeilo. Along the way, two budding gardens have sprung up in the last few years: one completely new in the form of the **National Botanic Garden of Wales**; the other a faithful restoration of the original walled gardens around the long-abandoned house of **Aberglasney**.

The tourist office in Carmarthen (see opposite) and a smaller one at Llandeilo (see p.177) have lots of **information** about the Tywi Valley and surrounding area, including the ever improving array of quality accommodation: we've listed the best of these under the Carmarthen and Llandovery accounts. Regular **buses** run along the A40 between Carmarthen and Llandeilo giving access to Aberglasney and Dinefwr: the #166 runs twice daily from Carmarthen train station to the National Botanic Garden.

The National Botanic Garden of Wales

Though only opened in 2000, the great glass "eye" of the **National Botanic Garden of Wales** (daily: April–Oct 10am–6pm; Nov–March 10am–4.30pm; £7, discounts for groups and those arriving by bike or public transport; Ⓦwww.gardenofwales.org.uk) has quickly become the centrepiece of the Tywi Valley. Located one mile north of the A48 and seven miles east of Carmarthen, it was conceived in the mid-1990s as a way of transforming the 500-acre remains of the once-immense estate owned by William Paxton, an early nineteenth-century London banker. The garden has gradually come to warrant its considerable hype, and although it will be years before it's anything like complete, enough of the elements are in place to see its huge potential.

A central walkway leads past lakes, sculpture and geological outcrops from all over Wales, with walks down towards slate bed plantings and different wood and wetland habitats. Paxton's double-walled garden has been teased back to life (providing vegetables for the good on-site café/restaurant), and enhanced by the addition of a small but exquisite Japanese garden, and a bee garden that's home to a million bees.

At the top of the hill is the garden's most audacious feature: the vast oval **glasshouse** designed by Norman Foster, a stunning piece of architecture that justifies a visit on its own. Inside are plants from regions with a Mediterranean

△ National Botanic Garden of Wales

climate: the Cape region of South Africa, southwestern Australia, Chile, California and the Mediterranean itself. Not far away are the remains of **Middleton Hall**, which burnt down in 1931, whose old estate forms the centrepiece of the gardens. A nearby group of buildings house a restaurant, an excellent exhibition about the Welsh herbalists known as the Physicians of Myddfai and the new Theatre Botanica, all focused around **Millennium Square**, the venue for open-air concerts and performances. The entire garden has been designed around principles of sustainability: rainwater is caught and used for irrigation; the glasshouses are heated by burning wood coppiced on the grounds; and human waste is transformed into essentially pure water by means of a series of reed beds. A large tract of the surrounding land is being turned over to organic farming using Welsh breeds of cattle and sheep, and the estate's outer edges are re-creations of moorland, spring wood, prairie and native Welsh habitats.

Aberglasney

A natural twin to the Botanic Garden can be found five miles northeast at **Aberglasney** (daily: April–Sept 10am–6pm; Nov–March 10.30am–4pm; £6; ⓦwww.aberglasney.org), half a mile south of the A40 near Broad Oak. While a partly ruined manor house dating back to the fifteenth century is the estate's centrepiece, it is the stunning **gardens** that have caused all the excitement. Locals had always known about the decaying and abandoned house – which even had Listed Building status – but it was only in 1994, when the grand eight-columned portico came up for sale at Christie's for £13,000, that the authorities took notice. The portico was withdrawn from the sale and reattached to the house as part of the major restoration undertaken by the Aberglasney Trust, although the stabilized shell of the building seems destined to play second fiddle to its all-but unique set of gardens. Once massively overgrown, these mostly sixteenth- to eighteenth-century walled gardens have regained much of their original formal splendour, while archeological work has uncovered their history. Especially noteworthy is the replanted kitchen garden and what is thought to be the only secular cloister garden in Britain. A walkway leads around the top of the cloister giving access to a set of six Victorian aviaries, and great views over the Jacobean Pool garden and the mature woodlands beyond. The highlight, though, is the yew tunnel, a line of five yews planted three centuries ago, and trained over to root on the far side.

In 2005, the central courtyard of the manor house was glassed in to form an atrium populated with subtropical plants – tree ferns, cycads, orchids and more. Dubbed a Ninfarium (after gardens at Ninfa, forty miles outside Rome) it already makes a beautiful counterpoint to the outdoor gardens, and should develop nicely over the next few years.

Dinefwr Castle

The strategic importance of the Tywi Valley is underlined by the tumbledown ruins of **Dinefwr Castle** (unrestricted access; CADW), a mile west of Llandeilo, reached through the extensive Dinefwr Park, a spectacular isolated spot on a wooded bluff over the river a few miles east of Aberglasney. The castle was built in the twelfth century by Lord Rhys, who united the warring Welsh princes against the Normans.

By 1523 the castle had become ill suited to the needs of Lord Rhys's descendants, who aspired to something more luxurious, and eventually built a new residence in 1660. Now named **Newton House** (mid-March to Oct Mon & Thurs–Sun 11am–5pm; house & park £3.80, park only £2.60; NT), it was given a new limestone facade in the 1860s and is currently being restored by the National Trust and should open in 2006 complete with new interpretive exhibition and tearoom. The lovely **park** was mostly landscaped in the 1770s by George Rhys, whose work was much admired and slightly enhanced by Capability Brown. It now contains rare white cattle, fallow deer and a woodland nature reserve.

Llandeilo, Carreg Cennan Castle and around

A mile east of Dinefwr, beautifully situated on the edge of the magnificent uplands of the Black Mountain, the small, rustic town of **LLANDEILO** is a place in transition. It remains a quiet market town, but has recently begun to fashion itself as an upscale rural retreat for the aspirational of Swansea, Cardiff and beyond, with a boutique hotel (see below), some fancy shops and galleries, and a handful of delis, cafés and restaurants. Though there's little to actually do in town, these assets make it a good base for exploring the region.

Llandeilo's few streets cluster around its main thoroughfare, Rhosmaen Street, and the parish **church of St Teilo** with its unusual raised graveyard (split by the main road). There's a small local **tourist office** (Tues–Sat 10.30am–5pm; ☎01558/823960) in the Artwerks craft gallery beside the Crescent Road car park, or you can pick up information on alternative local happenings at the excellent Friends of the Earth-run Green House shop, opposite the Barclays bank on Rhosmaen Street.

Llandeilo's new focal point is its **hotel**, the *Cawdor Arms*, 70 Rhosmaen St (☎01558/823500, ⓦwww.thecawdor.com; ⑤–⑨), a former coaching inn that has been given a major postmodern makeover and boasts chic, simply decorated rooms and stunning attic suites. It also has an excellent semi-formal **restaurant** serving three-course lunches (£10) and dinners (£20), while good wine, guest ales and deep leather sofas attract a broad clientele just for a **drink**.

If you can't stretch to the prices at the *Cawdor Arms*, there are several appealing accommodation options in the surrounding countryside (see below), though nothing much in town. There are plenty of places to **eat**, though, including *Barita*, 139 Rhosmaen St, for good coffee and cakes, and *The Angel Inn*, 62

Rhosmaen St (☎01558/822765), for modestly priced bistro meals. Llandeilo is positively stuffed with **pubs**: try the *White Horse*, a nice old coaching inn serving beer from the local brewery.

Carreg Cennen Castle

Isolated in the rural hinterland four miles southeast of Llandeilo is the most magnificently sited castle in Wales. **Carreg Cennen Castle** (daily: mid-March to Oct 9.30am–6.30pm; Nov to mid-March 9.30am–dusk; £3; CADW) was constructed on its fearsome outcrop in 1248 (though Sir Urien, one of King Arthur's knights, is said to have built a fortress here earlier), and stayed a Welsh stronghold until it fell to the English in 1277, during Edward I's first invasion. It remained in use until 1462, when it was partly destroyed by the Earl of Pembroke, for being a rebel base.

The castle's most striking aspect is its vertiginous location, three hundred feet above a sheer drop into the green valley of the Cennen River. The car park and **farm**, with rare breeds of cows and sheep, are at the bottom of a long path that climbs sharply upwards, with astounding **views** towards the severe purple lines of the Black Mountain, in utter contrast to the velvet greenery of the Tywi and Cennen valleys. The castle seems impenetrable, its crumbling walls merging with the limestone on which it defiantly sits. The highlights of a visit are the views down into the valley and the long descent into a watery, pitch-black cave that is said to have served as a well. Torches are essential (£1 rental from the tearoom near the car park), although it's worth continuing as far as possible and then turning them off to experience absolute darkness. The tearoom has a superb selection of home-cooked Welsh dishes, while a stone's throw away from the castle there's *Penhill* (☎01558/823060, ⓦwww.penhill.org.uk; ❷), a simple but very pleasant **B&B**.

Near the village of **TRAP**, a mile below the castle, you'll find a nice pub, the *Cennen Arms,* and the **Trapp Arts & Craft Centre** (March–Christmas daily except Mon 10.30am–6pm; free), a family-run showcase for local artisans, where imaginative temporary exhibitions complement the main business of selling.

Towards Llandovery

The railway and the A40 head northeast from Llandeilo through a pastoral landscape in which biblical reminders, attesting to fervent Welsh Christianity, can be seen in the hamlets of **BETHLEHEM**, where the friendly village shop and tearoom will keep your Christmas cards ready to be franked with the blessed postmark, and **SALEM**, an otherwise nondescript place with a good B&B and gastropub (see below). These places lie a couple of miles off the main road (south and north respectively), flanking **LLANGADOG**, which sits just off the A40 at the six-mile mark, a pretty little village beneath the glowering bluff of the Black Mountain.

The massive Iron Age hillfort of **Garn Goch**, which rises up above Bethlehem and spreads over fifteen acres, is as impressive for its bleak isolation as for the remaining earthworks and stone rampart. Against the brooding backdrop of the Black Mountain, this area is a more dramatic place to **stay** than the Tywi Valley. Good bets include the relaxing *Camomile House*, Gors Road, Salem (☎01558/822139; ❷); the comfy B&B accommodation at *Cynyll Farm* (☎01550/777316; £40 ❷), on the A4069 two miles southeast of Llangadog; and the imposing guest suite at the sixteenth-century *Cefn Cilgwyn* (☎01550/779066, ⓦwww.pasturefarm.com; ❸), near Garn Goch. On the main A40, just north of the Llangadog turning, there's a decent **campsite** at *Abermarlais Caravan Park* (☎01550/777868, ⓦwww.ukparks.com; closed

Dec–Feb; £9 per pitch). For **eating**, head to Salem and *The Angel Inn* restaurant (☎01558/823394), formerly a village pub which still does great bar meals, but partly transformed into a gastropub with superb if slightly pricey meals all beautifully prepared and presented.

Llandovery and around

Twelve miles northeast of Llandeilo, the town of **LLANDOVERY** (Llanymddyfri) makes a natural base for exploring the Tywi Valley, with the breathtaking countryside around the Dolaucothi Gold Mine to the west and tranquil Llyn Brianne to the north. The town's architecture and layout have changed little for centuries, the main Broad Street widening as it nears the cobbled Market Square, with its clocktower. This thoroughfare is lined with solid early nineteenth-century townhouses and older inns, much as it was when itinerant writer George Borrow visited in 1854 during his grand tour of Wales, remembering it as the "pleasantest little town in which I have halted in the course of my wanderings". Llandovery retains its ancient cattle market (every other Tuesday), but like so many other mid-Wales settlements, an influx of New Agers since the 1960s has had a discernible effect on the town. Alternative-type bookshops and wholefood stores abound.

On a grassy mound on the south side of Broad Street, the scant ruins of a **castle** afford fine views over Llandovery's huddled grey buildings and the Bran River, branching off the Tywi outside town, but the real draw is a stunning stainless-steel sculpture of local lord Llywelyn ap Gruffydd Fychan, the "Welsh Braveheart", who was executed in front of the English king Henry IV, for supporting the rebel prince Owain Glyndŵr in 1401.

Above the tourist office (see below), the community-run **Llandovery Heritage Centre** (Easter–Sept daily 10am–5pm, Oct–Easter Mon–Sat 10am–4pm, Sun 2–4pm; donation appreciated) contains a fine section on the legend of the Lady of the Lake from Llyn y Fan Fach, the outlaw Twm Sion Cati, the "Welsh Robin Hood", and seventeenth-century vicar Rhys Prichard, author of *Canwyll y Cymry* ("The Welshmen's Candle"). There's also material on the cattle drovers and their Black Ox bank which became a part of the present-day LloydsTSB bank.

Practicalities

The **train station** sits on the main A40 just before it becomes Broad Street; **buses** leave from Broad Street and Market Square. On Kings Road, the continuation of Broad Street, the joint **tourist office** and Brecon Beacons National Park visitor centre (Easter–Sept daily 10am–5.30pm; Oct–Easter Mon–Sat 10am–4pm, Sun 2–4pm; ☎01550/720693) is well stocked with leaflets on local walks and natural history and has an interpretive centre on the Black Mountain. Also on Broad Street, you can buy local guides and books at the Old Printing Office near the war memorial, or obtain details of alternative events at the Iechyd Da health-food shop.

The swankiest **place to stay** is the colonnaded *Castle Hotel* on Broad Street (☎01550/720343, ⓦwww.llandoverycastlehotel.co.uk; ❸), but there's cosier accommodation across the road at *The Drovers*, 9 Market Square (☎01550/721115, ⓦwww.droversllandovery.co.uk; ❸), an eighteenth-century townhouse full of antique furniture, with a guests' bar. With your own transport, two superb choices are the Gothic-styled en-suite rooms at *Cwm Rhuddan Mansion* (☎01550/721414, ⓔcwmrhuddan@hotmail.com; ❹), a mile southwest on the A4069, and the charming *Cwmgwyn Farm* on Llangadog Road

(T01550/720410, Wwww.cwmgwyn-holidays.co.uk; ❷), a mile further on. The nearest **campsite** is Erwlon (T01550/720332, Wwww.ukparks.com; £10 per pitch), a mile east of Llandovery off the A40.

Easily the best daytime **eating** is at *The Kitchen Garden*, inside the Craft Centre at the corner of Kings Road and Stone Street. The *Blue Bell* pub, 19 High St, does a good curry and very reasonable steaks, and outside town, the *Royal Oak Inn* in Rhandirmwyn (see opposite), is well worth the trip for its imaginative menu of nicely cooked classics. For **drinking**, the eccentric and bizarrely old-fashioned *Red Lion*, a red, colonnaded house nestled in an easy-to-miss corner at 2 Market Square, can't be beaten. If, as often happens, the landlord has chosen to close early, try the upscale *King's Head* nearby.

The Dolaucothi Gold Mine, Talley Abbey and Brechfa Forest

West of Llandovery the countryside is blissfully quiet, with a handful of main roads and lanes that rarely carry much traffic. The principal route off the A40 between Llandeilo and Llandovery is the A482 which heads six miles to the **Dolaucothi Gold Mine** (Easter–Oct daily 10am–5pm; site £3.20, Roman & Victorian underground tours £3.80 each, level-access Long Adit tour £2.50; NT).

This is the only place in Britain where it's certain that the Romans mined gold, laying astoundingly advanced systems to extract the precious metal from the rock; the remains of their workings – a few water channels and an open cast mine – can still be seen around the site. After the Romans left in 140 AD, the mine lay abandoned until 1888, when new shafts were sunk and sporadically exploited until 1938. The site appears much as it would have in the late 1930s, and there are good displays in the exhibit room, but you'll get a much better appreciation by joining one of the hard-hat underground tours deep into the workings, and try your hand at gold panning.

Near the entrance to the mine is a stone marked with indentations supposedly left by five sleeping saints who rested here one night. The event gives its name to the straggling village of **PUMSAINT** (Five Saints), located a mile to the west, where you'll find pleasant farmhouse B&B at *Dolaucothi Farm* (T01558/650261; ❶). The *Brunant Arms* (T01558/650483; ❶), a mile east of the gold mine at **CAIO**, offers bags of character, board games and debates.

Five miles south of Pumsaint, the crumbling twelfth-century tower of Wales' only Premonstratensian **abbey** dominates the village of **TALLEY**, also home to the serene **church of St Michael**, intact from its foundation in 1773 and still including its original box pews. Talley's more recent claim to fame is as the home of Wales' famous **Tipi Valley**, a hippy encampment that was set up in the 1970s near Cwmdu, just south of the village. Controversy has dogged the place ever since, but these days there seems to be a fairly stoic truce between the locals and the tipi dwellers.

A further ten miles southwest are the towering conifers of the **Brechfa Forest**, where solitude is assured and there are many fine walks. The best base is the unspoilt village of **BRECHFA**, with the gorgeous, oak-beamed **accommodation** at ⚑ *Tŷ Mawr* (T01267/202332, Wwww.wales-country-hotel.co.uk; ❻), which also serves superb meals to guests, *Glasfryn* B&B (T01267/202306, Wwww.glasfrynbrechfa.co.uk; ❸), and a great pub, the *Forest Arms*.

Towards Llyn Brianne

The land to the north of Llandovery is equally remote and even more spectacular, with walks following the River Tywi valley and over the hills. As a base, there's the old lead-mining hamlet of **RHANDIRMWYN**, above the winding river, which has some of the best views hereabouts and is accessible by a daily postbus from Llandovery. Here, the popular *Royal Oak Inn* (☎01550/760201, Ⓦwww.rhandirmwyn.com; ❸) offers great food, drink and B&B **accommodation**; just below the village, there's also a riverside **campsite** (☎01550/760257; closed Nov to mid-March; £6.50 per person). A few miles east, towards the viaduct and train station at Cynghordy, the delightful farmhouse B&B *Llanerchindda* (☎01550/750274, Ⓦwww.cambrianway.com; ❸) is used by many people walking the Cambrian Way (see p.473).

Three miles beyond Rhandirmwyn, there's a car park (£1) at the Ystradffin chapel for the RSPB's **Dinas Nature Reserve**, deep within which is the reputed hideout cave of Twm Sion Cati (see p.179). You're discouraged from seeking out the bandit's lair lest you disturb the red kites, woodpeckers, nuthatches, redstarts and pipits, but even so, this is a delightful spot: wooden walkways traverse the ancient woodland, a burst of flowers, butterflies, water and twisted trees. Once through, you can walk along the banks of the fast-flowing Tywi up to its confluence with the River Doethie.

A mile beyond Dinas, lanes widen for the traffic that bustles towards **Llyn Brianne**, at whose southern end are a car park and visitor facilities. Considering the reservoir was only built in the 1970s (to supply Swansea), it has folded well into the contours of the land and there are some peaceful shoreline walks. Walks beyond the lake link up to isolated youth hostel and campsites along the Abergwesyn Pass (see p.262).

Southern Carmarthenshire

Frequently overlooked in the stampede towards the resorts of Pembrokeshire, southern Carmarthenshire is a quiet part of the world, with few of the problems of mass tourism suffered by more popular parts of Wales. Its coastline is broken by the triple estuary of the Tywi, Taf and Gwendreath rivers, and between the Tywi and Taf is a knotted landscape of hills and tiny, winding lanes, penetrated by one decent road, the B4312, which ends at **Llansteffan**, with its ruined hilltop castle.

On the other side of the Taf estuary, **Laugharne** is the sole big tourist attraction, a place of pilgrimage for Dylan Thomas lovers. A curious and insular village, it was the last home of the Thomases, whose boathouse has been turned into a loving museum to the writer, and whose regular drinking hole is as much a part of the pilgrimage as the house.

Beyond Laugharne, the coast is formed by a seemingly endless sweep of sand, once used for various land speed record attempts orchestrated from the seasonally busy resort of **Pendine**. Back on the A40, **Whitland** is an architecturally unremarkable town, but historically significant as the site of the first parliament in Wales.

Regular trains connect Carmarthen with Whitland and the west, and buses fill in the gaps, with a service from Carmarthen and St Clears to Laugharne and Pendine. Another service leaves Carmarthen for Llansteffan.

Llansteffan

The neglected-looking village of **LLANSTEFFAN**, on the Tywi estuary ten miles southeast of Carmarthen, is overshadowed by a dramatic ruined **castle** (free entry). This prime example of Norman fortifications was built between the eleventh and thirteenth centuries by the Anglo-Norman de Camille family. The entrance used today is not the original gatehouse, which was converted into living quarters in the fourteenth century: its bricked-up entrance is obvious from outside. In both gatehouses, however, the portcullis and murder holes can still be seen. From atop the towers, it's easy to appreciate the site's defensive position, with far-reaching views in all directions; long before the present castle, there was an Iron Age promontory fort, known to have been occupied from 600 BC.

Returning from the castle to where the path doubles back to the right near a house, continue straight ahead past the house to *Parc Glas* (formerly a milk-and-rum tavern), and left down the lane towards the beach. The door in the wall on the right conceals **St Anthony's Well** (Bwthyn Sant Antwn), with its supposed powers of healing for lovesickness.

Around the Taf estuary, west of Llansteffan, are numerous ancient standing stones and a couple of ruined churches, with some awesome tombs, at **Llandeilo Abercywyn** and **Trefenty**, either side of the river. The stones and the churches were all part of a long-established pilgrims' route to west Wales, and St David's in particular.

Llansteffan is pretty enough to justify an overnight stay, perhaps at *On the Seafront*, a decent enough B&B on The Green (℡01267/241262, ⓦwww .llansteffan.net/accommodation; ❷). Two miles back towards Carmarthen, the *Pantyrathro Country Inn* (℡01267/241014, ⓦwww.pantyrathrocountryinn .co.uk; £12 per bunk) offers slightly pokey hostel-style accommodation but has its own bar and Mexican restaurant.

For **snacks** and Welsh teas try *The Beach Shop*, by the beachside car park, or for meals and **real ales** head to the *Sticks Inn* on Llansteffan's Main Street, which has a beer garden. The nearby *Yr Hen Dafarn* serves robust food – including excellent fish – at moderate to high prices.

Laugharne

When quiet, the village of **LAUGHARNE** (Talacharn), across the Taf estuary from Llansteffan, is a delightful spot, with a ragged castle looming over the reeds and tidal flats and narrow lanes snuggling in behind. Catch it in high season, though, and you're immediately aware that Laugharne has increasingly been taken over by the legend of Dylan Thomas, the nearest thing Wales has to a national poet. Wherever you go you'll meet people who knew him; some genuine, others gently milking the memory.

At the end of an excruciatingly narrow lane (unsuitable for cars) beside the estuary, you'll stumble across the **Dylan Thomas Boathouse** (daily: May–Oct & Easter weekend 10am–5.30pm; Nov–April 10.30am–3.30pm; £3; ⓦwww .dylanthomasboathouse.com), the simple home of Thomas, his wife Caitlin and their three children from 1949 until he died from "a massive insult to the brain" (spurred by numerous whiskies) on a lecture tour in New York four years later. It's an enchanting museum with a feeling of inspirational peace above the ever-changing water and light of the estuary and its "heron-priested shore". Upstairs is given over to a video on Thomas's life and a selection of local artists' views of the estuary and the village – none so rewarding as the one from the windows. Downstairs, the family's living room has been preserved intact, with the rich tones of the man himself reading his work via a period wireless set. Numerous artefacts are encased or on display, and contemporary newspaper reports of his demise show how he was, while alive, a fairly minor literary figure: the *Daily Mirror* manages a small obituary on page five, while even the

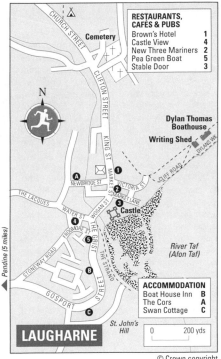

RESTAURANTS, CAFÉS & PUBS

Brown's Hotel	1
Castle View	4
New Three Mariners	2
Pea Green Boat	5
Stable Door	3

ACCOMMODATION

Boat House Inn	B
The Cors	A
Swan Cottage	C

LAUGHARNE

© Crown copyright

Carmarthen Journal relegates the story to second place behind the tale of a missing local farmer. A small tearoom and outdoor terrace afford views over the water and welcome refreshments. Back along the lane, you can peer into the green garage where Thomas wrote: a gas stove, curling photographs of literary heroes, pen collection and numerous scrunched-up balls of paper on the cheap desk suggest quite effectively that he is about to return at any minute. Thomas and Caitlin, who died in 1994, are buried together in the graveyard of the parish church in the village centre, marked by a simple white cross.

Laugharne is probably the closest to the fictional Llareggub, Thomas' town of darkly rich characters in *Under Milk Wood* – an honour, it is believed, shared with New Quay in Cardiganshire. The village exploits its Thomas connections with curiously disgruntled aplomb – none more so than his old boozing hole, **Brown's Hotel** on the main street, where, in the nicotine-crusted front bar, Dylan's cast-iron table still sits in a window alcove overlooked by low-key memorabilia. You're left in no doubt, though, that this is foremost a pub, not a shrine.

The main street courses down to the ornate ruins of **Laugharne Castle** (mid-March to Sept daily 10am–5pm; £2.75; CADW). Built in the twelfth and thirteenth centuries, most of the original buildings were obliterated in Tudor times when Sir John Perrot transformed it into a splendid gentleman's mansion. The mix of medieval might and Tudor finery is an intriguing one, especially in the impressive Inner Ward, dominated by two original towers, one of which you can climb for some good interpretive displays and, from the domed roof, sublime views over the huddled town. Built as an Anglo-Norman lookout on the sea, Laugharne was, like so many of these, taken by the Welsh princes Llywelyn the Great (1215) and Llywelyn the Last (1257), who also captured the then lord of the manor, Guy de Brian IV. The "castle brown as owls" (Dylan Thomas) has a connection with another famous Welsh writer, Richard Hughes, who lodged in the adjoining Castle House between 1934 and 1942. His *Danger* (1924), about a disaster in a Welsh mine, was the world's first radio drama, although Hughes remains best known for his novel, *A High Wind in Jamaica*. There's a small exhibition on him in the shore-facing gazebo in the castle's delightful gardens, landscaped to original Victorian specifications.

Opposite the castle entrance is the tiny toytown **town hall**, topped by a whitewashed Italianate bell tower, which once served as a single-cell prison.

Dylan Thomas

Dylan Thomas (1914–53) was the quintessential Celt – fiery, verbose, richly talented and habitually drunk. Born into a snugly middle-class family in Swansea's Uplands district, Dylan's first glimmers of literary greatness came when he was posted, as a young reporter, on the *South Wales Evening Post* in Swansea, from which some of his most popular tales in *Portrait of the Artist as a Young Dog* were inspired. Thomas' wordy enthusiasm is well demonstrated in a passage describing his gulping down a pint of beer, waiting for the senior reporter to join him for a pub crawl: "I liked the taste of beer, its live, white lather, its brass-bright depths, the sudden world through the wet brown walls of the glass, the tilted rush to the lips and the slow swallowing down to the lapping belly, the salt on the tongue, the foam at the corners."

Rejecting the coarse provincialism of Swansea and Welsh life, Thomas arrived in London as a broke 20-year-old in 1934, weeks before the appearance of his first volume of poetry, which was published as the first prize in a *Sunday Referee* competition. Another volume followed shortly afterwards, cementing the engaging young Welshman's reputation in the British literary establishment. He married in 1937 and the newlyweds returned to Wales, settling in the backwater of Laugharne, and uprooting to New Quay for some of World War II. Short stories – crackling with rich and melancholy humour – tumbled out as swiftly as poems, further widening his base of admirers, although they remained numerically small until well after his death. Like so many writers, he only gained star status posthumously. Despite his evident streak of hedonism and his long days boozing in *Brown's Hotel*, Thomas was a self-disciplined writer, honing his work into some of the most instantly recognizable poetry of the twentieth century, mastering both lyrical ballads of astounding simplicity and rhythmic metre, as well as more turgid, densely layered poetry. Perhaps better than anyone, he writes in an identifiably Celtic, rhythmic wallow in the language. Although Thomas knew little Welsh – he was educated in the time when the native language was stridently discouraged – his English usage is definitively Welsh in its cadence and bold use of words.

Thomas, especially in public, liked to adopt the persona of an archetypal stage Welshman: sonorously loquacious, romantic and fond of a stiff tipple. This role was particularly popular in the United States, where he made lucrative lecture tours; it was on one in 1953 that he died of a massive whisky overdose. Just one month earlier, he had put the finishing touches to what many regard as his masterpiece: *Under Milk Wood*, the "play for voices". Describing the dreams, thoughts and lives of a straggling Welsh seaside community over 24 hours, the play has never dipped out of fashion and has lured Wales' greatest stars, including Richard Burton and Anthony Hopkins, into the role of chief narrator. The small town of Llareggub (mis-spelt Llaregyb by the prudish BBC, who wouldn't sanction the usage of the expression "bugger all" backwards) is loosely based on Laugharne, New Quay in Cardiganshire, and a vast dose of Thomas' own imagination.

Practicalities

Laugharne has no tourist office but is small enough that you'll quickly get your bearings. **Accommodation** includes the welcoming *Swan Cottage*, 20 Gosport St (☏01994/427409; ❷), which has only one en-suite room; the stylish *Boat House Inn*, 1 Gosport St (☏01994/427263, ✉theboathousehotel@tiscali.co.uk; ❻); and *The Cors*, Newbridge Road (☏01994/427219; ❺), a small, gracious country house that doubles as a classy restaurant (see below). The nearest **campsite** is *Ants Hill Caravan Park* (☏01994/427293, ⦿www.antshill.co.uk; £14 per pitch), a few hundred yards north of Laugharne, off the St Clears road.

There's good **eating** too, but the limited number of places means you should reserve in advance in summer. For lunches and Welsh teas make for the *Pea Green Boat*, on the central square, while for something more substantial, go for ⅄ *The Cors*, which serves excellent modern Welsh cuisine (Thurs–Sat evenings only, bookings essential) with mains around £15. Alternatively, try the *Stable Door*, Market Lane (☎01994/427777; closed Mon–Wed), a relaxed conservatory restaurant and wine bar with an upmarket menu featuring the likes of pepper-crusted monkfish (£15). *Brown's Hotel* (see above) serves large, stodgy meals at lunchtime and early evening, while down on the square, there's tasty fish and chips at the *Castle View*. The best **drinking** hole is the cheery *New Three Mariners*.

Pendine and Whitland

Follow the road five miles southwest from Laugharne, and you'll reach the tatty seaside resort of **PENDINE** (Pentywyn), home to a mass of caravan parks, souvenir shops, cheap cafés and vast tracts of out-of-bounds military land. The crowning glory here is the six-mile-long stretch of sand sweeping away to the east, which, for a frenetic few years in the mid-1920s, was the scene of a series of attempts at the world land speed record. In 1927, Malcolm Campbell reached 174.88 miles per hour, a mark that former record holder and Welsh rival J.G. Parry-Thomas thought he could better. A month later, his 27-litre, aircraft-engined and chain-driven *Babs* hurtled along the beach only to explode: its chain decapitated Parry-Thomas. *Babs* was recovered but then buried in the sand for a respectful 42 years, until it was dug up in 1969 and restored. Each July and August *Babs* appears at the seafront **Speed Museum** (Easter & May–Sept daily 10am–5pm; free), which otherwise has mildly interesting panels on those heady times and a few motorcycles also used in record attempts. The headquarters for the speed attempts was the *Beach Hotel*, which still displays photographs and mementos of the glory days. Until 2004 you could even drive on Pendine Sands, but too much bad behaviour put a stop to that.

From Pendine, the A4066 leads back through Laugharne; you can also wind north through narrow lanes to the A40, the route to historically significant **WHITLAND** (Y Hendy Gwyn), today a small farming and light industrial town. It was here – in 930 AD – that Hywel Dda ("Hywel the Good"), king of Deheubarth, summoned representatives from all the other Welsh kingdoms to the first all-Wales assembly, to codify disparate local traditions into common laws for the whole of Wales. They drew up an elaborate code that was strikingly egalitarian, giving bastard children the rights of legitimate siblings, ensuring marriage by common consent, the equal division of land between spouses upon separation, and amongst all children after their parents' deaths. Many of these customs survived until the Tudors conquered Wales, and Welsh people today are still proud of the fairness and lack of oppression in that halcyon era, in stark contrast to the laws imposed after Wales' conquest by Edward I. The tales of Hywel Dda are told at a **commemorative centre** (Easter–Sept Tues–Sat 10am–1pm & 2–5pm; free), where his laws are inscribed on stone tablets around the walls. It's located 100m from the train station on St Mary Street.

Tenby and around

On a natural promontory of great strategic importance, the beguilingly old-fashioned **TENBY** (Dinbych-y-Pysgod) is everything a seaside resort should

Arrival, information and accommodation

The **train station** is at the western end of the town centre, at the bottom of Warren Street. Some **buses** stop at South Parade, at the top of Trafalgar Road, although most (including National Express coaches) call at the bus shelter on Upper Park Road, just along from the **tourist office** (daily: July & Aug 10am–6pm; rest of year 10am–5pm; ☎01834/842402, ✆tenby.tic@pembrokeshire .gov.uk). A nice way to explore the place is to join Marion Davies for her **Ghost Walk of Tenby** (mid-June to early Sept Mon–Sat; £3.75; reservations recommended ☎01834/845841), which leaves from the *Lifeboat Tavern* in Tudor Square at 8pm and spends an hour and a half exploring the town's past and the people who inhabited it. She also leads other themed walks and offers out-of-season specials – see the notices at the tourist office or contact her directly. For more esoteric information, including ads for gigs and festivals, check out Equinox on St Julian Street.

A word of warning to **motorists**: cars are banned in central Tenby throughout July and August (daily 11am–5pm). Free shuttle buses run from the Salterns and North Beach car parks (both pay-and-display), which are marked on our town map.

Accommodation

As a major resort, Tenby has dozens of hotels and guesthouses, all pressed from much the same mould. Prices are a little higher than elsewhere in west Wales, and in high summer the place is still full to bursting point, but at other times it's not hard to find decent, reasonable **accommodation**. If you don't find anything suitable, consider staying nearby in Saundersfoot, Manorbier or St Florence. There are caravan sites all around Tenby: most take **tents**, especially those around the village of New Hedges around a mile and a half north on the A478. In the peak summer season you'll also find tap-in-a-field sites which spring up for a couple of months.

Hotels and guesthouses

Atlantic Esplanade ☎01834/842881, ⊛www .atlantic-hotel.uk.com. The best – and priciest – hotel along the South Beach, with a high standard of rooms, a couple of good restaurants and a small indoor pool. Seafront rooms are much larger and costlier than the others. Rates include breakfast. ⑤ /⑥

Boulston Cottage 29 Trafalgar Rd ☎01834/843289. Consistently among the cheapest B&Bs in Tenby, it is always spotless, and run by a wonderful Spanish woman. ②

Castle View 14 The Norton ☎01834/842666, ⊛www.castleviewhotel.co.uk. Friendly and well-located hotel overlooking Castle Hill and the harbour, and with table d'hôte dinners for £15. ④

Coach Guesthouse 11 Deer Park ☎01834/842210. A welcoming hotel near the train station. Closed Dec & Jan. ③

Glenholme Picton Terrace ☎01834/843909, ⊛www.glenholmetenby.co.uk. Agreeable, friendly budget B&B near the town centre, with en-suite rooms. ②

Glenthorne Guest House 9 Deer Park ☎01834/842300. This large place is excellent value, with a well-deserved reputation. ③

Lyndale House Warren St ☎01834/842836. Small, well-maintained B&B near the train station, that's happy to cater for vegetarians. ④

Penally Abbey Penally, a mile west of Tenby ☎0871/995 8254, ⊛www.penally-abbey.com. Luxurious country-house hotel on the site of a sixth-century abbey, with great sea views. Standards are very high, yet the atmosphere's relaxed and the food unpretentious. ⑦

St Teresa's Old Convent South Parade ☎01834/844495. Appealing three-room B&B right by the Five Arches Gate but with parking. Two of the rooms have four-poster beds, and good vegetarian breakfasts are available on request. ④

Hostel and campsites

Manorbier YHA hostel Skrinkle Haven, near Manorbier ☎01834/871803 or 0870/770 5954, ✆manorbier@yha.org.uk. Bright, modern, corrugated-iron clad hostel overlooking the cliffs four

miles west of Tenby, near the Manorbier bus route from town. Open March–Oct. Dorm beds £12.50. **Meadow Farm** Northcliff ☎01834/844829. This small site on the northern edge of town is a great alternative to the family fun-park-style places, and far nearer to the centre. Closed Nov–March. £6 per person.
Trevayne Farm A mile or so north off the A478 ☎01834/813402. Family-oriented caravan and campsite with superb views over Saundersfoot and the great arc of sand that sweeps round to Amroth and Pendine. Closed Nov–March. £8 per pitch.
Well Park New Hedges, off the A478 ☎01834/842179. A high-class caravan and camping site one mile north of town. Its rates are reasonable, given the extensive facilities. Closed Nov–March. £14 per pitch.

The Town

Tenby's old centre is triangular, with two sides formed by the coast meeting at Castle Hill, and the third by the remaining **town walls**. South Parade runs alongside the massive twenty-foot-high wall, first built in the late thirteenth century and massively strengthened in 1457 by Jasper Tudor, Earl of Pembroke and uncle of the future king, Henry VII. It was further fortified in the 1580s, when Tenby was regarded as a likely target for the Spanish Armada. The only town gate still standing is **Five Arches**, a semicircular barbican used as an everyday entrance by citizens and peacetime visitors, with hidden lookouts and acute angles to surprise invaders. The wall continues south to the Esplanade, with a long line of snooty hotels facing out over the smarter and far less commercialized South Beach.

The centre's focal point is the 152-foot spire of the largely fifteenth-century **St Mary's church**, between Tudor Square and St George's Street. Its light interior shows the elaborate ceiling bosses in the chancel to good effect, while fifteenth-century tombs attest to Tenby's mercantile tradition. On the western side of St Mary's runs Upper Frog Street, replete with craft shops and an arcaded indoor **market**, containing craft stalls and gift shops.

Otherwise, it's a pleasure to explore the alleyways and steps in the old town, especially the medieval lanes in the immediate vicinity of the church. Due east, **Quay Hill** runs down towards the harbour past some of Tenby's oldest dwellings, including a **Tudor Merchant's House** (April–Oct daily except Sat 11am–5pm; £2.20; NT), built in the late fifteenth century, when Tenby was second only to Bristol as a west coast port. The compact house with its Flemish-style chimneypieces is on three floors, packed with furniture, either seventeenth- and eighteenth-century originals or Tudor repro made traditionally without glue or nails: notice especially the superb inlaid 1753 marriage chest.

Crackwell and Bridge streets run down to the **harbour**, which can look idyllic if it's not too crowded. Sheltered by the curving headland and fringed by pastel-hued Georgian and Victorian houses, it's a great place to stroll on a warm evening. By day, it's the departure point for numerous excursion boats, especially for the short trip to Caldey Island (see below). Above the harbour is the headland and **Castle Hill**, its grassy slopes rife with Victoriana in the form of huge flowerbeds (including an indigenous small daffodil in springtime), ornate benches, a bandstand and a pompous memorial to Prince Albert – upstaging the ruins of a Norman **castle**, mainly notable for its gatehouse and the all-round view from its windswept tower. The nearby **Tenby Museum & Art Gallery** (Easter–Oct daily 10am–5pm; Nov–Easter Mon–Fri 10am–5pm; £2.50), presents a moderately interesting trawl through topics of local interest, notably a broad history of the town and harbour since the tenth century with scale models and assorted artefacts from various excavations. The museum's geology section includes a five-foot mammoth tusk found near Milford Haven,

The *New Inn,* next to the beach, is an enjoyable place to eat and drink, if generally packed in summer.

The coast between Amroth and Tenby is one long line of caravan parks, broken only by the picturesque harbour of **SAUNDERSFOOT**, built originally for the export of local coal and anthracite. The town has been attracting visitors for centuries, and is a lively, good-natured place; now all the industry has folded, the harbour and the wide yawn of sand are used purely for recreational purposes, with a predictable clutch of cafés, tacky shops and boisterous fun pubs.

Saundersfoot's **train station** is located over a mile northwest up The Ridgeway from the harbourside **tourist office** (Easter–Oct daily 10am–5pm; plus winter weekends 10am-4pm; ℡01834/813672). If you want to **stay** in the village, try the lovely *Cliff House*, Wogan Terrace (℡01834/813931; ❹) which has great sea views, or *Valley Farm*, on Valley Road (℡01834/813388; ❷), about half a mile towards the train station from the harbour. High on the hill overlooking the beach the chic *St Brides Hotel*, St Brides Hill (℡01834/8112304, Ⓦwww.stbrideshotel.com; ❼), ranks as one of Pembrokeshire's finest hotels, recently remodelled along modern lines, with Welsh art in the public spaces and an elegant restaurant. There's handy **camping** a mile south at *Trevayne Farm* (see p.189)

Saundersfoot has plenty of **places to eat**: the best bets are the charming *Old Chemist Inn* on The Strand, right by the beach, and the *El Puerto* tapas bar on Wogan Terrace. Just south of town, the restaurant at the *Swallow Tree Gardens* caravan park (℡01834/812398) is a glorious surprise, offering imaginative fresh dishes with stylish twists. A mile and a half north of Saundersfoot towards Amroth, the thoroughly enjoyable *Wiseman's Bridge Inn* is a beachside pub that's good for a drink and a meal.

South Pembrokeshire coast

The southern zigzag of coast that darts west from Tenby is a strange mix of caravan parks and Ministry of Defence shooting ranges above some spectacularly beautiful bays and gull-covered cliffs. For Coast Path walkers it is constantly beguiling, but drivers will find themselves forever ducking inland then down narrow lanes to get to the next bay.

From Tenby, the A4139 passes through **Penally**, little more than an extended suburb of the town, before delving down past the **Lydstep Haven** beach. A road dips south here, past **Skrinkle Haven** and into the winding streets of **Manorbier**, where the ghostly castle sits above a small bay. Three miles inland from here is the quintessentially pretty village of **St Florence**, its narrow lanes crowned by a profusion of Flemish chimneys.

The coast nips and tucks in past some excellent, and comparatively quiet beaches to the National Trust's Stackpole Estate where the main attractions are diminutive **Stackpole Quay**, the beautiful sandy **Barafundle Bay** and the picturesque village of **Bosherston** and its lily lakes. Travelling west, the first of the area's many MOD artillery ranges lies between Bosherston and the coast, and you have to cross it in order to see the remarkable and ancient **St Govan's chapel**, squeezed into a rock cleft above the crashing waves.

On foot, you can get closer to the best of the scenery by way of a four-mile section of the Pembrokeshire Coast Path, walking west and brushing along the top of some of Wales' most dramatic cliff-side scenery, including **Stack Rocks** and limestone arch that mark the last point of access on this part of the coast. All

The Pembrokeshire National Park and Coast Path

Of the fourteen national parks in England and Wales, the **Pembrokeshire Coast National Park** is the only one that is predominantly sea-based, hugging the rippled coast around the entire southwestern section of Wales. Established in 1952, the park is not one easily identifiable mass, rather a series of occasionally unconnected patches of coast and inland scenery. Starting at its southeastern corner, the first segment clings to the coast from Amroth through to the Milford Haven waterway, an area of sweeping limestone cliffs and some fabulous beaches. The second (and by far the quietest) part courses around the inland pastoral landscape of the Daugleddau estuary, which plunges deep into the rural heart of Pembrokeshire southeast of Haverfordwest. Superb for scenic cliff walking, the third section is around the beaches and resorts of St Bride's Bay, where the sea scoops a great chunk out of Wales' westernmost land. In the north of the county, the boundary of the park runs far inland to encompass the Mynydd Preseli, a barren but invigoratingly beautiful range of hills dotted with ancient relics.

Crawling around almost every wriggle of the coast, the **Pembrokeshire Coast Path** winds 186 miles from Amroth in the south, to its northernmost point at St Dogmael's near Cardigan. For the vast majority of the time, the path clings precariously to clifftop routes, overlooking rocks frequented by sunbathing seals, craggy offshore islands, unexpected gashes of sand and shrieking clouds of sea birds. Only on the southwestern end of the Castlemartin peninsula, where the coast is given over to army training camps and rifle ranges, does the path veer inland for any major length; it also ducks briefly inland along the Milford Haven estuary, where the proximity of belching great oil refineries and the huge expanse of hill-backed water provide one of the route's many surprises.

The most popular and ruggedly inspiring segments of the Coast Path are around St David's Head and the Marloes peninsula, either side of St Bride's Bay; the stretch from the castle at Manorbier to the tiny cliff chapel at Bosherston along the southern coast; and the undulating contours, massive cliffs, bays and old ports along the northern coast, either side of Fishguard. These offer miles of windswept walking amongst great flashes of gorse, heather and seasonal plants, as well as the opportunity to study thousands of sea birds at close quarter. Basking seals are frequent visitors to some of the more inaccessible beaches, particularly around the time when pups are born in the autumn. This is reckoned to be a major cause of the occasional accidents along the route, as people try to gain better views of the creatures and consequently fall over the edge.

Of all the **seasons**, spring is perhaps the finest for walking: the crowds have yet to arrive and the clifftop flora is at its most vivid. There are numerous publications about the Coast Path, of which the best is Brian John's *National Trail Guide* (£13), which includes 1:25,000 section maps of the route. The national park publishes a handy *Coast Path Accommodation* guide (£2.50; available from the website), detailing B&Bs and campsites the entire length of the route, available from tourist and national park offices and bookshops. It also publishes the excellent free newspaper, *Coast to Coast*, detailing special walks, boat trips and other events, and which you can pick up from national park offices listed throughout this chapter. A further path has been created around the haunting Daugleddau estuaries, inland of Milford Haven. For details of both the national park and Coast Path, contact the Information Officer at the Pembrokeshire Coast National Park Authority, Llanion Park, Pembroke Dock, Pembrokeshire SA72 6DY (℗0845/3457275, ⓦwww.pembrokeshirecoast.org.uk).

around and to the west are **artillery ranges**, forcing the Coast Path inland in order to avoid shellfire. The next point of access on the coast is the west-facing **Freshwater West**, a wide beach popular with surfers, reached across windy spume-flecked sea for a magnificent close-up view of the precarious crags, caves and arches. **Accommodation** is available at the recently refurbished *St Govan's Country Inn* in Bosherston (☎01646/661311; ❹), an enjoyable place which caters mostly to rock climbers and serves mountains of inexpensive food (including good curries), plus a range of real ales.

Range West

All the land beyond the chapel is known as **Range West**, littered with dugouts, abandoned shells and tanks, and, apart from the narrow clifftop strip on which the Coast Path runs, entirely out of bounds. The path follows the top of the cliffs west for four miles, past a striking cleft known as **Huntsman's Leap** and two isolated beaches at **Bullslaughter** and **Flimston Bay**, to **Stack Rocks**. The only vehicle access to the coast is at the hamlet of **Merrion**, on the B4319, from where a lane (generally open Mon–Fri 9am–4.30pm and all day Sat & Sun; for details call ☎01646/662367) runs down to Stack Rocks past the mournful little chapel at **FLIMSTON**, a hamlet forcibly abandoned to the army.

Stack Rocks jut out of the sea here like a series of tall, lichen-spattered stepping stones. A hundred yards further west (as far as you're allowed to go), a graceful limestone arch rises from a wave-flattened rock platform, known as the **Green Bridge of Wales**. On a quiet day, the only company you will have are the shrieking gulls, guillemots and kittiwakes swooping to their perches on the limestone ledges. The land to the west, appropriated by the military, contains some of the most spectacular coastal scenery in Wales, as well as some superb dunes and important ancient remains.

Castlemartin, Freshwater West and Angle

Forced to turn inland, the Coast Path continues back up the lane to Merrion and follows the B4319 through the village of **CASTLEMARTIN** – whose church boasts an organ once owned by Mendelssohn. Here you can **stay** at the characterful *Old Smithy* (☎01646/661310, ✉paulineforsyth@bigfoot.com; ❸), peacefully set in over an acre of land, and with dinner available by arrangement. The Coast Path follows the B4319 a couple of miles to **Freshwater West**, a west-facing beach resort that's great for **surfing**, though the currents can be too strong for swimming. Behind the beach, desolate wind-battered dunes make for interesting walking.

The B4319 meets the B4320 from Pembroke near the **Devil's Quoit**, a Neolithic burial chamber topped by an impressive capstone. It continues down the final finger of the peninsula, to the remote village of **ANGLE** at the western end of a wide curve of mud known as **Angle Bay**. Angle consists of one long street, bounded by old, coloured cottages. **West Angle Bay**, a secluded spot a mile to the west of the main village, is better for swimming, and overlooks another of the Lord Palmerston protective forts (see p.203) on **Thorn Island**. An upmarket hotel chain has now bought the island and plans to reopen it as a luxury resort, linked to the mainland by a cable car. Meanwhile, there's no accommodation with a roof in Angle, but you can camp at *Castle Farm* (☎01646/641220; closed Oct–Easter; £3 per person) just behind the church. For **eating** and **drinking**, try the convivial *Hibernia Inn*, right in the centre; or it's ten minutes' walk east along the shore to the delightful, rustic *Old Point House* inn, whose fire is said to have burned continuously for over three hundred years until the mid-1990s, since when it has only been lit in winter. Quality meals come in large portions: go for the specials board which usually includes several examples of the day's catch.

The Pembrokeshire energy industries

On both sides of the magnificent Milford Haven waterway, the most prominent features on the landscape belong to the **refineries** that fringe the waters. Storage tankers, observation towers and security fences litter the Coast Path here, the most blighted stretch being the five miles between the west side of the Pembroke River estuary and Angle Bay.

As well as occasional disasters such as the grounding of the *Sea Empress* oil tanker in 1996, the presence of so much polluting and potentially hazardous industry in this rural corner of Wales has many ramifications. A few years ago, a huge fire at the Texaco refinery on the south side of the Haven prompted many residents of Rhoscrowther and Pwllcrochan to leave the area, and forced eviction of these villages occasionally surfaces as an option, hardly helping the remaining residents' confidence.

However, matters are improving. One of the three refineries has closed down and the two that remain have cleaned up their act considerably, while the neighbouring Pembroke power station is being dismantled after a major public campaign in the late 1990s forced its closure. Though designed as an oil-burning power station, the plant's owners, National Power, decided it would be more economic to convert it to burn orimulsion, a controversial fuel which even they admitted has a "kill factor" some 442 times greater than ordinary crude oil. Orimulsion had been burned elsewhere, notably at the now-closed Richborough station in Kent, England, where local crops suffered drastically, land was poisoned and car paint blistered – pure coincidence according to the owners. The company threatened to close Pembroke power station altogether, unless consent was given for its conversion, and consequently gained the support of some local trade unions and councillors, for whom the jobs and prosperity were paramount. Fortunately, though, public pressure won out in the end. Orimulsion stayed away and, as promised, the plant has now closed, heralding an unequivocal victory for the environment and the health of local people.

Pembroke and around

The old county town of **PEMBROKE** (Penfro) sits on the southern side of the Pembroke River, a continuation of the massive Milford Haven waterway that was described by Nelson as the greatest natural harbour in the world. Yet despite its location and its formidable **castle**, Pembroke is rather dull.

The town grew up solely to serve the castle, the mightiest link in the chain of Norman strongholds built across southern Wales. Drawn out along a hilltop ridge, the walled town flourished as a port for Pembrokeshire goods to be exported from the main quay, situated alongside the waters below the walls of the castle, to all parts of Britain, as well as Ireland, France and Spain. Though it managed to choose the winning side during the Wars of the Roses, Pembroke was less fortunate in the Civil War, when Cromwell besieged the town.

Though it subsequently became a centre of leather-making, weaving, dyeing and tailoring, Pembroke never regained its former importance, and by the twentieth century the small town was in grave decline, its port long since overtaken by neighbouring sites. One fortunate result of this is that Pembroke is mercifully free of postwar development in the centre, although the fringes around the main street are largely modern and bland.

The town's sole thoroughfare, **Main Street** stretches from the **train station** (as Station Road) in the east to the mighty walls of the castle. From the castle gates it widens out past some attractive Georgian- and Victorian-era shops,

600 yards or so from the ferry terminal. The *Welshman's Arms* on London Road has excellent **food**, while there's pricier continental fare at *La Brasseria* nearby on Laws Street (☎01646/686966).

Lamphey

The pleasant village of **LAMPHEY** (Llandyfai), two miles southeast of Pembroke, is best known for the ruined **Bishop's Palace** (daily 10am–5pm; £2.50; CADW) which stands off a quiet lane to the north of the settlement. Dating from at least the thirteenth century and abandoned at the Reformation in the mid-sixteenth century, the palace was built as a country retreat for the bishops of St David's, though it was in use as Crown apartments for a few decades afterwards. Stout walls surround the scattered ruins, with many of the palace buildings having long been lost under the grassy banks. Most impressive are the remains of the Great Hall that forms the eastern end of the complex, topped by the fourteenth-century Bishop Gower's hallmark arcaded parapets, similar to those that he built in the Bishop's Palace of St David's. Lit only by narrow slits, the gloomy hall beneath the Great Hall has the feeling of a crypt.

Lamphey is an agreeable enough place in which to linger: on the train line to Pembroke, and with a few **accommodation** options. The white Georgian *Lamphey Court Hotel* (☎01646/672273, ☜www.lampheycourt.co.uk;❼), opposite the Bishop's Palace ruins, is a bit over the top, but features an indoor pool and various ways to pamper yourself. The *Lamphey Hall Hotel* (☎01646/672394; ❺) by the church is more modest, or you can sleep well at the characterful Georgian *Lower Lamphey Park* (☎01646/672906, ☜www.lowerlampheypark .co.uk;❸). This last is located a few hundred yards north of the *Dial Inn*, on The Ridgeway, which offers a reliable menu and good beer.

Carew

The pretty, riverside village of **CAREW** (Caeriw), four miles east of Pembroke, is famed for its thirteen-foot **Celtic cross**, just south of the river crossing, by the main road. Erected as a memorial to Maredydd, ruler of Deheubarth, who died in 1035, the gracefully tapering shaft is covered in fine tracery of ancient Welsh designs.

Beyond the cross, an Elizabethan walled garden houses the ticket office for **Carew Castle and Tidal Mill** (Easter–Oct daily 10am–5pm; £3; ☜www .carewcastle.com). A hybrid of Elizabethan fancy and earlier defensive necessity, the castle is reached across a field. Explanatory models illustrate the development of the site, which is an excellent example of the organic nature by which castles grew, from the Norman tower believed to be the original gatehouse, through the thirteenth-century front battlements, to the Tudor gatehouse and the Elizabethan mansion grafted onto them all. A few hundred yards west of the castle is the **Carew French Mill**, last used in 1937 and the only extant mill powered by the shifting tides in Wales. The impressive eighteenth-century exterior belies the pedestrian exhibitions and self-guided audiovisual displays of the milling process at different stages.

Mid-Pembrokeshire

The central slab of Pembrokeshire is generally either ignored or actively avoided by visitors intent on reaching the more obvious coastal pleasures to the south

△ Celtic cross, Carew

and west. Certainly the waterfront petrochemical plants along this stretch are a far cry from the limestone cliffs and wheeling sea birds elsewhere, and none of the towns are especially exciting, but the villages dotting the arms of the **Daugleddau estuary** are delightful and almost entirely unspoilt.

Pembroke Dock lies on the southern banks of the magnificent Daugleddau River estuary, the continuation of one of the world's greatest natural harbours, the **Milford Haven**. This spawned an eponymous Quaker community on the northern bank, which now seems, rather sadly, to be searching for a new post-industrial identity by ploughing vast sums into the development of some dubious tourist features.

Seven miles to the north, the chief town of the region, **Haverfordwest**, makes an important market and transport centre that, despite some handsome architecture, remains rather soulless. It is made more palatable by its proximity to **Scolton Manor**, which houses the county museum, and **Picton Castle**. The latter sits above the wide, tidal waters of the Daugleddau, a river estuary flooding the valleys of inland Pembrokeshire and providing a surprisingly maritime feel amidst such rolling countryside. Dotted around the muddy estuary are creaky little villages and some fine walks and pubs. The stout little town of **Narberth** is the self-appointed capital of the **Landsker borderlands** – a revived name for the imaginary line that divides the anglicized corner of south Pembrokeshire from its Welsh-speaking neighbour – but is most widely known for the big-time tourist attractions nearby, among them the **Oakwood** theme park, home to Europe's largest wooden roller coaster.

A branch train line leaves the main Swansea–Fishguard route at Whitland, calling at Narberth and Tenby en route to Pembroke and Pembroke Dock. A second spur peels off the main line at Clarbeston Road bound for Haverfordwest and Milford Haven. A reasonable bus service throughout the area has most routes starting at either Pembroke or Haverfordwest.

Milford Haven

One of the most impressive sights in this part of Wales is the view from the 1970s **Cleddau Bridge** (car toll 75p) between Pembroke Dock and **Neyland** on the opposite bank. Pedestrians can also cross it: the views over the jutting headlands are magical, the masts of boats far below and the full skies reflected in the clear water. Even the refineries look attractive from this far up. Try to synchronize your journey over the bridge with a decent sunset, when the glowing sun dips into the estuary mouth. If you need to while away an hour or two before (or after) sunset, drop into the *Old Ferry Inn*, immediately below the bridge, for high-standard but relatively inexpensive meals and real ales.

The waterway below – the Milford Haven – has long been an important harbour, and was even recognized by William Shakespeare:

...how far it is
To this same blessed Milford; and, by the way,
Tell me how Wales was made so happy as
To inherit such a haven.

(Imogen in *Cymbeline*, Act III, scene 2)

Taking its name from the waterway, the town of **MILFORD HAVEN** (Aberdaugleddau), four miles west of Neyland, was founded in the late eighteenth century by a group of early American settlers from Nantucket who were imported as whalers. The grid pattern they imposed – principally three streets rising sharply parallel to the waterway – survives today amid new civic and religious buildings. Despite a magnificent site and interesting heritage, Milford Haven hasn't got much going for it. The town has seen hard times of late, with the dead-beat town centre receiving little of the development money pumped into the horribly sterile "marina". The waterside is impressive, though, with tugs

Palmerston's Follies

The coast of southern Britain, and particularly that of south Pembrokeshire, is littered with what are known as **Palmerston's Follies**, nineteenth-century naval defences that never saw action. During his second term as British Prime Minister in 1860, Lord Palmerston felt that Britain was ill-prepared to withstand any attack made by Napoleon III, who was newly equipped with iron-clad battleships. Britain's navy had been barely upgraded since Nelson's victory at Trafalgar half a century earlier, so a Royal Commission recommended building a series of forts to protect naval dockyards while the navy modernized.

Palmerston got wholeheartedly behind the recommendation and had forts built right along the south coast of England and around Milford Haven and Pembroke. By the time the defences were complete in the 1880s, Anglo-French relations had improved, and the forts were never attacked. Arguably, the forts had been an effective deterrent, but in the public eye they became known as Palmerston's Follies. Most remain inaccessible to the public, though you can visit the Gun Tower at Pembroke Dock.

The best examples around Pembrokeshire are at Tenby, West Angle Bay, West Blockhouse Point and Milford Haven.

and steamers ploughing up the glittering waters of the Haven that stretch out below the pleasant public gardens.

Hamilton Terrace skirts around the waterside to the revamped docks, now rebranded as a marina. Here you'll find an assortment of attractions, including a bowling alley, the **Dockside Gallery** and the genuinely interesting town **museum** (Easter–Oct Mon–Sat 11am–5pm, Sun during school holidays & bank holiday weekends noon–5pm; £1.50), housed in an eighteenth-century warehouse originally designed to store whale oil. Exhibits include photographs and mementoes from the fishing trade, an explanation of the modern oil industry, details of the Quaker beginnings of the town and some fascinating archive material of Milford Haven in wartime.

On the western side of the docks and estuary, **Fort Hubberston** is a Palmerston defence fort (see above) built between 1860 and 1865, that housed some 250 men in the late nineteenth century. It has recently become so rickety and vandalized that access is prohibited. Nearby is the ruined octagonal dome of the **Hakin Observatory**, the sole remaining relic of town founder Charles Francis Greville's dream to build a "mathematical college".

Practicalities

Milford Haven **train station** is located under the Hakin road bridge, next to the docks. The only reasons to stray from the docks area and into the town proper are to visit the **tourist office** at 94 Charles St (April–Sept Mon–Sat 10am–5pm; ☎01646/690866), or west Wales' only professional **theatre**, the Torch (☎01646/695267), on St Peter's Road, at the end of Charles Street.

Accommodation is handiest a few yards from the docks towards Hakin, at the well-kept *Cleddau Villa B&B*, 21 St Anne's Rd (☎01646/690313; ❶), or with *Mrs Williams*, 1 Pier Rd (☎01646/694531; ❶) in one of the oldest houses in town, where rooms all have sea views. There's a **campsite** at *Sandy Haven*, near Herbrandston, two miles west of town (☎01646/698844; £11 per pitch). Also consider the *Taberna Inn* (☎01646/693498; ❷) in Herbrandston, just over two miles west, with comfortable rooms above a convivial pub that serves real ales and quality, freshly prepared **meals**. Back in town *Martha's Vineyard* (☎01646/697083) on the Marina is a good option, particularly for fish lovers, or try *Hamiltons*, 26 Hamilton Terrace, a tearoom up by the tourist office, which opens some evenings.

Haverfordwest and around

Lying seven miles northeast of Milford Haven in the valley of the Western Cleddau, the ancient settlement of **HAVERFORDWEST** (Hwlffordd) grew up around the Gilbert de Clare castle that dominates the skyline to this day. The town prospered as a port and trading centre in the seventeenth and eighteenth centuries, and its command of local trade ensured that Haverfordwest deposed Pembroke as the county town of Pembrokeshire. However, despite its natural advantages, a slew of rich architecture from its glory days and some recent jazzing up along the river, Haverfordwest is scarcely a place to linger.

The diminutive Castle Square forms the heart of the town. From here, a small alleyway to the right of Woolworths ascends to the **castle**, which fails to live up to the expectations created by views of it from down below: all there is to see is a dingy shell of the thirteenth-century inner ward. Next to the castle, in the imposing governors' house, is the **town museum** (Easter–Oct Mon–Sat 10am–4pm; £1), a motley collection of minor art pieces and some fairly interesting local history. Back down below, the Riverside Shopping Centre follows the river from Castle Square up to the Old Bridge, next to the bus terminus and tourist office. The more architecturally appealing parts of Haverfordwest lie up the handsome High Street, rising from the River Cleddau towards the thirteenth-century St Mary's Church.

Practicalities

The **train** station is ten minutes' walk east of the centre, while **buses** come and go from the depot at the end of the Old Bridge, near the **tourist office** (May–Sept Mon–Sat 9.30am–5pm; Oct–April Mon–Sat 10am–4pm; ☎01437/763110, ✉haverfordwes.tic@pembrokeshire.gov.uk). Mike's Bikes (☎01437/760068), 17 Prendergast, does **bike rental**.

For B&B **accommodation** in town, try *College Guest House*, 93 Hill St (☎01437/763710; ❷), but if you've got wheels, drive three miles west to *East Hook Farmhouse*, Portfield Gate (☎01437/762211, ⓦwww.easthookfarmhouse.co.uk; ❸), which has delightful rooms, serves delicious breakfasts with style and does evening meals for under £20. There's a **campsite** two miles northwest on the A487, at the *Rising Sun Inn* in Pelcomb Bridge (☎01437/765171; £6 per pitch).

For daytime **food**, grab a freshly filled baguette in *Dylan's*, 23 High St, which is a cut above most of the town's cafés. A great option for lunch or evening meals at weekends is the inexpensive *George's*, 24 Market St (closed Sun), where you can eat in a lovely walled garden if the weather allows, or the cellar bistro if not.

Four miles northwest of town on the A487, the sublime *Keeston Kitchen* (☎01437/710440; closed Sun evenings and Mon), just before the village of Simpson Cross is superb for seasonal speciality dishes.

Picton Castle and Scolton Manor

The main A40 heads east out of Haverfordwest past the train station. After three miles, signs point two miles south towards **Picton Castle** (April–Sept daily except Mon noon–4pm; £6 including grounds), a somewhat graceless hybrid of architectural styles from the fourteenth to the eighteenth centuries, sited in glorious **grounds** (March–Oct daily 10.30am–dusk; £5) with views over the Eastern Cleddau and its valleys.

Four miles northeast of Haverfordwest, along the B4329, **Scolton Manor** (April–Oct daily 10.30am–5.30pm; £2) is a modest stately home, dating from 1840, which forms the nucleus of the Pembrokeshire County Museum. It's a good place to appreciate the lifestyle of a rich Victorian family: the gilt, brocade and fine furnishings upstairs in total contrast with the perfunctory cellar, larder and laundry below. Besides a fine collection of prints and maps detailing some of the lost picturesque estates of Wales, there's a Carriage House filled with traps and a wealth of local artefacts. Having refreshed yourself in the agreeable **café**, check out the surrounding **country park** (daily: April–Oct 9am–6pm; Nov–March 9am–4.30pm; parking £1), whose visitor centre emphasizes environmental awareness.

Narberth and the Landsker Borderlands

The area now known as the **Landsker Borderlands** forms a quiet, charming part of mid-Pembrokeshire, broken by some beautiful villages that are still well off the beaten tourist track. *Landsker* is an Anglo-Saxon word meaning "frontier", and is used in this sense as a definition of the division between Cymric north Pembrokeshire and the anglicized south. The division is ancient, going back to the Norman colonization of the south of the county, but despite its archaic tenor, the name is a comparatively recent sobriquet – first mentioned in this context in the 1930s. The "capital" of the borderlands is **NARBERTH** (Arberth), eight miles east of Haverfordwest, a pleasing and cheerful little town with a real community spirit and. According to The Mabinogion, a collection of ancient Celtic folk tales and legends, the town was the court of Pwyll, and its ruined **castle** was probably the old home of the Welsh princes. Today, though, its main draw is a growing reputation as Pembrokeshire's prime boutique shopping destination

The **train station** is at the far eastern end of the town. Station Road turns into Spring Gardens, along which you'll find one of Narberth's many artists' outlets, the enjoyable **Creative Café** (May–mid-Sept & school holidays daily 10am–6pm; other times Tues–Sun 10am–5pm; ☎01834/861651), where customers are encouraged to make a mess in the name of creating their own personalized ceramics. At the top of town, Spring Gardens meets High Street, where the **Queen's Hall** (☎01834/861212, ⓦwww.thequeenshall.com) is one of the best emerging venues in Pembrokeshire, hosting world music concerts, theatre, art exhibitions and more. Midway down High Street you'll see the curious, spiky **town hall**, built in the 1830s to mask the municipal water tank underneath, and now housing a design store.

Practicalities

Accommodation in Narberth is limited, though there are rooms at the comfy *Plas Hyfryd Country Hotel* (☎01834/869006, ⓦwww.plashyfrydhotel.com; ➎), on Moorfield Road at the top end of town. The hamlet of Robeston Wathen, just over a mile north on the A40, has two reliable guesthouses: *Highland Grange Farm* (☎01834/860952, ⓦwww.highlandgrange.co.uk; ➌), which serves meals; and the simpler *Canton House* (☎01834/860620; ➋) with shared bathrooms. *The Dingle* **campsite** (☎01834/860482; £8 per pitch), on Jessie Road 100 yards from the *Creative Café*, will usually fit in some tents. There are also a couple of nearby options around the Eastern Cleddau (see p.206).

Try to visit Narberth for **lunch**, best taken at ✲ *Café Ole*, 7 High St (☎01834/861491), a little slice of Spain tucked in behind the fabulous Ultracomida deli. Hams hang from the ceiling and the blackboard menu features summer-only greasy spoon that's usually full of board-riders, the yacht club's *The Moorings* (☎07792/592922), for good restaurant meals on the waterfront, and the adjacent *Griffin Inn* for real ales.

The calm waters of Dale are deceptive, and as you head south towards **St Ann's Head** the wind speed whips up, with waves and tides to match. Blasted by some of the highest winds in Britain (gale force on an average of 32 days per year) and buffeted by extraordinarily strong tide-races, the coastline here offers invigorating, walking. This was the site of the 1996 *Sea Empress* wreck, though thankfully all visible reminders of the oil slick have now vanished. The Coast Path sticks tight to the undulating coastline, passing tiny bays en route to the St Ann's lighthouse. Tucked in the eastern lee of St Ann's Head is **Mill Bay**, where Henry VII landed in 1485, marching the breadth of his native Wales and gathering a loyal army to face Richard III at Bosworth Field.

The coast turns and heads north from St Ann's Head, reaching the sandstone-backed **West Dale Bay**, less than a mile from Dale on the opposite side of the peninsula. Warnings are usually given about the unpredictability of the currents and hidden rocks in the sea here.

Marloes and around

A mile north of Dale, the village of **MARLOES** backs the great sandy curve of **Marloes Sands**, best known for its stunning cliffs of grey, gold and purple folds of rock, alternate layers of grey shale and old red sandstone. At **Three Chimneys**, two-thirds of the way along the beach, three vertical lines of hard Silurian sandstone and mudstone were formed horizontally and forced up by ancient earth movements. There was a fourth "chimney" which crumbled in a severe storm in 1954.

The beach is crowned at its western end by **Gateholm Island**, accessible at mid-tide and below (most easily accessed from the YHA hostel – see below, a hundred yards before which is a large National Trust car park). Over 130 Iron Age hut circles, pottery and pieces of jewellery have been found here, on what is thought to have been an ancient monastic community. Today, Gateholm is powerfully atmospheric and a great place to camp wild if you're prepared to carry your own water and undertake the tricky access scramble: head around the left side as you look at the island.

Next up is **MARTIN'S HAVEN**, a cluster of houses and a car park on a slim neck of the peninsula that faces out to Skomer island. Inexplicably bypassed by the Coast Path is the sublime headland of **Deer Park** the very western tip of this peninsula, reached by a small gateway in the wall just beyond the car park. The park has no deer, and probably never did, but paths radiate out all over the headland, all with stunning views over the offshore islands and St Bride's Bay: if you can catch a decent sunset here, you'll see none better. There's a small Wildlife Trust of South and West Wales information point at Martin's Haven, the principal departure point for **boats** to the offshore islands of Skomer, Skokholm and Grassholm (see below). North of Deer Park, the Coast Path continues less than half a mile from the village of Marloes round to **Musselwick Sands**, a beautiful and unspoilt beach that can be dangerous at high tide. Further north along the peninsula is the narrow **St Bride's Haven**, a tiny, sheltered inlet with a small beach at the end of the lane that peters out by the tiny chapel of St Bride. There are some good rock pools around the beach.

There's not much to the village of Marloes, but you can **stay** at the central *Lobster Pot Inn* (☎01646/636233; ❸), above Marloes' only real restaurant, which, unsurprisingly, serves up a good range of seafood. There are several **campsites**, among them *East Hook Farm* (☎01646/636291; £3 per person) a mile back from Martin's Haven. The *Marloes Sands YHA* **hostel** (℡01646/636667; ❶; open May to mid-Sept) consists of a series of converted farm buildings overlooking the northern end of Marloes Sands, with £8.50 bunks.

Skomer, Skokholm and Grassholm

One of the highlights of this stretch of coast is a boat trip out around the offshore islands, though the only one day-trippers can land on is **Skomer**, a 722-acre flat-topped island that dominates the near horizon. It has the finest **sea bird** colonies in northern Europe, the remains of hundreds of ancient hut circles, a stone circle, collapsed defensive ramparts and settlement systems and a Bronze Age standing stone known as Harold's Stone, near the narrow neck where boats land. The stars of Skomer are the 200,000-plus Manx shearwaters, which only leave their burrows at night, though there's a live video of one in a burrow for day visitors to see. There are also puffins (best May to early July), gulls, guillemots, storm petrels, cormorants, shags and kittiwakes. Land birds include buzzards, skylarks, jackdaws, chough, owls and peregrines. If you head to the north of Skomer, facing out over the Garland Stone, there's a good chance of seeing basking grey seals, especially in the autumn. In spring and early summer, wild flowers carpet the island.

Two miles south of Skomer is the 240-acre island of **Skokholm**, whose warm red sandstone cliffs are a sharp contrast to Skomer's grey severity. Britain's first bird observatory was founded here in the 1930s, and the island is still rich in birdlife.

Six miles west of Skomer, the tiny islet of **Grassholm** resembles a small icing-covered cake: the "icing" is, in fact, a swarming mass of 70,000 gannets, one of the largest colonies in the northern hemisphere, that covers well over half the island.

Boat trips to Skomer are run by Dale Sailing (℡0800/0284090 or 01646/603110, Ⓦwww.dale-sailing.co.uk) who operate landing trips on the

△ Skomer sea bird

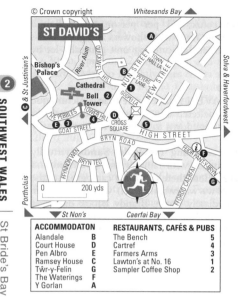

© Crown copyright   Whitesands Bay

ST DAVID'S

ACCOMMODATON		RESTAURANTS, CAFÉS & PUBS	
Alandale	B	The Bench	5
Court House	D	Cartref	4
Pen Albro	E	Farmers Arms	3
Ramsey House	C	Lawton's at No. 16	1
Tŵr-y-Felin	G	Sampler Coffee Shop	2
The Waterings	F		
Y Gorlan	A		

Conqueror included – and by 1120, Pope Calixtus II decreed that two journeys to St David's amounted to the spiritual equivalent of one pilgrimage to Rome. The settlement grew up around the cathedral, and St David's today still relies on the imported wealth of newcomers to the area, attracted by its savage beauty. With so many historical sites, outdoor pursuit centres, surf beaches, good cafés, superb walks, bathing and climbing, St David's and its peninsula are a must if you want to experience Wales at its wildest.

Arrival, information and activities

Entering St David's, the main road from Haverfordwest (here called High Street) passes the National Park **tourist office** (Easter–Oct daily 9.30am–5.30pm; Nov–Easter Mon–Sat 10am–4pm; ☎01437/720392, Ⓦwww.stdavids.co.uk), and carries on for two hundred yards to the **bus stop** in New Street. From May to September, an hourly *Celtic Coaster* shuttle bus connects the centre of St David's with Whitesands Bay, St Justinian's and Porth Clais. **Bike rental** is available from Voyages of Discovery, 1 High St (April–Oct; ☎01437/721911; £10 half-day, £15 full day). Cycle Hire Pembrokeshire, four miles north off the A487 (☎07875/775323), has slightly cheaper bikes and a range of tandems, kids' bikes and tag-a-longs that makes it ideal for families.

Several local companies run boat trips to the outlying islands (see p.209), as scheduled at their offices. There are a number of other **outdoor activities** available, most run through TYF, 1 High St (☎01437/721611, Ⓦwww.tyf .com), which pioneered **coasteering**, an exhilarating multi-sport combination of scrambling over rocks, jumping off cliffs and swimming across the narrow bays of St David's Peninsula. It is geared for just about anyone (even non-swimmers) and operates throughout the year, with two-and-a-half-hour sessions priced at £40. The company also offers surfing, kayaking and rock climbing (all £40 a half-day, £72 full day) and can organize multi-day sessions and longer courses.

Accommodation

There are numerous places to **stay** on and around the St David's Peninsula, with prices fairly high in season at the larger hotels, but coming down dramatically for the rest of the year. Campsites abound in and around the city.

Hotels and guesthouses

Alandale 43 Nun St ☎01437/720404. Small, friendly, central guesthouse with some en-suite rooms. A healthy breakfast is included. ➍

Crug Glas Abereiddl, 4 miles northeast of St David's ☎01348/831302, Ⓦwww .crug-glas.co.uk. Luxurious country house on a working farm. The five large rooms are elaborately decorated with gold fittings, tasselled cushions and either half-tester or four-poster beds. Breakfasts are excellent (great bacon) and delicious four-course evening meals are available for around £20. ➏

Cwmwdig Water Guesthouse Berea, 5 miles northeast of St David's ☎01348/831434,

@ andrewcwmwdig@aol.com. Welcoming B&B close to the Coast Path, also serving a four-course evening meal (£15). **③**

Pen Albro 18 Goat St ☎01437/721865. The cheapest B&B in town, with no en suites but a good breakfast, right beside the *Farmers Arms*. **①**

Ramsey House Lower Moor ☎01437/720321, ⓦwww.ramseyhouse.co.uk. Quality six-room B&B on the road to Porth Clais, recently redecorated and with excellent breakfasts: expect the likes of home-made apple and sage sausages and fresh bread. **⑤**

Tŵr-y-Felin Caerfai Rd ☎01437/721678, ⓦwww .tyf.com. Built around a converted windmill, this B&B is mostly given over to residential courses run by TYF (see opposite), but is open to all. Rooms are comfortable and there's a lively bar on site. **③**

The Waterings Anchor Drive ☎01437/720876, ⓦwww.waterings.co.uk. Luxurious en-suite rooms and suites in a former marine research establish-ment, which retains a maritime theme. There are lovely grounds and you can play pitch and putt on the lawn.

Y Gorlan 77 Nun St ☎01437/720837. Central guesthouse with en-suite rooms, in a converted Victorian residence. **④**

Hostels and campsites

Caerfai Farm Caerfai Bay ☎01437/720548. The best campsite around, based on an organic dairy farm 15 minutes' walk from the city. No caravans. Closed Oct–April. £5 per person.

Court House 20 Cross Square ☎01437/720811, ⓦwww.courthouse.org.uk. Convenient city-centre hostel with decent facilities and a Quaker bias. Mainly caters to groups; individuals should check for availability. Max 5 beds per room; £10 per person. **①**

Glan-y-môr Caerfai Rd ☎01437/721788, ⓦwww .glan-y-mor.co.uk. The nearest campsite to town, with a restaurant and budget bike rental. You can't book – just turn up on spec. Closed Nov–March. £5 per person.

Lleithyr Farm Whitesands Bay ☎01437/720245, ⓦwww.whitesands-stdavids.co.uk.. High-standard campsite and caravan park with heated shower rooms in winter, just off the B4583, half a mile short of Whitesands Bay. Closed Jan & Feb. £3.50 per person.

Rhosson Ganol St Justinian's ☎01437/720361. Popular year-round campsite, handy for the boats to Ramsey Island. Closed Nov–Easter. £5 per person.

St David's YHA hostel Llaethdy, White-sands ☎01437/720345 or 0870/770 6042, @ stdavids@yha.org.uk. Large and recently reno-vated hostel in a former farmhouse and outbuild-ings, two miles northwest of St David's near White-sands Bay. Closed Nov–March. Bunks £10.

The Town

St David's High Street courses down to the triangular Cross Square, with its centrepiece **Celtic cross**, and continues under the thirteenth-century **Tower Gate**, which forms the entrance to the serene **Cathedral Close**. The cathedral lies down to the right, hidden in a hollow by the River Alun. This apparent modesty is explained by reasons of defence: a towering cathedral, visible from the sea on all sides, would have been far too vulnerable. On the other side of the babbling Alun lie the ruins of the Bishop's Palace.

There are numerous small commercial **art galleries** and craft outlets throughout St David's: a few are dreadful, but most reflect the quality of the many artists attracted to this spirited corner of Wales, all of whom claim the area's unique light quality as their inspiration.

The cathedral

The gold-and-purple 125-foot stone tower of the **cathedral** (donation requested; ⓦwww.stdavidscathedral.org.uk) is approached down the Thirty-Nine Articles – steps named after Thomas Cranmer's key tenets of Anglicanism. They descend from beyond the doughty **Tower Gate** (£1 donation requested), the last of four medieval originals, which now houses an exhibition about the history of St David's.

The cathedral tower has clocks on only three sides (the people of the northern part of the parish couldn't raise enough money for one to be installed facing them), and is topped by pert golden pinnacles that seem to glow a different colour from the rest of the building. You enter via a porch in the south side of the low twelfth-century nave, the most striking feature of which is its intricate latticed oak **roof**, built to hide sixteenth-century emergency restoration work undertaken when the nave was in danger of collapse. The nave floor still has a discernible slope and the support buttresses inserted in the northern aisle of the nave look incongruously new and temporary.

At the crossing, an elaborate **rood screen** was constructed under the orders of fourteenth-century Bishop Gower, who envisaged it as his own tomb. Behind the rood screen and the organ, the choir sits directly under the magnificently bold and bright lantern ceiling of the tower, another addition by Gower. The round-headed arch over the organ was built in Norman times, contrasting with the other three underpinning the tower, which are pointed and date from the rebuilding work that took place in the 1220s. At the back of the right-hand choir stalls is a unique **monarch's stall**, complete with royal crest, for, unlike any other British cathedral, the Queen is an automatic member of the St David's cathedral Chapter. The misericords under the choir seats display earthy medieval humour; there's one of a chaotic wild boar hunt and another of someone being seasick. Behind the left-hand choir stalls, the **north transept** contains the tomb of St Caradoc, with two pierced quatrefoils, in which it is believed people would insert diseased limbs in the hope of a cure. Off the north transept, steps from St Thomas' chapel lead up to the **Chapter Library** (July & Aug Mon–Fri 11am–1pm & 2–4pm; Sept–June Mon only 2–4pm; £1), which includes the Royal Charter of 1995 that granted St David's city status.

Separating the choir and the presbytery is a finely traced, rare **parclose screen**. The back wall of the **presbytery** was once the eastern extremity of the cathedral, as can be seen from the two lines of windows. The upper row has been left intact, while the lower three were blocked up and filled with delicate gold mosaics in the nineteenth century, surrounded by over-fussy stonework. The colourful fifteenth-century roof, with its deceptively simple medieval pattern, was restored by Gilbert Scott in the mid-nineteenth century. Around the altar, the **sanctuary** has a few fragmented fifteenth-century tiles still in place. On the south side is a beautifully carved sedilla, a seat for the priest and deacon celebrating Mass. To its right are thirteenth-century tombs of bishops Iorwerth (1215–31) and Anselm de la Grace (1231–47), and on the other side of the sanctuary is the disappointingly plain thirteenth-century tomb of St David, largely destroyed in the Reformation.

Behind the filled-in lancets at the back of the presbytery altar is the Perpendicular **Bishop Vaughan's chapel**, crafted out of a soft honeyed stone, with an exquisite fan tracery roof built between 1508 and 1522. Bishop Vaughan's statue occupies the niche to the left of the altar. To the right is an effigy of Giraldus Cambrensis, Gerald of Wales, his mitre placed not on his head, but at his feet – a reminder that he never attained the status of bishop to which he evidently aspired. Opposite, facing west, a peephole looks into the presbytery. Around the opening, the four crosses may well predate the Norman church. The bottom cross is largely obscured by a casket, reputedly containing some of the intermingled bones of St David and his friend, St Justinian. Behind the chapel is the ambulatory and the simple **Lady Chapel** with its sentimental Edwardian stained glass. On either side are tombs in wall niches: the one on the left was originally believed to have been for Bishop Beck (1280–96), the builder of St David's Bishop's Palace, but now houses Bishop Owen (1897–1926), whose devoted service to the Church in Wales and the Welsh nation is symbolized by the roaring dragon above him.

Around the back of the cathedral, a new **cloister** is being built on the ruins of the fourteenth-century original, and by summer 2006 there should be a restaurant on site.

Guided tours of the cathedral (July & Aug daily except Wed & Sat 2.30pm, other times ℡01437/720691, ✉tours@stdavidscathedral.org.uk; £3) are arranged at the bookshop in the nave. Also worth noting is the cathedral's **evensong** (every Sun 6pm) when the girls' and men's choirs sing; and the superb annual **music festival** (℡01437/720271, ⓦwww.stdavidscathedral.org.uk/festivals), which takes place in late May/early June.

The Bishop's Palace

From the cathedral, a path leads over the River Alun to the splendid **Bishop's Palace** (mid-March to May & Oct daily 9.30am–5pm; June–Sept daily 9.30am–6pm; Nov–March Mon–Sat 9.30am–4pm, Sun 11am–4pm; £2.50; CADW), built by bishops Beck and Gower in the early fourteenth century. Its huge central quadrangle is enclosed by an array of ruined buildings in extraordinarily rich colours: the green, red, purple and grey tints of volcanic rock, sandstone and many other types of stone. The **arched parapets** along the top of the walls were a favourite motif of Gower, who did more than any of his predecessors or successors to transform the palace into an architectural and political powerhouse. Off the quadrangle, the ruinous yet still impressive **Bishop's Hall** and the enormous **Great Hall**, with its glorious rose window overlay a myriad of rooms adorned by eerily eroded corbels. Beneath the Great Hall are dank vaults containing an interesting exhibition about the palace and the indulgent lifestyles of its occupants. The destruction of the palace is largely due to Bishop Barlow (1536–48), who supposedly stripped the buildings of their lead roofs to provide dowries for his five daughters' marriages to bishops.

Eating, drinking and entertainment

With only one pub to its name, St David's might appear to be a quiet little backwater. Not so; the city is a real magnet for surfers, outdoor types and musicians. In the summer, and over Christmas/New Year, parties are likely to break out just about anywhere. It's also a great place to eat; there's something for all tastes and budgets.

The Bench 11 High St ⓦwww.bench-bar.co.uk. Classy but relaxed restaurant, café and wine bar. Pop in for a quick espresso and panini or to linger over pizza and fresh pasta dishes (£5–9). There's seating outside or in the sunny conservatory, Internet access, and Italian ice cream to go.
Cartref Cross Square ℡01437/720422. Reasonable, moderately priced restaurant serving family favourites in decent portions. Closed Jan & Feb.
Farmers Arms Goat St. The city's only real pub. Young, lively, very friendly and especially enjoyable on the terrace overlooking the cathedral on a summer's evening. Good pub food also available.
Lawton's at No. 16 16 Nun St ℡01437/729220, ⓦwww.lawtonsatno16.co.uk. Sleek, modern restaurant with a broad range of mains – from vegetable burrito (£14) to saffron monkfish (£18) and Ramsey Island lobster thermidore (£26). Evenings only; closed Mon.
Sampler coffee shop 17 Nun St. Slightly twee daytime coffee shop, serving delicious clotted-cream teas.

St David's Peninsula

Surrounded on three sides by inlets, coves and rocky stacks, St David's is an easy base for some excellent walking around the headland of the same name. A mile south, the popular **Caerfai Bay** is a sandy gash in the purple-sandstone cliffs, from which masonry for the cathedral was quarried. Half a mile to the west is the craggy indentation of **St Non's Bay**, reached from St David's down a tiny rhododendron-flooded lane leading off Goat Street, that's signposted to the *Warpool Court Hotel*. According to legend, St Non gave birth to St David at this spot during a tumultuous storm around 500 AD, when a spring opened up

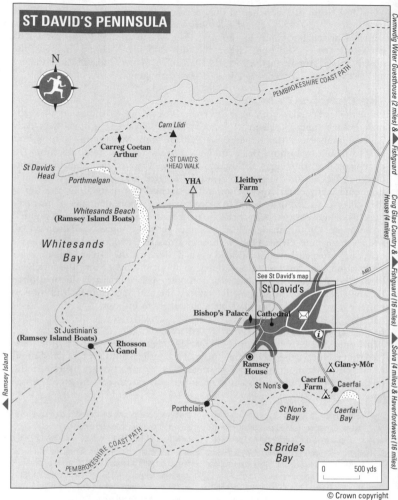

ST DAVID'S PENINSULA

N

Cwmwdig Water Guesthouse (2 miles) & ► Fishguard

*Crug Glas Country & ► Fishguard (16 miles) ►
House (4 miles)*

PEMBROKESHIRE COAST PATH

Carn Llidi

Carreg Coetan
Arthur

St David's
Head

Porthmelgan

ST DAVID'S
HEAD WALK

YHA

Lleithyr
Farm

Whitesands Beach
(Ramsey Island Boats)

*Whitesands
Bay*

A487

See St David's map

St David's

Solva (4 miles) & ► Haverfordwest (16 miles)

Bishop's Palace

Cathedral

St Justinian's
(Ramsey Island Boats)

Rhosson
Ganol

Ramsey Island

Ramsey
House

Glan-y-Môr

St Non's

Caerfai
Farm

Caerfai

Porthclais

*St Non's
Bay*

*Caerfai
Bay*

*St Bride's
Bay*

PEMBROKESHIRE COAST PATH

0   500 yds

© Crown copyright

between Non's feet, and despite the crashing thunder all around, an eerily calm
light filtered down onto the scene.

St Non's received pilgrims for centuries, resulting in the foundation of a tiny
chapel in the pre-Norman age, whose successor's thirteenth-century ruins now
lie in a field to the right of the car park, beyond the sadly dingy well and coy
shrine where the nation's patron saint is said to have been born. The 1934
chapel, built in front of the austere 1929 **Retreat House** (details of stays and
religious courses on ☎01437/720224), was constructed in simple Pembrokeshire style from the rocks of ruined houses, which, in turn, had been built from
the stone of ancient, abandoned churches.

Further west, **PORTH CLAIS**, is supposedly the place where St David was
baptized by the bishop of Munster, who went by the unlikely name of St Elvis.
Porth Clais was the city's main harbour, the spruced-up remains of which can

The great Welsh outdoors

With craggy mountains, large areas of moorland, a deeply indented coastline, wide beaches and fast-flowing rivers, Wales makes a fabulous outdoor playground. The short day-hikes are some of the best anywhere, while keen walkers can tackle the long-distance paths over a couple of visits or in one epic tramp. Mountain bikers whizz around the popular forest bike parks or peel off onto long off-road touring routes. Elsewhere the mountains and cliffs provide scope for fabulous rock climbing and even thrilling coasteering trips. Along gentler coasts, watersports prevail, particularly the growing sports of kiteboarding and wakeboarding. Whatever your activity, the great Welsh outdoors can handle it.

Mud hounds and mountain rides

Since the 1990s, the managed forests of Wales have gained an enviable reputation throughout Britain for top-class mountain biking. Miles of single-track now weave through the pines, and every weekend you'll spot mud-bespattered bikers recovering from their exploits in nearby cafés.

The key bike parks are dotted down the mountainous spine of the country – from the Gwydyr Forest just outside Betws-y-Coed on the fringe of Snowdonia to Cwm Carn in the Valleys northwest of Newport. They're free to use and brilliant fun, with routes for everyone from beginners to hardened speed freaks. Elsewhere, off-road cycling is allowed along designated bridleways, including the Snowdon Ranger, Rhyd Ddu and Llanberis paths up Snowdon (detailed on p.398), though in summertime you're limited to off-peak hours: slog up in the pre-dawn cool for that summit sunrise, or head up for sunset and a nerve-wracking dusk descent.

If you really fancy a challenge, make for Sarn Helen, an epic route across the country through Snowdonia and the Brecon Beacons loosely following an old Roman (and probably pre-Roman) route. At 270 miles long – running from Conwy to Gower (see pp.465 and 154) – it is reckoned to be the most ambitious off-road ride in Britain and is likely to take over a week.

For more on the practicalities of mountain biking, see p.65.

Going rockface climbing

Going cragging

Wales has some of the finest rock climbing in Britain, in fact the term "cragging" comes from *craig*, Welsh for cliff. The scale may not be huge (the highest route only takes you up 800ft) but the quality of the climbing is hard to beat and there's an astonishing variety of routes in a small area. Llanberis (see p.398), at the foot of Snowdon, is the home of Welsh climbing, and with over a century of climbing in the area the routes span the range from easy hands-on scrambles up mountain ridges to impossibly difficult climbs only achievable by a few dozen people in the world.

Much of the action is tucked away far from where non-climbers are likely to be, but stop on the roadside in Llanberis Pass any weekend (and weekdays through the summer) and you'll soon pick out small groups clustered at the bottom of the cliffs. The predominance of low-lying crags combined with easy accessibility make the area particularly popular.

In the south of the country, the pick of the crags are the limestone sea cliffs along the Pembrokeshire Coast (see p.193). There are pockets of activity all over, but the bulk of the action happens near Bosherston (see p.195), where the military ordnance testing areas of Range East and Range West give limited access to the coast. Permits for some areas require climbers to attend a bomb recognition course, but there are plenty of areas with much freer access. Further east, the Gower Peninsula (see p.154) is also ringed by tempting sea cliffs.

Heroic hikes and lengthy rambles

Wales is traced by a spider's web of over a dozen wonderful **long-distance paths** (LDPs). Three of these – the Pembrokeshire Coast Path, Offa's Dyke Path and Glyndŵr's Way – are additionally designated National Trails, waymarked at frequent intervals by an acorn symbol. These use a strong unifying theme for their route; others are a mite esoteric, though this seldom detracts from the quality of the walk. LDPs are usually well supplied with youth hostels, though you may need a tent for some of the more heroic hikes.

The following is a brief rundown of the most popular LDPs, all of which are also detailed in the Guide.

Cambrian Way (274 miles). The longest, wildest and most arduous of the Welsh LDPs, cutting north–south over the remote Cambrian Mountains. See p.473.

Glyndŵr's Way (123 miles). A lengthy meander amongst the remote mountains and lakes of midWales, visiting sites associated with the great fifteenth-century Welsh hero. From Welshpool to Knighton via Machynlleth. See p.277.

Landsker Borderlands Trail (60 miles). Gentle waterways, quiet villages and easy trails characterize this slightly contrived circular walk around the Landsker region, starting from Canaston Bridge in Pembrokeshire. See p.205.

Offa's Dyke Path (177 miles). The classic Welsh LDP, running from Prestatyn in the north to Chepstow in south Wales, largely tracing the line of the eighth-century earthwork along the English border. Mostly wooded lowland walking with demanding territory through the Black Mountains. See p.273.

Pembrokeshire Coast Path (186 miles). This quintessential Welsh coastal trail dips into quiet coves and climbs over headlands with sweeping ocean views, and plenty of birdlife on the cliffs and offshore islands. See p.193.

Wye Valley Walk (136 miles). A lovely, sylvan, sea-to-source trek following the River Wye from Chepstow to Plynlimon. It repeatedly crosses the English border past rolling countryside and dramatic limestone gorges. See p.83.

Offshore watersports

Whether you call it **kiteboarding** or kitesurfing, it is hot in Wales. The water may not be that warm, but great sweeping beaches lashed by strong steady winds off the Atlantic make for some excellent spots. Key centres are Rhosneigr on Anglesey, Aberdyfi along the Cambrian coast, Whitesands Bay in Pembrokeshire and Rhossili on the Gower peninsula near Swansea. All these places have shops selling gear and offering lessons. It isn't exactly an easy sport to learn, but a class can get you body-dragging (more fun than it sounds) inside a day, and actually riding a board in a couple of days.

If you'd prefer not to have to wait for ideal wind conditions, there are opportunities for wakeboarding, particularly on the Llŷn, where Abersoch hosts its annual wakeboarding festival, Wakestock (see p.434).

Coasteering

Wales is not normally considered to be at the cutting edge of adventure sports, but it led the way with coasteering, an exhilarating combination of hiking, coastal scrambling, swimming and cliff jumping. Clad in a wetsuit, helmet and buoyancy aid, the aim is to make your way as a group along the rugged, wave-lashed coastline. Home turf for the sport is the indented Pembrokeshire coast near St David's, where the pioneering TYF Adventure (see p.212) runs classic Blue Line trips for beginners, or White Line and Red Line trips conducted in progressively rougher conditions. For a bigger bite of the coast, the Flat Line trips cover about ten times the distance of a normal trip, and there are also eco-trips suited to families and those keen to explore the rock pools and inter-tidal zone.

Coasteering

For more details on all the outdoor activities mentioned here, see pp.63–68.

still be seen at the bottom of the turquoise river creek. Today, commercial traffic has long gone, replaced by a yachties' haven.

Running due west out of St David's, Goat Street ducks past the ruins of the Bishop's Palace and over the rocky plateau for two miles to the harbour at **ST JUSTINIAN'S**, little more than a ruined chapel, lifeboat station and ticket hut for the frequent **boats** over to **Ramsey Island** (see below).

Whitesands Bay (Porth Mawr), two miles to the north and reached from St David's via the B4583 off the Fishguard road, is lined with campsites and cafés, and as the beach faces west, **surfing** is good. The spectacularly beautiful **Porthmelgan**, a narrow slip of cove reached by a fifteen-minute walk north-west along the Coast Path from Whitesands car park, is far less crowded, largely

A circular walk around St David's Head

Note: OS 1:25,000 Outdoor Leisure map #35 (North Pembrokeshire) is advised for this walk.

The tapering finger of rock that tumbles down from the slopes of Carn Llidi, just over a mile north of St David's, is one of the most mysterious and magical places in Wales. Evidence of ancient civilization is everywhere, and numerous mystics and seers have pinpointed the area as a focus of the earth's natural energies.

Starting from the Whitesands Bay car park, double back up the lane to St David's. Go past the twin semi-detached houses and take the left track opposite the caravan park. Where the lane forks, take the right turning, signposted to Upper Porthmawr. Take the track between the two farmhouses and continue climbing, following the right track at the National Trust sign. Ascend to the rocky top of **Carn Llidi** (595ft) on the obvious track, passing two cromlechs – capped burial stones – on the lower slope. At the top, you get mesmerizing views over the whole of St Bride's Bay, the patchwork of the Dewisland peninsula, the cathedral, the rocky outcrops of Ramsey, Skomer and Grassholm, the dips of the coast north up to Strumble Head, White-sands Bay and miles of glittering sea.

Retrace your steps down the hill, past the cromlechs, and take the first obvious right path. This leads swiftly down to a hedge-backed green lane; turn right and keep walking as it curves gently round. On reaching the kissing gate, turn right into the peaceful little valley below the craggy cairns. The slope on the right has been excavated to reveal the extensive remains of an Iron Age field and settlement system, although this will be hard to see if the bracken is high. Take the first left path before the valley reeds and cross the peaty brook and bridleway, continuing up to meet a green road and then the main Coast Path. Turning left towards the headland brings you along and above some superb cliffs, speckled with wild flowers and squawking sea birds. After a few hundred yards, above the path to the left, you should spot **Carreg Coetan Arthur** (Arthur's Quoit), a 6000-year-old capstoned burial chamber. The path strikes on towards the end of the headland. Shortly, a line of broken wall indicates the first line of defence of Clawdd-y-Milwyr (The Warrior's Dyke), an Iron Age fort that occupied the very tip of this promontory. Although the Coast Path now ducks down to the other shore, you can continue over the dyke and see the three lines of defensive ditches crossing the headland.

Turning south, walk along the cliff top with the sandy cove of Porthmelgan down below. The path bumps gently down to the beach, a pleasant alternative to the crowds and ice creams of Whitesands. At mid-tide and lower, there are even some great caves to poke around in. From here, the Coast Path climbs back to Whitesands Bay. Just before the car park, a memorial stone records that a St Patrick's chapel once stood here, built between the sixth and tenth centuries. St Patrick, a Welshman who became the patron saint of Ireland, is said to have sailed from here for Ireland in the late fourth century AD.

on account of the dangerous swimming. The thin spit of rock and cliff that juts out into the ocean less than a mile to the west comprises **St David's Head**, site of an Iron Age coastal fortress, its outline most visible in spring. Rising behind Whitesands and Porthmelgan, the gnarled crag of **Carn Llidi** tops a pastoral patchwork of fields.

Ramsey Island and cruises

Less than two miles long, the dual-humped plateau of **Ramsey Island** has been under the able care of the RSPB since 1992 and is quite enchanting. Birds of prey circle the skies above it, but the island is better known for the tens of thousands of sea birds that noisily crowd the sheer cliffs on the western side. On the beaches, seals laze sloppily below the paths worn by a herd of red deer. There's something to see all year round, but spring is great for nesting birds (especially puffins and shearwaters), and autumn for seals with their pups.

The only operator that lets you **land** on the island is Thousand Islands Expeditions, based on Cross Square in St David's (April–Oct daily; ☎01437/721721, ⓦwww.thousandislands.co.uk; £14); boats depart at 10am and 1pm and return at 1 and 4pm, allowing you up to six hours' exploration. During the springtime nesting season (when you're not allowed to land), you see more from boats which just circle the island without landing. Try Thousand Islands' excellent evening Puffin & Shearwater Watch (£25), or the **round–Ramsey cruises** offered by Voyages of Discovery, also in St David's at 1 High St (☎0800/854367 or 01437/721911, ⓦwww.ramseyisland.co.uk; 1hr £18; 1.5hr evening trip £25), which uses fast rigid-inflatables to facilitate ducking into caves. The latter company also runs a trip around Grassholm Island (see p.209; 2.5hr £50).

These boats all leave from St Justinian's, while several other companies run similar trips from Whitesands Beach: pick up flyers around town.

North Pembrokeshire coast

The stretch of coast immediately north of St David's forms the very southern sweep of Cardigan Bay and is noticeably less commercialized than the touristy littoral of south and mid-Pembrokeshire. From the crags and cairns above St David's Head, the Coast Path perches precariously on the cliffs, where only the thousands of sea birds have access.

Although the major income from this part of west Pembrokeshire is now tourism, the remains of old mines, quarries and ports at **Abereiddi** and **Porthgain** bear witness to the slate and granite industries that once employed hundreds. Industry dies down towards **Trefin** and up to the more remote beaches and inlets that punctuate the coast as it climbs up to the splendid knuckle of **Strumble Head**. To the east is **Carregwastad Point**, the site of the last invasion of Britain in 1797. The event is also remembered in the port town of **Fishguard**, where local soldiers tricked the invading French into unconditional surrender at the *Royal Oak Inn*.

Abereiddi to Abercastell

A quiet lane leaves St David's and runs parallel to the coast across the rocky Pembrokeshire plateau, where the few trees have been blasted into spooky shapes by the relentless gusts off the Irish Sea. A small lane turns left five miles from St David's and tumbles down into the bleak hamlet of **ABEREIDDI**, at the head of its stony, black-sand beach. You can find tiny fossilized animals in

△ Porthgain harbour

the shale of the beach, which can become extremely crowded in midsummer. At the back of the beach are remains of workers' huts, industrial units and a tramway that once climbed over the hill to Porthgain, all part of the village slate quarry that closed in 1904. The quarry itself was dynamited for safety reasons, producing an inland lagoon where the seawater, combined with the minerals, has turned a violent shade of blue. The *Cwmwdig Water Guest House* (see p.212) is just half a mile inland.

The lane parallel to the coast passes the hamlet of Cwmwdig Water and leads to tiny **LLANRHIAN**, where a left turn takes you a mile down to the rambling village green of **PORTHGAIN**. This fascinating old port grew up around its slate works, the stumpy remains of which, together with an old brick-works, lime kiln and eerie ruins of workers' cottages, are huddled around the tiny quay. It also has a couple of small art galleries and the excellent *Sloop Inn*, an eighteenth-century stone house with good beer and food and numerous photographs of the port in its sepia heyday. There's also *The Shed* (℡01348/831518; closed Mon), a tearoom and classy evening bistro where £30 will get you three courses. The menu usually includes fish caught on the angling and potting **boat trips** that run from Porthgain Harbour (also ℡01348/831518, ⓦwww .porthgainboats.ndo.co.uk; from £12). Within walking distance of Porthgain is a brilliant **independent hostel**, 🏠 *Caerhafod Lodge* (℡01348/837859, ⓦwww .caerhafod.co.uk) on the north side of Llanrhian. It is self-catering with four-bedded rooms, sheets supplied, all for £12. There are also £10 bunks at the *Trefin YHA* **hostel** (℡01348/831414, ⒺAreservations@yha.org.uk) a couple of miles east at **Trefin** (Trevine).

The coastal lane continues east to **ABERCASTELL**, past the 4500-year-old **Carreg Samson** cromlech (burial chamber) at Longhouse, precariously topped by a sixteen-foot capstone. If you're walking, continue past the cromlech and down to the coast path to the attractive and popular harbour of Abercastell, once used for the export of limestone and coal. From Abercastell, one of the most scenic parts of the Coast Path zigzags east along the wild, vertiginous cliffs to the point at **Trwyn Llwynog**, about two miles away.

2

Strumble Head and Carregwastad Point

The headland – known as **Pen Caer** – that rises to the north of Aberscastell, peaking at **STRUMBLE HEAD**, is delightful: tiny hedge-backed lanes bump around between rocky cairns, with fields of wild flowers and sudden glimpses of the shimmering sea. This is the closest the Welsh mainland gets to Ireland, and from its lofty heights you can usually see ferries zipping across the waters to and from Fishguard.

From this remote and spectacular section of the Coast Path there's access to the sandy stretch of **Aber Mawr**, smaller **Aber Bach**, and the west-facing gash of **Pwllcochran**. Nearly two miles further north, there's the simple but fabulously positioned *Pwll Deri YHA* **hostel** (see p.222). Looming large on the inland side of the hostel are the three crags of **Garn Fawr** (699ft): by following a path from the car park at their eastern edge, on the lane up to Strumble Head, you can explore the vestiges of ditches, ramparts and hut circles from its days as an early Iron Age fort.

Strumble Head, just over a mile due north of Garn Fawr, is reached either by the rugged coast path – with astounding views over the two-mile long "wall" of cliffs to the south – or along a floral country lane. The last farm before the headland is *Fferm Tresinwen* (☎01348/891621; £3-5 per pitch), an ideal place to **camp** for great walks along the promontories and coves of this enchanting stretch of coast. At the headland, the 1908 **lighthouse** is perched atop **Ynys Meicel**, connected to the mainland by a metal footbridge that's closed to the public. It's a peaceful, invigorating spot that's great for sea bird spotting.

Almost three miles on, the hamlet of **LLANWNDA** merits a historical footnote as the site of the **last invasion of Britain** (see box below). The **church of St Gwyndaf** has no mementos of this bizarre episode, but it's well worth a visit for its charming setting, ancient history that winds back beyond the eighth century and collection of pre-Norman carved stones, embedded in its walls. The **walk** from Llanwnda to **Carregwastad Point** is fabulous, coasting gently

The last invasion of Britain

In 1797, while Napoleon was absent fighting in central Europe, a newly formed Franco-Irish revolutionary command was trying to make its mark in Paris. Believing that the oppressed countryfolk of Britain would sympathize with their revolutionary views and join their cause, a motley band of "liberators" – some just out of prison and still shackled – hatched a madcap plan to invade Britain. Winds blew their ships from their planned landing place at Bristol and they ended up at **Carregwastad Point**, just south of Fishguard, where the event is marked by a memorial stone. The disorganized army of 1400 made its base at Trehowel Farm, midway between Strumble Head and Llanwnda, which was stocked up with food and drink for an imminent family wedding. Indeed most local farms were full of contraband liquor plundered from a recent Portuguese shipwreck. The would-be conquerors set to the victuals with gusto, swiftly becoming too drunk to do anything except loot the silver plate in Llanwnda's church.

After two days the invasion had collapsed and the invaders surrendered to a local militia at the *Royal Oak* in Fishguard, claiming they had seen "troops of the line to the number of several thousand". No such army was in the vicinity and some say the bleary-eyed French mistook several hundred local women clad in stovepipe hats and red flannel shawls for British Redcoats. While that may not be true, it's a fact that fourteen soldiers were rounded up with a pitchfork by a 47-year-old cobbler's wife, Jemima Nicholas – dubbed ever since the "Welsh Heroine".

down fields and across the top of a craggy cwm. Go over the stile and along the path on the other side of the track from the church entrance.

Fishguard and Goodwick

Fishguard (Abergwaun), immediately north of Strumble Head, occupies a lofty headland, with the pretty Lower Town on one side and the adjoining port town of **GOODWICK** (Wdig) on the other. Though often seen only as a brief stopping-off place to the ferries and catamarans which run to Rosslare in Ireland, it's an enjoyable place in its own right, with fine sea views from the easy coastal walks around town.

Approaching from the south, you pass the Goodwick foreshore where the tourist office and a cybercafé share the foyer of **Ocean Lab** (daily: Easter–Oct 11am–5pm, Nov–Easter 10am–4pm; free), a child-oriented journey into the aquatic world. From there, the A487 becomes West Street, later meeting High Street and Main Street by the town hall and Market Square; it's along these three streets that most of the shops, banks, pubs and restaurants lie. In the centre of town, the **Royal Oak Inn** was the scene of the surrender of the "last invasion of Britain" in 1797 (see box, opposite). To mark the event's bicentennial in 1997, a wonderful pictorial record was created in the form of the **Fishguard Tapestry**, inspired by the famous Bayeux model; it's currently not on show, but by late 2006 it should be displayed in the town hall opposite the *Royal Oak*. The episode's heroine, Jemima Nicholas, is buried beside the Victorian **parish church** behind the pub.

Main Street winds northeast before plummeting down around the coast towards **Lower Town** (Cwm), a cluster of old-fashioned holiday cottages around a muddy, thriving pleasure-boat port. Views from Lower Fishguard over the town headland and to the Goodwick breakwater are superb. Lower Fishguard's moment of glory came in 1971, when it served as the set of Llareggub (see p.184) in the Richard Burton and Elizabeth Taylor movie of Dylan Thomas' *Under Milk Wood*, a film well worth catching if you get the chance.

Practicalities

Buses stop by the town hall in the central Market Square, right outside Fishguard's **tourist office** (July & Aug daily 10am–5pm; April–June, Sept & Oct Mon-Sat 10am–5pm; Nov–March Mon-Sat 10am–4pm; ☎01348/873484, ⓦwww.abergwaun.com); just steps away from Seaways bookshop on West Street, a source of books on Wales plus information on Ireland. There's a subsidiary tourist office in the foyer of the Ocean Lab in Goodwick (daily: Easter-Oct 11am–5pm, Nov–Easter 10am–4pm; ☎01348/874737). Half a mile east of here along Quay Road is the terminus for **ferries** and catamarans to Ireland (services are detailed on p.228) and the **train station**. Buses stop right outside the terminal, usually meeting ferries but seldom catamarans; a **taxi** (☎01348/873075) into town costs about £3.

Accommodation is plentiful, with most places used to visitors coming and going at odd times for the ferries. There's also a fair variety of places to **eat** and **drink**. If you're in the area in late July, the annual **Fishguard International Music Festival** (☎01348/873612) combines classical, choral, jazz and blues music.

Accommodation

Cefn-y-Dre a mile out of Fishguard following Hamilton Street ☎01348/875663, ⓦwww.cefnydre.co.uk. Recently renovated old farmhouse with a relaxed and understated elegance. Just three rooms, attractive grounds, tasty breakfasts, and home-cooked meals on request (£16). ❺

Glanmoy Lodge Tref-Wrgi Rd, Goodwick ☎01348/874333, ⓦwww.glanmoylodge.co.uk.

Comfy country B&B a couple of miles southwest off the A487 that caters to cyclists and walkers and has nightly badger watching in the garden. ❷

Gwaun Vale Caravan Park on the B4313, 1.4 miles southeast of town ☎01348/874698. Well-appointed site on the fringes of Cwm Gwaun that is relatively wind-free even when the coast path is getting battered. £10 per pitch.

Hamilton Backpackers Lodge 21–23 Hamilton St ☎01348/874797, ⓦwww.fishguard-backpackers .com. Cosy, very central and well set-up hostel with its own sauna. Dorm beds go for £13 and there are doubles and twins. ❶

Plain Dealings Tower Hill ☎01348/873655. Peaceful and attractive B&B half a mile from the centre, with views of the Lower Town. Closed Nov–Feb. ❷

Pwll Deri YHA hostel 4 miles south of Fishguard ☎01348/891385 or 0870/770 6004, ⓔpwllderi@yha.org.uk. A wonderful and superbly sited clifftop hostel above the strands of Pwll Deri. Dorms (£10) and a couple of private double rooms. ❶

Eating and drinking

Bar Five 5 Main St ☎01348/875050. Chic, modern non-smoking restaurant and wine bar with great harbour views and good meals (mains around £13). Closed Sun & Mon.

Bennett's Navy Tavern High St. Nautically themed pub with basic meals for around £5.

Corner Cafe Market Square ☎01348/874649. Standard daytime café that on summer evenings becomes *The Plaice*, serving seafood mains at modest prices (booking essential).

Royal Oak Main Square. Historic pub with good pub meals. Tuesday is folk night and participants are especially welcome.

Ship Inn Lower Town. Eccentric, unmissable pub with lots of interesting clutter all over the walls and ceiling, including black-and-white photos of Burton and Taylor shooting *Under Milk Wood* .

Three Main Street 3 Main St. Appealing wood-floored coffee house with good espresso, home-baked scones and cakes, and a range of meals including char-grilled vegetable ciabatta (£6). Daytimes only.

Mynydd Preseli

In a county celebrated for some of the most magnificent coastal scenery in Britain, Pembrokeshire's interior is frequently overlooked. The **Mynydd Preseli** (Preseli Mountains) occupy a triangle of land in the north of the county, flecked with prehistoric remains and roughly bounded by the coast in the north, the B4313 to the west and the A478 to the east.

The main A487 coast road is the only major **bus** route hereabouts, cruising from Fishguard to Cardigan through delightful **Newport**, handy for the historic peak of **Carn Ingli**, the bucolic church at **Nevern** with its "bleeding" yew, and the reconstructed Iron Age settlement at **Castell Henllys**. This is also the final (or initial) stretch of the Pembrokeshire Coast Path, the cognoscenti's favourite with awesome solitude, abundant natural life and stunning cliff formations.

Inland from Fishguard, the **Gwaun River** wriggles southeast through its green cwm, Europe's oldest glacial vale. It's a refreshing change from the sea bird-swirling coastline, with tiny villages and remote churches seemingly-untouched by the modern age.

The brooding mountains hereabouts shelter innumerable standing stones, stone circles, hillforts, cairns and earthworks, several linked by a hike along the **Golden Road**.

The 1:25,000 scale North Pembrokeshire Explorer Map (OS35; £7) is extremely useful for **route finding** in the area (even when driving), and local visitor centres stock leaflets (40p each) detailing walks, including the Golden Road.

Newport, Nevern and the coast

The A487 winds through **NEWPORT** (Trefdraeth), an ancient and proud little town that is without doubt the best base in north Pembrokeshire. Set on a gentle slope that courses down to the estuary of the Afon Nyfer, it is a quietly enjoyable place, with superb accommodation, food and drink, welcoming inhabitants and a selection of fine coastal and hill walks on its doorstep. Newport still elects a mayor annually, a legacy of its days as the capital of the Norman Marcher Lordship of Cemmaes. One visible manifestation of this heritage is the annual custom, in August, of "Beating of the Bounds", when the mayor marks out the town's boundaries on horseback.

The Town and Carn Ingli

From the main thoroughfare, **Bridge Street**, Long Street and Lower St Mary Street head down to the tidal banks of the Afon Nyfer. A path hugs the southern shore of the estuary, over which squawking sea birds circle and skim the water's edge. Turn east (or take the Parrog Road if you're driving) for a gentle stroll along to the **Parrog**, Newport's nearest beach, mostly shingle but with sandy stretches at low tide. A better beach is the vast dune-backed **Traethmawr**, on the other side of the estuary, reached over the town bridge down Feidr Pen-y-Bont. Just short of the bridge, on the town side, **Carreg Coetan Arthur**, a well-preserved capped burial chamber, can be seen behind holiday bungalows. The footpath that runs along the river either side of the bridge is marked as the Pilgrims' Way; follow it eastwards for a delightful riverbank stroll to Nevern (see below), a couple of miles away. Back on Lower St Mary Street, the old town school now contains the **West Wales Eco Centre** (Mon–Fri 9.30am–4.30pm, and often longer in summer; free), a venue for exhibitions, advice and resources on various aspects of sustainable living.

South of Bridge Street, a number of pretty thoroughfares rise up to the town's intriguing **castle** (private), a modern residence fashioned out of the medieval ruins. The other obvious landmark is the three-storied tower of the massive **St Mary's church**, an ancient site that was heavily "restored" by the Victorians. Fortunately, its original Norman font escaped the worst of their efforts. Follow Church Street, from the front of St Mary's, for the relatively easy two-hour ascent of **Carn Ingli** (Hill of Angels), once the core of an active volcano and, to many people, one of Wales' holiest mountains. It gets its name from St Brynach who supposedly lived here in quiet contemplation, with angels as his companions. More certainly, stone embankments of the Iron Age hillfort and the nearby Bronze Age hut circles prove that the hill once had a sizeable community.

The coast

Either side of Newport, the Coast Path runs through some sublime scenery. To the west, the trail edges around the nodule of Dinas Head (also known as Dinas Island), en route to Fishguard. Two miles west of Parrog beach, there's the popular strand at **Cwm-yr-Eglwys**, where the scant seafront ruins of the twelfth-century **St Brynach's church** are all that survived a huge storm on the night of October 25, 1859, when the rest of the church and some 114 ships at sea were wrecked.

The walk around Dinas Head offers splendid views over the huge cliffs, inhabited by thousands of nesting sea birds between May and mid-July. On the other side of the "island", three-quarters of a mile west of Cwm-yr-Eglwys via the path through Cwm Dewi, or two and a half miles around the Coast Path and the headland, is the grey-sand beach of **Pwllgwaelod**, accessible by car off the A487. Sadly, the *Sailors' Safety Inn*, where a light was kept burning to help the ships' navigation, closed after 401 years in 1994. Next door, the *Old Sailors* tearoom and restaurant is open throughout the summer season.

The segment of Coast Path to the east of Newport, running to the fringes of Cardigan at St Dogmael's, is perhaps the wildest stretch of the whole path. The only part accessible by car is at the spectacularly folded cliffs of **Ceibwr Bay**, eight miles from Newport near the pretty pastel village of **MOYLEGROVE** (Trewyddel). Any section along here is comparatively hard going: the path plummets and climbs along the ridged coast, passing rocky outcrops, blowholes, caves, natural arches, ancient defensive sites and thousands of sea birds.

Nevern, Pentre Ifan and Castell Henllys

Only a little more than a mile by road to the east of Newport, but about double that along the pleasant riverside walk, the straggling village of **NEVERN** (Nanhyfer) is darkly atmospheric, with a couple of intriguing sights. The ruined and overgrown **castle**, a thirteenth-century replacement of a Norman construction on the site of an earlier Welsh fortress, sits high above the village on a bluff. Below, the brooding bulk of the **church of St Brynach**, founded in the sixth century and with an intact Norman tower, has many features of interest. The churchyard is roofed by ancient yews, giving it a dank, dark presence. Note the second tree on the right, the famous "**bleeding yew**", so called for the brown-red sap that oozes mysteriously from its bark. Legend has it that it will continue to bleed until a Welsh lord of the manor is reinstated in the village castle – unlikely in the foreseeable future, given its tumbledown state. Also outside the church, just by the main doorway, is the stunning **Great Cross**, an inscribed tenth-century Celtic masterpiece standing some 13ft high. St Brynach's interior is no less interesting. If you stand at the back, you can easily divine how the chancel has been built slightly out of alignment with the nave, supposedly to represent Christ's inclined head on the cross. Built into the windowsills of the south transept are two ancient inscribed stones: the **Maglocunus Stone**, with Latin and Ogham inscriptions from about the fifth century AD, and the **Cross Stone**, marked with a very early Celtic cross.

Lanes to the south of Nevern lead to the well-signposted cromlech at **Pentre Ifan**. This vast burial stone – the largest in Wales – with its sixteen-foot arrowhead top-stone precariously balanced on large stone legs, dates back over four thousand years. The views from here are superb, situated as it is on the cusp of the stark, eerie Mynydd Preseli with the pastoral rolls of the countryside to the east. A couple of miles east of Nevern, signposted off the A487, the Iron Age hillfort of **Castell Henllys** (Easter–Oct daily 10am–5pm; £3) is undergoing archeological excavation that is turning up more and more of its past. Some re-created houses, complete with thatch, have been built on their 2000-year-old foundations and, throughout the summer, there are ample chances to try ancient skills like basket weaving and wool spinning, while children can play at being archeologists. A sculpture trail through the woods and river valley bring to life the tales of The Mabinogion. Free one-hour guided tours (11.30am and 2.30pm) come with a strong environmental message, looking at land usage, wood management and conservation.

Practicalities

The cheerful national park **tourist office** (April–Oct Mon–Sat 10am–5.30pm; ☎01239/820912) is on Long Street, as is the **post office**, outside which are boards full of local information. Bwydydd Cyflawn wholefood shop, on East Street, has news of less mainstream events.

There's plenty of **accommodation** in town. Tucked in behind the Eco Centre on Lower St Mary Street, the *Trefdraeth YHA* **hostel** (☎01239/820080 or 0870/421 2314 ©reservations@yha.org.uk; ❶) is a classy conversion of an old school with £12.50 bunks and a couple of private rooms. Other than that, *The Globe* B&B (☎01239/820296; ❷) is about the cheapest place around and serves continental breakfast. If your budget is a bit bigger, try *Tree Tops B&B*, West Street (☎01239/820048; ⓦwww.bandbtreetops.co.uk; ❹); or the superb ♣ *Cnapan Country House* on East Street (☎01239/820575, ⓦwww .online-holidays.net/cnapan; closed Jan & Feb; ❼), which by the time you read this should have beautifully modernized rooms. The nearest **campsite** is the *Morawelon* (☎01239/820565; £5–6 per person), just west of town at the Parrog, with pleasant gardens and its own café.

Food and **drink** is also plentiful. During the day head to *Café Fleur* on Market Street (☎01239/820131), which does fantastic sweet and savoury crepes, panini, smoothies and good coffee in a bright, modern room. In the evening go for the solid pub classics and a selection of good curries at the *Royal Oak* on Bridge Street or the exquisite meals, made from fresh local and even wild produce, at ♣ *Cnapan Country House* (see above; closed Mon & Tues). Expect to pay around £15 for mains in the restaurant, or in summer duck out the back for cheaper barbecue fare.

If you're going walking, stock up at the fabulous Yr Hen Bopty delicatessen on Market Street.

Cwm Gwaun and the inland hills

The valley of the burbling Afon Gwaun is one of the great surprises of Pembrokeshire – a bucolic vale of impossibly narrow lanes, surrounded by the bleak shoulders of bare mountains. It is a timeless place whose residents retain an attachment to the pre-1752 Julian calendar, celebrating New Year in the middle of January.

There is only a limited selection of **places to stay** and **eat** in the area, and we've mentioned some of the best. **Camping** is easy enough. There's loads of good common land watered by trickling springs, or, if you need your home comforts, retreat to the outskirts of Fishguard.

Llanychaer and Pontfaen

The B4313 leaves the skirts of Fishguard, heading two miles southeast to tiny **LLANYCHAER**, where the *Bridge End Inn* serves meals. Opposite, a lane runs almost half a mile steeply uphill to the **church** and **"cursing" well** of the lost settlement of **Llanllawer**. The well had a pre-Christian reputation for cementing curses and ill omens if you left a bent pin, although most pilgrims sought miraculous cures, particularly for eye conditions. The lane running east opposite the well and church leads to seven large standing stones – the longest megalithic alignment in Wales – in **Parc y Merw** (the Field of the Dead), just short of Trellwyn Farm.

Back on the B4313, nearly a mile beyond Llanychaer, a lane branches left and drops down into Cwm Gwaun, soon crossing the river near a picnic site from where there are some good walks up into the old oak forests that line the valley.

Three miles off the B4313 you reach the scattered settlement of **PONTFAEN**, complete with its time-warped pub, the rustic and remote *Dyffryn Arms* known as *Bessie's* after its ageing proprietor, where you can enjoy good company in an old-fashioned living room. By doubling back on yourself at the pub and following the lane that crosses the river and rises a quarter of a mile up a sharp hill, you'll reach Pontfaen's exquisitely restored **church**, dedicated, as are so many round here, to St Brynach. The circular graveyard indicates that this was a pre-Christian site of worship before the church was traditionally founded by the wandering Breton saint in 540 AD. In the graveyard, there are two impressive stone crosses, dating from between the sixth and ninth centuries. By the mid-nineteenth century, the church was in ruins and it took the initiative and wealth of the Arden family, who moved to the adjoining Pontfaen House in the 1860s, to restore it. The intricate interior is notable for a delicious early twentieth-century copy of a Fra Angelico painting of the Madonna, and the church's strange internal angles, known as a squint, that enabled all the congregation, including those in the "cheap" seats, to see what was going on.

Back on the lane that follows the Afon Gwaun, a further two miles brings you to the delightful **Gerddi Penlan-Uchaf** (March–Nov daily 9am–dusk; £2.50), a set of hillside gardens cut through by a stream with wonderful views over the valley. The gardens contain thousands of miniature flowering and alpine plants, and acres of herbs and wildflowers together with some impressive dwarf conifers.

Accommodation in the area is limited: try the very welcoming *Erw-Lon Farm* (℡01348/881297; ❸) on the B4313 overlooking Pontfaen, or for longer stays the self-catering cottages at *Tregynon Farmhouse Restaurant & Cottages*, east of Pontfaen (℡01239/820531, ⓦwww.tregynon-cottages.co.uk; from £300 a week), which offers the highest standards of comfort and has a wonderful members-only restaurant which has been earning the plaudits of foodies for two decades. It offers a four-course limited choice menu (£29) for which you need to reserve at least 24 hours in advance: one-night provisional "membership" costs £5.

Rosebush and the Golden Road

It is further east that the brooding nature of the Mynydd Preseli makes itself most apparent. This is bleak, invigorating countryside, the wild, open hills scattered with the relics of ancient civilizations and, more often than not, the remains of dead sheep that have succumbed to the harsh weather. The characteristic **Preseli blue stone**, which was used to construct Stonehenge, some 140 miles away, between 2000 and 1500 BC, came from these slopes. Slate is also found hereabouts, and was quarried into the twentieth century near the

△ Foeldrygarn

weird little village of **ROSEBUSH**, just off the B4313 around ten miles south-east of Fishguard. The nineteenth-century Klondike atmosphere of the place is partially explained by the fact that it was built quickly as a would-be resort by the Victorians on the arrival of the railway. The largest of several corrugated iron shacks contains *Tafarn Sinc* (*Zinc Tavern*), a good spot for a pint and a meal in the garden on a fine day. There's also great **food** at the licensed *Old Post Office* (℡01437/532205; closed Mon; ❶), which though noted for its vegetarian and vegan specialities, also does steaks and fish; it has one bargain, bathless **room**. There's **camping** up the road at the well-maintained, lakeside *Rosebush Caravan & Camping Park* (March–Oct; ℡01437/532206; £6.50 per pitch).

A good hike leads from Rosebush along the eastern edge of the coniferous Pantmaenog Forest to the 1760ft summit of **Foel Cwmcerwyn** (4 miles return; 2hr; 800ft ascent), the highest point in Pembrokeshire. This was the site of a legendary battle between King Arthur and his followers and the giant boar, Twrch Trwyth, as detailed in The Mabinogion. Topped by a Bronze Age cairn, the rounded hill sits above **Craig y Cwm**, the last glacial valley (c. 8000 BC) in the area.

The main range of the Preselis lies just northeast of the village, crossed by an ancient track, in use for at least 3500 years, known as the **Golden Road**. The best section to **hike** (8 miles one way; 4–5hr; 1000ft ascent) runs due north out of Rosebush past the old slate quarries through Pantmaenog Forest and up onto the Golden Road. Turn right to reach many of the Preselis' cairns and ancient sites, such as **Beddarthur**, an eerie stone circle that is supposed to be the great king's burial place, **Foeldrygarn** ("the Hill of Three Cairns") with its hugely impressive Iron Age ramparts and hut circles, and **Carn Menyn**, probably the quarry from which the majority of the Stonehenge boulders were mined. At the far end you can drop down to *Dolau-Isaf* (℡01994/419327; ❸), a cheerful farmhouse B&B within walking distance of Mynachlog-Ddu.

Travel details

Unless otherwise stated, frequencies for trains and buses are for Monday to Saturday services; Sunday averages 1–3 services, though the main routes are more frequent and some routes have no Sunday service at all.

Trains

Carmarthen to: Cardiff (3 daily; 1hr 30min–2hr); Ferryside (14 daily; 10min); Fishguard Harbour (2 daily; 1hr); Haverfordwest (11 daily; 45min); Kidwelly (11 daily; 20min); Llanelli (hourly; 30min); Milford Haven (8 daily; 1hr); Narberth (8 daily; 30min); Pembroke (7 daily; 1hr 10min); Swansea (hourly; 45min); Tenby (7 daily; 50min); Whitland (17 daily; 20min).

Fishguard to: Cardiff (2 daily; 2hr 30min); Swansea (2 daily; 1hr 30min).

Haverfordwest to: Cardiff (2 daily; 2hr 40min); Carmarthen (11 daily; 45min); Milford Haven (10 daily; 20min); Swansea (7 daily; 1hr 30min).

Llanelli to: Cardiff (8 daily; 1hr 10min); Carmarthen (hourly; 30min); Llandeilo (4 daily; 40min); Llandovery (4 daily; 1hr); Llandrindod Wells (4 daily; 1hr 50min); Llanwrtyd Wells (4 daily; 1hr 30min); Pembrey & Burry Port (hourly; 5min); Shrewsbury (4 daily; 3hr 20min); Swansea (hourly; 20min).

Milford Haven to: Carmarthen (8 daily; 1hr); Haverfordwest (10 daily; 20min); Swansea (6 daily; 2hr).

Pembroke to: Lamphey (7 daily; 3min); Manorbier (7 daily; 10min); Pembroke Dock (7 daily; 10min); Swansea (7 daily; 2hr); Tenby (7 daily; 20min); Whitland (7 daily; 50min).

Tenby to: Carmarthen (7 daily; 50min); Lamphey (7 daily; 20min); Narberth (7 daily; 20min); Pembroke (7 daily; 20min); Pembroke Dock (7 daily; 30min); Penally (7 daily; 3min); Saundersfoot (7 daily; 10min); Swansea (7 daily; 1hr 40min); Whitland (7 daily; 30min).

Whitland to: Carmarthen (17 daily; 20min); Haverfordwest (11 daily; 20min); Milford Haven (10 daily; 40min); Narberth (8 daily; 10min); Pembroke (7 daily; 50min); Swansea (16 daily; 1hr); Tenby (7 daily; 30min).

Buses

Carmarthen to: Aberaeron (hourly; 1hr 10min); Aberystwyth (hourly; 2hr 15min); Cardigan (6 daily; 1hr 30min); Cenarth (6 daily; 1hr 15min); Drefach Felindre (6 daily; 50min); Haverfordwest (3 daily; 1hr); Kidwelly (8 daily; 25min); Lampeter (hourly; 1hr); Laugharne (10 daily; 25min); Llandeilo (12 daily; 30–40min); Llandovery (8 daily; 1hr 25min); Llanelli (8 daily; 1hr 10min); Llansteffan (8 daily; 30min); Narberth (3 daily; 25min); Newcastle Emlyn (7 daily; 1hr); Pendine (10 daily; 45min); Swansea (every 30min; 1hr 20min); Tenby (2 daily; 45min); Trelech (2 daily; 45min).

Fishguard to: Cardigan (hourly; 50min); Haverfordwest (hourly; 40min); Newport, Pembrokeshire (hourly; 20min); Rosebush (2 on Tues only; 25min); St David's (7 daily; 50min); Trefin (5 daily; 30min).

Haverfordwest to: Broad Haven (2–5 daily; 20min); Cardigan (hourly; 1hr 20min); Carmarthen (3 daily; 1hr); Dale (3 daily; 1hr 15min); Fishguard (hourly; 40min); Manorbier (hourly; 1hr 10min); Milford Haven (every 30min; 25min); Narberth (hourly; 20min); Newgale (hourly; 25min); Newport, Pembrokeshire (hourly; 1hr); Pembroke (hourly; 45min); Rosebush (2 on Tues only; 45min); St David's (hourly; 45min); Solva (hourly; 40min); Tenby (9 daily; 1hr).

Llandeilo to: Carmarthen (12 daily; 30–40min); Llandovery (8 daily; 50min); Talley (Fri only 1 daily; 20min).

Llanelli to: Carmarthen (8 daily; 1hr 10min); Kidwelly (8 daily; 30min); Swansea (every 30min; 40min).

Llandovery to: Brecon (5 daily; 45min); Carmarthen (8 daily; 1hr 25min); Llandeilo (8 daily; 50min).

Milford Haven to: Broad Haven (2 daily; 1hr 20min); Dale (2 daily; 40min); Haverfordwest (every 30min; 25min); Marloes (2 daily; 30min); Pembroke (hourly; 40min); Solva (2 daily; 2hr); St David's (2 daily; 2hr).

Narberth to: Carmarthen (3 daily; 25min); Haverfordwest (hourly; 20min); Tenby (hourly; 1hr).

Newport (Pembrokeshire) to: Cardigan (hourly; 25min); Fishguard (hourly; 20min); Haverfordwest (hourly; 1hr 10min).

Pembroke to: Bosherston (2 daily; 1hr); Castlemartin (2 daily; 45min); Haverfordwest (hourly; 45min); Manorbier (every 30min; 20min); Milford Haven (hourly; 40min); Pembroke Dock (numerous; 10min); Stackpole (2 daily; 20min); Tenby (hourly; 40min).

Pembroke Dock to: Carew (4 daily; 10min); Pembroke (numerous; 10min).

St David's to: Broad Haven (2 daily; 40min); Fishguard (7 daily; 50min); Haverfordwest (hourly; 45min); Milford Haven (2 daily; 2hr); Solva (hourly; 10min); Whitesands Bay (June–Sept hourly; 40min).

Tenby to: Amroth (7–10 daily; 40min); Carmarthen (1 daily; 1hr); Haverfordwest (9 daily; 1hr); Manorbier (hourly; 20min); Narberth (hourly; 1hr); Pembroke (hourly; 40min); Pendine (6 daily; 1hr); Saundersfoot (every 30min; 15min).

Ferries

Fishguard to: Rosslare, Ireland (4–6 daily; 1hr 50min on a fast ferry, otherwise 3hr 30min).

Pembroke Dock to: Rosslare (2 daily; 4hr).

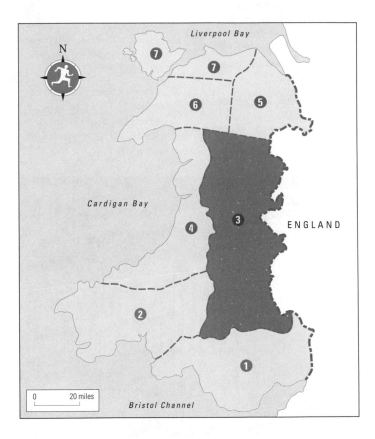

The Brecon Beacons and Powys

CHAPTER 3

Highlights

✳ **Ystradfellte waterfalls**
Whether you want to dive through, walk behind or swim in a waterfall, there are a host of superb options in the limestone country around Ystradfellte. See p.238

✳ **Abergavenny Food Festival**
If food is the new religion, then this lovely town in the Black Mountains is fast becoming a new Jerusalem. See p.252

✳ **Hay-on-Wye** Affectionately known as Way-on-High, this is the world capital of second-hand books, with an ebullient charm that is impossible to resist. See p.256

✳ **Offa's Dyke** Wales and England have been separated for thirteen centuries by this massive earthwork, large sections of which can be walked. See p.273

✳ **Llanidloes** A beguilingly self-assured mid-Wales town that knows how to have a good time. See p.274

✳ **Andrew Logan Museum of Sculpture** A surprising blast of high camp and glitter in bucolic Montgomeryshire. See p.281

△ Llanidloes market hall

The Brecon Beacons and Powys

The vast, inland county of **Powys** takes up a full quarter of Wales. Often viewed as little more than a corridor by which to reach the coast, it is easily an area worthy of languid exploration in its own right. The most popular area is the **Brecon Beacons National Park** at the county's southern end, an area of moody heights, boggy moors and awesome waterfalls. The main centres within the Beacons are **Abergavenny**, in the far southeast, and the small city of **Brecon**, a curious mix of traditional market town, army garrison and often very pretty tourist centre.

The bleaker part of the Beacons lies to the west, around the raw peaks of the **Black Mountain** and **Fforest Fawr**. A few roads cut through the glowering countryside, connecting popular attractions such as the immense **Dan-yr-ogof caves**, opera prima donna Adelina Patti's gilded home and theatre at nearby **Craig-y-nos** and the quite stunning caves and waterfalls around the walking centre of **Ystradfellte**. Walkers are equally well catered for in settlements like **Crickhowell** and **Talgarth**, small towns set in quiet river valleys.

At the northern corner of the national park, the border town of **Hay-on-Wye** draws in thousands to see the town's dozens of bookshops, housed in warehouses, the old castle and outdoor yards. West of Hay, the peaks of the **Mynydd Eppynt** now form a vast training ground for the British army, on the other side of which lie the old spa towns of Radnorshire – most notably **Llanwrtyd Wells** and the Powys county town, **Llandrindod Wells**. Crossed by spectacular mountain roads such as the **Abergwesyn Pass** from Llanwrtyd, the countryside to the north is barely populated and supremely beautiful – quiet, occasionally harsh country dotted with ancient churches and villages, from the lively border towns of **Presteigne** and **Knighton**, home of the flourishing **Offa's Dyke path** industry, to inland centres like **Rhayader**, the nearest centre of population for the grandiose reservoirs of the **Elan Valley**.

Montgomeryshire is the northern portion of Powys, similarly underpopulated and as remote as its two southern siblings. In common with most of mid-Wales, country towns such as the beautiful **Llanidloes** have a sizeable stock of old hippies amongst the population, resulting in a greater-than-expected presence of health-food shops, healing groups and arts activity. To

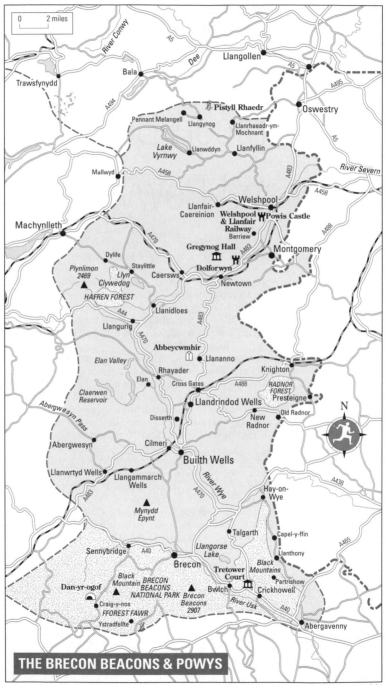

0   2 miles

River Conwy

A5

Dee

Llangollen

A495

Bala

Trawsfynydd

A494

Pistyll Rhaedr

Pennant Melangell

Llangynog

Oswestry

Llanrhaeadr-ym-
Mochnant

A5

Lake
Vyrnwy

Llanwddyn

Llanfyllin

A483

River Severn

Mallwyd

A458

A458

Llanfair-
Caereinion

Welshpool

A488

Machynlleth

A470

Welshpool
& Llanfair
Railway

Powis Castle

Berriew

A483

Dylife

Staylittle

Gregynog Hall

Montgomery

Plynlimon
2469

Llyn
Clywedog

Caersws

Dolforwyn

HAFREN FOREST

A44

Newtown

A483

Llanidloes

Llangurig

A470

Abbeycwmhir

Llananno

Elan Valley

Rhayader

Knighton

Elan

Cross Gates

A488

RADNOR
FOREST

Presteigne

Claerwen
Reservoir

Llandrindod Wells

Abergwesyn Pass

Disserth

Old Radnor

New
Radnor

N

Abergwesyn

Cilmeri

Builth Wells

Llanwrtyd Wells

Llangammarch
Wells

River Wye

Hay-on-
Wye

A438

A483

A470

Mynydd
Epynt

Capel-y-ffin

A465

Sennybridge

A40

Talgarth

Llangorse
Lake

Llanthony

Black
Mountains

Dan-yr-ogof

Black
Mountain

BRECON
BEACONS
NATIONAL PARK

Brecon

Tretower
Court

Partrishow

Craig-y-nos

Brecon
Beacons
2907

Bwlch

Crickhowell

FFOREST FAWR

Ystradfellte

River Usk

A40

Abergavenny

THE BRECON BEACONS & POWYS

© Crown copyright

the west, the inhospitable mountain of **Plynlimon** is flecked with boggy heathland and gloomy reservoirs, beyond which the popular and hearty town of Machynlleth is stranded out on a limb of Powys (though dealt with here in the Cambrian Coast chapter). The eastern side of Montgomeryshire is home to the anglicized old county town, **Montgomery**, between the robust towns of **Welshpool** and **Newtown**. The northern segment of the county is even quieter, with regional centres like **Llanfyllin** and **Llanrhaeadr-ym-mochnant** that are little more than villages, leaving the few crowds seen around here to cluster along the banks of **Lake Vyrnwy**, a flooded-valley reservoir which has harmoniously moulded itself into the landscape around it.

Getting around

Road transport in central Wales is fairly easy, with the swift A40 and A438 running from the English border to Carmarthen, Brecon and the west. Further north, the A44 heads into Radnorshire from Leominster in Herefordshire. The A458 heads off the north Wales-bound A5 at Shrewsbury down to Welshpool and Montgomeryshire.

Public transport takes more forward planning. **Train** services are restricted to the Heart of Wales line from Shropshire to Swansea via Knighton, Llandrindod Wells, Llanwrtyd Wells and smaller stops in between, and the Shrewsbury–Machynlleth route through Welshpool and Newtown. Larger centres such as Brecon, Llanidloes, Rhayader, Builth Wells and Hay-on-Wye have no stations. For them, and for the rest of this huge area, sporadic **bus** services (including school and post services) provide the only access, although with a bit of planning, most places are reasonably accessible. Staples of the mid-Wales bus scene include the three-times-daily #47, which runs up the spine of southern Powys from Brecon through Builth to Llandrindod Wells, where it meets connections for Newtown, Welshpool and the north. Nearby towns such as Wrexham, Abergavenny, Machynlleth and, over the border, Oswestry, provide useful intersection points. Available from libraries, tourist offices and main post offices, the most useful overview of all these services is the free *Wales Bus, Rail and Tourist Map & Guide*, which details operators and their different services.

Brecon Beacons National Park

With the lowest profile of Wales' three national parks, the **Brecon Beacons** are the destination of thousands of urban walkers from the industrial areas of south Wales and the West Midlands of England. Rounded, spongy hills of grass and rock tumble and climb around river valleys that lie between sandstone and limestone uplands peppered with glass-like lakes and villages

The western Beacons

The entire western half of the Brecon Beacons National Park is taken up by the western Beacons, a region comprising the bleak uplands of Black Mountain and Fforest Fawr, together with the sparsely populated valleys in between. It is in the valleys where most visitors congregate, chiefly at the **Dan-yr-ogof** showcaves, where some of Wales' finest limestone formations are given the son et lumière treatment. That this is limestone country is evident everywhere: caves, sink-holes and waterfalls dot the map, most spectacularly around the hills to the east at **Ystradfellte**, where a vast cavern swallows the River Mellte only to spew it out again in time for a series of waterfalls, one so undercut that you can walk behind it. From both valleys, wondrously lonely walks (or bike rides) thread their way up to the moors, and offer invigorating views across the Beacons.

Black Mountain

The most westerly expanse of upland in the national park is known as the **Black Mountain** (Mynydd Ddu), rising between the A4069 and A4067, at the very western end of the Brecon Beacons National Park. Despite being named in the singular, the "mountain" actually covers an unpopulated range of barren, smooth-humped peaks that break suddenly at rocky escarpments towering over quiet streams and glacial lakes. The area provides the most challenging and exhilarating walking in south Wales and has long been popular with trip-pers from the Valleys, just a few miles to the south. Paths cross the wet, wild landscape from Dan-yr-ogof in the east, and from the soaring ruins of Carreg Cennen Castle, just short of Llandeilo in the west. Other good starting points for forays into the open Black Mountain uplands are Tyhwnt, near Ystradg-ynlais, in the south and, in the north, the hamlet of **LLANDDEUSANT**, seven miles south of Llandovery, also home to a charming **YHA hostel** and **campsite** (☎0870/770 5930; closed Nov–Jan; £10) in the former village pub. Two miles west of Llanddeusant, you can camp at the pleasant *Pont Aber Inn* (☎01550/740202) on the main A4069. The best walk (see box below) from Llanddeusant runs along wooded gulches and moorland bluffs to the twin glacial lakes of **Llyn y Fan Fach** and **Llyn y Fan Fawr**. Llyn y Fan Fach features in one of Wales' most oft-told myths of a beautiful maiden, together with her herd of magic cattle, who rose from the lake to marry a local farmer.

A walk around Llanddeusant

Note: the OS Outdoor Leisure 1:25,000 map #12 (Brecon Beacons – Western & Central Area) is recommended for this walk.

Passing both Llyn y Fan Fach and Llyn y Fan Fawr, this bleak and lonely ten-mile circular walk from Llanddeusant weaves through classic glacial scenery: valleys slashed with tumbling streams cut between purple hills, while occasional mounds and moraines of rock debris indicate the force of the ice pushing through the valleys. Such heaps sometimes grew to a size large enough to form a natural dam, building up a lake, such as Llyn y Fan Fach, in its wake.

The walk (10 miles; 4–5hr; 1400ft ascent) starts in Llanddeusant and climbs steeply to Llyn y Fan Fach, from where a precarious path leads around the top of the escarpment, following the ridge to **Fan Brycheiniog** (2630ft), above the glassy black waters of Llyn y Fan Fawr. A remote path heads from here to the cross-moor road, two miles away.

The maiden's father had sanctioned the union only on the condition that if the farmer struck his daughter three times, she would return to the lake. Such occasions inadvertently occurred, the final blow being either when he slammed a gate and hit her or when he shook her at a funeral for laughing, depending on which version you hear. The maiden silently left the man and, with her cattle, disappeared beneath the lake's icy waters once more.

The Fforest Fawr

Covering a vast expanse of hilly landscape between the Black Mountain and the central Beacons southwest of Brecon, **Fforest Fawr** (Great Forest) seems something of a misnomer for an area of largely unforested sandstone hills dropping down to a porous limestone belt in the south. The "forest" tag refers more to the old definition of a forest as land used as a hunting ground.

The hills rise up to the south of the A40 west of Brecon, with the dramatic A4067 Sennybridge–Ystradgynlais road piercing the western side of the range and the A470 Brecon–Merthyr road defining the Fforest's eastern limit.

Dan-yr-ogof showcaves and Craig-y-nos

Coming south on the A4067, the road soon drops into the upper reaches of the valley of the Afon Tawe, Swansea's river. This is the beginning of the limestone belt, as seen in the hamlet of **Glyntawe** at the **Dan-yr-ogof showcaves** (April–Oct daily 10am–4pm; Nov–March call for details; ☎01639/730284, ⓦwww.showcaves.co.uk; £9.50). Only discovered in 1912, they claim to form the largest system of subterranean caverns in northern Europe. New attractions and a massive marketing campaign have turned the complex into something of an overblown theme park, but the extent and size of the caverns remains truly awe-inspiring.

In a self-guided tour, the path first leads you into the **Dan-yr-ogof** cave, the longest showcave in Britain, and a warren of caverns framed by stalactites and frothy limestone deposits. Although the whole cave is known to be around ten miles long, you'll be steered around a circular route of about a mile and a half. Back outside, you pass a downbeat re-created Iron Age "village", and walk through a hideous park of fibreglass dinosaurs to get to the **Cathedral Cave**, a succession of spookily lit caverns that lead into the "cathedral", a hugely impressive 150-foot-long, 70-foot-high cave, where a cheesy son et lumière performance provides unnecessary diversion. Reachable via a precarious path behind the dinosaur park is **Bone Cave**, the third and final cavern, known to have been inhabited by prehistoric tribes, with some 42 human (and many animal) skeletons found here. Elsewhere on site there's also a short **dry ski slope** and a **pony trekking centre**.

Unless you want to get an early start on the caves, or are using them as a base for walking, there's little reason to **stay** at the site, though it offers self-catering units (from £250 per week for a double) and **camping** (£5 per person). For £2.50, there's a very basic camping option half a mile north at *Maes-yr-eglwys Farm* (☎01639/730849), up the track behind the church by the *Tafarn-y-Garreg* pub. Between there and the showcaves, the *Gwyn Arms* serves decent meals.

A quarter of a mile south of the cave complex is the spiky, nineteenth-century **Craig-y-nos Castle** (☎01639/730205, evenings 731167, ⓦwww.craigynoscastle.com; ❸, dorm beds £20), a grand folly built in 1842 and fancifully extended from 1878, when it was bought by Adelina Patti, the celebrated Italo-American opera singer. In her forty years of residence, she turned the place into a Disneyesque castle, even adding a scaled-down version of the Drury

The central Beacons

Far more popular for walking and pony trekking than the sometimes desolate Black Mountain and Fforest Fawr are the **central Brecon Beacons**, after which the whole national park is named. The area, to the immediate south of Brecon town, is centred on the two highest peaks in south Wales, Pen y Fan and Corn Du. Although neither reaches 3000ft, the terrain is unmistakably, and dramatically, mountainous: classic old red-sandstone country with sweeping peaks rising up out of glacial scoops of land.

The highest peak in the Beacons, **Pen y Fan** (2907ft), together with **Corn Du** (2863ft), half a mile to the west, represent the most popular ascents in the park. The most direct route up is the well-trampled red-mud path that starts from Pont ar Daf, half a mile south of Storey Arms on the A470 midway between Brecon and Merthyr Tydfil. The ascent is a comparatively easy five-mile round trip gradually climbing up the southern flank of the two peaks. A longer and generally quieter route (see box below) leads up to the two peaks from the "Gap" route, the pre-nineteenth-century (and possibly Roman) main

---

A circular walk around Corn Du and Pen Y Fan

Note: The OS Outdoor Leisure 1:25,000 map #12 (Brecon Beacons West & Central) is recommended for this walk.

Few walkers visiting the Brecon Beacons for the first time can resist an ascent of the two highest peaks: Corn Du and Pen y Fan. Most take one of the shorter routes from the A470 south of Brecon, but connoisseurs prefer this longer and infinitely more rewarding **circular route** (8 miles; 4–5hr; 1400ft ascent) that describes a circuit around a ridge-top horseshoe of the Beacons.

The hike starts at the car park by the late-Victorian Neuadd reservoirs. Go through the gate and head down left through a gully and up onto the top of the grassy dam of the lower, smaller reservoir. Go to the end, through the muddy gap and up the hill in front, keeping the partly cleared plantation forest on your left-hand side. Keep to the fairly well-defined track and, when the forest ends, continue up the sharp gradient ahead, keeping the little stream gully on your left. This is the toughest, steepest and often boggiest part of the walk, but before too long you're up on the top of a windy ridge, commanding wide views over the reservoirs, the Beacons and way beyond. Head right along a well-defined path along the ridge top. The slope to the right becomes gradually sharper and more cliff-like as you continue over tiny streams that course down to the valley below. When the ridge on which you're walking narrows to a thin spit, views to the left down the completely uninhabited Cwm Crew are delightful. Corn Du and Pen y Fan are now looming in the foreground – follow the obvious path that strikes up the sandstone ridge to the first summit. Note how eroded the main path from the A470 is when you meet it just short of the peak.

Follow the obvious route from the summit of Corn Du down to a shallow saddle and up again to the peak of Pen y Fan, the highest point in south Wales. From both, the views over the mountains and valleys to Brecon are awesome. You can continue beyond Pen y Fan up to the next summit, Cribyn, and then descend to the Gap, where the wall of hills is breached by a track that may have been a Roman through route. Alternatively, without missing too much, you can take a right by the stream in the valley between Pen y Fan and Cribyn, following the rough track around the base of Cribyn to meet the Gap track. Turn right and continue along above the Neuadd reservoirs, turning right at the stream gulch to return to the car park.

road that winds its way north from the Neuadd reservoirs, through the only natural break in the sandstone ridge of the central Beacons to the bottom of the lane that eventually joins the main street in the Brecon suburb of Llanfaes as Bailihelig Road. Although the old road is no longer accessible for cars, car parks at either end open out onto the track for an eight-mile round-trip ascent up Pen y Fan and Corn Du from the east.

Brecon

BRECON (Aberhonddu) stands at the northern edge of the Beacons, its proliferation of handsome Georgian buildings bearing testimony to its past importance. Today, it's a lively base with lots of good accommodation, and places to eat and drink. As well as the obvious walking clientele, Brecon is also good for the more sedentary, with an appealing jumble of architecture, some great shops and a good social scene.

A Roman fort was built near here, but the town only started to grow with the building of a Norman castle and Benedictine monastery, founded in 1093 on the banks of the Honddu River, which gives the town its Welsh name. To the dual strands of military and ecclesiastical importance was added the status of regional market centre and cloth-weaving town. In the seventeenth-century Civil War, the townsfolk unequivocally demonstrated their neutrality between the forces of Parliament and the Crown by demolishing most of the castle and large sections of the town walls, dissipating the appeal for either side of seizing their town.

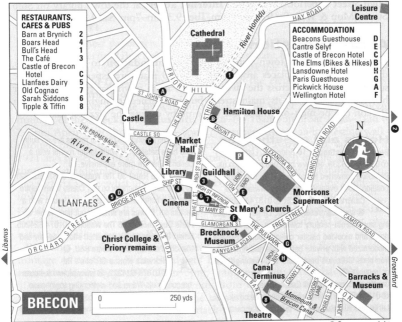

RESTAURANTS, CAFES & PUBS
Barn at Brynich 2
Boars Head 4
Bull's Head 1
The Café 3
Castle of Brecon Hotel C
Llanfaes Dairy 5
Old Cognac 7
Sarah Siddons 6
Tipple & Tiffin 8

ACCOMMODATION
Beacons Guesthouse D
Cantre Selyf E
Castle of Brecon Hotel C
The Elms (Bikes & Hikes) B
Lansdowne Hotel H
Paris Guesthouse G
Pickwick House A
Wellington Hotel F

BRECON

0   250 yds

© Crown copyright

Watton, a series of small streets runs down to the town's theatre and the northern terminus of the **Monmouth and Brecon Canal**, where afternoon cruises aboard the *Dragonfly* (☎07831/685222; £6) ease their way out of town for an enjoyably relaxed two-hour cruise. Longer and self-driven trips are available at nearby Talybont-on-Usk (see below).

North and west of The Bulwark are a cluttered grid of streets, packed with Georgian and Victorian buildings and containing many fine shops. The High Street Inferior is the main route northwest, passing the *Sarah Siddons* pub, converted from the 1755 birthplace of the great actress. High Street Inferior swiftly comes to a crossroads. Straight ahead, Ship Street descends down to the **River Usk**, the bridge crossing the Usk next to the point where the smaller Honddu River flows in from the north.

From the town centre crossroads, High Street Superior goes north, past the long **Market Hall**, home of a twice-weekly produce market (Tues & Fri) and, on the second Saturday of each month, an excellent **farmers' market**. The road becomes The Struet, passing **Hamilton House and Garden** at no. 13 (guided tour £3.50 per person, groups only, pre-booking essential; ☎01874/610200), a unique and very beautiful attempt to restore a timber merchant's Regency townhouse as accurately as possible. From here, the Struet continues up to become Hay Road.

Off to the left, over the rushing waters of the Honddu, Priory Hill climbs up to the stark grey buildings of the monastery settlement, centred on the **cathedral**, or Priory Church of St John the Baptist. The building's dumpy external appearance belies its lofty interior, graced with a few Norman features intact from the eleventh-century priory that was built here on the site of a probable earlier Celtic church. The hulking Norman font sits at the western end of the nave, near the entrance, from where the south aisle runs down to the most interesting of the many family memorials, the **Games monument** (1555), made up from three oak beds and depicting an unknown woman whose hands remain intact in prayer, but whose arms and nose have been unceremoniously hacked off. There's a mildly interesting **heritage centre** (March–Dec Mon–Sat 10.30am–4.30pm, plus May–Sept Sun noon–4pm; free) in a converted sixteenth-century tithe barn in the cathedral close. Among the gilded vestments lies the unusual Cresset Stone, a large boulder indented with thirty scoops in which to place torches.

Between the cathedral and the River Usk, the few remains of the town's **castle** are moulded into the walls of the *Castle Hotel*. The end result is a powerful, if bizarre, amalgam that looks its best from along **The Promenade** by the River Usk, reached from the town-centre side of the river bridge. In high summer, motor and rowing boats can be rented along the river bank.

Eating and drinking

Although Brecon's culinary status is rising, it's still a better place for a quick lunch than a proper dinner and many of the finest **restaurants** are out of town. As a lively and cosmopolitan town, there's broad scope for **drinking**, although some of the pubs in the near vicinity of the barracks are definitely worth avoiding.

Restaurants and cafés

Barn at Brynich Brynich Caravan Park, off the A470 island east of town ☎01874/623480. Cavernous, family-oriented truck stop, but worth investigating for hearty, home-cooked specialties.
The Café 39 High St. Great daytime café, with a warm, relaxed atmosphere and a good range of Free Trade coffees and hearty soups and sandwiches.

Castle of Brecon Hotel Castle Square. Worth investigating for the good-value fixed dinner menu in this enjoyable restaurant, contained in the town's smartest hotel.
Felin Fach Griffin Felinfach, 3 miles northwest of town ☎01874/620111. Superb modern Welsh cuisine in a smart gastro-pub just off the A470. Also has airy, classic rooms (❻).

Llanfaes Dairy 19 Bridge St. Just across the river, this wonderful homemade ice cream dairy is great for daytime indulgence.

Tipple & Tiffin Theatr Brycheiniog, Canal Basin. Tapas-style dishes to share, together with a few more substantial options, in this airy waterside bistro. Good for pre-theatre dinner whenever there's a show on.

White Swan Llanfrynach, 3 miles southeast of Brecon ☏01874/665276. Stylish village pub with a tremendous reputation for its local specialities and good wines.

Pubs

Boars Head Ship St. Two very different bars: the front is basic and the best place to meet locals, whereas the back bar is loud and resembles a youth club.

Bull's Head 86 The Struet. Small and cheery locals' pub, with views over the Honddu River and towards the cathedral. Good-value food (with vegetarian and vegan choices) and occasional live music.

Old Cognac High St Inferior. No-nonsense town pub, offering cholesterol-packed lunchtime and early evening food.

Sarah Siddons High St Inferior. Named after the famous actress, born here when the pub was known as the *Shoulder of Mutton*. A replica of Gainsborough's aloof portrait of her now forms the pub sign. A busy place, popular with off-duty soldiers.

Wellington Hotel The Bulwark. Surprisingly unstuffy hotel bar, a frequent venue for live music, especially jazz.

Activities and entertainment

Just off the A470 (turn off at Libanus), six miles southwest of the town, the **Brecon Beacons Mountain Centre** (daily: March–June & Sept–Oct 9.30am–5pm; July & Aug 9.30am–6pm; Nov–Feb 10.30am–4.30pm; ☏01874/623366) sits on a windy ridge amongst gorse heathland and overlooks some of the most inspiring scenery in the Beacons. As well as an excellent café, there are interesting displays on the flora, fauna, geology and history of the area, together with a well-stocked shop of maps, books and guides. Intentional lack of waymarking make these necessary for the walks that fan away from the centre around the lofty heath, and across the river valley to the more challenging peaks of Corn Du and Pen y Fan (see p.240). Buses leave Brecon for Merthyr and stop at Libanus school, from where it is a one-mile uphill walk along the lane next to the church up to the centre.

Brecon is well served for sports and recreational facilities: the old-fashioned Coliseum **cinema** is on Wheat Street near the central crossroads (☏01874/622501), while the **Theatr Brycheiniog** at the canal basin (☏01874/611622, ☻www.brycheiniog.co.uk) offers a good music and theatrical programme. There's an indoor **swimming pool** in the leisure centre a mile northeast of town on the Cerrigcochion Road (☏01874/623677). Brecon has several **bike rental** outlets: handiest to town are Brecon Cycle Centre, 9 Ship St (☏01874/622651) and Bikes & Hikes, 10 The Struet (☏01874/610071), both of which offer quality machines for around £15 a day.

The Usk Valley

The wide, fertile Usk Valley runs southeast from Brecon running parallel to the Monmouth and Brecon Canal and effectively dividing the Brecon Beacons proper from the Black Mountains to the northeast. The A40 provides the access through the region, connecting Brecon with Tretower, Crickhowell and Abergavenny, and providing a backbone for dozens of minor lanes which twist south over the Brecon Beacons or north into the bucolic headwaters of some of the Usk's tributaries. As the valley is home to the vast majority of the national park's church tower, constructed in the fourteenth century but harking back to Talgarth's position as a defence centre against the Norman invasion. The *Tower Hotel* on The Square (℡01874/711253; ❸) is the town's main centre for eating, drinking and **B&B**. The *Bridge End Inn*, over the bridge from the *Tower Hotel*, is good for live music and a cheerful atmosphere. There's independent **tourist information** and cheap Internet access at the Tower Shop (Easter–Sept daily 10am–4pm except Wed & Sun pm, Oct–Easter Mon–Sat 10.30am–3.30pm except Wed pm; ℡01874/712226), opposite the *Tower Hotel*.

Between Talgarth and the neighbouring village of **BRONLLYS** is **Bronllys Castle**, of which only a large twelfth-century cylindrical tower remains – climb to the top for stunning views up the Llynfi River valley and beyond to the light-washed peaks of the Black Mountains. There are some great places to **eat** and **sleep** around here: just north of Bronllys on the main road, the ⚑ *Honey Café*, open daily until 10pm, has been around since 1935 and is always popular, with a tasty Tex Mex evening menu. Heading up the A470 brings you to Llyswen and the superb fifteenth-century *Griffin Inn* (℡01874/754241; ❹), serving delicious local dishes. Continuing north on the A470 brings you to the luxurious *Llangoed Hall* (℡01874/754525, ⓦ www.llangoedhall.com; ❽), an ancient castle re-modelled in the early twentieth century by Portmeirion's Clough Williams-Ellis and now owned by Sir Bernard Ashley, widower of the late Laura.

Tretower and Pengenffordd

Twelve miles south of Talgarth, the solid round tower of the **castle and court** (daily: Easter–Sept 10am–5pm; Oct–Easter 10am–4pm; £2.50; CADW) at **TRETOWER** (Tre-twr̂) was built to guard the valley pass, and still rises out of the valley floor, dominating the view from both the A40 and A479 mountain road. The bleak, round thirteenth-century tower replaced an earlier Norman fortification, and in the late fourteenth century a comparatively luxurious manor house was built a couple of hundred yards away over a sheep-filled field, gradually being expanded more over the ensuing years. With restoration work still under way, exposed plaster and beams give a good insight into late medieval building methods. An open-air gallery and wall walk enable you to view the site on the upper level, while an enjoyable, self-guided headset tour takes you around the site.

Six miles north of Tretower, the hamlet of **PENGENFFORDD** is a good base for walks in the Black Mountains, including up to the vast nearby Iron Age hillfort of **Castell Dinas**, whose 2500-year-old ditches and grass ramparts sit 1500ft up in a magnificent position under an outlying crop of the mountain range, commanding views far down the valley of the Rhiangoll River. The *Castle Inn*, which sits at the base of Castell Dinas on the main road in Pengenffordd (℡01874/711353, ⓦ www.thecastleinn.co.uk; ❷), is a popular base for walkers, offering B&B, camping (£2 per person), bunkhouse accommodation (£12 per person, minimum group of 6), good food and drink. ⚑ *Upper Trewalkin Farm* (℡01874/711349; ❸), up in the lanes between Pengenffordd and Talgarth, is a brilliant farmhouse B&B with en-suite rooms, and staggering views over Castell Dinas and the Black Mountains.

Crickhowell

One of the liveliest bases in the vicinity of the Black Mountains, chipper **CRICKHOWELL** (Crucywel), on the northern shore of the wide and shallow Usk, has a grand seventeenth-century **bridge** with thirteen arches visible from the eastern end and only twelve from the west, spawning many a local myth. Bridge Street rises from the river and up to the uninspiring mound of the ruined **castle** and the wide **High Street**. New Road runs parallel to Bridge Street from the river, passing the steeple of the town's fourteenth-century **church of St Edmund**. There really isn't that much to see in the town, but its spectacular northern backdrop is **Table Mountain** (1481ft), whose brown cone presides over the rolling green fields below. The best access is along the path that goes off by the electricity substation past The Wern off Llanbedr Road. At the summit are remains of the 2500-year-old hillfort (*crug*) of Hywel, from which the town, tumbling down the slopes below into the Usk Valley, takes its name. An alternative, and far shorter, route to Table Mountain starts from the delightful village of **LLANBEDR**, some two miles north of Crickhowell, and heads up alongside the stream behind the *Perth-y-pia* bunkhouse (see below). The views are amongst the best in the area. Many walkers follow the route to the north from Table Mountain, climbing two miles up to the plateau-topped limestone hump of **Pen Cerrig-calch** (2302ft).

Practicalities

Crickhowell has many facilities in quite a compact space. The enthusiastic **tourist office** (April–Oct daily 9am–1pm & 2–4.30pm; ☎01837/812105) is in Beaufort Chambers on Beaufort Street. **Accommodation** is abundant, with a grandiose coaching inn, the *Bear Hotel*, on Beaufort Street (☎01873/810408, ⓦwww.bearhotel.co.uk; ❺); and the cheerfully relaxed *Dragon* on the High Street (☎01873/810362, ⓦwww.dragonhotel.co.uk; ❹). For B&B, try the budget *Greenhill Villas* on Beaufort Street (☎01873/811177; ❷) or the en-suite rooms at *Tŷ Gwyn* (☎01873/811625; ❷) an impressive stone gatehouse on Brecon Road, just beyond Porth Mawr. The only place to **camp** in town is the prissy *Riverside Caravan Park* on New Road (☎01873/810397; from £10 per pitch); far better – if you have transport or are prepared to walk 1.5 miles – is *Tŷ-Mawr* farm, under Table Mountain on the lane past the village of Llanbedr (☎01873/810164; from £6 per pitch).

There's no shortage of places to **eat** and **drink** in and around Crickhowell. Try the slightly twee *Cheese Press*, 18 High St, for daytime snacks – the quiches are great. There's heartier fare, including good curries, at the *Corn Exchange* bar opposite. Evening food is almost universally available in the town's pubs: the *Bear Hotel* (see above) wins legions of awards for its heavenly, pricier-than-average bar and restaurant food. Down by the town bridge, the *Bridge End* pub, part of which is an old tollhouse, is a very fine bet for food, including some impressive vegetarian selections. A mile along the A40 towards Brecon is the fabulous *Nantyffin Cider Mill* (☎01873/810775), where superb main courses are £10–15, but there is a fixed menu option at two courses for £10 or three for £12.50.

The Crickhowell Adventure Gear shop, opposite the market cross at 1 High St, sells caving and walking paraphernalia, while Mountain and Water (☎01873/831825, ⓦwww.mountainandwater.co.uk) offers boating, caving, climbing, orienteering and mountain activities.

Abergavenny

A world apart from its near neighbours in the Valleys, **ABERGAVENNY** (Y Fenni) is a slick and confident town with an ever-growing reputation for its fine cuisine, which reaches something of a zenith during the town's September **Food Festival**. The first main settlement was around the Norman castle, which

museum (Easter–Sept daily 11am–5pm though closed 1–2pm outside school summer holidays, Oct–Easter Mon–Sat 11am–1pm & 2–4pm; free). Displays cover the town's history, using photographs and billboards, and re-created interiors including a saddlery, a sanitized Border farmhouse kitchen of 1890 and Basil Jones' grocery shop, once on Main Street. After the death of Jones' son in 1989, the contents of the shop were transported to the museum lock, stock and biscuit barrel. Some of it was recent, but much of it dated from the 1930s and 1940s – World War II vegetable tins and decorations marked for the coronation of Edward VIII that never happened – and some dating back to the nineteenth century. You can get a good idea of how it might have looked *in situ* by visiting the outdated Saddler's stationers, on Main Street just uphill from the imposing *Angel Hotel* – even buying a newspaper here takes three times as long as normal.

Abergavenny's parish **church of St Mary**, on Monk Street, contains some superb effigies and tombs that span the entire medieval period. Originally built as the chapel of a small twelfth-century Benedictine priory, the existing building goes back only as far as the fourteenth century, although some of the monuments within predate the building itself. There are effigies of members of the de Braose family, along with the tomb and figure of Sir William ap Thomas, founder of Raglan Castle, and Dr David Lewis (died 1584), the first Principal of Jesus College, Oxford. Look too for the **Jesse Tree**, a recumbent, twice-lifesize statue of King David's father, which would once have formed part of an altarpiece tracing the family lineage from Jesse to Jesus. The Jesse Window at Llanrhaeadr in the Vale of Clwyd (see p.370) tells the same tale.

Eating and drinking

In the last fifteen years, **food** has become Abergavenny's main claim to fame – as well as numerous fine eateries, the town's annual **Food Festival** (℡01873/851643, Ⓦwww.abergavennyfoodfestival.co.uk), taking place in mid-September, is now one of the most prestigious in Britain. There are a clutch of cheap takeaways, of all varieties, at the bottom of Cross Street, towards the bus station.

Angel Hotel Cross St ℡01873/857121. Gracious dining room in the town's main hotel, serving excellent local cuisine.
Great George Cross St. Young and lively pub, especially appealing for good-value snacks, weekend discos and Sunday evening live music.
Greco Cross St. A classic café, great for piles of cheap cholesterol. Open until 7.30pm daily.
Greyhound Vaults Market St. Great for a wide range of tasty, moderately priced Welsh and English specialities, including the best vegetarian dishes in town.
Hen and Chickens Flannel St, off High St. Staunchly traditional pub, with the best beer in town and a regular programme of live music and other events.

Somerset Arms Victoria St, by the junction of Merthyr Rd. Bright and cheerful locals' pub with cheap, hearty food and excellent real ale.
Trading Post 14 Neville St. Trendy coffee house and bistro that's great for reading the paper over a cappuccino or tucking into £6–10 mains ranging from tortillas and chicken to tortellini and pizza. Open until 10pm Thurs–Sat.
Walnut Tree Inn on the B4521 at Llanddewi Sgyrrid, 2 miles north of town ℡01873/852797. Legendary foodies' paradise, drawing diners from all over Britain. It's exorbitantly expensive (especially in the evening), but the food, from the owner's native Italy, is astounding. Closed Sun & Mon.

The Black Mountains

The northeasternmost section of the Brecon Beacons National Park is known as the **Black Mountains**, not to be confused with its singular namesake forty miles west. Far quieter than the central belt of the Brecon Beacons, the Black

Mountains combine some of the awesome remoteness of Fforest Fawr with the dry terrain and excellent walking of the central Beacons. The wide valley of the River Usk – home to Tretower, Crickhowell and Abergavenny – divides the Beacons heartland from the Black Mountains, whose sandstone range rises to better defined individual peaks than can be found in the western end of the national park. The only exception to the unremitting sandstone is an isolated outcrop of limestone, long divorced from the southern belt, that peaks due north of Crickhowell at Pen Cerrig-calch.

Unlike the Black Mountain or Fforest Fawr to the west of the park, the Black Mountains have the feeling of a landscape only partly tamed by human habitation. Tiny villages, isolated churches and delightful lanes are folded into the undulating green landscape. Close to hand there is immediate access from the town to the three southernmost lumps of the Black Mountains, **Blorenge**, **Sugar Loaf** and **The Skirrid** – really only a taster for the remote beauty further north.

The most popular and rewarding areas to walk are in the east of the mountains, along the lane past Llanthony Priory and along the southern band of peaks, easily reached from Abergavenny and Crickhowell, notably Pen Cerrig-calch (see p.249), Table Mountain (see p.249) and the Sugar Loaf. The mass of rippling hills in the centre and to the north are less easy to reach, although a couple of good paths cross the contours.

Blorenge, Sugar Loaf and The Skirrid

From the grounds of Abergavenny Castle, the surrounding skyline is dominated by three southern outposts of the Black Mountains that climb out of the river plain. To the southwest is **Blorenge** (1834ft), a corruption of "Blue Ridge", accessible from the road that strikes off the B4246 a mile short of Blaenafon. The open road climbs the shale- and sheep-covered slopes to the car parks near the radio masts. An easy walk from here leads across boggy heathland to a long cairn at the summit, from which there are some glorious views south over the old mining region and north over the Usk Valley, Abergavenny and the Black Mountains. There is a steeper ascent of the Blorenge from **Llanfoist**, a mile southwest of Abergavenny, which cuts past the church and under the canal before zigzagging up the mountain.

The broad and smooth cone of **Sugar Loaf** (1955ft) commands the Black Mountains foothills to the northwest of Abergavenny. Falling away from its summit are paths that scour the windswept slopes before descending to tiny villages in the valleys of the Usk, the Grwyne Fawr and the Grwyne Fechan. The easiest ascent is from the south, taking the right fork of Pentre Lane off the A40, half a mile west of Abergavenny, and following the road that climbs Mynydd Llanwenarth.

At 1595ft, **The Skirrid** (Ysgyryd Fawr) is the most eye-catching mountain in the area. Shooting up from the Gavenny Valley, three miles northeast of Abergavenny, the hill almost seems man-made in its neatness: the gentle green fields climb about halfway, stopping suddenly in favour of purple scrub and bracken. The best path, although it is still a steep ascent, leads from the lay-by on the B4521 just short of the *Walnut Tree Inn* (see opposite). The Skirrid has long been held to be a holy mountain; the almighty chasm that splits the peak is said to have been caused by the force of God's will on the death of Christ, a theory that has drawn Saint Michael and legions of ensuing pilgrims to this bleak but breathtaking spot. At the summit, a few leaning boulders are the sole remains of a forbidden chapel built by persecuted Catholics.

The Vale of Ewyas

In total contrast to the urban Valleys just a few miles away, the northern finger of Monmouthshire and the extreme eastern boundary of the Brecon Beacons National Park, stretching along the English border, is one of the most enchanting and reclusive regions in Wales. The main A465 Hereford road leads north out of Abergavenny, passing the surreal mound of The Skirrid on the right-hand side. Six miles out of town, the road bypasses the village of **Llanfihangel Crucorney**, where a lane diverges off to weave through the Vale of Ewyas along the bank of the Honddu River, past the remote village of **Cwmyoy** with its wonky, subsided church, and on to the crumbling old religious institutions of **Llanthony Priory** and **Capel-y-ffin**. Parallel to the Honddu, a couple of miles and some impressive mountains to the west, is the **Grwyne Fawr**, a sparkling river that flows through the heart of some of Wales' most peaceful and gentle countryside. Folded amongst the contours is one of the country's most perfect small churches at **Partrishow**. Aside from the summer Sunday and Bank Holiday Monday Offa's Dyke Flyer service from Hay-on-Wye, there are no bus services in this area.

Llanfihangel Crucorney, Partrishow and Cwmyoy

A quiet dormitory village, **LLANFIHANGEL CRUCORNEY** (Llanfihangel Crucornau, the Sacred Enclosure of Michael at the Corner of the Rock) is named in honour of tales of St Michael's pilgrimage to The Skirrid. On the main village street are the odd fifteenth-century **church** and the **Skirrid Inn**, which makes bold claims to be the "oldest pub in Wales", a fact singularly difficult to prove.

From the village, the main road through the valley heads north into the beautiful Vale of Ewyas, along the banks of the Honddu River. After a mile, a lane heads west towards the enchanting valley of the **Grwyne Fawr**, lost deep in the middle of quiet hills. The road is well worth following, if only for the discovery of the hamlet of **PARTRISHOW**, where a bubbling tributary of the Grwyne Fawr trickles past the delightful **church** and **well** of St Issui. First founded in the eleventh century, the tiny church was remodelled in the thirteenth and fourteenth centuries, with major restoration work needed in 1908 to prevent it collapsing. The finest interior feature is the lacy fifteenth-century rood screen, carved out of solid Irish oak and adorned with crude symbols of good and evil, most notably in the corner, where an evil dragon consumes a vine, a symbol of hope and well-being – the rest of the whitewashed church breathes simplicity by comparison. Of special note are the wall texts painted over the apocalyptic picture of a skeleton and scythe. Before the Reformation, such images were widely used with the intent of teaching an illiterate population about the scriptures; however, King James I ordered that such "Popish devices" should be whitewashed over and repainted with scripture texts. Here, the ghostly grim reaper is once again seeping through the whitewash. Encased in glass by the pulpit is a rare example of a 1620 Bible in Welsh.

Back on the main road, the A465 winds its way on the valley's western side, past the fork at the *Queen's Head* pub (☎01873/890241), a great place to **camp** (£3 a head). It's well worth taking the little lane that peels off the main road here, as it dips down over the river and into the village of **CWMYOY**, where all eyes are drawn to the amazing spectacle of the **parish church of St Martin**, which has subsided substantially due to geological twists in the underlying rock. Nothing squares up: the tower leans at a severe angle from the bulging body of

△ Cwmyoy church

the church and the view inside from the back of the nave towards the sloping altar, askew roof and straining windows is unforgettable.

Llanthony

Four miles further into the Vale of Ewyas, the hamlet of **LLANTHONY** is nothing more than a small cluster of houses, an inn and a few outlying farms around the wide-open ruins of **Llanthony Priory** – a grander setting, and certainly a quieter one, than Tintern Abbey. Though on a far more modest scale than Tintern, Llanthony has the edge in many respects. Whereas Tintern has grown into a fully fledged tourist trap, Llanthony remains much as it has been for 800 years, retaining a real sense of spirituality and peace against a superior backdrop of river and mountain. Its origins are swaddled in myth and hearsay, but the priory is believed to have been founded on the site of a ruined chapel around 1100 by Norman knight William de Lacy, who, it is said, was so captivated by the spiritual beauty of the site that he renounced worldly living and founded a hermitage, attracting like-minded recluses and forming Wales' first Augustine priory. The church and outbuildings still standing today were constructed in the latter half of the twelfth century. Roving episcopal envoy Giraldus Cambrensis visited the emerging priory church in 1188, noting that "here the monks, sitting in their cloisters, enjoying the fresh air, when they happen to look up at the horizon behold the tops of mountains, as it were touching the heavens". A track behind the ruins winds up to the Offa's Dyke Path, straddling the England–Wales border on its lofty, windy ridge.

Fashioned out of part of the tumbledown priory, the *Abbey Hotel* here (℡01873/890487, Ⓦwww.llanthonypriory.supanet.com; ❸) was built in the eighteenth century as a hunting lodge and has a cellar bar with arches constructed in the twelfth century. It's usually closed on winter weekdays, and you'll be required to book in for both nights on summer weekends. At the other end of the ruins, *Court Farm* (℡01873/890359, Ⓦwww.llanthony .co.uk) offers great self-catering units in the farmhouse, together with a lovely bunkhouse (£8) in an old stone barn called *The Wain House*. Pre-booking is essential for both. It also offers basic camping (£2 per person) and pony trekking. A hundred yards north along the road from the priory is the thick-set *Half Moon Inn* (☎01873/890611; ❷), home of superb beer, bog-standard pub food and comfy beds.

Capel-y-ffin and the Gospel Pass

From Llanthony, the road climbs slowly alongside the narrowing Honddu River before coasting gently along by ruined farmhouses for four miles to the isolated hamlet of **CAPEL-Y-FFIN**, just yards over the Monmouthshire border in Powys. Locked in the middle of sheer hills, Capel-y-ffin has a strangely devotional feel, due principally to the fact that the village is made up of little more than two chapels and a curious ruined monastery. The minute, whitewashed eighteenth-century chapel on the main road has an apt text inscribed into one of its windows: "I will lift up mine eyes unto the hills from whence cometh my help" – at Capel-y-ffin, you can barely help doing anything else. A lane forks off by the phone box, leading up to the ruins of the privately owned (and confusingly named) **Llanthony Monastery**, founded in 1870 by the Reverend Joseph Lyne. The religious order failed to survive his death in 1908, but the place later became a self-sufficient outpost of the art world when, in 1924, it was bought by English sculptor, typeface designer and eccentric Eric Gill, whose commune, a motley collection of artists and their families, drew much of their creative inspiration from the area.

From Llanthony Monastery, the road narrows as it weaves a tortuous route up into the **Gospel Pass** and onto the glorious roof of the Black Mountains. A howling, windy moor by **Hay Bluff**, five miles up from Capel-y-ffin, affords vast views and terrific walking over spongy hills, punctuated by bleak crags and the distant view of tiny villages. The road drops just as suddenly as it climbed, descending five miles into Hay-on-Wye.

Facilities are scarce around here; *The Grange* (☎01873/890215; closed Nov–Easter; ❸) is a comfortable B&B with extensive gardens in which you can pitch a tent. Capel-y-Ffin **YHA hostel** (☎0870/770 5748; closed Dec & Jan, Nov & Feb weekends only; £10.50), which also has **camping**, lies a mile up the valley from the hamlet itself. This is a great area for **pony trekking**; available at both *The Grange* and *Court Farm* (see p.255).

Hay-on-Wye and around

The border town of **HAY-ON-WYE** (Y Gelli), at the northern tip of the Brecon Beacons, is known to most people for one thing – books. Hay saw its first second-hand bookshop open in 1961 and has since become a bibliophile's paradise, with just about every spare inch given over to the trade, including the old cinema, houses, shops and even the ramshackle stone castle. There are now nearly forty bookshops here – the largest containing around half a million tomes – alongside an increasing number of antique shops, galleries and fine food haunts. Inevitably, there has been a certain amount of cashing in on the town's popularity, and while you can almost always find what you want, you'll probably have to pay more than you'd expect. All the same, it's a fascinating and unique place to visit.

Always busy, Hay positively bursts at the seams in the last week of May, when all fashionable London literary life decamps here for the **Hay Festival of**

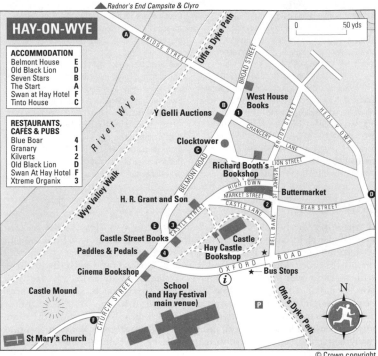

▲ Radnor's End Campsite & Clyro

HAY-ON-WYE

ACCOMMODATION
Belmont House	E
Old Black Lion	D
Seven Stars	B
The Start	A
Swan at Hay Hotel	F
Tinto House	C

RESTAURANTS, CAFÉS & PUBS
Blue Boar	4
Granary	1
Kilverts	2
Old Black Lion	D
Swan At Hay Hotel	F
Xtreme Organix	3

0   50 yds

BRIDGE STREET
Offa's Dyke Path
BROAD STREET
River Wye
Y Gelli Auctions
West House Books
CHANCERY LANE
HEOL Y DWR
BROOK STREET
Clocktower
BELMONT ROAD
LION STREET
Richard Booth's Bookshop
HIGH TOWN
JOHN PL
Wye Valley Walk
H. R. Grant and Son
MARKET STREET
CASTLE LANE
Buttermarket
BEAR STREET
BELL BANK
Castle Street Books
CASTLE STREET
Castle
Hay Castle Bookshop
Paddles & Pedals
ROAD
Cinema Bookshop
OXFORD
Bus Stops
CHURCH STREET
School (and Hay Festival main venue)
Offa's Dyke Path
Castle Mound
N
St Mary's Church

© Crown copyright

Literature (℡0870/787 2848, 🌐www.hayfestival.co.uk), when accommodation gets booked up sometimes years in advance. At any time of the year, the beauty of the countryside surrounding Hay makes staying in the town a sensible option. South of the town, one of the most awesome mountain roads in south Wales climbs up into the Black Mountains and under the glorious viewpoint at Hay Bluff before descending into the Gospel Pass and Vale of Ewyas. This is wonderful walking country, although the little ribbon of road laid seemingly casually across the springy moor can get horribly congested in high summer.

Arrival and information

Buses from Brecon and Hereford stop by the Oxford Road car park, next to the **tourist office** (daily: Easter–Oct 10am–5pm; Nov–Easter 11am–1pm & 2–4pm; ℡01497/820144, 🌐www.hay-on-wye.co.uk), which is housed in a grim craft centre and publishes an invaluable **free booklet** detailing the town's bookshops, galleries, restaurants and bars. Staff can also advise on and book local accommodation, which gets booked up long in advance for the festival.

Accommodation

As a major tourist venue, Hay is well served for accommodation, although prices are a little higher here than in other places nearby. There's **camping** five minutes' walk from town, across the Wye bridge and on the road to Clyro, where *Radnors End* campsite (℡01497/820780; £5 per person) enjoys a beautiful setting overlooking Hay, with showers and a washing machine on site.

Belmont House Belmont Rd ⓣ &
ⓕ 01497/820718, ⓦ www.hay-on-wye.co.uk/
belmont/welcome. Classy Georgian guesthouse
on the continuation of Broad Street with spacious
rooms, some en suite. ❷

🏃 **Old Black Lion** Lion St ⓣ 01497/820841,
ⓦ www.oldblacklion.co.uk. Excellent accommodation in a captivating thirteenth-century inn,
which favours candlelight in the evenings. ❺
Old Post Office Llanigon, 2 miles south of Hay
ⓣ 01497/820008, ⓦ www.oldpost-office.co.uk. A
wonderful vegetarian, non-smoking seventeenth-
century B&B which is well placed for local walks,
including the Offa's Dyke Path. ❸

Seven Stars Broad St ⓣ 01497/820886. Former
town pub near the clocktower, with a good range
of simple bedrooms, plus an indoor swimming pool
and sauna. ❸
The Start Hay Bridge ⓣ 01497/821391, ⓦ www
.the-start.net. Lovely renovation of a Georgian riverside house on the far side of the town bridge. ❸
Swan at Hay Hotel Church St ⓣ 01497/
821188, ⓦ www.swanathay.co.uk. The town's most
formal hotel, with high-standard if somewhat sanitized rooms and classy dining. ❻
Tinto House Broad St ⓣ 01497/820590, ⓦ www
.tintohouse.co.uk. Charming old house with a huge,
peaceful garden available to guests. ❸

The Town

If you don't like books, you'll probably want to avoid Hay, as the written word is the chief concern of this small market town. The best bookshop to start sampling the wares is up the track towards the castle that starts opposite the tourist office, where you'll find Richard Booth's **Hay Castle Bookshop**, with racks of overspill books under canopied covers outside, together with honesty boxes for payment. The shop itself specializes in an unlikely mix of photography, transport, humour and American Indians, along with bind-ings sold by the shelf-foot (anything from £8 to £200 per foot) which are popular with interior designers and theme pub developers. You can also find many a tract containing the thoughts of King Richard and even a record-ing of *The King of Hay's Greatest Hits*, which includes an address by Booth. Here – or from the tourist office – you can pick up the invaluable, *Hay-on-Wye Booksellers & Printsellers* leaflet (free), detailing all of the town's literary concerns. Just beyond the Castle Bookshop is the **castle** itself, a fire-damaged Jacobean mansion built into the walls of a thirteenth-century fortress, and owned – like just about everything in Hay – by Richard Booth. The ruling monarch lives in part of the castle, affected by fires in 1939 and 1978, and is planning to open his Throne Room, a kind of devotional museum complete with "Royal" balcony.

Walking from the tourist office to the bottom of Oxford Road and turning left into Castle Street, you'll come immediately to the **Hay Cinema Book-shop**, housed in the old town cinema and particularly good for new remain-dered editions at low prices. Most of the town's bookish activity takes place in the other direction along Castle Street, where **H.R. Grant and Son** at no. 6 and **Castle Street Books** at no. 23 are the best in town for contemporary and historical guides and maps, the former selling works pertaining to nine-teenth-century diarist Reverend Francis Kilvert and his winsome journals (see opposite). Beyond the open-sided, colonnaded **Buttermarket** at the top end of Castle Street, **Richard Booth's Bookshop**, 44 Lion St, is the largest shop in Hay, a huge, draughty warehouse of almost unlimited browsing potential. Lion Street dips down to Broad Street at the clocktower. Continue to **West House Books**, best for Celtic and women's works.

Around Hay

From Broad Street, Bridge Street passes over the River Wye and climbs the hill towards **CLYRO**, little more than a mile away. Sheltering behind the busy

Richard Booth and the Hay book business

Richard Booth, whose family originates in the area, opened the first of his Hay-on-Wye **second-hand bookshops** in 1961. Since then, he has built an astonishing empire and attracted other booksellers to the town, turning it into the greatest market of used books in the world. There are now over thirty such shops in the minuscule town, the largest of which – Booth's own flagship – contains around half a million volumes.

Whereas so many mid-Welsh and border towns have seen populations ebb away over the past fifty years, Hay is booming on the strength of its bibliophilic connections. Booth views this transformation of a hitherto ordinary little market town as a prototype for reviving an agrarian economy, depending on local initiatives and unusual specialisms instead of handouts from vast statutory or multinational corporations. He is unequivocal in his condemnation of bulky government organizations such as the Wales Tourist Board and the Development Board for Rural Wales, which, he asserts, have done little to stem the flow of jobs and people out of the region but which have succeeded instead in lining the pockets of a chosen few. This distaste for hefty bureaucracy, coupled with Hay's geographical location slap on the Wales–England border and Booth's own self-promotional skills, led him to declare Hay independent of the UK in 1977, with himself, naturally, as king. He appoints his own ministers and offers "official" government scrolls, passports and car stickers to bewitched visitors. Although such a proclamation of UDI carries no weight officially, most of the people of Hay seem to have rallied behind King Richard and are delighted with the publicity – and visitors – that the town's continuing high profile attracts.

King Richard continues to take his self-appointed role seriously, pumping out a series of tracts and pamphlets on subjects dear to his heart, from the predictable rallying cries against supermarket developments to criticism of the town's high-profile annual literary festival, founded on the basis of Hay's bibliophilic reputation. Amongst the egotism and occasional self-righteousness, Booth hits many targets accurately, and his criticism of the homogenization and consequent decline of rural communities due to crass actions by government and big business is a theme to which many have subsequently been drawn. Booth's ideas and the events surrounding the 1977 delaration are laid out in his very entertaining autobiography *My Kingdom of Books* (Y Lolfa); you can also consult his website at ⓦ www.richardbooth.demon.co.uk.

A438, the village is home to a couple of small commercial art galleries trading on the strength of Clyro's connections with nineteenth-century wandering parson Francis Kilvert. Although he was vicar of Clyro for only seven years (1865–72), the village, its idyllic surroundings and its precisely recorded inhabitants featured prominently in his published diaries, drawing a steady trickle of pilgrims to see the place ever since.

The A438 heads south, through the one-horse hamlet of **LLOWES**, whose dowdy church of St Meilig houses a superb three-ton seventh-century Celtic cross. A mile further, a lane to the right climbs to **MAESYRONNEN**, where the low-roofed barn chapel, built in 1696, is the oldest surviving Nonconformist worship house in Wales. If it's locked, and you want to see the whitewashed interior with its old benches and stacked wooden pulpit, get the key from the Old Post Office in Ffynnon Gynydd, a mile up the lane.

Eating, drinking and entertainment

As a centre for walking, as well as the ubiquitous book trade, Hay is very well served for **food and drink** outlets.

Blue Boar Castle St. Tasteful wood-panelled bar on the corner with Oxford Road. Excellent beer and reasonable summer food.

Granary Broad St. Unpretentious, moderately priced café and bistro, with a wide range of excellent vegetarian and meat-based meals, many made from local produce. Save space for wonderful desserts, ice cream and good espresso.

Kilverts Bull Ring at the corner of Market St and Bell Bank ☎ 01497/821042. Warm and friendly locals' pub, with an imaginative, moderate to expensive menu which might extend to crab and prawn terrine or chargrilled sirloin with brandy and mushroom sauce. In summer, there's live music outdoors in the marquee most Thursdays and occasional weekends.

Old Black Lion Lion St ☎ 01497/820841. Beautiful, olde-worlde pub that avoids any hint of kitsch. Superb, award-winning meals in the bar, or more robust fare in the pricier restaurant.

Swan at Hay Hotel Church St. Good downstairs bar, popular for its pool tables and games machines. Bar snacks are hearty and good value, and more substantial meals are served at the formal and expensive *Cygnet* restaurant.

Xtreme Organix 10b Castle St. Takeaway, deli and small sit-in café for hearty snacks from local farms, nowhere near as pofaced as the name might suggest. Open Mon–Sat 9am–11pm.

Radnorshire and Montgomeryshire

Even quieter than the Brecon Beacons, the northern tranche of Powys – the old counties of Radnorshire and Montgomeryshire –is a hugely rewarding area to explore. This is farming country, where urban life comes no bigger than a few small market towns, many of which make for excellent bases. Between the towns, the contours of the impossibly green, sheep-flecked farmland are shaped by the glassy lakes and lively rivers that run down from the open moorland of the Cambrian Mountains, which form Wales' spine.

Over the years, the quality and pace of life in Powys has proved irresistible to successive waves of hippies and "alternative" lifestylers, mostly English. Some have settled into their new communities very well, though many others seem to prefer to live apart. For a visitor, however, the wholefood cafés and quirky festivals are, for the most part, an attractive addition to the area. Combine that with the luscious landscape and the detritus of ten centuries of Anglo-Welsh conflict, and it's plain to see what makes this Powys heartland so appealing.

In the south of **Radnorshire**, four distinctly different communities jointly form the **Wells towns**, each grown up around a reputedly health-giving spring. There's more water still in the magnificent **Elan Valley**, where four interlocking reservoirs form the focus of countryside noted for its abundance of red kites. To the east, close to the English border, **Presteigne** is a charming little place with a great museum, while **Knighton** makes much of its position midway along the eighth-century border defence of **Offa's Dyke**.

The northernmost section of Powys is mellow **Montgomeryshire**. Good bases include the cheerily offbeat little town of **Llanidloes**, the laid-back northern outpost of **Llanfyllin,** the old county town of **Montgomery** and its much larger and more boisterous replacement, **Welshpool**. Although technically on a western limb of Montgomeryshire, **Machynlleth** is dealt with in the Cambrian Coast chapter.

The Wells towns

Straddling the old border of Brecknockshire and Radnorshire, around fifteen miles north of Brecon, mid-Wales' four spa towns are strung out along the Heart of Wales rail line and the main A483. Up until the eighteenth century, all were obscure villages, but then came the great craze for spas, and anywhere with a decent supply of apparently healing water joined in on the act. Royalty and nobility spearheaded the fashion, though once the railways arrived, the four Welsh spas became the domain of everyone, each developing its own distinct clientele and atmosphere.

Today, best of the bunch is undoubtedly the westernmost spa of **Llanwrtyd Wells,** hunkered down beneath stunning mountain scenery and with a real pulse to the place. Blink and you'd miss tiny **Llangammarch Wells,** though robust **Builth Wells** is definitely worth a stop. The most famous of the four – **Llandrindod Wells** – attracted the international elite in its Victorian heyday, but it's been a steady slide downhill since then, and the place is struggling these days.

Llanwrtyd Wells and around

Of the four spa towns, **LLANWRTYD WELLS,** around twenty miles northwest of Brecon, is the most appealing, especially for visitors. This was the spa to which the Welsh – farmers of Dyfed alongside the Nonconformist middle classes from Glamorgan – came to great eisteddfodau in the valley of the Irfon. Nowadays, it's the Welsh capital of wacky events – from the world bog-snorkelling championships to a Man versus Horse race and numerous biking/walking/beer-drinking combination weekends. Call the tourist office for more information or see ⓦwww.green-events.co.uk.

Main Street runs through the centre of town, crossing the Irfon River just below the main square, Y Sgwar, dominated by a stunning sculpture of a red kite by one Sandy O'Connor. On the opposite side of Main Street, Dolecoed Road winds for half a mile along the river to the *Dolecoed Hotel,* built near the original sulphurous spring. Although the distinctive aroma had been noted in the area for centuries, it was truly "discovered" in 1732 by the local priest, Theophilus Evans, who drank from an evil-smelling spring after seeing a rudely healthy frog pop out of it. The spring, named **Ffynnon Drewllyd** (Stinking Well), bubbles up amongst the dilapidated spa buildings a hundred yards behind the hotel.

Practicalities

Llanwrtyd's **tourist office** is in Tŷ Barcud just off the main square (daily 10am–5pm; ☎01591/610666, ⓦwww.llanwrtyd-wells.powys.org.uk). **Accommodation** is plentiful and of a high standard, but should be booked well in advance when there are festivals on. Options include the lively *Neuadd Arms* in the main square (☎01591/610236, ⓦwww.neuaddarmshotel.co.uk; ❸), which also offers good bar **food,** with some great curries; the lovely *Carlton House* (☎01591/610248, ⓦwww.carltonrestaurant.co.uk; ❹), yards away on Dolecoed Road, which also has a handful of cheaper rooms (including two bargain singles) across the street at its brasserie; and the fairly grand *Lasswade* on Station Road (☎01591/610515, ⓦwww.lasswadehotel.co.uk; ❺). The marvellous ⅄ *Drover's Rest* **restaurant** by the river bridge (☎01591/610264, ⓦwww.food-food-food.co.uk; ❸) serves wholesome, traditional Welsh dishes and snacks, and has some classy, cosy B&B accommodation, both above the restaurant and in the nearby *High View House.* Finally, the ⅄ *Stonecroft Inn* on

Dolecoed Road (☎01591/610332) is a superb pub with great food and regular live folk, R&B and rock music as well as beds (£13.50) in a small, self-catering **hostel** annexe. There's very basic tent-only **camping** (£1 per person) on the Dolwen Fields, 200m off the main road south from the town square, although 48 hours' notice is required (☎01591/610626, ✉g.jones@virgin.net).

Bike rental is available at Cycles Irfon (☎01591/610710, or 610668 out of hours) on the Maesydre industrial estate off the Beulah Road to the north of town. Llanwrtyd claims to have invented **pony trekking**: modern exponents include *Ffos Farm* (☎01591/610371) on Ffos Road, northeast of town.

Mynydd Eppynt and Llangammarch Wells

The gorgeous scenery around the town of Llanwrtyd Wells is one of its biggest attractions, and nowhere is this more evident than in the country to the south, where the remote **Crychan Forest** and the doleful mountains of the **Mynydd Eppynt** make up the northern outcrops of the Brecon Beacons and are most dramatically viewed from along the roads that snake across the moors from the towns of Garth and Builth. The bulk of the Eppynt has been appropriated by the British Army, as evidenced by the many red flags flying stiffly, signs warning you not to stop or touch anything and, saddest of all, the spooky **Drovers' Arms**, midway between Garth and Upper Chapel on the B4519, once a welcome respite for those droving cattle across the mountains and now a boarded-up wreck.

The B4519 descends dramatically from the Eppynt above a beautifully isolated valley, the **Cwm Graig Ddu**, from where the views over miles of soft farmland and rippling hills are overwhelming. At the bottom of the hill, a lane forks left, soon to join the River Irfon as it winds to **LLANGAMMARCH WELLS**, four miles east of Llanwrtyd. A mile before the village is the exquisite black-and-white-timbered **Lake Country House** (☎01591/620202, ⊛www .lakecountryhouse.co.uk; ❽), the home of the now-defunct barium well that attracted Lloyd George and foreign heads of governments searching for cures, and probably the best reason to come here. The village is excellent for fishing and walking, but singularly dull otherwise.

Abergwesyn and the Pass

Although the drovers' roads and inns across the Mynydd Eppynt are now forbidden territory, the most spectacular of the drovers' routes is thankfully still open. The lane from Llanwrtyd meets up with another road from Beulah at the riverside hamlet of **ABERGWESYN**, five miles north of Llanwrtyd. From here, a quite magnificent winding thread of a road – the **Abergwesyn Pass** – climbs up alongside the dwindling river, leaving it at the perilous **Devil's Staircase** and pushing up through dense conifer forests to wide, sparse valleys bereft of any sign of human habitation, framed by craggy peaks, bubbling waterfalls and blotches of gorse and heather. At the little bridge over the tiny Tywi River, a track heads south past an isolated, gaslit **YHA hostel** (☎0870/770 5796; closed Oct–April) at **DOLGOCH**. On the other side of the river, a new road channels past the thick forest on to Llyn Brianne (see p.180), a couple of miles further on. This is as remote a walking holiday as can be had in Wales – paths lead from Dolgoch, through the forests and hillsides to the exquisitely isolated chapel at **SOAR-Y-MYNYDD** and beyond, over the mountains to the next YHA hostel, *Tŷ'n-y-cornel* (☎0870/770 8868 closed Oct to late March), five strenuous miles from Dolgoch.

From Dolgoch, the Abergwesyn Pass continues over the massive, wide terrain, before dropping down along the rounded valley of the Berwyn River and into

Tregaron. Although the entire Llanwrtyd–Tregaron route is less than ˅ miles in length, it takes a good hour to negotiate the twisting, narrow ₁ safely. The old drovers, driving their cattle to Shrewsbury or Hereford, woul̲ have taken at least a day or two over the same stretch.

Builth Wells and around

Very much the spa of the Welsh working classes, **BUILTH WELLS** (Llanfair ym Muallt) still caters to local people, although visitor amenities are improving. It's a useful centre for transport, cheap accommodation and entertainment, and can make a reasonable base for exploring the area around.

The most pleasant area in Builth is the stretch along the Wye, below the architecturally jumbled High Street, home of some great local shops. Foreman's Emporium at nos. 25–27 is a superb stationer and bookshop, including many old and new works on Wales. High Street becomes Broad Street descending to the town bridge, where, opposite the eye-catching mural of Prince Llywelyn, you'll find the multipurpose **Wyeside Arts Centre** (℡01982/552555), converted out of the town's Victorian Assembly Rooms. On the other side of the river, Builth's major modern source of prosperity, the **Royal Welsh Showground** (℡01982/553683, ⓦwww.rwas.co.uk), hosts numerous agricultural events, together with monthly flea markets and occasional specialized collectors' fairs. The massive and utterly absorbing **Royal Welsh Show**, Britain's biggest rural jamboree, takes place in mid-July.

Practicalities

Builth Road **train station** is nearly three miles north of the town and inaccessible by public transport – a taxi (℡01982/553142) will cost about £3. **Buses** depart from the car park alongside the river bridge, in which the **tourist office** (Easter–Sept Mon–Sat 9.30am–5pm, Sun 9.30am–4pm; ℡01982/553307, ⓔbuiltic@powys.gov.uk) is to be found. **Bike rental** is from John Lloyd at Builth Wells Cycles on Smithfield Road (℡01982/552923).

Accommodation comes cheap: try the *Bron Wye* B&B at 5 Church St (℡01982/553587; ❷), the cheerful *Greyhound Hotel* (℡01982/553255; ❸), a few minutes west of the town centre or, if your budget stretches a bit further, the much revamped *Lion Hotel* (℡01982/553311; ❻), at the end of the bridge on Broad Street. For **food**, there are numerous cheap daytime cafés, though **pubs** are the only evening option. The *Greyhound* and the *Lion* hotels (above) are good, though for plain old drinking, try the *White Horse* or the *Fountain*, both on Broad Street/High Street.

Cilmeri

CILMERI, an unassuming village that straggles along the main A483 road and rail line between Builth and Llanwrtyd, is a place of pilgrimage for many Welsh people, as it was here that the last native Prince of Wales, Llywelyn ap Gruffydd, was slain by the English army in December 1282. On realizing whom they had killed, it is said that the English soldiers hacked off Llywelyn's head, whereupon it was dispatched to London and paraded victoriously through the city's streets. A large, pointed granite boulder on a small hillock to the side of the main road marks the spot. The English tablet by the monument calls Llywelyn "our prince". Its Welsh equivalent, tellingly, describes him as *ein llyw olaf* – "our last leader". Semantics aside, you are unlikely ever to see the monument without someone's fresh flowers ▸adorning it.

Llandrindod Wells and around

Once the most chichi spa resort in Wales, **LLANDRINDOD WELLS** (Llandrindod) is a pale imitation of its former self. Although many of the fine Victorian buildings still stand, the hotels do business and the flower boxes bristle with colour, there's something empty at the town's heart, and it will take more than a lick of paint to sort it out.

It was the railway that made Llandrindod, arriving in 1864 and bringing carriages full of well-to-do Victorians to the fledgling spa. Llandrindod blossomed, new hotels were built, neat parks were laid out and the town came to rival many of the more fashionable spas and resorts over the border. Like so many coastal resorts, however, Llandrindod has been on the slide for years. The hotels have come to rely on ever-ageing visitors, the grand old spa – the reason for the town's existence in the first place – is a mess, and nothing radical or new seems to have been tried in the town for decades. That all said, there is plenty of accommodation here, the surrounding countryside is lovely and transport links are good.

Arrival, information and getting around

Buses arrive outside the **train station**, in the heart of town between the High Street and Station Crescent. Follow Station Crescent to the right, then turn

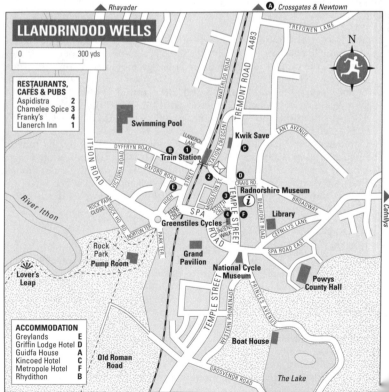

right onto Temple Street to reach the **tourist office** (April–Sept Mon–Fri 9.30am–5.30pm, Sat & Sun 9.30am–5pm; Oct–March Mon–Fri 10am–1pm & 2–5pm; ☎01597/822600, ✉llandtic@powys.gov.uk). The town's largest annual event is August's **Victorian Festival**, which culminates in a firework extravaganza over the town lake. The longer-established annual town **eisteddfod** takes place in early October. **Market day** is Friday. **Bike rental** costs £15 a day from Greenstiles Cyles (☎01597/824594) in Imperial Buildings, Temple Street, though it must be arranged in advance.

Accommodation

As rural mid-Wales' major tourist centre for the past 130 years, Llandrindod is well served for hotels, B&Bs, restaurants and cafés, even if its strait-laced past as a health resort is reflected in the notable lack of pubs. There's **camping** at *Disserth Farm* in Disserth, three miles southwest of Llandrindod (☎01597/860277; £10 per pitch) in a beautiful riverside setting, next to the lovely village church.

Greylands High St ☎01597/822253. Tall Victorian red-brick house in the town centre, near the station and all amenities. ❷

Griffin Lodge Hotel Temple St ☎01597/822432, ⓦwww.the-griffin-lodge-hotel.co.uk. Cheerful hotel in a sturdy Victorian house with some en-suite rooms. ❸

Guidfa House Crossgates ☎01597/851241, ⓦwww.guidfa-house.co.uk. Very comfortable Georgian guesthouse almost three miles north of Llandrindod on the A483, with mostly en-suite rooms and great meals made from local produce. ❸

Kincoed Hotel Temple St ☎01597/822656. Well-appointed old town-centre hotel, opposite Kwik Save supermarket. ❷

Metropole Hotel Temple St ☎01597/822881, ⓦwww.bw-metropole.co.uk. Large, faded but still elegant old spa hotel, the centrepiece of the town, with an excellent indoor swimming pool and a refined dining room open to non-residents. ❺

Rhydithon Dyffryn Rd ☎01597/822624. One of the smartest and friendliest guesthouses in town, just off the High Street. ❷

The Town

Llandrindod's Victorian heyday is still in evidence in the town's grandiose public buildings, even if many are in a sorry state these days. Plans are afoot to restore the lavish **spa pump room** in **Rock Park**, but little has come of this yet and the place continues to crumble. A free chalybeate fountain, in a glade to the front of the pump room, lets you sample more than enough of the town's metallic, salty spa water. A walk from the pavilion leads to "**Lovers' Leap**", a re-created bit of Victorian nonsense that's just a fake cliff with mediocre views over the river. The architecture around the park entrance is Llandrindod at its most confidently Victorian, with large, elaborately carved terracotta frontages and expansive gabling. From here, the **High Street** runs to the town centre, containing a few good antique and junk shops. Running parallel to the High Street is the Heart of Wales railway line, with the town's elegant train station (were it not for the incongruously modern footbridge ruining the view) two minutes' walk from the park. On the station platform is an old London North Western Railway **signal box** (June–Aug Fri & Sat 11am–3pm; free), which houses an interesting little display about the railway and its spirited survival in the face of repeated plans for closure over the last fifty years.

Behind the tourist office on Temple Street, you'll find the small **Radnorshire museum** (Tues–Thurs 10am–1pm & 2–5pm, Fri 10am–1pm & 2–4.30pm, Sat 10am–1pm; free), closed at the time of writing but due to be reopened by mid-2006. Next to the museum is a glutinous rockery **grotto**, a nineteenth-century whimsy built by a local doctor. West of Temple Street is Spa Road, from which a left turn leads down to the **Grand Pavilion**, home of tea dances and other genteel pursuits.

A town of water-taking and bridge tournaments seems an incongruous place for Britain's **National Cycle Exhibition** (March–Oct daily 10am–4pm, call ☏01597/825531 for winter hours; £2.50), unobtrusively located in the so-called Automobile Palace at the corner of Temple Street and Spa Road. Most items in the nostalgic collection of over 250 bikes are original, though the oldest style is a reproduction Hobbyhorse from 1818. From there, pretty much the whole spectrum is covered: boneshakers, Ordinaries (aka penny-farthings), an eight-foot-high "Eiffel Tower" advertising bike from 1899, trikes, tandems and styles that look way too uncomfortable to ever have been a success.

Cefnllys

One of the most popular walks from Llandrindod heads east from the town along Cefnllys Road and through some beautiful wooded pockets to the banks of the River Ithon at **CEFNLLYS**, just under two miles away. A car park by the river leads on to **Shaky Bridge**, whose name dates from when just two planks of wood connected the two banks – a more solid structure is in evidence today. On the other side of the Ithon, the castle mound rises to the right and you'll see the dumpy witch's-hat spire of the thirteenth-century **St Michael's church** ahead. In Victorian times, the rector removed the church roof to persuade the few remaining parishioners to travel into up-and-coming Llandrindod instead for worship. There was an outcry and a collection, and the roof was restored just two years later; photographs in the church show this strange period in its history. Back on the Llandrindod side of the river, **Bailey Einon Wood** is a designated nature reserve running three-quarters of a mile along the river.

Disserth

The other outlying former parish of Llandrindod is **DISSERTH**, lying a couple of miles to the south of the town, off the A483 at Howey, where the **church of St Cewydd** lies beside the Ithon in one of its most pastoral stretches. Resembling a fat medieval barn with a squat stone tower attached, the church escaped the restorative zeal of the Victorians, and its seventeenth-century wooden box pews were left intact, many with family names still discernible. The 1687 triple-decker pulpit, looking more like an auctioneer's lectern, also survives from pre-Victorian days.

Where the lane to Disserth heads west off the A483 at Howey, another lane also climbs up into the **Carneddau Hills**. About two miles after leaving the main road, a number of paths leave the lane and delve south into the rocky terrain, where glacial features such as moraines and abandoned blocks of stone litter the landscape.

Eating and drinking

Aspidistra Station Crescent. Decent daytime café serving cheap and wholesome sandwiches, snacks and meals.

Chamelee Spice Emporium Buildings, Temple St. Classy but not overpriced Bangladeshi and Indian restaurant, opposite the tourist office.

Franky's Temple St. Garish cellar bar-cum-bistro, compensated for by the good range of reasonable pizzas.

Llanerch Inn Llanerch Lane. Central Llandrindod's only pub, and a decent one at that. It's a cosy sixteenth-century inn that predates most of the surrounding town, with lots of pub games and a solid menu of good-value, well-cooked classics.

The Radnor at the *Metropole Hotel*, Temple St (see "Accommodation"). Stuffy, and fairly pricey, restaurant in Llandrindod's premier hotel that nonetheless offers the best local cuisine in town.

North and East Radnorshire

Before the reorganization of British counties in 1974, Radnorshire was the most sparsely populated county in Wales or England, and it's still a remote area, especially to the north and east. In the northwest, **Rhayader** is the only settlement of any real size; it's an excellent base, with some great pubs. Most people stay here in order to explore the wild, spartan countryside to the west of the town, a hilly patchwork of waterfalls, bogland, bare peaks and the four interlocking reservoirs of the **Elan Valley**, built at the beginning of the twentieth century and displaying a grandiose Edwardian solidity.

The countryside to the northeast of Rhayader is slightly tamer, with lanes and bridlepaths delving in and around the woods and farms, occasionally brushing through minute settlements like the village of **Abbeycwmhir**, named for the deserted Cistercian abbey that sits below in the dank, eerie valley of the Clywedog Brook. From here, the hills roll eastwards towards the English border and some of the most intact parts of **Offa's Dyke**, the eighth-century King of Mercia's border with the Welsh princes. The handsome town of **Knighton**, perched right on the border, is at the centre of the 177-mile path that runs along the dyke and is well geared-up for walkers and cyclists, with good accommodation and cheery pubs and cafés. Seven miles south and inches from England, the dignified little town of **Presteigne** contains a few reminders of its former importance as the county capital. The River Lugg flows through Presteigne from the Radnorshire hills, passing the isolated church at **Pilleth**, where Owain Glyndŵr captured Sir Edmund Mortimer, agent of the English king, in 1402.

Rhayader and around

RHAYADER (Rhaeder Gwy, literally "waterfall on the Wye"), ten miles west of Llandrindod Wells, has boomed during the twentieth century as mid-Radnorshire's principal base for exploring the spectacular hills and reservoirs of the Elan Valley. Although the waterfall invoked by the town's name virtually disappeared when the town bridge was built in 1780, the Wye still frames the town centre, running in a loop around the western and southern sides. Rhayader was a centre of the mid-nineteenth-century "**Rebecca Riots**", when local farmers disguised themselves in women's clothing in order to tear down tollgates that were prohibitively expensive for itinerant and local workers.

Rhayader's four main streets – named North, South, East and West – meet at a small clocktower in the centre of town. Three miles north of town, just off the A470, is the lovely **Gilfach Farm nature reserve** (unrestricted access; free), showpiece of the Radnorshire Wildlife Trust. Within the 418 acres are meadows, oak forest, moorland, an old railway tunnel that's home to some bats, and river habitats supporting a huge variety of wildlife and flora. The restored longhouse barn has now been kitted out as a **visitor and exhibition centre** (April–Sept Fri–Mon 10am–5pm; £1.75), showing live video footage from ten birds' nests around the reserve. To watch **red kites feeding**, head to **Gigrin Farm** (£2.50), off South Road (the A470 from Builth) on the outskirts of town, where they are lured daily at 3pm (2pm in winter).

Practicalities

Buses stop in the main Dark Lane car park, opposite the **tourist office** (April–Oct daily 9.30am–12.30pm & 1.30–5.30pm; Nov–March Mon–Tues & Thurs–Sat 10am–4pm; ☎01597/810591, ⓦwww.rhayader.co.uk), which shares its building with a leisure centre. Rhayader has always been well serviced for visitors, and eighteenth-century coaching inns still line the main streets. More modern **accommodation** includes the enjoyable *Elan Valley Hotel*, two miles west of Rhayader (see opposite), the cheerful *Brynteg* B&B on East Street (℡01597/810052; ❷), and the *Elan Hotel* on West Street (℡01597/810109, ⓦwww.elanhotel.co.uk; ❸). The cheapest place in town is *Greenfields* on South St (℡01597/811101; ❶), which offers B&B and hostel beds (£13.50). Almost two miles northeast of town, off the Abbeycwmhir Road, is *Beili Neuadd* (℡01597/810211, ⓦwww.midwalesfarmstay.co.uk; ❶/❷), a very relaxing farmhouse B&B that also has a sixteenth-century stone barn **bunkhouse**. There's a **campsite** at *Wyeside* (℡01597/810183; £10 per pitch), a few hundred yards north of town off the A44, although a quieter and less flashy option is the red kite centre a fifteen-minute walk south of town at *Gigrin Farm* (℡01597/810243; £7.50 per pitch). Rhayader is an ideal base for a **biking** holiday: cycles can be rented, as well as all-inclusive cycling packages booked, through the redoubtable Clive Powell Mountain Bikes (℡01597/811343, ⓦwww.clivepowell-mtb.co.uk) on West Street.

During the day, *Carole's Old Swan* tearooms, at the junction of West and South streets, is the place to go for simple **food**. Evening meals are good at the moderate *Brynafon* restaurant (℡01597/810735), half a mile south on the road to Builth Wells, or the *Elan Valley Hotel* (see opposite). Despite having a population of less than two thousand, there are twelve **pubs** in Rhayader, most offering reasonable pub food. Try the lively *Crown Inn* on North Street, or, over Bridge Street in the small hamlet of **LLANSANTFFRAED CWMDEUD-DWR**, usually shortened to Cwmdeuddwr, the ancient *Triangle Inn*, whose toilets are on the other side of the street, and where darts players must stand in a special floor hole for fear of spearing the roof.

Elan Valley

Until the last decade of the nineteenth century, the untamed countryside west of Rhayader received few visitors, although the poet Shelley did holiday here: his honeymoon retreat at Nantgwyllt was amongst the couple of dozen buildings submerged by the waters of the **Elan Valley** reservoirs, a nine-mile-long string of four lakes created between 1892 and 1903 to supply water to the rapidly growing industrial city of Birmingham, 75 miles away; in the 1950s, a supplementary reservoir at Claerwen, to the immediate west, was opened (see opposite). Although the lakes enhance an already beautiful and idyllic part of the world, the colonialist way in which Welsh valleys, villages and farmsteads were seized and flooded to provide water for England is something the tourist boards prefer to gloss over. The natural resentment against this has perhaps been best expressed by poet R.S. Thomas in his soulful elegy, *Reservoirs*:

There are places in Wales I don't go:
Reservoirs that are the subconscious
Of a people, troubled far down
With gravestones, chapels, villages even;
The serenity of their expression
Revolts me, it is a pose
For strangers, a watercolour's appeal
To the mass, instead of the poem's
Harsher conditions. There are the hills,
Too; gardens gone under the scum
Of the forests; and the smashed faces
Of the farms with the stone trickle
Of their tears down the hills' side.

△ Craig Goch dam; Elan Valley

The "watercolour's appeal" of the Elan Valley is, nonetheless, extremely strong, not only for the landscape but the profusion of rare plants and birds in the area. **Red kites** are especially cherished – in the 1930s, when numbers were down to just a couple of breeding pairs, the Elan Valley looked set to enter the history books as their last outpost in Britain. Loss of habitat, along with nest robbing by collectors and poisoning at the hands of farmers were largely to blame, but conservation work undertaken by a few dedicated individuals saved the day. Since then, the kites have staged an impressive recovery (now numbering over five hundred individuals) and have become so common here they've started repopulating the rest of the country.

From Rhayader, the B4518 heads southwest four miles to **ELAN** village, a curious collection of stone houses built in 1909 to replace the reservoir constructors' village that had grown up on the site. Just below the dam of the first reservoir, **Caban Coch**, the **Elan Valley visitor centre** (mid-March to Oct daily 10am–5.30pm; ☎01597/810898), incorporates a tourist office and a permanent exhibition about the history and ecology of the area. Frequent guided **walks** and even **Land Rover safaris** head off from the centre. The best place to **stay** here is the *Elan Valley Hotel* (☎01597/810448, ⊛www.elanvalleyhotel.co.uk; ❸), an imposing neo-Colonial pile on the Rhayader side of Elan village, which offers great food, comfy rooms and a lively bar.

From the visitor centre, a road tucks in along the bank of Caban Coch to the **Garreg Ddu** viaduct, where a road winds along the bank for four spectacular miles to the vast, rather chilling 1952 dam on **Claerwen Reservoir**. More remote and less popular than the Elan lakes, Claerwen is a good base for the more determined walker; you can follow paths for eight to ten miles across the harsh terrain to the abbey of Strata Florida or the lonely **Teifi Pools**.

Back at the Garreg Ddu viaduct, a more popular road continues north along the long, glassy finger of **Garreg Ddu** reservoir, before doubling back on itself just below the awesome **Pen-y-garreg** dam and reservoir; if the dam is overflowing, the vast wall of foaming water is mesmerizing. At the top of Pen-y-garreg lake, it's possible to drive over the final, or more properly the first, dam on the system, at **Craig Goch**. This is the most-photographed of all the dams, thanks to its gracious curve, elegant Edwardian arches and neat little green cupola. The lake beyond it is fed by the Elan River, which the road crosses just short of a junction. A bleak, invigorating moorland pass heads west from here to drop into the eerie moonscape of Cwmystwyth (see p.318), while the eastbound road funnels into a beautiful valley back to Rhayader. On the way back, fork off the Elan Valley Road in Rhayader onto the smaller Aberystwyth Road.

The only **bus** route hereabouts is the #103 postbus from Llandrindod and Rhayader (Mon–Fri), which runs as far as the Elan Valley visitor centre. The two services allow you to spend around three hours in and around the visitor centre.

Abbeycwmhir

ABBEYCWMHIR (Abaty Cwm Hir) seven miles northeast of Rhayader, takes its name from the abbey whose sombre ruins (open access; free) lie beneath the village. Cistercian monks founded the abbey in 1146, planning one of the largest churches in Britain, whose 242-foot nave has only ever been exceeded in length by the cathedrals of Durham, York and Winchester. Destruction by Henry III's troops in 1231 scuppered plans to continue the building, however. The sparse ruins of what they did build – a rocky outline of the floorplan – lie in a conifer-carpeted valley alongside a gloomy green lake, lending weight, if only by atmosphere, to the site's melancholic associations. Llywelyn ap Gruffydd's body, after his head had been carted off to London, was rumoured to have been brought here from Cilmeri in 1282, and a new granite slab, carved with a Celtic sword, lies on the altar to commemorate this last native prince of Wales. It should look incongruous, but somehow it only adds to the eerie presence of the ruins and the village.

Presteigne and around

The architecture of tiny, old-fashioned **PRESTEIGNE** (Llanandras), twenty miles east of Llandrindod Wells, reeks of its former status as county town, but its contemporary feel has more to do with the sizeable community of rat-race refugees who first descended on the town in the 1960s and have continued to arrive ever since. There's a relaxed pace to the place, perfect for mooching around the centre – Broad, High and Hereford streets – dipping into some enjoyably musty second-hand book and antique shops in between the quality craft shops and laid-back cafés.

Presteigne lies snugly between the B4362 town bypass and the River Lugg, the border with England, which flows under the seventeenth-century bridge at the bottom of the handsome Broad Street. Just before the bridge, the solid parish **church of St Andrew** contains Saxon and Norman fragments, as well as a sixteenth-century Flemish tapestry. To the left of the main churchyard entrance are twin gravestones that give an insight into early nineteenth-century morals: the original stone commemorates one Mary Morgan, who in 1805 gave birth to an illegitimate child that her father persuaded her to murder; he then sat on the jury that condemned her to death. A sanctimonious inscription records that she was "unenlightened by the sacred truths of Christianity" and "became the victim of sin and shame and was condemned to an ignominious death". Opposite is a later stone erected in repentance by the townsfolk, inscribed "He that is without sin among you, let him first cast a stone at her".

Mary Morgan's trial would have taken place up the street at the **Judge's Lodging** (March–Oct daily 10am–6pm; Nov–Christmas Wed–Sun 10am–4pm;

£4.50), a beautifully interpreted trawl through the rooms where circuit judges stayed while presiding over the local assizes. The building spent long years as the district museum, and folk had forgotten that many of the original furnishings had been stashed in the attic, a boon when the decision was made to restore the place to its 1868 grandeur. You now follow an audio tour, being "introduced" to characters along the way but with the freedom to stop and inspect the furnishings and even lounge on the sofas. Nothing is roped off or hidden behind screens, and it feels more like visiting a private home than a museum. The oil lamps that light the upper floors and the gas-flame lighting in the servants' quarters provide a whiff of authenticity. You finally emerge in the courtroom, where an alleged thief that you've "met" in the cells is being tried.

From the museum, Broad Street heads up to the main crossroads, with the High Street forking west and Hereford Street to the east. On the corner of Hereford and Broad streets the nineteenth-century Italianate Assembly Rooms also house the town's library. High Street contains the town's most impressive building, though, the Jacobean **Radnorshire Arms**, built as a private home for John Bradshaw, a signatory on the death warrant of Charles I, and converted into an inn in 1792.

Practicalities

Buses from Knighton, Kington and Leominster stop outside the *Radnorshire Arms* or at the coach park on the bypass. The Judge's Lodging also contains the **tourist office** (same hours; ☏01544/260650) where you can get details of local **accommodation**, which ranges from period luxury at the classy *Radnorshire Arms* on Hereford Street (☏01544/267406; ❻) to the simpler charms of the B&B at *20 Church St* (☏01544/260688; ❷) or the great value *Carmel Court* (☏01544/267986; ❷), an old nunnery on King's Turning Road on the eastern entrance to town. There's some good options in the surrounding villages: the sumptuous Victoriana of the *Old Vicarage* (☏01544/260038; ❺) in Norton, two miles north on the road to Knighton and the homelier charms of *Gumma Farm* (☏01547/560243; ❸), nearly two miles west on the road to Discoed, where you can also **camp** (£2 per person). There's a fuller site, including caravans, at *Rockbridge Park* ☏01547/560300, £5 per person), half a mile nearer town on the banks of the River Lugg.

Presteigne has become a centre for folk and traditional music with excellent **festivals** in July and over the August bank holiday (details from the tourist office): the former (ⓦwww.sheepmusic.info) organized by the excellent free music paper *Broad Sheep*, available from venues around town.

The *Farmer's Inn* on Hereford Street is the town's liveliest pub, and serves decent **food**, though for something a little more formal, make for the *Radnorshire Arms* with a moderately priced restaurant and a wood-beamed bar. Alternatively, the cafés on the High Street are worth investigating, as is the old-fashioned *Barley Mow* pub on Hereford Street.

Old and New Radnor

Just off the A44 six miles southwest of Presteigne and looking like it's been hewn straight from the hillside, **OLD RADNOR** was once the home of King Harold, killed at the Battle of Hastings by William the Conqueror's troops. The site of his castle is down the lane running southeast from the large, very English-looking **church**, overlooking a wooded vale. Inside the church, a massive eighth-century font on four stone feet is the most remarkable legacy. Opposite, the rambling, fifteenth-century ⚑ *Harp Inn* (☏01544/350655; ❸) has been magnificently restored from its earlier use as a farm cottage.

NEW RADNOR, just over two miles to the west, was built as a small Norman settlement and then planned, in the thirteenth century, to be expanded into a major city and capital of Radnorshire. The project faltered, confirming Wales' antipathy towards large settlements in favour of the more common feature of scattered farmsteads. Today, you enter the village from the A44 to the southeast, past a Victorian steeple erected to honour local dignitary Sir George Cornewall Lewis. This is the only feature of the village that seems to suggest any kind of metropolitan status, as the couple of streets are deathly quiet with just the *Radnor Arms* on Broad Street to liven things up.

The Radnor Forest

North of New Radnor, the deep-clefted valleys and wooded hillsides of **Radnor Forest** offer some of the region's best walking. The most popular route is along the driveable track that forks north off the A44 just over a mile west of New Radnor, leading into a thick forest and to the rushing cascade of the **Water-break-its-neck** waterfall, at its foaming best in winter. The trackway that continues on leads past the heads of numerous steep valleys plunging down to the lowland, giving perhaps the best impression of the area's strange geology, before coming out at the village of **Llanfihangel Rhydithon** some five miles beyond Water-break-its-neck. Paths head off the track to the east, up and over the rounded peaks of the forest and down towards the hamlet of **Casgob**, deep in the northeastern corner. The tiny church here, complete with half-timbered tower, contains a remarkable sixteenth-century amulet, purporting to exorcize one Elizabeth Lloyd from "all witchcraft and from all evil spirits and from all evil men or women or wizardes", together with numerous gnostic symbols, astrological motifs and the word "abracadabra" written as a triangular pattern said by various Gnostics and mystics to have been devised from secret knowledge more powerful than Christianity.

Three miles east of Casgob along tiny lanes, the small village church at **Discoed** is fronted by a yew tree dated to around 5000 years old, making it amongst the oldest living organisms in Britain. It's an amazing sight: the centuries have split and cracked the bark, twisting the vast tree in all directions and creating a central chasm big enough to sit in, but fresh green shoots continue to sprout all the same.

The B4536 from Presteigne follows the River Lugg as it skirts the upper edge of the Radnor Forest and passes a delightful example of an unadorned Welsh country church at **PILLETH**. A quiet enough place these days, Pilleth had its moment in the spotlight on Midsummer Day in 1402 when it witnessed the bloodiest and most famous battle of Owain Glyndŵr's war of independence. The English forces, led by Edmund Mortimer, were routed by Glyndŵr's numerically fewer, but far sharper, troops. Mortimer was captured, and 1100 – about half – of the English troops were killed. The mass grave, a mound marked by four lonely pine trees above the church, can still be seen today.

Knighton

KNIGHTON (Tref-y-clawdd, "the town on the dyke"), six miles north of Presteigne, straddles King Offa's eighth-century border as well as the modern Wales–England divide, and has come into its own as the most obvious centre for those walking the **Offa's Dyke Path**. Located almost exactly halfway along

Offa's Dyke

George Borrow, in his classic book *Wild Wales* (see p.548), notes that once "it was customary for the English to cut off the ears of every Welshman who was found to the east of the dyke, and for the Welsh to hang every Englishman whom they found to the west of it". Certainly, **Offa's Dyke** has provided a potent symbol of Welsh–English antipathy ever since it was created in the eighth century as a demarcation line by King Offa of Mercia, ruler of the whole of central England. It appears that the dyke was an attempt to thwart Welsh expansionism.

Up to twenty feet high and sixty feet wide, the earthwork made use of natural boundaries such as rivers in its run north to south, and is best seen in the sections near Knighton in Radnorshire and Montgomery. Today's England–Wales border crosses the dyke many times, although the basic boundary has changed little since Offa's day. The glorious **long-distance footpath**, opened in 1971, runs from Prestatyn on the north Clwyd coast for 177 miles to Sedbury Cliffs, just outside Chepstow in Gwent, and is one of the most rewarding walks in Britain – neither too popular to be unpleasantly crowded, nor too similar in its landscapes. The path is maintained by the Offa's Dyke Association, whose headquarters are in the Offa's Dyke Centre in Knighton (see below).

the route, Knighton, although without many specific sights, is a lively, attractive place that easily warrants a stopoff.

So close is Knighton to the border that the town's **train station** is actually in England. From here, Station Road crosses the River Teme into Wales and climbs a couple of hundred yards into the town, joining the pretty Broad Street at Brookside Square. Further up the hill is the town's Victorian clocktower, where Broad Street becomes West Street and the steep High Street soars off up to the left, past rickety Tudor buildings and up to the mound of the old **castle**. In West Street, the excellent **Offa's Dyke Centre** (Easter–Oct daily 9am–5.30pm; Nov–Easter Mon–Fri 9am–5pm, Sat & Sun 11am–3pm; ☎01547/528753, ⊛www.offasdyke .demon.co.uk) also houses the **tourist office** (same hours; ☎01547/529424). Looming high above Knighton, a mile off the A4113, the **Spaceguard Centre** is housed in the former Powys County Observatory (open year-round, Wed–Sun & bank holiday tours at 10.30am, 2pm & 4pm; evening tours pre-bookable on ☎01547/520247, ⊛www.spaceguarduk.com; £5 day, £6 evening) and has a planetarium, camera obscura and solar telescope.

Accommodation in Knighton is plentiful and generally good value: there's the revamped *Knighton Hotel* right in the middle on Broad Street (☎01547/520530; ❸), *Fleece House* B&B, at the top of High Street (☎01547/520168, ⊛www .fleecehouse.co.uk; ❷), with en-suite twin rooms; and the bargain *Jenny Stothert's*, behind the imposing parish church at 15 Mill Green (☎01547/520075; ❶), where you can also **camp** for £3. There's another low-cost tent field at *Panpwnton Farm* (☎01547/528597), over the river and half a mile up the lane that forks left at the station.

For **eating and drinking**, it's hard to beat the comfortable ⚔ *Horse and Jockey* at the town end of Station Road, which has a vast menu for lunch and early evening, serves huge, tasty pizzas until 11pm and packs in live music and discos as well. The *Red Lion* has large, inexpensive portions of basic pub food, and for a cheap breakfast or lunch, try *JD's* café on Church Street.

The local **bike rental** firm, Wheely Wonderful (☎01568/770755), is over the border in Shropshire at Petchfield Farm, Elton, near Ludlow; it will deliver to Knighton if you're without a car.

Montgomeryshire

The northern part of Powys is made up of the old county of **Montgomery-shire**, an area of enormously varying landscapes and few inhabitants. The best base for the spartan and mountainous southwest of the county is the solid little town of **Llanidloes**, a spirited place and a base for ageing hippies ten miles north of Rhayader on the River Severn (Afon Hafren), which arrives in the town after rising nearby in the dense **Hafren Forest** on the bleak slopes of **Plynlimon**.

From Llanidloes, one of Wales' most dramatic roads rises past the chilly shores of the **Llyn Clywedog** reservoir, squeezed into sharp hillsides, and up through the remote hamlets of **Staylittle** and **Dylife**. This stark, uplifting scenery contrasts with the gentler, greener contours that characterize the east of the county, where the muted old county town of **Montgomery**, with its fine Georgian architecture, perches above the border and Offa's Dyke. The Severn runs a few miles to the west, near the impeccable village of **Berriew**, home of the splendid **Andrew Logan Museum of Sculpture** and below the dank hilltop remains of **Dolforwyn Castle**. Further south, the Severn runs in a muddy channel through drab **Newtown**, good only as a transport interchange and for followers of **Robert Owen**, the pioneer socialist.

In the north of the county, **Welshpool** forms the only major settlement, packed in above the wide flood plain of the Severn. An excellent local museum, the impossibly cute toy rail line that runs to **Llanfair Caereinion**, good pubs and reasonable hotels make the town a fair stop for a day or two. On the southern side of Welshpool is Montgomeryshire's one unmissable sight, the sumptuous **Powis Castle** and its exquisite terraced gardens. The very north of the county is pastoral, deserted and beautiful. The few visitors that there are throng **Lake Vyrnwy** and make their way down the dead-end lane to the **Pistyll Rhaeadr** waterfall, leaving the leafy lanes and villages like **Llanfyllin** and **Llanrhaeadr-ym-mochnant** intact for those searching for peace, cheerful pubs and good walking.

Llanidloes and around

Thriving when so many other small market towns seem in danger of atrophying, the secret of success for **LLANIDLOES** seems to be in its adaptability, from rural village to weaving town and, latterly, a centre for artists, craftsfolk and assorted alternative lifestylers. One of mid-Wales' prettiest and most welcoming towns, Llanidloes' four main streets meet at the black-and-white **market hall**, built on timber stilts in 1600, allowing the market – now long since moved – to take place on the cobbles underneath. Running parallel along the length of the market hall are China Street and Long Bridge Street, the latter good for interesting little shops. Off Long Bridge Street to the left is Church Street, which opens out into a yard surrounding the dumpy parish **church of St Idloes** (daily 10.30am–3.30pm), whose impressive fifteenth-century hammerbeam roof is said to have been poached from Abbey Cwmhir.

Going west from the market hall is Short Bridge Street, a line of fine architecture that runs down to the River Severn, past two imposing nineteenth-century chapels – one Zionist, one Baptist – staring across the road at each other. Heading the other way from the market hall is Great Oak Street, the town's most important and attractive thoroughfare. At the bottom of the street is the **town hall**, originally built as a temperance hotel to challenge the boozy **Trewythen Arms** opposite. A plaque on the closed hotel commemorates Llanidloes as an

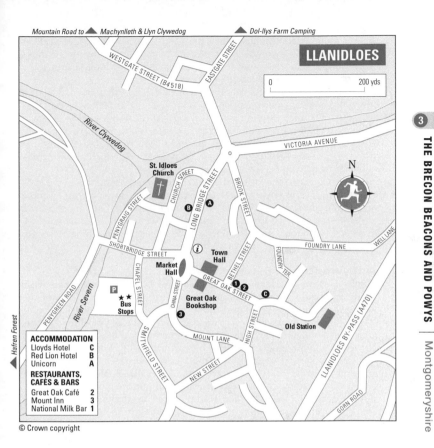

Within the map:

Mountain Road to ▲ Machynlleth & Llyn Clywedog   ▲ Dol-llys Farm Camping

LLANIDLOES

WESTGATE STREET (B4518)

EASTGATE STREET

0   200 yds

River Clywedog

VICTORIA AVENUE

N

St. Idloes Church

CHURCH STREET

LONG BRIDGE STREET

BROOK STREET

PENYGRAIG STREET

B **A**

SHORTBRIDGE STREET

FOUNDRY LANE

WELL LANE

i Town Hall

Market Hall

CHAPEL STREET

CHINA STREET

BETHEL STREET

FOUNDRY TER

PENYGREEN ROAD

River Severn

P ★★ Bus Stops

GREAT OAK STREET

1 2

C

Great Oak Bookshop

3

Old Station

SMITHFIELD STREET

MOUNT LANE

HIGH STREET

LLANIDLOES BY-PASS (A470)

▲ Hafen Forest

NEW STREET

GORN ROAD

ACCOMMODATION
Lloyds Hotel   C
Red Lion Hotel   B
Unicorn   A

RESTAURANTS, CAFÉS & BARS
Great Oak Café   2
Mount Inn   3
National Milk Bar   1

unlikely seeming place of industrial and political unrest, when, in April 1839, Chartists stormed the hotel, dragging out and beating up special constables who had been dispatched to the town in a futile attempt to suppress the political fervour of the local flannel weavers. The town's wonderfully eclectic **museum** (Easter–Sept daily except Wed 11am–1pm & 2–5pm; Oct–Easter Mon, Tues, Thurs & Fri 11am–1pm & 2–5pm, Sat 10am–1pm; £1) forms part of the town hall complex. The diverting collection of old local prints and mementos, including pictures of boomtown Dylife (see p.276), pale beside the stuffed two-headed lamb, born locally in 1914. Great Oak Street is also home to a branch of **Laura Ashley**'s empire, whose mission to wrap the world in floral fabric started just up the road in **Carno**.

Practicalities

Llanidloes is a good base, with friendly pubs and restaurants and plenty of places to stay. China Street curves down to the car park from where all **bus** services operate. The **tourist office** (April–Sept daily 9.30am–5pm, Oct–March Mon–Sat 9.30am–5pm; ☎01686/412605, ✉llantic@powys.gov.uk) is at 54 Long Bridge St, near the market hall. For news of alternative events – like the **Fancy Dress Night**, on the first Friday of July, when the pubs open late, the streets are cordoned off and virtually the whole town gets kitted out – pick up the free monthly community paper, the *Llani Gazette*, or visit the excellent Resource Centre on Great Oak Street. At the bottom of the road is the area's best **bookshop**, Great Oak, with loads of Celtic and Welsh-interest stuff and a barn full of good new and second-hand fiction.

Accommodation spans the delightful *Red Lion Hotel* (℡01686/412270; ❷) and the more modest *Unicorn* (℡01686/413167, ℱ413516; ❶), both on Long Bridge Street. The nicest option is ⚜ *Lloyds Hotel* (℡01686/412284, ⓦwww .lloydshotel.co.uk; ❸), on Cambrian Place, which is also a superb restaurant – booking is essential. You can **camp** around fifteen minutes' walk north of town at *Dol-llys Farm* (℡01686/412694; £4 per person), which allows campfires down by the infant River Severn.

Among the many options for **food**, there's wholesome veggie fare in the laid-back *Great Oak Café* on Great Oak Street, or a few doors down, a great example of that Welsh daytime caff institution, the *National Milk Bar*. For a bit of a treat, go to *Lloyds* (see above). Most of the **pubs** here serve food – the inexpensive *Unicorn* hotel (see above) and the olde-worlde *Mount Inn* on China Street are the best options.

Llyn Clywedog, Plynlimon, Dylife and Staylittle

Four miles northwest of Llanidloes, the beautiful **Llyn Clywedog reservoir** was built as recently as the 1960s and has settled well into the folds of the Clywedog Valley. At its southern end, the modern concrete dam is Britain's tallest (237ft), towering menacingly over the remnants of the **Bryntail lead mine**, through which a signposted path runs. The roads along the southern shores of Clywedog wind around into the dense plantation of **Hafren Forest**, the only real sign of life and vegetation on the bleak, sodden slopes of **Plynlimon** (Pumlumon Fawr, 2469ft). There's a car park at **RHYD-Y-BENWCH**, in the heart of the forest, from where **walking paths** fan out, the most popular being a six-mile round trip following the River Severn up through the trees, past a waterfall and out to its source, a saturated peat bog in some of the harshest terrain in Wales.

Plynlimon is bleak and difficult walking if you venture beyond the fairly well-trodden path to the Severn's source. Water oozes everywhere in this misty wilderness, with four other rivers – the Wye included – rising on its tufted slopes. The rivers Hengwm, Llechwedd-mawr and Rheiddol have been dammed on Plynlimon's western side to form the desolate, black-watered reservoir of **Nant-y-Moch**, reached by road via Ponterwyd (see p.317). There is little sympathetic landscaping here, the lake looking nothing more than the flooded valley that it is.

The hamlet of **STAYLITTLE** (Penfforddlas) – whose English name comes from a village blacksmith who was so quick at shoeing horses his smithy became known as Stay-a-little – is above the Clywedog River at the northern end of Llyn Clywedog. Just north of the village, the mountain road to Machynlleth forks left, running past the plunging ravine of the Twymyn River to the north. Old mine workings herald the approach to **DYLIFE** (pronounced duh-levah), a lead-mining community of almost two thousand people in the mid-nine-teenth century, with a reputation as a lawless, licentious gambling pit. The mine closed in 1896, and the population has since dwindled to around just twenty, although thankfully the village pub – the marvellous ⚜ *Star Inn* – is still there. It's a wonderful, unpretentious place to stay (℡01650/521345; ❷), eat and drink. There are plenty of wild places to pitch a tent for the night nearby too. Good walks from Dylife include up to Pen-y-crocbren, the mine-pocked slope that rises to the south of the village, and west to **Glaslyn**, or "blue lake", and the

Glyndŵr's Way

A fairly new long-distance footpath, **Glyndŵr's Way** weaves its 123 miles through Montgomeryshire and northern Radnorshire countryside well reputed for the solitude that it offers. Running from Knighton in the south, the path climbs up into the remote hills to the northwest before turning south four miles south of Newtown. From here, the path plunges through the pastoral hills and past only occasional settlements towards Abbey Cwmhir, where it again turns and heads north towards Llanidloes and Llyn Clywedog, passing the 103 lofty turbines of the Penrhyddlan and Llidiartywaun Windfarm, the largest in Europe. From Llyn Clywedog, the path heads across the mine-scarred mountains around Dylife and down into Machynlleth. It then ducks back inland, along the A489 for a few miles before dipping down into the hills, up over the A470 and across its bleakest stretch: the wet and wild upland moor south of the A458. Through the Dyfnant Forest, Glyndŵr's Way zigzags down to the shores of Lake Vyrnwy, eastwards along the River Vyrnwy and over its last few miles to Welshpool.

Well signposted all the way, though depending rather a lot on lane and road walking, Glyndŵr's Way is far quieter than Offa's Dyke path, both in the number of settlements en route and the number of people attempting it. Varied scenery includes barren bog, exhilarating uplands, reservoirs, undulating farmland and sections of river-valley walking.

reedy shores of **Bugeilyn**. The superb **Glyndŵr's Way** footpath (see box above) crosses this patch on its way to Machynlleth. A popular viewpoint on the road two miles west of Dylife has been furnished with a cheery memorial to broadcaster and author **Wynford Vaughan-Thomas** (1908–87), whose outstretched slate hand points out to the dozens of rippling peaks and verdant valleys.

Newtown and around

Despite its name, **NEWTOWN** (Y Drenewydd), thirteen miles northeast of Llanidloes, was founded in the thirteenth century, growing steadily until its population explosion in the nineteenth century as a centre for weaving and textiles. Today, it's a sadly charmless kind of place, but useful as a transport interchange and for shopping.

Of Newtown's sights, the High Street is home to the original base of the **W.H. Smith** chain of newsagents, now housing a small and reasonably interesting **museum** (Mon–Sat 9.30am–5.30pm; free) about the company and its growth since it was established in 1792. A block west, the car park where you'll find the bus depot and tourist office is also home to **Oriel 31** (Mon–Sat 10am–5pm; free), a great gallery of imaginative temporary exhibitions, with a decent café too. On Severn Street, opposite the nineteenth-century red terracotta **clocktower**, is the house in which early socialist **Robert Owen** was born in 1771, now open as a **Memorial Museum** (Mon–Fri 9.30am–noon & 2–3.30pm, Sat 9.30–11.30am; free) that explains this remarkable man's life (see box overleaf). The museum's visitors' book indicates just how much of a shrine the place has become, with a roll call of socialist politicians and trade unionists scrawling their thanks for Owen's work in its pages.

Over the river at 5–7 Commercial St, the **Textile Museum** sits above six cramped old weavers' cottages (May–Sept Mon–Tues & Thurs–Sat 2–5pm; free). Exhibits show the dramatic ebb and flow of the town's staple trade, from the flannel and handloom factories of the 1790s, through the social unrest and

Robert Owen

Born in Montgomeryshire in the late eighteenth century, **Robert Owen** (1771–1858) left Wales to enter the Manchester cotton trade at the age of 18 and swiftly rose to the position of mill manager. His business acumen was matched by a strong streak of philanthropy towards his subordinates. Fundamentally, he believed in social equality between the classes and was firmly against the concept of competition between individuals. Poverty, he believed, could be eradicated by co-operative methods. Owen recognized the potential of building a model workers' community around the New Lanark mills in Scotland and joined the operation in 1798, swiftly setting up the world's first infant school, an Institution for the Formation of Character and a model welfare state for its people.

Owen's ideas on co-operative living prompted him to build up the model community of New Harmony in Indiana, USA, which he had established between 1824 and 1828, before handing the still struggling project over to his sons. Before long, and without the wisdom of its founder, the idealistic tenets of New Harmony collapsed under the weight of greed, ambition and too many vested interests. Undeterred, Owen, by now back in Britain, was encouraging the formation of the early trade unions and co-operative societies, as well as leading action against the 1834 deportation of the **Tolpuddle Martyrs**, a group of Dorset farm labourers who withdrew their labour in their call for a wage increase. Owen's later years were dogged by controversy, as he lost the support of the few sympathetic sections of the British establishment in his persistent criticism of organized religion. He gained many followers, however, whose generic name gradually changed from Owenites to socialists – the first usage of the term. Owen returned to Newtown in his later years, and died there in 1858.

industrial decline of the 1830s and 1840s (Wales' first Chartist demonstration took place here in 1838), the revival of trade thanks to local entrepreneur Pryce Jones' world-first mail order service and its subsequent dwindling to nothing by 1935. Pryce Jones' **Royal Welsh Warehouse** – an industrial cathedral that dominates the eastern approach to the town centre – is now a deadbeat shopping centre.

Five miles north of Newtown, the mock-Tudor **Gregynog Hall** was the home from 1920 of Gwendoline and Margaret Davies, aesthete sisters who inherited a vast fortune from their port-building father and spent much of it on a world-class art collection, most of which now resides in Cardiff's National Museum of Wales. Gregynog became the headquarters for their artistic revival, including the establishment of a world-famous small press, which is up and running once more. It's now an extramural outpost of the University of Wales, offering public courses in Welsh language and culture and hosting an annual music **festival** in late June (@www.wales.ac.uk/gregynog): the hall is not generally open to the public, though groups can book a tour and you can wander through the grounds at any time.

Practicalities

Newtown's **train station** is on the southern edge of the town centre, and a path heads straight up past the ugly Victorian parish church of St David and up Back Lane to the **bus station** and **tourist office** (Easter–Sept daily 9.30am–5pm; Oct–Easter Mon–Sat 10am–5pm; ☏01686/625580, @newtic@powys.gov.uk).

If you have to **stay** in Newtown, your best bets are the *Plas Canol* guesthouse, between the station and the town centre at 32 New Rd (☏01686/625598; ❷), and *Yesterdays* (☏01686/622644, @www.yesterdayshotel.com; ❷), behind the clocktower in Severn Square, which also offers super Welsh speciality **food** in its pleasant restaurant. Otherwise, eating revolves around numerous cheap daytime cafés – you can get something a little classier at *Oriel 31* (see above). You won't be stuck for **pubs** – there are loads, even if most are eminently avoidable. The *Lion Inn*, near the clocktower, is good for live music, late drinking and discos, while Commercial Street's *Bell Hotel* and Severn Street's *Sportsman* host regular live folk, R&B and blues.

Dolforwyn Castle

The A483 continues northeast from Newtown, affording occasional glimpses of the River Severn and in almost constant proximity to the reed-filled **Montgomery Canal**. Three miles from Montgomery, there's a small left turn leading up to the *Dolforwyn Hotel* and the gaunt remains of **Dolforwyn Castle** (free access). Described by Jan Morris as "the saddest of all the Welsh castles", this was the very last fortress to be built by a native Welsh prince on his own soil – Llywelyn ap Gruffydd in 1273 – as a direct snub to the English king, Edward I, who had expressly forbidden the project. Llywelyn built his fortress and started to construct a small adjoining town as a Welsh fiefdom to rival the heavily anglicized Welshpool, just up the valley. Dolforwyn only survived for four years in Welsh hands before being overwhelmed after a nine-day siege by the English, and the castle was left slowly to rot. In the past twenty years, the remains have been excavated, and significant portions of the fragile old castle have emerged on the wind-blown hilltop, with its astounding views over the Severn Valley, four hundred feet below.

Montgomery and around

Eight miles northeast of Newtown, the tiny town of **MONTGOMERY** (Trefaldwyn) is Montgomeryshire at its most anglicized. It lies at the base of a dilapidated **castle** on the Welsh side of Offa's Dyke and the present-day border. The castle was started in 1233 by the English king, Henry III, and today's remains are not on their own worth the steep climb up the lane at the back of the town hall, although the view over the lofty church tower, handsome Georgian streets and the vast green bowl of hills around the town is wonderful. The impressively symmetrical main thoroughfare – well-named Broad Street – swoops up to the perfect little red-brick **town hall**, crowned by a pert clocktower. Facing the town hall, Arthur Street goes down to the right and the **Old Bell Museum** (April–July & Sept Wed–Fri & Sun 1.30–5pm, Sat 10.30am–5pm; Aug Mon–Fri & Sun 1.30–5pm, Sat 10.30am–5pm; £1), an unusually enjoyable local history collection of artefacts from excavations, scale models of local castles, an old workhouse exhibition and mementos from Montgomery civic life.

At the other end of Broad Street, the rebuilt tower of Montgomery's parish **church of St Nicholas** dominates the snug proportions of the buildings around it. Largely thirteenth-century, the highlights of its spacious interior include the 1600 canopied tomb of local landowner, Sir Richard Herbert, and his wife, Magdalen. They lie in prayer on top, with their eight (apparently angelic) children (including Elizabethan poet George Herbert) in beatific kneeling positions behind them. Under the couple lurks a shrouded cadaver. The two medieval effigies on the floor at the end of the tomb are of uncertain origin, although the farther one is thought to be of Sir Edmund Mortimer ("revolted Mortimer", as Shakespeare had him), son-in-law of Owain Glyndŵr, brother-in-law of Hotspur and once Constable of Montgomery Castle. Equally impressive are the elaborately carved fifteenth-century double screen and accompanying loft, believed to have been built from sections removed from a priory over the border in Cherbury.

Montgomery is near one of the best-preserved sections of **Offa's Dyke**, which the long-distance footpath shadows either side of the B4386 a mile east of the town. Ditches almost twenty feet high give one of the best indications of the dyke's original look and, to the south of the main road, the England–Wales border still exactly splices the dyke, twelve hundred years after it was built. If you want to **stay** here, the rambling *Dragon Hotel* (℡01686/668359, Ⓦwww .dragonhotel.com; ❺), by the town hall, has an indoor pool and is dependable, if

△ Andrew Logan Museum of Sculpture

rather pompous. Better options are *Brynwylfa* (☎01686/668555; ❷), a beautiful townhouse at 4 Bishops Castle St, or *Little Brompton Farm* (☎01686/668371, ⓦwww.littlebromptonfarm.co.uk; ❷), two miles south of town and handy for the Offa's Dyke path. You can also **camp** there (£3 per person). For **food** and **drink**, head for the *Checkers* pub, on Broad Street, livelier and younger than the *Dragon*.

Berriew

Three miles northwest of Montgomery, the neat village of **BERRIEW** (Aberrhiw) is more redolent of the black-and-white settlements over the English border than anywhere in Wales, with its Tudor houses grouped prettily around a small church, the shallow waters of the Rhiw River and the posh half-timbered *Lion Hotel* (☎01686/640452; ❺), which serves excellent home-cooked meals.

Just over the river bridge, the diverting **Andrew Logan Museum of Sculpture** (Easter weekend noon–6pm; May–Oct Wed–Sun noon–6pm; Nov–Christmas Sat & Sun noon–4pm; ⓦwww.andrewlogan.com; £2) seems an improbably camp addition to the tidy Berriew landscape. In the 1970s, British sculptor Logan inaugurated the great drag-and-grunge ball known as the Alternative Miss World Contest, launchpad of the late Divine's career. A "Divine Shrine" and some dazzling outfits from the contests form a large chunk of the exhibits at the museum, sharing space with Logan's oversized horticultural sculptures, gaudy model goddesses and a twelve-foot-high encrusted glass "cosmic egg".

A mile further down the lane from the museum, where it meets the main A493, you'll find **Glansevern Hall Gardens** (May–Sept Thurs–Sat & bank holidays noon–6pm; £3.50), a beautifully cool collection of plants, trees and follies gathered around a gorgeous Georgian mansion.

Welshpool

Three miles from the English border and five miles north of Berriew, eastern Montgomeryshire's chief town of **WELSHPOOL** (Y Trallwng) was formerly known as just Pool, its prefix added in 1835 to distinguish it from the English seaside town of Poole in Dorset. The town's bypass has cleared its streets of excessive traffic, and left a number of well-proportioned roads crowned with some Tudor and many good Georgian and Victorian buildings. But it's for sumptuous **Powis Castle**, one of the greatest Welsh fortresses, that Welshpool is on most people's agenda.

Arrival, information and accommodation

The pompous neo-Gothic turrets of the old Victorian **train station** (its modern replacement is directly behind) sit at the top of Severn Street, which leads down into the town centre, formed by the intersection of Severn, Berriew, Broad and Church streets. The **tourist office** (daily 9.30am–5.30pm; ☎01938/552043, Ⓔweltic@powys.gov.uk), is fifty yards up Church Street in the Vicarage Gardens car park. There's cheap **bike rental** at Brooks Cycles, 9 Severn St.

There is plenty of **accommodation** in town, though in the centre, the only place with en-suite rooms is the *Royal Oak* (☎01938/552217; ❺), a traditional coaching inn at the main crossroads. Dozens of **B&Bs** line Salop Road; of them all, *Montgomery House* (☎01938/552693; ❷) is the surest bet. If you've got transport, you're far better off out of town: there are some fabulous options including the splendid Georgian luxury of *Trefnant Hall Farm* (☎01686/640262; ❷), a couple of miles further up the lane to Powis Castle, and, two miles to the

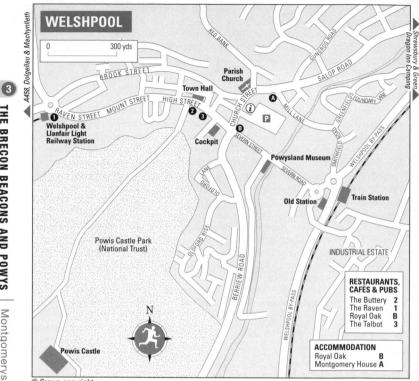

WELSHPOOL

A458, Dolgellau & Machynlleth

Shrewsbury & Green
Dragon Inn Camping

0   300 yds

BROOK STREET

RED BANK

GUNSROG ROAD

SALOP ROAD

Parish
Church

Town Hall

RAVEN STREET   MOUNT STREET   HIGH STREET

CHURCH STREET

❶

Welshpool &
Llanfair Light
Railway Station

❷❸

Cockpit

SEVERN STREET

MILL LANE

GREENFIELDS ROAD

FOUNDARY LANE

WELSHPOOL BY-PASS

A
ⓘ
P
B

Powysland Museum

SMITHFIELD ROAD

SEVERN ROAD

OLFORD LANE

OLFORD RISE

Powis Castle Park
(National Trust)

BERRIEW ROAD

N

Powis Castle

Old Station   Train Station

INDUSTRIAL ESTATE

WELSHPOOL BY-PASS

RESTAURANTS,
CAFÉS & PUBS
The Buttery   2
The Raven   1
Royal Oak   B
The Talbot   3

ACCOMMODATION
Royal Oak   B
Montgomery House   A

© Crown copyright

north of town, the beautiful *Lower Trelydan Farm* (℡01938/553105, ⓦwww
.lowertrelydan.com; ❸). **Camping** is good at the *Green Dragon Inn*, a mile along
the Shrewsbury road at Buttington (℡01938/553076; £4 per person).

The Town

Arriving at Welshpool's modern **train station** gives a false sense of what to
expect from the town, which is much more attractive than the modern mess
around the rail lines and the kitsch stores in the old station would lead you to
believe. Two hundred yards along Severn Street, a humpback bridge over the
much-restored **Montgomery Canal** hides the **canal wharf** and a wharfside
warehouse that has been carefully restored as the **Powysland Museum** (all
year Mon, Tues, Thurs & Fri 11am–1pm & 2–5pm; May–Sept also Sat & Sun
10am–1pm & 2–5pm; Oct–April also Sat 11am–2pm; £1), an impressively
wide collection looking at the history of the local area. Of particular interest
are Andrew Logan's blue spangly outsized handbag heralding the entrance, the
displays showing archeological finds from a local neolithic timber circle, Sarn-
y-bryn-caled, and Roman remains from the now obliterated Cistercian abbey
of Strata Marcella. More recent exhibits show the changing patterns of domestic
and civic life, as well as some surprises – most notably an intricate model of a
guillotine carved from mutton bones, left behind by prisoners of war from the
Napeolonic Wars of the early nineteenth century.

Right at the centre of town are the crossroads, where the Georgian **Royal Oak Hotel** acts as a firm reminder of the junction's importance on the old coaching route. Broad Street is the most architecturally interesting of the streets leading off from here, with the ponderous Victorian town hall and its dominating clocktower overlooking some fine Tudor and Jacobean townhouses. On New Street, behind the NatWest bank, you can wander around an early eighteenth-century circular **cockpit** (bank hours; free). Broad Street changes name five times as it rises up the hill towards the tiny Raven Square terminus station of the **Welshpool & Llanfair Railway**, half a mile beyond the town hall. The eight-mile narrow-gauge line (April to late May & Sept–Oct weekends only; Easter & late May to Aug daily; generally 2–3 trains a day; £9.90 return; ☎01938/810441) was open to passengers for less than thirty years, closing in 1931 – these days, scaled-down engines once more chuff along the appropriately modest valleys of the Sylfaen Brook and Banwy River to the quiet village of **LLANFAIR CAEREINION**, a good daytime base for walks and pub food at the *Goat Hotel*. The **post office**, opposite the church, stocks free leaflets of some good local circular walks.

Powis Castle

In a land of ruined castles, the sheer scale and beauty of **Powis Castle** (April–Oct Mon & Thurs–Sun castle 1–5pm, gardens 11am–6pm; July–Aug Tues–Sun, same times; castle £8.80, gardens and museum only £6.20; NT), a mile from Welshpool up Park Lane, is quite staggering. On the site of an earlier Norman fort, the castle was started in the reign of Edward I by the Gwenwynwyn family; to qualify for the site and the barony of De la Pole, they had to renounce all claims to Welsh princedom. In 1587, Sir Edward Herbert bought the castle and began to transform it into the Elizabethan palace we see today.

Inside, the **Clive Museum** – named after Edward Clive, son of Clive of India, who married into the family in 1784 – forms a lively account of the British in India, through diaries, notes, letters, paintings, tapestries, weapons and jewels, although it is the sumptuous period rooms that impress most, from the vast and kitsch frescoes by Lanscroon above the balustraded staircase to the mahogany bed, brass and enamel toilets and decorative wall hangings of the state bedroom. The elegant Long Gallery has a rich sixteenth-century plasterwork ceiling overlooking winsome busts and marble statuettes of the four elements, placed in between the glowering family portraits.

Designed by Welsh architect William Winde, the **gardens** are spectacular. Dropping down from the castle in four huge stepped terraces, the design has barely changed since the seventeenth century, with a charmingly precise orangery and topiary that looks as if it is shaved daily. Summertime outdoor concerts, frequently with firework finales, take place in the gardens.

Eating and drinking

Welshpool's four main streets are home to most of the town's **eating** and **drinking** establishments. The best food in town is at the *Royal Oak* pub (see above), which has managed to retain its olde-worlde grandiosity while including a contemporary all-day café-bar. Cheap and filling breakfasts, lunches and teas are served in the *Buttery*, opposite the town hall on the High Street. Many of the town's **pubs** do lunchtime food, with some, notably the *Talbot* in the High Street and the *Raven* up by the narrow-gauge train station, serving decent evening meals as well.

Llanfyllin and around

The hills and plains of northern Montgomeryshire conceal a maze of deserted lanes and farm outposts along the contours that swell up towards the north and the foothills of Denbighshire's Berwyn Mountains. The only real settlement of any size is **LLANFYLLIN**, a handsome and friendly hillside town, ten miles northwest of Welshpool in the valley of the River Cain. The High Street is a busy centre of bright pubs, cafés, shops and a weekly Thursday market. The striking red-brick parish church is a rare example of eighteenth-century church building in Wales.

Llanfyllin is short on places to **stay**, with only an ancient and somewhat over-priced coaching inn, the *Cain Valley Hotel*, on the High Street (℡01691/648366; ❹). On the whole, you're better off in Llanrhaeadr-ym-mochnant (see below) or some five miles southwest at the tranquil, ivy-draped seventeenth-century *Cyfie Farm* (℡01691/648451, ℱ648363; ❺), in a beautiful garden setting just south of the tiny village of Llanfihangel-yng-Ngwynfa. There's a fine **restaurant** on the Llanfyllin High Street in the shape of ⚷ *Seeds* (℡01691/648604), with a three-course set dinner menu including good vegetarian options for £24. Alternatively, there's cheap eating at *Eagles* bar on the High Street and the *Tŷ Coffi* café on the main square, and decent snacks in the bar of the *Cain Valley Hotel*.

The Tanat and Rhaeadr valleys

Parallel to the valley of the River Cain, three or four miles to the north, are the luscious valleys of the Afon Tanat and its tributary, the Rhaeadr. A sparsely populated, little-changed backwater, this is a beguiling area set against the looming Berwyn Mountains.

For a place so near the English border, **LLANRHAEADR-YM-MOCHNANT** is surprisingly Welsh. Six miles north of Llanfyllin, this small, low-roofed village is best remembered as the serving parish of Bishop William Morgan, who translated the Bible into Welsh in 1588 (see p.457), an act which ensured the survival of the old tongue. The village has three great **pubs** – the *Three Tuns*, *Hand Inn* and *Wynnstay Arms* – and excellent-value **B&Bs**: next to the post office on the central square is *Powys House* (℡01691/780201, ⓦwww .llanrhaeadrym.co.uk; ❷); alternatively, try the plusher *Bron Heulog* on Waterfall Street (℡01691/780521,ⓦwww.kraines.enta.net; ❸).

Llanrhaeadr lies at the foot of the wild walking country of the southern Berwyn Mountains. From the middle of the village, Waterfall Street becomes a lane that courses northwest for four miles to a dead end at the enchanting **Pistyll Rhaeadr**, Wales' highest waterfall at 240ft. The river tumbles down the crags in two stages, flowing under a natural stone arch known as the Fairy Bridge. Don't miss out on walking to the top of the fall, for vertiginous views down the valley, and paths up into the moody Berwyns. Pistyll Rhaeadr is a place rich in legend, which you can gen up on in the cute riverside ⚷ *Tan-y-Pistyll* licensed café. The owners also offer B&B (℡01691/780392; ❸) and a lovely **campsite** (£5 per person) in the back field, and operate various retreats and spiritually inclined groups.

The B4396 runs east from Llanrhaeadr, along the Tanat Valley and through the village of **LLANGEDWYN**. A mile or so after the village, few visitors make it up one of the left turns leading to **SYCARTH**, only a mile from the English border, but one of the most Welsh of all shrines: a grass mound marks the site of Owain Glyndŵr's ancestral court, reputedly a palace of nine grand halls. Bard Iolo Goch immortalized this Welsh Shangri-la as a place of "no want, no hunger, no shame/ No-one is ever thirsty at Sycarth".

Just to the east of Sycarth, the English–Welsh border tightly encircles the 740-foot limestone crag of **Llanymynech Rocks** (now a nature reserve), before cutting down to run right through the middle of the village's **LLANY-MYNECH**. Indeed, the divide runs slap through the village's rundown *Lion Hotel* – not so long ago, thanks to the now dead Welsh ban on licensing on the Sabbath, half the pub had to remain "dry" on Sunday, while the other (English) half downed beer with gusto.

The B4391 hugs the river as far as soporific little **LLANGYNOG**, where it heads north into the Berwyn Mountains and Denbighshire. Cowering under the rocky screes of Craig Rhiwarth, the village is a former mining centre, as evidenced in the scars on the hillsides around. A lane by the bridge leads to a stunning four-mile hike over the top of Y Clogydd and down to the elfin charms of Pistyll Rhaeadr (see above). Less strenuously, you can walk (or drive) two miles further up the Tanat Valley to the hamlet of **PENNANT MELANGELL**, sitting low in a quiet valley of sheer sides and sparkling brooks, the site of one of Wales' most enduring sites of pilgrimage. Legend has it that the eighth-century saint Melangell was praying in the valley when a hare being chased by a hunt pack led by Prince Brochwel took refuge in her skirts. The hounds drew to a sudden stop before her and fled howling. The prince drew his horn to his lips to call them, only to find himself unable to remove it. The prince was so moved by Melangell's gentle humanity that he granted her the valley, in which she built a religious community. The gorgeous little **church** (daily: May–Oct 10am–6pm; Nov–April 10am–4pm) that sits here today dates from the eighth century, although the site was one of worship and spiritual significance way before. Inside, a twelfth-century shrine (the oldest known in Britain) and supposed effigy of St Melangell lie beneath an exquisite barrel roof. Melangell's grave is in the semicircular *cell y bedd* at the back of the church. Intact Norman features include a window in the main church, the south door porch and the font.

Lake Vyrnwy

A monument to the self-aggrandizement of the Victorian age, the four-mile-long **Lake Vyrnwy** (Llyn Efyrnwy) combines its functional role as a water supply for Liverpool with a touch of architectural genius in the shape of the huge nineteenth-century dam at its southern end and the Disneyesque turreted straining tower which edges out into the icy waters. It's a magnificent spot, and a popular centre for walking and bird-watching. A commemorative stone at the eastern end of the dam arrogantly celebrates "taking and impounding the waters of the Rivers Vyrnwy, Marchnant and Cowny", which flooded a village of four hundred inhabitants in the process.

Constructed during the 1880s, Vyrnwy was the first of the massive reservoirs of mid-Wales. The village of **Llanwddyn** was flattened and rebuilt at the eastern end, its people receiving compensation of just £5 for the loss of their homes. The story is told, somewhat apologetically, in the **Vyrnwy Visitor Centre** (April–Oct daily 10.30am–5.30pm; Nov–March Sat & Sun only; free), which is located on the western side of the dam and coexists with an **RSPB Visitor Centre** (same hours). RSPB staff here are in charge of a small hide across the road, where you can sit and watch forest birds (and cheeky squirrels) attacking the feeders outside the windows. A few yards down the road, there's a **tourist office** (Easter–Oct daily 10am–5pm; Nov–Easter daily except Wed 10am–3pm; ☎01691/870346) and *Artisans Coffee Shop* (☎ 01691/870377), from where you can **rent bikes**. The Bethania Adventure Centre (☎01691/870615), in the boathouse near the dam, also rents bikes, offers **river rafting** and **sailing** trips, and doles out leaflets detailing modest walks through the woods around Llanwddyn.

Lake Vyrnwy's immediate surroundings boast some of the best **accommodation** in the region, notably the grand *Lake Vyrnwy Hotel* (☎01691/870692, 🖤www.lakevyrnwy.com; ❼), overlooking the waters above the southeastern shore. It's pricey, and a bit frayed around the edges, but dinners are worthwhile, B&B deals are a few pounds more than the room rate, and the full afternoon tea, served in a chintzy lounge overlooking the lake, is perfect if you just want to have a look around. There's a great **B&B** just beyond the visitor centre at *The Oaks* (☎01691/870250, 🖤www.vyrnwyaccommodation .co.uk; ❸), and daytime snacks and full evening meals are available at ⅌ *Lake View* (☎01691/870286), on the lakeside road beyond the *Lake Vyrnwy Hotel*. If you're **camping**, there are five tent pitches at the rather scruffy *Fronheulog* (☎01691/870662; £2.50 per person), at the top of the hairpin bends on the road to Llanfyllin, or, down the hill in Llanwddyn itself at the more informal *Bryn Fedwen* (☎01691/870288; £2 per person).

Travel details

Unless otherwise stated, frequencies for trains and buses are for Monday to Saturday services, Sunday averages 1–3 services, though the main routes are more frequent and some routes have no Sunday service at all.

Trains

Abergavenny to: Cardiff (hourly; 40min); Hereford (hourly; 20min); Newport (hourly; 30min); Pontypool (hourly; 10min).

Knighton to: Llandrindod Wells (4 daily; 40min); Llanwrtyd Wells (4 daily; 1hr 10min); Shrewsbury (4 daily; 1hr); Swansea (4 daily; 3hr 10min).

Llandrindod Wells to: Knighton (4 daily; 40min); Llanwrtyd Wells (4 daily; 30min); Shrewsbury (4 daily; 1hr 40min); Swansea (4 daily; 2hr 20min).

Welshpool to: Aberystwyth (6 daily; 1hr 30min); Birmingham (6 daily; 1hr 30min); Machynlleth (6 daily; 1hr); Newtown (6 daily; 20min); Pwllheli (4 daily; 3hr); Shrewsbury (6 daily; 20min).

Buses

Abergavenny to: Brecon (7 daily Mon–Sat; 1hr); Cardiff (hourly; 1hr 20min); Clydach (hourly; 30min); Crickhowell (7 daily Mon–Sat; 20min); Llanfihangel Crucorney (6 daily; 15min); Merthyr Tydfil (hourly; 1hr 30min); Monmouth (6 daily; 40min); Newport (hourly; 1hr 10min); Pontypool (hourly; 25min); Raglan (6 daily; 20min).

Brecon to: Aberdulais (2–3 daily; 1hr 30min); Abergavenny (every 2hr Mon–Sat; 1hr); Builth Wells (1–3 daily Mon–Sat; 40min); Cardiff (1 daily; 1hr 25min, otherwise change at Merthyr); Craig-y-nos/Dan-yr-ogof (2–3 daily; 30min); Crickhowell (7 daily Mon–Sat; 25min); Hay-on-Wye (7 daily; 45min); Hereford (7 daily; 1hr 45min); Libanus (9 daily; 10min); Llandrindod Wells (3 daily Mon–Sat; 1hr); Merthyr Tydfil (10 daily; 40min); Newport (5 daily; 1hr 50min); Pontypool (6 daily; 1hr 20min); Sennybridge (2–3 daily; 20min); Swansea (2–3 daily; 1hr 30min); Talgarth (6 daily; 30min); Talybont (7 daily Mon–Sat; 20min).

Builth Wells to: Llandrindod Wells (hourly Mon–Sat; 20min); Rhayader (2 daily Mon–Sat; 30min).

Hay-on-Wye to: Brecon (7 daily; 50min); Hereford (6 daily; 1hr); Llandrindod Wells (1 daily Wed & Sat; 1hr).

Knighton to: Ludlow (3 daily; 1hr 10min); Presteigne (7 daily; 30min).

Llandrindod Wells to: Abbeycwmhir (1 postbus daily Mon–Fri; 2hr); Aberystwyth (1 daily; 2hr); Brecon (3 daily Mon–Sat; 1hr); Builth Wells (hourly; 20min); Disserth (2 daily; 15min); Elan Village (1 postbus daily Mon–Fri; 40min); Hay-on-Wye (1 daily Wed & Sat; 1hr); New Radnor (2 daily Mon–Sat; 30min); Newtown (3 daily; 1hr 10min); Rhayader (3 daily; 30min).

Llanfyllin to: Llanwddyn for Lake Vyrnwy (3–4 daily Mon–Sat; 30min); Oswestry (3 daily Mon–Sat; 45min); Welshpool (1 daily Mon–Sat; 40min).

Llanidloes to: Aberystwyth (5 daily; 1hr); Dylife (1 postbus daily; 30min); Newtown (9 daily; 30min); Ponterwyd (1 daily; 40min); Shrewsbury (4 daily; 2hr); Welshpool (5 daily; 1hr 10min).

Llanwrtyd Wells to: Abergwesyn (1 daily postbus; 20min); Builth Wells (3 daily; 45min).

Oswestry (Shropshire) to: Chirk (hourly; 30min); Llanfyllin (3–4 daily; 50min); Welshpool (5 daily; 1hr); Wrexham (hourly; 1hr).

Shrewsbury (Shropshire) to: Llanidloes (4 daily; 2hr); Welshpool (7 daily; 50min).

Welshpool to: Berriew (6 daily Mon–Sat; 20min); Llanidloes (5 daily; 1hr 10min); Llanfyllin (1 daily Mon–Sat; 40min); Llanymynech (5 daily; 30min); Montgomery (4 daily Mon–Sat; 25min); Newtown (7 daily; 40min); Oswestry (5 daily; 1hr); Shrewsbury (7 daily; 50min).

The Cambrian coast

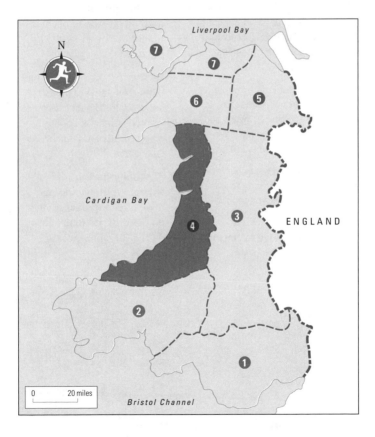

Liverpool Bay

N

Cardigan Bay

ENGLAND

0   20 miles

Bristol Channel

CHAPTER 4 # Highlights

* **South Ceredigion coast**
One of the finest coastlines in Wales, with gorgeous beaches, soaring cliffs and great villages. See p.295

* **Aberystwyth** Quintessentially Welsh seaside town complete with the National Library and a strong student presence. See p.308

* **Hafod** A sublime example of Picturesque landscaping, all sculptured walks and tumbling falls, being teased back to life. See p.318

* **Yny-shir bird reserve** Not just for birders: the Dyfi-side site is magnificently moody. See p.320

* **Machynlleth** Wales' ancient capital is bursting with good-natured life and plenty to see and do. See p.321

* **Cadair Idris** Hike up southern Snowdonia's highest peak for fabulous coastal and estuary views and the chance to become a poet . . . or go mad. See p.320

* **Dyffryn Ardudwy beach** An eight-mile yawn of golden sand, Wales' finest beach also contains the country's only official naturist section. See p.339

* **The Rhinogs** The wild side of Welsh hillwalking in an area approached on an old drovers' road known as the Roman Steps. See p.340

△ Ceredigion coast

4

The Cambrian coast

C ardigan Bay (Bae Ceredigion) takes a huge bite out of the west Wales coast, leaving behind the Pembrokeshire peninsula in the south and the Llŷn in the north. Between them lies the Cambrian coast, a loosely defined mountain-backed strip periodically split by tumbling rivers, which stretches up from Cardigan to Harlech and the shores of Tremadog Bay. Before the railway and improved roads were built during the nineteenth century, the awkward barrier of the Cambrian Mountains served to isolate this stretch of coast from the rest of Wales, with only narrow passes and cattle-droving routes pushing through the rugged terrain to get to the markets in England. Today, large sand-fringed sections are peppered with low-key coastal resorts, peopled in the summer by families from the English Midlands. The presence of English-dominated resorts and the influx of rat-race refugees to this staunchly nation-alistic part of the country has, on occasion, fuelled local antipathy, although visitors are unlikely to see anything more controversial than the odd piece of graffiti or flyposting. The Cambrian coast starts where the rugged seashore of Pembrokeshire ends, continuing in much the same vein of great cliffs, isolated beaches and swirling sea birds, punctuated with *sarnau*, stony offshore reefs largely exposed at low tide. North of the spirited town of **Cardigan**, the coast breaks at some popular seaside resorts – the best being **Llangrannog** and **New Quay** – before the tiny and ordered Georgian harbour town of **Aberaeron**, now designated the headquarters of the county of Ceredigion.

A bucolic **inland** alternative to the coastal resorts follows the **River Teifi**, which meets the sea at Cardigan and meanders through lush meadows past a clutch of small towns, prominent among them the stalwart market centre of **Newcastle Emlyn**, the lively university town of **Lampeter** and the charm-ingly old-fashioned community of **Tregaron**.

The coastal and inland routes connect at the robust and cosmopolitan "capital" of mid-Wales, **Aberystwyth**, built on the estuary of the **Rheidol**, a fast-falling river with dramatic ravines that make for great walking country. A narrow-gauge railway, an attraction in itself, climbs out of Aberystwyth to the popular tourist honeypot of **Devil's Bridge**, where three bridges, one on top of the other, span a turbulent chasm of waterfalls.

Although on a western limb of Powys, this chapter includes **Machynlleth**, at the head of the Dyfi estuary and a magical place, the seat of Owain Glyndŵr's putative fifteenth-century Welsh parliament and still a thriving market centre. Just outside the town is the **Centre for Alternative Technology**, Britain's most famous showpiece for sustainable living and renewable energy resources.

The main road continues due north from Machynlleth into the old county of **Meirionydd**, now part of Gwynedd. Trains and the smaller coast road skirt west

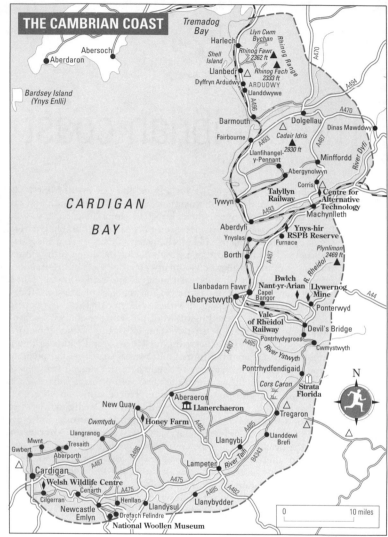

around **Cadair Idris**, the monumental mountain that dominates the southern third of the **Snowdonia National Park**. Each of its crag-fringed faces invites exploration, but it is best approached from the south where the narrow-gauge Talyllyn rail line reaches the tiny settlement of **Abergynolwyn**, a great base for the unhurried delights of the **Dysynni Valley**. Cadair Idris' northern flank slopes down to the market town of **Dolgellau**, at the head of the scenic Mawddach estuary and linked by waterside path to the likeable resort of **Barmouth**. The coastal strip then broadens out with complex dune systems protecting the approaches to **Harlech** and its virtually intact castle, the southernmost link in

Edward I's chain of thirteenth-century fortresses, perched high on its rocky promontory. Views from the fractured battlements sweep north towards the mountains of Snowdonia and west to the Llŷn.

Getting around

The most relaxing way to get fairly swiftly to and along the Cambrian coast is on the mid-Wales **train** line from Shrewsbury in England through to Machynlleth. At Machynlleth, the line splits: one branch runs south to Aberystwyth, from where you can pick up the Vale of Rheidol line to Devil's Bridge; the other swings north, calling at 25 stations in under sixty miles before terminating at Pwllheli on the Llŷn. The Day Ranger and Evening Ranger (see Basics, p.43) tickets make travel flexible and relatively cheap.

Buses run almost parallel to the trains, also extending south to Cardigan and inland to all towns of any size. There's also the express TrawsCambria service from Bristol (in England), Cardiff and Swansea to Bangor and Llandudno through Aberystwyth, Machynlleth, Dolgellau and Porthmadog. Many of the villages bypassed by the regular services rely on a skeletal network of **postbuses** (see Basics, p.45) working out of Aberystwyth and Machynlleth, though the most remote aren't served by public transport at all.

Detailed information on bus and train services as far south as Machynlleth appears in the Gwynedd and Ceredigion regional transport guides, available at tourist offices.

From Cardigan to Aberaeron

The southern section of Ceredigion coastline is enormously popular, combining safe beaches, lively market towns, Wales' highest sea-cliffs, great coastal walking and a resident pod of bottlenose dolphins. Although some of the larger towns, particularly **Aberporth**, have lost much of their scenic splendour to relentless waves of holiday homes and caravan parks, many of the coast's other settlements manage to cling on to some of the salty charm that makes them so popular: **New Quay** is a delightful hillside town, while smaller places like **Llangrannog**, **Penbryn**, **Mwnt** and **Tresaith** neatly juxtapose superb countryside and sweeping beaches. The primly ordered **Aberaeron**, with its fine harbour, is quite unlike anywhere else on the coast.

Just inland, at the mouth of the Teifi, is the old county town of **Cardigan**, scarcely thrilling but pretty, cheerful and with an excellent range of pubs, shops and accommodation.

The main A487 road runs parallel to the coast, meeting the sea at Aberaeron, and forms the basis of the regular #550 bus service linking the larger seaside villages and towns along this stretch. The summer-only Cardi Bach bus (#600) connects all the villages and coves between Cardigan and New Quay.

Cardigan and around

Until the River Teifi silted up in the nineteenth century, **CARDIGAN** (Aberteifi) was one of the greatest sea-ports in Britain, although these days there's little evidence of its former status. It is, however, a perky little town, with some great diversions and a relaxed ambience. The town's castle, slowly being teased out of dereliction, was founded by the Norman lord Roger de Montgomery in 1093 and was the site of the first Welsh eisteddfod in 1176. On the south side of the river, away from the town centre, an old granary houses

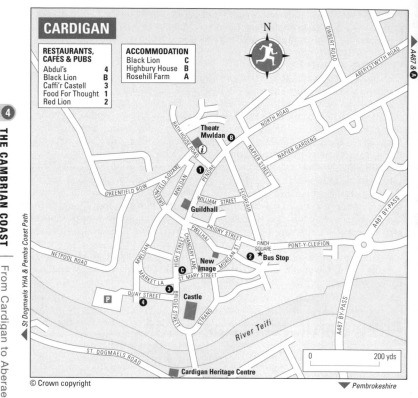

Pembrokeshire

the **Cardigan Heritage Centre** (Canolfan Hanes Aberteifi; March–Oct daily 10am–5pm; £2). It's free to go into the first section, a coffee shop and exhibition about the rise and fall of the port of Cardigan, including shipping history and memories of the emigration boats that left the port bound for Canada and the USA. The entrance fee covers the excellent second section, which takes many diverting looks at nuggets of Cardigan's long history. There's usually a temporary exhibition or two to finish off the tour.

Across the river towards the town centre, the currently out-of-bounds castle mound, shored up by unsightly steel buttresses, sits bulging at the town end of the medieval bridge. Sweeping up a hill all around the site, Bridge Street becomes the picturesque High Street – leading off from here are several narrow thoroughfares, crammed with Georgian and Victorian buildings. High Street snakes past pubs and shops to the spiky turrets of the **Guildhall**. Through the Guildhall courtyard is the town's superb **covered market** (daily except Wed & Sun), a typically eclectic mix of fresh food and plenty of browsable oddities. A couple of hundred yards up High Street (at this point called Pendre) from the Guildhall, Bath House Road dips down to the left and to the excellent **Theatr Mwldan** (℡01239/621200, 🌐www.mwldan .co.uk), a great place for exhibitions and performances alike. It's also home to the tourist office (see below) and a very good café. Priory Street leads down the hill from the Guildhall, past the council offices and on to Finch Square, where buses terminate.

When you are done with town, consider visiting the charming village of Cilgerran or the Welsh Wildlife Centre (see p.302), four miles by road but just a mile or so by riverside bike- and footpath; ask the tourist office for directions.

Practicalities

The helpful **tourist office** (Easter–Aug daily 10am–6pm; Sept–Easter Mon–Sat 10am–5pm; ☎01239/613230, ✉cardigantic@ceredigion.gov.uk) is in the foyer of Theatr Mwldan on Bath House Road, and there's **bike rental** from New Image Bicycles on Pwllhai (£15 for the first day, subsequent days £5; ☎01239/621275).

For **accommodation**, try the sturdy rooms in the old-fashioned *Black Lion* (*Llew Du*) pub (☎01239/612532; ❸) on the High Street or the basic but decent *Highbury House*, the old county gaol, on Pendre (☎01239/613403; ❶). With your own transport, try the sixteenth-century *Rosehill Farm* in Llangoedmor, a mile and a half east of town (☎01239/612019, ⓦwww.rosehillfarm.co.uk; closed Nov–March; ❸), which boasts a gorgeous riverside setting and excellent evening meals. Cardigan is just beyond the northern end of the Pembrokeshire Coast Path, which terminates four miles from town on the other side of the Teifi estuary at Poppit Sands, site of the nearest **YHA hostel** (☎0870/770 5996, ✉poppit@yha.org.uk; closed Nov–Feb), a newly renovated place with beds for £10.50. From mid-July to late September the Poppit Rocket bus service (2–3 daily) will take you there, and year-round the #407 stops within half a mile. **Camping** is allowed in the hostel grounds. Slightly nearer to Cardigan is the *Brongwyn Mawr Farm* caravan park (☎01239/613644; £9 per pitch), which also takes tents. It's just north of the village of Penparc, which itself is two miles north of Cardigan on the A487.

Cardigan has a glut of great daytime **eating** options: the café at *Theatr Mwldan* (open until 9pm Fri & Sat) is superb, the homemade cawl at the *Caffi'r Castell*, on the corner of Quay and High streets, is great on a chilly day, or the *Food For Thought* café, 13 Pendre, offers a good range of hearty snacks and coffees. The café at the Welsh Wildlife Centre (see p.302) is also good. In the evenings, either go for a fine curry at *Abdul's* on Quay Street (☎01239/621416) or hit the **pubs** – the *Black Lion* and the *Red Lion* on Pwllhai near Finch Square are good for food and beer, though not a patch on some in the surrounding villages, most notably the *Crown Inn* at Llwyndafydd (see p.297) or the *Nag's Head* at Aber-Cych (see p.303).

The southern Ceredigion coast

One of the most spectacular stretches of coastline in Wales, the rippled cliffs, expansive beaches and hedged lanes of the southern Ceredigion coast attract thousands of visitors every year.

The Gwbert Road heads out of the neat Cardigan suburbs before descending to the estuary edge and the straggling seaside village of **GWBERT**, a pleasant spot with good sea views best enjoyed from the **Cardigan Island Coastal Farm Park** (Easter–Oct daily 9.30am–6pm or dusk; £3.20), a great place for kids who will be thrilled to spot dolphins and fur seals on a coastal walk.

A mile or so to the east, tiny lanes bump down to the delightfully isolated hamlet of **MWNT**, where the exquisite sandy beach and cliffs are under the custody of the National Trust (parking £1.50). Set in windswept solitude above the cliffs, the tiny, whitewashed church is the oldest in Ceredigion – its foundation dates back to the sixth century, although most of today's thick-set building dates from the thirteenth century. Mwnt's most notable hour came in 1155,

△ Mwnt church

when invading Flemings landed here, only to be soundly routed by the Welsh. The occasion, which became known as *Sul Coch y Mwnt*, the Bloody Sunday of Mwnt, has been periodically remembered through the whole skeletons and other human bones that have been unearthed en masse in the vicinity. There's some good **camping** at Mwnt, though come supplied, as there are no shops nearby. Further along the track from the church is *Tŷ Gwyn*, a fairly basic site. Alternatively, a walk up through the wooded ravine behind the church brings you to the plusher *Blaenwaun Farm* site (☎01239/613456; £12 per pitch), also reached on the back lane from Felinwynt.

Four miles further east, the most popular stopping-off point on this stretch of coast has to be **ABERPORTH**, an elderly resort built around two adjoining bays, neither of them particularly pretty. The town's holiday resort status has long since robbed it of charm, and though it's packed full of places to stay, you're far better off pushing on to the infinitely preferable hamlet of **TRESAITH**, a mile east. This rewarding spot has a compact beach and, just around the rocks, a sandy cove with its own natural after-sea shower – a waterfall crashing down from the River Saith above. There is often good surf, **dinghy races** on calmer summer Sundays, and at low tide you can walk around to the wide, sandy, National Trust beach at **PENBRYN**. Once the coast path and the beach have exhausted you, don't miss a pint in the bustling *Ship Inn*. For **accommodation**, there's the superb Georgian ambience of *Glandŵr* (☎01239/811442, Ⓦwww.glandwrtresaith.co.uk; ❺) at the top of Tresaith village on the road to Aberporth, and a little further along, a wonderful tent-only clifftop **campsite** at the far end of the *Llety Caravan Park* (☎01239/810354, £10.50 per pitch), from where a pretty footpath descends straight to the beach. For something a little different, you can camp in a tipi for £15 at *Tipi West* on Hendre Farm, just south of Aberporth (☎07813/672336, Ⓦwww.tipiwest.co.uk).

Just along the coast, three miles northeast of Tresaith, **LLANGRANNOG** is the most attractive village on the Ceredigion coast, wedged in between hills covered with bracken and gorse. The very narrow streets wind their way to the tiny seafront, catering for visitors with a couple of cafés and pubs and assorted sporting activities. The beach can become horribly congested in midsummer – a quieter alternative is to head north over to **Cilborth Beach**, reachable in ten minutes along the coast at low tide or via a cliff path leading along the glorious National Trust headland towards **Ynys Lochtyn** and a couple of other remote strips of sand – a circuit that can be completed in about an hour. In Llangrannog, you can **stay** at the seafront *Pentre Arms* (☎01239/654345; ❸), where you can also dine, though you may prefer to stroll across to the excellent 350-year-old *Ship Inn* (☎01239/654423; ❹). Between Penbryn and Llangrannog is the *Maes-glas* caravan park (☎01239/654268; £7–10 per pitch), which takes tents.

Signs around Llangrannog point to an unlikely seeming local activity: **skiing**. There's a decent artificial slope a mile east of the village at the Urdd Centre (☎01239/654473), just off the B4321. This outward-bound centre, owned by the Welsh-language youth organization, opens its slope up to the public for both skiing and snowboarding; lessons are also available. There are numerous other outdoor activities on offer at the centre.

From Llangranog, you can walk along the coast path towards New Quay Head, where seasonal flowers swath wind-blasted hillsides and cliffs that drop dramatically into clear seas. The next bay north is the glorious cave-walled beach at **CWMTYDU**, approached along tiny lanes winding steeply down from above. Here you'll find Cwmtydu Trekking Centre (May–Oct daily; ☎01545/560494), which runs well-priced one- or two-hour hacks. Two miles inland is the village of **LLWYNDAFYDD**, where the excellent ⚓ *Crown Inn* (closed Sun evening in winter) is deservedly noted for its food. There's also very good accommodation nearby on the A487 in Pentregat at the comfortable, welcoming *Grange Country House* (☎01239/654121; ❺), a lovely Georgian building in its own grounds.

New Quay

Along with Laugharne in Carmarthenshire, **NEW QUAY** (Cei Newydd) lays claim to being the original Llareggub in *Under Milk Wood* (see p.184). Certainly, it has the little tumbling streets, prim Victorian terraces, cobblestone harbour, pubs and dreamy isolation that **Dylan Thomas** so successfully evoked in his "play for voices", as well, perhaps, as the darkly eccentric characters he excelled in describing. Furthermore, the poet's own experience in New Quay (he and his young family lived here during the last half of World War II) showed him the odder side of human nature. Thomas's metropolitan ways and poetic demeanour did not go down too well in such a close-knit little town, particularly so with an ex-commando officer, fresh home from the war, with whom he had a row in the *Black Lion* pub. The soldier, convinced that his wife was in a *ménage à trois* with Thomas and his wife Caitlin, followed the writer home and shot at his rented bungalow, the *Majoda*, with a machine gun, while the family was inside. The officer was charged with attempted murder in June 1945, and acquitted. Dylan Thomas and family left the area soon afterwards. These days, New Quay is a more orderly place, but perhaps only just so. Summer nights, fuelled by a huddle of pubs and a transient young population, can get boisterously good-natured. It's a great base at any time of the year, with coastal walks, beaches and the odd boat trip to fill the days. **New Year's Eve** here is legendary, when virtually the whole town gets kitted out in fancy dress and spends most of the night locked in the pubs or dancing out in the streets.

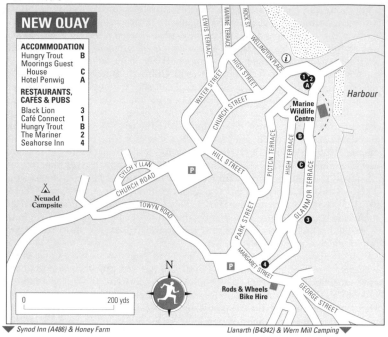

For decades New Quay made little of its Dylan Thomas connection, but has now woken up to the tourism potential and publishes a pair of leaflets: *Dylan Thomas' Ceredigion*, which guides you through local villages where the poet spent time, and the more diverting *Dylan Thomas' New Quay* **walking trail** concentrating on places he lived and his favourite pubs. If nothing else, pop into the *Black Lion* on Glanmor Terrace with its collection of Thomas memorabilia, and *The Seahorse*, known to Thomas as the *Commercial* and the model for *Under Milk Wood's Sailor's Arms*.

The Town and around

New Quay's main road cuts through the upper, residential part of town, past Uplands Square, from where acutely inclined streets swoop down to a pretty **harbour**, formed by its sturdy stone quay, and with a small, curving **main beach**. Back from the sand, the higgledy-piggledy lines of multicoloured shops and houses comprise the **lower town**, the more traditionally seaside part of New Quay, full of standard-issue cafés, pubs and beach shops. A good stop is the **Marine Wildlife Centre** (April–Oct daily 10am–5pm; donation requested), tucked away down the slipway above the main harbour beach, which contains some interesting exhibits on the dolphins, sea birds and seals that inhabit Cardigan Bay. Staff will also point you to the best spots on land from which to see dolphins.

It's easy to escape the town's bustle, such as it is. The northern stretch of beach soon gives way to a rocky headland, **New Quay Head**, where an invigorating path steers along the top of the sheer drops to **Bird Rock**, aptly named for the profusion of razorbills and guillemots nesting here, and beyond to Cwmtydu. A route plan is available from the tourist office (see below).

Dolphin-watching and **fishing** boat trips (see box below) ply the local waters. Courses in **kayaking**, **windsurfing** and **sailing** are offered by New Quay Watersports (℡01545/561257) down by the main beach. **Bike rental** (together with sea fishing equipment) is available from Rods & Wheels on Margaret St (℡01545/560931).

Two miles inland at Cross Inn, the well-signposted **New Quay Honey Farm** (May–Oct daily 10am–5.30pm; £2.95) does a great job of illustrating the life and works of bees, together with chances to sample the honey and mead produced here.

Practicalities

Buses stop at the top end of town on Park Street, from where any roads heading downhill will bring you to the harbour and the **tourist office**, on the corner of Church Street and Wellington Place (April–Sept daily 10am–6pm; ℡01545/560865, ✉newquay@ceredigion.gov.uk). **Accommodation** is patchy: the *Hungry Trout*, above the harbour on South John Street, (℡01545/560680; ❸) has two pleasant rooms; failing that, the *Moorings Guest House* a couple of doors up (℡01545/560375; ❸) is dependable, if nothing special. Down the street towards the harbour, the *Hotel Penwig* (℡01545/560910; ❸) has been nicely refurbished. There's a quiet caravan and tent **campsite** a mile down the B4342 at *Wern Mill* (℡01545/580699; £5-8 per pitch), just outside the lacklustre village of **Gilfachreda**, although the nearest to town is the *Neuadd* (℡01545/560709; £6–10 per pitch), behind the *Penrhiwllan Inn* at the top of the hill on the main road (A486) to Synod Inn.

Several **cafés** huddle around New Quay's harbour, the choicest being *The Mariner*, with its wide range of well-priced dishes, and the adjacent *Café Connect*, which has Internet access and the town's finest coffee. For restaurant food, your best bet is the *Hungry Trout* (see above), with locally caught fish on the menu

---

Dolphins and danger

One of only two pods in Britain, the Cambrian coast's **bottlenosed dolphins** are one of New Quay's major attractions, and can often be seen frolicking by the harbour wall, particularly when the tide is full and the weather calm. A mile-wide strip of the coastal waters forms the Ceredigion Marine Heritage Coast, in summer plied by boat trips geared around potential sightings. The pleasure jaunts run by New Quay Boat Trips, based at The Moorings on Glanmor Terrace (April–Oct daily ℡01545/560800 daytime, 560375 evenings; 1hr £5, 2hr £10), are the cheapest, but chances of a sighting are better on the Wildlife Cruises trips (℡01545/560032; £14 for 2hr, £28 4hr, £48 8hr), which go further offshore and up along the heritage coast on data-gathering exercises. These have a ranger on board and are bookable from the Marine Wildlife Centre (see opposite). Trips from the pier aboard a rigid-hull inflatable are available from the New Quay Boat Company (℡07989/175124): there's the choice of a half-hour fast ride (£9) or ninety-minute fishing trip (£15).

Although this stretch of coast is comparatively clean, Cardigan Bay's sea creatures are in constant danger from PCBs, inadequately treated sewage, monofilament fishing nets and noise from jet skies and powerboats. To get some idea of the results, make an appointment to visit the **Bird and Wildlife Hospital** (℡01545/560462; donations), a couple of miles inland of New Quay at Cross Inn, half a mile down the lane opposite the *Penrhiwgaled Arms*. A voluntary organization working with oil-soaked birds and diseased and injured seals and dolphins, the hospital is run by a team of dedicated volunteers who are usually happy to answer questions and show you their work.

and an imaginative vegetarian selection. Food is good at the *Black Lion*, which also has a great garden overlooking the bay, while the *Seahorse Inn*, on Margaret Street, is easily the town's best **pub**, where you'll find good food, a friendly crowd and regular live music.

Aberaeron and around

After the hugger-mugger streets and salty atmosphere of New Quay, **ABER-AERON**, seven miles up the coast, comes of something of a surprise. It's a sea town that's turned away from the ocean, its colourful Georgian houses preferring to look in on themselves and the town's internal harbour.

Aberaeron's unusual look comes from its odd pedigree, being built in one fell swoop during the early nineteenth century by the Reverend Alban Gwynne. After the 1807 Harbour Act paved the way for port development, Gywnne spent his wife's inheritance dredging the Aeron estuary as a new port for mid-Wales and constructing a formally planned town around it – reputedly from a design by John Nash.

Georgian planning is most evident around the central **Alban Square**, with graceful terraces of quoin-edged buildings and the odd pedimented porch, all writ small in keeping with the Ceredigion coast. From there, the grid of narrow streets stretches away to the sea at **Quay Parade**, the neat line of ordered, colourful houses on the seafront.

Sadly, despite its architectural attractiveness, Aberaeron is almost unique amongst the Ceredigion resorts for its unappealing **beach** – its north end all stones and rubbish, its south end only marginally better. Consequently, the most agreeable activity in Aberaeron is just to amble around the streets and waterfront and graze in its cafés and pubs. Overlooking the harbour, the old Sea Aquarium is the place from which to book **boat trips** around the bay aboard the *Atlantic Leopard* (April–Oct; 1hr for £10; 2hr £20; 3hr £25; book on ☏01545/570142), though these may be discontinued. Off the main road at the southern end of town, a cluster of ageing stone buildings house **Clôs Pengarreg** (summer daily 10am–6pm; rest of year Mon–Fri 10am–4pm), a better than average collection of craft shops.

Stunning (and steep) walks extend along the **cliff path** south to Cei Bach and New Quay – pick up a route plan from the tourist office (see below).

Llanerchaeron

Aberaeron's essential sight lies three miles east along the A482 at **Llaner-chaeron** (house and gardens late March to Oct Wed–Sun 11am–5pm; £5.20; parkland all year dawn–dusk; free; NT), the substantially restored remains of a late eighteenth-century Welsh country estate. Bequeathed to the National Trust in 1989, Llanerchaeron is a remarkable example of a type of holding once common in these parts, and over the last decade or so, a century of gentle decline has been arrested and partially reversed, leaving the Nash-designed main house in pristine shape. The original, mostly Edwardian furnishing and fittings are in place, along with an extensive and eclectic collection of small antiques – glassware, spectacles, fans, etc – amassed by London dealer Pamela Ward who left her life's work to the Trust.

The set-piece rooms only hint that this was someone's home just two decades ago, something better illustrated in the servants' quarters and the serviced courtyard which acted as laundry, dairy, salting room and home brewery. The intention is to have the estate operational as a self-supporting organic farm, and already there's considerable vegetable- and fruit-growing enterprise in the walled garden, a fascinating time capsule of horticultural history, featuring early greenhouses and hotbeds with underground heating styled on Roman hypocausts.

Little around the house is signed, so it is wise to buy the *Short Guide to Llanerchaeron* (£1) or join the weekly **guided tour** (Thurs 1.30pm; £1).

The #X40 bus from Aberaeron to Lampeter passes within half a mile of the site, though you might find it just as easy to ride (or walk) the two miles along the **cycle path** connecting Aberaeron with Llanerchaeron. Apart from a small hill in town, the route is flat, as it follows the old railway line: access is off South Road in Aberaeron.

Practicalities

Buses stop on the A487, here known as Bridge Street, from where it's a five-minute walk along Market Street to the **tourist office** on Quay Parade (July & Aug daily 10am–6pm; Easter–June & Sept daily 10am–5pm; Oct–Easter Mon–Sat 10am–5pm; ☎01545/570602, ✉aberaeron@ceredigion.gov.uk). There is a good supply of decent **accommodation** in and around Aberaeron. Overlooking the harbour on Cadwgan Place are the *Coedmor*, at no. 2 (☎01545/571615, ⓦwww.coedmorbandb.co.uk; ❸) and, better still, the *Arosfa*, at no. 8 (☎01545/570120, ⓦwww.arosfaguesthouse.co.uk; ❹). If money's not a problem, though, the best place in town is the central ☆ *Harbourmaster Hotel*, Pen Cei (☎01545/570755, ⓦwww.harbour-master.com; ❻), with ultra-modern rooms, great breakfasts, endless creature comforts and a relaxed, informal atmosphere.

The closest **campsite** is the *Aeron Coast Caravan Park* (☎01545/570349, £11–15 per pitch), just north of town on the A487, next to the petrol station. Much less fussy is the shoreline site next door at *Drefnewydd Farm* (☎07971/402201; £10 per pitch).

Far and away the best place to **eat** in Aberaeron is the laid-back bistro at the *Harbourmaster Hotel* (see above; closed Sun eve & Mon lunch), with delicious lunches, imaginative evening dishes (mains £13–18) and an abundance of Antipodean wines; it doubles as a convivial bar. Book ahead though: otherwise try the great little *Tŷ Thai* on Regent Street (☎01545/570578). Daytime alternatives include the very good *Hive on the Quay*, Cadwgan Place (☎01545/570445; closed mid-Sept to April), which serves fine local seafood in its airy conservatory, and scrumptious **honey ice cream** to eat in or take away. Of the many cafés in town, *Friends*, in the old post office on Alban Square, is the pick of the bunch.

For **drinking**, there's the *Prince of Wales* on Queen Street, which also offers a meaty menu, the *Monachty Arms* at 7 Market St, with its harbourside beer garden, and the *Black Lion*, Alban Square, which has a good range of guest real ales. A five-minute stroll around town will reveal if there is any live music happening, though the town's finest hour is the annual **Seafood Festival**, held on a Sunday in mid-July, with street entertainment and loads of free food and drink; contact the tourist office for details.

The Teifi Valley

The Teifi is one of Wales' most eulogized rivers – for its rich spawn of fresh fish, its otter population, its meandering rural charm and the coracles that were a regular feature from pre-Roman times – and flows through some gloriously green and undulating countryside to its estuary at Cardigan. Small towns have grown up along its course, each hubs of enterprise and industry in their day, and now pleasant little market towns with a very strong Welsh ambience.

The river is tidal almost as far up as the massive ramparts of **Cilgerran Castle**, and the nearby **Welsh Wildlife Centre**, though it has narrowed appreciably by the time it reaches the rapids at **Cenarth**, four miles beyond. Further upstream, it flows around three sides of another fortress at **Newcastle Emlyn**, and also takes in the quirky university town of **Lampeter**. Beyond here, the river passes through harsher scenery for eleven miles to **Tregaron**, a town Welsh in its language, feel and flavour, and a good base for nearby **Llanddewi Brefi**, with some spectacular walks up into the Abergwesyn Pass (see p.262) and the reedy bogland of **Cors Caron**. The river's infancy can be seen in the solid village of **Pontrhydfendigaid**, famous for its annual eisteddfod, and the nearby ruins of **Strata Florida Abbey**, beyond which the river emerges from the dark and remote **Teifi Pools**.

Cilgerran and the Welsh Wildlife Centre

Just a couple of miles up the Teifi from Cardigan (or a four-mile drive) is the attractive village of **CILGERRAN**. Behind the wide main street are the massive ramparts of the **castle** (daily: April–Oct 9.30am–6.30pm; Nov–March 9.30am–dusk; £2.50; CADW), founded in 1100 at a commanding vantage point on a high wooded bluff above the river, then still navigable for seagoing ships. This is the legendary site of the 1109 abduction of Nest (the "Welsh Helen of Troy") by a lovestruck Prince Owain of Powys. Her husband, Gerald of Pembroke, escaped by slithering down a toilet waste chute through the castle walls.

The massive dual entry towers still dominate the castle, and the outer walls are some four feet thicker than those facing the inner courtyard. Walkways high on the battlements – not for vertigo sufferers – connect with the other towers. The outer ward, over which a modern path now runs from the entrance, is a good example of the evolution of the keepless castle throughout the thirteenth century. Any potential attackers would be waylaid instead by the still-evident ditch and the outer walls and gatehouse, of which only fragmentary remains can be seen. Another ditch and drawbridge pit protect the inner ward underneath the two entry towers.

A footpath runs down from the castle to the river's edge, flanked by display boards telling the story of the emigrants to America, for whom Cardigan was the last sight of home, and the history of the Teifi Valley industries, particularly quarrying, brick-making and coracle fishing. If you want to see coracles in action, the best bet is Cilgerran's fun annual **coracle races**, which take place in August – contact Cardigan tourist office (see p.295) for details.

A mile or so north of Cilgerran, a long driveway leads to the extensive **Teifi Marshes Nature Reserve** (unrestricted access; parking £3), encompassing several important habitats – reed beds, meadows, marshes and untouched oak woodland – for otters, badgers, butterflies and birds, including Wales' largest resident group of Cetti's Warblers. Wandering incongruously amongst the native inhabitants is a herd of **buffalo**, brought in to control invasive bulrushes, and now an attraction in its own right, seen from the various trails which access viewing hides. All is surveyed from the modern timber-and-glass **Welsh Wildlife Centre** (Easter–Oct daily 10.30am–5pm; free), with informative displays and a good, spacious café with expansive views over the reserve. There's an adventure playground to keep the children happy, and three-hour **kayak** or canoe trips (£20; call ☎01239/613961 to book) through a wooded valley upstream as far as Cilgerran Castle.

Though four miles from Cardigan by road, the reserve is only a little over a mile upstream and can be easily reached on foot or bike along a riverside path.

Cenarth

A tourist magnet since the nineteenth century and still chock-full of tearooms and gift shops, **CENARTH**, seven miles upstream from Cardigan, is a pleasant spot, but hardly merits the mass interest it receives. The secret is that the village's main asset, its **rapids**, are close to the main road, ideal for lazy visitors. The low but attractive cataracts are a result of the Teifi being split by rocks as it tumbles and churns its way over the craggy limestone. The path to the rapids runs from opposite the *White Hart* pub and past the **National Coracle Centre** (Easter–Oct daily except Sat 10.30am–5.30pm; £3; other times by appointment on ☎01239/710980), a small museum with intriguing displays of original coracles from all over the world, half of them from Wales. The adjacent *Three Horseshoes* pub serves good beer and bar meals, though there's an even better range of food and real ales at the *Nag's Head*, two miles southwest along the B4332 at Aber-Cych.

Newcastle Emlyn and around

An ancient farming and droving centre, **NEWCASTLE EMLYN** (Castell Newydd Emlyn) still retains a robustly agricultural feel, particularly on Fridays, the busy and bellowing market day. The swooping meander of the Teifi River made the site a natural defensive position, first built on by the Normans. The "new" **castle**, of which only a few stone stacks and an archway survive, replaced their fortress in the mid-thirteenth century. Although the ruins aren't impressive, the site, surrounded on three sides by the river flowing through a valley of grazing sheep and rugby fields, is gently uplifting and quintessentially Welsh. The castle is tucked away at the bottom of dead-end Castle Terrace, which peels off the main street by a squat little stone **market hall**, topped by a curiously phallic cupola. Unsurprisingly, Bridge Street (Heol yr Bont), heads down from here to the stone bridge over the Teifi. That's about it for sights, but there are at least some great pubs and decent enough places to eat, and with its strong sense of community, eclectic range of shops, unhurried charm and fabulous scenery, Newcastle Emlyn is a decent base from which to explore the surrounding area.

Practicalities

There's no tourist office in town, but posters everywhere will give you the lowdown on local events. The town website (ⓦwww.newcastle-emlyn.com) has some good stuff on it; there's free Internet access at the library on Church Lane, which spurs off Bridge Street opposite the market hall.

The only real **hotel** in town is the *Emlyn Arms* on Bridge Street (☎01239/710317, ⓦwww.emlynarmshotel.co.uk; ❹), an old coaching inn with comfortable modern rooms. Further out, the *Maes-y Derw* guesthouse (☎01239/710860; ❸), half a mile towards Cardigan on the A484, has spacious Edwardian rooms, a restaurant and private fishing.

The best place to **eat and drink** is the deservedly popular *Bunch of Grapes*, a stylish bar on Bridge Street, with guest real ales and live Celtic music most Thursdays in summer. Next door, the cosy *Blue Bell* bistro is a good bet for fresh fish and has a weekly Thai night on Tuesdays. Straightforward boozing is best at the *Ivy Bush*, a gnarled old local on Emlyn Square.

Museum of the Welsh Woollen Industry

The lower Teifi's prolific past as a weaving centre is best seen in the village of **DREFACH FELINDRE**, five miles southeast of Newcastle Emlyn. At the beginning of the twentieth century, this was at the heart of the Welsh wool trade, with 43 working mills in and around the village. One of these, the Cambrian Mills, has been turned into the National Museum's customarily excellent **Museum of the Welsh Woollen Industry** (daily: April-Sept 10am–5pm; Oct–March Tues- Sat 10am–5pm; free). The museum takes the visitor through the whole process – from the different wools produced by Wales' eleven million sheep, through working presses and looms to stunning examples of the finished flannels, shawls and blankets. Throughout, museum staff working the machines, video footage and informative wall displays put the industry into its social and cultural contexts. There's also a real working mill, the *Melin Teifi* (generally Mon–Fri 10am–4pm), on site, which sells its produce. The museum is at the hub of twenty miles of paths, packed into a two-mile radius, along which workers walked to the mills. Regular buses (#460/461) between Cardigan and Carmarthen, via Newcastle Emlyn, pass nearby.

Llandysul and Llanybydder

The pace slows down even further as the lanes reach **LLANDYSUL**, sitting pretty above the Teifi some eight miles east of Newcastle Emlyn. Two main streets run parallel through the village, the lower one brushing past the massive Early English-style **church of St Tysul**. Two centuries back, the church porch served as a goalpost in the annual match of *cnapan*, an anarchic and extremely rough, day-long football-like game that ran the length of the village. Inside the church, there's an inscribed altar stone, thought to date from the sixth century, in the Lady Chapel.

Most of Llandysul's shops and pubs are on the upper main street, which changes name four times in a couple of hundred yards. If you want to **stay**, the *King's Arms* on that street (℡01559/362265; ❷) is good.

While Llandysul's fortnightly livestock market (Tues) is a reminder of the area's strong agricultural pedigree, the biggest, smelliest reminder comes in the shape of the monthly **horse market** in the otherwise sleepy village of **LLANYBYDDER** (sometimes anglicized to Llanybyther on old road signs), some ten miles east of Llandysul along the Teifi. Held on the last Thursday of every month, the market is one of the biggest in Britain, bringing buyers and sellers together from all over. Amongst the hubbub of spoken Welsh and English, together with the noise of neighing horses, there's little to remind you that you're in the twenty-first century.

Lampeter

Five miles further along the Teifi from Llanybydder, the old-fashioned town of **LAMPETER** (Llanbedr Pont Steffan, often known as Llambed) is best known as a remote outpost of the British university system. St David's University College was Wales' first, founded in 1822 by the Bishop of St David's to aid Welsh theological students who could not afford to travel to England for their education; it only became part of the University of Wales in the 1970s. Though the town has less than three thousand residents, it's an eclectic mix of current students, graduates who forgot to leave, the obligatory hippies and a multitude of farmers.

While Lampeter is a lively town with frequent gigs and theatre performances, there's not a great deal to actually see, and what you are able to visit is fairly low-key. A decent heritage trail, with plaques marking out historical places of interest, is accompanied by a leaflet that you can pick up at the library (see below). The town's three main streets – High, Bridge and College – meet at **Harford Square**, named after the local landowning family who were responsible for the construction of the early nineteenth-century **Falcondale Hall**, now an opulent hotel, on the northern approach to Lampeter.

The main buildings of the **University College** lie off College Street, and include C.B. Cockerell's original stuccoed quadrangle of buildings, dating from 1827 and modelled along the lines of an Oxbridge college. Tucked right underneath the main buildings, the motte of Lampeter's long-vanished **castle** forms an incongruous mound amidst such order. On the other side of Harford Square, the High Street is the most architecturally distinguished part of town, its eighteenth-century coaching inn, the *Black Lion*, dominating the streetscape; you can see its old stables and coach house through an archway. Go through the archway of the former town hall and past the Somerfield supermarket to reach the **library** (Mon 9am–4pm, Tues 2–6pm, Wed 10am–noon, Thurs 2–5pm, Fri 1–4pm, Sat 10am–1pm), its foyer containing a supply of local tourism leaflets and a minute civic **museum** (free), mainly comprising curly old photographs of the town. You can also get there from Harford Square by taking the alley by the Spar shop.

Practicalities

Leaflets in the library foyer (see above) are the closest Lampeter gets to a tourist office, though notice boards in the *Mulberry Bush* wholefood shop at 2 Bridge St carry information about local B&Bs and longer lets. For central **accommodation** try: *Haulfan*, 6 Station Terrace (T01570/422718, Wwww.haulfanguesthouse .co.uk; ❷), a good B&B behind University College; the recently refurbished *Black Lion* on High Street (T01570/422490; ❹), or Best Western's Italianate *Falcondale Mansion Hotel* (T01570/422910, Wwww.falcondalehotel.com; ❻), a Victorian pile surrounded by fourteen acres of parkland located a third of a mile west along High Street then twice that along a long drive.

The best places to stay, though, lie slightly out of town. *Pentre Farm* (T01570/493313; ❸), near Llanfair Clydogau, five miles north of Lampeter, offers very comfortable rooms in a former carthouse and tasty evening meals (£9–12) on a working farm. Best of all is the hospitable ✴ *Abermuerig Mansion* (T01570/470216, Wwww.abermuerig-mansion.co.uk; ❸), an early eighteenth-century squire's manor house surrounded by formal lawns, woodland inhabited by red kites and a stretch of the River Aeron where there's private trout fishing. Inside, the period furniture includes ancient (but firmly upholstered) half-tester and four-poster beds. It's over seven miles northwest of Lampeter and equally handy for Aberaeron. If you're more interested in self-catering **holiday cottage** accommodation in these parts, look no further than the superb collection of beautifully restored properties run by *Under the Thatch* (T01239/851410, Wwww.underthethatch.co.uk); as the name suggests, three are traditional Ceredigion thatched cottages (from £200 a week), but there's also a Romany caravan (from £175 a week) and an outrageous 1970s woodland "love shack" (from £200 a week) for rent: lets are weekly or half-weekly.

Lampeter's restaurant scene is fairly lacklustre, though there's decent daytime **eating** at the *Sosban Fach*, 1 Bridge St, opposite the classy chippy *Lloyds*, which stays open until 9pm. In the evenings, it's either pub food (the *King's Head* on Bridge Street is best) or the *Shapla* on College Street, which does the best curries for miles around. Make sure you at least stick your head into *Conti's Café* on Harford Square – the food is cheap and none too spectacular, but the surroundings are wonderfully decayed, plastered with ageing accolades for the café's rich homemade ice cream.

Drinking is better, with the friendly and fairly studenty *King's Head* on Bridge Street serving very well-kept beer, and the *Cwmann Tavern*, half a mile up the road out of town, which is the best local bet for beery **live music** gigs and sessions. A further half-mile up the hill is the excellent *Ram Inn*, a sixteenth-century drovers' inn that wins national accolades for its real ales and convivial atmosphere.

The Lampeter area is rich in festivals, groups and **women's events** – check notice boards (see above) or the website of August's Women in Tune music camp (Ⓦ www.womenintune.org.uk).

Tregaron and around

On the cusp of the lush Teifi Valley and the gloomy moors rising above it, the neat small town of **TREGARON**, ten miles northeast of Lampeter, is an enchanting spot. It feels almost untouched by the twenty-first century, and remains a bastion of the Welsh language and culture in an area that has experienced galloping anglicization over recent decades.

All roads to Tregaron lead into the spruced-up market square, hemmed in by solid eighteenth- and nineteenth-century buildings, of which the most impressive is the **Talbot Hotel**, a classically symmetrical old drovers' inn. The square and the inn were the very last points of civilization seen by drovers before heading out of town on the wild Abergwesyn Pass (see p.292), which rises above the Tregaron en route to Llanwrtyd Wells and beyond. The **statue** in the centre of the square is of Tregaron-born Henry Richard (1812–88), the founder of the Peace Union, forerunner of the League of Nations and, subsequently, the United Nations. On the corner of the market square and Dewi Road (the B4343 to Llanddewi Brefi) is the **Rhiannon Welsh Gold Centre**, a classy shop stocking jewellery in Celtic designs fashioned partly from Welsh gold and other materials. Overlooking the square is the squat bulk of the much-restored **St Caron church**, which sits in a large, circular churchyard – an indication that the religious settlement here predates Christianity.

It is a hundred yards along Dewi Road to the community-run **Tregaron Red Kite Centre and Museum** (April–Sept daily 10.30am–4.30pm; Oct–March Sat & Sun noon–4pm; donation requested), housed in an old Victorian school and exhibiting an eclectic mixture of local memorabilia, much inevitably drawn from the area's farming tradition.

The river running through the middle of Tregaron is the Brennig, a babbling tributary of the Teifi which meanders through a wide, flat valley into the eerie wetland of **Cors Caron** (Tregaron Bog), two miles north. This national nature reserve of peat bog is one of the most prodigious wildlife areas in Wales, home to rare marsh grasses, black adders, buzzards and red kites. There's a limited walkway along the disused rail line, but to really see the bog you'll need to follow the three-mile circuit along both the railway and the river; call the Countryside Council for Wales warden (Ⓣ 01974/298480, Ⓦ www.ccw.gov.uk) to reserve the necessary permit; it can be sent to you by post or collected in Tregaron.

Practicalities

Buses arrive at the market square, by the Henry Richard statue. There's no tourist office, but the Rhiannon Welsh Gold Centre and the Kite Centre (see both above) have leaflets and can provide some assistance. Local **accommodation** is severely limited, though the *Talbot Hotel* on the square (℡01974/298208; ❸) is good. A more atmospheric bet is the remote Blaencaron **YHA bunkhouse hostel** (April–Sept; ℡0870/770 5700, ⒺReservations@yha.org.uk), three miles east and perfectly positioned for walks on the towering moorland above a tiny stream, the Nant-y-groes Fawr; beds cost £10. Otherwise head a mile and a half northwest on the A485 to *Neuaddlas* guesthouse (℡01974/298965; ❷), or five miles south to *Pentre Farm* (see p.305).

Options for **eating** are few, but decent. In the daytime, pick from delicious homemade local specialities in ⚑ *Tŷ Sara Bara* on Heol Dewi, just off the square. For evening food, the *Talbot Arms* is perfectly adequate, though you're better off visiting the *Black Lion* six miles northeast in Pontrhydfendigaid (see overleaf).

For plain **drinking**, hit *Y Llew Coch* (The Red Lion) by the river bridge, a youthful pub with a pool table and bar games, but the *Talbot* excels with live roots music (folk, blues and so on), often featuring surprisingly big names (details Ⓦwww.cambriaarts.org.uk).

Llanddewi Brefi

Heol Dewi, the road from Tregaron runs three miles south past a cottage hospital and along the Teifi to the gorgeous little village of **LLANDDEWI BREFI**, latterly famous as the fictitious home of the "only gay in the village" from the BBC comedy *Little Britain*. Souvenir T-shirts nodding to this unlikely notoriety are available in the village shop.

Llanddewi Brefi's previous claim to fame was the legend of a convocation of 118 Welsh churchmen meeting here in 519 AD and summoning Dewi Sant (Saint David). On appearing, Dewi began to speak to the men, but had trouble being heard, until the ground beneath him shuddered ominously and suddenly rose, giving him a natural platform from which he was able to continue speaking – the massive **parish church** of St David sits on the mound to this day. Part of the church wall consists of two discernible stones inscribed with fragments of Latin script. These were originally part of a single memorial that dated from within a century of David's death – the first recorded mention of the Welsh patron saint – but they were broken up by an illiterate eighteenth- or nineteenth-century mason. Either of the village's two **pubs** – the *Foelallt Arms* and the ancient *New Inn* – are great places to booze away an evening.

Pontrhydfendigaid, Strata Florida and the Teifi Pools

Six miles northeast of Tregaron, the last village on the Teifi is austere **PONT-RHYDFENDIGAID** ("Bridge near the ford of the Blessed Virgin"), a grey-stoned cluster remarkable for its annual May eisteddfod in the enormous village pavilion, recently rebuilt and accommodating up to 3000 spectators. The infant Teifi flows in from the east, followed by a road that, after a mile, reaches the atmospheric ruins of the mighty **Strata Florida Abbey** (May–Sept daily 10am–5pm; £2; Oct–April unrestricted entry), originally located in Ystrad Fflur, "the valley of the flowers" two miles away, but relocated in its early years to this equally bucolic spot. This Cistercian abbey was founded in 1164, swiftly growing into a centre for milling, farming and weaving, and becoming an important political centre for Wales. In 1238, a dying Llywelyn the Great, fearful that his work of unifying Wales under one ruler would disintegrate, summoned the lesser Welsh princes here to command them to pay homage to his son, Dafydd.

The church here was vast – larger than the cathedral at St David's and although very little survived Henry VIII's dissolution of the monasteries, the huge, Norman west doorway gives some idea of its dimensions. Fragments one-time side chapels include beautifully tiled medieval floors, and there's also a serene cemetery, but it's really the abbey's position that impresses most, in glorious rural solitude against wide open skies and fringed with a scoop of sheep-spattered hills. A yew tree in the neighbouring graveyard shades the spot where Dafydd ap Gwilym (see p.313), fourteenth-century bard and contemporary of Chaucer, is said to be buried.

The narrow lane running due east from Strata Florida leads to Tyncwm, a farm with bridleways to the drenched grass and craggy outcrops around the **Teifi Pools**, a series of sombre lakes where the Teifi River rises. This is stern, but rewarding, walking country where you may be tempted to strike out over the rocky, squelchy moorland down to the Claerwen Reservoir (see p.269). More direct access to the pools can be had from the lane that forks off the B4343 in the village of **Ffair-Rhos**, a mile north of Pontrhydfendigaid.

The best bet for **accommodation**, **eating** and **drinking** in the area is Pont-rhydfendigaid's ﾈ *Llew Du* (Black Lion) pub (☎01974/831624, ⓦblacklionhotel .co.uk; ❹), which is particularly welcoming to cyclists and walkers and has a roaring fire when the weather cools.

Aberystwyth

The liveliest seaside resort in Wales, and capital of the sparsely populated middle of the country, bustling **ABERYSTWYTH** is an essential stop along the Ceredigion coast. With one of the most prestigious colleges of the University of Wales and the National Library both in the town, there are plenty of cultural and entertainment diversions here, as well as an array of Victorian and Edwardian seaside trappings. As a town firmly rooted in all aspects of Welsh culture, it's an enjoyable and relaxed place to gain a clear insight into the national psyche. Historically, Aberystwyth has always been a little anti-establishment, and its anarchic soul shines through in many diverse ways. Pubs – and there are loads – stay

△ Aberystwyth

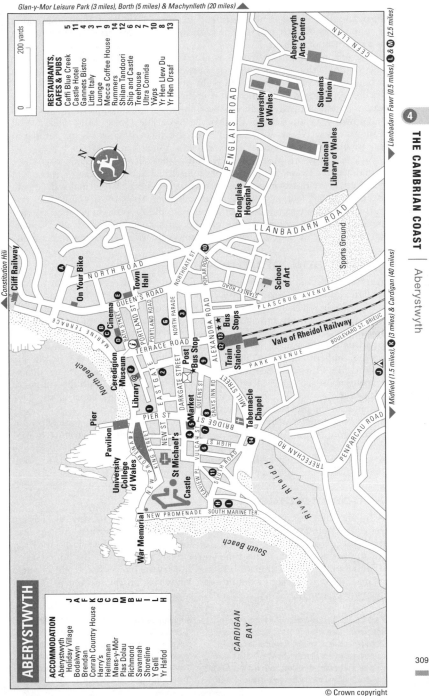

Glan-y-Mor Leisure Park (3 miles), Borth (5 miles) & Machynlleth (20 miles) ▲

Llanbadarn Fawr (0.5 miles), ⓁⒷ & Ⓜ (2.5 miles) ▶

Midfield (1.5 miles), Ⓚ (3 miles) & Cardigan (40 miles) ▶

ABERYSTWYTH

ACCOMMODATION

Aberystwyth Holiday Village	J
Bodalwyn	A
Brendan	F
Conrah Country House	K
Harry's	G
Heimsman	C
Maes-y-Môr	D
Plas Dolau	M
Richmond	B
Savannah	E
Shoreline	I
Y Gelli	L
Yr Hafod	H

RESTAURANTS, CAFES & PUBS

Caffi Blue Creek	5
Castle Hotel	11
Gannets Bistro	4
Little Italy	3
Lounge	1
Mecca Coffee House	9
Rummers	14
Shilam Tandoori	12
Ship and Castle	6
Treehouse	2
Ultra Comida	7
Ywps	10
Yr Hen Llew Du	8
Yr Hen Orsaf	13

0   200 yards

4

309

© Crown copyright

open late, the political scene is distinctly green-tinged and radically Welsh, and in a country that still struggles to cope with an inherent conservatism, Aberystwyth is a salty blast of fresh air.

The precursor of Aberystwyth is the inland village of **Llanbadarn Fawr**, the seat of Wales' oldest bishopric between the sixth and eighth centuries, whose massive parish church still reeks of past power. Aberystwyth and Llanbadarn grew together around the church and the seafront thirteenth-century castle, minting its own coins and becoming a major headquarters for Owain Glyndŵr's revolutionaries in the Middle Ages. The *Cymdeithas yr Iaith* (Welsh Language Society) was founded in Aberystwyth in 1963 and is still located in the town, and the National Library was established here in 1907.

As a seaside resort, Aberystwyth is hard to beat. Two long, gentle bays curve round between twin rocky heads: Constitution Hill to the north, and Pen Dinas to the south above the town harbour's marina, where both the Rheidol and Ystwyth rivers end their journeys through the valleys of Aberystwyth's hinterland (see p.315). The town rises up towards the east from the flat plains in between the two, peaking at Penglais, where the graceful Portland stone buildings of the National Library and the modernist blocks of the university gaze over the town's rooftops.

Arrival and information

Aberystwyth's twin **train stations** (one for main-line trains and one for the Vale of Rheidol line) are adjacent to each other on Alexandra Road, a ten-minute walk from the seafront on the southeastern side of the town centre. **Local buses** stop outside the main-line station, with **long-distance** ones thirty yards to the north along Alexandra Road. In addition, Aberystwyth acts as the hub of three **postbus** services that penetrate the town's hinterland. One service runs inland up the southern side of the Vale of Rheidol to Devil's Bridge, Cwmystwyth and towards the Elan Valley (see p.268); a second follows the Vale's northern side to Capel Bangor and Capel Dewi; and the third runs southeast into the villages of Llangwyryfon and Blaenpennal. All leave from Chalybeate Street at the back entrance to the post office at around 7.30am and 2.30pm.

The busy **tourist office** (July & Aug daily 10am–6pm, Sept–June Mon–Sat 10am–5pm; ℡01970/612125, Ⓔaberystwythtic@ceredigion.gov.uk) is a ten-minute stroll from Alexandra Road, straight down Terrace Road towards the seafront: staff will help with accommodation and can sell you tickets for local events. Bike rental, Internet access and more are listed on p.315.

Accommodation

As in all major seaside towns, there are dozens of **places to stay**, so beds are generally quite reasonable and easy to find, though everywhere fills up over graduation week, which usually falls in the second or third week of July. Even if you can find a room at this time you're likely to pay above the odds. Guesthouses and B&Bs predominate, but there are several budget hotels and a couple of nice, more upmarket establishments. Anywhere on the seafront is likely to charge a premium.

Hotels and guesthouses

Bodalwyn Queens Ave ℡01970/612578, Ⓦwww .bodalwyn.co.uk. A spacious, stylishly decorated guesthouse where all rooms have well-appointed en-suite bathrooms. Breakfast is served in a sunny conservatory and special diets are catered for. ❹

Brendan 19 Marine Terrace ℡01970/612252, Ⓔivor.williams@virgin.net. One of the better budget seafront guesthouses; most rooms have sea views and many have en-suite bathrooms. ❸

Conrah Country House Rhydgaled, Chancery ℡01970/617941, Ⓦwww.conrah.co.uk. Elegant

Georgian country-house hotel four miles south of town along the A487, with luxurious rooms, comfortable lounges, sauna, heated indoor pool and superb restaurant, all set amid 22 acres of beautifully tended grounds. ❽

Harry's 40–46 North Parade ☏01970/612647, ⓦwww.harrysaberystwyth.com. The best of the mid-range places, converted from four terraced houses in the heart of town and with a very good restaurant and bar downstairs. All rooms are en-suite and some have recently been remodelled. ❻

Helmsman 43 Marine Terrace ☏ & ⒻF01970/624132, Ⓔhelmsman_ guesthouse@hotmail.com. Tall seafront guesthouse in the middle of the curving Promenade. Book early for a sea view. ❹

Richmond 44–45 Marine Terrace ☏01970/612201, ⓦwww.richmondhotel.uk.com. Comfortable, family-run seafront hotel, with a full complement of en-suite rooms, plus a restaurant, bar and small garden. ❻

Savannah 27 Queens Rd ☏01970/615131, ⓦwww.savannahguesthouse.co.uk. Well-priced guesthouse close to the town centre and with some en-suite rooms. ❸

Shoreline 6 South Marine Terrace ☏01970/615002. About the cheapest guesthouse in town; slightly dingy but still bright enough and with sea views from some rooms. ❷

Y Gelli at *Plas Dolau*, Lovesgrove ☏01970/617834, ⓦwww.dolau-holidays.co.uk. Comfortable B&B three miles east of town along the A44, with rooms (one with spa bath) in a modern Scandinavian-style house and others next door at the *Plas Dolau* hostel (see below). Some en-suite rooms. ❸/❹

Yr Hafod 1 South Marine Terrace ☏01970/617579, Ⓔjohnyrhafod@aol.com.

Spacious, well-maintained and tastefully decorated guesthouse south of the castle; the best of the bunch on the seafront. ❸

Hostels, campsites and self-catering

Aberystwyth Holiday Village Penparcau Rd ☏01970/624211. A 10-min walk over the Trefechan River bridge and up the hill, this is the closest campsite to town – large and family-oriented with restaurant, bar and amusements. From £10 per pitch.

Glan-y-mor Leisure Park Clarach Bay ☏01970/828900. The best of the caravan parks in Clarach Bay, on the other side of Constitution Hill, to the north of Aberystwyth. It has caravans for rent and tent pitches. £12 per pitch.

Maes-y-Môr 25 Bath St ☏01970/639270. With adjoining launderette, this is a brightly painted and very central hostel with a good guests' kitchen. The mostly twin rooms are let at £15 per person, and at busy times lone travellers may be required to share.

Midfield Southgate, Penparcau ☏01970/612542. Pleasant family campsite just off the A4120 (A487) a couple of miles south of town. Free showers and games area. £12–13 per pitch.

Plas Dolau (see above). Well-run hostel, specializing in groups, in a characterful Victorian mansion. The bunks (£14) come equipped with linen and there are extensive cooking facilities. ❶

University of Wales Penglais ☏01970/621960, ⓦwww.aber.ac.uk/visitors. Single-bed rooms in eight-room self-contained flats go for £17.50 a night during the university's summer recess (mid-June to mid-Sept). Bed linen is supplied, there are full cooking facilities and you get free access to the university facilities, including two sports halls and a heated pool.

The Town

On a warm summer afternoon there's nothing better than strolling along the increasingly spruced up **Promenade**, where waves lap the jagged tideline rocks and beach. Stroll from **Constitution Hill** with its **cliff railway** right along to the **castle ruins** before nipping through town to the **Vale Of Rheidol Railway** or up to the **National Library** and university.

Along the Prom

The 430-foot **Constitution Hill** (Y Graig Glais) overshadows the northern end of the long Promenade, where it rises sharply away from the rocky beach. The focal point of genteel Victorian pursuits, it is accessible on foot, but if you don't fancy the invigorating walk up, you can take the clanking 1896 **cliff railway** (daily: July & Aug 10am–6pm, mid-March to June, Sept & Oct 10am–5pm; £2.50 return) from the grand terminus building at the top of Queen's Road, behind the Promenade. Once water-balanced, it is now electrically driven and creeps up the crooked tracks at just over walking pace.

The summit is crowned with a tatty jumble of amenities that include a café, picnic area, telescopes and an octagonal **camera obscura** (hours as for railway; free), a device popular in the pre-TV era using a mirror and hefty lens to project close-up and long-shot views over the town, the surrounding mountains and bays, plus a vista of the hordes of caravans to the north, looking like legions of tanks poised for battle. The existing structure was built in the 1980s on the ground plan of the original, but expanded to make it the largest of its type in the world.

From the bottom of Constitution Hill, the **Promenade** – officially Marine Terrace – arcs away to the south, past ornate benches decorated with snakes, a continuous wall of hotels and guesthouses, a prim bandstand and a shingle beach. Terrace Road peels off to the left after a couple of hundred yards, almost immediately reaching the tourist office and the **Amgeuddfa Ceredigion** (Ceredigion Museum), atmospherically housed in the ornate Edwardian Coliseum music hall (Mon–Sat 10am–5pm; free). Mementos of the building as a theatre and cinema give a sense of place to an otherwise disparate collection, on three floors, including cosy reconstructed cottages, dairies complete with all manner of separating and churning equipment, a nineteenth-century pharmacy, exhibits on the local geology and a surprisingly interesting look at the history of weights and measures.

Marine Terrace continues round to the spindly **pier**, beyond which a John Nash-designed turreted **villa** dominates the seafront. Dating from 1790, the villa was massively extended in the 1860s, as a hotel designed to soak up the anticipated masses arriving on the new rail line. The venture failed, though, and in 1872, it was sold to the fledgling university, whose property it remains. The Promenade cuts around the front of the building to a rocky headland, where the **castle** ruins (unrestricted access) stare blankly out to sea. Built by Edward I as part of his conquest of Wales, the thirteenth-century fortress is more notable for its breezy position than for the buildings themselves, of which the two outer gates are the most impressive remains. South of the castle is the quieter, sandy beach along South Marine Terrace, which peters out by the wide **harbour**, the mouth of the Rheidol and Ystwyth rivers. The quietest beach of all is further south still, across the other side of the rivers' mouth, at **Tanybwlch**. Rising high over the shingle strand is the Iron Age hillfort of **Pen Dinas** (413ft), crowned with what looks like a chimney, actually an 1853 memorial to the Duke of Wellington. Paths snake their way to the top from the car park at Tanybwlch or from opposite the *Aberystwyth Holiday Village* on Penparcau Road.

The rest of town

A couple of blocks inland from the Promenade, you'll find the terminus of the **Vale of Rheidol Railway** (see p.315), next to the main-line train station on Alexandra Road. A hundred yards north of the station, Stanley Road forks off to the right, leading down to the splendid **School of Art** (Mon–Fri 10am–5pm; free) at Buarth Mawr. Originally bequeathed to the university by the Davies sisters of Gregynog Hall (see p.278), this impressive Edwardian building, topped with a distinctive cupola, has been the home of the art department since 1995. The public galleries on the ground floor house both touring exhibitions and those culled from the university's extensive permanent collection, with an emphasis on Welsh art.

North Parade meets up with Queen's Road at the bottom of Northgate Street; the latter winds east, becoming Penglais Road as it climbs the hill towards the university's main campus and the **National Library of Wales** (Mon–Sat 9.30am–5pm; free; ⓦwww.llgc.org.uk), an essential and enjoyable stop for anyone with an interest in matters Welsh. Housed in a massive white stone Edwardian building overlooking the town, the library's fine manuscripts include the oldest extant Welsh text, the twelfth-century *Black Book of Carmarthen*, and the earliest manuscript of The Mabinogion. Temporary exhibitions are held in the corridors near the entrance, the upstairs Gregynog Gallery and the downstairs Peniarth Gallery, and are invariably excellent. Elements of the library's permanent collection of books, manuscripts and papers are also on display, most notably in the exhibition downstairs, the **World of the Book**, which looks at the history of the written word and publishing in Wales. Free tickets need to be obtained in advance for entry into the **Reading Rooms**, which boast an enormous range of texts, maps, photos and documents, including, as one of the UK's six copyright libraries, copies of every new book published in Britain. Download and print an application form for a Reader's Ticket from the library website, or turn up and fill in the form in person. Either way, you'll need two forms of validating ID, including one that shows your current address. The National Library is also home to the impressive new exhibition and perform-ance space, the **Drwm**.

While in the Penglais area, you might want to check out the excellent **Aber-ystwyth Arts Centre**, a quarter of a mile further up the hill from the National Library in the middle of the university's main campus. A curious mix of 1960s brutalism and postmodern elegance, the Arts Centre is a great place to while away an hour or two, taking in the various temporary art and ceramics exhibi-tions, browsing the designer crafts and book shops, catching a movie or enjoy-ing a drink in the café, which affords sublime views over the town and bay.

Llanbadarn Fawr

A mile inland from the main resort is **LLANBADARN FAWR**, the original settlement from which Aberystwyth grew. Barely distinct from Aberystwyth proper, it's a fairly humdrum knot of busy roads that would warrant little attention were it not for the stunning sight of the massive **St Padarn parish church**. Today's structure was completely rebuilt in the thirteenth century, but religious association with the spot goes back to the Breton St Padarn establish-ing a monastic settlement here in the second half of the sixth century, decades before even St Augustine's mission to the English of 597 AD.

Inside the church, opposite the main door, hangs an enlargement of a page from *Rhygyfarch's Psalter* of 1079, one example of the beautifully decorated texts for which the monks of Llanbadarn became renowned. In the south transept, there's a fascinating exhibition on St Padarn's monastic foundation and the area's history that includes two beautiful tenth-century crosses, moved inside from the churchyard in 1916. The taller one, about eight feet high, is woven with exquisite Celtic tracery. Perhaps the most entertaining part of the exhibi-tion deals with poet Dafydd ap Gwilym (c. 1320–70) and his upbringing in Llanbadarn parish. His poem *Merched Llanbadarn*, the Women of Llanbadarn, tells of his frustration at sitting in the church watching the beautiful parish girls, as this opening extract demonstrates:

Plygu rhag llid yr ydwyf,
Pla ar holl ferched y plwyf!
Am na chefais, drais drawsgoed,
Onaddun'yr un erioed,
Na morwyn fwyn ofynaig,

Na merch fach, na gwrach, na gwraig.
Passion doubles me over,
Plague take all the parish girls!
Because, frustrated trysting,
I've had not a single one.
No lovely, longed-for virgin,
Not a wench nor witch nor wife.

Eating, drinking and entertainment

Aberystwyth's cultural and gastronomic life is an ebullient, all-year-round affair, thriving on students in term time and visitors in the summer. As well as a varied range of **pubs** and **restaurants**, the town is a good place to hear Welsh **music** and a lively centre for theatre and cinema. For a slice of Edwardian gentility, take afternoon tea in any of the seafront hotels along the Promenade. Daytime **café** culture is booming in the town centre.

Restaurants and cafés

Caffi Blue Creek St James Square. Relaxed small daytime café with comfy sofas and cheerful vibe. Open until 7pm Mon–Fri.

Gannets Bistro 7 St James Square ☎01970/617164. Small and long-established restaurant reliably producing delicious and imaginative dishes from local farm and sea produce. Open Wed–Sat.

Harry's 40–46 North Parade ☎01970/612647. One of the best restaurants in town, though not overly formal, serving the likes of salmon and prawn rillette (£4.50) and roasted half duck (£14.50), with a board of daily specials.

Little Italy 51 North Parade ☎01970/625707. Cosy and popular little pasta and pizza restaurant with most mains £6–10. Good seafood antipasti too.

Lounge 31 Pier St ☎01970/626444. Student-oriented bar-cum-bistro with decent atmosphere and a dependable menu of good-value steaks, burgers, salads and bruschetta. Closed Sun & Mon.

Mecca Coffee House 26 Chalybeate St. Comfy sofas, daily papers and Aberystwyth's best espresso coffee, along with a range of savoury dishes and tasty cakes.

Shilam Tandoori Station Building, Alexandra Rd ☎01970/615015. Superb modern Indian restaurant with unusual specialities and good vegetarian choices.

Treehouse 14 Baker St ☎01970/615791. Upbeat, mostly vegetarian organic food shop and restaurant, good for vegetarian rissoles, pizza slices, fruit smoothies, good coffee and a range of daily specials. Closed Sun.

Ultra Comida 3 Bridge St. Small, classy deli specializing in cheese, olives, Spanish tortilla, stuffed baguettes, panini, smoothies and very good coffee, all to take away or consume downstairs where there's a sofa, music and newspapers.

Pubs

Castle Hotel 37 South Rd. Pub built in the style of an ornate Victorian gin palace. Live local bands at weekends and a good bar menu with vegetarian specialities.

Rummers Bridge St, by the River Rheidol bridge. Late-opening, popular pub and wine bar with sawdust on the floor, outside seating by the river and live music Thurs–Sun.

Ship and Castle cnr of Vulcan and High streets. Nautical-style bar, with a good range of beer, cider and food. Hosts regular Welsh and Irish folk music, best on Wed.

Y Cŵps (*Coopers Arms*), Llanbadarn Rd. Firmly Welsh local; fun and friendly, with regular folk and jazz nights and jam sessions.

Yr Hen Lew Du (*The Old Black Lion*), Bridge St. Boisterous, very Welsh and hugely enjoyable pub. Easily the best place in Aberystwyth to catch an international match on the big screen.

Yr Hen Orsaf Alexandra Rd. Part of the Wetherspoons chain, well sited in a large section of the train station with outside seating on the platform. Cheap drinks, non-smoking areas and decent bar meals at good prices.

Entertainment

Aberystwyth Arts Centre the University, Penglais ☎01970/623232, ⓦwww.aber.ac.uk/artscentre. The town's main venue for arthouse cinema, touring theatre, classes, events and wide-ranging temporary exhibitions. From late July through August there's always some kind of musical extravaganza on.

Commodore Cinema Bath St ☎01970/612421. Screens mainstream current releases.

Drwm National Library, Penglais ☎01970/632548. Funky new centre for film, lectures and concerts.

Listings

Banks Most major banks are along Great Darkgate Street and North Parade.

Bike rental Summit Cycles, 65 North Parade (☎01970/626061), is the best spot for spares, bike repair and info about local rides and off-road trails, but bike rental is only available from On Your Bike in the Old Police Yard, Queen's Road (Mon–Fri 9am–5.30pm, Sat 10am–5.30pm; ☎01970/626996), which charges a bargain £10 a day for rigid mountain bikes and also rents out tandems.

Books Siop y Pethe, on North Parade, has a huge array of Welsh-interest books, magazines and music in both Welsh and English. There is also a good bookshop in the Aberystwyth Arts Centre, though Galloway, on Pier Street, has a wider range. Ystwyth Books, near the Market Hall on Princess Street, buys and sells second-hand books.

Internet access Free access at the public library (see below) and low-cost connections during business hours at Biognosis, 21 Pier St.

Library The public library is on Corporation Street (Mon–Fri 9.30am–8pm, Sat 9.30am–5pm).

Male Voice Choir Visitors are welcome to the rehearsals of the Côr Meibion Aberystwyth group, held at the Tabernacle Chapel on Mill Street (Thurs 7.45–9.30pm except in Aug; ☎01970/624494).

Post office 8 Great Darkgate St.

Sport Plascrug Leisure Centre (☎01970/624579), off the Llanbadarn Road, has two indoor pools, sauna, solarium, squash and tennis courts, indoor pitches and multigym. The Glan-y-Mor Leisure Park (see "Accommodation", p.311) is open to the public.

Around Aberystwyth

Aberystwyth's sights run out long before it's time to hit the restaurants and nightlife, so there is every reason to go exploring beyond the town. Immediately inland is the **Vale of Rheidol**, a region of forested glades and remote villages, easily accessed by road or, more enjoyably, rail – the narrow-gauge steam train which serves the area is a draw in itself. Tourist attractions like **Devil's Bridge**, where the line terminates, are also obviously popular, although there are numerous other lesser-known beauty spots whose charms require only a little more imagination to discover.

The coast north of Aberystwyth also has its devotees, principally sunseekers drawn to the beach at **Borth** and the dunes close to the mouth of the Dyfi estuary. Nature buffs will prefer to head further northeast to the RSPB's **Ynys-Hir Nature Reserve**, with its complex series of bird habitats.

The Vale of Rheidol

Inland from Aberystwyth, the Rheidol River winds its way up to a secluded, wooded valley, where occasional old industrial workings have moulded themselves into the contours, rising up past waterfalls and minute villages. It's a glorious route, and by far the best way to see this part of the world is on board one of the trains of the **Vale of Rheidol Railway** (2–4 services daily April–Oct; £12.50 return; ☎01970/625819, ⊛www.rheidolrailway .co.uk), a narrow-gauge steam train that wheezes its way along twelve miles of sheer rock faces, climbing six hundred feet in the process. It was built in 1902, ostensibly for the valley's lead mines but with a canny eye on its tourist potential. For many years it operated as part of British Rail's network, running steam trains into the late 1980s (some twenty years after steam locos had ceased operating elsewhere), then was sold to the private group which now operates it using authentic Rheidol rolling stock. Today it offers a gorgeous journey, best seen from the comfortable first-class observation carriage (£1 extra each way) or the open-sided "summer car", but the timetable and limited interest at any of the wayside halts conspire to keep you on the train for the full hour-long one-way trip.

If you'd rather drive, the easiest way is to take the A4120 along the south side of the valley direct to Devil's Bridge (see opposite) or the A44 along the north side; the two meet at Ponterwyd. You can also explore the valley by bike using the **Rheidol Cycle Trail**, a combination of designated cycle paths and quiet country lanes which runs eighteen miles from Aberystwyth to Devil's Bridge: the tourist office in Aberystwyth has a free leaflet outlining the route.

The tiny hamlet of **CAPEL BANGOR**, five miles east of Aberystwyth along the A44, has little to recommend it other than the Rheidol Riding School (℡01970/880863), from where you can book hacks for around £10 an hour; the 300-year-old *Tynllidiart Arms*, notable for its homebrew beer and summertime draught cider; and the nearby **Cwm Rheidol Reservoir**, reached by a narrow riverside route off the main road. This is the final element in a small, showpiece hydroelectric scheme that starts high in the headwaters of the Rheidol River at the Nant-y-moch Reservoir. An **information centre** (Easter & May–Sept 10.30am–4.15pm; free), run by privatized electricity generator e-on, explains the scheme's significance, and a visit is essential to appreciate the free 45-minute tour of the **power station**, where you can see the impressive sluices and channels that funnel the water according to need, and the neighbouring **fish farm** (April–Oct daily 10.30am–4.30pm) a stone's throw up the road. Most gimmicky of all, but fun all the same, the reservoir dam and weir are floodlit nightly, from dusk until 11pm in the summer, 10pm in the winter. Behind the visitor centre, the **Magic of Life Butterfly House** (Easter–Oct daily 10am–5pm; £4) houses dozens of beautiful butterflies and moths in a wild garden and tropically heated polytunnel.

Slight remains of old lead workings are evident on the banks of the reservoir, although the valley's mining legacy is better seen further along, as the road begins to narrow before finally disappearing into a wood as a mud track. From here, paths rise either side of the river to overlook the burned orange spoil, vividly coloured water and bright plants, fitted snugly into their green landscape. A sharp path on the south side of the river climbs up to Rhiwfron halt on the Rheidol Railway (see above).

Llywernog Mine Museum and Ponterwyd

Travelling eastbound, the A44 winds up into **galena** country, tucked between the bleak moorland of Plynlimon (see p.276) and the rugged mountains to the south. The silver-rich lead ore was found throughout the region and scores of mines sprang up, each plugging away at the lode until waterlogging made the mines uneconomic. In the boom years, the latter half of the 1800s, the whole of northern Ceredigion was a mini-Klondike, attracting speculators and opportunists by the trainful. The remains – waste tips scarring hillsides and shafts pockmarking former sites – lie all around, most now hidden amongst the exotic evergreens of the Rheidol Forest. They can be visited on wonderful walks and mountain bike rides from the **Bwlch Nant-yr-Arian visitor centre** (daily: Easter–Sept 10am–5pm, Oct–Easter generally 10am to dusk; entry free, parking £1; ℡01970/890694), perched above a magnificent valley scooped out of the wooded hillsides, seven miles east of Capel Bangor. Here you can pick up a free leaflet detailing a half-hour all-access walkway around a small lake and a couple of longer hikes (1hr & 2.5hr), and visit the café which has a terrace that's perfect for viewing the **red kite feeding** which takes place at 3pm (2pm when the clocks go back). The woods also offer top-class **mountain biking**, notably on the 16km Summit Trail, which is classed as difficult and will take at least an hour and a half. You can buy a £1 route map from the visitor centre but will need to bring your own bike – or rent one in Aberystwyth (see p.315).

The soft contours of the forest make it difficult to imagine how stark the valley once looked. A truer picture unfolds a mile further east with the impressive barrenness around the **Llywernog Mine Museum & Caverns** (Easter–Aug daily 10am–6pm; Sept–Oct daily 11am–5pm; £5.95; Ⓦwww .silverminetours.co.uk), which opened in the 1740s and closed in the early years of the twentieth century. Decay was well advanced when the place reopened in the early 1970s, but the site has expanded consistently over the years in a satisfyingly rough manner. A low-key mock-up of a working mine, housing an interesting museum, leads on to a collection of rusted machinery and the dank, dark mine itself, visitable on a great thirty-minute underground tour. Topside, you can pan for "fool's gold" or dowse for veins of galena.

The largest settlement to spring up around the mines was **PONTERWYD**, a mile from Llywernog on the banks of the Rheidol. Walking aside, there's little of interest here; indeed, one of the funniest sections in George Borrow's *Wild Wales* tells of his night in the inn at Ponterwyd – now the *George Borrow Hotel* – when the pompous Englishman met his match in a pugnacious landlord, who, even in 1854, was complaining about the numbers of unimaginative tourists ignoring his and other local villages and flocking instead to Devil's Bridge.

Devil's Bridge

Folk legend, perfect Picturesque scenery and travellers' lore combine at **DEVIL'S BRIDGE** (Pontarfynach), a tiny settlement twelve miles east of Aberystwyth – reached by road (A4120) or the Vale of Rheidol Railway – built largely for the growing visitor trade of the last few hundred years.

The main attraction is the Devil's Bridge itself, where three roads (the A4120, the B4343 and the B4574) converge and cross the churning River Mynach yards above its confluence with the Rheidol to form three bridges, one on top of the other. The road bridge in front of the Alpine *Hafod Arms* hotel (see p.318) is the most modern of the three, dating from 1901. Immediately below it and wedged between the rock faces are the stone bridge from 1753, and, at the bottom, the original bridge, dating from the eleventh century and reputedly built by the monks of Strata Florida Abbey. To see the bridges – and it is well worth it – you have to enter the turnstiles on either side of the modern road bridge. With your back to the hotel, the right-hand side (£1) is the shorter route, signposted to the Punch Bowl. Slippery steps lead down to the deep cleft in the rock, where the water pounds and hurtles through the gap crowned by the bridges. The Punch Bowl is the name given to a series of rock bowls scooped by the sheer power of the thundering river, which rushes through past bright-green mossy rocks and saturated lichen.

On the opposite side of the road is a ticket office (Easter–Oct daily 9.45am–5pm) – pay £2.50 or pass through turnstiles (£2) when closed – which opens out onto a path leading down into the valley and ultimately to the crashing **Mynach Falls**. The scenery here is magnificent: sharp, wooded slopes rising away from the frothing river, with distant mountain peaks surfacing on the horizon. A platform overlooks the series of falls, from where a set of steep steps takes you further down to a footbridge dramatically spanning the river at the bottom. Be warned, however, that Devil's Bridge has been a seriously popular day excursion for centuries; to escape some of the inevitable congestion, it is wisest to come here at the beginning or end of the day, or out of season.

The railway terminates half a mile away at a tinpot brown-and-cream shack, just by Devil's Bridge **post office**, which has some worthwhile booklets on local walks. For **accommodation**, there's the comfortable and friendly *Mount Pleasant* (Ⓣ01970/890219, Ⓦwww.mpleasant.co.uk; ❷/❸), 200 yards to the right as you leave the station, where you get a continental breakfast (or pay a bit extra for a cooked one) and can order a candlelit evening meal (£11.95). The only hotel is the revamped *Hafod Arms* (☎01970/890232, ⓦwww.hafodarms .co.uk; ④/⑥), midway between the station and the bridges, but there is reasonably priced **camping** at *Woodlands Caravan Park* (☎01970/890233; £9 per pitch) by the petrol station, just beyond the bridges.

The *Hafod Arms* serves **food**, as do a couple of simple cafés, but none are brilliant and you're better off five miles west along the A4120 at the ☆*Halfway Inn*, just beyond the spectacularly positioned village of **PISGAH**, which does a decent pint and tasty bar meals. If you're not driving or cycling, you could use the Vale of Rheidol narrow-gauge railway and get off at Nantyronen halt, from where it's a steep half-mile trek up to the village.

The Vale of Ystwyth

The Ystwyth River runs pretty much parallel to the Rheidol, a couple of miles to the south. Four miles south of Devil's Bridge is the dour village of **PONTRHYDYGROES**, the former centre of local lead-mining activity. The B4574 climbs out of the village and past the delightful country estate of **Hafod**, once the seat of a great house belonging to the wealthy Johnes family. In the late eighteenth century, Thomas Johnes commissioned a mansion here in the Picturesque style; it was added to by John Nash, amongst others, and contained a library full of Welsh manuscripts, but was ravaged by a terrible fire in 1807. The sumptuous replacement house was demolished in 1958 as an unsafe ruin, and all that remains is the beautiful estate Johnes landscaped and forested two hundred years ago. The church, off the B4574, is the best place to embark on the waymarked **trails** that lead through the estate and down to the river. Johnes' larch forest, broken by trickling streams, monumental relics and planted glades, swoops down to the Ystwyth River, less than a mile from the church car park. A bridge spans the river, where paths fan out either way along its banks or up through the tiny valley of the Nant Gau. In many ways, the estate has all of the beauty of nearby Devil's Bridge, but with a fraction of the crowds.

Continuing east, a small road grinds up the hill into the bizarre moonscape surrounding **CWMYSTWYTH**, a small, semi-derelict village at the bottom of a valley of old lead mines, deserted in the late nineteenth century when the mines were exhausted. As the river shimmers past, the view is one of abandoned shafts, tumbledown cottages, twisted tramways and grey heaps of spoil littering spartan hillsides. The isolated road continues to climb the uninhabited slopes, before dropping down into the Elan Valley and its reservoirs.

North from Aberystwyth

The A487 runs north from Aberystwyth towards Machynlleth, slicing between the mountains to the east and the flat lands bordering the vast Dyfi estuary. The seaward plain is one of the most surprising landscapes in Wales, at its heart a raised bog, **Cors Fochno**, visible from the main road but seen much better from the rail line or the coastal B4353. This road sneaks through **Borth**, an end-of-the-world resort stretching for nearly two miles along the seafront, to the **nature reserve** at **Ynyslas**, the best place to explore the sand dunes.

Inland, attractions worth heading off the A487 for include the roadside village of **Furnace** with its eighteenth-century iron foundry and access to the lovely **Artists' Valley**, and nearby **Ynys-hir**, an RSPB nature reserve with an impressive range of bird habitats.

Borth and Ynyslas can be reached from Aberystwyth on buses #511 and #512. The #28 and #X32 to Machynlleth run through Furnace and Ynys-hir. You can also get to Borth and Machynlleth by train.

Borth and Ynyslas

People either love or hate **BORTH**, five miles north of Aberystwyth. It's a strange, otherworldly place, a linear village strung along one ruler-straight street (High Street) that regularly gets battered by weather fronts from the Atlantic. With the sea on one side, and a vast peat bog on the other, Borth feels strangely vulnerable, yet surprisingly robust. It's an old fishing village that gradually adapted to tourism, mainly in the shape of the caravan parks that fringe the village. The shallow **beach**, some three miles in length, is excellent: swimming is fine as long as you don't go too far up towards the mouth of the Dyfi. If you've got kids you could take them to see the creatures at the **Animalarium** zoo half a mile off High Street (daily: Easter–Oct 10am–6pm; Nov–Easter 11am–4pm; £6.50). The Ceredigion **coast path** from Borth (start by the war memorial on the headland south of the village) to Aberystwyth (5 miles; 3hr) is a wonderful up-and-down route with some great beach stops. You can also easily return by bus or train.

For a seaside resort, there are surprisingly few **B&Bs**: *Pebbles*, on the High Street overlooking the beach, is decent (℡01970/871362; ❷), as is *Tŷ Gwylan* on Francis Road up the hill in Upper Borth (℡01970/871925; ❷). There's an Edwardian **YHA hostel** at the northern end of the High Street (℡0870/770 5708, ℮borth@yha.org.uk; ❶; open Easter–Oct) with £12.50 dorm beds and some double rooms, and the central *Ynys Fergi* **campsite** (℡01970/871344; £8 per pitch) on the road to the Animalarium. There are a few cafés and three pubs: the beachside *Victoria Inn* is the best, with decent food including good-value carveries.

To the north, the flat landscape meets the formidable sand dunes that line the southern side of the Dyfi estuary. The road follows the coast a couple of miles to **YNYSLAS**, entrance to the dramatic estuary-side **Ynyslas nature reserve** (£1 per car), most notable for its birdlife. In winter, wading and sea birds feed amongst the dunes and mud flats, while in summer, butterflies flit around vibrant sand plants growing in the grass. The views here are wonderful: to the mountains inland, along the estuary and coast, and over the river to the colourful huddle of Aberdyfi. Staff at the Countryside Council for Wales **visitor centre** (Easter–Sept daily 10am–4pm; ℡01970/871640), the starting point for guided walks and tours that take place most summer weekends, can point you to the short circular dune walk or half a mile along the beach to the **fossilized forest**. At low tides, the sands near the water's edge are studded with the petrified stumps of a dozen or so 5000-year-old trees, a reminder that the coast was some twelve miles away when these trees were in their prime. A less prosaic explanation tells of a drowned land known as Cantre'r Gwaelod which was protected by sea walls and floodgates. Their keeper, Seithenyn, happened to get drunk the night of an almighty storm and the sea burst through, drowning a thousand people and fourteen settlements.

Furnace and Ynys-hir

The Borth road rejoins the A487 a couple of miles south of the hamlet of **FURNACE** which, as its name suggests, grew principally as an industrial centre, firstly around silver refining and then iron smelting. Both activities centred around the **Dyfi Furnace** (unrestricted access), a barn-like building constructed to harness the power of the Einion River, with a vast water wheel driving the bellows. Take five minutes to stroll around the back to a picturesque waterfall.

The adjacent narrow lane follows the river through a forest and out into the idyllic **Cwm Einion**, known as "Artists' Valley" because of its popularity with nineteenth-century landscape painters. A parking area about a mile and a half along the lane gives access to footpaths which head up into the deserted foothills of Plynlimon (see p.276), across the spongy moors and through conifer forests to the remote glacial lakes of **Llyn Conach** and **Llyn Dwfn**, three miles away.

Half a mile north of Furnace, a short lane runs seaward to *Ynyshir Hall* hotel and restaurant (see p.325) and the RSPB's **Ynys-hir Nature Reserve** (reserve daily 9am–9pm or dusk; visitor centre April–Oct daily 10am–5pm, Nov–March Wed–Sun 10am–4pm; £3.50). The thousand-plus-acre site, comprising five rich and distinct habitats, drips with diversity. Redstarts, pied-flycatchers and warblers flit about the ancient hanging oak woodland so typical of mid-Wales; cormorants flock to the estuarine salt marshes; red-breasted mersangers and elusive otters inhabit the freshwater streams and pools; remnant peat bogs are a riot of wild flowers in spring; and winter brings water rails to the reed beds to join the herons. The attractions are obvious to the birders who return time and again to the network of hides, but there's enough along the one- or two-hour designated trails to interest anyone, and most weekends there are special-interest guided walks (call for details on ☎01654/700222).

Southern Cadair Idris and the Dyfi and Talyllyn valleys

The southern coastal reaches of Snowdonia National Park are almost entirely dominated by **Cadair Idris** (2930ft), a five-peaked massif standing defiant in its isolation. Tennyson claimed never to have seen "anything more awful than the great veil of rain drawn straight over Cader Idris", but catch it on a good day, and the views from the top – occasionally stretching as far as Ireland – are stunning. During the last Ice Age, the heads of glaciers scalloped out two huge cwms from Cadair Idris' distinctive dome, leaving thousand-foot cliffs dropping away on all sides to cool, clear lakes. The largest of these amphitheatres is Cwm Gadair, the **Chair of Idris**, which takes its name from a giant warrior poet of Welsh legend, although some prefer the notion that Idris' Chair refers to a seat-like rock formation on the summit ridge, where anyone spending the night (specifically New Year's Eve, say some) will become a poet, go mad or die.

Cadair Idris' southern limits are lapped by the broad expanse of the Dyfi estuary, which in turn bleeds into the grand scenery of the **Dyfi Valley**, "one of the greenest corners of Europe". Focal point for the valley is the genial town of **Machynlleth**, a candidate for Welsh capital in the 1950s and site of Owain Glyndŵr's embryonic 1404 parliament. The area is rife with the B&Bs and businesses of New Agers who have flocked to this corner of Wales since the late 1960s, and in the hills to the north, the renowned, co-operatively run **Centre for Alternative Technology** makes for a spirited day out.

Small-time coastal resorts are sprinkled around the region, the pick of them being **Aberdyfi**, though many prefer to press on to **Tywyn** and ride the **Talyllyn Railway**, justly one of Wales' most popular narrow-gauge lines, running seven miles up the **Talyllyn Valley** to **Abergynolwyn** at the foot of Cadair

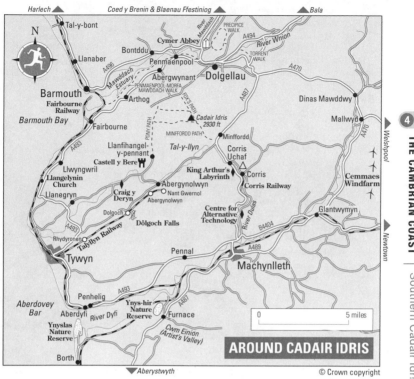

AROUND CADAIR IDRIS

© Crown copyright

Idris, and only a short distance from the brooding thirteenth-century **Castell-y-Bere** and the inland cormorant colony at **Craig yr Aderyn**.

A well-coordinated network of bike routes, trains, steam rail lines and buses make **getting around** the area easy. The very useful, summer-only Dyfi Sherpa ticket (£10; ☎01654/710472) allows a circuit from Tywyn using the Talyllyn Railway to Abergynolwyn, the #30 bus to Machynlleth and the bus or mainline train back to Tywyn.

Machynlleth and around

Shortlisted for Welsh capital in the 1950s and site of Owain Glyndŵr's totemic fifteenth-century Welsh parliament, handsome **MACHYNLLETH** (pronounced Mah-hun-cthleth) is at the pivotal crossroads of Wales. It's long been a town to which visitors have come, none more so than in the last few decades, when its reputation as the "green" capital of Wales has been growing. Well-heeled hippies mix easily enough with the local, largely farming, population, a combination evident in the town's eclectic shops and market. With a good range of places to stay, eat and drink, together with great transport links to both beaches and mountains, Machynlleth makes a fine base.

It is difficult to imagine a nation's capital consisting essentially of just two intersecting streets, but that is the basis of Machynlleth. The A489 enters the town from the east becoming the wide main street, **Heol Maengwyn**, busiest on Wednesdays when a lively **market** springs up out of nowhere. Heol Maengwyn comes to an end at a T-junction, under the fanciful gaze of a fussy **clock-tower**, erected

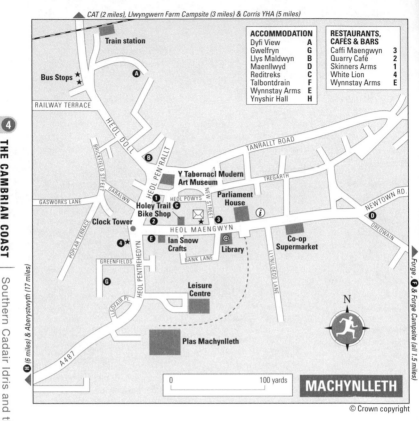

ACCOMMODATION

Dyfi View	A
Gwelfryn	G
Llys Maldwyn	B
Maenllwyd	D
Reditreks	C
Talbontdrain	F
Wynnstay Arms	E
Ynyshir Hall	H

RESTAURANTS, CAFÉS & BARS

Caffi Maengwyn	3
Quarry Café	2
Skinners Arms	1
White Lion	4
Wynnstay Arms	E

Train station

Bus Stops

RAILWAY TERRACE

HEOL DOLL

TANRALLT ROAD

BRICKFIELD STREET

GARSIWN

GASWORKS LANE

HEOL PENRALLT

Y Tabernacl Modern Art Museum

TREGARTH

HEOL POWYS

NEW STREET

Parliament House

NEWTOWN RD.

DROWAIN

Holey Trail Bike Shop

Clock Tower

POPLAR TERRACE

HEOL MAENGWYN

Ian Snow Crafts

Library

BANK LANE

Co-op Supermarket

LLYNLLOEDD LANE

GREENFIELDS

HEOL PENTREHEDYN

LLFAIR PL.

Leisure Centre

Plas Machynlleth

A487

N

0   100 yards

MACHYNLLETH

© Crown copyright

H (6 miles) & Aberystwyth (17 miles)

Forge, F & Forge Campsite (all 1.5 miles)

in 1873 by local landowner, the Marquess of Londonderry, to commemorate his son and heir's coming of age.

The Town

Glyndŵr's partly fifteenth-century **Parliament House** (Easter–Sept Mon–Sat 10am–5pm; other times by arrangement on ☏01654/702827; free) sits halfway along Heol Maengwyn, a modest looking black-and-white-fronted building concealing a large interior. Displays chart the course of Glyndŵr's life, his military campaign, his downfall, and the 1404 parliament in the town, when he controlled almost all of what we now know as Wales and even negotiated international recognition of the sovereign state. The sorriest tales are from 1405 onwards, when tactical errors and the sheer brute force of the English forced a swift retreat and an ignominious end to the great Welsh uprising.

Opposite the Parliament House, a path leads into the landscaped grounds of **Plas Machynlleth**, the elegant seventeenth-century mansion of the Marquess of Londonderry. Its solitude is entirely intentional: in the 1840s the Marquess bought up all the surrounding buildings and had them demolished, and rerouted the main road away from his grounds. For the last decade, the Plas has been home to the **Celtica** museum, a resource for all matters Celtic, though this is scheduled to close in 2006 and plans for the building's future are currently unclear.

No name is so frequently invoked in Wales as that of **Owain Glyndŵr** (c. 1349–1416), a potent figurehead of Welsh nationalism ever since he rose up against the occupying English in the first few years of the fifteenth century.

Little is known about the man described in Shakespeare's *Henry IV, Part I* as "not in the roll of common men". There seems little doubt that the charismatic Owain fulfilled many of the mystical medieval prophecies about the rising up of the red dragon. He was of aristocratic stock, and had a conventional upbringing, part of it in England of all places. His blue blood – he was directly descended from the princes of Powys and Cyfeiliog – furthered his claim as Prince of Wales, and as a result of his status, he learned English, studied in London and became a loyal, and distinguished, soldier of the English king, before returning to Wales and marrying a local woman.

Wales in the late fourteenth century was a turbulent place. The brutal savaging a century earlier of Llywelyn the Last and Edward I's stringent policies of subordinating Wales had left a discontented, cowed nation where any signs of rebellion were sure to attract support. Glyndŵr became the focus of the rebellion through a parochial problem: his neighbour in Glyndyfrdwy, the English Lord of Ruthin, seized some of his land and when the courts failed to back him, Glyndŵr took matters into his own hands. With four thousand supporters and a new declaration that he was Prince of Wales, he attacked Ruthin, and then Denbigh, Rhuddlan, Flint, Hawarden and Oswestry, before encountering an English resistance at Welshpool. However, whole swaths of north Wales were his for the taking. The English king, Henry IV, dispatched troops and rapidly drew up a range of severely punitive laws against the Welsh, even outlawing Welsh-language bards and singers. Battles continued to rage, with Glyndŵr capturing Edmund Mortimer, the Earl Marcher, in Pilleth in June 1402. By the end of 1403, he controlled most of Wales.

In 1404, Glyndŵr assembled a parliament of four men from every *commot* (community) in Wales at Machynlleth, drawing up mutual recognition treaties with France and Spain. At Machynlleth, he was also crowned ruler of a free Wales. A second parliament in Harlech took place a year later, with Glyndŵr making plans to carve up England and Wales into three as part of an alliance against the English king: Mortimer would take the south and west of England, Thomas Percy, Earl of Northumberland, would have the Midlands and North, and Glyndŵr himself Wales and the Marches of England. The English army, however, concentrated with increased vigour on destroying the Welsh uprising, and the Tripartite Indenture was never realized. From then on, Glyndŵr lost battles, ground and castles and was forced into hiding; dying, it is thought, in Herefordshire. The draconian anti-Welsh laws stayed in place until the accession to the English throne of Henry VII, a Welshman, in 1485. Wales became subsumed into English custom and law, and Glyndŵr's uprising became an increasingly powerful symbol of frustrated Welsh independence. In modern times, the shadowy organization that surfaced in the early 1980s to burn the holiday homes of English people and English estate agents dealing in Welsh property took the name Meibion (the sons of) Glyndŵr. More prosaically, the figure of Glyndŵr, his trademark double-pointed beard to the fore, can usually be seen gracing Welsh pub signs of inns called the Prince of Wales – a far better option than the various playboys and whingers who, by dint of being the first-born son of the reigning British monarch, have occupied the title ever since.

Back into town, past the clocktower and up Heol Pen'rallt towards the station, is the **Museum of Modern Art, Wales** (MOMA Cymru: Mon–Sat 10am–4pm; free; ☎01654/703355; ⓦwww.momawales.org.uk). Housed in Y Tabernacl, a beautifully serene old chapel converted into a cultural centre, it hosts an ongoing programme of temporary exhibitions, including some from

△ Owain Glyndŵr

its own growing collection. It is also the place to go for films, theatre, comedy, concerts and the August Gŵyl Machynlleth festival, which combines classical and some folk music with theatre and debate.

Practicalities

The **train station** is a five-minute walk up Heol Pen'rallt from the town's central clocktower, which is the main **bus stop**, though many also call at the train station. **Postbus** services which loop inland pick up (at 7.20am and 3.55pm) from outside the Spar supermarket on Heol Maengwyn, just a few steps from the **tourist office** (daily: Easter–Sept 9.30am–6pm; Oct–Easter 10am–5pm; ℡01654/702401, ⓔmactic@powys.gov.uk) and the neighbouring Parliament House. If you're after information of a more "alternative" ilk, try the boards in the CAT-run *Quarry Cafe*, near the clock tower on Heol Maengwyn. The library (Mon & Fri 9.30am–1pm & 2–7pm, Tues & Wed 9.30am–1pm & 2–5pm, Sat 9.30am–1pm) on Heol Maengwyn has free **Internet access**.

Machynlleth has become something of a **mountain biking** mecca, with some excellent purpose-built routes in the vicinity. Best place for information and **cycle rental** is The Holey Trail at 31 Heol Maengwyn (℡01654/700411). Guided biking holidays can be booked through *Reditreks* (℡01654/702184) at their bunkhouse (see below).

Accommodation is plentiful and of a high standard. At the top end, there's the laid-back grandeur of the *Wynnstay Arms* on Heol Maengwyn (℡01654/702941; ❻). Mid-range B&Bs include the squeaky-clean *Dyfi View* on Ffordd Mynydd Griffiths (℡01654/702562; ❸) and the *Maenllwyd* on Newtown Road, the eastward extension of Heol Maengwyn (℡01654/702928; ❸). Cheaper are *Gwelfryn* at 6 Greenfields, off Bank Street behind the central Dragon garage (℡01654/702532; ❷) and the *Llys Maldwyn* B&B in the old Vale infants school on Heol Doll (℡01654/703001; ❷). If you've got your own transport, the fantastically welcoming *Talbontdrain* is four miles south of town, in stunning countryside beyond the village of Forge (℡01654/702192, ⓦwww.talbontdrain .co.uk; ❷). If money's no object, the Michelin-starred luxury of *Ynyshir Hall*, near the Ynys-hir Nature Reserve (see p.320) at Eglwysfach, six miles southwest on the A487 (℡01654/781209, ⓦwww.ynyshir-hall.co.uk; ❽/❾) is wonderful.

There's a shiny new *Reditreks* **bunkhouse** off Heol Powys in central Machynlleth (℡01654/702184, ⓦwww.reditreks.com), with beds for £15. They'll also let you **camp** for £5, though it's little more than a grassy yard you'll be in; otherwise, the nearest site is three miles north near the Centre for Alternative Technology (CAT) at *Llwyngwern Farm* (℡01654/702492; £8 per pitch).

There are plenty of **cafés**, **restaurants** and **pubs** in the town, including a popular veggie wholefood café, the CAT-run *Quarry Café*, near the clocktower on Heol Maengwyn. For good-value meatier fare, try the *Caffi Maengwyn*, along the street across the side road from the Spar supermarket. Lunch and dinner are great at the ✻ *Wynnstay Arms*, which also has a superb pizzeria in its courtyard bar. The *Skinners Arms*, round the corner on Heol Pen'rallt, is cheaper but cosy and good for food or beer. Liveliest pub is either the *Skinners* or the *White Lion*, by the clocktower.

Centre for Alternative Technology and Corris

Regular buses head north from Machynlleth up the A487, through the Dulas Valley towards Dolgellau. Since its foundation in the middle of the oil crisis of 1974, the **Centre for Alternative Technology** (CAT) or *Canolfan y Dechnoleg Amgen* (daily: Easter–Sept 10am–5.30pm; Oct–Easter 10am–dusk; £8 summer, £6 winter, £1 discount to those arriving by bike or public transport; ℡01654 705950, ⓦwww.cat.org.uk), three miles along the road, has become one of the biggest attractions in Wales. Over almost three decades, seven acres of a once-derelict slate quarry have been turned into an almost entirely sustainable community, generating eighty percent of its own power from wind, sun and water. But this is no back-to-the-land hippie commune. Right from the start, the idea was to embrace technology – much of the on-site equipment was developed and built here, reflecting the centre's achievements in this field – and, most importantly, to promote its application in urban situations.

CAT's earnest education is leavened with flashes of pzazz, particularly in the water-balanced **cliff railway** (Easter–Oct only), which whisks the visitor 200ft up to the main site from the car park. It is also a beautiful site, sensitively landscaped using local slate and wood, and you can easily spend half a day sauntering around. There's plenty for kids to do, including a children's theatre (mainly mid-July to Aug), the wholefood restaurant turns out delicious food, and the excellent bookshop stocks a wide range of alternative literature along with crafts and intriguing toys.

Primarily, though, this is a working community which exists more to educate by example than entertain, partly facilitated by the new environmental information centre housed in a rammed earth building. Residential courses are offered, the most popular being a guide to building your own energy-efficient home, and for £5.50 per night to cover bed and board, you can get a week-long taster of life and work at the centre between March and September – see the website for details.

Corris

The spirit of CAT is carried three miles higher up the valley to **CORRIS**, a small former slate-quarrying settlement in the middle of the Dyfi Forest. In the centre of the village is the **Corris Railway and Museum** (generally weekends April–Sept and daily in school holidays; £3; ☎01654/761303, ⓦwww.corrisco.uk). The line currently shuttles passengers a mere half-mile and back, though there are plans to restore a further two miles. It's part of the old narrow-gauge railway that linked the slate quarries of the Dulas Valley with the main line at Machynlleth. Corris station is a short signposted walk from the former village school, now operating as the holistically minded *Canolfan Corris* **hostel**, Old Road (mid-Feb to Oct & weekends Nov–Feb; ☎01654/761686, ⓦwww.canolfancorris.com). It's the kind of place where people stay longer than they intended – in large subdivided dorms (£12.50 a bed, £15 with breakfast), family rooms and even tents; reasonably priced, healthy meals are available and there are kitchen facilities. There's also food and drink at the village's lovely old **pub**, the *Slaters' Arms*, right at the central crossroads. Up on the main road above Corris, there's another **bunkhouse** in the old *Braich Goch* pub (☎01654/761229, ⓦwww.braichgoch.co.uk; £13.50), which can arrange all manner of sporting and outward bound activities.

Half a mile further up the valley, the **Corris Craft Centre** occupies a former slate mine, and houses the local **tourist office** (Easter–Oct daily 10am–5.30pm; ☎01654/761244, ⓔcorris.tic@gwynedd.gov.uk), a few run-of-the-mill craft shops, a decent enough café, a good children's playground, and a couple of modest attractions. **King Arthur's Labyrinth** (late March to Oct daily 10am–5pm, call for winter hours; £5.15, or £7.05 with Bard's Quest; ☎01654/761584, ⓦwww.kingarthurslabyrinth.com) is based deep with the tunnels of a former quarry. Led by someone dressed as a monk, the boat trip into the heart of the mountain is huge fun, but the son et lumière tableaux, illustrating various Welsh legends, occasionally verge on the cheesy. The new **Bard's Quest** (£3.80, or £7.05 with Labyrinth) is an outdoor floral maze which reveals "mystical stories echoing across the ages".

Aberdyfi

With a south-facing aspect across the Dyfi estuary, backed by lush mountains, **ABERDYFI** has been well blessed by its position. A proud maritime heritage has largely vanished to be replaced by the life of a well-heeled resort, with one of the highest proportions of holiday homes anywhere on this coast – and with some of the highest prices for those holiday homes too. But it's a likeable enough place, with a good stretch of coast and estuary, plus numerous outdoor pursuits to occupy a day or two. There's a rather sporadic rental service of canoes and sailboards on the beach, but there isn't much else to do here. Swimming is possible, but tidal currents make it potentially hazardous so aim to swim close to high tide, or keep in the shallows. If you've got your own windsurfing or sailing equipment, you can become a temporary member of the Dovey Yacht Club (℡01654/767607) on the wharf.

In the mid-nineteenth century, the town, with its seamlessly joined eastern neighbour **Penhelig**, built shallow-draught coastal traders for the inshore fleet, a past remembered in the small historic and **maritime display** in the tourist office, Wharf Gardens (see below).

Practicalities

Aberdyfi is served by two equally inconvenient **train** stations, the request-only Penhelig, half a mile east, and Aberdyfi, half a mile west of the **tourist office** at Wharf Gardens (Easter–Oct daily 10am–5pm; ℡01654/767321, Ⓔticaberdyfi@hotmail.com), near where the #28 **bus** stops.

None of the **accommodation** here is terribly cheap: the nearest to budget is the very welcoming, non-smoking *One Trefeddian Bank*, about a third of a mile north along the A493 (℡01654/767487; closed Nov–Feb; ❸) and the *Cartref Guest House*, Penrhos, near Aberdyfi train station (℡01654/767273, Ⓦwww.cartref-guesthouse.co.uk; ❸). The swankiest options are the luscious seafront designer hotel *Llety Bodfor* (℡01654/767475, Ⓦwww.lletybodfor .co.uk; ❼) and the fabulous ⚑ *Penhelig Arms Hotel*, near Penhelig train station (℡01654/767215, Ⓦwww.penheligarms.com; ❼), which boasts an excellent restaurant with an extensive wine list.

Lighter **meals** are offered at the good-value *Old Coffee Shop*, 13 New St, built into the cliff behind the *Britannia Inn*, with homemade cakes and inexpensive lunches, and the *Grapevine Restaurant*, 1 Chapel Square (℡01654/767448), which offers bistro-type fare. In the evening, the *Dovey Inn*, a few doors along, has the best bar meals and, along with the *Britannia*, the liveliest atmosphere.

Tywyn and the Talyllyn Railway

Despite four miles of sandy beach, **TYWYN** ("the strand"), four miles north of Aberdyfi, is really only of interest as a base for the Talyllyn and Dysynni valleys (see pp.328–331). It's a traditional sort of seaside resort, but spread out thinly and devoid of much atmosphere. At the east end of the long High Street, the Norman nave of the **Church of St Cadfan** (daily 9am–5pm, later in summer) houses one of the town's few real sights – the five-foot-high **St Cadfan's Stone** bears the earliest example of written Welsh, dating back to around 650 AD.

Tywyn's saving grace is the **Talyllyn narrow-gauge railway** (April–Oct & late Dec daily plus some winter weekends; ℡01654/710472, Ⓦwww.talyllyn .co.uk; £10 unlimited one-day travel), which belches seven miles inland through the delightful wooded Talyllyn Valley to Nant Gwernol. From 1866 to 1946, the rail line was used to haul slate from the Bryn Eglwys quarry near Nant Gwernol to Tywyn Wharf station; then just four years after the quarry's closure, rail enthusiasts took over the running of services, making this the world's first volunteer-run railway. The round trip (at a maximum 15mph) takes two hours, but you can get on and off as frequently as the schedule allows, taking in some fine broadleaf **forest walks**. The best of these starts at Dôlgogh Falls station, where three trails (maximum 1hr; leaflet 30p) lead off to the lower, mid- and upper cascades. At the end of the line, more woodland walks take you around the site of the old slate quarries. In mid-August each year, the schedule is disrupted by the "Race the Train" event, when runners attempt to beat the train on its fourteen-mile trip to Abergynolwyn and back. Some do.

The new **Narrow-Gauge Museum** (open when trains are running; free) at Tywyn Wharf station contains displays about the railway, other narrow-gauge lines in Britain and much about Thomas the Tank Engine, loosely inspired by the Talyllyn line. Of the original Talyllyn rolling stock, two steam engines and all five of the oak and mahogany passenger carriages still run up to Nant Gwernol.

Practicalities

The three main roads in Tywyn – the High Street, Pier Road and the Aberdyfi road – meet at the **train station**, which also acts as the main **bus** stop. The **tourist office** is in front of the Leisure Centre on High Street (Easter–Oct daily 9.30am–1pm & 2–5pm; ☎01654/710070, ✉tywyn.tic@gwynedd .co.uk), Pier Road makes for the beach, and the Aberdyfi road heads south past the Talyllyn narrow-gauge train station (Tywyn Wharf) two hundred yards away.

The cheapest **accommodation** is the basic *Llys Maldwyn* B&B, opposite the tourist office on High Street (☎01654/711058; ❷), while the *Monfa*, 4 Pier Rd (☎01654/710858; ❸), between the seafront and the High Street, is a more comfortable alternative. For something smarter, there's the *Corbett Arms Hotel* on Corbett Square, just a little further up the main street from the parish church (☎01654/710264; ❻), or, better still, head out to neighbouring Aberdyfi. The handiest **campsite**, ten minutes' walk from town on the Aberdyfi road, is the *Vaenol Camping Park* (☎01654/710232; £10 per pitch).

Good daytime food is served up at the *Town & Gown* on Marine Parade (the prom), where you can eat while browsing thousands of second-hand books. There are plenty of cafés in the town centre, and staple bar **meals** are dished up at the *Tredegar Arms*, a welcoming High Street pub. The *Proper Gander* on High Street (☎01654/711270) serves imaginative lunches, teas and great desserts all day, as well as à la carte evening meals (£18–23; Wed–Sat only). There's occasional live music at the *Corbett Arms* and Wurlitzer concerts (🌐www.organ .co.uk/tywyn) at the nearby Neuadd Pentre on Brook Street.

The Talyllyn and Dysynni valleys

The **Talyllyn and Dysynni valleys** form a two-pronged fork pointing southwest towards the sea. The handle is formed by the Talyllyn Valley, which starts at the northeast by Minffordd and is followed by the A river Dysynni as far as Abergynolwyn. Here the valley splits into two, some ancient geological upheaval having forced the river to abruptly switch its course north, forming the Dysynni Valley and leaving its original course beside the Talyllyn Railway all but dry. Although a quick tour around the sites won't take more than a half a day, the area is monumentally beautiful, and the superb lowland or mountain walking (particularly on Cadair Idris) warrants more time.

The Talyllyn Valley is served by the #30 bus, running from Tywyn to Abergynolwyn, continuing to Minffordd (where you can catch #32 to Dolgellau or Machynlleth). The Talyllyn narrow-gauge railway runs from Tywyn to Abergynolwyn

A walk on Cadair Idris from Minffordd

Note: The OS Explorer 1:25,000 map #OL23, "Cadair Idris & Llyn Tegid", is recommended.

The most dramatic ascent of Cadair Idris follows the **Minffordd Path** (6 miles; 5hr; 2900ft ascent), a justifiably popular route that makes a full circuit around the rim of **Cwm Cau**, probably the country's most impressive mountain cirque.

The path starts just west of the *Minffordd Hotel* at the junction of the A487 and the B4405. From the car park, follow the signs along an avenue of horse chestnuts and up through the woods, heading north. You will reach a fork: take the left path that wheels around the end of Craig Lwyd into Cwm Cau, and before you reach the lake, fork left and climb onto the rim of Cwm Cau, following it round to **Penygadair** (2930ft; see also p.335), the highest point on the massif. Here, there's a circular shelter and a tin-roofed hut originally built for dispensing refreshments to thirsty Victorians, and now affording none-too-comfortable protection from wind and rain.

The shortest descent follows the summit plateau northeast, then down to a grassy ridge before ascending gradually to **Mynydd Moel** (2831ft), from which you get a magnificent view down into a cwm containing the waters of Llyn Arran. The descent starts beside the fence which you cross just before the summit – you follow the fence south all the way to fork below Cwm Cau described above.

station half a mile short of the village, or to Nant Gwernol, just past the village but off the road. **Accommodation** is scattered throughout the two valleys, but the only **pubs** or **restaurants** are by the lake and in Abergynolwyn. Campsites tend towards the simple: farmers' fields with or without showers.

The Talyllyn Valley

From Tywyn, the B4405 up the **Talyllyn Valley** runs parallel to the Talyllyn Railway (see p.327), meeting it at **Dolgoch Falls**, the site of some delightful wooded walks. A few hundred yards further, there's a superb farmhouse B&B, *Tan-y-Coed-Isaf* (☎01654/782639; ❸; March–Oct), just two miles short of the twin valleys' only real settlement, **ABERGYNOLWYN**. Here a few dozen quarry workers' houses crowd around the ☀ *Railway Inn*, which serves the best range of real ales for miles, together with some great food. There's also the *Riverside Guesthouse* (☎01654/782235; ❷), which has a limited number of bargain **tent sites**.

The Dysynni Valley branches northwest here, but the Talyllyn Valley continues northeast for a couple of miles to the serene **Tal-y-Llyn Lake** (Llyn Mwyngil). The chief interest here is the fifteenth-century **St Mary's church** on the southern shores of the lake, a fine example of a small Welsh parish church, unusual because of its chancel arch painted with an alternating grid of red and River white roses, separated by grotesque bosses.

The lake itself is frequently stocked with brown trout and, occasionally, it's the resting place of migratory sea trout and salmon. Talyllyn Fisheries, beside the lake, issues fishing permits (£18 per day), and rents out boats with outboard engines (£20) and tackle (£10). It is part of the angling-oriented *Tynycornel* hotel (☎01654/782282, ⊛ www.tynycornel.co.uk; ❼), which also offers a sauna, mountain bikes for guests and an excellent range of bar lunches (£6–11), plus à la carte evening meals (from £13). On a tighter budget, try the nearby sixteenth-century *Pen-y-Bont* (☎01654/782218; ❺), next to the church, with a good bar and an affordable restaurant. Better value still, there's a lovely B&B

a mile further on near the top of the lake at *Dolffanog Fawr* (℡01654/761247, Ⓦwww.dolffanogfawr.co.uk; ④).

Just before the B4405 meets the A487 at **MINFFORDD** is the access point for the finest ascent of Cadair Idris (see box, p.329), together with a great **campsite**: *Dôl Einion* (℡01654/761312; £5–12 per pitch).

The Dysynni Valley

The **Dysynni Valley** has more to offer in the way of sights, even though a lack of public transport makes it difficult to explore. A mile and a half northwest of Abergynolwyn, a side road cuts northeast to the hamlet of **LLANFIHAN-GEL-Y-PENNANT** and the scant ruins of the native Welsh **Castell-y-Bere** (unrestricted access; CADW), a fortress built by Llywelyn ap Iorwerth (Llywelyn the Great) in 1221 to protect the mountain passes. After being besieged twice in the thirteenth century, this castle – one of the most massive of the Welsh castles – was consigned to seven centuries of obscurity and decay. Like so many of the native fortresses, Castell-y-Bere seems to rise almost imperceptibly out of the rock upon which it was built. With large slabs of the main towers still standing, there's plenty to poke around, but it's primarily a great place just to sit or picnic, with good views to Cadair Idris and Craig y Deryn (see below). A few hundred yards beyond the castle, you'll come to the centre of Llanfihangel, where the thick-set little **church of St Michael** is well worth seeing. Sitting snug in its circular graveyard, the church contains a couple of interesting exhibits in its vestry. One is a fabulous 3-D map of the valley, some fourteen feet long and built to a scale of one foot to one mile from patchwork and cloth. There are also some exhibits centred on one Mary Jones, including photos from 1921 detailing the unveiling of her monument, which can be found a little further up the lane at the ruined **Tŷn-y-ddôl** (unrestricted access). Jones' fame rested with her 1800 Bible-buying walk to Bala (see box on p.417), an event commemorated by a plaque in the remains of the house. Tŷn-y-ddôl marks the beginning of a path (10 miles; 7hr; 2900ft ascent) up Cadair Idris, though a longer and far less exciting one than that described in the box on p.329.

Three miles seaward from Tŷn-y-ddôl, along the Dysynni Valley road, around thirty breeding pairs of cormorants colonize **Craig y Deryn** (Birds' Rock), a stunning 760-foot-high cliff four miles from the coast. As the sea has gradually withdrawn from the valley, the birds have remained loyal to their home, making this Europe's only inland cormorant nesting site. It's reachable via a path (2 miles; 1hr; 750ft ascent) from two miles west of Abergynolwyn – conveniently, the *Llanllwyda* **campsite** (℡01654/782276; £8 per pitch) is at the start of the path.

The lane snakes back towards the coast, reaching the village of **LLANE-GRYN** three miles on. Half a mile northwest of the village, the little hilltop church (open daily) has an unexpectedly beautifully rood screen, probably carved in the fifteenth century, which is said to have been carried overnight from Cymer Abbey (see p.334) after its dissolution.

Just over two miles west of Llanegryn, where the northbound A493 swings dramatically around to hug the coast, there's a wonderful cliff-top campsite at *Cae Du* (℡01654/711234; £8 per pitch), half a mile short of the hamlet of **LLANGELYNIN**. There, a track descends seawards off the main road to another ancient church (open daily): a mainly eleventh-century building on the foundations of an eighth-century structure, and bare but for a few basic pews and a horse bier. Just outside the porch is the grave of Abram Wood, patriarch of Y Teulu Wood, a clan of Romanies who settled in Wales at the beginning of the eighteenth century. Continue along the main road for the cheerful village of **LLWYNGWRIL** and its excellent tearoom-cum-**gallery** (Ⓦwww.llwyngwril-gallery.co.uk), housed in an old chapel and regularly hosting events such as music nights.

Northern Cadair Idris and the Mawddach Estuary

In 1824, Wordsworth found the Mawddach "a sublime estuary". Some years later, John Ruskin concurred, deeming the waterside road he followed here "the most beautiful walk in the world". Romantic hyperbole perhaps, but these broad tidal flats gouging deep into the heart of the mid-Wales mountains create dramatic backdrops from every angle. With the sun low in the sky and the tide ebbing, the constantly changing course of the river trickles silver through the golden sands.

But the colour of the sands isn't just an illusion: they really do contain gold, albeit in tiny amounts, as the abandoned mines littering the hills around testify. Spasmodic outbursts of gold fever still occasionally hit the region's main town, **Dolgellau**, but most people are content to come here for some excellent walking up Cadair Idris and along the estuary, or to hit the beaches. The moribund **Fairbourne** and tatty but lively **Barmouth** are the main resorts.

Fairbourne

The tiny, stagnant resort of **FAIRBOURNE**, on the southern side of the Mawddach Estuary, was developed in the late nineteenth century as the country estate of the chairman of the McDougall's flour company. There's a decent beach and sublime views along along the coast and across the estuary, but little else to detain you. The one attraction is the steam-hauled **Fairbourne Railway** (Easter & May to late Sept 4–9 trains daily; £6.50 return), with a gauge of just one foot. The railway makes a pleasant alternative route across the estuary to Barmouth, starting across the road from the **train station** and running a mile to a connecting **passenger ferry** (Easter–Sept; £1.50 single, £2 return) which takes you the rest of the way.

Midway between Fairbourne and the ferry's departure point, a halt on the railway line boasts a name to outdo even Llanfairpwll on Anglesey. No doubt hopeful that a ridiculously contrived station name might bring Fairbourne the same kudos and visitors, it has been officially named Gorsafawddacha'idraigodanheddogleddollônpenrhynareurdraethceredigion ("The station on the Mawddach with dragon's teeth on the north Penrhyn Drive on the golden Cardigan sands"). If only to show how tortuously overblown the name is, the "dragon's teeth" are a set of grim concrete defences left over from World War II. And that's about as good as Fairbourne gets.

Dolgellau

The old county town of Meirionethshire, **DOLGELLAU** still maintains an air of unhurried importance, never more so than when all the area's farmers pile into town for market. It's a handsome place indeed, though its dark buildings, seemingly hewn from the one rock, can appear foreboding when gleaming in the frequent downpours. In fine weather, with the lofty crags of Cadair Idris framing the grey squares and streets, Dolgellau feels as Welsh and exotic as is possible.

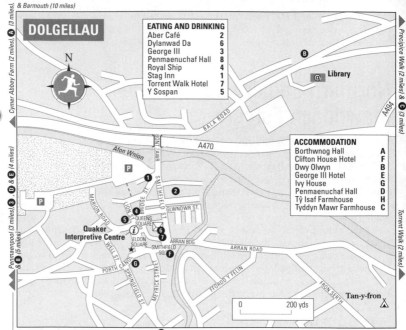

& Barmouth (10 miles)

Cymer Abbey Farm (2 miles) ◀ ④ (3 miles)

Precipice Walk (2 miles) & ⑥ (3 miles)

THE CAMBRIAN COAST | Northern Cadair Idris and the Mawddach Estuary

④

Penmaenpool (3 miles) ③ & ⑩ & ⑤ (4 miles) ◀ & ⑧ (5 miles)

Torrent Walk (2 miles) ▶

DOLGELLAU

EATING AND DRINKING
Aber Café	2
Dylanwad Da	6
George III	3
Penmaenuchaf Hall	8
Royal Ship	4
Stag Inn	1
Torrent Walk Hotel	7
Y Sospan	5

@ Library

ACCOMMODATION
Borthwnog Hall	A
Clifton House Hotel	F
Dwy Olwyn	B
George III Hotel	E
Ivy House	G
Penmaenuchaf Hall	D
Tŷ Isaf Farmhouse	H
Tyddyn Mawr Farmhouse	C

Quaker Interpretive Centre

0   200 yds

Tan-y-fron

Bryn-Y- Gwyn Campsite(0.5 miles), Ty Nant Campsite, ⑪ & Cadair Idris: Pony path (3 miles)   © Crown copyright

It is a much older town than appearances suggest, lying at the junction of three Roman roads which converged on a now-vanished military outpost. It was here that Owain Glyndŵr assembled the last Welsh parliament in 1404, and later signed an alliance with Charles VI of France for providing troops to fight against Henry IV of England. Seventeenth-century Quakers sought freedom from persecution here, and in the 1860s, Dolgellau became the focus of numerous **gold rushes**, drawing wave after wave of prospectors to pan the estuary or blast levels into Clogau shale or mudstone sediment under the Coed y Brenin Forest. The quartz veins yielded some gold, but in quantities too small to make much money.

As the most convenient access point to the southern reaches of the Snowdonia National Park, Dolgellau is a decent and enjoyable base today. As well as offering some wonderful walks, notably an easy stroll along the Mawddach Estuary and a strenuous hike up Cadair Idris, Dolgellau offers plenty of evening diversions in the form of good pubs and restaurants and a fair bit of live music, none more so than during the superb annual **Sesiwn Fawr** (see p.334).

Arrival, information and accommodation

Dolgellau has no train station but is well served by **buses** (except Sun when services are sparse) from Bala, Barmouth and Machynlleth, which all pull into Eldon Square. The building on the square known as Tt Meirion houses the **tourist office** (Easter–Oct daily 9.30am–5.30pm; Nov–Easter Mon & Thurs–Sun 9.30am–4.30pm; ☎01341/422888, ℮ticdolgellau@hotmail.com), along with the Quaker Interpretive Centre (see p.334). There's **Internet access** at the library (Mon & Fri 10am–7pm, Tues & Thurs 10am–5pm, Wed 10am–1pm, Sat 10am–noon) on the northeastern edge of town on the Bala Road. **Bike rental** is available at Dolgellau Cycles on Smithfield Street (☎01341/423332).

△ Dolgellau

Though there is some commendable **accommodation** in Dolgellau itself (several places catering to the legions of mountain bikers frequenting Coed-y-Brenin), there are more appealing options scattered around the district, some so close to Cadair Idris that you can start your hike at the back door.

Hotels and guesthouses

Borthwnog Hall 3 miles west of Dolgellau on the A496, towards Bontddu ☎01341/430271, ⓦhomepages.enterprise.net/borthwnoghall. Small country house with its own art gallery superbly located on the northern shores of the Mawddach Estuary, with log fires and great meals. Take the #94 bus. ❻

Clifton House Hotel Smithfield Square ☎01341/422554, ⓦwww.clifton-house-hotel .co.uk. Good-value hotel built in an ex-police station and jail – the basement cells are used as a restaurant. Some rooms are en suite. ❸/❹

Dwy Olwyn Coed y Fronallt, Llanfachreth Rd ☎01341/422822, ⓦwww.dwyolwyn.co.uk. Peaceful guesthouse in landscaped gardens and with Cadair Idris views. A 10-min walk from the centre – cross Bont Fawr (Big Bridge) and turn right. ❷

George III Hotel Penmaenpool, 4 miles west of Dolgellau ☎01341/422525, ⓦwww.landmark-inns .co.uk. Superb seventeenth-century hotel right by the Mawddach Estuary (bus #28). Some rooms are in former train station buildings and the restaurant (see p.336) is excellent. ❻

Ivy House Finsbury Square ☎01341/422535, ⓦwww.ukworld.net/ivyhouse. Fairly basic licensed guesthouse a few yards southeast of Eldon Square, with some en-suite rooms, a cellar bar and plenty of bike storage. ❸

Penmaenuchaf Hall Penmaenpool, 4 miles west of Dolgellau ☎01341/422129, ⓦwww.penhall .co.uk. Grand house formerly home to a Lancashire cotton magnate and now operating as a classy country hotel, with beautiful decor, a full-size billiard table and free angling for trout and salmon. It's pricey for one night but quite competitive for short breaks. ❽

Tan-y-Fron Arran Rd ☎01341/422638, ⓦwww .tanyfron.co.uk. Non-smoking B&B with en-suite rooms and an associated campsite, a 10-min walk east along Arran Road. Closed Dec & Jan. ❸

Tŷ Isaf Farmhouse Llanfachreth ☎01341/423261, ⓦwww.tyisaf78.freeserve .co.uk. Small, comfortable seventeenth-century guesthouse in three acres of grounds close to the Precipice Walk. Great £15 communal dinners and generous breakfasts. ❹

Tyddyn Mawr Farmhouse, Islawrdref, 3 miles southwest of Dolgellau ☎01341/422331, ⓦwww .lokalink.co.uk/dolgellau/tyddynmawr. Eighteenth-century farmhouse on the slopes of Cadair Idris at the foot of the Pony Path. Very welcoming and great value, with all rooms en suite. Closed Nov to mid-March. ❸

Hostels and campsites

Bryn-y-Gwyn Campsite Cader Rd ☎01341/422733. A basic tents-only site less than a mile southeast of Dolgellau. £5 per pitch.

Kings YHA Hostel Penmaenpool, 4 miles west of Dolgellau ☎01341/422392 or 0870/770 5900, ✉kings@yha.org.uk. Large country house a mile up a wooded valley off the #28 Tywyn bus route (last bus around 7pm), with 6-bed rooms at £9.50 per person. An ideal base for the Pony Path up Cadair Idris. Open April–Aug.

Tan-y-Fron Campsite Arran Rd ☎01341/422638. Well-appointed and reasonably priced camping and caravan site next to the B&B of the same name. £6 per pitch.

Tŷ Nant Cader Rd, Islawrdref, 3 miles southwest of Dolgellau ☎01341/423398. Simple field campsite (£5 per pitch) with shower facilities shared by a simple bunkhouse. £8 gets you a bunk space (bring your own mat and bedding) and the use of a gas cooker, pots and pans.

The Town

Its decent shops aside, Dolgellau's only central diversion is the **Quaker Interpretive Centre**, above the tourist office (see above), which uses a series of explanatory panels to tell of the local Quakers' (the Society of Friends) well-recorded sufferings before the 1689 Act of Toleration that put a stop – at least legally – to persecution for their pacifist Nonconformist views, non-attendance at church and non-payment of its tithes. At a trial in Bala in 1679, this last sin earned a group of Friends a prison term, a further encouragement to those thinking of following the two thousand Welsh Quakers who had already fled to the United States and started the Pennsylvania towns of Bangor, Bryn Mawr and others. The building also houses a **national park exhibition** concentrating on southern Snowdonia.

Around Dolgellau

Gold frenzy hit Dolgellau long before its heyday in Victorian times: flecks of gold were discovered in the Mawddach silt by the Romans, while the thirteenth-century Cistercian monks based at **Cymer Abbey** (open access; free; CADW), two miles north of Dolgellau, were given "the right in digging or carrying away metals and treasures free from all secular exaction". The fine location at the head of the Mawddach Estuary is typical of this austere order, but unfortunately the surrounding caravan site mars the effect of the remaining Gothic slabs. A path beside the abbey makes an alternative approach to the Precipice Walk (see box opposite).

Precious metal was also the raison d'être for the village of **BONTDDU**, four miles west along the A496 towards Barmouth. This is the source of gold used in royal wedding rings, and if you walk up the wooded valley north of the village, you'll come across mine workings past and present.

To see something of the local landscape without having to foot it, head to Penmaenpool, four miles west of Dolgellau on the A493, where the **Abergwynant Farm Pony Trekking Centre** (☎01341/422377; £15 for 2hr) offers superb year-round pony trekking.

Eating, drinking and entertainment

Dolgellau and the surrounding area are blessed with some good **eating** options, particularly in the daytime. Evening life focuses on the numerous pubs, together with odd concerts and performances – see local notice boards. The public are welcome at weekly rehearsals for the town's male voice choir, Côr Meibion Dolgellau, at Ysgol Gynradd (Wed 8pm). The annual **Sesiwn Fawr** (literally "Big Session"; booking hotline ☎08712/301314, ⓦwww.sesiwnfawr.co.uk) is just that: a long weekend of bands and musical shenanigans taking place on

Note: The OS Explorer 1:25,000 map #OL23, "Cadair Idris & Llyn Tegid", is recommended, particularly for the ascent of Cadair Idris.

Torrent Walk

The attractive lowland **Torrent Walk** (2 miles; 1hr; 100ft ascent), follows the course of the Clywedog River as it carves its way through the bedrock. Stroll downstream past the cascades and through some gnarled old woodland that drips with antiquity. Bus #32/X32 can take you the 2.5 miles east along the A470, from where it's a couple of hundred yards or so down the B4416 (signposted to Brithdir) to a sign on the left-hand side marking the beginning of the walk.

Precipice Walk and New Precipice Walk

Though the path is narrow in places and there are some steep banks, the **Precipice Walk** (3–4 miles; 2hr; negligible ascent) can hardly be called precipitous. In fact it is very easy-going, simple to follow and has great views to the 1000-foot ramparts of Cadair Idris and along the Mawddach Estuary – best in late afternoon or early morning sun. The path makes a circuit around Foel Cynwch, starting three miles north of Dolgellau from a public car park on the road to Llanfachreth. For those without a vehicle, there's access from a path beside Cymer Abbey (see p.334). Even less precipitous, the **New Precipice Walk** (4 miles; 2hr; 700ft ascent) combines luscious views of the estuary with a ramble along the old tramways of the Foel Ispri gold mine. Access is easiest from the signed path at the very western end of Llanelltyd village, two miles northwest of Dolgellau.

Penmaenpool–Morfa Mawddach Walk

Beside the Mawddach Estuary's broad sands, a disused rail line makes for easy going on the **Penmaenpool–Morfa Mawddach Walk** (8 miles one way; 3hr; flat), starting in Dolgellau at the car park by Bont Fawr (Big Bridge). The first two miles are the least interesting, so it makes sense to catch the #28 bus to the **RSPB Nature Information Centre** (Easter & late May to Sept daily 11am–5pm; Easter to late May Sat & Sun noon–4pm; free) in an old rail signal box at Penmaenpool, just by a wooden toll bridge (daily 8am–7pm; cars 50p, pedestrians 20p) linking the two banks of the estuary. From there the path (also a popular cycle trail) hugs the estuary bank all the way to Morfa Mawddach, from where you can walk across the bridge to Barmouth or catch the bus back to Dolgellau. Another good scheme is to take the bus to Morfa Mawddach and walk back to Penmaenpool, or use the Cambrian Coast railway to Morfa Mawddach.

Pony Path

If the weather is good and you are well kitted out, don't miss the classic **Pony Path** (6–7 miles; 4–5hr; 2500ft ascent), a straightforward and enjoyable route up Cadair Idris which starts from the car park at Tŷ Nant, three miles southwest from Dolgellau along the Cadair Road. Turn right, then right again at the telephone box, following the path to "Cader Idris". Already, the views to the craggy flanks of the massif are tremendous, but they disappear as you climb steeply to the col, where you turn left on a rocky path to the summit shelter on **Penygadair** (2930ft; see also p.329). The descent is either by the same route or (with some care and considerable efforts to minimize erosion) by taking the first part of the Fox's Path down to Llyn y Gadair. From the summit, go northeast to a grassy plateau then north to a couple of cairns and down to Llyn y Gadair. By the lake, forsake the rest of the Fox's Path in favour of a less obvious route heading off from the northwest corner of the lake, eventually meeting the Pony Path again. Note that there are no buses up Cadair Road.

the riverside meadows below the bridge, with plenty more music and mayhem to be found in the town's pubs. Taking place in mid-July, this is undoubtedly Dolgellau's finest hour.

Aber Café Smithfield St. One of Dolgellau's nicest daytime cafés.

🏃 **Dylanwad Da** 2 Smithfield St ☎01341/422870. The best restaurant in town, with creative, affordable dishes – like Thai seafood soup (£5) and cumin-spiced salmon or Moroccan lamb stew (£12) – and great desserts served in simple surroundings. Also open for good coffee and cakes 10am–4pm. Closed Feb.

George III Penmaenpool (see p.333). Superb spot for an afternoon drink, a bar meal or something gamey and expensive from the à la carte menu.

Penmaenuchaf Hall Penmaenpool (see p.333). High-quality modern British cuisine in tasteful surroundings, complete with crystal and candle-light. Expect to pay £40 for a full meal.

Royal Ship Queens Square. Large and cheerful old coaching inn, with good beer and decent food too.

Stag Inn Bridge St. Straightforward town-centre pub with good beer and a garden.

Torrent Walk Hotel Smithfield Square. Currently the liveliest pub in town, though with some quiet corners for more reflective drinking.

Y Sospan Queen's Square ☎01341/423174. Dependable café/bistro behind the tourist office, serving reasonable coffee, decent daytime meals and better dinners (booking necessary), all at modest prices.

Barmouth and around

The best approach to **BARMOUTH** (Abermaw) is the 2253-foot-long rail bridge created for the nineteenth-century English Midlands sea-bathers who popularized the town; from the south, the bridge traverses over 113 rickety-looking wooden spans across the Mawddach River estuary. On the face of it, this tight little town, tucked into the shadow of steep cliffs and lapped by both estuary and sea, should be the jewel of the Cambrian coast, but years of shabby development have lumbered it with too many heavy buildings and charmless pleasure-beach attractions. Keep your eyes out to sea or make for the hills behind the town, though, and it's a fine stop for a night or two.

Barmouth was once a shipbuilding centre, and a maritime air lingers around the quay at the south end of town, departure point for a **passenger ferry** to Fairbourne (Easter–Oct; as frequently as custom demands; £1.50 single, £2 return) as well as several sea angling and sightseeing trips (enquire on the quay). In late June each year, the highly competitive **Three Peaks Race** (Ⓦwww .threepeaksyachtrace.co.uk) starts here, a two-to-three-day amateur monohull yachting event entailing navigation to Caernarfon, the English Lake District and Fort William in Scotland, and a run up the highest peak in each country. The current record, set in 2002, is two days, fourteen hours and 22 minutes.

The quay is also where you'll find the **RNLI Lifeboat Museum** (Easter–Sept daily 10.30am–4.30pm; free), with its workaday exhibition of lifesaving paraphernalia, and the **Tŷ Gwyn Museum** (July–Sept daily 10.30am–5pm; free), a medieval tower house where Henry VII's uncle, Jasper Tudor, is said to have plotted Richard III's downfall. First recorded in a poem around the middle of the fifteenth century, the house was thought to have been destroyed until renovations in the 1980s revealed its identity. It now contains displays on the Tudor dynasty, as well as explanatory panels on local shipwrecks

On the hill behind, the **Tŷ Crwn Roundhouse** (same hours as Tŷ Gwyn museum) acted as a lockup for drunken sailors in the eighteenth century, and was reputedly built circular to prevent the devil lurking in any corners and further tempting the incarcerated mariners. It now houses some old photos of Barmouth.

One shipwreck not mentioned in the museum is that of the 700-ton Genoese galleon the *Bronze Bell*, which sank in 1709 five miles northwest of

Walks from Barmouth

The best lowland walk on the Cambrian coast, the **Barmouth–Fairbourne Loop** (5 miles; 2–3hr; 300ft ascent) makes a superb circuit around Barmouth and Fairbourne, with fine mountain, estuarine and coastal views all the way. The route can be done with almost no walking at all using the rail line to Fairbourne, the Fairbourne narrow-gauge railway and the ferry across the mouth of the estuary, but walking allows for seemingly infinite variation. The route first crosses the rail bridge (60p return toll) to Morfa Mawddach station, follows the lane to the main road, crosses it onto a footpath that loops around the back of a small wooded hill to Pant Einion Hall, then follows another lane back to the main road near Fairbourne. Turn north for 400 yards, then left down the main street of Fairbourne to the sea, walk north along the beach and you can catch the ferry back to Barmouth. Any desired extension to the walk is best done from Morfa Mawddach, where the route described meets the Penmaen-pool-Morfa Mawddach Walk (see box on p.335). Follow it for a mile to Arthog where a small road and a mesh of paths lead up past waterfalls to the beautiful **Cregennan Lakes** (NT).

The **Panorama Walk** (10min) is more famous, but apart from the fine estuary view, its chief quality is its brevity, the viewpoint being only yards away from the nearest road. By taking in **Dinas Oleu** (Fortress of Light), the cliffs immediately above Barmouth, which became the National Trust's first property in 1895, it can be turned into a decent walk (3 miles; 2hr; 400ft ascent). Essentially the route follows Gloddfa Road opposite Woolworth's on High Street onto the exposed clifftops, where there is a map of the reserve. Go through the metal gate and follow the path past French-man's Grave to a road where you turn left to the Panorama Viewpoint. Return by the same route.

here, complete with its cargo of Carrara marble virtually identical to the stuff Michelangelo was using at the time. Forty or so two-ton blocks of marble still lie on the seabed but one piece was raised in the 1980s, and fashioned by local sculptor Frank Cocksey into "**The Last Haul**", a sculpture which stands at the junction of The Quay and Church Street. Three centuries of undersea corrosion have left the surface fabulously pockmarked, though the quality of marble comes through in the carved section which depicts three fishing generations working together to haul in a catch.

Practicalities

Buses from Harlech and Dolgellau stop on Jubilee Road, near the **train station** and just a few yards from the **tourist office**, Station Road (Easter–Oct daily 10am–6pm; ☏01341/280787, ⓦ www.barmouth-wales .co.uk). Free **Internet access** is available at the library on Talbot Square, and there's basic **bike rental** from Birmingham Garage on Church Street (☏01341/280644).

In winter, the tourist office displays a list of available **accommodation**; in summer, there's plenty to go round except for July and August when booking ahead is advised. There are also loads of places to **camp**, the closest – and least afflicted with fixed caravans – being the plush *Hendre Mynach*, Llanaber Road (closed Jan & Feb; ☏01341/280262, £12 per pitch), just off the beach a mile north of town. Among the usual cheap cafés that populate every seaside resort, there are quite a few decent places to **eat**, the majority clustered at the south end of town where The Quay meets Church Street, which is also the best area for **pubs**. The **entertainment** scene has less to offer, with only a couple of decent pubs and a notoriously iffy nightclub.

Hotels and guesthouses

Bae Abermaw Hotel Panorama Hill
☎01341/280550, ⓦwww.baeabermaw.com.
Very un-Barmouth, this former Victorian hotel has
gone all contemporary, with minimalist white-on-
white rooms, a spacious and elegant bare-boards
lounge and a good restaurant, almost all with
superb Cardigan Bay views. **❼**

Bryn Melyn Hotel Panorama Rd ☎01341/280556,
ⓦwww.brynmelynhotel.co.uk. Comfortable, traditional,
mountainside hotel noted for its fine estuary views and
proximity to the Cambrian Way walking route. **❺**

Endeavour Marine Parade ☎01341/280271.
Basic but reasonable B&B with sea views from all
rooms. **❷**

Llwyndû Farmhouse Llanaber, 2 miles
north of Barmouth ☎01341/280144, ⓦwww
.llwyndu-farmhouse.co.uk. One of the finest farmhouse B&Bs in Wales, with en-suite rooms in the
seventeenth-century farmhouse building – complete
with mullioned windows and inglenook fireplace
– and adjacent converted barn, plus delicious
evening meals in the candlelit dining room (Mon–Sat;
from £21). **❺**

Wavecrest Hotel 8 Marine Parade
☎01341/280330, ⓦwww.lokalink.co.uk/
wavecrest. One of the better beachfront B&Bs,
with antique-furnished en-suite rooms and a good,
budget restaurant. **❸**

Eating, drinking and entertainment

Bae Abermaw (see "Accommodation", above).
Comfy chairs, wooden floors, white walls and a

wintertime fire make dining here a pleasure – and
the food's good, too, with mains around the £20
mark. The wine list is reasonable but there's little
choice by the glass.

The Bistro Church St ☎01341/281009. Ging-
ham tablecloths, bentwood chairs and a menu of
bistro favourites, with starters £4–6 and mains
£10–15.

Indian Clipper Church St
☎01341/280252. A great South Asian
balti house which serves well-prepared and
tasty meals including plenty of vegetarian
dishes. Unlicensed, but you can bring your own
booze.

Isis The Quay. The pick of the quayside places with
good stuffed baguettes, a limited range of pizzas
(£5–8) and straightforward low-cost meals, including vegetarian options, and good espresso. Closed
Oct–Feb.

Last Inn Church St ☎01341/280530. A cosy bar
in a former cobbler's shop where you can also get
good pub meals – like Thai red chicken curry (£8)
and sirloin steak (£11). The outdoor tables catch
the afternoon sun.

Llwyndû Farmhouse (see "Accommodation", above). Lovely two- and three-course
table d'hôte meals (£21/25) utilizing local produce
but with Mediterranean influences. You'll be served
in an intimate wood-beamed room, but arrive early
for pre-dinner drinks around the vast inglenook
fireplace.

Tal y Don High St. Traditional and friendly pub with
well-kept real ales.

Ardudwy

North of Barmouth, the coast opens out to a narrow coastal plain running a
dozen miles towards Snowdonia and flanked by the heather-covered slopes
of the Rhinog Mountains, five miles inland. This is **Ardudwy**, a land which
Giraldus Cambrensis described as "the rudest and roughest of all the Welsh
districts", a contention hard to reconcile with a fertile strip used as a fattening
ground for black Welsh cattle on their way to the English markets, and now
tamed by caravan sites and golf courses.

No modern road crosses the Rhinogs to the east, but until the early nineteenth-century building of coach roads, the existence of two mountain passes
(see box on p.340) made this a strategic and populous area, as the number of
minor Neolithic burial chambers and small Iron and Bronze Age forts demonstrate. Further up the coast, the town of **Harlech** was built as one link in
Edward I's chain of magnificent fortresses. It is the only sizeable town in the
region, followed in importance by **Llanbedr**, from where a road runs west to
the dune-backed camping resort on Shell Island, and another rises east, splitting
into two delightful remote valleys.

Bus #38 services the coast from Barmouth to Harlech, then inland to Blaenau

Ffestiniog. The Cambrian coast train line covers the same route to Harlech, from where it makes for Porthmadog on the Llŷn.

Llanddwywe and Dyffryn Ardudwy

Two of the most accessible and impressive Neolithic sites in Ardudwy are in the contiguous twin villages of **LLANDDWYWE** and **DYFFRYN ARDUDWY**, five miles north of Barmouth. Turn right opposite the church in Llanddwywe and continue for a mile to get to **Cors-y-Gedol Burial Chamber** (unrestricted entry), a large capstone on deeply embedded uprights. It's currently unsignposted, but follow the path to the right at the far end of Ffordd Gors; the one straight ahead leads to the old drovers' bridge at **Pont Scethin** and the Roman Steps (see p.341). More substantial than Cors-y-Geddol, the **Dyffryn Ardudwy Burial Chambers** (unrestricted entry; CADW) are signposted just off the main road behind the school. Two supported capstones lie amongst a bed of small boulders, the base stones of a mound thought to have been a hundred feet long. Finds from a dig here in the 1960s – including pottery, finely polished stone plaques and bones – are on display at the National Museum in Cardiff.

If you're travelling by train, get off at Talybont, walk north to visit the two sites and rejoin the line at Dyffryn Ardudwy, a walk of three miles in all. Just beyond Dyffryn Ardudwy station is the southern entrance to the **Morfa Dyffryn National Nature Reserve**, a coastal dune system stretching up to Shell Island (see below) notable for its flora, particularly the marsh helleborine. This is a fragile zone and large areas are fenced off, but there's beach access across a boardwalk. Follow the path from Dyffryn Ardudwy station through the caravan parks and the dunes to the splendid, vast **beach**, possibly the finest in Wales. A section of shore a few hundred yards to the north serves as Wales' only official nudist beach.

Llanbedr and around

LLANBEDR, three miles north of Dyffryn Ardudwy, is home to more Neolithic sights There are two imposing **standing stones** at the northern end of the village, in the field to the northwest of the petrol station; sadly, though, they and an oak tree are incarcerated behind a rusty fence. Across the road from the stones is the parish **church of St Peter**, which contains an ancient stone grooved with a spiral pattern, a common design from other pre-Christian sites. Other than that, its **YHA hostel**, *Plas Newydd* (℡0870/770 5926, ellanbedr@yha.org.uk; open April–Oct), right in the centre and with dorm beds at £10.50, makes Llanbedr a reasonable place to stay, as does the central ⚔ *Victoria Inn* (℡01341/241213; ❹) with its beer garden, good bar meals and à la carte dinners.

Though Llanbedr itself offers limited excitement, there are plenty of things to do in the area. A lane forks off the main road in the village centre, snaking its way alongside the babbling Afon Artro, past the train station and redundant airfield to **Shell Island**, or Mochras, two miles away (£5 per car). A peninsula at anything other than high tide, you reach the island by a tidal causeway, then you can swim, sail, examine the wildflowers or scour the beach for some of the two hundred varieties of shell found here. The Shell Island complex houses a restaurant, deservedly popular for Sunday roast lunch, and forms the centrepiece of the huge caravan-free **campsite** (℡01341/241453, ❂www.shellisland .co.uk; £6 per person), which spreads its way along the beach from the harbour down to the vast dunes of Morfa Dyffryn. Although it can get crowded during the school summer holidays and warm bank holiday weekends, at any other

The northern **Rhinogs** offer some surprisingly tough walking. At under 2500ft, they're hardly giants, but the typically large, rough, gritstone rocks hidden in thick heather make anything but the most well-worn paths hard-going and potentially ankle-twisting. The rewards for your efforts are long views across Cardigan Bay, a good chance of stumbling across a herd of feral goats and a strong sense of achievement. The two walks described here start at the head of different valleys (see opposite), but share a common summit, that of Rhinog Fawr. Ambitious walkers might try combining the two (10 miles; 7hr; 3700ft ascent), using paths that only approximately follow those marked on the OS Landranger #124 1:50,000 "Porthmadog & Dolgellau" map or the 1:25,000 Explorer #OL18 "Harlech, Porthmadog & Bala" map.

Cwm Bychan Walk #1

The **Cwm Bychan walk** (5 miles; 3–4hr; 1900ft ascent) starts at the car park in Cwm Bychan, following signs up through a small wood then out onto the open moor and up to the misnamed **Roman Steps**. These guide you up to a pass, Bwlch Tyddiad, giving views east to Bala and beyond. Continue a couple of hundred yards past a large cairn to a smaller one signalling a much less well-defined path leading south and steeply up. Beyond Llyn Du, the terrain gets steeper still, and you may have to use your hands to finally reach **Rhinog Fawr** (2362ft). The standard route is then to retrace your steps, but in good weather you can descend the same way you came for a few hundred yards and seek out a line running northwest from the shoulder towards Gloyw Llyn. From there, with some effort, you can pick up a path by following the obvious watercourse along a small stream to the head of Llyn Cwm Bychan.

Cwm Bychan Walk #2

The second walk (6–7 miles; 5–6hr; 2900ft ascent) starts by the Maes-y-Garnedd farmhouse at the head of Cwm Nantcol and makes a fairly rugged circuit over Rhinog Fawr and Rhinog Fach. Follow the track north from the car park to the house, into the fields and over the stile, then turn northeast and walk gradually towards the base of the rocky southwest ridge, following the white marker posts. Eventually, the path turns north to a cairn on the skyline, then east following more cairns up the ridge to the summit trig point of **Rhinog Fawr** (2362ft).

To approach Rhinog Fach you first have to make an arduous descent into Bwlch Drws Ardudwy (The Pass of the Door of Ardudwy). From the summit of Rhinog Fawr head southeast towards a couple of cairns, then with Rhinog Fach ahead of you keep left, descending on whatever looks like it has had the most use. Eventually you'll reach the col, where you cross the stone wall and start on a fairly clear line up **Rhinog Fach** (2236ft). Explore the summit ridge to get the best views either way, then descend to Cwm Nantcol by first walking to a rocky ledge overlooking Llyn Hywel to the south. From here you should be able to see a scrappy path running very steeply down to the lake on the right-hand edge of the ledge. You'll have to use your hands at times, and there are sections of scree, but you're soon on a clear path that skirts north around the base of Rhinog Fach towards Bwlch Drws Ardudwy. When you reach the path through the pass, turn left and follow it back to Cwm Nantcol.

---

time, you're virtually guaranteed solitude amongst quite spectacular scenery, with some of the best sunsets in north Wales. At low tide you can see a line of rocks in the sea leading out towards Ireland, known as Sarn Badrig (St Patrick's Causeway) and traditionally thought to be the road to a flooded land known as the Cantre'r Gwaelod ("The Low Hundreds").

East of Llanbedr, a narrow road dives through gorgeous woods as it follows the Afon Artro six miles to the waters of **Llyn Cwm Bychan**, deep in the heather and angular rocks of the Rhinog range. Park (£2) at the farm here, to take the path up to the **Roman Steps** – most likely a medieval packhorse route, made of flat slabs cutting through the range – onto Rhinog Fawr (see box, opposite). Branching off the Cwm Bychan road a mile out of Llanbedr, another delightful road leads to **Cwm Nantcol**, the next valley south. Two hundred yards up the lane, **Capel Salem** was where Sidney Curnow Vosper's famous 1908 painting of the same name was modelled – a copy hangs inside. Further up the lane, follow the signs to the Nantcol Waterfalls for a lovely basic **campsite** (£3 per person) by the river.

North of Llanbedr the A496 climbs gently for a mile or so to **Chwarel Hên Slate Caverns** (Easter to Sept daily 10am–5pm; Oct daily 11am–4pm; £3.95) at Llanfair, a small slate quarry visited on a self-guided underground tour. A few yards further on, a small road branches down to the hamlet of **Llandanwg**, a great place to get out onto the dunes, with a small church that has to be periodically dug out of the sand by youth scheme workers so that the occasional service can be held. From the top road in Llanfair, a lane to the right ascends into spectacular hill country, a crisscross of dry stone walls, sheep and prehistoric relics.

Harlech

One of the undoubted highlights of the Cambrian Coast is charming **HARLECH**, three miles north of Llanbedr. Clinging to a rocky outcrop, the time-worn castle alone dramatically raises Harlech above its neighbours, and the town behind commands one of Wales' finest views: over the Morfa Harlech dunes across Cardigan Bay and beyond to the Llŷn, and north to the jagged peaks of Snowdonia. The castle's bulky intactness, and its seemingly impregnable position, dominate the surroundings, but don't miss the narrow streets and buildings of this small, friendly town, cloaking the hill behind the fortress. With some superb places to stay, eat and drink, together with wonderful walking country behind and superb beaches in front, Harlech is an excellent option for a few nights' sojourn.

Arrival, information and accommodation

Harlech's **train** station is on the main A496 under the castle. Most **buses** call both here and at the southern end of High Street,

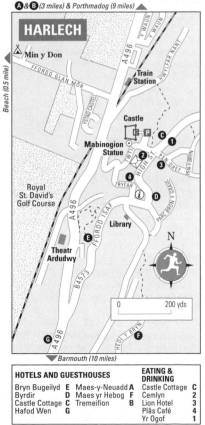

HOTELS AND GUESTHOUSES		EATING & DRINKING	
Bryn Bugeilyd **E**	Maes-y-Neuadd **A**	Castle Cottage	**C**
Byrdir **D**	Maes yr Hebog **F**	Cemlyn	**2**
Castle Cottage **C**	Tremeifion **B**	Lion Hotel	**3**
Hafod Wen **G**		Plâs Café	**4**
		Yr Ogof	**1**

© Crown copyright

a couple of hundred yards from the **tourist office** (Easter–Oct daily 10am–5pm; ☎01766/780658, ✉ticharlech@hotmail.com). Theatr Ardudwy (☎01766/780667, ⓦ www.theatrardudwy.co.uk), on the A496, occasionally puts on decent plays and shows recent releases at the only cinema in the district. There's **accommodation**, in town and around, to suit all pockets, and a reasonable summer-only **campsite**, *Min y Don* (☎01766/780286; £10 per pitch), only three minutes' walk towards the beach (left out of the station then first right).

Hotels and guesthouses

Bryn Bugeilyd B&B Ffordd Isaf ☎01766/780617. Two rooms in a 1920s stone house with stunning seaward views. ❷

Byrdir High St ☎01766/780316, ⓦ www.byrdir. com. Reliable small hotel with some en-suite rooms and meals available, 200 yards from the tourist office. Closed Nov. ❷/❹

Castle Cottage Pen Llech ☎01766/780479, ⓦ www.castlecottageharlech.co.uk. Cosy informal "restaurant with rooms", and often booked well ahead. Inevitably, the excellent meals are a feature and there's a comfortable bar. ❺

Hafod Wen A496 half a mile south of town ☎01766/780356, ⓦ www.harlechguesthouse .co.uk. A lovely guesthouse set in well-tended grounds and with stupendous coastal views. Some of the spacious, comfy en-suite rooms have sunny verandas, and all are imaginatively furnished and dotted with original artwork. ❺

Maes-y-Neuadd Talsarnau, 3 miles north of Harlech ☎01766/780200, ⓦ www.neuadd. com. One of the region's finest places to stay, in a substantially modernized country-house hotel (parts of which date from the fourteenth century) set in beautiful grounds. The expensive meals have garnered all manner of accolades. ❾

Maes yr Hebog Heol y Bryn ☎01766/780885, ⓦ www.harlechholidays.co.uk. Comfortable and well-appointed rooms in a large modern house on the outskirts of Harlech, plus a hearty dinner for £13. Closed Nov–Feb. ❸

Tremeifion Talsarnau, 3 miles north of Harlech ☎01766/770491, ⓦ www.vegetarian-hotel.com. Luxury, non-smoking vegetarian guesthouse in three acres of grounds sweeping down to the coast with views of Portmeirion. Rates (£56–65 per person), are for dinner, bed and breakfast, including substantial vegetarian or vegan meals made almost entirely from organic produce (much of it grown in the garden), and served with organic wine.

The Town

Although blessed with some of the coast's best beaches, it is the substantially complete **castle** (June–Sept daily 9.30am–6pm; April–May & Oct daily 9.30am–5pm; Nov–March Mon–Sat 9.30am–4pm, Sun 11am–4pm; £3; CADW), squatting on its 200-foot bluff, that is Harlech's showpiece. Intended as one of Edward I's Iron Ring of monumental fortresses (see p.468), construction of Harlech castle began in 1283, just six months after the death of Llywelyn the Last. It was built of a hard Cambrian rock, known as Harlech grit, hewn from the moat where sheep now peacefully graze. One side of the fortress was originally protected by the sea – the waters have now receded, though, leaving the castle dominating a stretch of duned coastline.

The castle has seen a lot of action in its time: it withheld a siege in 1295, was taken by Owain Glyndŵr in 1404, and the youthful, future Henry VII – the first Welsh king of England and Wales – withstood a seven-year siege at the hands of the Yorkists from 1461 to 1468, when the castle was again taken. It fell into ruin, but was put back into service for the king during the Civil War, and in March 1647 it became the last Royalist castle to fall.

The first defensive line comprised the three successive pairs of gates and portcullises built between the two massive half-round towers of the **gatehouse**, where an exhibition now outlines the castle's history. Much of the outermost ring has been destroyed, leaving only the twelve-foot-thick curtain walls rising up 40ft to the exposed battlements, and only the towering gatehouse prevents you walking the full circuit. Outside the castle, a modern equestrian **statue** by Ivor Roberts depicts a scene from The Mabinogion, recalling a semi-mythical era long before Edward's conquest. The heroic giant and king of the British, Bendigeidfran (Brân the Blessed), ruled the court at Harlech, which needed to ally itself with the Irish. Bendigeidfran's sister Branwen (White Crow) married the king of Ireland and bore him a son, Gwern, but war soon broke out and Gwern was killed. Sorrowful uncle and dead nephew are **The Two Kings** of the sculpture's title.

Although there are no specific sights in town aside from the castle and the obligatory cluster of attendant craft shops, Harlech is a cheerful enough place in which to wander, admiring the splendid views in all directions. Reachable via Beach Road, which shoots off the main road through Harlech, directly below the castle, the town's **sand dunes** and **beach** are superb. On the way to the sands, you'll brush past the rather snooty **Royal St David's golf course**, venue of many a championship.

Eating and drinking

For a place of its size, there are some good pubs, cafés and restaurants in Harlech, even if they do tend towards the slightly chintzier end of the market.

Castle Cottage High St ☎01766/780479. Limited choice dinner menu (£24.50–27.50) featuring the likes of duck liver and Cointreau parfait and roasted suckling pig, all beautifully cooked and served informally in snug surroundings.

Cemlyn High St ☎01766/780637. By day, an upscale café serving the best loose-leaf teas and espresso coffees around, by night a quality restaurant for which booking is advised.

Lion Hotel Pen Dref, just up from the central crossroads. About the liveliest pub in Harlech, with handpumped ales and good home-cooked bar meals.

Plâs Café High St ☎01766/780204. Unpretentious licensed café and restaurant with well-prepared lunches and afternoon tea served in a glass-fronted dining room or on a garden terrace with sensational views. Also open for inexpensive to moderately priced evening meals. Closed Jan.

Yr Ogof High St ☎01766/780888. Highly commendable bistro-style place a few yards north of the centre, with bentwood chairs and a good-value range of inventive vegetarian and meaty dishes, with mains around £10.

Travel details

Unless otherwise stated, frequencies for trains and buses are for Monday to Saturday services; Sunday averages 1–3 services, though the main routes are more frequent and some routes have no Sunday service at all.

Trains

Aberdyfi to: Barmouth (10 daily; 30min); Machynlleth (8–10 daily; 20min); Porthmadog (7 daily; 1hr 20min); Pwllheli (7 daily; 1hr 40min); Tywyn (10 daily; 5min).
Aberystwyth to: Borth (9 daily; 12min); Machynlleth (9 daily; 30min).
Barmouth to: Aberdyfi (10 daily; 30min); Harlech (7 daily; 25min); Machynlleth (8–10 daily; 50min); Porthmadog (7 daily; 45min).
Harlech to: Barmouth (7 daily; 30min); Machynlleth (6 daily; 1hr 20min); Porthmadog (7 daily; 20min).
Machynlleth to: Aberdyfi (8–10 daily; 20min); Aberystwyth (9 daily; 30min); Barmouth (10 daily;

50min); Birmingham (7 daily; 2hr 15min); Harlech (7 daily; 1hr 20min); Porthmadog (7 daily; 1hr 45min); Shrewsbury (7 daily; 1hr 20min).
Tywyn to: Aberdyfi (10 daily; 5min); Barmouth (7 daily; 25min); Harlech (7 daily; 1hr); Machynlleth (7 daily; 30min); Porthmadog (7 daily; 1hr 10min).

Buses

Aberaeron to: Aberystwyth (every 30min; 40min); Cardigan (8 daily; 50min); Carmarthen (10 daily; 1hr 40min); Lampeter (10 daily; 40min); New Quay (hourly; 20min).
Aberdyfi to: Machynlleth (8 daily; 20min); Tywyn (8 daily; 10min).

Aberystwyth to: Aberaeron (every 30min; 40min); Borth (hourly; 20min); Caernarfon (4 daily; 3hr); Cardigan (9 daily; 1hr30min–2hr); Carmarthen (mostly hourly; 2hr 20min); Devil's Bridge (2 daily Mon–Sat; 50min); Lampeter (Mon–Sat hourly; 1hr15min); Machynlleth (hourly; 45min); New Quay (hourly; 1hr); Ponterwyd (7 daily Mon–Sat; 30min); Pontrhydfendigaid (3 daily Mon–Sat; 45min); Tregaron (7 daily; 45min); Ynyslas (hourly; 30min).

Barmouth to: Bala (mostly hourly; 1hr); Blaenau Ffestiniog (5 daily; 1hr); Dolgellau (hourly; 30min); Harlech (hourly; 30min); Llangollen (mostly hourly; 2hr); Wrexham (mostly hourly; 2hr 30min).

Cardigan to: Aberaeron (8 daily; 50min); Aberporth (hourly; 25min); Aberystwyth (9 daily; 1hr 30min–2hr); Carmarthen (hourly; 1hr 30min); Cenarth (10 daily; 25min); Cilgerran (8 daily; 10min); Drefach Felindre (hourly; 30min); Newcastle Emlyn (10 daily; 25min); New Quay (hourly; 1hr).

Dolgellau to: Bala (10 daily; 35min); Barmouth (hourly; 30min); Llangollen (mostly hourly; 1hr 30min); Machynlleth (mostly hourly; 30min); Porthmadog (6 daily; 40min); Tywyn (8 daily; 55min).

Fairbourne to: Dolgellau (8 daily; 20min); Tywyn (8 daily; 35min).

Harlech to: Barmouth (hourly; 30min); Blaenau Ffestiniog (4 daily; 35min); Dyffryn Ardudwy (mostly hourly; 15min).

Lampeter to: Aberaeron (10 daily; 40min); Aberystwyth (Mon–Sat hourly; 1hr15min); Carmarthen (mostly hourly; 1hr); Llanddewi Brefi (6 daily Mon–Sat; 25min); Tregaron (Mon–Sat 8 daily; 20–35min).

Machynlleth to: Aberdyfi (8 daily; 20min); Aberystwyth (hourly; 45min); Corris (hourly; 15min); Dolgellau (mostly hourly; 30min); Tywyn (8 daily; 35min).

New Quay to: Aberaeron (hourly; 20min); Aberporth (hourly; 40min); Aberystwyth (hourly; 1hr); Cardigan (hourly; 1hr).

Tregaron to: Aberystwyth (9 daily; 1hr); Lampeter (Mon–Sat 8 daily; 20–35min); Llanddewi Brefi (Mon–Sat 6 daily; 10min).

Tywyn to: Aberdyfi (8 daily; 10min); Abergynolwyn (3 daily; 18min); Corris (3 daily; 30min); Dolgellau (8 daily; 55min); Fairbourne (8 daily; 35min); Machynlleth (8 daily; 35min).

5

The North Wales borderlands

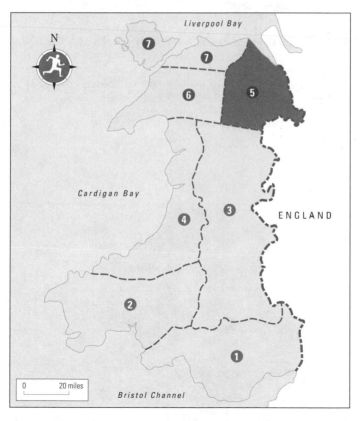

CHAPTER 5 # Highlights

✳ **Plas Newydd, Llangollen** An elegant monument to romantic friendship, Plas Newydd always inspires. See p.358

✳ **Castell Dinas Brân, Llangollen** Hike up to this ragged ruin of a Welsh castle for a breath of air and great views. See p.361

✳ **Llanarmon Dyffryn Ceiriog** Great accommodation and food in a tiny village on the edge of bleak moors. See p.354

✳ **Capel Rûg and Eglwys Llangar, Corwen** One ticket, two small churches, and a finer pair you couldn't hope to find. See p.363

✳ **Ruthin** This compact hilltop town with its cluster of diverting sights also has easy access to gentle walks on the Clwydian hills. See p.367

✳ **Holywell** Once one of Britain's most important pilgrimage sites, St Winefride's Well is now a serene spot where you can still take the waters. See p.373

△ Plas Newydd

The North Wales borderlands

The **North Wales borderlands** is a schizophrenic region encompassing both industrialized flatlands that spill over the border from England and attractive folds of green hill country that are as Welsh as anywhere. There is plenty to see here, but few of the sights top most people's list and visitors often travel through with their minds set firmly on the more obvious destinations further west.

The three main routes through the region – the Dee Valley, the Vale of Clwyd, and Deeside – all start in the English border country known as the **Marches**, an area long contested by the Welsh and English. At its heart is the borderlands' largest conurbation, **Wrexham**, where the light industrial hinterland is leavened by the packaged mining and smelting heritage along the **Clywedog Valley**.

The only extant Marcher fortress of note is **Chirk Castle**, a potent reminder of the centuries after the Norman conquest of England, when powerful barons fought the Welsh princes for control of these fertile lands. It is a fine introduction to the **Dee Valley**, the umbilical cord through to the rugged mountains of Snowdonia. The Dee Valley remains more firmly Welsh than the Marches, and three hundred years after the arrival of the Normans, the area was the site of the first big revolt against them. From his base near **Corwen**, Wales' greatest hero, Owain Glyndŵr, attacked the property of a nearby English landowner, sparking a fourteen-year campaign which, at its height, saw Glyndŵr ruling most of Wales. Little remains to commemorate the era, and most people drive through oblivious of its heritage. **Llangollen** is the valley's main draw, with an international eisteddfod folk music festival each July and a broad selection of ruins, rides and rambles to tempt visitors throughout the rest of the year.

The bucolic lands to the north reward a leisurely approach. The historic but dull market town of **Mold** is the gateway to the bald tops of the **Clwydian Range**, easy walking country that overlooks the pastoral **Vale of Clwyd**. Its gentle contours and minor sights take time to appreciate, something seldom afforded the valley by visitors to the largest towns, appealing **Ruthin** with its fine medieval buildings and gaol tour; and **Denbigh**, surmounted by its craggy castle.

The fastest route through the borderlands follows the A55 close to the coast. This initially runs through **Deeside**, a wedge of former mining communities set between the salt marshes of the Dee estuary and the Clwydian Range.

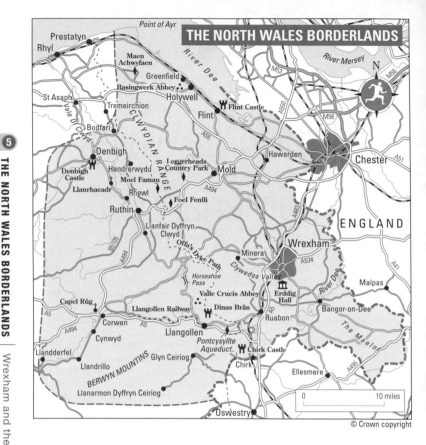

THE NORTH WALES BORDERLANDS

© Crown copyright

The area has its share of modest and varied offerings: the bucolic village of **Hawarden**; **Flint**, the first link in Edward I's Iron Ring of castles; and understated **Holywell**, whose quiet attractions include St Winefride's Well, a pilgrimage site of varied fortunes during the last 1300 years.

Getting around

The region is best explored by car, but public transport will get you most places. **Trains** are good for Deeside and Wrexham, but otherwise you'll be reliant on **buses**. The main routes to Snowdonia are from Wrexham to Llangollen, where you can pick up a bus to either Betws-y-Coed or Bala. Further north, the #51 links Ruthin and Denbigh with the Rhyl on the north coast, and the #11 visits Flint and Holywell on its run between Chester and Rhyl.

Wrexham and the Clywedog Valley

While not a classically pretty place, **WREXHAM** (Wrecsam), the largest town in North Wales, has a boisterous charm and some fine older buildings amidst the identikit chainstores. Having long looked more to the industrial northwest of England than its own Welsh hinterland, Wrexham's Welshness is only loudly and proudly flaunted when the Welsh football team plays international matches at the town's Racecourse Ground (home for the rest of the time of one of the three Welsh sides in the English Football League).

Once a medieval marketplace for the fertile lands all around, Wrexham developed as an administrative centre before the discovery of iron ore, coal and lead combined to jettison the town into the industrial age. The legacy of these times is best seen to the south and west of town in the **Clywedog Valley**, which played a key role in the early part of the Industrial Revolution. Its sites have recently been smartened up as Wrexham's chief attractions, the finest being the National Trust's splendidly evocative **Erddig Hall**.

The Town

Though it is pleasant enough wandering around the recently smartened up centre, complete with Edwardian arcades and two Victorian market halls, you'll soon want to head for the imposing **St Giles' Church** (daily 11am–3pm; free), whose Gothic tower gracefully rises above the knot of lanes at the end of Hope Street. Topped off with a steeple in the 1520s, the tower's five tiers, rising to four hexagonal pinnacles, is replicated at America's Yale University in homage to the ancestral home of the college's benefactor, Elihu Yale, whose tomb is here

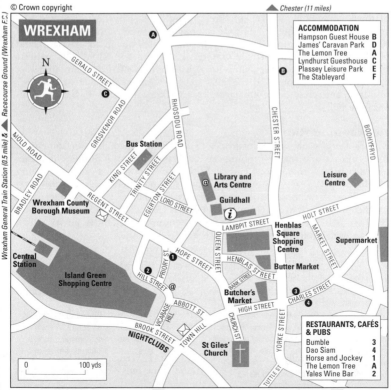

© Crown copyright — ▲ Chester (11 miles)

WREXHAM

N

GERALD STREET

GROSVENOR ROAD

RHOSDDU ROAD

MOLD ROAD

BRADLEY ROAD

Wrexham General Train Station (0.5 mile) & ▲ Racecourse Ground (Wrexham F.C.)

CHESTER STREET

BODHYFRYD

ACCOMMODATION
Hampson Guest House **B**
James' Caravan Park **D**
The Lemon Tree **A**
Lyndhurst Guesthouse **C**
Plassey Leisure Park **E**
The Stableyard **F**

Bus Station

KING STREET

TRINITY STREET

REGENT STREET

EGERTON STREET

LORD STREET

Library and Arts Centre @

Guildhall ℹ

Leisure Centre

Wrexham County Borough Museum ✉

LAMBPIT STREET

HOLT STREET

MARKET STREET

Henblas Square Shopping Centre

Supermarket

Central Station

QUEEN STREET

PRIORY ST.

HOPE STREET

HILL STREET

Island Green Shopping Centre

HENBLAS STREET

BANK STREET

Butter Market

Butcher's Market

VICARAGE HILL

ABBOTT ST.

BROOK STREET

TOWN HILL

NIGHTCLUBS

CHURCH ST.

St Giles' Church ✝

HIGH STREET

CHARLES STREET

YORKE STREET

TUTTLE ST.

RESTAURANTS, CAFÉS & PUBS
Bumble **3**
Dao Siam **4**
Horse and Jockey **1**
The Lemon Tree **A**
Yales Wine Bar **2**

0   100 yds

Ⓓ (5 miles) & Llangollen (11 miles) ▼   Erddig (1 mile), **Ⓔ** (4 miles) & **Ⓕ** (4 miles) ▼

at the base. The engraved stone in the tower wall near his grave came from the university, replacing one that now holds up a replica tower there. The spacious interior boasts the scant remains of a late-fifteenth-century mural of *The Last Judgement* above the entrance to the chancel, and an abundance of Victorian and contemporary stained glass. The church is approached through wrought-iron gates installed between 1718 and 1724 by famed Welsh ironworkers Robert and John Davies of Bersham, also responsible for the striking gates at Chirk Castle and St Peter's Church in Ruthin.

From St Giles' you can head up Hope Street to Regent Street, one of Wrexham's main shopping thoroughfares, to reach the small but quite engaging **Wrexham County Borough Museum** (Mon–Fri 10am–5pm, Sat 10.30am–3pm; free). Its central room exhibits a ramshackle array of artefacts from the town's nineteenth-century boom years, alongside Roman nuggets and the remarkable remains of the Bronze Age Brymbo Man, who was unearthed from a local sandstone burial cist complete with his pottery beaker and flint knife. Two smaller galleries house temporary exhibitions, usually on local themes.

Practicalities

Wrexham has two **train stations**, half a mile apart. Chester, Chirk and Shrewsbury trains call only at Wrexham General on Regent Street, ten minutes' walk northwest of the centre, while services from Liverpool (change at Bidston on the Wirral line) call there on request before Wrexham Central, incorporated into the Island Green shopping centre behind Hill Street, in the middle of town. Midway along Regent Street, King Street branches off to the **bus station**, where infrequent National Express buses (tickets from Key Travel on King Street) arrive from Manchester, Birmingham, London and Glasgow, and regular **local buses** depart for Chester, Llangollen and Mold. The **tourist office** is on Lambpit Street (Mon–Sat: April to mid-Oct 10am–5pm; mid-Oct to March 10am–4pm; ☎01978/292015, ✆www.borderlands.co.uk). There's free **Internet** access at the library and pay facilities at @rrow CyberWorld on Vicarage Hill.

Accommodation

There's a reasonable choice of places to stay in Wrexham, but for something more upscale it's worth pushing on to Llangollen or Ruthin. The nearest **campsite** is the pricey *Plassey Leisure Park*, four miles south at Eyton (☎01978/780277, ✆www.theplassey.co.uk; £19 per pitch), with tent and caravan facilities, a swimming pool and microbrewery. There's a cheaper alternative another mile south at the comfortable *James' Caravan Park*, Llangollen Road, Ruabon (☎01978/820148, eray@carastay.demon.co.uk; £8 per pitch), which boasts a heated toilet and shower block.

Hampson Guest House 6 Chester Rd ☎01978/357665, ✆www.wrexhamhotels .com. Pleasant, central, renovated B&B with some en-suite rooms, full breakfast and nice lawns for a relaxing sundowner. ❷

The Lemon Tree 29 Rhosddu Rd ☎01978/261211, ✆www.lemon-tree.net. Modernized hotel converted from an old priory, with small and simple yet tasteful en-suite rooms (some with canopy beds and DVD players), and a good restaurant where breakfast is served. ❹/❺

Lyndhurst Guesthouse 3 Gerald St, off Grosvenor Rd ☎01978/290802, ✆lyndhurst1@supanet.com. Cosy and central, with a very warm welcome and good breakfasts. ❷

The Stableyard High St, 4 miles southeast in Bangor-on-Dee ☎01978/780642, ✆www .stableyard.co.uk. Attractive rooms and superb meals in a seventeenth-century tavern, in an appealing, ancient village. ❷

Eating, drinking and entertainment

Wrexham has a tolerable range of places to **eat**. There are a few cheap cafés on Bank Street, a narrow passage off Hope Street, and around the markets. While you're here, don't forget to sample Wrexham Lager, the UK's oldest lager, first brewed in 1882 using the town's naturally soft water supply.

At weekends, the area around the junction of Brook Street and Vicarage Hill features a handful of reasonable **nightclubs**; and there's more highbrow diversion in the form of the Brymbo **Male Voice Choir**, who rehearse (Thurs 7.30pm & Sun 8pm) at the Brake Chapel in Moss, three miles northwest of central Wrexham.

Bumble 2 Charles St. Café above a gift shop, good for sandwiches and more substantial meals. Closed Sun.

Dao Siam 13 Charles St ☎01978/351071. Good-quality Thai restaurant, with most mains £6–8. Takeaways available.

The Lemon Tree (see "Accommodation", above). Bustling, brightly decorated Italian restaurant, café and bar with an extensive menu of ciabattas and pasta dishes for lunch (£6–7) and a

wider range of vegetarian and meaty mains from £9–13. Save room for tiramisu or chocolate truffle ice cream. Closed Sun lunch.

Horse and Jockey corner of Hope and Priory streets. Thatched, characterful old cottage, long since converted into a convivial low-beamed pub serving Wrexham Lager and decent food.

Yales Wine Bar Hill St. The best bet in town for live bands or special entertainment; look out for posters around town advertising events.

The Clywedog Valley

The **Clywedog Valley** – forming an arc around the western and southern suburbs of Wrexham – was the crucible of industrial achievement in the northern Welsh borders during the eighteenth century. Iron production boomed here, thanks to an abundance of ore deposits and cheap waterpower harnessed from the River Clywedog. As the Industrial Revolution forged ahead, coal became a more important energy source than water and factories moved closer to their raw materials, leaving the valley barely disturbed. The restored sites are now stations on the seven-mile-long **Clywedog Trail**. It is all a bit over-packaged, but no less interesting for that, and you can see all the sights in one long, varied day, making use of the free *Clywedog Valley Trail* leaflet available from tourist offices and any of

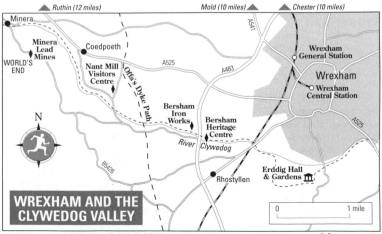

WREXHAM AND THE CLYWEDOG VALLEY

Ruthin (12 miles) ▲ Mold (10 miles) ▲ Chester (10 miles) ▲

Minera

Minera Lead Mines

WORLD'S END

Coedpoeth

Nant Mill Visitors Centre

Offa's Dyke Path

A525

A541

A483

Wrexham General Station

Wrexham

Wrexham Central Station

A525

N

Bersham Iron Works

Bersham Heritage Centre

River Clywedog

B5426

Rhostyllen

Erddig Hall & Gardens 🏛

0   1 mile

A483 to Llangollen (8 miles) & Welshpool (30 miles) ▼

© Crown copyright

the sites. Aside from Minera and Nant Mill, all the sites are within a couple of miles of the centre of Wrexham, and can be visited on foot. The easiest way to see the whole valley is to catch a #10 or #11 bus to Minera, walk the full length of the trail to Erddig Hall, then wander the mile and a half back into Wrexham.

There isn't a lot to see at the **Minera Lead Mines** (mid-July to early Sept daily except Tues & Wed 10am–5pm; free), four miles west of Wrexham. Many of the surface workings are still incompletely excavated, but the engine house and a pithead derrick have been largely rebuilt, together with some ore-processing machinery by the small museum in the former ore house. For a better impression of the site's layout, walk up onto the hill behind – a heather-clad moor on the fringe of an area called **World's End** – and look back on the valley. In the eighteenth century it was full of mines extracting galena, a silver-and-zinc-rich lead ore, from shafts over 1200ft deep.

From the lead mines, a path leads for almost a mile east along the River Clywedog to the wildlife and local history centre at **Nant Mill** (Easter–Aug Tues–Sun 10am–5pm; Sept–Easter Sat & Sun 10am–4pm; free), where you can pick up leaflets for nature trails leading to a very visible section of **Offa's Dyke** in the woods nearby. The Clywedog Trail runs through the wood to **Bersham Ironworks** (Easter & mid-July to early Sept daily except Tues & Wed noon–5pm; free), established in the seventeenth century and expanded by Cumbrian ironmaster John "Iron-Mad" Wilkinson who, in 1775, patented his new method for horizontally boring out cylinders. This produced the first truly circular, smooth bore, perfect for highly accurate cannons – hundreds were made here for the American Civil and Napoleonic wars – and the production of fine tolerance steam-engine cylinders. Engineer James Watt was a big customer, producing steam engines that made water-powered sites unprofitable and eventually put Bersham out of business.

After nearly two centuries of neglect, the remains are now being unearthed, revealing a broad area of knee-high foundations around the old foundry. This survived largely intact though it saw service as a corn mill and still retains its huge water wheel. The foundations really only serve to help you visualize the layout, which is better explained inside the foundry and put in context ten minutes' walk away at the **Bersham Heritage Centre** (April–Sept Mon–Fri 10am–5pm, Sat & Sun noon–5pm; Oct–Easter closes 4pm; free), which has a room dedicated to Wilkinson.

Erddig Hall

Despite the closure of the ironworks, coal continued to be mined around Bersham until 1986. After World War II, coal tunnels were pushed under **Erddig Hall**, just south of Wrexham (daily except Thurs & Fri: house April–Sept noon–5pm, Oct & Nov noon–4pm; garden March–June & Sept 11am–6pm, July & Aug 10am–6pm, Oct & Nov 11am–5pm; £7.40, outbuildings & gardens only £3.80; NT), adding subsidence to the troubles of an already decaying building. Ever since it was built in the late seventeenth century, its owners – all seemingly called Simon or Philip Yorke – had a hands-off attitude; especially the fourth Simon Yorke, who inherited Erddig in 1922; he failed to install electricity, running water, gas or a phone, and ignored the chronic damp that had the Chinese hand-blocked paper peeling off the walls. The National Trust took charge in the 1970s, since when it has restored the house to its 1922 appearance and returned the jungle of a garden to its formal eighteenth-century plan.

The house itself isn't distinguished, but, as nothing was ever thrown away, the collection of fine furniture and portraits – including one by Gainsborough of the first Philip Yorke – is unusually complete. The real interest, however, lies in

the servants' quarters, particularly the Servants' Hall, where specially commissioned portraits of eighteenth- and early nineteenth-century staff members are accompanied by personalized dedications in verse written by a Yorke – an extraordinary display of benevolence. You can also see the blacksmith's shop, stables, laundry, the still-used bake house and kitchen.

Reserve an hour for the **walled garden**, saved from the worst excesses of the eighteenth-century landscaping craze despite the attentions of William Emes, a contemporary of Capability Brown, who worked on the surrounding parkland. Manicured box hedges delineate beds planted with pleached lime trees, the walls support some 150 species of ivy, and apple trees produce fruit celebrated during an annual apple festival in early October.

To return to Wrexham from Erddig Hall, head half a mile or so northeast to *Squire Yorke Inn*, from where it's about a mile along the road.

The Dee Valley

The **Dee Valley** has long been the main transport route from the English Marches to Snowdonia, and it remains the most interesting route west. The course of the River Dee is traced by Thomas Telford's A5 road between London and Holyhead which approaches the region past **Chirk**, with its fine Marcher castle. From Chirk, the bucolic Glyn Ceiriog is a peaceful alternative to the more bustling charms of **Llangollen** with its hilltop castle ruins, broken-down abbey and medieval bridge over the river. Upstream, Owain Glyndŵr's stronghold, **Corwen**, deserves a stop to explore a couple of beautiful small churches.

Chirk and Glyn Ceiriog

The peaceful vale of **Glyn Ceiriog**, which runs parallel to the Dee Valley three miles to the south, is a blissfully quiet and starkly beautiful part of the country billed as the "Little Switzerland of Wales" (though that's more than a little optimistic). Other than **Chirk Castle** at the entrance to the valley, there are no compelling sights to draw you here, but the area makes a perfect getaway from the rigours of touring Wales.

Chirk and Chirk Castle

The Normans founded **CHIRK** (Y Waun) almost a thousand years ago, their motte remaining as a small tree-covered mound at the southern end of this pleasant enough village with long views up the valley to the Berwyn hills. Pick up the *Chirk Bridges Trail* (available free from tourist offices in the region), which details a circular route (2 miles; 1hr; negligible ascent) around Thomas Telford's towering 1801 aqueduct, built to carry the Llangollen Canal 70ft above the river. The route is sporadically indicated by a red hand, the principal element on the local lairds' coat of arms and the source of all the "Hand" hotels which dot the region.

For the last 400 years, the Myddleton family have occupied the massive drum-towered **Chirk Castle** (mid-March to Sept Wed–Sun noon–5pm, Oct Wed–Sun noon–4pm; £6.40; NT), squatting ominously on a rise half a mile to the west of Chirk. Roger Mortimer began the construction of this Marcher fortress at the behest of Edward I during the thirteenth century, and it eventually fell to the Myddletons. The approach to the castle is guarded by a magnificent Baroque **gatescreen**, the finest work done by the Davies brothers of Bersham, who wrought it between 1712 and 1719. The ebullient floral designs are capped by the Myddleton coat of arms, with a pair of wolves reproduced atop the cage-like gateposts (perhaps a memorial to one of the last wolves in Wales, said to have kept watch over the moat in the 1680s). From the gates, a mile-and-a-half-long avenue of oak leads up to the castle, an austere-looking place softened only by its mullioned windows. The original plan was probably to mimic Beaumaris Castle, started just a couple of months earlier, but Chirk lacks Beaumaris's purity and symmetry. The east and west walls are both incomplete, stopping at the half-round towers midway along the planned length, and the towers have been cut down to wall level, probably after the Civil War when taller towers would have been vulnerable to mortar attack. Internal modifications have been no less extensive, leaving a legacy of sumptuous rooms reflecting sixteenth- to nineteenth-century tastes, many returned to their former states after some Victorian meddling by Pugin in the 1840s.

After touring the house, spend an hour exploring the beautiful ornamental gardens (which open an hour earlier than the castle and close an hour later) or tracing the section of Offa's Dyke that runs across the front of the house, though it was flattened in 1758 for use as a cart track.

Glyn Ceiriog

Chirk Castle guards the entrance to the Glyn Ceiriog Valley, for centuries an important route into the heart of Wales and over the Berwyns into Snowdonia. These days it is the minor B4500 which runs beside the river for five miles through the hamlet of Pontfadog to the slightly larger Glyn Ceiriog, then on a further four miles to **LLANARMON DYFFRYN CEIRIOG** (usually referred to as Llanarmon DC), an appealing small village consisting of nothing but a church, a post office and some excellent accommodation catering to walkers. From February to November, the mountain-leader owners of *Gwynfa* (see below) run Hillwalk Wales, offering guided hillwalks for people of all abilities and a series of residential weekend courses.

Practicalities

Though **trains** on the Shrewsbury to Wrexham line stop at Chirk's station on Station Avenue, and **buses** infrequently penetrate the Glyn Ceiriog Valley as far as Llanarmon DC, you really need your own transport to explore the valley. The many high-quality country **inns** in the region are an attraction in themselves, and all serve good **food**. For **camping**, try *Ddol-Hir* (℡01691/718681; £10 per pitch), a small riverside caravan and campsite on the B4500 a mile west of Glyn Ceiriog.

Golden Pheasant Hotel Llwynmawr ℡01691/718281, ⓦwww.goldenpheasanthotel .co.uk. Traditional eighteenth-century rod-and-gun country hotel with pleasant B&B rooms. Formal and bar meals are served in separate non-smoking dining rooms, plus there's a wood-beamed bar where smoking is allowed. ❺

Gwynfa Llanarmon DC, 200 yards along the Llanrhaeadr road ℡01691/600287, ⓦwww .hillwalkwales.co.uk. Attractive, comfortable non-smoking B&B, the home base for Hillwalk Wales (see opposite). Great breakfasts, and four-course evening meals for just £12. ❷

Hand Hotel Llanarmon DC ℡01691/600666, ⓦwww.thehandhotel.co.uk. Converted

sixteenth-century farmhouse with a convivial wood-beamed bar and relaxed dining room with top-quality food. Try to get one of the older, more atmospheric but less well-appointed rooms rather than those in the modern extension. ❹/❻

West Arms Llanarmon DC ℡01691/600665, ⓦwww.thewestarms .co.uk. Ancient farmhouse-turned-inn with stone-flagged floor and a gorgeous inglenook fireplace. There are a couple of cheaper, more modest rooms, but you'll really want one of the older rooms with bags of character. Stay for the sumptuous dinners (£33 for three courses) and affordable bar meals. ❻/❽

Llangollen and around

Clasped tightly in the narrow Dee Valley between the shoulders of the Berwyn and Eglwyseg mountains, **LLANGOLLEN** is the embodiment of a Welsh town in both setting and character. Along the valley's floor, the waters of the River Dee (Afon Dyfrdwy) cut a wide arc around the base of **Dinas Brân**, a conical tor surmounted by the ruins of a native Welsh castle. At the apex of the bend, the Dee licks the angled buttresses of Llangollen's weighty Gothic bridge, which has spanned the river since the fourteenth century. On its south bank, half a dozen streets, their houses harmoniously straggling up the rugged hillsides, are labelled in both Welsh and English, and form the core of the scattered settlement flung out across the low hills. With its wealth of historical sights, Llangollen is very popular throughout the summer, particularly in early July when the town struggles to cope with the thousands of visitors to Wales' celebration of worldwide folk music, the **International Music Eisteddfod** (see box on p.359).

As the only river crossing point for miles, Llangollen was an important town long before the early Romantics arrived at the end of the eighteenth century, when they were cut off from their European Grand Tours by the Napoleonic Wars. Turner came to paint the swollen river and the Cistercian ruin of **Valle Crucis**, a couple of miles up the valley; John Ruskin found the town "entirely lovely in its gentle wildness"; and writer George Borrow made Llangollen his base for the early part of his 1854 tour detailed in *Wild Wales* (see "Books" in Contexts, p.548). The rich and famous came not only for the scenery, but to visit the celebrated **Ladies of Llangollen**, an eccentric couple who became the toast of society from their house, **Plas Newydd**. But by this stage, some of the town's rural charm had been eaten up by the works of one of the century's finest engineers, Thomas Telford (see box overleaf), who squeezed both his **London–Holyhead trunk road** and

Thomas Telford (1767–1834)

The English poet Robert Southey dubbed **Thomas Telford** the "Colossus of Roads" in recognition of his pre-eminence as the greatest road builder of his day, if not the greatest ever. Throughout the early years of the nineteenth century, he managed some of the most ambitious and far-reaching engineering projects yet attempted, and was seldom a public work on which his opinion wasn't sought.

Born in Scotland, he was apprenticed to a stonemason in London where he taught himself engineering architecture, eventually earning himself a position working for the Ellesmere Canal Company, which was planning a canal to link the Severn, Dee and Mersey rivers. His reputation was forged on the **Pontcysyllte Aqueduct**, part of the **Llangollen Canal** which, though one of his earliest major projects, was recognized as innovative even before he had completed it. Though lured away to build the Caledonian Canal in Scotland and St Katherine's Docks in London, he continued to work in Wales, reaching the apotheosis of his road-building career by pushing the London–Holyhead Turnpike through Snowdonia.

After the 1800 Act of Union between Britain and Ireland, a good road was needed to hasten mail and to transport the new Irish MPs to and from parliament in London. What is now the A5 was wedged into the same valley as Telford's Llangollen Canal, then driven right through Snowdonia with its gradient never exceeding 1:20. The combination of its near-level route and the high quality of its well-drained surface cut hours off the journey time, but the Dublin ferries left from Holyhead on the island of Anglesey, separated from the mainland by the Menai Strait. Telford's solution and his greatest achievement was the 580-foot-long **Menai Suspension Bridge**, strung 100ft above the strait to allow tall ships to pass under. Though the idea wasn't completely novel, the scale and the balance of grace and function won the plaudits of engineers and admiring visitors from around the world.

the **Llangollen Canal** alongside the river. Canal trips run east to his majestic nineteen-span **Pontcysyllte Aqueduct** over the Dee, while steam-hauled trains now ply the reconstructed track west beyond the head of the canal at the Horseshoe Falls. If none of this is energetic enough, try the panoramic day-long walk along the limestone escarpment to the north of town (see box on p.360).

Arrival, information and getting around

Buses are the only form of public transport to reach Llangollen, with local services (and the daily Wrexham–London National Express coach) stopping on Market Street. The nearest **train station** is five miles away at Ruabon, and passed by frequent buses on the Llangollen–Wrexham run. With your own vehicle, the most spectacular way to approach Llangollen is over the 1350-foot Horseshoe Pass (A542) from Ruthin.

The **tourist office** (Easter–Oct daily 9.30am–5.30pm; Nov–Easter daily 9.30am–5pm; ☎01978/860828, ✉llangollen@nwtic.com) is in The Chapel on Castle Street, just south of the bridge and less than a hundred yards from the bus stop on Market Street. There's a smart art gallery in the same building, along with the town's library (closed Thurs & Sun) with free Internet access.

Buses in the immediate locality are fairly infrequent, so you might as well resign yourself to **getting around** on foot – no great hardship as Valle Crucis, the most distant sight, is only a mile and a half along the towpath. **Bike rental** is available from ProAdventure on Parade Street (☎01978/861912, ⓦwww .proadventure.co.uk), with mountain bikes for £12 a half-day.

Accommodation

Llangollen is a fine place to **stay**, with some very pleasant B&Bs (mostly £50 per room and up) and a few luxury options, though no really useful **hostel**. Finding rooms can be a chore in the middle of summer, especially during the eisteddfod (the week beginning the first or second Tuesday of July), though this is alleviated by people letting out one or two bedrooms in the peak period. The tourist office can book you into these as well as the ordinary guesthouses that are dotted all over the valley.

Hotels and guesthouses

Bryn Howel Trevor, 2 miles east off the A539 ☏01978/860331, ⊛www.brynhowel.com. One of Llangollen's best hotels, set in beautiful grounds and good facilities including sauna, solarium, free trout fishing and a top-class restaurant. Two-night deals are cheaper. **❻**

Cornerstones 15 Bridge St ☏01978/861569, ⊛www.cornerstones-guesthouse.co.uk. Deluxe B&B with just two en-suite rooms, one heavy with oak beams, the other overlooking the river below. **❹**

Gales 18 Bridge St ☏01978/860089, ⊛www.galesofllangollen.co.uk. Very comfortable and central guesthouse above the restaurant of the same name (or in the house next door), some with brass beds and oak beams. Rates are lowest at weekends. **❸**

Greenbank Victoria Square ☏01978/861835, ⊛www.greenbank.uk.com. Refurbished and good-value guesthouse with clean, bright, simply furnished rooms. **❸**

Hafren Berwyn St ☏01978/860939. Good non-smoking B&B with shared bathroom and minimal single supplement. **❷**

Hillcrest Hill St ☏01978/860208, ⊛www.hillcrest-guesthouse.com. Appealing licensed Victorian guesthouse up towards Plas Newydd with excellent breakfasts. **❸**

Maesmawr Church St ☏01978/860477. Central, budget guesthouse with off-street parking and (a rarity at the bottom end) some rooms dedicated to smokers. **❶**

Plas Tegid Abbey Rd ☏01978/861013, ⊛www.llangollen.com/plastegid.html.

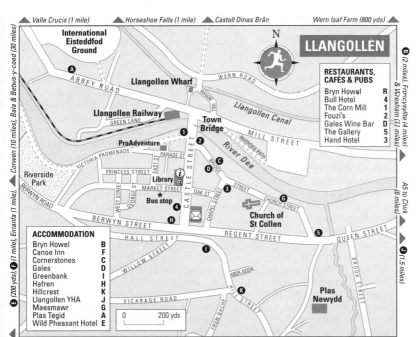

Spacious B&B close to the eisteddfod site, with bathless rooms, great breakfasts and negligible single supplements. ➋

Wild Pheasant Hotel Berwyn Rd, half a mile west along the A5 ☎01978/860629, ⓦwww.wildpheasanthotel.co.uk. Venerable hotel with an older wing of standard rooms and a luxurious, tastefully decorated new wing, plus spacious suites. Guests have free use of the modern spa pool, steam room and sauna (£10 day pass for non-guests). ➍/➐

Hostels and campsites

Canoe Inn Mile End Mill, Berwyn Rd ☎01978/869043. Clean, basic accommodation in three- or four-bed dorms for £18 overlooking the canoe slalom site a mile west of town, and with a simple café.

Eirianfa Berwyn Rd ☎01978/860919. Fully equipped riverside campsite and holiday park almost a mile west of the town on the A5. £8 per pitch.

Llangollen YHA Tyndwr Rd ☎0870/770 5932, ⓔllangollen@yha.org.uk. High-standard hostel in a Victorian manor a mile and a half east of town. Technically open to individuals who book at least two days in advance, though often booked months ahead by groups. Dorms £11.

Wern Isaf Farm ☎01978/860632. Simple farmhouse campsite just under a mile up Wern Road. Turn right over the canal on Wharf Hill. £4 per person.

The Town

Few visitors can resist admiring the view up the valley from the parapet of the **town bridge** which, though widened and strengthened over the years, has spanned the river since the fourteenth century. Below it, the Dee pours through the fingers of shale which make up the unimaginatively dubbed "Town Falls" rapids. The bridge runs onto Castle Street, which heads due south past the tourist office. Bibliophiles should cross the road to *Maxine's* café, above which there's a cavernous second-hand **bookshop**.

Llangollen takes its name from the **Church of St Collen** on Church Street, off Castle Street (May–Sept Tues–Sat 2–6pm; free). Dedicated to a sixth-century saint, the church features a fine fifteenth-century oak hammerbeam roof, said to have come from Valle Crucis (see p.261). The graveyard is of equal interest for the triangular, railed-off monument to Mary Carryll erected by her mistresses, the Ladies of Llangollen (see below), who are also buried with her in the churchyard and commemorated on the other two sides of her pillar.

Plas Newydd

Standing in twelve acres of formal gardens, half a mile up Hill Street from the southern end of Castle Street, the two-storeyed mock-Tudor **Plas Newydd**, Butler Hill (Easter–Oct daily 10am–5pm; £3) was, for almost fifty years, home to the celebrated **Ladies of Llangollen**. Lady Eleanor Butler and Sarah Ponsonby were a lesbian couple from Anglo-Irish aristocratic backgrounds, who tried to elope together at the end of the eighteenth century. After two botched attempts dressed in men's clothes, they were grudgingly allowed to leave in 1778 with an annual allowance of £280, enough to settle in Llangollen, where they became the country's most celebrated lesbians – though apparently they were affronted by the suggestion that their relationship was anything other than chaste. Regency society was captivated by their "model friendship" in what Simone de Beauvoir called "a peaceful Eden on the edge of the world". Despite their desire for a "life of sweet and delicious retirement", they didn't seem to mind the constant stream of gentry who called on them. They found the Duke of Wellington a "charming young man, hansom, fashioned tall and elegant" and commemorated his visit in typically self-absorbed manner by engraving "E.B & S.P. 1814" over the mantelpiece in the Oak Room. Walter Scott was also well received, though he found them "a couple of hazy or crazy old sailors" in manner, and like "two respectable superannuated clergymen" in their mode of dress. Thomas de Quincey humoured the ladies, if only to bend

The Llangollen International Music Eisteddfod

Llangollen is heaving in summer, but never more so than during the second week of July, when for six days the town explodes into a frenzy of music, dance and poetry. The **International Music Eisteddfod** comes billed as "the world's greatest folk festival" but unlike the National Eisteddfod (see colour insert), which is a purely Welsh affair, the Llangollen event draws amateur performers from fifty countries, all competing for prizes in their chosen disciplines. Throughout the week, dances and choral performances take place at Plas Newydd, Valle Crucis and just about anywhere that a group of people can congregate, though competitive performances are concentrated in the main venue, the **Royal International Pavilion**, on the north bank just west of the town bridge. When the day's competition is over, headlining stars often pack out the pavilion: a few years back, Luciano Pavarotti and his 200-strong entourage fronted up on the fortieth anniversary of his first performance here.

The festival has been held in its present form since 1947, when it was started more or less on a whim by one Harold Tudor to soothe the social wounds of World War II. Forty choirs from fourteen countries performed at the first (entirely choral) event, and it expanded, drawing praise quickly from Dylan Thomas, who declared that "the town sang and danced, as though it were right". Today over 12,000 international musicians, singers, dancers and choristers descend on this town of 3000 people, further swamped by up to 150,000 visitors. While the whole setup can seem oppressive, there is an irresistible *joie de vivre* as brightly costumed dancers walk the streets and fill the restaurants and fish-and-chip shops.

Unless you are going specifically for the eisteddfod, the week beginning the first or second Tuesday of July is a good time to stay away. Accommodation should be booked (most easily through the tourist office) several months in advance, though **tickets** (T01978/862001, Wwww.international-eisteddfod.co.uk) for all but the headlining shows can be obtained much closer the time, often on the day itself. All-day access to the site, with no guarantee of a seat, costs as little as £6 a day.

Since the late 1990s the eisteddfod has been followed by the less frenetic **Llangollen Fringe** (T01978/860600, Wwww.llangollenfringe.co.uk) with a number of more "alternative" acts – music, dance, comedy and so on – performing in the town hall on Castle Street over the last two weeks in July.

their favour towards his friend Wordsworth, who had displeased them by referring to their house as "a low roofed cot" in an inelegant poem he had composed in the grounds.

An excellent, self-guided audio tour (free) guides you around the half-dozen rooms of the modest black-and-white timbered house, where most of the walls are covered in a riotous frieze of dark wood panelling. It is a wonderful if slightly oppressive effect set off by a mixed bag of furniture in a style similar to that owned by the ladies. As a counterpoint you can also visit the spartan attic room where their loyal housekeeper, Mary Carryll, lived. Outside, take time to wander through the formal **grounds** (always open) including the **knot garden** which perfectly complements the front of the house.

The north bank of the Dee

Wherever you are in Llangollen, the hills echo to the shrill cry of steam engines easing along the **Llangollen Railway** (April–Oct 3–7 services most days; call ahead at other times; £8 return; T01978/860979; Wwww.llangollen-railway .co.uk). Shoehorned into the north side of the valley, it runs west from Llangollen's time-warped station past Glyndyfrdwy, near the Horseshoe

A walk from Llangollen

Note: This walk is difficult to follow without the OS Landranger #117 map.

Climbing up to Dinas Brân, you get a fair idea of what is in store on Llangollen's **Precipice Walk** (14 miles; 7hr; 1800ft ascent), which traces the crest of the wonderful limestone escarpment formed by Trevor and Eglwyseg rocks. One of the most dramatic sections of the Offa's Dyke Path – though not the dyke itself – follows the base of these cliffs, but the tops make a far better walk, offering superb views down into the Vale of Llangollen and across the Berwyn Range to the south. Since the eastern half of what is effectively a circuit around Ruabon Mountain is the least interesting part, the walk is described anticlockwise so the best can be experienced when you're freshest. Although it is certainly a long walk, the worst of the climbing is quickly over and fine weather makes it a superb outing.

Start the walk on a narrow tarmac path over the canal from Llangollen Wharf signposted up towards the ruins of Castell Dinas Brân. From the castle the route ahead unfolds, down the north flank towards the tarmacked road that runs below the escarpment forming part of the Offa's Dyke Path. Turn right at the road and head east along it for three miles, always taking any left turns and keeping the open land of Ruabon Mountain on your left. Half a mile past Hafod Farm turn left to Bryn-Adda following a "Public Footpath" sign. The route then heads roughly north over dense heather to the forestry plantation at Newtown Mountain and on to the road near Mountain Lodge. Just past the entrance to the lodge, turn west up towards the top of the moor and the head of the valley known as World's End. Follow the southern perimeter of a plantation and pick up the path, which then follows the escarpment south back to Llangollen. The easiest way back is to continue past Dinas Brân to the end of Trevor Rocks, then follow the road down to town.

Falls, as far as Carrog, eight miles up the valley: eventually it will go a further two miles to Corwen. Operating along a restored section of the disused Ruabon–Barmouth line, belching steam engines creep along the river bank, hauling ancient carriages which sport the liveries of their erstwhile owners. A while back the railway gained some notoriety by offering steam train funerals, the body or ashes being loaded on a train equipped for a mobile wake. Local opposition – founded on fears that rail fanatics would have their ashes thrown in the fire box to be distributed over the valley – has scuppered plans for the time being. The occasional driver-experience courses, letting you behind the controls of a steam loco (from £150 for 2hr) are proving less controversial.

Across the road, **Llangollen Wharf** is the starting point for trips along the Llangollen Canal. Until the coming of the railway in 1865, the waterway was the only means to carry slates from the quarries on the Horseshoe Pass. Designed as a water supply for the Shropshire Union Canal, the Llangollen canal was one of Britain's finest feats of canal engineering: from the artificial **Horseshoe Falls**, a crescent-shaped weir built in 1806 to feed water into the canal, its architect, Thomas Telford, managed to avoid using locks for the first fourteen miles. He did this by building the thousand-foot-long **Pontcysyllte Aqueduct** 126ft above the river, at **Froncysyllte**, four miles east, employing long cast-iron troughs supported by stone piers – a bold move for its time. **Narrowboats** run from the Horse Drawn Boat Centre on Llangollen Wharf (Easter–Oct daily; ☎01978/860702, ⊛www.horsedrawnboats .co.uk), which offers a 45-minute ride in a horse-drawn narrowboat (£4.50) and a two-hour motorized trip down to and across the Pontcysyllte Aqueduct (£8.50). Alternatively, you can drive to the *Telford Inn* in Froncysyllte (which has a good garden bar) on the A542 – or walk the towpath – and take a 45-minute narrowboat ride with Aqueduct Cruises (℡01691/690322; hourly from 2pm most days in summer; £3.50) across the aqueduct and back.

Castell Dinas Brân

It's the view both ways along the valley which justifies a 45-minute slog up to **Castell Dinas Brân** (Crow's Fortress Castle), perched on a hill 800ft above the town, and reached by a signposted path from Llangollen Wharf. The lure certainly isn't the few sad but evocative vaulted stumps that stand in poor testament to what was once the district's largest and most important Welsh fortress. Built by the ruler of northern Powys, Prince Madog ap Gruffydd Maelor, in the 1230s, the castle rose on the site of an earlier Iron Age fort. Edward I soon took it as part of his first campaign against Llywelyn ap Gruffydd (see p.505), and the castle was left to decay. John Leland, Henry VIII's antiquarian, finding it "all in ruin" in 1540.

Although not much to look at, it's a great place to be when the sun is setting, imagining George Borrow sitting up here translating seventeenth-century bard Roger Cyffyn:

Gone, gone are thy gates, Dinas Brân on the height!
Thy warders are blood-crows and ravens, I trow;
Now no-one will wend from the field of the fight
To the fortress on high, save the raven and the crow.

The eisteddfod site, Valle Crucis Abbey and Eliseg's Pillar

Walking west from the town bridge, the eisteddfod site soon hoves into view, heralded by the architecturally controversial but nonetheless impressive **Royal International Pavilion**. The 6000-seat white plastic structure was designed to evoke the shape of the traditional marquee formerly erected on the site each year, but looks more like some giant armoured reptile dropped from a great height into the green valley. Outside the eisteddfod season, the auditorium acts as a concert venue and sports hall, the foyer operates as a **gallery** (Mon–Fri 10am–4pm; free) with reputable changing exhibitions of international fine art and north Welsh crafts, and side rooms host workshops ranging from alternative medicines to Chinese brush painting.

Following the A542 or the canal towpath a mile west, you pass Llangollen's **Motor Museum** (March–Oct daily 10am–5pm, winter by appointment ℡01978/860324; £3), a shed full of lovingly restored not-so-vintage cars and vans supplemented by a small **canal exhibition**, which admirably explains the construction of the Llangollen Canal in the context of Britain's canal building mania at the end of the eighteenth century.

Half a mile beyond, the gaunt remains of **Valle Crucis Abbey** (mid-March to Sept daily 10am–5pm, £2; Oct–Easter unrestricted access; CADW), stand in Glyn y Groes, the "Valley of the Cross". In 1201, Madog ap Gruffydd Maelor of Dinas Brân chose this majestic pastoral setting for one of the last Cistercian foundations in Wales, as well as the first Gothic abbey in Britain. Despite a devastating fire in its first century, and a complement of far-from-pious monks, it survived until the Dissolution in 1535. The church fell into disrepair, after which the monastic buildings, in particular the monks' dormitory, were employed as farm buildings. Later, Turner painted the abbey, imaginatively shifting Dinas Brân a couple of miles west onto the hill behind.

Though less impressive than Tintern Abbey, Valle Crucis does greet you with its best side, the largely intact west wall of the church pierced by the frame of a rose window. At the opposite end, the equally complete east wall guards a row of six graves, one of which is said to contain Owain Glyndŵr's resident bard, Iolo Goch. There are displays on monastic life upstairs, reached by a detour through the mostly ruined cloister and past the weighty vaulting of the chapterhouse.

The cross that gives the valley its name is the eight-foot-tall **Eliseg's Pillar** (unrestricted access; CADW), four hundred yards north by the A542. Erected to a Prince of Powys in the ninth century by his great-grandson, it originally stood 25ft high but was smashed during the Civil War in the 1640s. The stump remains, but you can now only see half of the full 31 lines glorifying the lineage of the Princes of Powys, which Celtic scholar Edward Llwyd translated from the remaining pieces in 1696.

Eating, drinking and entertainment

Though not extensive by city standards, Llangollen boasts a fairly good selection of **restaurants** and no shortage of daytime **cafés** around town. Picnic ingredients are best bought at Bailey's Delicatessen on Castle Street, next to the tourist office.

Outside the eisteddfod and its fringe, there's not a great deal of **nightlife**, but local bands (and occasionally bigger acts) do play from time to time, and it's always worth checking if there is anything going on at the eisteddfod site.

Bryn Howel Hotel Trevor ☎01978/860331. Formal, fairly pricey, award-winning restaurant, with great views of Dinas Brân across the lawns.

Bull Hotel Castle St. Lively and central town pub (with a beer garden) that's the main gathering place for Llangollen's youth.

The Corn Mill Dee Lane ☎01978/869555. Superb conversion of a town-centre mill, with riverside decking that catches the afternoon sun. Good all day for coffee, real ales and well-prepared café-bar food with mains (£9–13) such as chargrilled tuna with a Niçoise salad.

Fouzi's Castle St ☎01978/861340. Smart modern daytime café serving panini, stuffed baguettes (£4–5), plus a few mains (£6), daily specials and good espresso.

Gales Wine Bar 18 Bridge St ☎01978/860089. Old church pews and one of the most extensive cellars around make this a great place for an evening of wine glugging, with delicious, bistro-style food (mains £8–11) and great homemade ice cream.

The Gallery 15 Chapel St ☎01978/860076. Friendly evening-only restaurant serving a good range of medium-priced pizza and pasta dishes. Closed Sun & Mon.

Hand Hotel 26 Bridge St. Straightforward local pub where you can listen to the male voice choir in full song at 7.30pm on Mon & Fri.

Royal International Pavilion Abbey Rd ☎01978/860111. Year-round venue for anything from choral and classical concerts to pull-out-the-stops rock gigs.

Activities

The climb up to Dinas Brân and the Precipice Walk (see box on p.360) both make for excellent walks with magical valley views, but require considerably more effort than the gentle riverside walk along Victoria Promenade past the Town Falls. If the sight of all this white water gives you a taste for something more active, head a mile upstream to JJ Canoeing & Rafting at Mile End Mill on Berwyn Road (☎1978/860763, ⓦwww.jjraftcanoe.com), which offers modest **rafting trips** (£40 for 2hr session; £45 on Sat) on the bouncy but less-than-menacing waters of the Dee. It also offers a range of other outdoor activities (rock climbing, abseiling, gorge walking etc), and skilled kayakers can use the slalom course all day for £5, and they offer a range of rock climbing, abseiling and multi-activity packages.

Corwen and around

In the early fifteenth century, Welsh rebel Owain Glyndŵr set out from **CORWEN**, ten miles west of Llangollen, to wrest back all Wales from the English barons (see p.506). The new steel statue of Glyndŵr, right in the middle of town, is welcome, if already rusty and slightly unprepossessing. More impressive is **Glyndŵr's Sword**, the shape of a dagger incised into a grey-stone lintel of the south porch of the thirteenth-century **church of St Mael and St Julien**. The Welsh hero, local landowner and scourge of Henry IV is said to have cast the "sword" in anger at the townspeople from atop the hill behind, though it actually predates him by half a millennium. Look, too, around the churchyard with its well-preserved Celtic cross and gravestone with indentations for penitents' knees. Inside the church, there is a fine Norman font.

In Glyndŵr's time cattle droving routes from Anglesey and from Harlech met at Corwen for the final push to the English markets. Subsequently a major rail junction, Corwen is now a quiet market town with a couple of fine ancient churches nearby (see below). Glyndŵr aficionados will probably be interested in the thirty foot-high truncated cone of **Owain Glyndŵr's Mount**, on the south bank of the Dee just over three miles east on the road to Llangollen, where he is supposed to have stood on lookout for his enemies. He may well have done so, but the earthworks are more likely to be a Norman motte-and-bailey castle.

Corwen's charms don't justify stopping overnight, although the *Corwen Court*, London Road (closed Dec–Feb; ☎01490/412854; ❶), is a **B&B** with a difference: converted from a police station and courthouse, the cells are now single rooms, and the doubles are converted from the sergeant's family's quarters. If that doesn't suit, *Bron-y-Graig* (☎01490/413007, ⓦwww.north-wales-hotel .co.uk; ❸) is only a few yards east along the A5, and offers authentically renovated Victorian rooms in a house built for the Sheriff of Denbigh. It has its own restaurant and a holiday cottage let by the week. The welcoming *Powys House Estate* at Bonwm, a mile east on the A5 (☎01490/412367; ❸), has its own outdoor swimming pool and tennis court.

Buses on the Llangollen–Bala route stop in the centre of Corwen.

Capel Rûg and Eglwys Llangar

Taking its name from the Welsh word for heather, **Capel Rûg** (Easter–Sept Wed–Sun 10am–5pm; £2.50; CADW), a mile west of Corwen on the A494, is one of Wales' best examples of an unmolested seventeenth-century church. Along with the Gwydyr Uchaf Chapel, near Llanrwst (see p.393), it gives a charming insight into worship three hundred years ago, when Mass was a private clerical devotion, with the congregation kept behind rood screens.

Rûg didn't entirely escape, but much here is as it was built in 1637 by the former privateer and collaborator on William Morgan's Welsh Bible (see p.457), William Salusbury. The plain exterior design gives no hint of the richly decorated interior: wooden angels support a roof patterned with stars and amoebic swirls, and a painting of a skeleton said to represent the transient nature of life and the inevitability of death. Informative displays in the ticket office give more details of the building's use.

Your ticket to Capel Rûg also entitles you to an escorted visit from there to another little-changed church, **Eglwys Llangar** (normally locked, phone Capel Rûg on ☎01490/412025 for tour times, usually Easter–Sept Wed–Sun 2pm), a mile to the south off the B4401, which dates back to the fourteenth century or earlier. Parish boundary changes in 1853 made this church redundant, saving its extensive fifteenth-century wall paintings and seventeenth-century figure of death from obliteration. The interior woodwork is wonderful, from the beamed roof and minstrels gallery down to the eighteenth-century box pews.

The Vale of Edeyrnion

West of Corwen, the A5 provides the quickest route to Betws-y-Coed and the mountains of Snowdonia. An alternative route heads south through the Vale of Edeyrnion to the watersports centre of Bala, through the peaceful villages of Cynwyd, Llandrillo and Llandderfel and past a couple of the best country hotels in the area. Buses on the Llangollen–Bala route go right through the valley. None of the villages is particularly interesting, but any can act as a base for hikes on the largely undiscovered Berwyn Range to the east (see box below), where you can walk all day without seeing a soul.

The first village, two miles south of Corwen, is **CYNWYD**, home to the budget *Pen-y-Bont Fawr* B&B (℡01490/412663, ℮robert.wivell@btopenworld .com; ❶), in a converted barn behind the *Prince of Wales* pub. A further couple of miles south, *Hendwr Caravan Park* (℡01490/440210, ⓦwww.hendwrcaravanpark .freeserve.co.uk; £16 per pitch; closed Nov–Easter), is just one of several **camp-sites** which dot the river flats through the valley.

A walk on the Berwyns from Cynwyd or Llandderfel

Note: The OS 1:50,000 Landranger #125 map is recommended for this walk.

Henry II's 1165 expeditionary force encamped on the Berwyn Hills, until forced to flee back to England from the Welsh weather and the guerrilla tactics of Owain Gwynedd. Legend has it that the king beat his retreat along the ancient high-moor trackway, thereafter known as Ffordd Saeson (Englishman's Road). Whether he did or not, the path makes for a good route up onto these lonesome rocky heather-clad outcrops. The **walk** (10 miles; 5–6hr; 2500ft ascent) follows part of Ffordd Saeson starting from Cynwyd about a hundred yards north of *Y Llew Glas* (The Blue Lion) pub then up through a forest to the deep heather moorland pass of **Bwlch Cynwyd** (1700ft). From Bwlch Cynwyd, the circular route leads south, but if the skies are clear, the lone summit of **Moel Fferna** (2067ft), a mile or so to the north, makes a rewarding detour. South from Bwlch Cynwyd, follow the path beside the fence for a couple of miles across desolate, somewhat featureless land to the summit of **Pen Bwlch Llandrillo Top** (2037ft), then drop down the other side to an ancient drovers' road. Known locally as the Maid's Path, it was once the harvest-time route for girls heading east from Llandrillo, sometimes as far as Llanarmon Dyffryn Ceiriog, five miles from here (see p.354). If you don't have your own transport, try walking over the Berwyns from the Vale of Edeyrnion into Glyn Ceiriog: it is the closest you'll get to experiencing what the drover's life must have been like.

Near where you meet the drovers' road, a much later traveller is commemorated by a stone to "A Wayfarer 1877–1956, a lover of Wales". In the days before knobbly tyres and gas mono-shock suspension systems, one W.M. Robinson rode up here by bicycle, unwittingly laying the groundwork for scores of mountain bikers now following his lead along the bridleways. A metal box nearby contains a book to record your visit. The cairned summit of **Cadair Bronwen** (2575ft), a mile and a half south of the memorial, is the only place in Wales where you can pick cloudberries (sharp-tasting orange blackberries); otherwise head east for Glyn Ceiriog or west for the Vale of Edeyrnion. After half a mile on the westerly path, a sign points to Llandrillo, while an unsigned path forks right to Cynwyd. The track to Llandrillo heads downwards and under the lip of the hill on which **Moel Tŷ Uchaf**, a quite stunning 3500-year-old stone circle, can be found.

The Berwyns are equally accessible from **LLANDRILLO** where, after a day in the hills, you can rest your head at the excellent *Y Llwyn Guesthouse* (℡01490/440455; ❷), in the centre near the post office; alternatively, luxuriate in the elegant Georgian surroundings of *Tyddyn Llan Country House*, on the B4401 towards Bala (℡01490/440264, ⓦwww.tyddynllan.co.uk; ❼) and eat in its highly rated, expensive restaurant. For sheer grandeur, and the opportunity to stay in a house once frequented by Queen Victoria, you can't beat the hand-painted and intricately carved nineteenth-century interiors of *Palé Hall*, three miles south of Llandderfel (℡01678/530285, ⓦwww.palehall .co.uk; ❼), located in peacock-inhabited grounds beside a trout stream available for guests' use. Superb meals (£40 for three courses) are also served to non-residents: tartlet of goats' cheese and leeks and breast of wood pigeon are typical dishes.

If your budget won't stretch to these kind of prices, continue along the B4401 past **LLANDDERFEL** to *Melin Meloch*, just two miles short of Bala (March–Nov; ℡01678/520101, ⓦwww.melochmill.com; ❸), a B&B partly built from a converted thirteenth-century water mill beside the Dee.

Mold and the Vale of Clwyd

One of the least-travelled paths through northwest Wales leaves the English Marches at the market town of **Mold**, crosses the soft contours of the **Clwydian Range** – along whose tops runs a section of the **Offa's Dyke long-distance path** – and approaches the north coast through the wide and fertile **Vale of Clwyd**, which follows the sandstone course of the barely noticeable River Clwyd (Afon Clywedog). Nineteenth-century poet Gerard Manley Hopkins eulogized the valley where he studied for the priesthood, celebrating its beauty in some of his best-loved works, *The Windhover*, *In the Valley of the Elwy* and *Pied Beauty*. Linked by quiet roads through a patchwork of small farms, two attractive towns of warm-hued stone sit on hillocks above the valley. The ancient market town of **Ruthin** is the pick of the two, with its thirteenth-century castle, compact core of medieval buildings, intriguing gaol and a host of good places to stay. Four miles north, past the village church at **Llanrhaeadr** – the Vale's prime example of medieval ecclesiastical architecture, with a fine Jesse Window – is **Denbigh**, best known for its "hollow crown", the high-walled castle ruin that rings the hilltop behind the town.

The old rail line from Corwen to Rhyl has long gone, leaving regular **buses** along the A525 between Ruthin and Rhyl as the primary transport route – #51 is the most useful.

Mold

The slow pace of **MOLD** (Yr Wyddgrug) is only disrupted by its Wednesday and Saturday markets, when stalls supplant cars along the High Street. Despite a good deal of interesting history tied to the town, there's no great reason for a visit, except perhaps en route over the Clwydian Hills into the Vale of Clwyd.

Mold was founded during the reign of William Rufus, though only a bowling green and a copse of beeches atop a mound mark the site of the motte-and-bailey fortifications on **Bailey Hill**, at the top of High Street. Built for the local Norman lord, Robert de Montalt (who probably gave the town its English name, essentially the same as the Welsh, meaning "The Mound"), its commanding view over the River Alyn (Afon Alun) shows the strategic value of the site.

△ The Eyes of Ruthin

English. The castle went on to resist the Parliamentarians for eleven weeks during the Civil War, eventually falling to General Mytton in 1646, after which it was destroyed. In 1963, it was partially restored as a **hotel**, with Italian and rose gardens landscaped around the ancient moat and crumbling ruins. Strictly speaking, the grounds are open to residents and peacocks only, but you can wander through if attending one of the tacky medieval banquets or drinking in the panelled library bar.

St Peter's Square

Before making tracks for Ruthin Gaol it's worth spending a few minutes around **St Peter's Square**, the hub of the town's medieval street plan. **St Peter's Church** (daily 9am–4pm or thereabouts) is approached via a lovely pair of iron gates wrought by the Davies Brothers (who also made the gates of St Giles' church in Wrexham and those at Chirk Castle). The ceiling of its north aisle consists of 408 carved black oak panels with Tudor Rose bosses, reputedly donated by Henry VII from Basingwerk Abbey (see p.375), in gratitude to those who helped him take the English throne. Details are hard to make out in the gloom, so if any members of staff are about, ask them to turn on the lights. Alternatively simply rely on the grotesque faces and floral and geometric designs reproduced on a panel opposite the door. One of the busts on the north wall is of Gabriel Goodman, who, in 1574, while Dean of Westminster, re-founded the **grammar school** that had been closed by Henry VIII forty years earlier; the building still stands behind the church, next to the Christ's Hospital Almshouses, which Goodman built in 1590 as a gift to the town.

Goodman was born beside St Peter's Square in Exmewe Hall (now Barclays bank), outside which sits an unimpressive chunk of limestone known as **Maen Huail**. A less-than-convincing story has Arthur and Huail, brother of a Welsh chieftain called Gildas, fighting over the attentions of a woman. Huail pierced

Arthur's thigh, giving him a permanent limp, but promised never to mention Arthur's loss of face. Inevitably, though, Huail couldn't resist taunting him about it and an incensed Arthur had him beheaded on this stone.

Standing isolated on the other side of the square is one of the many half-timbered buildings around town. Now the NatWest bank, it was built in 1401 as a courthouse and prison and still retains under the eaves the barely visible stump of the **gibbet**, last used in 1679 to hang a Franciscan priest, Charles Meehan, who was later drawn and quartered. However, the most photographed building in town is the **Myddleton Arms pub**, built in 1657 in Dutch style and topped by seven dormer windows known as "The Eyes of Ruthin", which overlook the square.

There are all manner of Welsh-interest crafts and books at Elfair, 16–18 Clwyd St, but if Ruthin's huddle of buildings becomes too claustrophobic, you might want to take one of the nearby **walks** along the Clwydian Range to Moel Famau and Foel Fenlli (see box on p.367), or go **horse riding** at the Ruthin Riding Centre (℡01824/703470) in Pentre Coch, four miles north of town.

Ruthin Gaol

The town's latest attraction is the recently restored **Ruthin Gaol** (April–Oct daily 10am–5pm; Nov–March Tues–Sun 10am–5pm; ⊛www.ruthingaol.co.uk; £3), five minutes' walk down Clwyd Street from St Peter's Square. Though there was a prison on the site from 1654 to 1916, the so-called "Gruelling Experience" focuses on the Victorian era and the four-storey cell block (1866) inspired by London's Pentonville, designed to improve living conditions and penal correction, with one prisoner per cell and the requirement to work while incarcerated. Most upper floor cells are now used as council offices and county archives, but you can poke around elsewhere, perhaps following the free audio-guide which traces the prison life of a mythical "Will the Poacher". Informative panels in the lower cells and prison kitchen explain daily prison life and behind-the-scenes operations along with the real meaning of "screws" and "bobbies" and the source of the expression "money for old rope". One tale tells of John Jones, the "Welsh Houdini", who spent time here in 1913 before escaping then getting shot five days later.

Practicalities

Buses from Denbigh, Rhyl and Mold all stop on Market Street, which runs between St Peter's Square and the valley's best **tourist office** (June–Sept daily 10am–5.30pm; Oct–May Mon–Sat 10am–5pm, Sun noon–5pm; ℡01824/703992, ℮ruthin@nwtic.com), 300 yards away inside the Ruthin Craft Centre. There's **Internet** access at the library on Record Street. **Accommodation** should be reserved ahead at weekends, when rooms fill up with guests attending weddings at the castle. Ruthin's **food** scene has improved considerably in recent years. *Minffordd Campsite* (℡01824/707169; £6 per pitch) is a simple, tent-and-campervan-only site two miles north of Ruthin and just east of Rhewl: follow signs for Gellifor then turn right 150 yards after a pair of stone bridges.

Accommodation

Eyarth Station ℡01824/703643, ⊛www .eyarthstation.com. Attractive B&B in a former train station on the disused Corwen to Rhyl line; take bus #152 to Llanfair Dyffryn Clwyd,

from where it's a half-mile walk. Closed Nov–Feb. ❸

Firgrove Country House on the B5105 a mile southeast of Ruthin ℡01824/702677, ⊛www.firgrovecountryhouse.co.uk. A large Georgian the A543. It has its own woodland trail, and there are self-catering cottages let for short breaks. The handiest **campsite** is the *Station House Caravan Park* (☎01745/710372; £6 per pitch) at Bodfari, reached on bus #14.

Eating and drinking in Denbigh is limited: *Y Pantri* on High Street is the best bet for daytime snacks, the *Bull Hotel* does straightforward bar meals, and *Y Llew Aur* (the Golden Lion), on Back Row behind High Street, is a good local. Otherwise, head out to 🍴 *The White Horse Inn* (☎01824/790218, ⓦwww .white-horse-inn.co.uk), three miles southeast at Hendrerwydd, a superb country pub with top-quality meals (mains £11–13) and a cosy bar with an array of real ales and single malts.

Deeside

The industrial hinterland that spreads over the English border from Chester can best be avoided by heading directly for **Deeside**, a narrow littoral flanking the River Dee estuary. Most visitors shoot past on the A55 expressway, but a short detour onto the A548 is rewarded by a few mildly interesting sights such as the pretty village of **Hawarden**, one-time home of William Gladstone. The crumbling castle remains at **Flint** should only detain you briefly, though you may want longer to pay homage to St Winefride and her healing waters at **Holywell**, especially if you're drawn to the adjacent minor collection of historic industrial buildings of the **Greenfield Valley Heritage Park** or the gorgeous carved Celtic cross of **Maen Achwyfaen**.

The salt-soaked fields alongside the Dee estuary support huge numbers of waders and **wildfowl**, which come to feed on the sands and mud flats left by retreating tides. At the RSPB's **Point of Ayr** site (unrestricted access), around seven miles northwest of Holywell, plovers, oystercatchers and Europe's largest concentration of pintails winter here, pushing the bird population into six figures.

Hawarden

The interesting hilltop settlement of **HAWARDEN** (Penarlâg), just a couple of miles west of the English border, commands views over the Cheshire Plain and the Dee Estuary making it a site of strategic importance for a thousand years. By the busy village crossroads, a small door in an imposing castellated gateway leads into the rolling parkland (open daily until dusk) that surrounds the two Hawarden castles. The **Old Castle** (April to late Aug second & fourth Sun 2– 5pm) is a stone tower on a mound, all that remains of Edward I's border fortress; the other is a heavily gothicized eighteenth-century mansion (no access) that was renamed Hawarden Castle in the Victorian age.

In 1839, William Ewart Gladstone, Britain's long-serving Liberal prime minister, married into the castle's resident family. He and his wife Catherine later made the castle their home, and there's a memorial to them in the village **church of St Deiniol**. Rebuilt by Sir Gilbert Scott in the mid-nineteenth century, and rich in William Morris stained glass, it stands at the bottom of Church Lane, off the main street. Next door is the sumptuous **St Deiniol's Library**, a floridly extravagant neo-Gothic building constructed from a bequest after Gladstone's death. Britain's only residential library, St Deiniol's is mainly frequented by theological scholars, but you can go in to see the small **Gladstone Exhibition** (Mon–Fri 10am–4pm, Sat 10am–1.30pm; free), and eat in the café. Gladstone's legacy can also be seen in the memorial fountain by the main crossroads. Heading east along the main street, look out for a seventeenth-century **lock-up**, a small single cell built into a wall opposite a row of cottages.

The **train station** – on the line between Bidston and Wrexham – is a five-minute walk west of the main crossroads, and there are numerous daily **buses** to Chester, Flint and Holywell from outside the *Glynne Arms* in the centre of the village. There's little need to stay, though the *Glynne Arms* itself (℡01244/520323; ❷) is an atmospheric old coaching inn, serving a decent pint and a range of **meals**.

Flint

If you're travelling on the North Coast train line, take one of the regional services which stop at **FLINT** (Y Fflint), seven miles north of Mold, and spend the hour between trains rambling around the buff sandstone ruins of **Flint Castle** (unrestricted access; CADW), two minutes' walk over the footbridge from the station. Started in 1277, this was the first of Edward I's Iron Ring of fortresses (see p.468), standing sentinel over once-important shipping lanes into Chester. The ten-foot-thick pockmarked walls form a square with drum towers at all except the southeast corner, where a small moat and drawbridge separate the castle from the well-preserved Great Tower, or Donjon. Uniquely in Britain, this was intended as the castle's main accommodation and last place of retreat, and came equipped with its own well. Together with its large grassy outer ward and the adjoining town, the castle formed a unified enclave known as a "bastide" (see p.468). Though Conwy and Caernarfon subsequently received the same treatment, Flint can claim to be the first borough in Wales to receive its charter, in September 1284. Until then, towns didn't really exist in essentially rural Wales.

Flint's greatest hour came in 1399 when Richard II was lured here from the safety of Conwy Castle and captured by Henry Bolingbroke, the Duke of Lancaster and future Henry IV. Shakespeare dramatized the event in *Richard II*, when in response to Bolingbroke's, "My gracious Lord, I come but for mine own", the defeated king replies, "Your own is yours, and I am yours, and all". Even Richard's favourite greyhound is said to have deserted him at this point.

During the Civil War, Flint remained Royalist until taken in 1647 by General Mytton, who so effectively dismantled it that only six years later it was practically buried in its own ruins. It was in this condition when Celia Fiennes found it on the brief – and generally displeasing – Welsh leg of her journeys around Britain between 1698 and 1712. She described Flint as "a very ragged place", and things haven't changed much. Unless you have come to spot some of the hundred thousand wintering waders on the Dee Estuary, you'll probably want to move on by the hourly **trains** or the #11 Arriva **buses** which leave from outside the train station every half-hour, bound for Chester and Rhyl.

Holywell and around

A place of pilgrimage for thirteen hundred years, **HOLYWELL** (Treffynnon), just off the A55 four miles northwest of Flint, is fancifully billed as "The Lourdes of Wales", though without the tacky souvenir stalls selling Virgin Mary lighters. Instead, Holywell is a quiet little town that modestly plays down its ancient appeal. The source of all the fuss is **St Winefride's Well** (daily: April–Sept 9am–5.30pm; Oct–March 10am–4pm; 60p; ⓦwww.saintwinefrideswell .com), a sacred and ancient spring that was first recorded by the Romans, who used its waters to relieve rheumatism and gout. The Roman connection sheds considerable doubt on the veracity of local legends said to date back to 660 AD

(April–Oct daily 10am–4.30pm; free), which is effectively the entrance to the **Greenfield Valley Farm and Museum** (same hours; £2.75), a collection of reconstructed buildings from around North Wales, many saved from demolition. Particularly interesting are the Victorian school and the agricultural buildings, the latter preserved as a working farm where you can feed the animals. Come on Sunday afternoon, when there are workshops, demonstrations and guided countryside walks.

Maen Achwyfaen

If you've got your own transport, it's well worth making an excursion four miles west from Holywell to the impressive **Maen Achwyfaen** or "Stone of Lamentation" (unrestricted access; CADW), Britain's tallest **Celtic cross**. Though the shaft, incised with interwoven latticework, is over 10ft high and crowned with a wheel cross, this thousand-year-old monument is little celebrated and stands alone in a field. To get there, take the A5026 to the northwest of Holywell, turning right onto the A5151, then taking the third exit at the first roundabout and following signs to Treloyan for a little over a mile.

Travel details

Unless otherwise stated, frequencies for trains and buses are for Monday to Saturday services, Sunday averages 1–3 services, though the main routes are more frequent and some routes have no Sunday service at all.

Trains

Flint to: Chester (at least hourly; 15min); Llandudno Junction (at least hourly; 40min); Prestatyn (at least hourly; 15min).
Wrexham to: Hawarden (hourly; 25min); Shotton (hourly (30min).

Buses

Chirk to: Llangollen (7 daily; 20min); Oswestry (hourly; 20min); Wrexham (hourly; 40min).
Corwen to: Bala (13 daily; 40min); Denbigh (3 daily; 1hr); Llangollen (13 daily; 20min); Ruthin (7 daily; 30min).
Denbigh to: Corwen (3 daily; 1hr); Rhyl (every 30min; 45min); Ruthin (12 daily; 25min); St Asaph (every 30min; 20min).

Flint to: Mold (hourly; 20min); Prestatyn (every 30min; 50min).
Llangollen to: Bala (13 daily; 1hr); Chirk (7 daily; 20min); Betws-y-Coed (4 daily; 1hr); Corwen (13 daily; 20min); Wrexham (at least hourly; 40min).
Mold to: Chester (every 30min; 1hr); Flint (hourly; 20min); Ruthin (7 daily; 40min); Wrexham (at least hourly; 40min–1hr).
Ruthin to: Corwen (7 daily; 30min); Denbigh (12 daily; 25min); Mold (7 daily; 40min).
Wrexham to: Chester (every 15min; 40min); Chirk (hourly; 40min); Llangollen (at least hourly; 40min); Mold (at least hourly; 40min–1hr); Oswestry (hourly; 1hr).

6

Snowdonia and the Llŷn

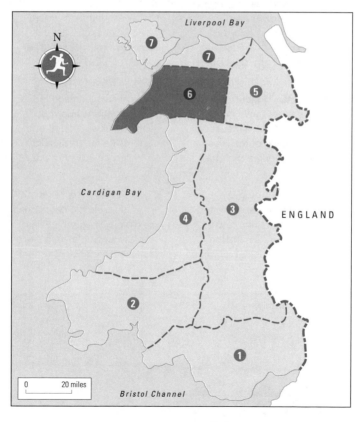

CHAPTER 6

Highlights

✳ **Gwydir Castle** Restored late fifteenth-century manor house, surrounded by formal gardens and offering Wales' best opportunity to stay in a castle. **See p.393**

✳ **Snowdon** Wales' highest mountain and the only one with half a dozen hiking paths and a cog railway converging on the summit-top café, bar and post office. **See p.404**

✳ **Welsh Slate Museum** Learn how slate was hewn from the hills around Llanberis and something of the lives of those who worked the quarries. **See p.403**

✳ **Blaenau Ffestiniog** Wales' slate capital – a tremendously atmospheric town, surrounded by mountains and rich in industrial heritage. **See p.410**

✳ **Ffestiniog Railway** The finest of Wales' narrow-gauge railways, running thirteen miles from the coast high into the heart of the mountains. **See p.424**

✳ **Portmeirion** This surreal seaside "village", made from bits of rescued architecture, was the setting for the cult TV series *The Prisoner*. **See p.425**

✳ **Bardsey Island** A point of Christian pilgrimage for centuries, this windswept sea-bird-strewn "Island of the Currents" is the destination for Wales' best offshore day-trip. **See p.436**

✳ **Clynnog Fawr** This large but wonderfully simple church on the old pilgrimage route lies near Clynnog dolmen, a site of much more ancient veneration. **See p.438**

△ Snowdon Mountain Railway

Snowdonia and the Llŷn

W hat the coal valleys are to the south of the country, the mountains of Snowdonia (Yr Eryri) are to the north: the defining feature, not just in their physical form but in the way they have shaped the communities within them. Trapped between the brash coastal resorts in the north and the thinly inhabited hill tracts of mid-Wales to the south, this mountainous kernel is north Wales' crowning glory, a tightly packed bundle of soaring cliff faces, jagged peaks and plunging waterfalls.

Snowdonia is the heart – and undisputed highlight – of the massive **Snowdonia National Park** (Parc Cenedlaethol Eryri), an 840-square-mile area which extends north and south, beyond the bounds of Snowdonia and this chapter, to encompass the Rhinogs, Cadair Idris (see p.340 and p.320 respectively) and 23 miles of superb Cambrian coastal scenery. It is this concentrated section, little more than ten miles by ten, that most people mean when they refer to Snowdonia: staggeringly beautiful and home to Wales' highest mountain, **Snowdon** (Eryri), where winter snows cling to 3000-foot peaks well into April.

Not surprisingly, the massif is the region's focus, and there are enough mountain paths to keep even the most jaded walking enthusiast happy for weeks. But Snowdonia isn't all walking. Small settlements are dotted in the valleys, making great bases or places to rest. Chief among them are **Betws-y-Coed** and **Llanberis**, the latter linked to Snowdon's summit by mountain rail, while others, like **Beddgelert** and **Blaenau Ffestiniog**, are former mining or quarry towns still brimming with interest. Over the barren hills on the eastern fringes of Snowdonia, **Bala** tempts with water sports: either lake sailing or whitewater rafting down the Tryweryn.

West of here, the mountain landscape bleeds gently into the softer contours of the **Llŷn**, which juts into the Celtic Sea at a near right angle to the Cambrian coast. Linked to Snowdonia by the magnificent, narrow-gauge **Ffestiniog Railway**, its first settlement is the harbour town of **Porthmadog**, best-known these days for its proximity to the Italianate dream village of **Portmeirion**. The Welsh castle at Cricieth and the museum devoted to Lloyd George a couple of miles away are amongst the good reasons to pause before Wales ends in a flourish of small coves around **Abersoch** and **Aberdaron**. Finally, roads loop back along the Llŷn to the tip of the north coast where **Caernarfon**, the heart

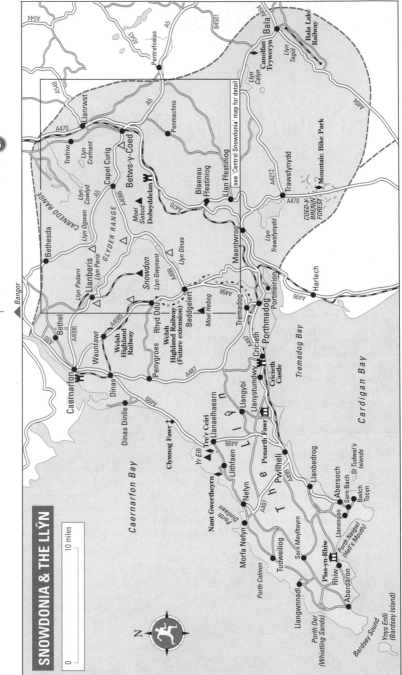

SNOWDONIA & THE LLŶN

N

0 —— 10 miles

© Crown copyright

of one of the most nationalist, Welsh-speaking areas in the country, is overshadowed by its mighty castle.

Getting around

Getting to the fringes of Snowdonia from elsewhere in Wales is easy: mainline **trains** run along the coast to nearby Bangor, while the Conwy Valley line branches at Llandudno Junction, penetrating to Betws-y-Coed and on to Blaenau Ffestiniog. Here, you can transfer to the useful and highly scenic Ffestiniog Railway for Porthmadog – the latter is also a stop on the Cambrian Coast line, shuffling daily around the coast to Pwllheli and to the heart of the Llŷn.

There are frequent **bus** services from Llandudno Junction (close to Llandudno and Conwy) up the Conwy Valley to Llanrwst, where you can change for Betws-y-Coed. From there, the Snowdon Sherpa services (see box, p.385) provide access to Bethesda, Llanberis, Beddgelert and Porthmadog, each with good connections to the coast. Pwllheli is the main transport hub for the Llŷn, with buses to most parts of the peninsula leaving from near the train station. Routes and times are all fully detailed on the free *Gwynedd Public Transport Maps and Timetables*, available from tourist offices and bus stations.

Current **discount fares** include the **Red Rover** (£4.95; buy on the first bus), good for one day's bus travel anywhere in northwest Wales as far south as Aberystwyth, and east to Llandudno and Corwen. Arriva Cymru buses (which cover north and much of mid-Wales) offer Rover tickets valid for one day (£5) or one week (£13), which can work out to be cost-effective. If you intend to travel by both bus and train, there's the **North and Mid-Wales Rover**, available from any staffed train station: a one-day pass costs £20; three days in any seven costs £30, and seven consecutive days £44.

Roads throughout the region are well surfaced but also well travelled, making **cycle touring** less appealing than it might seem. That said, the views are great, parking isn't a problem, and the quieter roads on the Llŷn are perfect for relaxed pedalling. You can also explore the ever expanding network of **cycle tracks** (see colour insert) and get off-road among the pines of Coed-y-Brenin south of Blaenau Ffestiniog and the Gwydir Forest near Betws-y-Coed.

Snowdonia

To Henry VIII's antiquarian, John Leland, **SNOWDONIA** seemed "horrible with the sight of bare stones"; these days, it's widely acclaimed as the most dramatic and alluring region in Wales, a compact, barren land of tortured ridges dividing glacial valleys where the sheer faces belie the fact that the tallest peaks only just top three thousand feet. It was to this mountain fastness that Llywelyn ap Gruffydd, the last true Prince of Wales, retreated in 1277 after his first war with Edward I; it was also here that Owain Glyndŵr held on most tenaciously to his dream of regaining the title for the Welsh. Centuries later, the English came to remove the mountains; slate barons built huge fortunes from Welsh toil and reshaped the patterns of Snowdonian life forever, as men looking for steady work in the quarries fled the hills and became town dwellers.

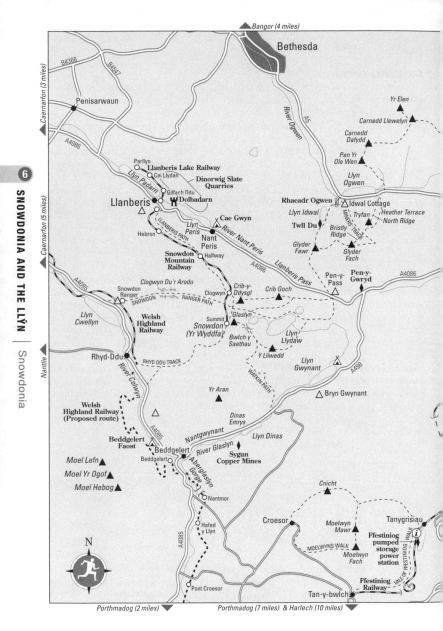

From the late eighteenth century, Snowdonia became the focus for the first truly structured approach to geological research. Early proponents of this new science pieced together the glacial evidence – scoured valley walls, scalloped mountainsides and hanging valleys – to come up with the first reliable proof of the last Ice Age and its retreat ten thousand years ago. These pioneers produced the rock-type classifications familiar to any students of

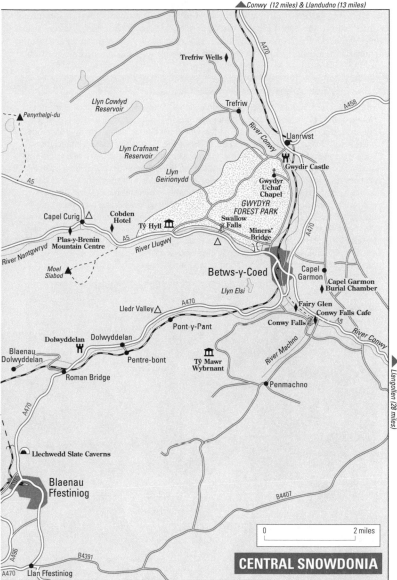

Conwy *(12 miles)* & Llandudno *(13 miles)*

Bala *(23 miles)*

© Crown copyright

the discipline: Cambrian rock takes its name from the Roman name for Wales, Ordovician and Silurian rocks from the Celtic tribes, the Ordovices and the Silures.

Botanists found rare alpine flora, writers produced libraries full of purple prose, and Richard Wilson, Paul Sandby and J.M.W. Turner all came to paint the landscape. Soon, those with the means began flocking here to marvel at the plunging waterfalls and walk the ever-widening paths to the mountaintops. Numbers have increased rapidly since then, and today, thousands of hikers arrive every weekend for some of the country's best walks over steep, exacting and constantly changing terrain. In recognition of the region's scientific importance,

Snowdonia National Park

The oldest and largest of Wales' national parks, **Snowdonia National Park** (*Parc Cenedlaethol Eryri*; ⓦ www.snowdonia-npa.gov.uk) was set out in 1951 over 840 square miles of northwest Wales – all the way from Conwy to Aberdyfi – to encompass the Rhinogs, Cadair Idris and 23 miles of the Cambrian coast. Jagged mountains predominate, but the harsh lines come tempered by broadleaf lowland woods around calm glacial lakes, waterfalls tumbling from hanging valleys and complex coastal dune systems. However, you won't find total wilderness: sheep and cattle farming supports many of the 27,000 people who live in the park (some 65 percent of them Welsh speakers) and another fourteen million people come here each year to tramp almost 2000 miles of designated paths. In apparent contradiction to its name, the national park is 75 percent privately owned by the Forestry Commission and National Trust. However, trespass isn't usually a problem as long as you keep to the ancient rights of way that conveniently cross private land where needed. Many of the most popular areas are National Trust land where access is unrestricted.

△ Snowdon National Park

as well as its scenic and recreational appeal, Snowdonia became the heartland of Wales' first, and still largest, national park (see box opposite).

The last Ice Age left a legacy of peaks ringed by cwms – huge hemispherical bites out of the mountainsides – while the ranges were left separated by steep-sided valleys, a challenge for even the most fly-footed climber. The most striking monument, and understandably the clear focus, is **Snowdon**, reached by superb hikes and a cog railway from the former slate town of **Llanberis**. But the other mountains are as good or better, often far less busy and giving unsurpassed views of Snowdon. The **Glyderau** and **Tryfan** are particular favourites and best tackled from the **Ogwen Valley**. The walkers' hamlets of **Capel Curig** and **Pen-y-Pass** have a suitably robust atmosphere, though many more prefer the comforts of the nearby Victorian resort, **Betws-y-Coed**. Elsewhere, settlements tend to coincide with some enormous mine or quarry. Foremost among these are **Beddgelert**, where the former copper mines are open to the public, and **Blaenau Ffestiniog**, the "Slate Capital of North Wales", where one of the mines has opened its caverns for underground tours.

If you're serious about doing some **walking** – and some of the walks described here are serious, especially in bad weather (Snowdon gets 200 inches of rain a year) – you need a good map, such as the 1:50,000 OS Landranger #115 or the 1:25,000 OS Explorer #OL17. Always check mountain weather conditions before setting out: latest reports are usually posted on the doors or notice boards of outdoor shops and tourist offices, while the Met Office (ⓦ www.metoffice.com) has a premium-rated mountain forecast for Snowdonia (ⓣ 09068/500449; 60p/min).

Accommodation inside the Snowdonia National Park is strictly limited, and most is on the fringes. The main exception is Betws-y-Coed, a village packed with guesthouses, all of them filling up early during the busy summer season. Elsewhere in Snowdonia are B&Bs, hostels, bunkhouses and basic campsites, mostly geared towards walkers and climbers. In all, there are six **YHA hostels** within five miles of Snowdon's summit, and a further half-dozen other budget places. Even with a medium-sized backpack, walking from one to another makes a welcome change from the usual circular walks.

Parking, buses and the Snowdon Sherpa

Throughout Snowdonia (and much of the rest of Wales) towns are often tucked into folds in the mountains or wedged between cliffs and the sea, giving little space for parking in the narrow streets. When you do find somewhere to park you'll usually have to pay, though it may only be 50p per hour or less. In the mountainous core around Snowdon, visitors are encouraged to park in surrounding towns and use the comprehensive bus system to get around. The **Snowdon Sherpa** is a catch-all name for a handful of interconnecting bus services plying the roads between Betws-y-Coed, Bethesda, Llanberis, Waunfawr and Porthmadog. They all meet at Pen-y-Pass, and a **Day Ticket** (£3; buy from the driver) will give you one day's unlimited travel within this region throughout the day. On summer weekends and school holidays, some services use open-top double-deckers.

Major routes through northern Snowdonia are:

#S1 Llanberis to Pen-y-Pass via Nant Peris.

#S2 Betws-y-Coed to Pen-y-Pass which occasionally runs in from Llandudno.

#S4 Caernarfon to Pen-y-Pass via Waunfawr and Beddgelert (day ticket not valid from Caernarfon).

#S6 Bethesda to Pen-y-Pass via Llyn Ogwen, Capel Curig and the *Pen-y-Gwryd Hotel*.

#S96 Betws-y-Coed to Porthmadog via Capel Curig, Pen-y-Pass and Beddgelert.

Betws-y-Coed and around

Sprawled out across a flat plain around the confluence of the Conwy, Llugwy and Lledr valleys, **BETWS-Y-COED** (pronounced "betoos-er-coyd") should be the perfect base for exploring Snowdonia. Its riverside setting, overlooked by the conifer-clad slopes of the **Gwydyr Forest Park**, is undeniably appealing, and the town boasts the best selection of hotels and guesthouses in the region, but after an hour mooching around the outdoor equipment shops and drinking tea you are left wondering what to do. The town is touted as "the gateway to Snowdonia", which makes it hard to avoid, but none of the serious mountain walks starts from here, just a couple of easy strolls (see box, p.389) to its two main attractions, the **Conwy Falls** and **Swallow Falls**. Despite its genteel pretensions, Betws-y Coed is something of a magnet for **bikers**, both those with polished chrome hogs parked outside the town's pubs and cafés, and mud-bespattered mountain bikers returning from the pleasures of the Gwydyr Forest.

The quieter valleys in the vicinity can often be a lot more appealing than the town itself. The rail line from the coast comes up the **Conwy Valley** past **Llanrwst**, five miles north of Betws-y-Coed, a town graced by a fine bridge attributed to Inigo Jones and a couple of beautifully decorated chapels. The train continues south from Betws-y-Coed up the **Lledr Valley**, a wonderfully scenic journey passing the lonely **Dolwyddelan Castle**, on its way to the slate town of Blaenau Ffestiniog. Further to the southeast, a minor road leads to **Penmachno** and the house of William Morgan, who first translated the Bible into Welsh. Walkers bound for the high hills will be heading west beside the **River Llugwy** to the mountain centre of Capel Curig and beyond to Llanberis and the Ogwen Valley. Most of the land around Betws-y-Coed and along the Conwy Valley was part of the Gwydyr Estate owned by the Wynn family, descended from the kings of Gwynedd and the most powerful dynasty in the region until the male line died out in 1678; several place names are reminders of the family's might.

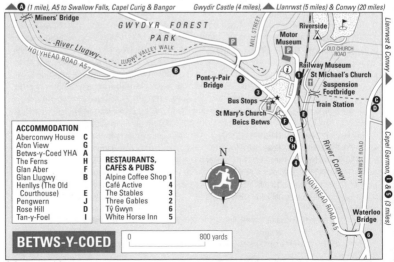

Arrival and accommodation

Betws-y-Coed is arranged in a flat triangle bounded by the Conwy and Llugwy rivers and the A5, which forms the town's High Street. Access is easy, either by train or bus from the north coast, or by car along the A5 from Llangollen. The **train station** is just across the lawn from the **tourist office** in Royal Oak Stables (daily: Easter to mid-Oct 9.30am–5.30pm; mid-Oct to Easter 9.30am–4.30pm; ☎01690/710426, ✉tic.byc@eryri-npa.gov.uk), where displays give a quick overview of Snowdonia.

Buses, which fan out towards the peaks around Snowdon (see box on p.385), and to Penmachno, Llanberis, Conwy and Llandudno, stop outside St Mary's Church on the main street. Some bus journeys will require a change at nearby Llanrwst, the hub for the local bus system.

Accommodation

Betws-y-Coed has plenty of **accommodation**, but has to cope with an even larger numbers of visitors pushing prices up in the summer. Expect to pay a pound or two more than in other towns in Snowdonia, and don't be surprised to find the places listed below full if you arrive late in the day. Even if rooms aren't in short supply it's worth considering staying just out of town in places we've listed under Llanrwst and Trefriw. Walkers and climbers who want direct access to the mountains need to make for Capel Curig or Llanberis.

There's also a YHA hostel just out of town (see below), another one six miles west at Capel Curig and an independent hostel four miles south in the Lledr Valley.

B&Bs and hotels

Aberconwy House Lôn Muriau, Llanrwst Rd ☎01690/710202, ⊚www.aberconwy-house.co.uk. A friendly and well-appointed Victorian guesthouse, with most rooms enjoying superb views over Betws-y-Coed and the Llugwy Valley. To get there on foot, cross the suspension bridge behind the train station; by car, take the A470 towards Llanrwst. ❸

Afon View Holyhead Rd ☎01690/710726, ⊚www.afon-view.co.uk. Non-smoking, quality B&B with off-street parking, a small garden and hearty breakfasts. ❹

The Ferns Holyhead Rd ☎01690/710587, ⊚www.ferns-guesthouse.co.uk. Beautifully appointed, licensed, non-smoking guesthouse. Closed Dec. ❸

Glan Aber Holyhead Rd ☎01690/710325, ⊚www.glanaberhotel.com. Reasonable town-centre hotel with bar and a separate room with hot tub and sauna (fee for both), plus a kind of hostel with two bunks to a room (£13 per head) but no self-catering facilities: optional £5 breakfast. Good bike storage. ❶/❹

Glan Llugwy on the A5 towards Capel Curig, 300 yards beyond Pont-y-Pair ☎01690/710592. One of the cheapest B&Bs around, with shared bathrooms. ❷

Henllys (The Old Courthouse) Old Church Rd ☎ & ☎01690/710534, ⊚www.guesthouse-snowdonia.co.uk. Guesthouse in a converted Victorian magistrates' courthouse with many original features, plus comfy rooms in the frilly tradition, many with views over the River Conwy. ❹

Pengwern Allt Dinas, a mile east on the A5 ☎01690/710480, ⊚www.snowdoniaaccommodation.com. Beautiful, welcoming and tastefully decorated country house set in two acres of woods with just three rooms plus a separate self-catering cottage let from around £300 a week in summer. ❺

Rose Hill Lôn Muriau, Llanrwst Rd ☎01690/710455, ⊚www.rosehill-snowdonia.co.uk. Next to *Aberconwy House* (see above), this welcoming guesthouse is run by keen walkers always happy to advise on planned routes. ❸

Tan-y-Foel Capel Garmon ☎01690/710507, ⊚www.tyfhotel.co.uk. Ultra-modern public spaces and stylish, luxurious rooms in a sixteenth-century farmhouse make this one of the best small country hotels in the district. Expect sweeping views across eight acres of grounds to the Conwy Valley, and outstanding three-course dinners for around £40. Take the A470 towards Llanrwst then turn right after two miles. ❼

Hostels and campsites

Betws-y-Coed YHA A5, 2 miles west of Betws-y-Coed ☎01690/710796, ⓦwww.swallowfallshotel.co.uk. Pleasant, modern hostel with dorms (from £12.50) and rooms, plus breakfasts and packed lunches available (both £4.25). It is next door to the otherwise nondescript *Swallow Falls Hotel* (which has a bar and restaurant), and a nice campsite (£5 per person). ❶

Riverside Caravan & Camping Park ☎01690/710310. The closest campsite to town, right behind the station, open to couples and families only. Closed Nov to mid-March. £6 per person.

Rynys Farm Camping Site 2 miles southeast of town on the A5 near the Conwy Falls ☎01690/710218, ⓦwww.rynys-camping.co.uk. Peaceful farm campsite catering mainly to tents. £4 per person.

The Town

Betws-y-Coed was founded in the fifth or sixth century, when a monastic cell earned the settlement the moniker of the "oratory in the forest". Apart from some lead mining, it remained a backwater until 1808, when road improvements brought the Irish Mail this way. As part of the A5 construction, Telford completed the graceful cast-iron **Waterloo Bridge** (Y Bont Haearn) in 1815, complete with spandrels that utilize the emblems of the four countries of the then newly formed United Kingdom (English rose, Scottish thistle, Irish shamrock and Welsh leek). The improved access lured landscape painters David Cox and J.M.W. Turner, who in turn alerted the leisured classes to the town's beauty. Anglers keen to exploit the richly stocked pools came too, but it was the arrival of the train line in 1868 that really lifted Betws-y-Coed's status to genteel resort, an air the town vainly tries to maintain. Sights in town are few, but include the **Pont-y-Pair Falls**, a low cataract where the waters of the River Llugwy thunder over assorted boulders and funnel under the adjacent Pont-y-Pair ("Bridge of the Cauldron"). Relaxing on the stone slabs which surround the falls, it's hard to generate much enthusiasm for the fourteenth-century **St Michael's church** (key from the Railway Museum in winter), most interesting for the twelfth-century font and a carved effigy of an armoured knight, whose inscription identifies him as Gruffydd ap Dafydd Goch, the grandson of Llywelyn ap Gruffydd's brother, Prince Dafydd. St Michael's obscure isolation, tucked away down the lane behind the train station, was one of the reasons why the rather plain **St Mary's** parish church was newly constructed on the main road in 1873.

Adjoining the train station, the **Conwy Valley Railway Museum** (daily 10.15am–5pm; £1.50) is a fairly dull collection of memorabilia and shiny engines, slightly enlivened by a model of a Welsh slate quarry and the opportunity for kids to take a short ride on a miniature train (£1.50) or tram (£1). If internal combustion interests you more than steam, the **Motor Museum** (Easter–Oct daily 10.30am–6pm; £1.50), a couple of hundred yards away behind the tourist office, is a marginally better bet. The half-dozen classic bikes and fifteen cars on display change frequently, but expect the likes of a 1934 Bugatti Straight 8 and a rare Riley MPA.

Activities

There are several easy to moderate walks around Betws-y-Coed (see box, opposite), but for more of a workout, go **mountain biking** in the Gwydyr Forest Park, one of the top trail-riding locales in Wales and among the best in Britain. Forest track ascents provide access to numerous single-track descents of varying difficulty, and the scenery is fantastic, particularly along the higher sections where there are mountain views. Trails are continually being built and improved, so to see the latest developments **rent a bike** from Beics Betws (☎01690/710766) in the street up behind the post office: front-suspension bikes (£14 half-day, £18 full day), and full-suspension machines (£20/35) come with a photocopied trail map marked with suggested routes.

The nearest **horse riding** is at Tŷ Coch Farm (℡01690/760248; 2hr £23), seven miles south of Betws-y-Coed in Penmachno. **Anglers** with a rod licence and their own tackle can try hooking salmon and sea trout on stretches of the Conwy and Llugwy within town (£18 a day; mid-March to mid-Oct), and brown and American brook trout on Llyn Elsi in the hills just south (£12.50 a day, late March to late Oct only). For details, pick up the free Betws-y-Coed Anglers Club leaflet from the tourist office or Pendyffryn Stores, by the post office on Holyhead Road, which also sells gear.

Eating and drinking

For a town so geared to tourism that it's hard to turn around without knocking someone's cream tea onto the floor, there are surprisingly few really good places to **eat**. Many of the more visible ones along the main road are quite mediocre, but better options do exist. **Entertainment** doesn't usually stretch much further than a beer in one of the pubs, though there are a couple of male voice choirs putting on performances through the summer: a different choir performs each week in St Mary's Church (Sun 8pm, £4) and there's usually a performance each Friday evening at *The Stables*.

Walks around Betws-y-Coed

An easy introduction to the countryside around Betws-y-Coed is to join a five- to six-hour **guided walk** from outside the tourist office (book on ℡07790/851333; £3.50). If you'd rather go it alone, choose from a couple of walks that follow narrow river gorges. Neither is circular, so unless you plan to hitch back to your base, consult bus timetables first to avoid a long wait for the infrequent services.

The **Conwy Gorge walk** (3 miles; 1hr 15min; descent only) links two of the district's best-known natural attractions, Fairy Glen and the Conwy Falls (see p.390), by way of a cool green lane giving glimpses of the river through the woods. Catch the #64 bus (8 daily) to the *Conwy Falls Café*, then after viewing the falls, walk a hundred yards back along the road towards Betws-y-Coed and follow a path parallel to the river through the trees. After about half an hour, you'll see the gate to Fairy Glen on your left. Returning to the main path, continue to the *Fairy Glen Hotel*, where you can cross the river by Beaver Bridge, turn right and follow a minor road a mile back to town.

The car park on the north side of the Pont-y-Pair bridge marks the beginning of the **Llugwy Valley walk** (6 miles; 2hr 30min; 600ft ascent), a forested path following the twisting and plunging river upstream to Capel Curig. With the A5 running parallel to the river all the way, there are several opportunities to cut short the walk and hitch or wait for the bus back to Betws-y-Coed. Less than a mile from Pont-y-Pair, you first reach a ford where the Roman road Sarn Helen crossed the river, then pass the steeply sloping Miners' Bridge, which linked miners' homes at Pentre Du on the south side of the river to the lead mines in the Gwydyr Forest. With its plunge pools and rocky diving platforms this is a wonderfully refreshing place to take a dip. The path follows the river on your left for another mile to a slightly obscured view of Swallow Falls. Detailed maps available from the tourist office in Betws-y-Coed show numerous routes back through the Gwydyr Forest, or you can continue half a mile to the road bridge by Tŷ Hyll and follow the right bank to Capel Curig, passing the scant remains of the Caer Llugwy, a Roman fort, and a couple more treacherous rapids: The Mincer and Cobden's Falls.

Alpine Coffee Shop in the train station. Bright, wooden-floored daytime café with art on the walls and an appealing range of sandwiches, wraps and vegetarian dishes as well as speciality teas and espresso.

🏃 **Café Active** Holyhead Rd, ⓦwww .cafeactive.co.uk. Convivial café above the Cotswolds Outdoor Rock Bottom shop, with the town's only Internet access and good espresso. The café owners and staff are a good source of outdoor advice and offer a free activity booking service.

The Stables *Royal Oak Hotel*, High St ☎01690/710219. The town's liveliest bar, with good beer, outdoor seating, jazz on summer Thursdays,

and a good range of bar food, pizzas and grills at reasonable prices.

Three Gables Holyhead Rd. Simple meals well cooked and in respectable proportions for £7–12. The best bet if you aren't devoting your evening to dining.

🏃 **Tŷ Gwyn** on the A5 ☎01690/710383, ⓦwww.tygwynhotel.co.uk. Convivial wood-beamed bar that's a great place to tuck into decent bar meals (£8 mains) over a pint or two. They also serve tasty and well-presented restaurant meals (£13–15) either in the restaurant or bar.

White Horse Inn Capel Garmon (see p.392). An excellent evening retreat, with cosy bars, good beer, home-cooked bar meals and a restaurant serving fine meals (mains £9–12).

Conwy Falls, Fairy Glen and Tŷ Mawr Wybrnant

None of the attractions of Betws-y-Coed can compete with getting out to the gorges and waterfalls in the vicinity, and **walking** is the ideal way to see them (see box on p.389). A few miles upstream of Betws-y-Coed, the River Conwy plunges fifty feet over the **Conwy Falls** into a deep pool. After slotting £1 into the turnstile beside the *Conwy Falls Café* (reached by the #64 bus 8 times daily), you can view the falls on the right and a series of rock steps to the left, originally cut as a kind of primitive fish ladder, which is now superseded by a tunnel through the rock on the far side.

A mile or so downstream, after negotiating a continuous series of tortuous rapids, the churning waters of the Conwy negotiate a staircase of drops and enter **Fairy Glen**, a cleft in a small wood which takes its name from the Welsh fairies, the Tylwyth Teg, who are said to be seen hereabouts. Take the A470 towards Blaenau Ffestiniog and turn up the lane beside the *Fairy Glen Hotel*. From the car park here (£1) a short path (20min each way; 50p) leads to the glen.

Just above Conwy Falls is the river's confluence with the River Machno, which drains the hills around the small village of **Penmachno**, a couple of miles upstream. Some two and a half miles beyond Penmachno stands the isolated and little-visited cottage of **Tŷ Mawr Wybrnant** (late March–Sept Thurs–Sun noon–5pm, Oct Thurs–Sun noon–4pm; £2.60; NT). Here, Bishop William Morgan, the man who first translated the Bible into Welsh (see p.457), was born in 1545 and lived until his teenage years when he decamped to Gwydir Castle to pursue his education. The original cottage has been restored to something like its sixteenth-century appearance: all bare stone and beams, with a gaping fireplace supporting a huge, sagging beam dating back to the thirteenth century. Its star attraction is the collection of Bibles and prayer books, including a Morgan original.

The Llugwy Valley: Swallow Falls and the Gwydyr Forest

The **Swallow Falls** (a mistranslation of *Rhaeadr Ewynnol* or "foaming cataract") lie two miles west of Betws-y-Coed along the A5 towards Capel Curig. Such easy access makes this one of the region's most-visited sights, but it is no more than a straightforward, pretty waterfall with the occasional mad kayaker scraping down the precipitous rock. Pay your £1 and you can walk down to a series of viewing platforms.

Less than a mile beyond, the road crosses the river passing **Tŷ Hyll** (Easter–Oct daily 9.30am–5pm; Nov–Easter Mon–Fri variable hours; ℡01690/720287, Ⓦwww.snowdonia-society.org.uk; £1), known as the "Ugly House" for its chunky appearance. Decked out with period furniture and surrounded by a cottage garden, wildlife pond, and forest full of easy paths, it is also the head-quarters of the Snowdonia Society, an environmental campaigning group which lobbies to preserve the region's ecological and social integrity.

From here, a small side road climbs north into the evergreens of the **Gwydyr Forest**, an area best explored by mountain bike but pleasant enough on foot. Starting from a lakeside parking area a mile or so northeast of Tŷ Hyll, the **Miners' Trail** (3 miles; 2hr; minimal ascent) gives a focus to a forest walk, though you would have to be pretty keen on defunct lead workings to get much out of it. From Tŷ Hyll, the A5 follows the River Llugwy upstream past a number of roadside cataracts – most notably opposite *Cobden's Hotel* – and on to Capel Curig.

The Lledr Valley

The train line up the Conwy Valley from Betws-y-Coed follows the twists of the beautiful **Lledr Valley** to Blaenau Ffestiniog, the river flowing through deciduous and pine forests that give way to the smooth, grassy slopes of the Moel Siabod before the route bores through over two miles of slate – the long-est rail tunnel in Wales. Take this trip while you can: the line is always under threat of closure, especially since the demise of its principal funder, the Traws-fynydd nuclear power station.

The A470 runs parallel to the river from Betws-y-Coed to Blaenau Ffes-tiniog. Four miles south of Betws-y-Coed, you come to Pont-y-Pant station, where the Roman road Sarn Helen crosses the river on a clapper bridge and follows its banks to Dolwyddelan. The *Lledr House* **independent hostel** (℡01690/750202, Ⓦwww.ukyh.com; ❶), across the river from the station, is an ideal starting point for a walk up Moel Siabod (see box on p.395). It offers beds in double, twin and family rooms with self-catering facilities for £10 a head, and accommodates **campers** for half that.

A mile further on is **DOLWYDDELAN**, a village well placed for the south-ern approach to Moel Siabod and only a mile east of lonely **Dolwyddelan Castle** (April–Sept daily 10am–6pm; Oct–March Mon–Sat 10am–4pm, Sun 11am–4pm; £2; CADW), commanding the head of the valley. Llywelyn ap Iorwerth ("the Great"; see p.505) may well have been born here, since his father was reputedly responsible for its construction at the end of the twelfth century. The strategic site, on the important route from Aberconwy to the north and Ardudwy to the south, was soon turned against him when Edward I took the castle, refortified it and used it to further subdue the Welsh. By the end of the fifteenth century, it had become redundant and lay abandoned until the Wynns of Gwydyr treated it to a suitably Victorian reconstruction, complete with fanciful battlements and a new roof. Today, it shelters only a small exhibition on native Welsh castles, but affords a panoramic view of Snowdonia from between its castellations.

If you want to stay around here, the castle custodian runs the neighbouring *Bryn Tirion Farm* B&B (℡01690/750366; ❸), a **campsite** (closed Nov–Feb; £3 per person;) and a comfortable, self-catering **bunkhouse** (open all year; £10 per person), with bedding supplied. Back in the centre of Dolwyddelan, *Elen's Castle Hotel* (☎01690/750207, ⓦ www.elenscastlehotel.co.uk; ❸) has cosy rooms and serves good, inexpensive bar food and pricier meals. The best **pub** is the welcoming *Y Gwydyr*, on the main road in Dolwyddelan, where Sunday lunch is served.

The Conwy Valley: Capel Garmon, Llanrwst and Trefriw

Fed by the water of the Machno, Lledr and Llugwy rivers, the Conwy River leaves Betws-y-Coed along its broad pastoral corridor to the sea at Conwy flanked on the left by the bald tops of Snowdonia's northern and eastern bulwark, the mighty Carneddau range. More manageable hills lie to the east, where Neolithic dwellers left their mark at the **Capel Garmon Burial Chamber** (unrestricted access; CADW), a heavily reconstructed, multichambered burial site built between 2500 and 1900 BC. It is an atmospheric spot comprising some rough stones lining a series of linked pits, with a central chamber covered by an enormous capstone. The site is a five-minute signposted walk across farmland two miles southeast of Betws-y-Coed, half a mile south of the tiny hilltop village of **CAPEL GARMON**. There's top-notch refreshment in the village at the excellent *White Horse Inn* (see p.390).

Llanrwst

Five miles north of Betws-y-Coed, **LLANRWST** is neither particularly striking, nor especially large, but does have a lively working-town feel. It was once the largest wool market in north Wales, had a spell as a centre for harp manufacture in the eighteenth century, and is still the most economically important town in the valley, retaining Wednesday and Friday livestock **markets**, and a general one each Tuesday.

Inigo Jones is said to have spent his early years here, so it isn't entirely unlikely that the great seventeenth-century architect was at least partially responsible for the town's most noted sight, the slender humpback **Pont Fawr** (Big Bridge). It undoubtedly bears Jones' mark: three graceful arches and beautifully proportioned symmetry, combined with engineering techniques that were extremely advanced for their time. In summer, its single lane struggles to cope with the traffic across it to **Tu Hwnt i'r Bont**, a photogenic, fifteenth-century, ivy-clad former courthouse that's now a National Trust tearoom.

Denbigh Street links the main **train station** to the central **Ancaster Square**, lined with some cheerfully unpretentious pubs and the odd eatery. **Buses** stop on Watling Street which branches off midway along Denbigh Street. Since it's so close to Betws-y-Coed, few people choose to **stay** in Llanrwst, but consider B&B at ⚑ *Gwydir Castle* (see opposite; ☎01492/641687, ⓦ www.gwydir-castle .co.uk; ❻) where two spacious rooms have been fitted out in baronial style with four-poster beds, deep baths and elegantly eclectic decor. There's no TV but you can relax in the oak-panelled parlour where breakfast is served.

Llanrwst has recently made huge gastronomic strides and now offers several good **places to eat**. The long-standing *Tu Hwnt i'r Bont Tearooms* (see above; Easter–Oct), is still good for traditional afternoon teas, but for something more modern visit ⚑ *The Tannery* on Willow Street (☎01492/640172; closed Mon, Tues & Sun evenings), where tables indoors and a sunny riverside deck make a welcome spot to enjoy the likes of lamb and bean nachos or salami, smoked bacon and four-cheese bruschetta (both £7), washed down with wine or good espresso. Back in Ancaster Square the non-smoking Italian-oriented *La Barrica* bistro (Tues–Sun lunch plus Thurs & Fri evenings; ☎01492/642297), is especially good for snacks and evening specialities.

Gwydir Castle and Gwydyr Uchaf Chapel

Across the river, half a mile west of Llanrwst, is Richard Wynn's ancestral home, **Gwydir Castle** (March–Oct daily 10am–4.30pm; £3.50), actually a low-slung manor house begun around 1490 on the site of a fortified house a century older. Despite additions in the sixteenth and nineteenth centuries, with parts plundered from the post-dissolution Maenan Abbey, the ivy- and wisteria-covered building is a fabulous model of early Tudor architecture.

Its core is a three-storey solar tower, whose windows relieve the gloom of the great halls, each with enormous fireplaces and stone-flagged or heavy timber floors. Most of the original fittings and Tudor furniture were sold in 1921, by the then owner, the Earl of Carrington, and much of the rest of the house was ruined in a fire a few months later. A major restoration of the house is largely complete, and, in line with its baronial nature, the furnishing is kept simple – tapestries cover the solid stone walls, a few tables and chairs are scattered about and there's some fine painted glass. Fortunately, some of the original furnishings have been tracked down, including the heavily carved oak panels, Baroque door-case and fireplace, and abundant gilded Spanish leather of the magnificent **Dining Room**. This was initially installed by Richard Wynn around 1642, and is again attributed to Inigo Jones. The complete set was bought during the 1921 sell-off by American newspaper magnate William Randolph Hearst and shipped across the Atlantic. New York's Metropolitan Museum acquired it in 1956 and kept it boxed up for forty years until it was sold back to the castle in 1996 and re-installed.

Outside, the main attraction is the **Dutch Garden**, with its fountain, peacocks and Cedars of Lebanon dating back to 1625. Since its owners have made two splendid bedrooms available to bed and breakfast guests (see opposite), Gwydir represents one of the best opportunities in Wales to stay in an authentic castle that still maintains the air of a family home.

A few hundred yards from his home, Richard Wynn built his own private **Gwydyr Uchaf Chapel** (key from the adjacent Forest Enterprise office, Mon–Fri 8.30am–5pm; free; CADW) in 1673. The plain exterior is in striking contrast to the unashamedly Baroque interior, with its roof beams cut into angelic figures. The inward-facing pews are unusual, but it's the painted ceiling that's really outstanding, depicting the Creation, the Trinity and the Day of Judgement.

Trefriw and Llyn Crafnant

The small village of **TREFRIW**, two miles north of Llanrwst, is home to the **Trefriw Woollen Mills** (mill Easter–Oct Mon–Fri 10am–5pm, shop daily all year; free), whose demonstrations of late nineteenth-century weaving methods, using power from the stream outside, make for a more compelling visit than other mills around north Wales. In the second century, Romans garrisoned on the banks of the Conwy recognized the restorative properties of the iron-rich waters of **Trefriw Wells** (Easter–Sept daily 10am–5.30pm; Oct–Easter Mon–Sat 10am–5pm, Sun noon–5pm; £3), a mile and a half north of the village. An interesting, if laboured, twenty-minute self-guided tour visits a robust pair of gentlemen's and ladies' bathhouses, complete with slate tubs built around 1700. You can also sample the waters – they taste a little like sucking a rusty nail, but their invigorating, curative powers are extolled by the numerous testimonials kept in the café.

A signposted road back in the village close to the woollen mills leads three miles southwest to **Llyn Crafnant**, a calm reservoir hemmed in by mountains, and one of the more popular local beauty spots. Alternatively, take the steep lane south of the village towards the neighbouring lakes of **Llanrhychwyn** and **Llyn Geiri-onydd**. There are numerous other small pools in the vicinity, many bordered by forest, and it's a lovely area for a picnic, a gentle walk or a swim. If you want to **stay**, there are a couple of places that easily match anything in Betws-y-Coed. The tastefully appointed *Crafnant Guesthouse* (☎01492/640809, ⓦwww.trefriw .co.uk; ❷; closed Dec & Jan), is right in the village on the B5106, while the lovely ⚡ *Yr Hafod Country House* (☎01492/640029, ⓦwww.hafodhouse.co.uk; ❹), is just a few hundred yards to the south.

⑥ Capel Curig and the Ogwen Valley

Tantalizing glimpses of Wales' highest mountains flash through the forested banks of the Llugwy as you climb west from Betws-y-Coed on the A5. But Snowdon, the mountain that more than any other has become a symbol of north Wales for walkers, mountaineers, botanists and painters alike, eludes you until the final bend before **Capel Curig**. This tiny walkers' village makes a perfect base for the two valleys that plunge westwards deep into the mountains. The A4086 follows Nant Gwryd southwest to the Snowdon massif while the A5 prises apart the Carneddau and Glyder ranges to the northwest, forging through the **Ogwen Valley** to tatty **Bethesda**, home to one of Wales' last surviving slate quarries.

As you cross the watershed between the Llugwy and Ogwen rivers, the frequently mist-shrouded Carnedd range to the north glowers across at the Glyder range and its triple-peaked **Tryfan**, arguably Snowdonia's most demanding mountain. This forms a fractured spur out from the main range and blocks your view down the valley, the twin monoliths of Adam and Eve that crown Tryfan's summit picked out on the skyline. The courageous or foolhardy make the jump between them as a point of honour at the end of every ascent. West of Tryfan, the road follows a perfect example of a U-shaped valley, carved and smoothed by rocks frozen into the undersides of the glaciers that creaked down **Nant Ffrancon** ten thousand years ago.

Capel Curig

There's scarcely a building in tiny **CAPEL CURIG**, six miles west of Betws-y-Coed, that isn't of some use to hikers, whether as inexpensive accommodation, a mountain-gear shop or just a place to replenish the body. Foremost among them is **Plas-y-Brenin: The National Mountain Centre** (☎01690/720214, ⓦwww.pyb.co.uk), a quarter of a mile along the A4086 to Llanberis from the town's main road junction. Built around a former coaching inn and hotel, the centre runs internationally renowned residential courses in orienteering, kayaking, skiing and rock climbing (see p.70). Daily mountain weather forecasts are available from reception. If you're just passing through and don't have your own equipment, the two-hour indoor climbing, lake canoeing and dry-slope skiing sessions held during August and other school holidays (£10) may be of interest. Kids who want a full-day taster of canoeing, skiing and abseiling can be left on the "3 in a Day" adventure session (£25), where adults are welcome too. There is also a climbing wall (daily 10am–11pm; £3), a dry ski slope (daily 10am–4pm; £5 per hour including ski rental, £20 per hour for instruction; call for availability) and the opportunity to hear talks or watch slide shows of recent expeditions (usually Mon, Tues & Sat 8pm; free). Plas-y-Brenin also rents out all kinds of hiking, camping and mountaineering gear at reasonable prices, but for **mountain bikes** you'll need to visit Beics Betws in Betws-y-Coed (see p.388).

A walk from Capel Curig

Note: the 1:50,000 OS Landranger #115 map or the 1:25,000 OS Explorer #OL17 map are recommended for this walk.

If you approached **Capel Curig** from the west, you won't have looked twice at the rounded grassy back of **Moel Siabod** (2862ft), but its eastern aspect is another matter – a challenging ridge rising up to afford a magnificent summit view of the Snowdon Horseshoe.

The mountainous section of the east ridge walk (5 miles; 4hr; 2200ft) is circular and brings you back into the Llugwy Valley. The route starts from opposite the YHA hostel in Capel Curig, crossing the concrete bridge and following the right bank downstream past the falls by *Cobden's Hotel* to the Pont Cyfyng road bridge (30min), an alternative starting point for the walk. Taking the road south, turn right on the second path signposted to Moel Siabod. This quickly rises out of the valley and keeps to the left of the mountain, past a disused slate quarry and across some boggy land, before the long scramble up the east ridge. Once found, the path is fairly clear, but it weaves around outcrops where a moment's inattention could be perilous. The summit is flat and uninteresting, so once you've admired Snowdon, turn northeast and follow the craggy summit ridge, which eventually starts to drop across grass to the moors below, soon rejoining your ascent route for the hike back to Pont Cyfyng.

Despite Capel Curig's popularity, the only major **walk** from here is up Moel Siabod (see box above), but the village acts as a base for the Ogwen Valley and Snowdon. The road A4086 runs four miles southwest to the *Pen-y-Gwryd Hotel* (see p.408). The A498 continues south to Beddgelert, past the best view of Snowdon's east face, while the A4086 branches west to Llanberis, passing Pen-y-Pass, the start for the best-known Snowdon walks.

Practicalities

The only **buses** servicing Capel Curig are the Snowdon Sherpa services (see box on p.385). If none are suitable, you can always walk the six miles along the River Llugwy from Betws-y-Coed (see box on p.389) – a pleasant three-hour walk in good weather.

Once here, there are lots of **places to stay**, though none is especially luxurious. *Bron Eryri* (☎01690/720240, ⓦwww.eryriguesthouse.fsnet.co.uk; ❸) is a comfortable and welcoming B&B half a mile outside the village towards Betws-y-Coed, while the wonderful *Bryn Tyrch Hotel* (☎01690/720223, ⓦwww.bryntyrch-hotel.co.uk; ❸/❹) is also on the A5 but closer to the main road junction, with some en suites. There's also the simple yet comfortable *Bryn Glo* (☎01690/720215, ⓦwww.bryn-glo.com; ❷/❸), a mile towards Betws-y-Coed, also with some en suites, and the *Capel Curig YHA* **hostel** (☎01690/720225 or 0870/770 5746, ⓔcapelcurig@yha.org.uk; £16; March–Oct), 500 yards along the A5 towards Betws-y-Coed.

During the day, walkers tend to patronize either the *Pinnacle Café* and general store at the main road junction, or the superior *Snowdonia Café*, next to the YHA, which has better food at low prices, garden seating and a wonderful view of Snowdon. In the evenings, most retire to the warm and lively bar at the ⚔ *Bryn Tyrch Hotel*, where the inexpensive **meals** are huge, delicious and predominantly vegetarian – indeed, this is one of the very few establishments in the whole of Snowdonia to make any real attempt to please vegans. Everyone who isn't at the *Bryn Tyrch* heads for the bar at Plas-y-Brenin.

The Ogwen Valley

Five miles west of Capel Curig the gentle **Ogwen Valley** fills with the waters of Llyn Ogwen, a post-glacial lake formed behind time-compacted moraine left by the retreating ice. At its western end stands **IDWAL COTTAGE**, the only settlement in the valley and so small it isn't named on most maps.

Walks from Ogwen: The Glyderau and the Carneddau

Note: The OS 1:25,000 map #OL17 ("Snowdon & Conwy Valley") is highly recommended for all these walks. The 1:50,000 Landranger #115 also covers the whole area. For a general layout see our Snowdonia map, pp.382–383.

The Glyderau

"Tourists" climb Snowdon, but mountain connoisseurs almost invariably prefer the sharply angled peaks of the **Glyderau**, with their challenging terrain, an entertaining high-level jump, cantilevered rocks and views back to Snowdon. The sheer number of good paths make it almost impossible to choose one definitive route. The individual sections have therefore been defined separately giving the greatest flexibility. All times given are for the ascents: expect to take approximately half the time to get back down.

Tryfan

If you've got the head for it, the North Ridge of **Tryfan** (1 mile; 1hr–1hr 30min; 2000ft ascent) is one of the most rewarding scrambles in the country. It's not as precarious as Snowdon's Crib Goch, but you get a genuine mountaineering feel as the valley floor drops rapidly away and the views stretch further and further along it. The route starts in the lay-by at the head of Idwal Lake and goes left across rising ground, until you strike a path heading straight up following the crest of the ridge to the 3002-foot summit. Anyone who has seen pictures of people jumping the five-foot gap between Adam and Eve, the two chunks of rhyolitic lava which crown this regal mountain, will wonder what the fuss is about until they get up there and see the mountain dropping away on all sides. In theory the leap is trivial, but the consequences of overshooting would be disastrous.

There are two other main routes up Tryfan. The first follows the so-called Miners' Track (2 miles; 2hr; 1350ft ascent) from Idwal Cottage, taking the path to Cwm Idwal then, as it bears sharply to the right, keeping straight ahead and making for the gap on the horizon. This is Bwlch Tryfan, the col between Tryfan and Glyder Fach, from where the South Ridge of Tryfan (800 yards; 30min; 650ft ascent) climbs past the Far South Peak to the summit. This last section is an easy scramble. The second route, which is more often used in descent, follows Heather Terrace (1.5 miles; 2hr; 2000ft ascent), which keeps to a fault in the rock running diagonally across the east face. The start is the same as for the north ridge, but instead of following the ridge, you cut left, heading south until you arrive between the South and the Far South peaks. A right turn then starts your scramble for the summit.

Glyder Fach

The assault on **Glyder Fach** (3260ft) begins at Bwlch Tryfan, reached either by the Miners' Track from Idwal Cottage or by the South Ridge from Tryfan's summit. The trickier route follows Bristly Ridge (1000 yards; 40min; 900ft ascent), which isn't marked on OS maps but runs steeply south from the col up past some daunting-looking towers of rock. In good conditions, it isn't so difficult, and saves a long hike southeast along a second section of the Miners' Track (1.5 miles; 1hr 30min; 900ft ascent), then west to the top. The summit is a chaotic jumble of huge grey slabs that many people don't bother climbing up, preferring to be photographed on a massive cantilevered rock a few yards away.

Comprising just a mountain rescue centre, a snack bar and a YHA hostel clustered around a car park, the main reason to come here is to tackle some of Wales' most demanding and rewarding hikes (see box below), or start the easier twenty-minute walk to the magnificent, classically formed cirque, **Cwm Idwal**.

Glyder Fawr

From Glyder Fach, it is an easy enough stroll to the 3280-foot summit of **Glyder Fawr** (1 mile; 40min; 200ft ascent), reached by skirting round the tortured rock formations of Castell y Gwynt (the Castle of the Winds) then following a cairn-marked path to the dramatic summit of frost-shattered slabs angled like ancient headstones.

Glyder Fawr is normally approached directly from Idwal Cottage, following the Devil's Kitchen Route (2.5 miles; 3hr; 2300ft ascent) past Idwal Lake, then to the left of the Devil's Kitchen, zigzagging up to a lake-filled plateau. Follow the path to the right of the lake; then, where paths cross, turn left for the summit.

A southern approach to Glyder Fawr (3 miles; 2hr 30min; 2100ft ascent) leaves from beside the YHA hostel at Pen-y-Pass (see p.408), following a "courtesy path" marked at key points by faint red flashes of paint. It rises steeply behind the hostel heading northwest, but turns north for the summit to avoid straying onto the screes on the flanks of the neighbouring mountain, Esgair Felen.

The Carneddau

The appearance of the **Carneddau** could hardly be in greater contrast to the jagged edges of the Glyderau. These peaceful giants, which present the longest stretch of ground over three thousand feet in England and Wales, form a rounded plateau stretching to the cliffs of Penmaenmawr on the north coast. The sound of a raven in the neighbouring mist-filled cwms, and the occasional wild pony, can often be your only company on inclement days, but in fine weather the easy walking and roof-of-the-world views make for a satisfying day out.

Though the tops are fairly flat once you're up there, getting to them can be a hard slog. The start from Idwal Cottage is the most strenuous, requiring a long push up the shaley south ridge from the stile beside the road bridge at the foot of Ogwen Lake. If you can, avoid this in favour of the fine Carneddau loop (9 miles; 5hr; 3500ft ascent), starting from the lay-by at the head of the lake near Tal y Llyn Ogwen farm and taking in the range's four mighty southern peaks. The path keeps to the right of the farm, then follows boggy land by a stream towards its source, Ffynnon Lloer, before turning left up the east ridge of Pen yr Ole Wen (3212ft), with its magnificent view down into Nant Ffrancon and back to Tryfan. In clear weather, you can see the route running north past Carnedd Fach, and what looks to be a huge artificial mound, to Carnedd Dafydd (3425ft). After a short easterly descent, the path skirts the steep Ysgolion Duon cliffs, then climbs over stones to the broad, arched top of Carnedd Llywelyn (3491ft), the highest of the Carneddau and surpassed in Wales only by two of Snowdon's peaks, Yr Wyddfa and Crib-y-ddysgl.

For little extra effort, enthusiasts can conquer Yr Elen (3152ft), a short distance to the northeast, but most will be content with the easterly descent to Craig yr Ysfa, a sheer cliff which drops away into the vast amphitheatre of Cwm Eigiau to the north. Continuing with care, skirt around the north of Ffynnon Llugwy reservoir and climb to the grassy top of Penyrhelgi-du (2733ft), from where there's a steady broad-ridged descent to the road near Helyg. The mile-long trek back west to the starting point is best done on the old packhorse route running parallel to the A5, and linked to it occasionally by footpaths.

The evidence of glacial scouring is so clear here that you wonder why it took geologists so long to work out the process that created these hollowed faces and scored rocks. In 1842, Darwin wrote of his visit with the geologist Alan Sedgewick eleven years earlier, recalling "Neither of us saw a trace of the wonderful glacial phenomena all around us". The cwm's scalloped floor traps the beautifully limpid **Llyn Idwal**, which reflects the precipitous grey cliffs behind, split by the jointed cleft of **Twll Du**, the Devil's Kitchen. Down this channel, a fine watery haze runs off the flanks of **Glyder Fawr**, soaking the crevices where early botanists found the rare arctic-alpine plants (see Contexts, p.530) that were the main motivation for designating Cwm Idwal as Wales' first **National Nature Reserve** (NT) in 1954. More common species can be seen in the luxuriant fenced-off control areas, though the proposed removal of sheep from Cwm Idwal should see the whole place blanketed in wildflowers in early summer.

Geomorphologists pay more attention to the twisted rocks beside the Devil's Kitchen, one of the few places where you can see the downfolded strata of what is known as the Snowdon syncline, evidence that the existing mountains sat between two much larger ranges some 300 million years ago. To their left, the smooth inclines of the Idwal Slabs act as nursery slopes for budding rock climbers.

An easy, well-groomed path leads up to the reserve from the car park, where the *Ogwen Falls* café (daily 8.30am–5pm; later on summer weekends) will provide a free nature trail leaflet. A five-minute walk down the valley from the car park, the road crosses a bridge over the top of **Rhaeadr Ogwen** (Ogwen Falls), which cascades down this step in the valley floor. Before you put your camera away, look under the road bridge, where you'll see the simple mortarless arch of a bridge, part of the original packhorse route that followed the valley before Telford pushed the Holyhead road through.

Practicalities

Six **buses** a day run along the valley between Bethesda and Capel Curig with connections to Betws-y-Coed and Bangor. A **footpath** parallel to the fast and busy road follows a five-mile-long packhorse route that runs the length of the valley from Capel Curig to Idwal Cottage. **Accommodation** in the valley is limited. Three miles west of Capel Curig, Gwern Gof Isaf Farm is home to *Williams Camping Barn* (℡01690/720276, ⊛www.gwerngofisaf.co.uk; NT), with a primitive bunkhouse (£5; bring a sleeping bag and your own pots and pans) and cheap **campsite** (£3 per person). A mile further west, ⚐ *Gwern Gof Uchaf* campsite (℡01690/720294, ⊛www.tryfanwales.co.uk) is superbly sited right at the base of Tryfan, and offers £3 camping, a brand-new shower block, drying room and a good bunkhouse (£6 per person) with a fully equipped kitchen converted from an old farm building. At the western end of Llyn Ogwen, five miles from Capel Curig, the *Idwal Cottage YHA* **hostel** (℡01248/600225 or 0870/770 5874, ℮idwal@yha.org.uk; Feb–Oct and some winter weekends) has bunks for £12.50 and is right by the only other amenity in the valley, the *Ogwen Falls* café (see above).

Llanberis and Snowdon

Mention **LLANBERIS**, ten miles west of Capel Curig, to any mountain enthusiast and **Snowdon** immediately springs to mind. The two seem inseparable, not

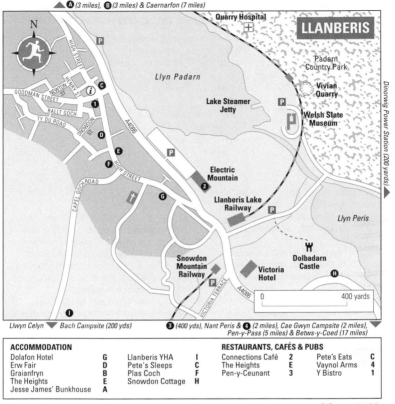

LLANBERIS

Quarry Hospital

Llyn Padarn

Lake Steamer Jetty

Pàdarn Country Park

Vivian Quarry

Welsh Slate Museum

Dinorwig Power Station (200 yards)

Electric Mountain

Llanberis Lake Railway

Llyn Peris

Snowdon Mountain Railway

Dolbadarn Castle

Victoria Hotel

Llwyn Celyn ▼ Bach Campsite (200 yds)

Ⓒ(400 yds), Nant Peris & Ⓓ (2 miles), Cae Gwyn Campsite (2 miles), Pen-y-Pass (5 miles) & Betws-y-Coed (17 miles)

SNOWDONIA AND THE LLŶN | Llanberis and Snowdon

ACCOMMODATION				RESTAURANTS, CAFÉS & PUBS			
Dolafon Hotel	G	Llanberis YHA	I	Connections Café	2	Pete's Eats	C
Erw Fair	D	Pete's Sleeps	C	The Heights	E	Vaynol Arms	4
Graianfryn	B	Plas Coch	F	Pen-y-Ceunant	3	Y Bistro	1
The Heights	E	Snowdon Cottage	H				
Jesse James' Bunkhouse	A						

least because of the five-mile-long umbilical cord of the **Snowdon Mountain Railway** (see p.401), Britain's only rack and pinion railway, that bonds the town to the summit, and the popular path running parallel to the tracks (see box on p.406). Llanberis is the nearest you'll get in Wales to an alpine climbing village, its single main street thronged with weather-beaten walkers and climbers decked out in Gore-Tex and fleece, high fashion for what is otherwise a dowdy town. Most are Snowdon-bound, others are just making use of abundant budget accommodation and the best facilities this side of Betws-y-Coed.

At the same time, Llanberis is very much a Welsh rural community, albeit a depleted one now that slate is no longer being torn from the flanks of Elidir Fawr, the mountain separated from the town by the twin lakes of Llyn Padarn and Llyn Peris. The **quarries**, which for the best part of two centuries employed up to three thousand men to chisel out the precious slabs, closed in 1969, leaving a vast staircase of sixty-foot-high terraced platforms as a testament to their labours. At much the same time, proposals were tabled for a power station to be built on the former quarry sites. Environmentalists were incensed that this fragile spot on the fringes of the national park could be desecrated. The people of Llanberis, still reeling from the closure of the quarries, had no such qualms, and in the end both parties were pacified: the project went ahead underground.

Arrival, information and accommodation

With no train or National Express services, the easiest way to get here is by **bus**: #85 or #86 from Bangor, #88/9a from Caernarfon or the #S1 Sherpa service. All stop along High Street outside either of the two outdoor equipment shops, both just a few steps from the town's **tourist office**, 41b High St (Easter–Oct daily 9.30am–5pm; Nov–Easter Mon & Fri–Sun 11am–4pm; ☎01286/870765, ✉llanberis.tic@gwynedd.gov.uk).

There's a wealth of low-cost **accommodation** and **campsites** in or close to town, as well as up at Pen-y-Pass (see p.408). Luxurious places are harder to find, so if you have your own transport and don't mind being a few miles further from the mountain, you might prefer to stay in places listed under Caernarfon or Bangor.

Hotels and guesthouses

Dolafon Hotel High St ☎01286/870993, Ⓦwww.dolafon.com. Appealing, well-priced non-smoking B&B in its own grounds, with spacious, comfortable rooms. ❸

Erw Fair High St ☎01286/872400, Ⓦwww.erwfair.com. Large house with rooms upgraded to a high standard, some with en-suite bathrooms. ❷/❸

Graianfryn Penisarwaun, 3 miles north west of Llanberis ☎01286/871007, Ⓦwww.fastasleep.me.uk. An exclusively vegetarian and vegan wholefood, non-smoking B&B in a Victorian farmhouse. Home-grown vegetables are used in the three-course evening meals. ❷

The Heights 74 High St ☎01286/871179, Ⓦwww.heightshotel.co.uk. B&B catering primarily to the walking and climbing set, with comfortable en-suite rooms with TV, and dorms (see "Hostels"). Downstairs is the liveliest bar and restaurant in town. ❸

Plas Coch High St ☎01286/872122, Ⓦwww.plas-coch.co.uk. One of the nicest places in town, tastefully renovated and maintained to a high standard, with all en-suite rooms plus a separate bathroom with tub for post-hike soaks. Great breakfasts too. There's one cheaper attic room. ❸/❹

Snowdon Cottage A4086, half a mile southeast of central Llanberis ☎01286/872015. Small B&B in a renovated eighteenth-century cottage with a cosy guest lounge and open fire that's perfect after a blustery day in the hills. ❷

Hostels, bunkhouses and campsites

Cae Gwyn Campsite Nant Peris, 2 miles southeast of Llanberis ☎01286/870718. Fairly basic campsite and primitive bunkhouse with showers, almost opposite the *Vaynol Arms* pub towards Pen-y-Pass. Budget-minded climbers and mountain bikers make up the bulk of the clientele. Camping £3.50 per person, bunkhouse £7.

Jesse James' Bunkhouse Buarth y Clytiau, Penisarwaun ☎01286/870521. The original bunkhouse, large, clean, non-smoking and efficiently run since 1966 by a mountain guide. Beds £9 a night (sleeping bag and towel required) or separate, slightly comfier self-contained accommodation. Take the A4086 two miles towards Caernarfon, turn right onto the A4244 and continue for a mile. ❶

The Heights (see "Hotels" above). Accommodation in eight-bed dorms with bedding and towels provided but no self-catering facilities. Bed only £14; B&B £19.

Llanberis YHA Llwyn Celyn ☎01286/870280 or 0870/770 5928, ✉llanberis@yha.org.uk. Well-appointed but not especially atmospheric YHA hostel with £12.50 bunks and some twin rooms, a 700-yard uphill slog along Capel Goch Rd. ❶

Llwyn Celyn Bach Capel Coch Rd ☎01286/870923. Farmer's field site 200 yards beyond the *Llanberis YHA* hostel, with showers and toilets. £3 per person.

Pete's Sleeps 40 High St ☎01286/872135, Ⓦwww.petes-eats.co.uk. Fairly basic dorm-style accommodation (£12 per bed) above *Pete's Eats* café (see p.404), plus a couple of twin rooms (£30 without breakfast) with access to self-catering facilities. ❶

The Town and around

At first acquaintance Llanberis isn't a stunning-looking place. Snowdon's summit isn't visible from most of the town and the hillside on the northern side to Llyn Padarn and Llyn Peris has been chewed away by decades of slate mining, leaving tiers of blue-grey rubble covering the mountainside. Yet it's an oddly compelling scene, especially when low cloud shrouds the workings and the hilltop Dolbadarn Castle looms from the murk like a lonely sentinel.

Though such days are great for exploring the Dinorwig Slate Quarries and the Welsh Slate Museum, if the weather is really bad you're better off underground visiting the Dinorwig Power Station. When the sun breaks out there's a choice of two narrow-gauge railways, the most celebrated being the wonderful Snowdon Mountain Railway to Wales' highest point.

Llanberis also offers myriad activities – from playing around in boats on the lake to scrambling, mountain biking and paragliding.

Snowdon Mountain Railway

The **Snowdon Mountain Railway** (mid-March to Oct 6–25 trains daily; ☏0870/458 0033, ⓦwww.snowdonrailway.co.uk; summit return £20) was completed in 1896, and carriages – some dating back to the nineteenth century, and sometimes pushed by seventy-year-old steam locos – still climb to the summit in just under an hour. The three-thousand-foot, mostly one-in-eight struggle up five miles of the most heavily maintained track in Britain follows the shallowest approach to the top of Snowdon.

Times and type of locomotive vary with demand and season, but whether hauled by steam or diesel, the full round trip takes two and a half hours, with half an hour on top. In summer (especially July, Aug and weekends in Sept) trains are often full, so book a day or so in advance. Those who reserve a day in advance and travel on the 9am train go for half price. If you walk up by one of the routes detailed in the box on pp.406–407, you can still take the train down. Standby tickets back to Llanberis (£14) are sold at the summit if there are seats, but round-trippers get priority.

The railway **starts** at the southeastern end of Llanberis opposite the *Royal Victoria Hotel*, and climbs past the summertime swimming hole at Bishop's Falls to the **summit** café designed in 1935 by Portmeirion architect Clough Williams-Ellis on what must have been a rough Monday morning. There are plans to replace it with a nicer looking structure, but nothing will happen until the Snowdon Summit Appeal (ⓦwww.snowdon-summit.co.uk) raises enough cash.

The **café** (mid-May to Oct) has a bar and a post office where you can buy a "Railway Stamp" (13p) to affix to your letter – along with the Royal Mail one – thereby entitling you to use the highest postbox in the UK and enchant your friends with a "Summit of Snowdon – Copa'r Wyddfa" postmark. In bad weather, trains terminate at **Clogwyn station**, thirty minutes' walk from the summit.

For a full description of Snowdon and walks on the mountain, see pp.404-408.

Dolbadarn Castle and the Dinorwig Power Station

Perched on a rock between Llyn Padarn and Llyn Peris, where it once guarded the mouth of the Llanberis Pass, a single dramatic tower and some scattered masonry are all that remain of **Dolbadarn Castle** (unrestricted access; CADW). Built in the thirteenth century, its construction is usually attributed to Llywelyn ap Iorwerth ("the Great"), even if its circular keep is more redolent of a Norman Marcher fort than a native Welsh castle. Close up, there's not a lot to look at, but, viewed across Llyn Padarn and framed by the grey crags of the Pass behind, it is easy to see why both Richard Wilson and Turner came to paint it.

10am–10pm; ☎01286/650045, ⓦwww.beaconclimbing.com; £5), which offers taster sessions (£45 total for 1–3 people).

As well as being one of the most popular walking routes up Snowdon, the **Llanberis Path** (see box, p.406) is designated a bridleway, making it, the Snowdon Ranger Path and the Pitt's Head Track to Rhyd-Ddu, open for **cyclists**. A voluntary agreement restricts access to and from the summit between 10am and 5pm from May to September, but otherwise these paths are open. Currently, there is no bike rental in Llanberis: Caernarfon is the closest.

You can also take a **horse** up onto Snowdon's lower slopes for £15 an hour from the Dolbadarn Pony Trekking Centre at the *Dolbadarn Hotel* on High Street (☎01286/870277), or rent **rowboats** on Llyn Padarn from Padarn Boats (Easter–Sept sporadically when weather permits).

Eating, drinking and entertainment

While Llanberis isn't spilling over with good places to **eat**, it does have something to suit all pockets. Pretty much all there is lies on High Street, where you'll find a couple of likeable **pubs**. To broaden the choice, Bangor and Caernarfon are both only eight miles away.

Connections Café Electric Mountain building. Cheesy name but a good spacious café with outdoor seating and a range of espresso coffees, jumbo rolls and baguettes, Welsh rarebit, daily specials (£5) and rich ice cream.

The Heights 74 High St. One of the liveliest bars in town, also popular with outdoor types, who fill up on hearty low-cost meals such as lime-soaked chicken wrap, lasagne and chips, veggie burgers and daily specials (mostly £5–7).

Pen-y-Ceunant Snowdon Path. ⓦwww.ceunant. co.uk. Snug, slate-floored eighteenth-century cottage, 400 yards steeply uphill along the Llanberis Path serving hikers and all comers with Welsh teas, coffee and snacks until 9pm daily. Visit if only to see the cottage, decorated with paintings and prints by Kyffin Williams and other Welsh artists.

Pete's Eats 40 High St. Climbers fortify themselves on Pete's large portions of top-value caff food and a few more delicate dishes. Free jukebox and cheap Internet access. Daily 8am–8pm or later for most of the year.

Vaynol Arms Nant Peris, 2 miles east of Llanberis. Cosy pub, the only one before Pen-y-Gwryd, with good beer, decent meals and a convivial atmosphere. Full of locals midweek, and climbers and campers at weekends.

Y Bistro 43–45 High St ☎01286/871278, ⓦwww.ybistro.co.uk. Dinner-only restaurant that has been attracting foodies for twenty years. The menu is modern with strong French and Welsh influences, with mains costing around £16. Booking recommended. Generally closed Sun & Mon.

Snowdon

The highest British mountain south of the Scottish Grampians, the **Snowdon** massif (3650ft) forms a star of shattered ridges with three major peaks – Crib Goch, Crib-y-ddysgl and Y Lliwedd – and the summit, **Yr Wyddfa**, crowning the lot. If height were its only quality, it would be popular, but Snowdon also sports some of the finest walking and scrambling in the park, and in the winter, the longest season for ice climbers. Its Welsh name, Eryri, is derived from either *eryr* (land of eagles) or *eira* (land of snow); since the eagles have long gone, the latter is more appropriate, with winter snows lingering well into April.

Some hardened outdoor enthusiasts dismiss Snowdon as overused, and it certainly can be crowded. A thousand visitors a day press onto the postbox-red carriages of the Snowdon Mountain Railway (see p.401), while another fifteen hundred pound the well-maintained paths to make this Britain's most-climbed mountain. Opprobrium is chiefly levelled at the train for its mere existence, and at the abominable concrete-bunker **café** (see p.401) on the summit for selling the country's highest pint of beer. But at least there's a warm place for walkers to rest, and those unable to walk up have the chance of seeing the **view** over most of north Wales – and even across to Ireland on exceptionally clear days.

There is no longer a tumulus on the top of Snowdon, but the Welsh for the highest point, Yr Wyddfa, means "The Burial Place" – near proof that people have been climbing the mountain for millennia. More recently, early ascents were for botanical or geological reasons – 500-million-year-old fossil shells can be found near the summit from when Snowdon was on the sea bottom – but the Welsh naturalist Thomas Pennant came up here mainly for pleasure, and in 1773, his description of the dawn view from the summit in his *Journey to Snowdon* encouraged many to follow. Some were guided by the Snowdon Ranger, Evan Roberts, from his house on the south side (now a YHA hostel), but the rapidly improving facilities in Llanberis soon shifted the balance in favour of the easier Llanberis Path, a route later followed by the railway. This remains one of the most popular routes, though many prefer the three shorter and steeper ones from the Pen-y-Pass car park at the top of the Llanberis Pass. By far the most dramatic, if also the most dangerous, is the wonderful Snowdon Horseshoe, which calls at all four of the high peaks.

Snowdon in legend, poetry and art

From the departure of the Romans until the tenth century, Welsh history is pervaded by **legends** of King Arthur (see p.96), Gwrtheryn (Vortigern) and Myrddin (Merlin; see p.173). Arthur's British (as opposed to Anglo-Saxon) blood gives him a firm place in Welsh hearts, and while Caerleon in southeast Wales lays a powerful, though not incontestable, claim to being the site of Arthur's court, Snowdon is often held to be his home.

It was atop Dinas Emrys, the seat of Gwrtheryn's realm beneath the south ridge (near Beddgelert), that the most potent symbol of Welsh independence, the Red Dragon, earned its colours. The Celtic king, Gwrtheryn, was trying to build a fortress to protect himself from the Saxons, but each night the earth swallowed the masonry. Myrddin divined this to be caused by two dragons sleeping underground: one white, the other red. When woken, they fought unendingly, symbolizing the Red Dragon of Wales' perpetual battle with the White Dragon of the Saxons.

Arthur's domain was higher up the mountain. Llyn Llydaw aspires to being the lake into which Bedivere cast Arthur's sword, Excalibur, after Arthur was mortally wounded by an arrow while on the point of vanquishing his nephew Modred at Bwlch-y-Saethau (The Pass of the Arrows), thirteen hundred feet above the lake. The remains of Carnedd Arthur, just below Bwlch Ciliau on the Watkin Path (see box on p.407), are claimed as Arthur's burial site, but it is probably a fairly modern cairn. Another burial place is that of one of Arthur's victims, Rhita Gawr, whose now-vanished tumulus gave Snowdon's highest point, Yr Wyddfa, its name.

In the eighteenth and nineteenth centuries anywhere with Arthurian associations proved irresistible to writers and painters. Thomas Gray enhanced the mystery of the place and its Celtic symbolism in his ode *The Bard*, in which the last Welsh bard hurls himself from the summit while fleeing Edward I's army, but the painter Richard Wilson's *Snowdon from Llyn Nantlle* had already planted the pre-Romantic seeds from which grew a vast, still growing, body of work capturing the mountain's changing moods. Two of the best places to see some of the artwork inspired by Snowdonia are the National Trust information centre in Beddgelert (p.409) and the National Museum in Cardiff (p.125).

Note: All paths are easy to follow in good weather, but the 1:25,000 OS Explorer #OL17 map ("Snowdon & Conwy Valley") is still recommended. There's also a series of leaflets (40p each) detailing the individual routes up the mountain.

Llanberis Path

The easiest and longest route up Snowdon, the **Llanberis Path** (5 miles to summit; 3hr; 3200ft ascent), following the rail line, is widely scorned by the sort of serious hiker who wouldn't use the railway or deign to visit the summit café. Victoria Terrace runs off the A4086 opposite the *Royal Victoria Hotel* and becomes a path which soon passes the *Pen-y-Ceunant* tearoom (see p.404). The summit gradually comes into view as you rise towards the midway point and the *Halfway House Café* (June–Sept daily 10am–5pm; Easter–June & Sept–Dec weekends only). From here there are views of Clogwyn Du'r Arddu (The Black Cliff, or "Cloggy" to its friends), an ominous sheet of rock which frames a small lake. Today, climbers virtually sprint up the face, which caused an early exponent to lament, "No breach seems either possible or desirable along the whole extent of the west buttress. Though there is the faintest of faint hopes for a human fly rather on the left side." The path next passes Clogwyn station, from where you get a great view down onto the Llanberis Pass. This soon disappears as the path gets steeper, passing the low remains of stables where mule trains used to rest. Bwlch Glas (Green Pass) is marked by the "Finger Stone" where the Snowdon Ranger Path (see opposite) and three routes coming up from Pen-y-Pass join the Llanberis Path for the final ascent to Yr Wyddfa. Llanberis Path is the route used by the annual Snowdon Race which takes place on the second Saturday in July, with the leading runners recording times of only a little over an hour for the combined ascent and descent.

The Miners' Track

The **Miners' Track** (4 miles to summit; 2hr 30min; 2400ft ascent) is the easiest of the three routes up from Pen-y-Pass. Leaving the car park, a broad track leads south then west to the former copper mines in Cwm Dyli. Dilapidated remains of the crushing mill perch on the shores of Llyn Llydaw, a tarn-turned-reservoir with one of the worst eyesores in the park, an overground pipeline slicing across Snowdon's east face to the power station in Nantgwynant. Skirting around the right of the lake, the path climbs more steeply to the lake-filled Cwm Glaslyn, then again to Upper Glaslyn, from where the measured steps of those ahead warn of the impending switchback ascent to the junction with the Llanberis Path.

Pig Track

The stonier **Pig Track** (3.5 miles to summit; 2hr 30min; 2400ft ascent) is really just a shorter and steeper variation on the Miners' Track, leaving from the western end of the Pen-y-Pass car park and climbing up to Bwlch y Moch (the Pass of the Pigs), which gives the route its name. Ignore the scramble up to Crib Goch (part of the Snowdon Horseshoe) and traverse below the rocky ridge looking down on Llyn Llydaw and those pacing the Miners' Track, content that you're already 500ft up on them. They'll soon catch up, as the two tracks meet just before the zigzag up to the Llanberis Path. The path is also known as the PYG track, supposedly after the nearby *Pen Y Gwryd Hotel*: no one seems able to settle the argument.

Snowdon Horseshoe

Some claim that the **Snowdon Horseshoe** (8 miles round; 5–7hr; 3200ft ascent) is one of the finest ridge walks in Europe. The route makes a full anticlockwise circuit around the three glacier-graven cwms of Upper Glaslyn, Glaslyn and Llydaw. Not to be taken lightly, it includes the knife-edge traverse of Crib Goch. Every summer's day, dozens of people find themselves straddling the lip, empty space on either side, and wishing they weren't there. In winter conditions, an ice axe and crampons are the minimum requirement. The path follows the Pig Track to Bwlch y Moch, then pitches right for the moderate scramble up to Crib Goch. If you balk at any of this, turn back. If not, wait your turn, then painstakingly pick your way along the sensational ridge to Crib-y-ddysgl (3494ft), from where it's an easy descent to Bwlch Glas and a stiffer one to Yr Wyddfa. Having ticked off Wales' two highest peaks, turn southwest for a couple of hundred yards to a marker stone where the Watkin Path (see below) drops away to the east. Follow it down to the stretched saddle of Bwlch-y-Saethau (Pass of the Arrows), then onto the cairn at Bwlch Ciliau from where the Watkin Path descends to Nantgwynant. Ignore that route, continuing straight on up the cliff-lined northwest ridge of Y Lliwedd (2930ft), then descend to where you see the scrappy but safe path down to Llyn Llydaw and the Miners' Track.

Snowdon Ranger Path

Many of the earliest Snowdon climbers engaged the services of the Snowdon Ranger, who led them up the comparatively long and dull but easy **Snowdon Ranger Path** (4 miles to summit; 3hr; 3100ft ascent), on the now unfashionable south side of the mountain. The path starts from the *Snowdon Ranger YHA Hostel* (see p.410) on the shores of Llyn Cwellyn, five miles northwest of Beddgelert. To the left of the hostel, a path leads up a track then ascends, steeply flattening out to cross sometimes boggy grass, eventually skirting to the right of the impressive Clogwyn Du'r Arddu cliffs (see Llanberis Path, opposite). This is another steep ascent that eventually meets the Llanberis Path at Bwlch Glas.

Rhyd Ddu Track

The **Rhyd Ddu Track** (4 miles to summit; 3hr; 2900ft ascent) has two branches, one starting from Pitt's Head Rock, two and a half miles northwest of Beddgelert, the other from the national park car park in Rhyd Ddu, a mile beyond that. They join up after less than a mile's walk across stony, walled grazing land, and after crossing a kissing gate continue to the northwest up to the stunning final section along the rim of Cwm Clogwyn and the south ridge of Yr Wyddfa. The Welsh Highland Railway (or the #S4 bus) makes it easy to turn this and the Snowdon Ranger Path into a loop.

Watkin Path

The most spectacular of the southern routes up Snowdon, the **Watkin Path** (4 miles to summit; 3hr; 3350ft ascent), is also the one with the greatest height gain. From Bethania Bridge, three miles northeast of Beddgelert in Nantgwynant, the path starts on a broad track through oaks opening up to long views of a series of cataracts. Ascend beside these to a disused inclined tramway where the track narrows before reaching the natural amphitheatre of Cwm Llan. The ruins of the South Snowdon Slate Works only briefly distract you from Gladstone Rock, at which, in 1892, the 83-year-old Liberal statesman, then in his fourth term as British Prime Minister, officially opened the route. A narrower path wheels left around the base of Craig Ddu, then starts the steep ascent past Carnedd Arthur to Bwlch Ciliau, the saddle between Y Lliwedd (see Snowdon Horseshoe opposite) and the true summit (Yr Wyddfa), then turning right for the final climb to the top. The Watkin Path can be easily turned into a loop by descending the top section of the Pitt's Head Track then continuing down Bwlch Main to the saddle and cutting east into Cwm Llan and down.

The Llanberis Pass and Pen-y-Pass

The steady Llanberis Path which grinds up Snowdon's gentlest ascent may be the most popular single route up the mountain, but more walkers start from the lofty saddle at the top of the **Llanberis Pass**, the deepest, narrowest and craggiest of Snowdonia's passes, running five miles east from Llanberis itself. At its head is the YHA hostel, café and car park that make up **PEN-Y-PASS**, the base for the Miners' Track, the Pig Track and the demanding Snowdon Horseshoe (see box, p.406). These all leave from the car park, while a route up Glyder Fawr (see box, p.397) follows a "courtesy path" to the west of the hostel.

Frequent #S1 Sherpa **buses** travel daily to Pen-y-Pass, worth catching even if you have a car, since the Pen-y-Pass car park is almost always full and costs £4 (£2 after noon). Use the "park and ride" facility at the bottom of the pass close to the *Vaynol Arms*: parking is free and the bus costs £1.50 each way.

The only **accommodation** at Pen-y-Pass is the **YHA hostel** (☎01286/870428 or 0870/770 5990, ⓔpenypass@yha.org.uk; £12.50; open all year), which has full daytime access, free parking, a few two-bedded rooms, plus videos on climbing and kayaking. A mile east is the nearest **pub** with accommodation, the ☀ *Pen-y-Gwryd Hotel* (☎01286/870211, ⓦwww.pyg.co.uk; no credit cards; ❺; closed Nov & Dec, open weekends only Jan & Feb), a wonderfully rustic place with ageing furniture, magnificent Edwardian bathrooms, an outdoor sauna, and a lot of muddy boots in the bar. Amongst others, the first successful expedition up Mount Everest in 1953 stayed at the hotel while doing final equipment testing, and took time out to sign the ceiling: Edmund Hillary, Chris Bonnington, Doug Scott and Portmeirion designer Clough Williams-Ellis are all there. The Everest team also brought back a piece of the mountain, which now sits in pride of place in the bar. If you stay, expect a congenial though somewhat regimented atmosphere and lots of plain home cooking (£22 for a five-course meal).

Beddgelert and around

Almost all of the vast quantity of rain that falls on Snowdon spills down the valleys on its south side – into the Glaslyn River in Nantgwynant or the Colwyn River in Nant Colwyn – then crashes down the bony **Aberglaslyn Gorge** towards Porthmadog. Amid the majestic mountain scenery at the rivers' confluence, a few dozen hard grey houses make up **BEDDGELERT**. It's a curiously enchanting place, its front gardens and window boxes bursting with award-winning flowers, and lots of spots to mooch, eat and drink. When the Welsh Highland Railway (see p.442) project reaches completion, Beddgelert will be the principal halt between Caernarfon and Porthmadog.

If you tire of the view from the village, it's easy enough to embark on one of the longer walks described in the box (see p.411). A shorter and more celebrated excursion takes you four hundred yards south, along the right bank of the Glaslyn, to the spot that gives the village its name, **Gelert's Grave** (bedd means "burial place"). A railed-off enclosure in a field marks the final resting place of Prince Llywelyn ap Iorwerth's faithful dog, Gelert, who was left in charge of the prince's infant son while he went hunting. On his return, the child was gone and the hound's muzzle was soaked in blood. Jumping to conclusions, the impetuous Llywelyn slew the dog, only to find the child safely asleep beneath its cot and a dead wolf beside him. Llywelyn hurried to his dog, which licked his hand as it died. Sadly, the story is an eighteenth-century invention by a local publican, that has lured punters ever since. The real source

Festivals
and events

There's no better way to get a take on Wales than by hanging out at one of the country's many festivals. Ranging from the epic to the absurd, all life is here and partying somewhere in a muddy field. Many events are uniquely Welsh, whether in the high-blown pomp and circumstance of an eisteddfod or in the grittier, grungier rock festivals that showcase music from Wales and other minority nations. Not surprisingly, there are also plenty of events with a distinctly surreal edge – from parading around Llangynwyd villages with a horse's skull to welcome in the new year (the Mari Lwyd), or snorkelling through peat bogs in Powys.

For more on Welsh festivals and annual events, see our events calendar on pp.61–62. Music festivals are also listed on p.537.

◀ The eisteddfod

Procession of the Bards

The centrepiece of Welsh culture is the eisteddfod (plural eisteddfodau), a term that originally meant "a meeting of bards". Nowadays it covers anything from a small village festival, where prizes of a couple of pounds are awarded for poetry and song, to two vast cultural orgies: the International Music Eisteddfod, held on a purpose-built fixed site at Llangollen in early July and open to competitors from all over the world, and the roving Royal National Eisteddfod, a much more Welsh affair in the first week of August. Venues for forthcoming National Eisteddfodau are Swansea (2006), Mold, Flintshire (2007) and Cardiff (2008). The National is *the* Welsh festival: the huge *maes* (field) includes pavilions for art and craft, literature, rock music, Welsh learners, theatre and the huge main pavilion, where all the big music and poetry competitions, as well as the nerve-tingling crowning and chairing ceremonies, take place. Also on the maes are scores of stalls, bars and cafés. Rock bands, DJs, camping and binge drinking occupy the youth-oriented Maes B, and wherever the Eisteddfod lands, bands, party nights, plays, poetry slams and debates break out in every available local meeting place – especially the pubs.

The similar Urdd Eisteddfod ("urdd" means youth) takes place in late May; venues for forthcoming events are Ruthin, Denbighshire (2006), Carmarthen (2007), Conwy (2008) and Cardiff (2009). The National and the Urdd Eisteddfodau are the largest indigenous cultural festivals of their ilk in Europe, and are without doubt one of the best ways to jump into Welsh life. Although everything is conducted in the Welsh language, simultaneous translation exercises make it easy for anyone to join in, and if you've picked up a bit of *Cymraeg*, this is the place to give it a go. See p.359 for more on the International Music Eisteddfod, and p.62 for all eisteddfodau contact details.

▼ Royal Welsh Show

Proportionately, Wales is far more agricultural than Britain as a whole, and the Royal Welsh Show, held in July at the massive showground near Builth Wells, is the UK's biggest farming jamboree. Even if your interest in matters rural goes no further than a nice Sunday afternoon stroll, the *sioe fawr* ("big show") is a top day out: as well as dropping in on the ultra-serious contests for cows, pigs, chickens, horses or sheepdogs, you can watch competitive sheep-shearing or

Winning cattle on parade

pole-climbing, displays of falconry and rural crafts or just gorge yourself silly in the showpiece food halls. There are also hundreds of stalls offering retail opportunities for the most jaded of shoppers, and, if you stay overnight (the vast campsites are legendary), nearby Builth is hopping with boisterous action come the evening. See p.263 for more details.

▶ Hay-On-Wye Literature Festival

Hay-on-Wye ("is that some kind of sandwich?" – Arthur Miller) is unique. Outside of the festival, the town's forty second-hand bookshops are enough for any serious print junkie. Throw in ten days of authors, critics and a rout of punters, and you're in literary hog heaven, even if it is all a bit Islington-on-the-Hill at times. Bill Clinton, who charmed the pants off the festival a couple of years back, called it "the Woodstock of the mind", though whether he inhaled or not is a moot point. Hay is a great place to appreciate the *raison d'être* of literary festivals, which is quite simply to hear a writer give voice

Taking it easy at Hay-on-Wye

to his or her own words, with all of the pauses, nuances and inflections that only the author can know. For more details, see p.256.

On stage at Sesiwn Fawr

◀ Sesiwn Fawr

Although it's outgrown the streets and squares of its beautiful host town Dolgellau, Sesiwn Fawr (literally "big session"), now located on the town's riverbank meadows, remains one of the liveliest rock festivals in Wales. To get the full experience, you need a weekend ticket, a tent and an iron constitution, as well as a limitless ability to party hard. Bands and DJs from Wales, the other Celtic countries and beyond perform on a variety of stages, with more entertainment – organized and spontaneous – in the town's many pubs. For more details, see p.334.

▶ Gwyl Y Faenol

Opera superstar Bryn Terfel still lives in his *milltir sgwar* ("square mile") near Caernarfon, and has bequeathed it one of Wales' most popular annual events. Held in the sylvan surrounds of the Faenol Park, on the edge of the Menai Strait, every August, his four-day festival has rapidly acquired the tag of the "Welsh Glyndebourne". It's not, however, half as stuffy as that moniker suggests: international orchestras and opera divas mingle happily with rock gods and native Welsh talent, although, like Glyndebourne, it can still get rather competitive over who's packed the poshest picnic. For more details, see p.62.

Bryn Terfel

▶ Wakestock

Now attracting around twenty thousand punters every July, Wakestock (see p.434) is proof of just how far, and how quickly, the whole watersports scene has come on in recent years. Mixing wakeboarding contests and surfing on the beaches of the Llŷn peninsula with BMX-riding, cutting-edge music acts and DJs, the event is a magnet for bleach-haired beauties of both sexes from all over Europe.

Wakeboarder in action

◀ Glorious food

Jelly on a plate, Abergavenny Food Festival

If food is the new religion, then Abergavenny (see p.252) could claim to be the new Jerusalem, never more so than during its phenomenally successful September Food Festival. Wild food guru Hugh Fearnley-Whittingstall is a fan, as are many other celebrity chefs who showcase their talents in numerous cookery events around the town. Specialist markets and children's events also feature, with the emphasis firmly on local produce. There are dozens of other culinary events around the country, some with great specialisms, such as the Aberaeron Seafood Festival, the Big Cheese in Caerphilly, the Welsh Cider Festival near Abergavenny and the Anglesey Oyster Festival. See p.000 for more about Welsh food and drink.

Weird and wonderful

Welsh capital of strange events is **Llanwrtyd Wells** (see p.261), a laid-back sort of place that manages to host an annual **Man versus Horse** race, a gathering of **Morris Dancers** and the **World Bog-Snorkelling Championship**, as well as a host of boozy walking events, including one that traces old drovers' routes and re-opens an old drovers' pub just for the day.

The Welsh have an inordinate fondness for **dressing up**: anything goes at the Llanidloes fancy-dress night in early July or on New Year's Eve in New Quay. For more traditional and ancient events, catch a **Mari Llwyd** procession at New Year; most are in south Wales (see Llangynwyd, p.113), but there's a few in the rest of the country too. Alternatively, you could celebrate New Year all over again two weeks later in Pembrokeshire's **Cwm Gwaun** (see p.000), where they still prefer to use the pre-1752 calendar, get to a Christmas **plygain** service, the massed screech of the **Pencader Pipe Festival** (see p.537), the **Samhain/Calan Gaeaf lantern procession** in Machynlleth or see folk-dancing-a-go-go at Cardiff's **Gwŷl Ifan**. March 1 is **St David's Day**, when mams force their little girls into stovepipe hats and everyone sports a daffodil and feels the warmth of their Welshness.

Competitor in the annual World Bog Snorkelling Championships of the name is probably the grave of Celert, a sixth-century British saint who supposedly lived hereabouts, possibly near **Dinas Emrys**, a wooded mound a mile up Nantgwynant on the A498, where Vortigern's fort once stood and, legend has it, dragons fought.

Beddgelert makes less of its other legendary animal, **Rupert the Bear**. Arthur Bestall, who wrote and illustrated the *Daily Express* cartoon strip for thirty years from 1935, spent much of his later years in Beddgelert, and "The Followers of Rupert Bear" have recently contributed to the planting of Cae Gel, a picnic meadow near the banks of the River Glaslyn, just over the footbridge in town.

A sixteenth-century former farmhouse, inn, general store and tearoom right in the heart of the village known as Llewelyn Cottage is now **Tŷ Isaf** (Easter–Oct Wed, Sat & Sun 1–4pm; ☎01766/510129; NT), a tiny exhibition centre that puts on good displays, usually on some aspect of Snowdonia's cultural history. Staff will also tell you about National Trust activities in the area including the ongoing work at **Craflwyn**, almost a mile north on the A498 (daily 8am–6pm; free), where an overgrown and neglected Victorian estate is being wrestled back into the Oriental woodland garden it once was.

Almost across the road, the red-brown stain on the hillside opposite identifies the **Sygun Copper Mine** (daily: Easter–Oct 10am–5pm; Nov–Easter 10.30am–4pm; Ⓦwww.syguncoppermine.co.uk; £8), whose ore drew first the Romans, then nineteenth-century prospectors. The dilapidated remains of what was once the valley's prime source of income have now been restored and made safe for the cool (9°C) 45-minute self-guided **tour** up through the multiple levels of tunnels and galleries. At stations along the way the disembodied voice of a miner describes his working life. Afterwards, you're free to potter around the ore-crushing and separation equipment.

For something more active, there's good **mountain biking** for all abilities in the Beddgelert Forest a mile out on the Caernarfon Road and a mile uphill from the *Beddgelert Forest Campsite* (see below). On-site **bike rental** is available from Beics Beddgelert (☎01766/890434, Ⓦwww.bikeworld.uk.com) at £8 for two hours, £24 a full day.

Practicalities

Beddgelert straddles two **bus** routes: the #S4 Sherpa between Caernarfon and Pen-y-Pass, and the #S96 between Betws-y-Coed and Porthmadog. All stop on the main street just yards from the **tourist office** (Easter–Oct daily 9.30am–5.30pm; Nov–Easter Fri, Sat & Sun 9.30am–4.30pm; ☎01766/890615, Ⓦwww.beddgelerttourism.com). There's a **post office** in the centre of the village, but no banks and only limited grocery shopping.

Accommodation

Accommodation is limited and quite expensive, though most of the houses near the bridge and along Caernarfon Road let rooms. If you're wanting to make an early start on the Snowdon walks you'll find the hostels better sited.

Hotels and guesthouses

Beddgelert Bistro & Antiques Waterloo House ☎01766/890543. Three attractive en-suite rooms, some with TV, above the restaurant and tearoom, directly opposite the bridge. ❷

Colwyn ☎01766/890276. Central 300-year-old cottage guesthouse with comfortable, recently renovated rooms, a beamed lounge and an open fire. ❸

Plas Colwyn ☎01766/890458, Ⓦwww.plascolwyn .co.uk. Non-smoking guesthouse by the bridge, with large rooms in a 300-year-old house. ❸

Sygun Fawr three-quarters of a mile northeast off the A498 ☎01766/890258,

@ www.sygunfawr.co.uk. This partly seventeenth-century country house in its own grounds is the pick of the local hotels. Some of its comfy rooms have views of Snowdon, and at weekends there are two-night deals which include dinner at the superb restaurant (see below). ❺

Hostels and campsites

Beddgelert Forest Campsite ☏01766/890288, @ www.forestholidays.co.uk. Excellent, reasonably priced campground a mile out on the Caernarfon road with two-person pitches for £8–12 (depending on time of year) and hiker/biker sites for £5–7. Closed Nov to mid-Dec.

Bryn Dinas Bunkhouse Nantgwynant ☏01766/890234, @ www.bryndinasbunkhouse .co.uk. Fully self-catering cabins sleeping one to six (£10 per person, Fri & Sat £12), at the foot of the Watkin Path (see box on p.407), three miles northeast of Beddgelert on the A498. A sheet and cabin heating are provided; showers, blankets and drying room cost extra.

Bryn Gwynant YHA hostel ☏01766/890251 or 0870/770 5732, @ bryngwynant@yha.org.uk.

Beautifully sited in a former mansion in Nantgwynant, on the A498 four miles northeast of Beddgelert, near the start of the Watkin Path. Meals are served, there are family rooms and also a campsite where you can use the hostel's facilities for half the adult rate of £11. Daily mid-Feb to Oct, phone for other times.

Cae Du Camping ☏01766/890345. Spacious, summer-only site with showers, less than a 10-min walk towards Capel Curig on the A498. £12 per pitch.

Hafod y Llan Nantgwynant ☏01766/890473. Tent-only site on a farm purchased by the National Trust and managed to enhance the landscape and for nature conservation. £2.50 per person.

Snowdon Ranger YHA Hostel, Rhyd Ddu ☏01286/650391 or 0870/770 6038, @ snowdon@yha.org.uk. A former inn five miles northwest of Beddgelert on the Caernarfon road, at the foot of the Snowdon Ranger Path (see box on p.407). Bunks (£11) are mostly in two- and four-bed rooms. Meals available. Open April–Aug daily; call for other times.

Eating and drinking

Beddgelert Bistro & Antiques (see "Accommodation"). Scones with clotted cream by day; wild goose breast in triple sec, Anglesey lobster or leek and mushroom pie (£11–19) by night. There's a cosy cellar bar, too. Book ahead for dinner.

Glaslyn Ices/Cafe Glyndŵr on the south side of the river bridge. Great ice-cream shop with three dozen flavours to take away, and a

surprisingly good family-style restaurant tucked in behind.

River Garden Restaurant ☏01766/890551. Centrally located with a waterside terrace serving hearty breakfasts, meals (£8–10) and cream teas.

🏃 **Sygun Fawr** (see "Accommodation"). Beautifully prepared four-course evening meals (£20) are served to guests and non-residents in a snug dining room. Worth booking ahead.

Blaenau Ffestiniog and around

Snowdonia's most southerly major settlement, **BLAENAU FFESTINIOG** cowers at the foot of stark thousand-foot mountains strewn with heaps of splintered slate. *Blaenau* means "head of the valley", in this case the lush Vale of Ffestiniog, in stark contrast to this forbidding-looking place. Blaenau Ffestiniog attracts some of Snowdonia's worst weather, and when clouds hunker low in the great cwm and rain lashes the grey roofs, walls and paving slabs it looks terrifically gloomy. Fortunately, on days when every tourist office in north Wales is packed with wet visitors wondering what to do, Blaenau Ffestiniog is at its most dramatic, and besides, its slate mine will keep you dry.

Thousands of tons of slate a year were once hewn from the labyrinth of caverns beneath the town, and exported worldwide. Nowadays, only two mines manage to keep ticking over (one of them aided by earnings from tours) and the loss of a steady income has hit the town hard. Its population has dropped to less than half its 1910 peak of 12,000; unemployment is high; almost all the Nonconformist chapels are empty shells, and *Ar Werth* (For Sale) signs have

Two fine hikes up Snowdon start near Beddgelert and there are a couple of good ones closer to town: all are covered by OS 1:25,000 #17 "Snowdon & Conwy Valley" and 1:50,000 #115 "Snowdon" maps.

The Aberglaslyn Gorge

This fairly easy walk follows the short but very picturesque **Aberglaslyn Gorge** (4 miles; 2hr 30min; 600ft ascent), and returns to the copper mines (see p.409) on a path up Cwm Bychan between Mynydd Sygun and Moel y Dyniewyd. Cross a foot-bridge over the Glaslyn River in the village and follow the left bank downstream until you join the track-bed of the Welsh Highland narrow-gauge rail line, which is currently being prepared for relaying of the track. Half a mile on, a couple of train tunnels are now closed to pedestrians so you're forced near to the river on the more adventurous Fisherman's Path, which affords a closer look at the river's course through chutes and channels in sculpted rocks. You'll need confident footing on a few short sections of this path.

The path meets the road at Pont Aberglaslyn – the tidal limit before The Cob was built at Porthmadog – where you can either retrace your steps, or head north up Cwm Bychan on a path near the exit of the disused railway tunnel. It's about a two-mile valley walk to the copper mines, from where a track follows the left bank of the River Glaslyn to Beddgelert.

Moel Hebog

From Beddgelert, you are unlikely to have missed the lumpish **Moel Hebog** (Bald Hill of the Hawk; 2569ft) to the west of the village. It forms the highest point on a fine panoramic ridge walk (8 miles; 5hr; 2800ft ascent) which also takes in the lesser peaks of Moel Lefn, and Moel yr Ogof (Hill of the Cave), named after a refuge used by Owain Glyndŵr when fleeing the English in 1404, after his failed attempt to take Caernarfon Castle. The final forest section can be a bit disorientating, even in good weather, so be sure you have a compass.

Start half a mile northwest of the centre of Beddgelert on the A4085, where Pont Alyn crosses the river to Cwm Cloch Isaf Farm. Follow the signs to a green lane, which soon leads up onto the broad northeast ridge, all the time keeping left of the Y Diffwys cliffs. The summit cairn is joined by two walls, the one to the northwest leading down a steep grassy slope to Bwlch Meillionen, from where you can ascend over rocky ground to Moel yr Ogof, or descend to the right, and then skirt left in a probably fruitless attempt to find the elusive Glyndŵr's Cave. From the top of Moel yr Ogof, it's a clear route north to Moel Lefn, then down to a cairn from where you can plan your descent. The easiest line is to Bwlch Cwm-trwsgl, near the highest point of the Beddgelert Forest, where a stile over a wire fence leads into the forest. Both the maps cited above show a clear, though not always easy-to-follow, route to *Beddgelert Forest Campsite*, where you turn right and tramp a mile along the A4085 to reach Beddgelert.

sprouted everywhere. For now, the town's economy leans on tourism, generated by its mine tour and the fact that it's the junction of two of the finest train journeys in Wales: the narrow-gauge **Ffestiniog Railway** which winds up from Porthmadog, and the Lledr Valley rail line to Betws-y-Coed.

Arrival and accommodation

By **car**, Blaenau Ffestiniog is most dramatically approached from the north via the Lledr Valley, climbing over the Crimea Pass between the Manod and

The curse of the Rhododendron

It is against the pervasive greyness of Blaenau Ffestiniog that Snowdonia's **rhododendron** (specifically *Rhododendron ponticum*) invasion is most evident. Come in June and July, and many of Snowdonia's valleys are a riot of lilac and purple blooms. There's no doubting their aesthetic appeal, but these choking mats of foliage block footpaths and are high on ecologists' hate lists. In their native Himalayas they grow into trees, but in Britain, where they've spread from the cultivated gardens of grand houses, they've become a noxious weed. Native flora can't compete with the dense canopy that cuts out so much sunlight that nothing can grow underneath – a major threat to native birds and insects which thrive in more open scrub. Volunteer action groups periodically target particular areas, blitzing a valley by digging out all the plants, but the rhododendron is proving difficult to contain.

Moelwyn mountains and plunging down into the town's shattered landscape. The **train station**, where High Street becomes Church Street, serves both the Ffestiniog narrow-gauge line from Porthmadog and main-line train services from Betws-y-Coed and Conwy. Beside the station is the *Queen's Hotel*, while the **tourist office** (Easter–Oct daily 9.30am–12.30pm & 1.30–5.30pm; ℡01766/830360) stands virtually opposite. **Buses** stop either in the station car park or along High Street.

The Welsh slate industry

Slate is as much a symbol of north Wales as coal is of the south: it too peaked around the beginning of the twentieth century and shaped society throughout the period of British mass industrialization, drawing thousands from the impoverished hills to the relative wealth of the new towns which sprang up around the quarries.

Slate derives its name from the Old French word *esclater*, meaning "to split" – a perfect description of its most highly valued quality. Six hundred million years ago, what is now north Wales lay under the sea, gradually accumulating a thousand-foot-thick layer of fine-grained mud. In the collision zone of converging continental plates, the deposits were subject to immense pressures which caused the massive folding and mountain-building; the shale then metamorphosed into the purplish Cambrian slates of the Penrhyn and Dinorwig quarries and the hundred-million-year-younger blue-grey Ordovician slates of Ffestiniog.

The Romans recognized the potential of the substance, and used it as **roofing material** for the houses of Segontium (see p.442), and Edward I used it extensively in his Iron Ring of castles around Snowdonia (see box on p.468). But it wasn't until around 1780 that Britain's Industrial Revolution took hold, leading to greater urbanization and a demand for roofing slates. As cities grew during the nineteenth and early twentieth centuries, millions of tons of slate were shipped around the globe, primarily for use as a cheap and durable roofing material. Hamburg was re-roofed with Welsh slate after its fire of 1842, and it is the same material that still gives that rainy-day sheen to interminable rows of English mill-town houses.

By 1898, Welsh quarries – run by the English, like the coal and steel industries of the south – were producing half a million tons of dressed slate a year (and ten times as much slate waste), almost all of it from Snowdonia. At Penrhyn and Dinorwig, mountains were hacked away in terraces, sometimes rising 2000ft above sea level, with teams of **workers** negotiating with the foreman for the choicest piece of rock and the selling price for what they produced. They often slept through the week in

Many of Blaenau Ffestiniog's visitors ride the train up from Porthmadog, visit a slate mine and leave, so **accommodation** is limited, but excellent value. In town, *Isallt Guest House* on Church Street (℡01766/832488; ❷), is very reasonable, or step up to the *Queen's Hotel*, 1 High St (℡01766/830055,🆆www.queens-snowdonia.co.uk; ❹), handily sited by the station. A couple of miles out along Manod Road (the A470), *Cae Du* (℡01766/830847, 🆆www.caedu.co.uk; ❷) is a comfy, sixteenth-century beamed farmhouse, beautifully situated at the end of a long drive, serving fine three-course dinners at bargain prices. A very popular option is 🕱 *Bryn Elltyd* (℡01766/831356, 🆆www.accommodation-snowdonia.com; ❷), an environmentally friendly, sustainable house overlooking Llyn Ystradau a mile from Blaenau in Tanygrysiau, run by a mountain leader. Excellent evening meals are available from £12.

The nearest **campsite** is the low-priced *Bryn Tirion* four miles north in the Lledr Valley (p.391).

The Town and mine tours

It's hard to get a real feeling of what slate means to Blaenau Ffestiniog without a visit to the town's only remaining visitable slate mine, which presents entertaining and informative insights into the rigours of a miner's life. It's a mile or so north of town on the Betws-y-Coed road and accessible by a special bus that meets the Ffestiniog trains.

damp dormitories on the mountain, and tuberculosis was common, exacerbated by slate dust. At Blaenau Ffestiniog, the seams required mining underground rather than quarrying, but conditions were no better; miners even had to buy their own candles, their only light source. Few workers were allowed to join *Undeb Chwarelwyr Gogledd Cymru* (the North Wales Quarrymen's Union), and in 1900, the workers in Lord Penrhyn's quarry at Bethesda went out on **strike**. For three years they stayed out – one of Britain's longest-ever industrial disputes – but failed to win any concessions. Those who got their jobs back were forced to work for even less money as a recession took hold, and although the two World Wars heralded mini-booms as bombed houses were replaced, the industry never recovered its nineteenth-century prosperity, and most quarries and mines closed in the 1950s.

Welsh slate was firmly established as the finest in the world at the 1862 London Exhibition, where one skilled craftsman produced a sheet 10ft long, 1ft wide and a sixteenth of an inch thick – so thin it could be flexed. Slate is now produced worldwide, and although none beats the quality of north Wales' output, this is little compensation as the region struggles to compete with inferior but half-priced Spanish slate. Until recently, the Snowdonia National Park Board insisted on local slate for roofing, but pressure from the European Union now forces them to accept slate "equivalent in colour, texture and weathering characteristics". The last criterion is a moot point, as the Spanish industry is barely thirty years old, but in the meantime, slate is being shipped from Spain while Welsh slate lies in the ground and unemployed quarrymen kick their heels. The remaining quarries produce relatively small quantities, much of it used for floor tiling, road aggregate or an astonishing array of ashtrays and coasters etched with mountainscapes. More memorable are the roadside fences made from lines of broken, wafer-thin slabs, the beautifully carved slate fire surrounds and mantelpieces occasionally found in pubs and houses, as well as Westminster Abbey's memorial to Dylan Thomas which is made entirely of Penrhyn slate.

around Tanybwlch train station, Snowdonia National Park's study centre, **Plas Tan y Bwlch** (☎0871/841 4004, ⓦwww.plastanybwlch.com), runs numerous courses throughout the year. Many are taught in Welsh or bilingually, and suitable for beginners (see Basics, p.70).

Heading south from Blaenau Ffestiniog, the A470 runs through the village of **LLAN FFESTINIOG** (Ffestiniog on maps, just Llan locally), three miles away, broadly following the remains of the old Great Western Railway route which ran across the broad open moors of the Migneint to Bala. **Walks** from Llan's former station run parallel with the old railway down into the wooded valley of the Afon Cynfal: follow the signposts to the lovely Rhaeadr Cynfal waterfalls, below a great rock known as Huw Llwyd's Pulpit, after a local seventeenth-century wizard and bard.

Rusted rails run four miles further south to the greatest blot on the national park's landscape, the defunct **Trawsfynydd Nuclear Power Station**. Trains removed the last of the fuel rods back in 1995, but it's going to take 130 years to safely clear and landscape the area. Just over a mile to the east, a small lane off the A470 bumps down to the **Tomen-y-Mûr Roman fort**, straddling the trans-Wales route known as Sarn Helen. This bleak, inhospitable place must have been a hardship posting for any Roman soldier, more used to comparatively metropolitan comforts. The "tomen", or motte, from which the place takes its name, is a Norman addition to the site. Nearby are the scant remains of a Roman amphitheatre.

A mile or two south, the main road bypasses the low-key village of **TRAWS-FYNYDD**, where the **Llys Ednownian Heritage Centre** (March–Nov daily 10am–5pm; Dec–Feb Mon–Fri 10am–5pm; £2.50) explores the area's history, including the tale of Ellis Evans, the poet awarded the Chair at the 1917 National Eisteddfod, held some six weeks after he had been killed in action during World War I. His bardic pseudonym, Hedd Wyn ("beautiful peace"), became the title of a Welsh-language movie about his life and death, which was nominated for the foreign language Oscar in 1994. A statue of Evans stands in the village main street (which was also the set for much of the film), and the Eisteddfod Chair – draped in black and empty, as it was when it was awarded – still sits in the family farmhouse down the road. The heritage centre is also home to a spruce new self-catering **hostel** (☎01766/770324, ⓦwww.trawsfynydd.com; £12 per bunk with bedding provided), which caters to mountain bikers.

The A470 continues south to Dolgellau, past the evergreen **Coed y Brenin** (The King's Forest), Wales' premiere **mountain-biking** destination. Its dreamy single-track trails have become so popular that a new **visitor centre** (expected hours April–Oct daily 10am–5pm; Nov–March Sat & Sun 10am–5pm; ☎01341/440666; parking fee applies) is due to open in 2006 four miles south of Trawsfynydd. Here you'll be able to pick up a map (£2) of the main tracks, graded for difficulty. It is uncertain whether the centre will offer **bike rental**, so call first. Otherwise rent bikes (£13 for 4hr, £20 a day) from Trawsfynydd Holiday Village (☎01766/540555, ⓦwww.logcabins-skiwales.co.uk), two miles north along the A470.

Bala

East of Trawsfynydd, the A4212 climbs twenty miles over open moors, past Canolfan Tryweryn (see below) to the little town of **BALA** (Y Bala). Located at the northern end of Wales' largest natural lake, **Llyn Tegid** (Bala

Lake), Bala is a major water-sports centre with a modest sideline in remote walks on little-visited hills. Thankfully, the tourist hype about "Teggy", a legendary beast lurking in the lake's waters, hasn't yet done to Bala what the Nessie industry has done in Scotland. The four-mile-long body of water is perfect for **windsurfing**, with buffeting winds whipping from the coast up the Talyllyn Valley and between the Aran and Arenig mountains that flank the lake.

Bala's second lake, **Llyn Celyn**, five miles west of town, isn't that much smaller than Llyn Tegid, but is very much an artificial affair created amid huge controversy in the 1960s, to supply Liverpool, in England, with its drinking water. A modern chapel on the shore commemorates the valley-bottom village of Capel Celyn (flooded to create the reservoir) and there are plans to erect a stunning memorial sculpture too.

The Town

The narrow town sits slightly back from the lake edge, perhaps to avoid the catastrophe which, according to two legends, drowned the old town which stood where the lake now is. One tells of someone forgetting to put the lid on

Thomas Charles and Michael D. Jones

During the seventeenth and eighteenth centuries, the religious needs of the Welsh were being poorly met by the established Church. None of the bishops were Welsh, few were resident, and most regarded their positions as stepping stones to higher appointments. The preachings of the newly emerging Nonconformists – Quakers, Baptists and, later, Calvinist and Wesleyan Methodists – were therefore welcomed by the people. Congregations swelled from the middle of the eighteenth century, but conversion didn't get into full swing until the effects of itinerant religious teachers improved literacy and the strident sermons of native Welsh-speakers fired their enthusiasm. There were already over twice as many chapels as Anglican churches when the chief protagonist of Methodism in Wales, **Thomas Charles**, gave the movement a massive boost through the founding of the British and Foreign Bible Society, a group committed to distributing local-language Bibles worldwide.

He had already reprinted Bishop Morgan's 1588 original Welsh translation (see p.457), but was down to his last copy when 16-year-old Mary Jones (see p.330), the daughter of a poor weaver from the other side of Cadair Idris, arrived on his doorstep. She had saved money for six years to buy a Bible from Thomas Charles and, in 1800, walked the 25 miles to Bala, barefoot some of the way, prompting Charles to found the society.

Despite the rise in Nonconformism, many of the more pious converts sought greater freedom to worship as they pleased, in a land where they felt free; something denied them in Wales by the oppression of both the English Church and State. The reformist preacher **Michael D. Jones** came to Bala enlisting recruits for his model colony outside Wales, and accordingly, he helped them found Y Wladfa, "The Colony", a Welsh enclave in Chubut Valley, Patagonia: in 1865 he transported 153 Welsh settlers to Argentina, to set up a radical colony where Nonconformism and the Welsh language kept a tight rein. This was the start of a 3000-strong community (and the world's first society to give women the vote), which grew until 1912, when immigration stopped and linguistic assimilation accelerated, although the area still has many Welsh connections. Jones stayed in Wales, setting up the Bala-Bangor Theological College and leading campaigns for Welsh causes, and many now regard him as "the father of modern Welsh nationalism".

△ Tryweryn rafting

The Llŷn

An undulating spur from Snowdonia's mountainous heartland, the **Llŷn** takes its name from an Irish word for "peninsula", an apt description for this most westerly part of north Wales, which, until the fifth century, had a significant Irish population and which still maintains an atmosphere reminiscent of parts of western Ireland. The Llŷn's cliff-and-cove-lined finger of land juts out south and west, separating Cardigan and Caernarfon bays, its hills tapering away along the ancient route to **Aberdaron** where pilgrims sailed for **Ynys Enlli (Bardsey Island)**. Ancestors of those last Irish inhabitants may have been responsible for the numerous hillforts and cromlechs found on the Llŷn, particularly the hut circles of the **Tre'r Ceiri** hillfort. But these days, it's the beaches that lure people to the south-coast family resorts of **Cricieth**, **Pwllheli** and **Abersoch**, and unless you want to rent windsurfers or canoes, it's preferable to make for the far quieter coves punctuating the north coast, or press on along the narrow roads that dawdle down towards Aberdaron.

The Llŷn is approached through one of two gateway towns linked by the A487, an effective boundary between Snowdonia proper and the peninsula. **Porthmadog** is primarily of interest for its proximity to the private dream village of **Portmeirion**, reached on Wales' finest narrow-gauge train line, the **Ffestiniog Railway**. The Llŷn's northern coast comes to an abrupt end at the mouth of the Menai Strait, guarded by the awesome fortress that forms the centrepiece of **Caernarfon**, a good base for both the Llŷn and central Snowdonia.

Not even Snowdonia feels more remote than the tip of the Llŷn, and nowhere in Wales is more staunchly Welsh; defiantly so, nearly eight decades after the meeting in Pwllheli that saw the formation of the Welsh nationalist party, Plaid

For decades the biggest threat to rural Wales was **depopulation**, as workers and their families fled the declining quarry, pit and farming villages. Now repopulation is the hot issue as self-appointed guardians of both the language and the rural way of life fight a rearguard action against incomers – predominantly wealthy English, buying up coastal cottages as weekend getaways.

During the 1980s, north and west Wales witnessed a spate of **arson attacks** on holiday homes conducted by the shadowy Meibion Glyndŵr, or "Sons of Glyndŵr". Though their campaign petered out by the 1990s, newcomers keep arriving and and pushing house prices beyond the reach of locals.

Some **incomers** are permanent migrants sympathetic to the Welsh way of life, but others – particularly the second-home owners who might only spend the odd weekend there – make little attempt to integrate. It is the latter contingent that enrages Cymuned (literally "Community"; ⓦ www.cymuned.org), a pressure group formed in 2000 to campaign for the preservation of rural communities and the Welsh language. Its slogan "Dal dy dir" appears daubed around north Wales, encouraging residents to "Stand your ground". It advocates a minimum ten-year residency clause for home buyers; planning permission to turn a permanent dwelling into a second home; investment in schemes to help residents buy property locally; and a Welsh-learning requirement for residents. Opponents suggest this would create a divided Wales and effectively a "language ghetto" in the north and west, but such talk is bending ears in Gwynedd County Council.

Plaid Cymru, the Welsh nationalist party, takes a broader view, citing economic deprivation as the main issue. After all, being unable to afford property isn't restricted to rural Wales; people in Cardiff (let alone London) have more trouble buying a house than most in Gwynedd. Some argue that communities might do better embracing incomers, exploiting any economic spin-off and using that to help preserve the culture and language.

Cymru (see Contexts, p.520). In most local shops you'll only hear Welsh spoken, Stryd Fawr is used instead of High Street, and everywhere you'll see street signs with any words in English daubed out. To some extent it is a reaction (or over-reaction) to the increasing number of English speakers moving here or buying second homes (see box above).

The Llŷn's bountiful caravan parks can seem unappealing to campers and often only accept families and couples, but a local ruling allows anyone with a field to run a **campsite** for one month a year, and through the summer they spring up everywhere.

Trains and National Express **buses** both serve Cricieth and Pwllheli, leaving an extensive network of infrequent buses to cover the rest. Better still, the peninsula's quiet narrow lanes through rolling pastoral land are ideal for cycling, and you can **rent bikes** in Pwllheli and Porthmadog.

Porthmadog and around

The Vale of Ffestiniog and Beddgelert's Glaslyn River meet the sea at Tremadog Bay, where the Cambrian coast (see Chapter Four) makes a sharp left to become the south side of the Llŷn. The bustling town of **PORTHMADOG** drapes itself around the northern shore of Traeth Bach, the mountain-backed common estuary, sadly making little of its wonderful position. It was once the

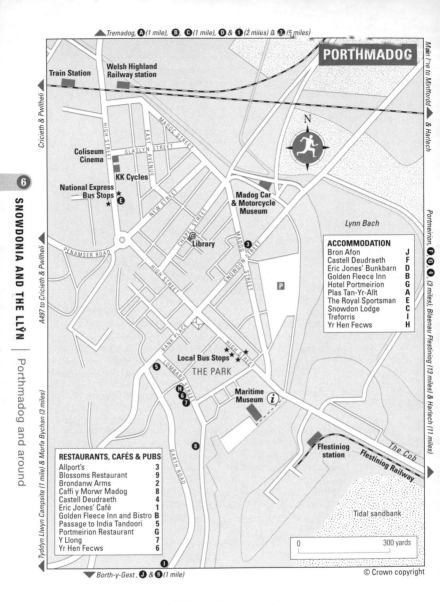

PORTHMADOG

Train Station

Welsh Highland
Railway station

Cricieth & Pwllheli

HIGH STREET

Coliseum
Cinema

GLASLYN STREET

KK Cycles

National Express
Bus Stops

EAST AVENUE

MADOC STREET

N

Madog Car
& Motorcycle
Museum

Lynn Bach

NEW STREET

A497 to Cricieth & Pwllheli

PENAMSER ROAD

CHAPEL STREET

@
Library

MADOC STREET

SNOWDON STREET

❸

P

ACCOMMODATION

Bron Afon	J
Castell Deudraeth	F
Eric Jones' Bunkbarn	D
Golden Fleece Inn	B
Hotel Portmeirion	G
Plas Tan-Yr-Allt	A
The Royal Sportsman	E
Snowdon Lodge	C
Treforris	I
Yr Hen Fecws	H

HIGH STREET

BANK PLACE

Local Bus Stops

LOMBARD STREET

❺

THE PARK

HIGH STREET

H
❻
❼

Maritime
Museum ⓘ

Tydyn Llwyn Campsite (1 mile) & Morfa Bychan (3 miles)

❽

GARTH ROAD

Ffestiniog
station

Ffestiniog Railway

The Cob

Tidal sandbank

0		300 yards

RESTAURANTS, CAFÉS & PUBS

Allport's	3
Blossoms Restaurant	9
Brondanw Arms	2
Caffi y Morwr Madog	8
Castell Deudraeth	4
Eric Jones' Café	1
Golden Fleece Inn and Bistro	B
Passage to India Tandoori	5
Portmeirion Restaurant	G
Y Llong	7
Yr Hen Fecws	6

Main line to Minffordd & Harlech

*Portmeirion, **F ❸ ❹** (3 miles); Blaenau Ffestiniog (13 miles) & Harlech (11 miles)*

© Crown copyright

▼ *Borth-y-Gest*, **❶** & **❾** *(1 mile)*

busiest slate port in north Wales, and is now a pleasant enough town to use as
a base for visiting the Italianate folly of **Portmeirion**, two miles east of Porthmadog, and the wonderful **Ffestiniog Railway** that originally carried down
slates from Blaenau Ffestiniog.

Arrival, information and accommodation

The main-line **train** station and the Welsh Highland Railway station are at
the north end of the High Street; the Ffestiniog station is located down by the

harbour, about half a mile to the south. In between, the helpful **tourist office** is at the southern end of High Street (Easter–Oct daily 9.30am–5.30pm; Nov–Easter daily except Wed 10am–5pm; T01766/512981, Wwww.porthmadog. co.uk). A little further up High Street are the stops for both National Express **buses** from Chester, Liverpool, Manchester and London, and local bus services. Note that Dolgellau buses go inland through Coed-y-Brenin: take the train if you want to stick to the coast.

While budget and high-end **accommodation** is strong, those seeking mid-range places might try pressing on to Cricieth or Harlech.

Hotels and guesthouses

Bron Afon Borth-y-Gest, 1 mile southwest of Porthmadog T01766/513918, Whomepages .tesco.net/~amanda.williams3. Attractive, en-suite B&B rooms in this pretty village with fabulous views across the bay to the mountains. Also self-catering facilities. ❸

Castell Deudraeth Portmeirion T01766/770000, Wwww.portmeirion-village.com. Chic designer hotel in a remodelled Victorian "castle" decorated in muted tones with the finest fittings, including widescreen TVs with episodes of *The Prisoner* on DVD. Only ten minutes' walk from Portmeirion village, where you're free to roam and use the outdoor heated pool. So classy you'll want to stay a week. ❽

Golden Fleece Inn Tremadog, a mile north of Porthmadog T01766/512421. The best bet for pub accommodation, with pleasant rooms above an excellent bar. ❸

Plas Tan-Yr-Allt 1 mile north of Porthmadog and immediately east of Tremadog on the Beddgelert road T01766 514 545, Wwww.tanyrallt .co.uk. Cool and stylish conversion of a small Georgian mansion (once the home of the poet Shelley), with quirky, comfortable rooms, optional dinners and exquisite breakfasts overlooking Tremadog Bay. ❺

Hotel Portmeirion Portmeirion T01766/770000, Wwww.portmeirion-village.com. Elegant suites in the hotel or in serviced cottages throughout Portmeirion village, meeting international hotel standards but with little of the quirkiness you'd hope for (the choicest ones are booked months in advance at peak times). While the dearer suites will strain your credit, it's worth asking about low-season, midweek and weekend breaks. Tennis and a heated outdoor pool. ❽

The Royal Sportsman 131 High St T01766/512015, Wwww.royalsportsman.co.uk.

Porthmadog's only full-service hotel, recently remodelled and close to the station. ❹

Treforris Garth Rd T01766/512853. Pleasant rooms in a large house overlooking the harbour to the west. Take Bank Place off High Street then left onto Garth Road – a 15-min walk in all. ❶

Yr Hen Fecws 15 Lombard St T01766/514625. Relaxed, pleasant B&B with comfy, uncluttered rooms, beside a popular restaurant of the same name (see p.427). ❸

Hostel, bunkhouse, self-catering and campsite

Eric Jones' Bunkbarn Tremadog T01766/512199. Two miles north of Porthmadog on the A498 to Beddgelert, opposite *Eric Jones' Café* (see p.427), this is a rock climbers' bunkbarn where you can get a mattress for about £4 a night, and there's basic camping for £3 per person.

Hotel Portmeirion (see p.426). The hotel also lets luxurious self-catering cottages by the week, or half-week in winter. The cottages sleep two (£500–660 a week), four (£700–856), or up to eight people (£1000–1150).

Snowdon Lodge Church St, Tremadog, 1 mile north of Porthmadog T01766/515354, Wwww.snowdonlodge.co.uk. A well-organized and welcoming activity-oriented backpackers hostel in the house where T.E. Lawrence was born. Clean, well-kept four- to ten-bed dorms (£14 including continental breakfast), en-suite and shared-bath doubles (two with four-poster beds), plus a bar. ❶ / ❷

Tyddyn Llwyn Black Rock Rd T01766/512205, Wwww.tyddynllwyn.com. A superior family camp-site on a grassy hillside, with all facilities and a bar, a 15-min walk along the road to Morfa Bychan following Bank Place southwest off High Street. Closed Nov–Feb. £12 per tent.

The Town and around

Porthmadog would never have existed at all without the entrepreneurial ventures of a Lincolnshire MP named **William Alexander Madocks**. He named the town and its elder brother Tremadog, a mile to the north, after both himself and the Welsh Prince Madog, who some say sailed from the nearby Ynys Fadog (Madog's Island) to North America in 1170. In 1805, Madocks fancied he could get himself some good grazing land by draining a thousand acres of estuarine mud flats here; he bought Ynys Fadog, built an earth embankment, then started on Tremadog. The towns prospered and, buoyed by their success, Madocks embarked on a project to enclose a further 7000 acres by sealing off the Glaslyn estuary with a mile-long embankment known as The Cob, southeast of present-day Porthmadog. Madocks died before the project came to fruition, but the Glaslyn River was rerouted and soon scoured out a deep watercourse close to the north bank, ideal for a slate wharf. This was the first of several which, boosted by the completion of the Ffestiniog Railway in 1836, spread along a waterfront thick with orderly heaps of slate and the masts of merchant ships. The slate traffic ceased by the middle of the twentieth century, and today only a few dozen yachts grace the harbour.

The waterfront is still the most interesting place to wander, not least because the last surviving slate shed contains the **Maritime Museum** (Easter & June–Sept daily 11am–5pm; £1), a modest collection of ships in glass cases, with panels telling of the town's shipbuilding role and its importance in carrying slate around the world.

Just across the harbour, the Ffestiniog Railway (see below) begins its ascent, but Porthmadog has a second narrow-gauge line, the far less interesting **Welsh Highland Railway** (Easter & May to mid-Oct 5–6 services daily; £5; ☎01766/513402, ⓦwww.whr.co.uk), running from nearby the train station along a mile of track. Fans can ride the footplate (£3 extra for diesel, £6 for steam), though you need to be over 18. Plans are afoot to rebuild the railway all the way to Beddgelert and Caernarfon, a venture not without its controversies and problems (see p.443).

If the weather is fine, and particularly towards sunset, you can't go far wrong with a gentle stroll along The Cob, the occasional steam-hauled Ffestiniog service adding atmosphere to views up the estuary towards Snowdon.

The Ffestiniog Railway

The **Ffestiniog Railway** (April–Oct 4–8 services daily; Nov–March services several days a week; return to Blaenau Ffestiniog £16; return to Tan-y-Bwlch £9.60; discounts on first and last trains of the day; a £27.50 combo ticket gets you to Blenau Festiniog and back, a ride on the Porthmadog branch of the Welsh Highland Railway and includes a round trip on the Caernarfon branch of the Highland Railway; ☎01766/516000, ⓦwww.festrail.co.uk) is Wales' finest narrow-gauge rail line, twisting and looping up 650ft from Porthmadog to the slate mines at Blaenau Ffestiniog, thirteen miles away. The gutsy little engines make light of the steep gradients and chug through stunning scenery, from broad estuarine expanses to the deep greens of the Vale of Ffestiniog, only fading to grey on the final approaches to the slate-bound upper terminus at Blaenau Ffestiniog.

When the line opened in 1836, it carried slates from the mines down to the port with the help of gravity, horses riding with the goods before hauling the empty carriages back up again. Steam had to be introduced to cope with the 100,000 tons of slate that Blaenau Ffestiniog was churning out each year in the late nineteenth century, but after the slate-roofing market collapsed between the wars, passengers were carried instead until the line was finally abandoned in 1946. Most of the tracks and sleepers had disappeared by 1954, when, encouraged by the success of the Talyllyn Railway (see p.327), a bunch of dedicated volunteers began to reconstruct the line, only completing the entire route in 1982.

Leaving Porthmadog, trains cross The Cob then stop at Minffordd, an interchange point for the Cambrian coast main line and the mile-long walk to Portmeirion (see below). A mile further on, Penrhyn station presents the possibility of a four-mile walk through the woods of Coed Llyn y Garnedd to either the third station, Plas Halt, from where it is a short stroll to the *Grapes* pub at Maentwrog (see p.414), or the nearby fourth station at Tan-y-Bwlch. Short **nature trails** spur off from Tan-y-Bwlch, as does the longer Vale of Ffestiniog walk (see box on p.414) which passes Dduallt station by the spiral on its way to Tanygrisiau, the start of the Moelwyn/Cnicht walk (see p.414). The full round trip to Blaenau Ffestiniog takes almost three hours, but you can get on and off as frequently as the timetable allows, and the journey is included in the North and Mid Wales Rover ticket (see Basics, p.43). You must pay £2.50 each way for bikes, but call first to confirm that there's room for them. Sit on the right of the carriage going up to get the best view of the scenery; for more legroom or to sit in the observation carriage you'll need to pay £3 each way for a first-class upgrade.

At the Ffestiniog Railway's imposing station in Porthmadog's High Street, *Spooner's* café and pub contains a few museum pieces from the railway's long history, including a complete locomotive wedged in one corner.

Tremadog, Borth-y-Gest and Morfa Bychan

Even without your own vehicle it's easy to explore a couple of local villages. A mile north of Porthmadog, **Tremadog** was founded by William Madocks around 1805 and though really just the intersection of three streets is a good example of early town planning. Budget travellers may wish to stay at *Snowdon Lodge* (see p.423), in the house where T.E. Lawrence ("of Arabia") was born in 1888.

Almost equally handy is **BORTH-Y-GEST**, a small former boat-building village enveloping a picturesque harbour a mile south of Porthmadog. There's nothing to do here but enjoy the estuary views, maybe stay at *Bron Afon* (see p.423) and eat at one of the waterfront cafés, or more formally at the delectable *Blossoms Restaurant* (see p.427). The #99 bus (5 daily) runs here from Porthmadog, but the coastal walk (20min: follow Lôn Cei) makes a particularly nice summer evening stroll.

If all the sand and water around Porthmadog leaves you hankering for a swim, **Black Rock Sands**, three miles west of Porthmadog at **MORFA BYCHAN**, is the best beach: a two-mile swath of golden sands with sublime views down to Harlech and up to the peaks of Snowdonia. It's also a popular boy racers' spot, as it's possible to drive a car straight on to the beach. Behind the beach, the vast Greenacres Holiday Park is home to **The Ropeworks** (daily 9.30am–5pm; booking essential ☎01766/515316, ⊛www.ropeworks.co.uk). A two-hour session (£15) on its combined **ropes course**, trapeze, zip wire and basic climbing wall can be as challenging as you want. It also rents bikes (£8 half-day, £12 full day).

The #99 **bus** runs here (hourly or better in summer) from Porthmadog.

Portmeirion

Porthmadog's other major attraction is the unique Italianate private village of **PORTMEIRION** (daily 9.30am–5.30pm; ⊛www.portmeirion-village.com; £6), set on a small rocky peninsula in Tremadog Bay, three miles east near Minffordd. You can walk there in an hour from Porthmadog, or catch the Express #98

Giraldus Cambrensis and his journey through Wales

Through his books *The Journey Through Wales* and *The Description of Wales*, Norman-Welsh **Giraldus Cambrensis** (Gerald of Wales or Gerallt Cymro) has left us with a vivid picture of life in Wales in the twelfth century. Gerald worked his way up the ecclesiastical hierarchy, but failed to achieve his lifelong goal, the bishopric of St David's, mainly because of his reformist ideals.

Gerald's influence in Wales made him the first choice when Baldwin, the Archbishop of Canterbury, needed someone to accompany him on his 51-day tour around Wales in 1188, preaching the cross and recruiting for a third Crusade that was designed to dislodge the Muslim leader Saladin from Jerusalem. Three thousand signed up for the Crusade on Baldwin's circular tour from Hereford in England across south Wales, up the Cambrian coast to Caernarfon, along the north coast and back down the Marches, during which time he said Mass in each of the four cathedrals: Llandaff, St David's, Bangor and St Asaph, the first Archbishop of Canterbury to do so.

During the tour, Gerald amassed much of the material for his books, where he sensitively portrayed the landscape and its people, judging that "Welsh generosity and hospitality are the greatest of all virtues", but warning "If they come to a house where there is any sign of affluence and they are in a position to take what they want, there is no limit to their demands". But on the whole, he shows sympathy for the Welsh, coming up with a conclusion that has an oddly contemporary ring: "if only Wales could find the place it deserves in the heart of its rulers, or at least if those put in charge locally would stop behaving so vindictively and submitting the Welsh to such shameful ill-treatment".

There's not much to see or do here, though, apart from visiting David Lloyd George's childhood home a mile or so to the west at Llanystumdwy (see opposite), and the battle-worn **Cricieth Castle** (daily: mid-March to May & Oct 10am–5pm, June–Sept 10am–6pm, £2.90; Nov to mid-March 10am–4pm, free; CADW), dominating the coastline with what remains of its twin, D-towered gatehouse. The castle was started by Llywelyn ap Iorwerth in 1230, but strengthened and finished by Edward I, who took it in 1283. During his 1404 rebellion, Owain Glyndŵr grabbed it back, only to raze it and leave little remaining besides an outline of broken walls and the gatehouse. It is a great spot to sit and look over Cardigan Bay to Harlech or down the ripples of the Llŷn coast in the late afternoon, but leave time for the fairly workaday exhibition on Welsh castles and a wonderful animated cartoon based on the twelfth-century Cambrian travels of Giraldus Cambrensis (see above) in the ticket office. If all you want are glorious views, clamber up the neighbouring hill behind Marine Terrace. The view there is just as good and is set off by the hulking castle.

Practicalities

Both National Express **buses** from the north Wales coast, and frequent local buses from Porthmadog and Pwllheli stop at Y Maes, the open square at the centre of town flanked by The Green, just a couple of hundred yards east of the Cambrian coast **train station**. As Cricieth has no tourist office, call at Porthmadog or Pwllheli in advance. For such a small town, good **restaurants** are surprisingly abundant in Cricieth, which boasts the widest range of eating on the peninsula. It also hosts the annual **Cricieth Festival** (℡01766/522778, Ⓦwww.cricciethfestival.co.uk) which takes place over the third week of June in venues all over town, and features jazz and classical music, lectures, art shows and plenty for kids.

Hotels and guesthouses

Bron Eifion ☎01766/522385, ⓦwww.broneifion
.co.uk. Beautiful Victorian country-house hotel with
fittings of carved Oregon pine and a fine restaurant,
set in five acres nearly a mile west of the centre
of town. ❼

Cantref 9 Marine Terrace ☎01766/522287. Very
nice en-suite B&B with great rates. ❷

Craig-y-Môr West Parade ☎01766/522830.
Highly rated guesthouse with well-appointed
rooms, some with fine sea views. Closed Nov–Feb.
❷

Moelwyn 27–29 Mona Terrace ☎01766/522500,
ⓔmoelwyn@aol.com. Unfussy en-suite rooms with
sea views and TVs. Above one of the better restaurants in town, with discounted meals for guests.
Closed Dec–Feb. ❹

Mynydd Ednyfed Caernarfon Rd, a mile north on
the B4411 ☎01766/523269, ⓦwww.criccieth
.net. Elegant, recently renovated country house
with gym and solarium set in attractive grounds.
There's also a very good restaurant with an extensive wine list. ❺

Seabank Hotel 25 Marine Terrace
☎01766/522255, ⓦwww.theseabankhotel.co.uk.
One of Cricieth's cheapest waterfront guesthouses,
200 yards west of the castle and with a good bar. ❷

Hostel, bunkhouse and campsites

Budget Accommodation 11 Marine Terrace
☎01766/523098. Hostel-style self-catering in
twin rooms for £12 per person (breakfast £1.50

extra). On Cricieth seafront below the castle. Closed
Oct–April.

Mynydd Du ☎07747/033035. Simple campsite
a mile towards Porthmadog on the A497. Closed
Nov–Feb. £8 per pitch.

Tyddyn Morthwyl Farm and Caravan Park
☎01766/522115. Not the closest but the nicest
campsite, on the Caernarfon road, a mile and a half
north of Cricieth. The bargain price (£7 per pitch)
includes hot showers, and there's a spacious bunkhouse in converted farm buildings for £6 a night.
Book ahead and bring a sleeping bag.

Eating and drinking

Blue China Tearooms Marine Terrace. Down by
the sea, this is the pick of the bunch for daytime
coffee and cake.

Bron Eifion (see above). Expensive, innovative and
highly rated cuisine served in a candlelit conservatory with a choice of à la carte and table d'hôte
dining.

Moelwyn (see above). International menu
with superb seafood and a comprehensive
wine list in airy, non-smoking and slightly formal
surroundings with great sea views. Expect to pay
£11–15 for mains.

Poachers Restaurant 66 Stryd Fawr
☎01766/522512. Highly commendable French-
style café-restaurant with a full menu and good-
value set meals.

The Prince of Wales Stryd Fawr. The best of the
town's pubs: a multi-room local with a few guest
beers, inexpensive bar meals and live music most
Tues and some weekend evenings.

Llanystumdwy

Though born in Manchester, the Welsh nationalist, social reformer and British
Prime Minister David Lloyd George (1864–1945) lived in his mother's home
village of **LLANYSTUMDWY**, a mile west of Cricieth, until 1881, when he
was nearly eighteen. He grew up in Highgate House, the home of his uncle, the
village cobbler, which is now part of the **Lloyd George Museum** (Easter–May
Mon–Fri and bank holiday weekends 10.30am–5pm; June Mon–Sat 10.30am–
5pm; July–Sept daily 10.30am–5pm; Oct Mon–Fri 11am–4pm; £3), a fairly
pedestrian collection of gifts, awards and caskets honouring Lloyd George
with the freedom of various cities illustrate the great man's popularity, and the
displays are full of anecdotes and little-known facts about him, with weighty
and hagiographic explanatory panels and a couple of short films giving a broad
sweep of his life.

The video presentations demonstrate some of his talent as a witty and
powerful orator, but only hint at the figure described by Churchill as "a
man of action, resource and creative energy, [who] stood, when at his zenith,
without a rival". Read between the lines to get a sense of the betrayal felt
by many Welsh nationalists as his interest turned from the politics of Wales to
those of Westminster.

△ Lloyd George

Rustic late nineteenth-century beds and dressers furnish Lloyd George's wooden-floored two-up, two-down house, in a garden laid out much as it would have been in Lloyd George's day. Before ambling through the garden, walk down the path towards the River Dwyfor, beside which Lloyd George is buried under a memorial – a boulder and two simple plaques designed by Portmeirion's creator Clough Williams-Ellis (see p.426). **Bus** #3 runs from Porthmadog and Cricieth, through the village on its way to Pwllheli.

Penarth Fawr and Llangybi

Five miles west of Cricieth along the A497, signposts point down a tiny lane half a mile inland towards **Penarth Fawr** (Easter–Sept Tues–Fri 10am–5.30pm Sat & Sun 10–5.30pm; free), a compact fifteenth-century hallhouse built to a common standard for the Welsh gentry. Constructed in 1416, the rare aisle truss hall was originally heated by a huge central hearth, replaced in the seventeenth century by the large fireplace you see today. Alterations at that time included the insertion of an upper floor – a dismantled beam from this work is on display and bears the date 1656.

Adjoining the house is the lovely **Penarth Fawr Gallery** and café (Tues–Sun 1.30–5.30pm) run by the custodians who live at Penarth Fawr – examples of their potting and bookbinding skills are on display. These days, the bookbinding business specializes in producing fake TV and film accessories – you can see Bergerac's false passport and a notebook and the Holy Grail from the movie *Indiana Jones and the Last Crusade*.

Confusing lanes run a couple of miles north of Penarth Fawr to the charming little village of **LLANGYBI**, best known for its **healing well**, said to cure warts, lameness, blindness, rheumatism and other disorders. St Cybi, a sixth-century Cornish healer, was believed to have discovered the curative properties of the waters which, in the eighteenth century, were encased in spa buildings, the ruins of which stand today.

Pwllheli and around

The undoubted "capital" of the Llŷn, **PWLLHELI** (pronounced something like "Poothl-heli") is a strange place: not quite a seaside resort despite its best efforts, nor yet a town that exploits its illustrious history. Its principal function is as the area's main market and transport hub, making it refreshingly down to earth. Even in the height of summer, you'll hear far more Welsh spoken here than English. It was at the *Maesgwyn Temperance Hotel* (now a pet shop on Y Maes, Pwllheli's central square, marked with a plaque) during the National Eisteddfod in August 1925 that six people, three from *Byddin Ymreolwyr Cymru* (the Army of Welsh Home Rulers) and three from *Y Mudiad Cymreig* (The Welsh Movement) met to form Plaid Cymru (see Contexts, p.520). Pwllheli also has one of the few exclusively Welsh-language bookshops in the country, Llên Llŷn, on Y Maes, owned by writer Alun Jones.

Although the town appears largely Victorian, Pwllheli's market charter dates back to 1355. The **market** (each Wed) is held on Y Maes and is a great time to browse and eavesdrop on the *Cymraeg* chatter of youngsters and rainhat-clad old ladies. From Y Maes, Ffordd-y-Cob leads south, past the spruce new **marina**, packed with yachts where once thriving shipbuilding and fishing industries held sway. Continue down Ffordd-y-Cob to Pwllheli's ghostly **West End**, a forlorn Victorian seaside development of pastel-shaded villas that seem ripe for renovation.

Pwllheli marina is lively all summer, with **boat trips** leaving for Bardsey Island and the *Shearwater* (Easter–Oct only; ☎01758/613000, ⓦwww.shearwater.info) running a morning cruise (2hr; £19) along an impressive section of coast, an afternoon cruise (3hr; £29) that includes a non-landing circuit of Bardsey Island, and an evening cruise (2hr; £23).

Practicalities

The town spreads out from Y Maes, the central square where National Express and local **buses** pull in. The **train station**, northern terminus of the Cambrian coast line, stands a few yards to the east, opposite the **tourist office** on Station Square (April–Oct daily 9am–5pm; Nov–March Mon–Wed, Fri & Sat 10.30am–4.30pm; ☎01758/613000, ⓔpwllheli.tic@gwynedd.gov.uk).

There is a wider choice of good **accommodation** elsewhere on the Llŷn but Pwllheli offers some decent places to stay. Unless you're off to *Plas Bodegroes*, **dinners** are probably better served eight miles east in Cricieth or four miles west in tiny Llanbedrog.

Accommodation

Bank Place Stryd Fawr ℡01758/612103. Simple B&B with shared bathrooms. ❶

Gwynfryn Farm ℡01758/614324, ⓦwww .gwynfryn.freeserve.co.uk. Mostly self-catering cottages, but also comfy B&B, with access to the indoor pool, sauna and hot tub on an organic dairy farm. It's just over a mile north of Pwllheli up Gaol Street, left of the Salem Chapel – branch left, then straight on until the entrance is signposted on the left. ❸

Llys Gwyrfai 14 West End Parade ℡01758/614877. A comfortable guesthouse with sea views, en-suite rooms and home-cooked meals, located 400 yards from Y Maes. ❷

🏃 **Plas Bodegroes** Efailnewydd, 2 miles northwest of Pwllheli on the A497 ℡01758/612363, ⓦwww.bodegroes.co.uk. The finest accommodation on the Llŷn, in a very swish Georgian country house set in wonderful parkland. Gorgeous rooms, and you'll want to stay in for dinner. Closed Sun & Mon and all of Dec–Feb. ❻

Victoria Hotel Embankment Rd ℡01758/612843. A cosy pub with comfortable rooms. ❷

Eating and drinking

Barn Eating House Gaol St. Pub-style food served both inside or out, beside the *Whitehall* pub, one of the best in town.

The Mariner Station Square. Inexpensive bistro churning out steak and fish staples.

Penlan Fawr 3 Penlan St ℡01758/612864. Four-hundred-year-old pub that's always lively, serves cask ales and does decent meals, especially the Sunday lunches.

🏃 **Plas Bodegroes** (see above). Sumptuous dining in Wales' only Michelin-starred restaurant, which serves modern interpretations of traditional dishes for lunch and dinner (£40 for three courses). Sunday lunch costs a modest £18. Closed Sun evening and Mon.

Polash 28 Penlan St. Reliable for tandooris and baltis from £5.

Llanbedrog

LLANBEDROG, four miles west of Pwllheli, is a delightful village with a wonderful beach and one of the most impressive arts centres in north Wales. Until it was washed away in storms in 1927, a little tram railway, connecting the village with Pwllheli's West End, disgorged holiday-makers into **Plas Glyn-y-Weddw** (daily except Tues 11am–5pm; ⓦwww.oriel.org.uk; £2.50), one of Wales' oldest public art galleries. Solomon Andrews, the Cardiff entrepreneur who built Pwllheli's West End, bought the Victorian Gothic mansion in 1896 and turned it into a genteel centre for the arts, with pleasure gardens and legendary tea dances. It's an impressive building: all rooms peel off a spectacular galleried hallway under a huge stained-glass window and a gorgeous hammerbeam oak roof, topped with a lantern. Don't miss the two sixth-century basalt columns in the hallway windows, once of Llanor church and latterly returned to the area from the Ashmolean Museum in Oxford. The exhibitions combine pieces from the gallery's permanent collection with touring works, often with a Welsh theme. There's also a lovely conservatory tearoom in which to sit and gaze out at the sea.

It's a short stroll from Glyn-y-Weddw down to **Traeth Llanbedrog**, a charming strand whose restored, pastel-hued beach huts attest to its ownership by the National Trust. From the southern end of the beach, a steep, fairly rough path climbs through a wooded glen onto a towering headland known as Mynydd Tir-y-Cwmwd, where the sweeping views are shared by the **Iron Man**, a contemporary wrought-iron sculpture designed and built locally to replace an eight-foot ship's figurehead erected there in 1919.

The village is also blessed with some excellent **places to eat**. Besides the tearoom at Plas Glyn-y-Weddw, there's the *Gallery*, an appealing bistro down by Traeth Llanbedrog with a cosy interior, beachside seating and a good range of snacks (£4–6) and mains (£9–14). Nearby, two of the finest **pubs** in the area both serve tasty, inexpensive meals: the *Glyn-y-Weddw Arms* at Ty Du on the A499; and the friendly (and generally superior) *Ship Inn* at Bryn-y-Gro, half a mile further on, which has a very popular summertime beer garden.

Abersoch and around

After the distinctly Welsh feel of Pwllheli, **ABERSOCH**, seven miles southwest along the coast, comes as a surprise. This former fishing village pitched in the middle of two golden bays has, over the last century, become a largely anglicized resort, catering to affluent boat-owners and holidaying families. Abersoch now ranks as one of the country's major **dinghy-sailing** centres, the odd foreign entrant to the numerous regattas throughout the summer lending a mildly cosmopolitan air to the place and fuelling its haughty opinion of itself.

Such high self-esteem isn't really justified, but at high tide the harbour is attractive and the long beach is a fine spot even if it's barely visible under beach towels at busy times. A short walk along the shore shakes off most of the crowds, except for surfers drawn to **Porth Neigwl** (Hell's Mouth), two miles to the southwest, which is one of the finest **surf** beaches in Wales – beware of the undertow if you're swimming. In town, the needs of yachties and surfers are catered for with a couple of chandlers and more surf shacks than anywhere north of the Pembrokeshire coast. Sun-seekers should head a mile north to a fine stretch of beach backed by *The Warren* holiday park.

If baking on the beach isn't active enough, you might fancy trying your hand at **water sports**. The West Coast Surf Shop, Lôn Pen Cei (℡01758/713067, ⓦwww.westcoastsurf.co.uk), one of several shops renting surfing and wind-surfing gear, is well informed about surfing events, competitions and parties. Throughout summer, Offaxis, right in the centre of town (℡01758/713407, ⓦwww.offaxis.co.uk), runs a wakeboarding and surfing academy (£30 per lesson) and rents gear, while Abersoch Sailing School (March–Oct; ℡01758/712290, ⓦwww.abersochsailingschool.com) runs lessons and rents Lasers and other craft on the town's main beach.

For something a bit less outdoorsy, bus #18 can take you two miles to **Llanengan**, a short walk from the beach of Porth Neigwl, where you can also visit the gorgeous twin-aisled fifteenth-century **St Engan's Church** (instructions for obtaining the key are inside the porch). Its twin altars and rood screens are integral parts of decoration, unchanged by the eighteenth- and nineteenth-century reformist zeal that altered most other churches. Llanengan is also home to the *Sun Inn*), a cosy pub serving reasonable bar meals, with a pleasant beer garden.

Practicalities

Buses from Pwllheli loop through the middle of Abersoch, stopping near the **tourist office** on Lôn Pen Cei (April–Sept daily 10.30am–4.30pm; Oct–March Sat & Sun 11am–1pm; ℡01758/712929, ⓦwww.abersochtouristinfo.co.uk). To continue to Aberdaron by bus, you must take a Pwllheli-bound service as far as Llanbedrog, then change onto the #17.

There are lots of places to stay in and around Abersoch, but **accommodation** can be tight over summer and at weekends during spring and autumn. Almost all the **campsites** in villages around Abersoch are family-oriented places, so groups need to look reputable to be admitted. Ask the tourist office for a list of places with a freer regime. One such place is *Rhydolion Llangian* (℡01758/712342, ⓦwww.rhydolion.co.uk; camping £4–7 per person), a small, welcoming tent and caravan site a mile or so northwest of Abersoch and fifteen minutes' walk from Porth Neigwl beach. It also has a couple of very well-appointed, self-contained units.

Abersoch is increasingly well supplied with decent **places to eat**. Almost all along Lôn Pen Cei, most are packed in summertime and seldom open

the western end of Porth Neigwl. The house was derelict in 1938 when it was bought by Thomas' moneyed friends, the Keating sisters, who restored it with the help of Portmeirion architect Clough Williams-Ellis, whose offbeat touch is evident in the flattened arches and a Gothic doorway rescued from a castle being demolished. Unlike many National Trust mansions, this is a manageable and relaxed place, filled with rustic furniture like a 1920s oil stove used by Honora Keating until her death in 1981, and her accomplished watercolours. The upstairs sitting room is notable for its six-foot-thick wall containing a fireplace, a spiral staircase and a window nook overlooking gorgeous gardens almost overgrown with fuchsias, hydrangeas, roses and wildflowers.

Having made your way out as far as Aberdaron, it's worth using the village as a base for exploring the narrow lanes at the end of the peninsula, leading to the National Trust property around **Mynydd Mawr**, the hill overlooking Bardsey Sound. A minor road weaves west to the headland of **Braich-y-Pwll**, two miles west of Aberdaron, from where a short path heads down the cliffs to the ruins of St Mary's church, the crossing point at the end of the Pilgrim's Way. The road continues from here to the top of Mynydd Mawr, from where the medieval patchwork of ancient fields which make up the tip of the Llŷn are clearly visible.

Alternatively, head two miles north to the clean, safe and secluded bay of **Porth Oer** (NT), known as "Whistling Sands" for the white sands which squeak as you walk on them. Barring a small beach shop in high summer, the only amenities are the clifftop and coastal paths leading away.

Practicalities

Without your own transport, the only way to reach Aberdaron is the fairly infrequent #17 **bus** from Pwllheli. There's no tourist office, but information is available on Ⓦwww.aberdaronlink.co.uk. **Accommodation** is quite limited and hard to get in summer. The cheapest options are *Brynmor* (Ⓣ01758/760344; ❷), a hundred yards up the road to Porth Oer, and *Pennant* (Ⓣ01758/760610; ❷), a mile further out along the same road. More central and comfortable is the *Tŷ Newydd Hotel* (Ⓣ01758/760207; closed Sun–Tues & Jan; ❺), with some rooms overlooking the sea.

The nearest of many decent **campsites** is *Dwyros*, up the hill on the way to Mynydd Mawr; a little further afield, the seasonal *Mur Melyn* (no phone), midway between Aberdaron and Porth Oer off the eastbound B4413, is quieter. Both cost around £3 per person.

For light **meals**, try the tearooms behind Hen Blas Crafts in the middle of the village. For bar snacks and full dinners, there's the *Tŷ Newydd Hotel* (see above).

Ynys Enlli (Bardsey Island)

Bardsey Island or **Ynys Enlli** (The Island of the Currents) rises out of the ocean two miles off the tip of the Llŷn, separated from it by a strait of churning, unpredictable water. This national nature reserve has been an important pilgrimage site since the sixth century, when St Cadfan set up the first monastery here: three visits were proclaimed equivalent to one pilgrimage to Rome. Legend claims Bardsey as "The Isle of Twenty Thousand Saints", most likely remembering not saints, but huge numbers of pilgrims who came to die at this holy spot. By the twelfth century, Giraldus Cambrensis was already claiming that "the bodies of a vast number of holy men are buried there", and that "no one dies there except in extreme old age, for disease is almost unheard of". Numerous other stories tell of the burial place of Myrddin (Merlin) and the former Bishop of Bangor, St Deiniol, but the only hard evidence is the remaining **bell tower** of the thirteenth-century Augustinian Abbey of St Mary and a few Celtic crosses scattered around it. After the dissolution of the monasteries in 1536, piracy became the focus of the island's economy for over a century, gradually giving way to agriculture and fishing.

Interesting though the abbey ruins and later buildings are, most visitors come to watch **birds**. Among the dozen or so species of nesting sea birds are Manx shearwaters, fulmars and guillemots, and an amazing number of vagrants turn up after being blown off course by storms. Few other people bother to make the journey, as **boats** are dependent on sea conditions and a viable load of passengers. The Bardsey Island Trust runs one from Pwllheli (daily except Sat 8am; £30; book on ☎01758/760667), giving six hours on the island, and if tides permit also picks up from Porth Meudwy, a tiny cove half a mile south of Aberdaron, giving four hours on Bardsey (except Sat 10am; £20). For details of the few **houses** rented by the week (April–Oct only), contact the Bardsey Island Trust (☎01758/112233, ⓦwww.enlli.org). There are no facilities on the island and only one family of residents.

The north Llŷn coast

Sprinkled with small coves and sweeping beaches between rocky bluffs, the **north Llŷn coast** is a dramatic contrast to the busier south. It has few settlements of any size, leaving quieter beaches – Porth Towyn by Tudwei-liog and Traeth Penllech by Llangwnnadl – accessible via the #8 bus from Pwllheli and a short walk. Even at the best of times, services are infrequent and badly timed, so you're far better off with your own car or bike – the north Llŷn coast is particularly suited to cycling. Amenities are also thinly scattered hereabouts – a few campsites dotted around, and the odd shop and pub in a village.

Nefyn and Porth Dinllaen

There isn't much to recommend **NEFYN**, the largest of the peninsula's northern communities, though if the **Maritime Museum** inside St Mary's Church is open you can learn about the village's herring-fishing past.

Neighbouring **MORFA NEFYN**, a mile to the west, and the adjacent shoreline hamlet of **PORTH DINLLAEN**, both benefit from having lost the 1839 battle to become the terminus for ferries to Ireland. A single Parliamentary vote swung the decision in favour of Holyhead, thus saving tiny Porth Dinllaen from that town's fate. Recently bought lock, stock and a mile of beach by the National Trust, Porth Dinllaen is now just a pristine sweeping bay backed by the popular waterside *Tŷ Coch Inn* (closed Sun evening) a beautiful spot for a beer. Easiest access is to walk half a mile along the beach from the National Trust's Porth Dinllaen car park in Morfa Nefyn.

The smartest option for **accommodation** is the welcoming *Caeau Capel Hotel* on Rhodfa'r Môr in Nefyn village (☎01758/720240; ❹), though you might prefer B&B at *Llys Olwen* in Morfa Nefyn (☎01758/720493, ⓦwww .llysolwen.co.uk; ❸), which serves evening meals for £18. There's also the summer-only *Greenacres* **campsite** along the road between the two villages (£3 per person).

Nant Gwrtheyrn and Tre'r Ceiri

Northeast of Nefyn the mountains of Yr Eifl rise steeply only to plummet into the sea to the north. A fold in the mountains called **Nant Gwrtheyrn** (Vortigern's Valley) is supposed to be the final resting place of the Celtic chieftain Vortigern, who was responsible for inviting the Saxons to Britain after his magician, Myrddin (Merlin), had seen the struggle of the two dragons – the red of the ancient Britons and the white of the Saxons. Vortigern should be pleased to know that his valley is now doing its best to atone for his error, by keeping the ancient British language alive at the impressive **Nant Gwrtheyrn: The Welsh Language and Heritage Centre** (☎01758/750334, ⓦwww.nantgwrtheyrn .org), in rows of converted granite quarry cottages at the foot of the valley. The centre is primarily set up for residential courses entirely in Welsh (see p.70) but is also a beautiful spot to spend a couple of hours exploring the three-mile **nature trail**, strolling through old mine workings and learning all about the place at the new Heritage Centre (Mon–Thurs 11am–5pm Fri 11am–4.30pm; free), adjacent to the language centre. You can even **stay** here in restored quarrymen's cottages (self-catering from £65 for three), which are ideal for small groups. The centre is reached down a narrow, precipitous two-mile track from **Llithfaen**, three miles east of Nefyn: look for signs to "Canolfan Genedlaethol Iaith".

Back on the northern coast road (B4417) it's less than two miles northeast to reach the steep path (4km return; 2hr; 800ft ascent) to the **Tre'r Ceiri** or "Town of the Giants" hillfort (unrestricted access), easily the finest prehistoric remains on the Llŷn. Crowning the entire rounded top of the second-highest of the three Yr Eifl mountains, the hillfort is a massive tumble of rocks, mostly formed into the waist-high walls of about 150 dry-stone hut circles surrounded by a rampart twelve feet high in places. The site is Bronze Age, but the huts are probably only a couple of thousand years old. Locals refer to them as *Cytiau Gwddelod* or "Irishmen's Huts", possibly recalling the Irish immigrant population on the Llŷn in the first few centuries AD, when five hundred people lived on this inhospitable site. Today, the ruins command a stunning **view** over the whole peninsula. The infrequent #14 bus from Tudweiliog passes the foot of the main path up, near a lay-by on the B4417 0.6 miles west of **Llanaelhaearn**, itself reached by the hourly bus #12 from Pwllheli.

Clynnog Fawr

The last worthwhile stop on the #12 bus route to Caernarfon is **CLYNNOG FAWR**, four miles beyond Llanaelhaearn. Rich in ancient spiritual connections, its large, airy, early sixteenth-century **Church of St Beuno** (generally Easter–Oct 9am–6pm) is built on foundations laid by Saint Beuno in the sixth century. This monastic settlement would have been an important stop for pilgrims bound for Ynys Enlli, ensuring a hefty income that probably financed this impressive church. The interior combines spartan whitewash and limestone flags with wealthier flourishes like the fine hammerbeam roof with ornamental bosses, lovely choir stalls and imposing chancel. St Beuno's stone, a boulder used as a prayer stone or a boundary marker around the eighth century, can be seen in the chapel adjacent to the bell tower, while St Beuno's Well bubbles forth on the other side of the main road, about two hundred yards southwest of the church. Between church and well, a lane to Bach Wen Farm heads seawards – park by the entrance to the farm and follow a grassy lane turning off southwest to the spectacularly situated **Clynnog dolmen**. Lying beneath the peaks of Bwlch Mawr and Gyrn Goch, it's a perfect little cromlech, topped with a superbly hewn capstone featuring 110 mysterious cupped hollows.

The road to Caernarfon passes the gates of Parc Glynllifon and close by the Inigo Jones Slateworks (for both see p.445).

Caernarfon and around

It was in **CAERNARFON** in 1969 that Charles, the current heir to the throne, was invested as Prince of Wales, a ceremony that reaffirmed English sovereignty over Wales in the midst of one of the most nationalist of Welsh-speaking regions. Since 1282, when the English defeated Llywelyn ap Gruffydd, the last Welsh Prince of Wales, the title has been bestowed on heirs to the English throne, usually in a ceremony held either at Windsor Castle or in Westminster Abbey in London. However, in 1911, the machinations of Lloyd George – MP for Caernarfon, Welsh cabinet minister and future Prime Minister – ensured that the investiture of the future King Edward VIII would take place

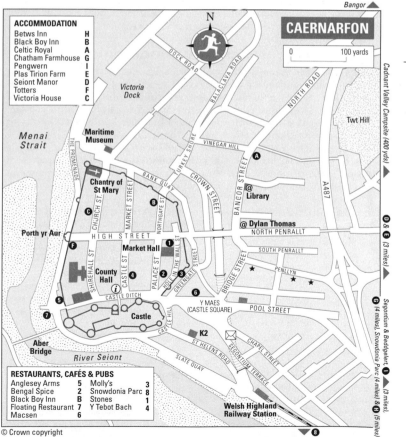

ACCOMMODATION
Betws Inn	H
Black Boy Inn	B
Celtic Royal	A
Chatham Farmhouse	G
Pengwern	I
Plas Tirion Farm	E
Seiont Manor	D
Totters	F
Victoria House	C

CAERNARFON

0   100 yards

Bangor

N

Victoria Dock

Menai Strait

Twt Hill

Maritime Museum

Cadnant Valley Campsite (400 yds)

DOCK ROAD

BALACLAVA ROAD

NORTH ROAD

VINEGAR HILL

TURKEY SHORE

BANK QUAY

CROWN STREET

BANCOR STREET

A487

Ⓐ

Chantry of St Mary

CHURCH ST

MARKET STREET

NORTHGATE ST

Ⓑ

@ **Library**

Ⓖ

@ **Dylan Thomas**

NORTH PENRALLT

Porth yr Aur

HIGH STREET

SOUTH PENRALLT

Ⓕ

Market Hall

CASTLE ST

PALACE ST

HOLE IN THE WALL ST

GREENGATE STREET

BRIDGE STREET

PENLLYN

❶

❷ ❸

County Hall

SHIREHALL ST

ⓘ

❹

❻

D & E (3 miles) ▶

Segontium & Beddgelert (3 miles) ▶

CASTLE DITCH

Ⓖ (4 miles), Snowdonia Parc ▶

❺

Castle

CASTLE HILL

Y MAES (CASTLE SQUARE)

POOL STREET

Segontium & Beddgelert (4 miles), Snowdonia Parc (4 miles) & Ⓗ (5 miles) ▶

❼

Aber Bridge

River Seiont

K2

ST HELENS ROAD

SLATE QUAY

CHAPEL STREET

SEGONTIUM TERRACE

Welsh Highland Railway Station

❽

RESTAURANTS, CAFÉS & PUBS
Anglesey Arms	5	Molly's	3
Bengal Spice	2	Snowdonia Parc	8
Black Boy Inn	B	Stones	1
Floating Restaurant	7	Y Tebot Bach	4
Macsen	6		

© Crown copyright

in the centre of his constituency: a paradoxical move for a nationalist, but one that undoubtedly helped to advance Lloyd George's career.

By the time it was Charles' turn, nationalist activism was on the rise and two of the more militant cadres of the so-called Free Wales Army tried to blow up the Prince's train but succeeded only in killing themselves, an event still mourned by their successors Meibion Glyndŵr, the Sons of Glendower (see p.323 & p.421). Charles' 25-year commemorative return visit in the summer of 1994 was less than triumphant, a low-key affair most significantly characterized by the local constabulary ruling that the local joke shop risked committing a public-order offence by selling "wingnut" ears and Prince Charles masks.

Caernarfon is a town where ardent support for Plaid Cymru guarantees the party a seat in Westminster, and the local dialect is barely intelligible even to other Welsh-speakers. It is also the county town of Gwynedd, a suitable title for what is one of the oldest continuously occupied settlements in Wales, once the site of the Romans' most westerly legion post. Today, Caernarfon is primarily of interest for its awesome castle and town walls, though there's little else to see or do here. The rest of town (bisected by a dual carriageway) is nothing special, and fails to exploit its magnificent setting, where the tidal mouth of the River Seiont meets the Menai Strait. That said, good bus connections to the Llŷn and Snowdonia make it a useful base, and there's something of an edge to deeply individualistic Caernarfon which, when approached sensitively, could well provide you with some of the more memorable encounters of a Welsh tour.

Arrival, information and accommodation

With no main-line train station, the hub of Caernarfon's public transport system is Penllyn, where both National Express and local **buses** arrive just a few steps from the central Y Maes (Castle Square). The **tourist office** (Easter–Oct daily 9.30am–5pm; Nov–Easter Mon–Sat 10am–5pm; ☎01286/672232, ©caernarfon.tic@gwynedd.gov.uk) is on Castle Street, and there's **Internet** access both at the **library** on Bangor Street (Mon, Tues, Thurs & Fri 10am–7pm, Wed 10am–1pm, Sat 9am–1pm), and at the *Dylan Thomas* cybercafé, 4 Bangor St.

Central Caernarfon has decent **accommodation** for all pockets, and there are some lovely farmhouse B&Bs in the vicinity, particularly *Tŷ Mawr Farm* in Llanddeiniolen, halfway between Caernarfon and Bangor (see p.475).

Hotels and guesthouses and hostels

🏃 **Betws Inn** Betws Garmon, 5 miles south-east on the A4085 ☎01286/650324, ⓦwww.betws-inn.co.uk. A low-beamed former drovers' inn (some parts from 1620) with some stylish modern touches. Guests share a cosy lounge with huge inglenook fireplace (not used), and there are excellent three-course dinners by arrangement (£15). ❸

Black Boy Inn Northgate St ☎01286/673604, ⓦwww.welsh-historic-inns.com. Characterful but bathless low-beamed rooms in what is said to be the town's oldest building (bar the castle). Newer en-suite rooms and good-value singles are also available. ❸/❹

Celtic Royal Bangor St ☎01286/674477, ⓦwww.celtic-royal.co.uk. Smart town-centre hotel, with a fine, formal restaurant, and an excellent leisure suite with a decent-sized indoor pool. ❼

Chatham Farmhouse Llandwrog, 4 miles south of Caernarfon just beyond Saron ☎01286/831257. Welcoming country guesthouse with a fine inglenook fireplace and nice decorative touches. Evening meals are made with organic vegetables from the garden and you can bring your own wine. Closed Nov–Feb. ❸

Pengwern Llanwnda, 3 miles southwest of Caernarfon ☎01286/831500, ⓦwww.pengwern.net. Friendly, top-quality, non-smoking B&B in a rural setting, with characterful rooms and farm-fresh evening meals. Take the A487 south across the river then turn right towards Saron – *Pengwern* is just over two miles down on the right. Closed Nov–Feb. ❹

Plas Tirion Farm Llanrug, 3 miles east of Caernarfon on the A4086 ℡01286/673190, ⊛www .plas-tirion.co.uk. Welcoming Welsh farmhouse B&B, furnished with exquisite antiques. ❸

Seiont Manor Llanrug, 3 miles east of Caernarfon on the A4086 ℡01286/673366. Rustic edifice converted into the region's finest hotel, complete with indoor pool, sauna and considerable pampering. ❽

Victoria House 13 Church St ℡01286/678263. Good-value B&B within the town walls. ❸

Hostel and campsites

Cadnant Valley ℡01286/673196. Campsite ten minutes' walk east of town near the start of the

A4086 to Llanberis. Closed Nov–Feb. £9–12 per tent.

Snowdonia Parc Waunfawr ℡01286/650218, ⊛www.snowdonia-park.co.uk. Attractive year-round campsite four miles southeast on the A4085, right by a station on the Welsh Highland Railway and a good brewpub. £10 per pitch.

Totters Plas Porth Yr Aur, 2 High St ℡01286/672963, ⊛www.applemaps.co.uk/totters. Caernarfon's only backpacker hostel is one of the best in Wales. Centrally located, with clean dorms (£12 including continental breakfast) and some lovely communal spaces, including a fourteenth-century cellar kitchen. Staff can direct you to all manner of local activities and lend you a bike. ❶

The Town

Caernarfon may not match Conwy for the sheer pleasure of simply wandering around, but it's slowly getting its act together. Buses no longer clog the central square, and though large sections of the waterfront are taken up by car parks, there's a lot to be said for meandering among the seventeenth- and eighteenth-century buildings in the knot of streets wedged between the **town walls**. These are as complete as those at Conwy, but so boxed-in by modern buildings that they're far less striking, and there's currently no way to get onto them.

Caernarfon Castle

In 1283, Edward I started work on **Caernarfon Castle** (June–Sept daily 9.30am–6pm; Easter–May & Oct daily 9.30am–5pm; Nov–Easter Mon–Sat 9.30am–4pm, Sun 11am–4pm; £4.75; CADW), the strongest link in his Iron Ring (see p.468) and the decisive hammerblow to any Welsh aspirations of autonomy. Until Beaumaris Castle was built to guard the other end of the Menai Strait, Caernarfon was the ultimate symbol of Anglo-Norman military might and political wrangling. With the Welsh already smarting from the loss of their Prince of Wales, Edward reputedly rubbed salt in their wounds by justifying his own infant son's claim to the title, having promised them "a prince born in Wales who could speak never a word of English", and subsequently presenting them with the newborn baby that had arrived after his pregnant wife had been forced to take up residence in the castle. The story is almost certainly apocryphal, since Edward's son, though born at Caernarfon, wasn't invested until seven years later.

However, Edward attempted to woo the Welsh with gestures to certain local legends. The Welsh had long associated their town with the eastern capital of the Roman Empire: Caernarfon's old name, Caer Cystennin, was also the name used for Constantinople, and Constantine himself was believed to have been born at Segontium. Edward's architect, James of St George, exploited this connection in the distinctive limestone and sandstone banding and polygonal towers, both reminiscent of the Theodosian walls in present-day Istanbul. The other legend to influence the castle was the medieval **Dream of Macsen Wledig**, in which the eponymous Welsh hero (the Roman legionnaire Maximus) remembers "a fair fortress at the mouth of a river, in a land of high mountains, opposite an island, and a tower of many colours at the fort, and golden eagles on the ramparts". When it came to finishing off the turrets in 1317, Edward III perfected the accuracy of this description by adding eagles

Caernarfon and Denbigh Herald, issued on Thursdays, has gig information for both Bangor and Caernarfon. For news of alternative social occasions, check out the notice boards in the old **Market Hall** on Palace Street, home to a number of interesting shops and stalls.

Anglesey Arms The Promenade. The sea wall outside makes this the best pub for soaking up the afternoon sun, though it also rates with good real ales and decent bar meals.

Bengal Spice 11 Palace St ☎01286/676797. Reliable curry restaurant and takeaway with fab balti dishes (£6–8).

Black Boy Inn (see p.440). The closest Caernarfon comes to an old-fashioned British pub, with a choice of two low-beamed bars and the best bar meals in town.

Floating Restaurant Slate Quay ☎01286/672896. Enjoyable eaterie in a boat moored below the castle, whose locally caught fish dishes (about £7) are spot on. June–Aug only.

Macsen 11 Y Maes. Modern licensed café right on the square that's a notch or two above the average lunch spot. Great for breakfasts, tasty club sandwiches, baguettes and burgers (£4–6) plus pasta specials, cakes and reasonable espresso.

Molly's 23–25 Hole in the Wall St ☎01286/673238. Smart but relaxed dinner-only bistro with an eclectic menu stretching to Cantonese roast duck (£13), Thai seafood curry (£9), halibut in chilli and lemon butter (£13) plus a host of daily specials and yummy desserts. Closed Tues.

Snowdonia Parc Waunfawr ☎01286/650409. Rural pub four miles southeast of town by a station on the Welsh Highland line, with beer brewed on site and decent pub meals. Bus #95 to Beddgelert goes right by.

Stones 4 Hole in the Wall St ☎01286/671152. Simply decorated brick-walled place serving quality bistro-style meals such as fresh salmon or pork escalopes (£10–13). The Welsh lamb is famed and there's a choice of vegetarian dishes. Closed Sun & Mon.

Y Tebot Bach 13 Castle St. Modern food with old-fashioned attention to detail in this smoke- and chip-free tearoom that's good for sandwiches, salads, home-baked cakes and cream teas throughout the day. Closed Sun & Mon.

Around Caernarfon

One of the most enjoyable ways to get out into the Caernarfon surrounds is to follow either of two walking and **bike paths** along the route of a disused railway: Lôn Las Menai, accessed from Victoria Dock and running north for four miles to Y Felinheri (Port Dinorwig) and thence via lanes to Bangor. In the other direction and leaving town alongside the line of the restored Welsh Highland Railway on St Helen's Road, Lôn Eifion heads twelve miles south to Bryncir, and then via lanes to Cricieth. There's **bike rental** for around £13 a day from Beics Menai, 1 Slate Quay (☎01286/676804). You might also consider catching the Welsh Highland Railway to Dinas then walking the three miles back along Lôn Eifion.

Spectacular **scenic flights** (£39 per person for 20min; ☎08707/541500) over Snowdonia and Anglesey are available from Caernarfon's tiny airport, eight miles south of town at Dinas Dinlle (bus #91; not Sun).

North of Caernarfon

Three miles northeast of Caernarfon, just west of the village of Bethel on the B4366, the **Greenwood Centre** (mid-March to Aug daily 10am–5.30pm; Sept & Oct daily 11am–5pm; ☎01248/670076, ⓦwww.greenwoodforestpark.co.uk; £7.50, reduced prices in winter;) is primarily a family fun park geared around keeping kids happy with small boats, slides, longbow shooting, adventure playgrounds and the like. Located on the fringe of a copse of managed woodland, it has grown from a desire to celebrate the life of trees, and its roots are still evident. You enter though a large barn built using ancient methods and forty tons of green Welsh and English oak trees, its gargantuan beams held together with pine struts and wooden pegs. Tree and forest ecology is explored through a blend of the scientific, the spiritual (due attention is paid to Celtic tree spirits and the like) and the sensory: you're invited to punch the bark of a redwood to see how "soft" it is, identify aromatic woods from their smell and try out an Ethiopian wood pillow.

A few miles due west at Llanfairisgaer, the shores of the Menai Strait hold **Plas Menai: The National Watersports Centre** (℡01248/670964, Ⓦwww .plasmenai.co.uk), a largely group-oriented complex with two- to seven-day courses (see p.70) in sailing, windsurfing, canoeing and powerboating.

South of Caernarfon

The Lôn Eifion bike path runs south from Caernarfon right by the **Inigo Jones Slateworks**, Groeslon (daily 9am–5pm; Ⓦwww.inigojones.co.uk; £4), on the A487 six miles south of Caernarfon. Slate has been fashioned in roadside sheds here since 1861, when the factory was started by one Inigo Jones, a local man apparently unrelated to the seventeenth-century architect. Many of the inscribed slate plaques adorning public buildings around north Wales were cut here, ample excuse for an interesting calligraphy exhibition that forms part of the 45-minute self-guided audio tour. You can even try your hand at chiselling out a few random chips of slate to appreciate the skill of the carvers here. A mile west, off the A499 near Llandwrog, **Parc Glynllifon** (daily 10am–5pm; craft workshops and café free; grounds £3) occupies the grounds of the sombre nineteenth-century Glynllifon Hall (not open to the public), once home of the Lord Newborough. Easy trails weave through a pleasant woodland garden complete with arboretum, but time is equally well spent at the former workshops now given over to well-respected craftspeople including one of Wales' top artistic blacksmiths, Ann Catrin Evans. The *Black Cat Café* is particularly good and has outside seating.

Travel details

Unless otherwise stated frequencies for trains and buses are for Monday to Saturday services; Sunday averages 1–3 services, though the main routes are more frequent and some routes have no Sunday service at all.

Trains	Buses
Betws-y-Coed to: Blaenau Ffestiniog (6 daily; 30min); Llandudno (6 daily; 40min); Llandudno Junction (6 daily; 30min).	**Aberdaron** to: Pwllheli (9 daily; 40min).
	Abersoch to: Pwllheli (10 daily; 15min).
Blaenau Ffestiniog to: Betws-y-Coed (6 daily; 30min); Llandudno (5 daily; 1hr 10min); Llandudno (6 daily; 1hr 10min); Llandudno Junction (6 daily; 1hr); Porthmadog by Ffestiniog Railway (Easter–Oct 4–8 daily; 1hr).	**Bala** to: Corwen (13 daily; 40min); Dolgellau (13 daily; 40min); Llandrillo (13 daily; 20min); Llangollen (13 daily; 1hr).
	Beddgelert to: Caernarfon (10 daily; 30min); Pen-y-Pass (9 daily; 20min); Porthmadog (7 daily; 25min).
Cricieth to: Porthmadog (7 daily; 10min); Pwllheli (7 daily; 15min).	**Betws-y-Coed** to: Bangor (3 daily; 1hr 15min); Capel Curig (every 30min; 10min); Idwal Cottage (6 daily; 20min); Llangollen (4 daily; 1hr); Llanrwst (roughly hourly; 10min); Penmachno (8 daily; 10min); Pen-y-Pass (every 30min; 20min).
Porthmadog to: Barmouth (7 daily; 45min); Blaenau Ffestiniog by Ffestiniog Railway (Easter–Oct 4–8 daily; 1hr); Harlech (7 daily; 20min); Machynlleth (7 daily; 1hr 40min); Pwllheli (7 daily; 25min).	**Blaenau Ffestiniog** to: Caernarfon (roughly hourly; 1hr 30min); Harlech (4 daily; 40min); Porthmadog (hourly; 30min).
Pwllheli to: Cricieth (7 daily; 15min); Porthmadog (7 daily; 25min).	**Caernarfon** to: Bangor (every 20min; 30min); Beddgelert (10 daily; 30min); Blaenau Ffestiniog

CHAPTER 7

Highlights

✳ **The Great Orme** Ride the San Francisco-style cable car or aerial gondola to the summit of Llandudno's limestone hummock, before delving into Bronze Age copper mines. See p.462

✳ **Conwy** The pick of North Wales towns with its imposing castle and intact ring of medieval walls enclosing a fascinating centre. See p.465

✳ **Menai Strait** Look back from Anglesey across the Menai Strait, with the great bridges framing long views of Snowdonia. See p.480

✳ **Penmon Priory** Lovely twelfth-century church containing yet more ancient stonework, hidden in an almost forgotten corner of Anglesey. See p.485

✳ **Newborough Warren** Easy strolls through ecologically important dune systems to the lovely peninsula known as Llanddwyn Island. See p.488

✳ **South Stack** Wheeling sea birds, stunning sea cliffs, a picturesque lighthouse on a small island and some great coastal walking. See p.492

△ South Stack

The north coast and Anglesey

W ales' north coast and its natural extension, Anglesey, encompass both the geographical extremities of the country and the extremes of Welsh life. Walking around most of the brash seaside towns along the eastern section of the coast, only the street signs give any indication that you are in Wales at all: further west, there are places where English is seldom spoken other than to visitors. Scattered along the coast, dramatically situated castles work as a superb antidote to the lowbrow hedonism of the resorts.

Two major forces shaped the region into what it is today. In the thirteenth century, the might of English king Edward I all but crushed the Welsh princes and forced their armies out of the area, whereupon Edward set about building the Norman castles that finally subjugated them.

Though there were earlier castles, the first major success was at **Conwy** where the castle was surrounded by a "bastide" town and the garrison and burghers were interdependent. Economically and politically marginalized by this English entity, the Welsh retreated west to Anglesey, where the English wielded less influence. In response, Edward sited his final castle at **Beaumaris**, a highly advanced concentric design, protecting the entrance to the **Menai Strait**, the treacherous channel that separates the Isle of Anglesey from the mainland.

The second sweeping change came in the late nineteenth and early twentieth centuries, when the benefits of the Industrial Revolution finally loosened the shackles on English mill-town factory workers enough for them to take holidays. Beachfront towns sprang up, catering to the summer visitors who arrived by the trainload. The setup isn't so different today, but cars have all but taken over from the train, caravans are as popular as guesthouses and amusement arcades rule. The stretch of coast from **Prestatyn** to **Colwyn Bay** epitomizes the image of the shabby, tacky British seaside resort – whereas Victorian **Llandudno** was always a posher resort and remains a cut above the rest. With no real beach, Llandudno's neighbour, **Conwy**, is a different proposition with its tight kernel of ancient buildings overshadowed by a fine castle.

If it's beaches you're after, you'll find that more discerning swimmers and windsurfers shun the mainland coast, heading instead through the university

The north coast

Wales' northern seaboard elicits strong reactions. The ranks of detractors citing brash resorts at its eastern end are matched by files of advocates who swear by the low-cost charms of these same towns or who are drawn to the more high-brow attractions further west. Either way, the initial strip of the **north coast** proper is the ugliest in Wales, an endless array of caravan parks with barely an arm's length between adjacent vehicles – packed each year with fun-seekers from Merseyside and the rest of northern England. The amusements scattered along the promenades and beachfronts seem designed to keep you off the beaches: wise counsel even in the hottest weather since the sea here is none too clean. Of the resorts, **Prestatyn**, though uninspiring, is at least notable as the starting, or finishing, point of the Offa's Dyke long-distance path. **Rhyl** is the largest, loudest and tackiest, although it's full of good budget accommodation, and enjoys proximity to three inland attractions: the second of Edward I's castles at **Rhuddlan**, the tiny cathedral city of **St Asaph** and the National Portrait Gallery's Welsh outpost at **Bodelwyddan**. **Colwyn Bay** is smarter, but pales next to its far superior western neighbours, Conwy and Llandudno.

The great sweep of the north coast is interrupted by the **Great Orme**, a massive limestone hummock that rises above **Llandudno**, queen of the north Wales coast for over a hundred years. Neighbouring **Conwy** is more appealing still, packing more sights than the rest of the coast put together within the girdle of 700-year-old town walls which spur off from the mighty castle. The A55 expressway is held tightly to the coast by the northern fringes of Snowdonia's Carneddau range for the final fifteen miles to **Bangor**, home to north Wales' only university and consequently its liveliest town.

Prestatyn to Colwyn Bay

Almost all the vituperative comments aimed at the north coast land squarely on this heavily populated twenty-mile stretch of amusement arcades, bingo halls, caravan sites and negligible beach. Of the resorts, the best known is **Rhyl** – big, brash and ballsy but with more gentle attractions nearby including the cathedral at tiny **St Asaph**, one of Edward I's castles at **Rhuddlan** and the collection of Victorian portraits and furniture at **Bodelwyddan Castle**. There's little to keep you in **Prestatyn**, although it is significant as the starting point for the Offa's Dyke long-distance path, and the Neolithic mound of the **Gop** is nearby. The more architecturally coherent, if hardly exciting, **Colwyn Bay** is marginally the nicest of the main resorts.

Prestatyn and around

Immortalized in the scabrous verse of Philip Larkin, **PRESTATYN** is a likeable enough market town, struggling to compete with its neighbours further along the coast by building minor seaside attractions such as the **Nova Entertainment Centre**, a swimming and leisure complex (hours vary; £2; ℡01745/888021). Next door stands the joint **Offa's Dyke Path Centre** and **tourist office** (July–Sept daily 10am–4pm; Easter–June Sat & Sun 10am–4pm; ℡01745/889092), inside which is an interpretive diagram of the 177-mile

Windfarms in Wales

Even if the connection between greenhouse gases and global warming turns out to be overstated, few would deny that the world would be a better place if we reduced pollution caused by electricity production. Britain has hardly been a world leader in renewable energy, but in the last few years set the goal of producing ten percent of all energy from renewable resources, up from the roughly three percent at the turn of the millennium. In the 1990s, Welsh hillsides sprouted a dozen or so **windfarms** comprising some 400 graceful white wind turbines peeking from behind trees or dominating ridgelines.

As usual, everybody wants them, but nobody wants them where they live, nearby residents often complaining of a constant low drone from the blades. Others protest about the visual impact on some of Britain's most beautiful scenery, so there is general rejoicing over the thirty-turbine **North Hoyle Offshore Wind Farm**, five miles off the coast of Prestatyn. On grey days you can't see them from land, but on clear days they're a striking sight glistening white on the horizon. Commissioned in 2003 the 300-foot-high turbines now produce enough power for 40,000 homes. British electricity consumers can support offshore wind power by buying their power from Juice (ⓦ www.npowerjuice.com), a joint electricity supply venture between npower, who built North Hoyle, and Greenpeace.

route of the Offa's Dyke Path from Prestatyn to Chepstow (see box on p.273) and a stack of leaflets, maps and guides for walkers. The more committed traditionally start at least ankle-deep in the water, then cross the beach onto Bastion Road. The path then follows High Street, through the main shopping area, to the *Cross Foxes* pub, from where acorn-marked signs guide you up to the hills behind. You won't come across any of the Offa's Dyke earthworks until the path gets south of the River Dee, the route planners rightly preferring the Clwydian Range to the scrappy industrial towns of Trevor and Ruabon on the dyke's route. On a good day, though, the view is tremendous – east to

△ Wind turbines near Prestatyn

Important though the castle was, Rhuddlan earns its position in Welsh history as the place where Edward I signed the **Statute of Rhuddlan** on March 19, 1284, consigning Wales to centuries of subjugation by the English that many insist still continues. The ceremony took place on the site of **Parliament House**, on the main street 200 yards to the north. A sign on the building cynically claims that the Statute secured Welsh "judicial rights and independence", despite the fact that Edward laid down the laws by which the Welsh should be governed, including the outlawing of the native language in any official capacity.

Rhuddlan is served by the frequent #51 **bus** from Rhyl.

St Asaph

Six miles south of Rhyl, a single main street forms the heart of Britain's second smallest city, **ST ASAPH** (Llanelwy). While the city of St David's in Pembrokeshire is slightly less populous, St Asaph boasts the country's smallest **cathedral** (open daily 8am–dusk) – an edifice no bigger than many village churches, standing on a rise above the River Elwy (Afon Elwy), with its squat square tower at the crossing of a broad, aisled nave and a well-lit transept.

The town's Welsh name translates as "the church on Elwy River", a title that dates back to the sixth century when St Asaph succeeded the cathedral's founder, St Kentigern, as abbot in 570, and became its first bishop. Both are commemorated in the easternmost window in the north aisle of the cathedral. In 1282, Edward I's men ravaged the church, leaving the incumbent bishop Anian II (whose effigy is in the south aisle) with the task of building the present structure, which itself was attacked in 1402 by Owain Glyndŵr, though only the woodwork was lost and soon replaced.

From 1601 until his death in 1604, the bishopric was held by **William Morgan** (see box opposite), who was responsible for the translation of the first Welsh-language Bible in 1588. An octagonal monument in the churchyard on the north side of the cathedral commemorates the work of Morgan and his fellow translators, including William Salusbury and Gabriel Goodman (see p.368). This is Morgan's only memorial; his grave under the presbytery has been unmarked since Giles Gilbert Scott's substantial restoration in the 1870s. Around a thousand Morgan Bibles were printed – one for every church in the land – of which only nineteen remain, one of them displayed in the south aisle along with Elizabeth I's 1549 copy of *The Book of Common Prayer* that only slightly predated Salusbury's New Testament translation of 1567. In the south transept you'll find a handsome collection of psalter and prayer books; an exquisite sixteenth-century ivory Madonna, said to have come from the Spanish Armada; and a plaque commemorating native son and explorer, Henry Morton Stanley (of "Dr Livingstone, I presume?" fame).

In a similar vein, the churchyard of St Kentigern and St Asaph's Church, a couple of hundred yards down High Street, contains the tombstone of Richard Robert Jones, the nineteenth-century compiler of a Welsh-Greek-Hebrew dictionary. Usually known as Dic Aberdaron, after the fishing village (see p.434) where he was born in 1780, he lived more or less as a tramp whilst acquiring command of fifteen languages and smatterings of another twenty. His tombstone is engraved with a few lines by Ellis Owen, which translate as:

A linguist eight times above other linguists – truly he was
A dictionary of every province.
Death took away his fifteen languages.
Below he is now without a language at all.

William Morgan and the first Welsh Bible

Until 1588 only English Bibles had been used in Welsh churches, a fact which rankled Welsh-born preacher **William Morgan**, who insisted: "Religion, if it is not taught in the mother tongue, will lie hidden and unknown". This was the professed reason behind Elizabeth I's demand for a translation, though her subjects' disaffection could be most conveniently controlled through the church. Four clergymen took up the challenge over a period of 25 years, but it is Morgan who is remembered: working away in Llanrhaeadr-ym-Mochnant (see p.284), he so neglected his other duties that he needed an armed guard to get to his services and was said to preach with a pistol at his side.

The eventual translation was so successful that the Privy Council decreed that a copy should be allocated to every Welsh church. Though it was soon replaced by a translation of the Authorized Version, Morgan's Bible differs little in style from the latest edition used in Welsh services today. More than just a basis for sermons, The Welsh Bible (*Y Beibl*) served to codify the language and set a standard for Welsh prose. Without it the language would probably have divided into several dialects or even followed its Brythonic cousin, Cornish, into history.

Practicalities

The A55 runs close by St Asaph, but without your own transport you're reliant on local **buses**, which all stop outside the cathedral. There's comfortable **accommodation** at the non-smoking *Chalet* (℡01745/584025; ❷) and the plush *Plas Elwy* (℡01745/582263; ❹), both on The Roe – down High Street from the cathedral, across the river bridge then right. For something special head four miles west to the picturesque hamlet of **St George** and the ℀ *Kinmel Arms* (℡01745/832207, ⊛www.thekinmelarms.co.uk; closed Sun & Mon; ❼), a lovely seventeenth-century pub with chic, modern, well-furnished rooms.

You can get snacks, coffee and picnic supplies from the Farm Shop, halfway down High Street. For more substantial **meals**, try the *Plough Inn*, The Roe, home to a lively bar with several real ales on tap and a wide selection of bar meals (£6–8). Alternatively, head out to the ℀ *Kinmel Arms* (closed Mon) for a wide selection of fine beer and wine, great espresso, classy brasserie lunch mains (£7–9) and fancier dishes à la carte (£10–17).

Marble Church and Bodelwyddan Castle: the National Portrait Gallery

There's nothing of interest in the small town of **BODELWYDDAN**, two miles west of St Asaph along the A55 expressway, but from miles around you can pick out the slender 202-foot limestone spire of **Marble Church**, standing as a beacon over the flat coastal plain. The spire's finely worked Gothic tracery is its most impressive feature, and is continued inside around the marble arcades that give the church its name.

Half a mile to the south amid landscaped grounds, **Bodelwyddan Castle** (late July to early Sept daily 10.30am–5pm; late March to late July and early Sept to Oct daily except Fri 10.30am–5pm; Nov–March Thurs 9.30am–6pm, Sat & Sun 10.30am–4pm; £4.50, gardens £2; ⊛www.bodelwyddan-castle .co.uk) is the finest art showcase in north Wales. Although crenellated and edged with turrets, the castle is essentially a nineteenth-century country mansion, its opulent Victorian interiors re-created during its restoration in the 1980s, after sixty years as a girls' school. The Williams Hall wing of the building now houses one of four provincial outposts of the **National Portrait Gallery**, specializing in works contemporary with the castle. The entry fee includes an audio tour replete with its tiresome anecdotes, but you may prefer to rely on the *Visitor Guide* (£2) or the fact sheets in each room.

Most of the two hundred paintings are on the ground floor, approached through the "Watts Hall of Fame", a long corridor lined with 26 portraits of eminent Victorians by G.F. Watts, among them Millais, Rossetti, Browning and Walter Crane. In the Dining Room, two portraits highlight the Pre-Raphaelite support for social reform: William Holman Hunt's portrayal of the vociferous opponent of slavery and capital punishment, Stephen Lushington; and Ford Madox Brown's double portrait of Henry Farell, prime mover in the passing of the 1867 Reform Bill, and suffragette Millicent Garrett. Works by John Singer Sargent and Hubert von Herkamer also adorn the room, which, like the others, is furnished with pieces from the Victoria and Albert Museum in London. The table and chairs originally belonged to one Alfred Waterhouse, who designed the superb walnut and boxwood grand piano.

More worthy Victorians line the Library, which leads on to the Ladies' Drawing Room where a beautiful Biedermeier sofa outshines the paintings of nineteenth-century society ladies. A Grand Staircase leads upstairs to further examples of nineteenth-century portraiture, such as daguerreotypes – including some of Queen Victoria and her brood – works by female artists, and animal painters (especially Landseer).

The rest of the castle is occupied by an expensive adults-only hotel complex, restricted to guests, though you can walk through the modest gardens and a bit of woodland. To get here, catch the #51 **bus** from Rhyl or Rhuddlan, bringing you within ten minutes' walk of both the castle and the church.

Colwyn Bay and Rhos-on-Sea

COLWYN BAY (Bae Colwyn), twelve miles west of Rhyl, has marginally more charm than its eastern neighbours, with its hilly setting, architecturally intact Victorian main street and old-fashioned seafront enhanced by a semi-working pier. Like many other British piers, Colwyn Bay's suffered decades of neglect as Britons opted for foreign holidays, but a small pier renaissance in the mid-1990s saw a number of new shops open along its first few yards. As a whole, though, it is better viewed from the shore, and the Prestatyn to Rhos-on-Sea **cycle path** offers excellent opportunities – you can rent a bike from West End Cycles (☎01492/530269) at 121 Conwy Rd in Colwyn's West End. Alternatively, head a mile inland and steeply uphill to the **Welsh Mountain Zoo** (daily: Easter–Sept 9.30am–5.30pm; Oct–Easter 10am–4pm; £7.50; ⓦwww.welshmountainzoo.org), which touts Californian sea lions, "Chimpanzee World" and free-flying eagle displays as the main attractions. If you're not cycling, a free shuttle bus runs every twenty minutes (Easter and late May to mid-Sept) between the zoo and the town's train station.

Colwyn Bay merges into **RHOS-ON-SEA**, whose seaside **Harlequin Puppet Theatre** (July, Aug and most school holidays daily 3pm & Wed 8pm; £5; ☎01492/548166) is one of the very few remaining marionette acts in the British tradition, with a ninety-minute daytime family show. At Rhos Point, half a mile further on, the minuscule **St Trillo's chapel** has seating for just six worshippers, but may be standing room only during the service at 8am on Fridays. The chapel stands over an ancient healing well and was reputedly the launch point of Prince Madoc ap Owain Gwynedd's voyage to America in 1170 – Welshmen and women the world over like to claim that he was the first European to visit the New World, over three hundred years before Christopher Columbus.

Trains stop on the Colwyn Bay seafront, almost opposite the **tourist office** in Imperial Buildings, Princes Drive (Mon–Sat 9am–5pm; ℡01492/530478, ✉colwynbaytic@conwy.gov.uk). Although you're probably better off staying in nearby Llandudno or Conwy, there's budget **accommodation** at the *Grosvenor Hotel* B&B, 106 Abergele Rd (℡01492/530798; ❶, en-suite ❷), and at the friendly *Marine Hotel* on the Promenade (℡01492/530295, ⓦwww.marinehotel.co.uk; ❸), while for more luxury go for the classy and central *Rathlin Country House*, 48 Kings Rd (℡01492/532173, ⓦwww.rathlincountryhouse.co.uk; ❺). There's simple **camping** at *Dinarth Hall Farm* (℡01492/548203; £8 per person) on Dinarth Hall Road in Rhos-on-Sea.

Chip shops and takeaways abound, but **foodies** make straight for the Provencal 🍴 *Café Niçoise*, 124 Abergele Rd (℡01492/531555, ⓦwww.cafe-nicoise.co.uk; closed Sun evening, Mon, and Tues lunch), with its two- or three-course tourist menu (£12/£16). The best of the local **pubs** is the historic *Rhos Fynach* pub in Rhos-on-Sea, which serves excellent food.

Llandudno

The twin limestone hummocks of the 680-foot **Great Orme** and its southern cousin the Little Orme provide a dramatic frame for the gently curving

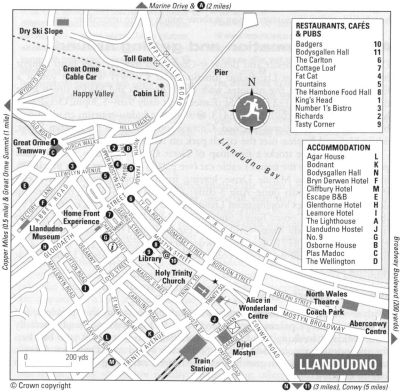

RESTAURANTS, CAFÉS & PUBS

Badgers	10
Bodysgallen Hall	11
The Carlton	6
Cottage Loaf	7
Fat Cat	4
Fountains	5
The Hambone Food Hall	8
King's Head	1
Number 1's Bistro	3
Richards	2
Tasty Corner	9

ACCOMMODATION

Agar House	L
Bodnant	K
Bodysgallen Hall	N
Bryn Derwen Hotel	F
Cliffbury Hotel	M
Escape B&B	E
Glenthorne Hotel	H
Leamore Hotel	I
The Lighthouse	A
Llandudno Hostel	J
No. 9	G
Osborne House	B
Plas Madoc	C
The Wellington	D

LLANDUDNO

© Crown copyright

works by artists of international renown with a particular leaning towards the current Welsh arts scene.

If you have children to entertain, head down Charlton Street from the gallery to the **Alice in Wonderland Centre**, 3–4 Trinity Square (April–Oct daily 10am–5pm; Nov–March closed Sun; £2.95; @www.wonderland.co.uk). Here, a twenty-minute taped tour guides you through the "Rabbit Hole", full of amateurish animated models of Mad Hatters and March Hares, and treats you to excerpts from Lewis Carroll's books. Carroll's association with Llandudno is tenuous but assiduously milked by the town's tourism machine. The writer never visited the town, but Alice Liddell, the inspiration for his books, did – her parents' holiday home now forms the core of the *Pen Morfa Hotel*, on the West Shore.

Towards the Orme, the **Llandudno Museum**, 17 Gloddaeth St (Easter–Oct Tues–Sat 10.30am–1pm & 2–5pm, Sun 2.15–5pm; Nov–Easter Tues–Sat 1.30–4.30pm; £1.50), exhibits items unearthed in local copper mines (see below), Roman artefacts and a rural kitchen from Llanberis. Behind the museum on New Street, the **World War II Home Front Experience** (March–Nov daily 10am–4.30pm; £3) pays a nostalgic and informative visit to early 1940s Britain, with wartime shopfronts, wardens' huts, bomb shelters and the like all packed into one small room. Ration books, children's toys and the efforts of the Women's Land Army are all given evocative treatment.

Otherwise, Llandudno is a supremely easy place in which to wander: on a sunny day, join the ranks of folk on the seafront deckchairs or down on the beach, or head inland to explore the gracious shopping streets, clustered with the best upmarket and speciality **shops** in north Wales.

The Great Orme

The views from the top of the **Great Orme** (Y Gogarth), an ancient mountain almost surrounded by sea, are magical. They combine the seascapes towards Rhyl and over the sands of the Conwy estuary to the shores of Anglesey with the brooding, quarried northern limits of the Carneddau, where Snowdonia crashes into the sea. Take a short walk across the rounded summit of the Orme to escape from the crowds around the car park – it's easy to find somewhere to admire the view as fulmars wheel on the thermals, but less easy to see the feral goats which roam all over the mountain.

Formed about 300 million years ago at the bottom of a tropical sea, this huge lump of carboniferous limestone was subject to some of the same stresses that folded Snowdonia, producing fissures filled by molten mineral-bearing rock. Though there are a few minor Neolithic sites on the hill, it was in the Bronze Age that the settlement really developed, when the people began to smelt the contents of the malachite-rich veins, supplying copper throughout Europe, according to current thinking. The Romans seemingly ignored the Orme's potential – leaving it to early Christian Celts like St Tudno, but the Vikings later gave the place its name, which derives from Old Norse meaning "worm" or "sea serpent" – just how it might have appeared in the mist to those approaching by sea.

Today it is favoured not just by day-trippers here for the view, but also by botanists drawn by the profusion of rare or endangered maritime species: goldilocks aster, spotted cats-ear and spiked speedwell. You can learn more about this intriguing place at the informative **Great Orme Country Park Visitor Centre** (Easter–Oct daily 10am–5pm) by the cafés and bar at the **Summit Complex** (Easter–Oct daily noon–11pm; Nov–Easter Sat & Sun only, same hours).

Apart from walking, there are three other ways to explore the Orme. The traditional favourite is **Marine Drive**, a four-mile circuit cut into the rock high above the coastal cliffs. You can freely walk or cycle around, or make the anticlockwise circuit from near Llandudno's pier in your own car (£2.50 toll summer roughly 9am–8pm, winter 9am–4pm, otherwise free). A summit road leads off Marine Drive and your ticket entitles you to free parking at the top.

A separate route – Old Road – leads directly from Llandudno to the Summit Complex, running parallel to the mile-long route of the vintage, San Francisco-style **Great Orme Tramway** (Easter–Oct 10am–6pm; £4.50 return, £3.40

single; ⓦ www.greatormetramway.com), creaking up from the bottom of Old Road much as it has done since 1902. The third route starts at the base of the pier, close to the start of Marine Drive, where an Italianate colonnade flanks the short road to the **Happy Valley** formal gardens and the **Cable Car** (awaiting reopening) which, when operational, lifts people up to the Summit Complex in open four-seater cabins. At the start it swings over **Llandudno Ski & Snowboard Centre** (variable hours, but generally 10am–10pm), where £16 will get you a couple of hours on the dry slopes (including all equipment), or for a quarter of the price you can make a couple of runs down a 700-yard-long snow-free **Toboggan Run**.

The Great Orme Copper Mines

From the tramway's halfway station, it's a five-minute walk to the long-disused **Great Orme Copper Mines** (Feb–Oct daily 10am–5pm; £5; ☎01492/87047, ⓦ www.greatormemines.co.uk). The Victorians, who last mined the area, were aware of earlier workings, and until the late 1970s these were assumed to be Roman. Digs in the 1980s, however, uncovered 4000-year-old animal bones that had been used as scrapers up to 200ft down. This is one of the few sites in Britain where mineral veins were accompanied by dolomitization, a rock-softening process that permitted the use of the simple tools available in the Bronze Age. Ease of extraction led to this becoming the pre-eminent copper mine in Europe, and with more excavations continuing in the off-season, it may well turn out to have been the world's largest.

Hard hats are provided on the **self-guided tour**, which, after an explanatory video, takes you down through a small portion of the four miles of tunnels so far uncovered – enough to get a feel for the cramped working conditions, and see the burial site of one of three cats thought to have been sacrificed by superstitious miners. Topside, you can see some of the ongoing dig and get a idea of how the copper ore was smelted to form tools.

Eating, drinking and entertainment

Llandudno is blessed with the best choice of **restaurants** in north Wales, ranging from budget cafés to one of the most expensive places in the country. Most cluster at the foot of the Great Orme around Mostyn Street, where numerous **pubs** cater to most tastes. Llandudno's pubs can get chaotically crowded at weekends when the normally genteel atmosphere slides into raucous hedonism: if that's your bag, head for the bars of Upper Mostyn Street.

A century ago all the best music-hall performers clamoured to play Llandudno. After a lull of several decades, the early 1990s saw the opening of the North Wales Theatre which has put Llandudno back on the formal **entertainment** scene: look for flyers around town to see who's on. Otherwise, there's a nightclub that draws in revellers from miles around, and movies at Llandudno Junction.

Restaurants and cafés

Badgers Victoria Centre, Mostyn St. Slightly twee but excellent café and lunch spot, the higher prices justified by the food quality, attentive service and a range of eight blends of cafetière coffee.

Bodysgallen Hall 3 miles south of town on the A470 ☎01492/584466. Top-notch traditional and modern British fare in one of Britain's best country hotels. Go for the full three-course dinner (£38;

jacket and tie for gents) or a sumptuous lunch overlooking the gardens (£18–20). The Sunday lunches (£24) here are superb.

The Hambone Food Hall Lloyd St. Excellent deli producing great takeaway sandwiches to order along with a wide range of meat pies, pâtés and salads.

Number 1's Bistro 1 Old Rd. One of Llandudno's finer low-key restaurants, with a simple dark-wood and burgundy decor, it serves imaginative, moderately priced French-styled bistro meals (two courses for £12 and three for £15 between 5.30 & 6.30pm; otherwise £18/£22). Only open for dinner; closed Sun.

Richards 7 Church Walks ☎01492/875315. Intimate dinner-only basement bistro with slate-tiled floor and an intriguing modern British menu that borrows from east Asia. Expect the likes of seafood platter in a saffron broth, and some mouthwatering traditional desserts. Three courses £25. Closed Sun & Mon.

Tasty Corner Lloyd St ☎01492/873333.Modern daytime café serving bruschetta (£5), mushroom stroganoff (£7) and good coffee. On Fri and Sat evenings they run Greek nights (booking suggested) with mousakka, stifado and other Greek specialities (£8–9).

Bars and pubs

The Carlton 121 Mostyn St, cnr of Gloddaeth St. Lively town-centre pub with a pool table, good beer and fine iron-and-glass verandas.

Cottage Loaf Market St. Flag-stoned pub built from ships' timbers atop an old bake house, that's popular for lunchtime eating and drinking all day.

Fat Cat 149 Upper Mostyn St. Frantic and fun café-bar with an eclectic clientele and heated pavement section for year-round alfresco drinking and people-watching.

Fountains 114 Upper Mostyn St. Hugely popular early evening meeting point that's good for shots and cocktails.

King's Head Old Rd, by the bottom of the tramway. Llandudno's oldest pub, where Edward Mostyn and his surveyor mapped out the town, it contains some interesting photos and serves substantial, tasty bar meals, ranging from Welsh rarebit to noisettes of lamb.

Entertainment

Broadway Boulevard Grand Theatre, Mostyn Broadway, on the corner of Ty'n y Ffridd Rd ☎01492/879614. Llandudno's liveliest club, with a host of party nights.

Cineworld ☎01492/574910. The closest cinema is three miles south in Llandudno Junction, but boasts nine screens.

North Wales Theatre (Theatr Gogledd Cymru) The Promenade ☎01492/872000, ⊛www.nwtheatre. co.uk. North Wales' premier live entertainment centre, this modern 1500-seat theatre lures touring companies and occasional international acts.

Conwy and around

Since the completion of the A55 bypass tunnel under the river reduced traffic on its streets, **CONWY**, four miles southwest along the coast from Llandudno, has blossomed. In the last decade, asphalt has been replaced with cobbles and shop fronts have been prettified, but it has, for the moment, resisted becoming a heritage museum town. There's a huge amount to see and do here, all the same: a stunning early-medieval castle and a complete belt of accompanying town walls enclosing some fascinating glimpses into the past of north Wales. The town remains one of the highlights of the north coast, its setting on the Conwy estuary, backed by a forested fold of Snowdonia, irresistible to painters and photographers ever since Englishman Paul Sandby published his *Views of North Wales* in 1776. Even if you're a little weary of castle-hopping, Conwy is still worth a stop, whether for the wondrous Elizabethan townhouse, Plas Mawr, the three estuary bridges, or cutesy treats like Britain's smallest house and the Butterfly Jungle.

In Sandby's day, the Conwy estuary still produced a good living for the families who had held mussel-gathering rights on the sands for centuries, a heritage going back long before the foundation of the Cistercian monastery of Aberconwy in 1172. The monastery, where Llywelyn ap Iorwerth ("the Great") died in 1240, was on the present site of the parish church of St Mary and All Saints, but a century later was moved eight miles upriver to Maenan, near Llanrwst, to make way for one of the doughtiest links in Edward I's chain of fortresses.

Barring a brief siege during the Welsh uprising of 1294, the castle saw little action until 1399, when Richard II stayed there on his return from Ireland, until lured from safety by the Earl of Northumberland, Bolingbroke's vassal.

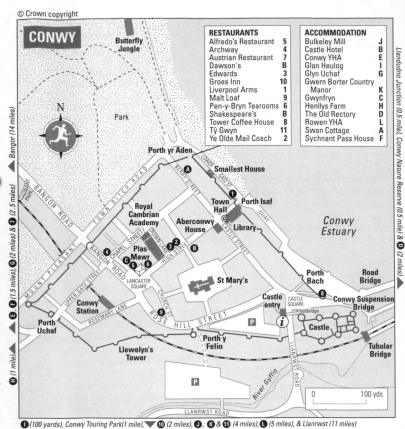

CONWY

RESTAURANTS	
Alfredo's Restaurant	5
Archway	4
Austrian Restaurant	7
Dawson's	B
Edwards	3
Groes Inn	10
Liverpool Arms	1
Malt Loaf	9
Pen-y-Bryn Tearooms	6
Shakespeare's	B
Tower Coffee House	8
Tŷ Gwyn	11
Ye Olde Mail Coach	2

ACCOMMODATION	
Bulkeley Mill	J
Castle Hotel	B
Conwy YHA	E
Glan Heulog	I
Glyn Uchaf	G
Gwern Borter Country Manor	K
Gwynfryn	C
Henllys Farm	H
The Old Rectory	D
Rowen YHA	L
Swan Cottage	A
Sychnant Pass House	F

Bangor (14 miles)

Butterfly Jungle

Park

N

(1.5 miles), (2 miles) & (2.5 miles)

(1 mile)

BANGOR ROAD

MOUNT PLEASANT

TOWN DITCH ROAD

Porth yr Aden

Smallest House

Royal Cambrian Academy

CHAPEL STREET

CROWN LANE

BERRY STREET

LOWER GATE ST

Town Hall

Porth Isaf

QUAY

Aberconwy House

HIGH STREET

Library

CASTLE STREET

Conwy Estuary

Plas Mawr

LANCASTER SQUARE

St Mary's

Porth Bach

Road Bridge

Conwy Station

UPPER GATE STREET

BANGOR ROAD

ROSEMARY LANE

CHURCH STREET

ROSE HILL STREET

Castle entry

CASTLE SQUARE

footbridge

Conwy Suspension Bridge

Porth Uchaf

Porth y Felin

P

i

Castle

Tubular Bridge

Llewelyn's Tower

LLANRWST ROAD

P

River Gyffin

LLANRWST ROAD

0   100 yds

LLANRWST ROAD

Llandudno Junction (0.5 mile), Conwy Nature Reserve (0.5 mile) & (2 miles)

(100 yards), Conwy Touring Park(1 mile), (2 miles), , & (4 miles), (5 miles), & Llanrwst (11 miles)

Northumberland swore in the castle's chapel to grant Richard safe passage, but imprisoned him at Flint (see p.373), enabling Bolingbroke to become Henry IV. Two years later, on Good Friday, Owain Glyndŵr's cousins, Gwilym and Rhys ap Tudor, seized Conwy castle while the guards were at church and razed the town for Glyndŵr's cause. Harry Hotspur, Chief Justice of north Wales, rushed from Denbigh to recapture the fortress and eventually struck a deal whereby nine Welsh were handed over to be hanged, drawn and quartered, in return for the Tudors' freedom. After this, the castle fell into disuse, and was bought in 1627 for £100 by Charles I's Secretary of State, Lord Conway of Ragley, who then had to refortify it for the Civil War, when it held out until 1646, only surrendering to Mytton after the town had fallen. At the restoration of the monarchy in 1665, the castle was stripped of all its iron, wood and lead, and left substantially as it is today.

Arrival and information

Llandudno Junction, less than a mile across the river to the east, serves as the main **train station** for services from Chester to Holyhead, as well as for trains heading south to Betws-y-Coed and Blaenau Ffestiniog; only slow, regional services stop in Conwy itself (on request). National Express **buses** on the north coast run mostly stop in Llandudno, though usually one service a day pulls up outside the town walls on Town Ditch Road, as do open-top double-deckers to Llandudno. Local buses to Bangor and points west stop on Lancaster Square, while those to Betws-y-Coed, Llandudno and points east stop on Castle Street.

Walking south from either Conwy station or the Lancaster Square bus stops, skip the Conwy Visitor Centre in favour of the **tourist office** (mid-March to May & Oct daily 9.30am–5pm; June–Sept daily 9.30am–6pm; Nov–March Mon–Sat 9.30am–4pm, Sun 11am–4pm; ☎01492/592248), which shares the same building and hours as the castle ticket office. Bikes can be rented from the Conwy Outdoor shop, 9 Castle St (☎01492/593390, ⓦwww.snowdoniacyclehire.co.uk), for £16 a day.

Accommodation

Although the Conwy region offers a fair range of **accommodation** – including the only town-centre YHA hostel in the vicinity – the choice is a bit thin in the heart of town, and those without the transport to reach the less central places should book ahead in summer.

Hotels and guesthouses

Bulkeley Mill Rowen, 4 miles south of Conwy ☎01492/651052, ⓦwww.bulkeley-mill.co.uk. Olde-worlde B&B in a converted seventeenth-century water mill surrounded by gardens with two en-suite rooms; very peaceful and relaxing. ➋

Castle Hotel High St ☎01492/582800, ⓦwww.castlewales.co.uk. Former coaching inn in the heart of town, now restored to the exalted standard it deserves. There's a very good restaurant on site where substantial breakfasts are served. ➐

Glan Heulog Llanrwst Rd ☎01492/593845, ⓦwww.snowdoniabandb.co.uk. One of the best small guesthouses in easy walking distance, on the outskirts of town. ➌

Glyn Uchaf Conwy Old Rd, Capelulo, 2 miles west of Conwy ☎01492/623737. One of the finest secluded B&Bs around, backing onto the hills just over Sychnant Pass. ➍

Gwern Borter Country Manor Barker's Lane, Rowen ☎01492/650360, ⓦwww.snowdoniaholidays.co.uk. Comfortable manor house on a Conwy Valley farm just north of Rowen (bus #19), with sauna, gym and pony trekking available and easy access to walks into the nearby Carneddau range. ➍

Gwynfryn 4 York Place ☎01492/576733. Recently converted B&B with five tastefully decorated rooms, each boasting a small fridge and DVD player, with access to a movie library. ➌

Henllys Farm Llechwedd, 1.5 miles west of Conwy ☎01492/593269. Appealing guesthouse on a working farm. Turn up Upper Gate Street, bear left along St Agnes Road, then follow signs for Llechwedd – *Henllys* is on the right. ➋

The Old Rectory Llansantffraid Glan Conwy ☎01492/580611, ⓦwww.oldrectorycountryhouse.co.uk. Georgian-style country house, opulently furnished with antiques and fine paintings, overlooking the Conwy estuary, a mile up the Conwy Valley. Rates (starting around £200) include breakfast and a fabulous evening meal. ➒

🏃 **Swan Cottage** 18 Berry St ☎01492/596840, ⓦwww.swancottage.btinternet.co.uk. Central B&B with small but attractive rooms, one with en-suite facilities, and two with great estuary views. ➊

🏃 **Sychnant Pass House** 1.5 miles up Sychnant Pass ☎01492/596868, ⓦwww.sychnant-pass-house.co.uk. More like a welcoming family home than a hotel, with comfortable rooms, a new indoor pool, relaxing lounges stocked with games, books and cats, and extensive grounds where dogs play (guests' dogs are welcome). Dinner (£25–28) is available nightly except Mon. ➏

Hostels and campsites

Conwy Touring Park ☎01492/592856. A fully equipped campsite taking tents, just over a mile south along the B5106 (bus #19). It operates a strict "families and couples only" rule, so you'll have to look reasonably respectable to get in. Closed Nov–March. £9 per tent.

🏃 **Conwy YHA** Lark Hill ☎01492/593571 or 0870/770 5774, ⓔconwy@yha.org.uk. Spacious, modern hostel a 10-min walk from town up the Sychnant Pass road with double rooms and small dorms (£14). The place is open all day, serves good-value meals and rents bikes to guests (£8 a half-day). Open mid-Feb to Oct and winter weekends. ●

Rowen YHA Rowen, half a mile up a steep hill above the village ☎ 0870/770 5774. Simple YHA hostel on the flanks of the Carneddau range, with superb views over the Conwy Valley. Bunks cost £10. Reached by turning right 200 yards past Rowen's pub, and served by bus #19 from Conwy. Open Easter & May–Aug.

The Town

Nothing within Conwy's core of medieval and Victorian buildings is more than two hundred yards from the irregular triangle of protective masonry formed by the town walls, which makes the town wonderfully easy to potter around. Though you'll get to see everything you want to in a day, you may well want to stay longer.

Conwy Castle

During their incursions along Wales' north coast, Edward I's Anglo-Norman ancestors had all but destroyed the castle at Deganwy, near Llandudno, but maintaining a bridgehead west of the Conwy River had always eluded them. Accordingly, once over the river in 1283, Edward set about establishing another of his bastide towns. He chose a strategic knoll at the mouth of the Conwy River and set James of St George to fashion a castle to fit its contours. With the help of 1500 men, James took just five years to build **Conwy Castle** (hours as for tourist office, last entry half an hour before closing; £4, joint ticket with Plas Mawr £6.50; CADW), now entered through a ticket office and over a modern bridge.

Overlooked by a low hill, the castle appears less easily defended than others along the coast, but James constructed eight massive towers in a rectangle

---

The Iron Ring

Dotting the north Wales coast, a day's march from each other, Edward I's fearsome **Iron Ring** of castles represents Europe's most ambitious and concentrated medieval building project, designed to prevent the recurrence of two hugely expensive military campaigns (see Contexts, p.506). After Edward's first successful campaign in 1277, he was able to pin down his adversary, **Llywelyn ap Gruffydd** ("the Last") in Snowdonia and Anglesey, gaining space and time to build the now largely ruined castles at **Flint**, **Rhuddlan**, **Builth Wells** and **Aberystwyth**, and consolidate his grip by confiscating and upgrading several Welsh castles.

Although Llewellyn's second uprising (1282) also ultimately failed, Edward was determined not to have to fight a third time for the same land, and set about extending his Iron Ring in an immensely costly display of English might, which – together with the Treaty of Rhuddlan (1284) – effectively crushed Welsh resistance. **Harlech**, **Caernarfon** and **Conwy** are nearly contemporaneous, yet manifest a unique progression towards the later, highly evolved concentric design of **Beaumaris**, for all these castles (and the town walls of Caernarfon and Conwy) were built by **James of St George d'Espéranche** – the master military architect of his age – whose work is now recognized with **UN World Heritage Site** status.

Each castle was integrated with a **bastide town** – an idea borrowed from Gascony in France, where Edward I was duke – the town and castle being mutually reliant on each other for protection and trade. The bastides were always populated with English settlers, and the Welsh were only permitted to enter during the day, but not to trade and certainly not carrying arms. It wasn't until the eighteenth century that the Welsh would have towns they could truly call their own.

around the two wards, the inner one separated from the outer by a drawbridge and portcullis, and further protected by turrets atop the four eastern towers. Strolling along the ramparts, you can look down onto something unique in the Iron Ring fortresses, a roofless but largely intact interior. The outer ward's 130-foot-long Great Hall and the King's Apartments are both well preserved, but the only part of the castle to have kept its roof is the **Chapel Tower**, named for the small room built into the wall whose semicircular apse still shows some heavily worn carving. On the floor below, there's a small exhibition on religious life in medieval castles, that won't detain you from exploring the passages for long.

The rest of the town

Anchored to the castle walls as if it were a drawbridge, Telford's slender **Conwy Suspension Bridge** (mid-March to Oct daily 11am–5pm; £1, joint ticket with Aberconwy House £3.50; NT) was part of the 1826 road improvement scheme, prompted by the need for better communications to Ireland after the Act of Union. Contemporary with his far greater effort spanning the Menai Strait (see p.481), it mimics the crenellations of the battlements above, to compensate for spoiling the view of the castle immortalized by J.M.W. Turner. The bridge was used until 1958, was briefly threatened with demolition, and has now been restored to approximately its original state. It serves as a footbridge linking the town to a **tollhouse**, furnished as it would have been circa 1900, complete with period toll charges on a board outside.

The approach to the newer road bridge has created the only breach in the thirty-foot high **town walls** that branch out from the castle into a three-quarter-mile-long circuit, enclosing Conwy's ancient quarter. Inaccessible from the castle they were designed to protect, the walls are punctuated by 21 evenly spaced horseshoe towers, as well as twelve latrines bulging out from the wall-walk. At present, only half of the distance can be walked, the best section being from Porth Uchaf to Porth yr Aden (unrestricted access), with great views over the town to the castle and estuary beyond.

Here, you come down off the walls by brightly rigged trawlers, mussel boats and the self-proclaimed **smallest house in Great Britain** (Easter to mid-Oct daily 10am–5pm and often later in good weather; 75p), which was built wedged between two terraces, one of them now demolished. The two tiny rooms combined are only nine feet high and six wide, the door taking up a quarter of the frontage. Most people will have to duck to get in, a problem that vexed the last resident, a six-foot-three fisherman, until he left around 1900.

Porth Isaf, the nearby gate in the town walls, leads up Lower High Street to the fourteenth-century timber and stone **Aberconwy House** on Castle Street (mid-March to Oct daily except Tues 11am–5pm; £3, joint ticket with suspension bridge £3.50; NT), the oldest house in Conwy and the sole surviving medieval building, dating from about 1300. Built for a wealthy merchant, it saw service as a bakery, antique shop, sea captain's house and temperance hotel, somehow managing to survive numerous fires and Victorian improvements. Its various incarnations are re-created in rooms furnished with a simple yet elegant collection of rural furniture on loan from the Museum of Wales. Tours start with an introductory video in the attic, winding up in a kitchen complete with fireside settle, pewter plates and a few hunks of stale bread.

Conwy's grandest residence is the splendid **Plas Mawr**, or "great mansion" (June–Aug Tues–Sun 9.30am–6pm; mid-March to May & Sept Tues–Sun 9.30am–5pm; Oct Tues–Sun 9.30am–4pm; £4.50, joint ticket with castle £6.50; CADW), just up the High Street at no. 20. One of the best-preserved Elizabethan townhouses in Britain, it was built in a Dutch style for Robert

△ Plas Mawr and Conwy Castle

Wynn of Gwydir Castle (see Llanrwst, p.393), who was one of the first native Welsh to live in the town, returning to the area after mixing at European courts. The main part of the house dates from 1576, with features such as the gatehouse added some ten years later to augment the grand effect. In the Great Hall, the impressive plaster over-mantel was designed to woo visitors with Wynn's noble credentials – especially his descent from the Princes of Gwynedd – and much of the superb plasterwork throughout the house relates to the Wynn dynasty, except in the Great Chamber, where he demurred, presumably so as not to upstage visiting royalty. The tour – aided by an excellent recorded commentary – concludes with an exhibition about Tudor and Stuart attitudes to disease and cleanliness that's compulsively gory, hilariously scatological and highly informative.

For over a century, Plas Mawr was home to the Royal Cambrian Academy, a group aiming to foster art in Wales. The **Royal Cambrian Academy Art Gallery** (Tues–Sat 11am–5pm, Sun 1–4.30pm; free; Ⓦ www.rcaconwy.org), is now located just behind Plas Mawr in a converted chapel on Crown Lane. At their best during the annual summer exhibition, the airy, well-lit galleries display work by the Academy members, almost all Welsh or working in Wales.

There's more lightweight entertainment ten minutes' walk north along Castle/Berry Street at the **Butterfly Jungle** (April–Aug daily 10am–5.30pm; Sept daily 10am–3.30pm; £3.50; Ⓦ www.conwy-butterfly.co.uk), a hothouse full of bougainvillea, hibiscus and oleander pollinated by some fifty breeds of tropical butterfly, most imported as chrysalises but several bred here.

If you're still stuck for something to do, **river cruises** on the *Queen Victoria* (30min; £4) or *Princess Christine* (45min; £5.50) leave from the quay, or visit the RSPB's **Conwy Nature Reserve**, across the river at Llandudno Junction. Entered by a **visitor centre** (daily 10am–5pm; £2.50) overlooking a pool, its reed beds sustain year-round breeding colonies of reed buntings, and reed and sedge warblers in season, plus skylarks and nesting plovers (spring), butterflies and dragonflies (summer & autumn), widgeons and red-breasted mersangers (winter).

Finally, the best **short walk** from Conwy is onto the gorse-, bracken- and heather-covered slopes of **Conwy Mountain** (Mynydd y Dref: 2 miles return; 1hr; 650ft ascent) and the 800-foot Penmaenbach and Alltwen peaks behind, all affording fantastic views right along the coast. Follow a sign up Cadnant Park off Bangor Road just outside the town walls, then take the road around until Mountain Road heads off on the right to a small parking area.

Eating and drinking

For a popular tourist town, Conwy has relatively few **restaurants**, and if you want to sample some really great pubs, you've got to get a few miles out into the Conwy Valley. **Drinking** in town is fairly perfunctory, with nightlife being limited to the odd pub gig. Most people head into Llandudno or Bangor for anything more exciting.

Restaurants and cafés

Alfredo's Restaurant Lancaster Square
ⓉⒸ 01492/592381. Good-value pizza and pasta dishes (£7) and respectable mains (£12–14) amongst the Chianti bottles. Evenings only.
Archway 12 Bangor Rd. Quality sit-in and take-out fish and chip restaurant also doing pizza and pies. On a fine evening take your haul to The Quay and wash it down with a pint from the *Liverpool Arms*.
Austrian Restaurant Conwy Old Rd, Capelulo Dwygyfylchi, 2.5 miles west over Sychnant Pass
ⓉⒸ 01492/622170. Worth making a journey for steaming helpings of goulash and paprika schnitzel (around £10), and great-value three-course Sunday lunches for £8.50. Closed Mon & Tues, & Sun evening.
Edwards 18 High St. A fine deli with a decent salad bar; the place to stock up for picnics.
Pen-y-Bryn Tearooms 28 High St. Slightly twee establishment in a sixteenth-century house, with

delicious lunches and the best artery-hardening Welsh teas around.
Shakespeare's is in the *Castle Hotel*. Easily the finest restaurant in town where linen and crystal set the tone for dishes such as beef fillet with oxtail ragout or roasted halibut (both £18), followed by iced berry soufflé or a Welsh cheeseboard (£6).
Tower Coffee House Castle Square. Quality café set in one of the town wall towers with estuary views. Come for panini, stuffed baguettes, espresso and good cakes.

Bars and pubs

Dawson's inside the *Castle Hotel*, High St. Refined lounge bar in an upmarket hotel with cask ales, good wine and bar meals a cut above the norm (mains £7–9).
Groes Inn Tyn-y-Groes, 2 miles south on B5106 to Llanrwst. Excellent bar meals and cask ales at an

atmospheric fifteenth-century pub which claims to be the oldest licensed house in Wales.

Liverpool Arms The Quay. Compact pub built into the town wall, whose dockside location makes it a hot venue on warm evenings.

Malt Loaf Rosehill St, opposite the station. Scruffily low-key pub, home to the town's folk club (Mon) and attendant jumper-wearers.

Tŷ Gwyn Rowen, 4 miles south of Conwy. Village pub in an idyllic setting, with a friendly atmosphere, decent bar meals and a nice garden.

Ye Olde Mail Coach 16 High St. Spacious neo-olde-worlde pub serving good real ale and bar meals, and hosting occasional live music.

Around Conwy

With its marvellous setting and plentiful accommodation, Conwy is the ideal base for a few days spent exploring the Lower Conwy Valley and the coast around its estuary. It's easy to make a day trip to Llandudno (see p.459), and there's a smattering of other attractive diversions within a few miles' radius. Thousands come here specifically to see **Bodnant Garden**, and tiny **Rowen** has a low-key appeal. Conwy also acts as a base for the **Cambrian Way** long-distance walking path to Cardiff (see box on opposite). The guesthouses and restaurants mentioned in the text are all listed on pp.467 and 471–2.

The Lower Conwy Valley: Bodnant Garden and Rowen

During May and June, the 160-foot laburnum tunnel flourishes and banks of rhododendrons are in glorious bloom all over **Bodnant Garden,** eight miles south of Conwy (mid-March to Oct daily 10am–5pm; £5.50; NT), Wales' finest formal garden and one of the loveliest in Britain. Laid out in 1875 around Bodnant Hall (closed to the public) by its then owner, English industrialist Henry Pochin, the garden spreads over eighty acres of the Conwy Valley. Divided into an upper terraced garden and lower Pinetum and Wild Garden, Bodnant catches the late afternoon sun as it sets over the Carneddau range, though the limited opening hours mean that visitors only experience this in October. Shrubs and plants provide a blaze of colour throughout the opening season, but autumn is a perfect time to be here, with hydrangeas still in bloom and fruit trees shedding their leaves. You'll need a minimum of two hours to fully appreciate the place. The #25 bus runs here from Llandudno roughly every hour, calling at Llandudno Junction, or it's a two-mile walk from the Tal-y-Cafn train station on the Conwy Valley line.

Across the valley on the eastern slopes of the Carneddau range, the tiny mountainside hamlet of **ROWEN** (also spelt Roewen) is one of the prettiest in the area, composed of a few cottages, a post office, a chapel and the lovely *Tŷ Gwyn* pub (see below). If you don't mind the short drive into Country, it makes a great base for exploring the area. Try *Bulkeley Mill, Gwern Borter Country Manor* or the *Rowen YHA* hostel (all listed on p.467). The #19 bus links Rowen with Conwy and Llanrwst every hour or better.

Heading west: Sychnant Pass and Penmaenmawr Mountain

When heading west towards Bangor it's worth taking a short detour inland through the narrow cleft of **Sychnant Pass**, which separates Conwy Mountain from the Carneddau range.

Old Conwy Road, served by the very infrequent bus #75, passes the *Conwy YHA* hostel (see p.467) and crosses the pass before dropping into the hamlet of **CAPELULO**, just over two miles west of Conwy, rejoining the A55 at workaday Penmaenmawr. If you have a decent map, Capelulo makes a good

The ultimate Welsh long-distance path, the **Cambrian Way** crosses the whole country, winding some 274 miles from Cardiff to Conwy. Its most salient feature is its isolation, passing through some of Wales' most spellbinding upland scenery, as the route climbs over the Carneddau, the Glyderau, the Snowdon massif, Cadair Idris and the Brecon Beacons before dropping down through the Valleys to Cardiff.

This is the most arduous long walk in Wales, and one of the most satisfying, requiring a high degree of commitment and good route finding (signposting is erratic en route), and while fit hikers might do the walk in one tough two-week push, most prefer to break it into manageable sections.

The experience is undoubtedly heightened by spending nights under canvas atop the moors, but with over a dozen YHA hostels scattered along the route and B&Bs selected from *Stillwell's National Trail Companion* (see Contexts, p.555), much of the way can be done with a roof over your head. A.J. Drake's *The Cambrian Way: A Mountain Connoisseur's Walk* (see Contexts, p.555) is also well worth acquiring.

The Cambrian Way Walkers Association organizes a number of guided and self-guided multi-day walks along sections of the route, providing GPS hand-sets, maps and mobile phones, and using minibuses to get walkers to and from the ends of each section. For details, and free information contact the association's effervescent Nick Bointon at Llanerchindda Farm, Cynghordy, Llandovery, Dyfed SA20 0NB (☏01550/750274, ⓦwww.cambrianway.com; see also p.181).

starting point for a walk across **Penmaenmawr Mountain**, an important source of stone for axe-making from around 3000 BC and still being quarried today. Not surprisingly, the area boasts several Neolithic remains, most notably the misnamed **Druid's Circle** (Y Meini Hirion) – marked on the map (grid reference 723746) simply as "Stone Circle".

Bangor and around

After a few days travelling through mid-Wales or in the mountains of Snowdonia, **BANGOR** makes a welcome change. It's not big; but, as the largest town in Gwynedd and home to the **University of Wales Bangor**, it passes in these parts for cosmopolitan. Students are the main reason for Bangor's vibrancy, and with only a trickle of summer visitors the city struggles to keep an active social life going outside term time. The presence of a large non-Welsh student population inflames the passions of the more militant nationalists in this overwhelmingly Welsh-speaking area, and though antagonism seldom results in anything more than drunken slanging matches, you'll notice a dramatic change if you've just arrived from one of the largely English-speaking north coast resorts.

While the slate industry and road and rail projects brought some urbanization to Bangor in the nineteenth century, for well over a millennium before that, the city was solely noted for its bishopric, founded as a monastic settlement by St Deiniol in 525 AD and thus the oldest continuous cathedral see in Britain, predating even Canterbury by some seventy years. At first, St Deiniol only cleared a space in the woods which became known as *Y Cae Onn* (The Ash Enclosure), later developing into the town's present name, a corruption of *bangori*, a type of interwoven wattle fence which presumably demarcated the monastic lands.

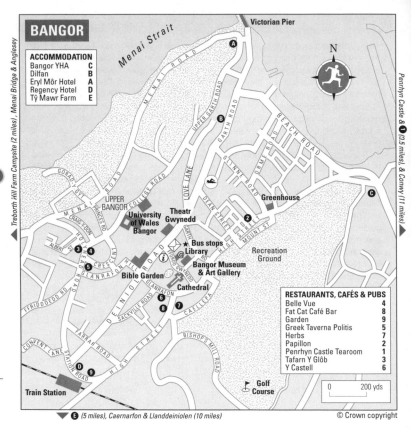

BANGOR

ACCOMMODATION
Bangor YHA   C
Dilfan   B
Eryl Môr Hotel   A
Regency Hotel   D
Tŷ Mawr Farm   E

Victorian Pier

Menai Strait

UPPER BANGOR

University of Wales Bangor

Theatr Gwynedd

Greenhouse

★ Bus stops
Library

Bangor Museum & Art Gallery

Bible Garden

Cathedral

Recreation Ground

Golf Course

RESTAURANTS, CAFÉS & PUBS
Belle Vue   4
Fat Cat Café Bar   8
Garden   9
Greek Taverna Politis   5
Herbs   7
Papillon   2
Penrhyn Castle Tearoom   1
Tafarn Y Glôb   3
Y Castell   6

Train Station

0   200 yds

Treborth Hill Farm Campsite (2 miles), Menai Bridge & Anglesey

Penrhyn Castle & (0.5 miles), & Conwy (11 miles)

▼ Ⓔ *(5 miles), Caernarfon & Llanddeiniolen (10 miles)*

© Crown copyright

Arrival and information

All trains on the north coast line between Chester and Holyhead stop at Bangor's **train station** on Station Road, at the bottom of Holyhead Road. From here, Deiniol Road, Bangor's main street, runs along the bottom of the valley, changing its name to Garth Road and continuing almost to the pier. The long High Street runs one block parallel to the south; to the north, the grandiose buildings of the university dominate the skyline of Upper Bangor. National Express and local **buses** stop on a short spur of Garth Road, a few steps from the **tourist office** on Deiniol Road (April–Sept Mon, Wed & Fri 9.30am–4pm, Tues, Thurs & Sat 9.30am–5pm; ☎01248/352786, Ⓔbangor .tic@gwynedd.gov.uk). **Alternative information**, on anything from the local green scene to women's and gay groups, is best found at the redoubtable **Greenhouse/Tŷ Gwydr** resource centre, 1 Trevelyan Terrace (Mon–Fri 9am–5pm; ☎01248/355821, Ⓦwww.tygwydr.com), at the northern end of High Street. If nothing else, you should be able to pick up a copy of the monthly *Network News* from here, which has details of New Age events in the locality. The **library**, opposite the tourist office on Ffordd Gwynedd (Mon, Tues, Thurs & Fri 9.30am–7pm, Wed & Sat 9.30am–1pm) has free **Internet** access.

Though you might be discouraged by the many hills in and around town, **bikes** can be rented from Snowdonia Surf and Mountain, 75 High St (☎01248/354321) for £25 a day, and at the youth hostel (see below).

Accommodation

With relatively few tourists, Bangor doesn't have a huge choice of accommodation, particularly mid-range and fancy hotels. Most of the cheaper options are at the northern end of Garth Road, about twenty minutes' walk from the train station. The nearest **campsite** is the cheap and cheerful *Treborth Hall Farm* (☎01248/364104; £5–8 per pitch), a mile or so out of town off the A487 between the two Menai Strait bridges and easily walkable from Upper Bangor (though #5 buses pass the entrance).

Bangor YHA Tan-y-Bryn ☎0870/770 5686, ⓔbangor@yha.org.uk. A large house with bunks (£12.50) signposted on the right of the A56, 10min east of the centre and reached either by walking along High Street or taking bus #5, #6 or #7 along Garth Road.

Dilfan Garth Rd ☎01248/353030. Marginally the best in a row of three serviceable, low-cost B&Bs. ❷

Eryl Môr Hotel 2 Upper Garth Rd ☎01248/353789, ⓦwww.erylmorhotel.co.uk. Quiet, comfy, fully licensed hotel with some rooms overlooking Bangor's pier and the Menai Strait. Some en-suites. ❷/❹

Regency Hotel Holyhead Rd ☎01248/370819. Good-value small hotel noted chiefly for its proximity to the train station. ❷

Tŷ Mawr Farm half a mile east of Llanddeiniolen, 5 miles southwest of Bangor on the B4366 ☎01286/670147, ⓦwww.tymawrfarm.co.uk. Cosy B&B on a working farm with views of Snowdonia and very good homemade food. Quality, well-equipped self-catering cottages also available for short lets outside the school holidays. ❸

The Town

Straddling the hill that separates the town centre from the Menai Strait, the university takes up much of **Upper Bangor**. The shape of the college's main building is almost an exact replica of the **cathedral**, directly below on the other side of Deiniol Road (daily 11am–5pm; free), which boasts the longest continuous use of any cathedral in Britain, easily predating the town's existence. Nowadays only a blocked-in Norman window gives any hint of the see's ancient origins. Though you won't want to spend a lot of time here, it's worth venturing into the spacious white-walled interior, particularly to see the sixteenth-century wooden **Mostyn Christ**, depicted bound and seated on a rock.

Little is recorded of the original cathedral until it was destroyed and then rebuilt by the Normans in 1071, only to be damaged by the Vikings two years later. Archbishop Baldwin preached here in 1188 while raising support for the Third Crusade, when his chronicler, Giraldus Cambrensis, was shown a double vault by the high altar containing Owain Gwynedd and his brother Cadwaladr. Owain was posthumously excommunicated by Archbishop Thomas for incest with his first cousin, and the Bishop of Bangor was asked to remove his body from the cathedral. Though it was probably re-interred in the churchyard, many believe it lies within the arched tomb in the south transept.

Trashed by King John (1211), Edward I (1277) and Owain Glyndŵr (1402), its reconstructions resulted in the present thirteenth- to fifteenth-century edifice, heavily restored by Gilbert Scott in 1866. Outside, there's a **Bible Garden** with a collection of all the biblical trees, shrubs and flowers capable of withstanding the local climate.

Across the road on Ffordd Gwynedd, the former Canonry now houses the **Bangor Museum and Art Gallery** (Tues–Fri 12.30–4.30pm, Sat 10.30am–4.30pm; free), where the standard regional museum fare and snippets of local history are enlivened by refurbished traditional costumes and an archeology room containing the most complete Roman sword found in Wales. The most insightful rooms are those devoted to a complete set of furniture from a moderately wealthy Cricieth farm, covering three hundred years of acquisitions, from brooding Welsh dressers to fine Italian pieces. Furniture also forms the basis of the museum's homage to Thomas Telford, whose favourite chair sits alongside a model of his bridge complete with the web of chains that were stripped off the bridge during strengthening in 1935, when they were found to be heavy and unnecessary. The art gallery downstairs has no permanent collection, its temporary displays concentrating on predominantly Welsh contemporary works.

Heading away from the centre, Telford's bridge is best appreciated by walking on to it, but there's also a fine view of it from Bangor's pristine **Victorian Pier** (Mon–Fri 8.30am–dusk, Sat & Sun 10am–dusk; 25p), which juts 1550 feet into the Menai Strait – over halfway across to Anglesey. Built in 1896, the pier lay derelict for years, but was restored in the mid-1990s, with a token amusement pavilion. It's just a fifteen-minute walk from the town centre and makes a good place to sit and watch the world drift idly by.

Eating, drinking and entertainment

Bangor has few really good **restaurants**, though as befits a university town there are lots of places to eat reasonably well at modest cost. These are scattered around town, several clustering around the student bedsit-land of Upper Bangor along Holyhead Road. High Street is the best zone for grazing or stocking up for a journey, with an abundance of cheap cafés, pasta and sandwich joints.

Restaurants and cafés

Fat Cat Café Bar 161 High St. Breezy modern decor and a moderately priced menu – from massive burgers to salmon-and-broccoli pasta quills – help pack this place out with students and locals.

Garden 1 High St. Good Cantonese restaurant offering a broad but not overwhelming menu; three-course weekday lunchtime specials for under £9.

Greek Taverna Politis 12 Holyhead Rd ☎01248/354991. Expect to pay £7–10 for souvlaki and stifado favourites and top-class Greek salads served around the fire, in the airy conservatory or outside in the courtyard. Cheaper meals at the bar and jazz every Mon.

Herbs 307–309 High St. Great daytime vegetarian café with a salad bar, serving two-course specials for £8. Closed Sun.

Papillon 347a High St ☎01248/360248. Casual café-bar decorated with flowers and local artwork, offering a range of breakfasts, bruschettas, light meals and desserts. Upstairs is more formal, serving tapas and an international range of mains (£9–13).

Penrhyn Castle Tearoom Penrhyn Castle (see below). When visiting Penrhyn be sure to leave time for lunch (or at least tea and cake), selecting from dishes based on recipes once used in the castle; the leek and cheese bread and butter pudding is very good as is the lamb pie (both around £6). Save room for desserts such as the rosemary and orange cake or a Welsh cream tea.

Pubs, entertainment and nightlife

Belle Vue Holyhead Rd. Bangor's big student pub, right next to the university and heaving at the weekend. Good real ales.

Tafarn Y Glôb 7 Albert St, Upper Bangor. If you've tried to learn any of the language, you can put it to good use at this traditional local where ordering in Welsh is pretty much *de rigueur*. For a pint of beer, try "Un peint o cwrw, os gwelwch yn dda" (pronounced "een paint o gooroo, os gweloch un tha").

Theatr Gwynedd Deiniol Rd ☎01248/351708, ⊛www.theatrgwynedd.co.uk. Along with its counterpart in Mold, Theatr Gwynedd is the most progressive art house in north Wales and is about

your only chance of seeing contemporary plays or even slightly offbeat movies.
University Students' Union Deiniol Rd ☎01248/353709. Fly posters around town almost all point you to the Students' Union as

the venue for touring rock/pop bands or the *Amser/Time* nightclub. Usually quiet over the summer break.
Y Castell/The Castle Glanrafon. Big, lively student pub, bang opposite the cathedral.

Penrhyn Castle

There can hardly be a more vulgar testament to the Anglo-Welsh gentry's oppression of the rural Welsh than the nonetheless compelling **Penrhyn Castle** (late March to June, Sept & Oct daily except Tues noon–5pm; July & Aug daily except Tues 11am–5pm; £7, £5 grounds, kitchens & railway museum only; NT), two miles east of Bangor, which overlooks Port Penrhyn from its acres of isolating parkland. Built on the backs of slate miners for the benefit of their bosses, this monstrous nineteenth-century neo-Norman fancy, with over three hundred rooms dripping with luxurious fittings, was funded by the quarry's huge profits.

The responsibility falls ultimately on Caribbean sugar plantation owner, slave trader and vehement anti-abolitionist Richard Pennant, First Baron Penrhyn, who built a port on the northeastern edge of Bangor in order to ship his Bethesda slate to the world. But it was his self-aggrandizing great-great-nephew George Dawkins who inherited the 40,000-acre estate added his ancestor's surname to his own, and with the aid of architect Thomas Hopper spent thirteen years from 1827 encasing the neo-Gothic hall in a Norman fortress complete with monumental five-storey keep.

Vulgar though it may be, the decoration is impressive, and fairly true to the Romanesque, with its deeply cut chevrons, billets and double-cone ornamentation. Hopper even looked to Norman architecture for the design of the furniture, but abandoned historical authenticity when it came to installing the central heating system, which piped hot air through ornamental brass ducts at the cost of twenty tons of coal a month.

Everything is on a massive scale and no more so than in the Great Hall with its pair of stained-glass zodiac windows by Thomas Willement. Three-foot-thick oak doors separate subsequent rooms: the Library, with its full-size slate billiard table, and the oppressive Ebony Room, which leads onto the Grand Staircase. Upstairs, the lightness of the original William Morris wallpaper and drapes around the King's Bed are in marked contrast to the Slate Bed, designed for Queen Victoria but declined by her in favour of the Hopper-designed four-poster in the State Bedroom. The family managed to assemble the country's largest private **painting collection**. Much of this remains, especially in the two dining rooms, where there's a Gainsborough landscape, Canaletto's *The Thames at Westminster,* and a Rembrandt portrait. During the Blitz of 1940, some 1800 masterpieces from Britain's National Gallery were sent here for safekeeping, though Lord Penrhyn's drunken clumsiness and demands for rental payments forced the then Prime Minister, Winston Churchill, to have the treasures moved to a former slate mine at Manod for the rest of the war.

Away from the pomp you can visit the enormous **kitchens** convincingly laid out as if about to cater to the 1894 visit of the Prince and Princess of Wales, and the **Industrial Railway Museum** (same hours; entry with castle or grounds tickets), packed with gleaming examples of rolling stock once used on the estate's quarry-to-port rail line. Leave time too for the sumptuous gardens and the excellent café (see opposite). **Buses** #5, #6 and #7 run frequently from Bangor to Penrhyn's gates, a mile-long walk from the house.

Vaynol Estate

On the other side of Bangor from Penrhyn, spend an hour or two on the waymarked walks through the mixed woods and parkland of **Vaynol Estate** (Glan Faenol; unrestricted access; NT), which look across the ever-changing waters of the Menai Strait to the gentle frontage of Plas Newydd (see p.487). Once the estate of the privately owned Vaynol Hall (no access), the grounds sport some curious follies, most obviously the round tower built to rival the Marquess of Anglesey's Column (see p.486) in Llanfairpwll on Anglesey. Access to Vaynol's car park and the walking trails is via the business park at the southern roundabout of the Britannia Bridge (A487/A5). Once inside Parc Menai, go down Ffordd y Parc and left into Ffordd y Plas, following the lane past Vaynol Hall and chapel.

Anglesey

The island of **Anglesey** (Ynys Môn) is a world apart from Wales, let alone the rest of Britain. After the mountains and hemmed-in settlements of Snowdonia, this green ripple of fields and farms comes as a bit of a shock. Seen from the four-lane A55 expressway which speeds across Anglesey towards Holyhead, the island can look dull, but take to the older A5, or the smaller roads, and you'll discover plenty to see and do.

Signs and slogans announce Anglesey as Mam Cymru, "The Mother of Wales", attesting to the island's former importance as the country's breadbasket. In the twelfth century, Giraldus Cambrensis noted that "When crops have failed in other regions, this island, from its soil and its abundant produce, has been able to supply all Wales". While feeding their less productive kin in Snowdonia is no longer a priority, the land remains predominantly agricultural, with small fields, stone walls and white houses reminiscent of parts of Ireland and England. Linguistically and politically, though, Anglesey is intensely Welsh, a Plaid Cymru stronghold with over seventy percent of its population using Welsh as their first language – one of the country's highest proportions of native speakers. Most residents will at least understand the lines of one of Anglesey's most famous poets, Goronwy Owen, whose eulogy on his homeland translates as "All hail to Anglesey/ The delight of all regions/ Bountiful as a second Eden/ Or an ancient paradise". Judging by the numbers who flock to the island's necklace of fine sandy coves and rocky headlands, many agree with Owen, but just as many charge straight through from Bangor to **Holyhead** and the Irish ferries, missing out on Wales' greatest concentration of pre-Christian sites and some superb coastal scenery.

The earliest people on Anglesey were Mesolithic hunters who arrived between 8000 and 4000 BC. Around 2500 BC, a new culture developed among the small farming communities, giving rise to the many henges and stone circles on the island, that held sway until the Celts swept across Europe in the seventh century BC, led by their priestly class, the druids. In the centuries prior to the Roman invasion, Anglesey – well positioned at the apex of Celtic sea traffic – became the most important druidic centre in Europe. The druids were so firmly established

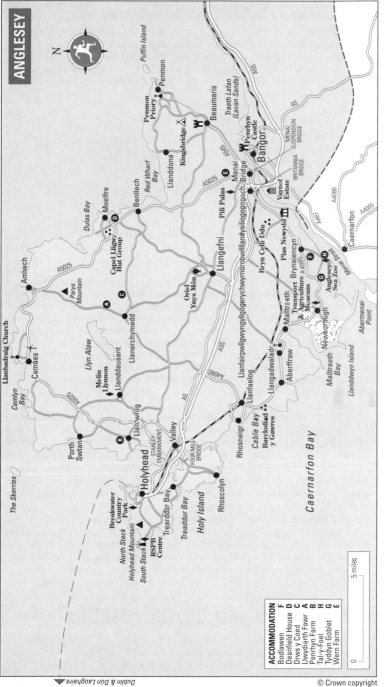

ANGLESEY

N

Dublin & Dún Laoghaire

The Skerries

Porth Swtan
Cemlyn Bay
Cemaes
Llanbadrig Church
Llyn Alaw
Amlwch
Parys Mountain
Melin Llynnon
Llanddeusant
Llanerchymedd
Llantrisant
Valley
STANLEY EMBANKMENT
FOUR MILE BRIDGE
Breakwater Country Park
North Stack
South Stack
Holyhead Mountain
RSPB Centre
Holyhead
Trearddur Bay
Treaddur Bay
Holy Island
Rhoscolyn
Rhosneigr
Cable Bay
Barclodiad y Gawres
Aberffraw
Llangadwaladr
Llangaffo
Llantaelog
Newborough
Malltraeth Bay
Llanddwyn Island
Caernarfon Bay
Abermenai Point
Malltraeth
Transport & Agriculture Museum
Brynsiencyn
Anglesey Sea Zoo
Plas Newydd
Bryn Celli Ddu
Llanfairpwllgwyngyllgogerychwyrndrobwllllantysiliogogogoch
Menai Bridge
Pili Palas
Llangefni
Oriel Ynys Môn
Capel Lligwy Hut Group
Dulas Bay
Moelfre
Benllech
Red Wharf Bay
Llanddona
Llanbedrgoch
Beaumaris
Kingsbridge
Penmon Priory
Penmon
Puffin Island
Traeth Lafan (Lavan Sands)
Penrhyn Castle
Bangor
Vaynol Estate
MENAI SUSPENSION BRIDGE
BRITANNIA BRIDGE
Caernarfon

A5025
A5025
A5
A5
A55
A55
A4080
A4080
A4080
A4085
A4086
A487
A5
A545
A5025

0   5 miles

© Crown copyright

7

THE NORTH COAST AND ANGLESEY | Anglesey

479

Anglesey's rural B&Bs

The island is so compact that, at least if you have your own transport, the choice of **accommodation** should be based on factors other than solely location. There are some excellent, moderately priced B&Bs and farmhouses, many relatively distant from any recognized sight, but no less appealing for it. Several of the better ones have been listed below and marked on our map of Anglesey; see the accounts on the following pages for details.

Bodlawen Brynsiencyn (see p.488). ❸
Drws-Y-Coed Llanerchymedd (see p.494). ❹
Llwydiarth Fawr Llanerchymedd (see p.494). ❹
Penrhyn Farm Llanfwrog (see p.494). ❸
Tal-y-Foel Dwyran (see p.488). ❹
Tyddyn Goblet Brynsiencyn (see p.488). ❷
Wern Farm near Menai Bridge (see opposite). ❺

that Anglesey was the last place in Wales to fall to the Romans. When the Romans finally invaded in 61 AD, the ensuing massacre and extirpation of drudic worship was described by the Roman historian Tacitus:

Women were seen rushing through the ranks of soldiers in wild disorder, dressed in black, with their hair dishevelled and brandishing flaming torches. Their whole appearance resembled the frantic rage of the Furies. The druids were ranged in order, calling down terrible curses. The soldiers, paralysed by this strange spectacle, stood still and offered themselves as a target for wounds. But at last the promptings of the general – and their own rallying of each other – urged them not to be frightened of a mob of women and fanatics. They advanced the standards, cut down all who met them and swallowed them up in their own fires. After this a garrison was placed over the conquered islanders, and the groves sacred to savage rites were cut down.

The vacuum left by the Romans' departure in the fifth century was soon filled by the greatest of all Welsh dynasties, the Princes of Gwynedd, who held court at **Aberffraw**. Under Rhodri Mawr, in the ninth century, their influence spread over most of Wales as he defeated the encroaching Vikings, earning thanks from Charlemagne for his efforts. Anglesey again fell to outsiders towards the end of the thirteenth century when Edward I defeated the Welsh princes, sealing the island's fate by forging the final link in his Iron Ring of castles at **Beaumaris**, nowadays by far the most absorbing town on the island.

Getting around the island is easy enough. The train line from Bangor crosses the Menai Strait, stopping at the station with the longest name in the world – usually abbreviated to **Llanfairpwll** or Llanfair PG – before continuing on to meet the ferries at Holyhead. The rest of the island is covered by a bus network, thoroughly detailed in the free *Ynys Môn* public transport timetable.

Menai Bridge and the approaches

Two bridges – both engineering marvels of their time – link Anglesey to the mainland over the **Menai Strait**, a perilous fourteen-mile-long tidal race that in places narrows to two hundred yards wide, forcing the current up to eight knots as it rushes between Conwy and Caernarfon bays. The view from the mainland over to Anglesey is impressive enough, but outdone by the eastward vistas from the Anglesey shore, where you can look over the rocky mid-channel islets, some adorned with jetties and small houses, and backed by the heartland of Snowdonia.

For centuries before the bridges were built, drovers used the Strait's narrow stretches to herd Anglesey-fattened cattle on their way to market in England. Travellers had to wait for low tide to cross Lafan Sands, northeast of Bangor, then find a boat to take them across to Beaumaris, in foggy weather guided only by the sound of church bells. So it's not surprising that Irish MPs, needing transport to Westminster and a faster mail service, pushed for a fixed crossing.

The first permanent link, in 1826, was Telford's graceful **Menai Suspension Bridge**, the world's first large iron suspension bridge, spanning 579 feet between piers and 100 feet above the water to allow high-masted sailing ships to pass. Almost everything about the project was novel, including the process of lifting the first 23-ton cable into place, which involved a pulley system and 150 men kept in time by a fife band. They celebrated their achievement by running across the nine-inch-wide chain from Anglesey to the mainland.

In 1850, Robert Stephenson also made engineering history with his **Britannia Tubular Bridge**, which carried trains across the strait in twin wrought-iron tubes. It burned down in 1970, however, leaving only the limestone piers that now support the twin-deck A5/A55 road and rail bridge to Llanfairpwll and Holyhead.

Nestling in the shadow of the older crossing, with a few private islands to break the view across the strait to the mainland, is the town of **MENAI BRIDGE** (Porthaethwy). A short bus ride (#53, #57 or #58) or just over half an hour's pleasant walk from Bangor affords views from the bridge over to the fourteenth-century **Church of St Tysilio** (open mid-July to Aug) on Church Island, where its patron saint founded his cell around 630 AD. Topped by a Celtic cross war memorial, the island has delightful views along the Strait and to both bridges. It can be reached through the woodland behind the car park on the approach to the Menai Bridge itself, or from the town along a causeway and waterside promenade named Belgian Walk (having been built by refugees during World War I).

If you have children to amuse, take the B5420 two miles northeast of the village to **Pili Palas** (mid-March to Oct daily 10am–5.30pm; Nov–Christmas Eve daily 11am–3.30pm; £5), a steamy walk-in butterfly house with up to seventy species, some as big as your hand. British butterflies that are becoming less common in the wild are bred for release here, a venture promoted in the educational material available for kids. An aviary and vivarium complete the set up.

Practicalities

If you plan to **stay** in Menai Bridge, be sure to book ahead at the amazingly hospitable *Wern Farm* (☎01248/712421, ⓦwww.angleseyfarms.com; ❺), two miles north of town, off the A5025, whose farmhouse dates from the early seventeenth century. Back in town, the choice of **places to eat** is surprisingly good, the best being *Tafarn y Bont* (☎01248/714864) right by the bridge on Telford Road, with refreshingly original wine-bar food in cosy rooms or an airy conservatory. Worthy alternatives include the pub grub and superb beer at the cosy *Liverpool Arms* on St George's Pier, and *Ruby* on Dale Sreet (☏01248/714999), a minimalist bistro with delicious food (mains £10–16).

Beaumaris

The original inhabitants of **BEAUMARIS** (Biwmares) were evicted by Edward I to make way for the construction of his new castle and bastide town, dubbed "beautiful marsh" in a ploy to attract English settlers. Today the place can still seem like the small English outpost Edward intended, with a grand Georgian terrace (designed by Joseph Hansom, of cab fame) and more plummy English accents than you'll have heard for a while. Many of their owners belong with the flotilla of yachts, an echo of the port's fleet of merchant ships, which disappeared with the completion of the Menai bridges and subsequent growth of Holyhead.

Beaumaris is not only attractive, it boasts more sights than the rest of Anglesey put together. This inevitably brings the crowds here in summer, though even then the evenings are peaceful, with day-trippers gone and overnighters ensconced in their hotel restaurants.

Arrival and accommodation

With no trains, long-distance coaches or proper tourist office, Beaumaris seems poorly served, but it has a regular **bus** service to Bangor (#53, #57 and #58), and the Town Hall, next to the *Bulkeley Hotel* on Castle Street, stocks leaflets and will advise on local amenities. There are no real budget **places to stay** except for the *Kingsbridge* campsite, two miles northeast towards Penmon (☏01248/490636; £11 per pitch).

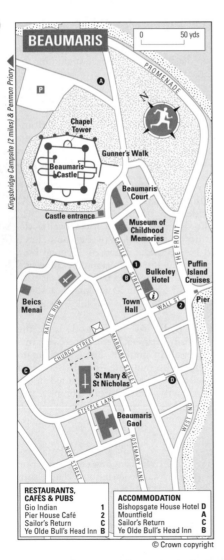

Kingsbridge Campsite (2 miles) & Penmon Priory

BEAUMARIS

0   50 yds

PROMENADE

Ⓐ

P

Chapel Tower

Gunner's Walk

Beaumaris Castle

Beaumaris Court

Castle entrance

Museum of Childhood Memories

THE FRONT

CASTLE STREET

❶ Bulkeley Hotel

Ⓑ

Puffin Island Cruises

Beics Menai

RATING ROW

Town Hall

ⓘ

WALL ST

❷

Pier

CHURCH STREET

MARGARET STREET

Ⓒ

'St Mary & St Nicholas

Ⓓ

STEEPLE LANE

Beaumaris Gaol

NEW STREET

ROSEMARY LANE

WEST END

RESTAURANTS, CAFÉS & PUBS	
Gio Indian	1
Pier House Café	2
Sailor's Return	C
Ye Olde Bull's Head Inn	B

ACCOMMODATION	
Bishopsgate House Hotel	D
Mountfield	A
Sailor's Return	C
Ye Olde Bull's Head Inn	B

© Crown copyright

△ Beaumaris

Hotels and guesthouses

Bishopsgate House Hotel 54 Castle St ☎01248/810302, ⓦwww.bishopsgatehousehotel .co.uk. High-standard, predominantly business-oriented hotel in an elegant Georgian townhouse with chintzy decor, all the expected facilities and a good restaurant. ❺

Mountfield immediately east of the castle ☎01248/810380. Attractive guesthouse an easy walk into town, with great views of Menai Strait and the castle. ❹

Sailor's Return Church St ☎01248/811314, ⓦwww.sailorsreturn.co.uk. Simple en-suite rooms above this good town pub, with decent food, and breakfast included in the price. ❹

🏃 **Ye Olde Bull's Head Inn** 18 Castle St ☎01248/810329, ⓦwww.bullsheadinn .co.uk. The best hotel in Beaumaris, this ancient and luxurious coaching inn was used as General Mytton's headquarters during the Civil War and, in more peaceful circumstances, by Dr Johnson and Charles Dickens. It has a fantastic restaurant and bistro (see p.486). ❻

The Town and around

While you can spend an hour or two mooching around Beaumaris's antique shops, enjoying the views across the Strait towards Bangor and along the coast to Llandudno's Great Orme from the stumpy pier, this shouldn't distract from the main attractions. The **castle** remains central to Beaumaris, its water-filled moat and loop-holed ramparts satisfying the British castle archetype more than any other in Wales. The law and order theme continues in the **court** and **gaol**, both offering their own angle on Welsh subjugation. In good weather, a cruise out around **Puffin Island** or a wander along the nearby coastline close to **Penmon Priory** may suit better.

The Castle

Beaumaris Castle (June–Sept daily 9.30am–6pm; mid-March to May & Oct daily 9.30am–5pm; Nov to mid-March Mon–Sat 9.30am–4pm, Sun 11am–4pm; £3; CADW) is the most picturesque of Edward's gargantuan fortresses, built in response to Madog ap Llywelyn's capture of Caernarfon in 1294. Its

Gio Indian 13 Castle St ☎01248/810623.
Reasonable curries at modest prices.
Pier House Café Bron Menai, The Front. Bright
and cheerful licensed café with sea views and
serving decent espressos, pastries and cakes as
well as all-day breakfasts (£5–6), bagels, grills and
daily specials.
Sailor's Return Church St. Town pub best known
for its excellent bar meals and therefore not too
smoky for eating at lunchtimes.

 Ye Olde Bull's Head Inn (see p.483).
Beaumaris's top hotel doesn't disappoint

when it comes to eating and drinking. There's a
cosy old-fashioned bar but a more modern angle
to the brasserie with bare boards and slate
interior where you might expect prosciutto,
sun-dried tomato and asparagus pasta (£8)
followed by white chocolate and summer fruit
terrine (£4.50). The upstairs restaurant is more
formal though no less contemporary and
serving three courses (£33) extending to the
likes of lamb and pistachio terrine, and pan-fried
venison.

Llanfairpwllgwyngyllgogerychwyrndro bwllllandysiliogogogoch and the south coast

When Robert Louis Stephenson wrote "to travel hopefully is a better thing than to arrive" he might have been thinking of **LLANFAIRPWLL**, the village with the longest place name in Britain and little else but for a wool shop and a small train station (request stop only) bearing the famed sign **Llanfair pwllgwyngyllgogerychwyrndrobwllllandysiliogogogoch**. Sadly, "St Mary's Church in the hollow of white hazel near a rapid whirlpool and the Church of St Tysilio near the red cave" is no authentic Welsh tongue twister; simply the fabrication of a Menai Bridge tailor in the 1880s, who added to the original first five syllables in an attempt to draw tourists – as indeed it has.

Coming from Bangor, half a mile before the town you'll probably notice the bronze figure atop the 91-foot-high Doric **Marquess of Anglesey's Column** (daily 9am–5pm; £1.50). The apocryphal story has him declaring to Wellington, on having a leg blown off at Waterloo, "Begod, there goes me leg", to which Wellington dryly replied, "Begod, so it do". There hadn't been much love lost between them since the Marquess ran off with Wellington's sister-in-law some years previously. You can climb the 115 steps up to the Marquess to share his view across the strait to Snowdonia, and see his replacement leg at Plas Newydd, close to Bryn Celli Ddu: two good reasons to spend time in the area.

Practicalities

The main reason to stop in Llanfairpwll itself is to visit the **tourist office** by the station (Mon–Sat 9.30am–5.30pm, Sun 10am–5pm; closes 5pm Oct–Easter; ☎01248/713177, ✉llanfairpwll@nwtic.com), the only one worth its salt on the island. It is packed with free leaflets: look out for ones detailing "Historic Anglesey" and a series of "Circular Walks on the isle of Anglesey".

Trains continue from Llanfairpwll to Rhosneigr and Holyhead, but to visit the rest of the **south coast** you're reliant on **buses**. In high summer the handiest is the hourly #42 **bus** that passes Plas Newydd and Bryn Celli Ddu, Brynsiencyn and Newborough on its way to Aberffraw and Llangefni (see p.496). No buses continue along the south coast, so services to Rhosneigr are limited to the infrequent #25 from Holyhead and the slightly more regular #45 from Llangefni.

Plas Newydd

A mile and a half along the A4080 southwest of Llanfairpwll is the approach to **Plas Newydd** (April–Oct daily except Thurs & Fri noon–5pm; gardens open an hour earlier; £5, garden only £3; NT). Though now owned by the National Trust, the house remains, as it has been since the eighteenth century, the home of the marquesses of Anglesey. A house had stood on this site since the sixteenth century, but it was the First Marquess's huge profits from Parys Mountain (see p.495) and other ventures that paid for its transformation by James Wyatt and Joseph Potter into a Gothic mansion in the late eighteenth century. Potter designed the pleasing, castellated stable block that almost upstages the modest-looking three-storey house with incongruous Tudor caps on slender octagonal turrets.

Inside, the Gothic Hall, with its Potter-designed fan-vaulted ceiling, leads to the longest and most finely decorated room in the house, the Music Room, originally the great hall. All available space is covered with oil paintings, including portraits of the First Marquess and Lady Paget, his first wife, both by John Hoppner. Despite the Gothic start, Wyatt was given free rein in the rest of the house, and there's a transition to the Neoclassical on entering the Staircase Hall with its cantilevered staircase and deceptively solid-looking Doric columns, actually just painted wood. Predominantly dull paintings line the gallery, mainly portraits of monarchs and most family members, though those of the Sixth Marquess and his sister are the work of Rex Whistler, who spent two years here in the 1930s. A minor exhibition in a former kitchen celebrates the artist, but it's in the **Rex Whistler Room** that you'll find Plas Newydd's glory and Whistler's masterwork: a whole 58-foot-long wall consumed by the magnificent trompe l'oeil painting of some imaginary seascape seen from a promenade. At first it seems utterly incongruous but you are soon drawn into the fantasy, your position seeming to shift by over a mile as you walk along, altering your perspective on the mountains of Snowdonia and a whimsical composite of elements. Portmeirion is there, as are the Round Tower from Windsor Castle and the steeple from St Martin-in-the-Fields in London. Whistler himself appears as a gondolier, and again as a gardener in one of the two right-angled panels at either end, which appear to extend the room further.

The **Cavalry Museum**, a few rooms further on, exhibits the world's first articulated leg, a synthesis of wood, leather and springs, designed for the First Marquess who lost his leg at Waterloo. By the time you've also visited the Neolithic **cromlech** located in grounds landscaped by Humphrey Repton in the early nineteenth century, you'll need to allow a couple of hours, plus an extra forty minutes for a **historic cruise** on the *Star Queen* (June to early Sept daily except Thurs & Fri noon-4pm; £5), which plies the Menai Strait. Recover in the former milking parlour, now a fine tiled tearoom serving tasty snacks and light meals (open daily in summer).

Bryn Celli Ddu

Almost a mile past Plas Newydd, a signposted side road leads half a mile north to **Bryn Celli Ddu** (unrestricted access; CADW), the "Mound of the Dark Chamber", one of the island's most significant prehistoric sites. It is an atmospheric spot, overlooked by a natural rock that may have been its precursor as a place of worship, and by the purple mountains of Snowdonia. Reached along a ten-minute path from the car park, it was built by Anglesey's late Neolithic inhabitants four thousand years ago. Several seasons of digs have shown it to be an extensive religious site, but today all you can see is a well-proportioned henge and stone circle, later built over to turn it into a passage grave beneath an earthen mound. The original entrance stone was whisked off to the National Museum in Cardiff, but a replica gives an idea of its carved spiral patterns. In the last chamber you'll find an impressive, smooth monolith under a rather less than impressive supporting concrete beam. The #42 **bus** passes within half a mile, as does the #4 (only when it goes to nearby Llanddaniel Fab); otherwise it's an hour-long walk from Llanfairpwll.

Anglesey Sea Zoo and Brynsiencyn

Facing Caernarfon across the Menai Strait, seven miles southwest of Llanfairpwll, **Anglesey Sea Zoo** (mid-March to Oct daily 10am–6pm; £6.95; ℡01248/430411, ⓦwww.angleseyseazoo.co.uk), is one of the most absorbing attractions on Anglesey. Local marine environments are simulated in wave tanks, and in shallow pools where plaice, turbot and dogfish, camouflaged against the shingle bottom, are barely visible from the catwalks above. They haven't entirely got away from glass-sided tanks, but most are large and the contents chosen to depict specific environments: tidal flats, quayside, wrecks and kelp forest amongst them. In keeping with the buildings' previous functions as an oyster hatchery and lobster breeding farm, the zoo uses aquaculture to give the lobsters a much greater chance of survival once released into the wild, and you can view an industrial-looking plant producing table salt from local seawater, which is sold in the shop and used in the zoo's café.

The only useful bus service (#42) stops in the unremarkable village of **BRYNSIENCYN**, two miles to the north. Between the Sea Zoo and Brynsiencyn there's **accommodation** at *Bodlawen* (℡01248/430379; ❸), a large modern guesthouse overlooking the Menai Strait and Caernarfon with a relaxed atmosphere and an acclaimed opera-singing owner, Marian Roberts. Alternatively, try the bargain *Tyddyn Goblet* (℡01248/430296; ❷), a characterful farmhouse just off the A4080, or *Tal-y-Foel* (℡01248/430977, ⓦwww.tal-y-foel.co.uk; ❹), a particularly nice farmhouse B&B just north of Brynsiencyn at Dwyran.

Newborough and Malltraeth

Three miles southwest of the Sea Zoo, the end of the Menai Strait is marked by Abermenai Point, a huge sand bar backed by the 600-acre **Newborough Warren** (unrestricted access), one of the most important dune systems anywhere in Britain. Rabbits are common here, as are the otherwise rare thick-horned Soay sheep, Britain's oldest native breed. Since 1948, much of the land has been clad in pines which stabilize the ground and provide habitat for goldcrests, warblers and rare native red squirrels, justifying the Warren's designation as a National Nature Reserve.

Three main trails, all well marked and none more than an hour or two's stroll, weave through the pines to **Llanddwyn Island**, a glorious peninsula of rocky coves and sandy beaches. On it stands Tŷr Mawr (the Great Tower), built in 1800 to warn the ships in Caernarfon Bay, later supplanted by the disused lighthouse, built in 1873 in the style of an Anglesey windmill. There's also a row of restored cottages and a thirteenth-century church ruin dedicated to the patron saint of lovers in Wales, St Dwynwen. In the fifth century, after her abortive affair with Welsh prince Maelon, Dwynwen became a nun at Llanddwyn and requested that hopeful lovers who make a supplication to God in her name should receive divine assistance.

Access to the Newborough Warren section of the reserve is from a free car park down a short track from the roundabout where the A4080 bends north. The main walk from here is out to Abermenai Point (2 miles), but be careful, as rapid tidal changes can quickly cover the broad sandy approach. To reach the reserve's main entrance (and Llanddwyn Island), continue north along the A4080 for half a mile to **NEWBOROUGH** (Niwbwrch), a town of limited appeal founded by Edward I to rehouse villagers displaced during the building of Beaumaris. From the village a road leads a mile down to a signposted toll barrier (have a couple of pound coins handy) and a second car park. A third of a mile down this access road it is worth stopping briefly at **Llys Rhosyr** (unrestricted access), the ruined footings of several buildings which represent the partially excavated remains of the pre-thirteenth-century court of the Princes of Gwynedd.

Family entertainments around Newborough extend to the **Anglesey Model Village**, a mile south on the A4080 (Easter–Sept daily 10.30am–5pm; £2.25), with its 1:12 scale models of Anglesey landmarks and a model railway; and the **Anglesey Transport and Agriculture Museum**, signposted a mile east of Newborough (April–Sept daily 11am–4pm; £3.50), with several dozen classic and vintage vehicles in a big shed.

From 1945 until his death in 1979, the estuarine beaches to the north and around **MALLTRAETH** were the haunt of **Charles Tunnicliffe**, who spent much of his days producing beautifully detailed wildlife drawings. Birds were always his chief subject, and throughout his fifty-year career he produced thousands of intricate illustrations for other people's works besides six books of his own, including *Shorelands Summer Diary*, largely researched around Newborough and named after his house on the shoreline just north of the bridge in Malltraeth. Examples of Tunnicliffe's work form a significant part of the Oriel Ynys Môn exhibition in Llangefni (see p.496).

Around Aberffraw

The area around Newborough and tiny **LLANGADWALADR**, three miles northwest, was once the seat of the great ruling dynasty of the Princes of Gwynedd who, from the seventh-century reign of Cadfan until Llywelyn ap Gruffydd's death in 1282, controlled northwest Wales, and often much of the rest of the country, from this now-quiet corner of Anglesey. The most substantial evidence lies in **Llangadwaladr Church** (usually closed except for Sun mornings; call ☎01407/840282 for the key), built in the thirteenth century with a memorial plaque, carved in Latin about 625, incorporated into an inside wall. It reads "Cadfan the King, wisest and most renowned of all kings". **CABLE BAY** (Porth Trecastell), two miles northwest of Aberffraw, was the eastern terminus of the first telegraph cable to Ireland, though it is now better known for its good sandy beach, popular with **surfers**. On the headland to the north, the heavily reconstructed remains of the 5000-year-old **Barclodiad y Gawres** burial chamber are more dramatic than nearby Bryn Celli Ddu but harder to see, as CADW have perversely seen fit to keep it locked at all times – to get inside, obtain the key from the Wayside Stores, a mile north in Llanfaelog (Mon–Sat 7am–7pm Sun 8am–6pm), and bring a torch. Without artificial light, you won't really see the stones carved with chevrons and zigzag patterns, similar to Newgrange and other Boyne Valley sites seventy miles across the water in Ireland. Bus #25 from Holyhead and Rhosneigr passes by.

Rhosneigr

The weekday roar of fighter jets from the nearby RAF Valley airfield deafens you long before you reach the otherwise peaceful Edwardian seaside resort of **RHOSNEIGR**, two miles further north along the coast. Rambling over consolidated dunes behind a series of small bays, Rhosneigr remains justifiably popular with English holiday-makers after a century of patronage, although space on the beach is these days contested by the dozens of devoted **windsurf-ers** who flock here when the wind is right. It's the sort of low-key place you might feel like joining in: rent a board and rig from Funsport, 1 Beach Rd (℡01407/810899, ⓦwww.buckys.co.uk; £16 per half-day, tuition £15/hr) and take to the sea or the small Maelog Lake, safer when the wind is offshore.

Rhosneigr has limited facilities, but you can **camp** at *Shoreside Camping* (℡01407/810279; £5 per person), by the train station a mile north of the town centre, and eat at *Sandy's Bistro* on the High Street, where mains cost around £9.

Holy Island

Holy Island (Ynys Gybi) is blessed with Anglesey's finest scenery and cursed with its most unattractive town. The spectacular sea cliffs around **South Stack**, and the Stone Age and Roman remains on **Holyhead Mountain** are just a few miles from downbeat **Holyhead**, whose ferry routes to Ireland and good transport links mean you'll probably find your way there at some stage. In many respects, you can taste Ireland hereabouts without even getting on the ferry. The rough stone walls, prehistoric tumps (mounds) and stones, ragged bays and whitewashed farms that characterize Holy Island are all redolent of the west of Ireland, as is the laid-back atmosphere.

This hourglass of land adjoins Anglesey's west coast at two points. The more ancient and picturesque approach turns west at Valley (Dyffryn), and passes the fine beaches at **Rhoscolyn** and **Trearddur Bay** before reaching Holyhead. Most road traffic now takes the fast A55 across a new bridge into Holyhead, though rail and the older A5 still follow Thomas Telford's 1200-yard-long Stanley Embankment. Along the way he constructed distinctive octagonal toll-houses, used until 1895 when the A5 was Britain's last major toll road. A couple have been converted to houses and one, at the northern end of the Stanley Embankment, now operates as the *Tollhouse Tearooms*.

Getting to Holyhead itself isn't difficult, as trains and a fair number of Anglesey's buses go there. Rhoscolyn and South Stack can be reached from Holyhead by the #23 and the #22 respectively. The #4 bus to Holyhead from Bangor and Llangefni is the only really useful service to Trearddur Bay.

Holyhead

HOLYHEAD (Caergybi; pronounced in English as "holly-head") is a place of dilapidated shopfronts and high unemployment, the local council's valiant attempts to brighten its streets with maritime relics such as anchors and buoys somehow only making it even more depressing. In 1727, Swift found it "scurvy, ill-provided and comfortless", while a century or so later, George Borrow called it "a poor, dull, ill-lighted town", and, apart from the scurvy and the light-ing, little has changed. Fortunately, recent modifications to the ferry terminal combined with the reasonably well-integrated train and ferry timings mean you shouldn't need to venture into the town proper, but if you do get stuck, there are a couple of things to see.

The town's makeover has only really worked along the Newry Beach seafront, north of the town centre. Besides great views over Britain's longest breakwater (7860ft – nearly 1.5 miles), you'll find, tucked down in the old lifeboat station, the recently upgraded **Holyhead Maritime Museum** (Easter–Oct hours yet to be decided; £2; ℡01407/769745). Amid the haunting memorabilia of local maritime

△ Holyhead

disasters, you'll find lovely models of the boats that have plied the Ireland route over the centuries and even some modelled whale's eardrums. In their natural state, these show a passing resemblance to a human head and face, and for no apparent reason, two on display here have been carved to portray Mussolini and Hitler.

The town's Welsh name indicates that this was the site of a Roman fort – an outpost of Segontium – and home of the sixth-century saint Cybi. His hermit's cell was built in the protection of the Roman walls and is now marked by the partly thirteenth-century **Church of St Cybi** (June–Sept Mon–Sat 11am–3pm). Both walls and church have undergone substantial reconstruction, the church gaining stained glass by Edward Burne-Jones and William Morris. The tiny chapel next door housed the town's first free school.

Breakwater Country Park (daily 9am–dusk; free), a couple of miles west along Beach Road, is one of the better ways to pass the time if you miss your boat. An old brickworks marks the starting point for a bracing clifftop **walk** to the foghorn station on North Stack (an hour or so return), or on to South Stack, an hour's walk beyond (see below).

Practicalities

The A55 Expressway spills you into central Holyhead right by the **train station**, local and National Express **bus stops**, passenger **ferry terminal** and **tourist office** (daily 8.30am–6pm; ☎01407/762622, ℮holyhead@nwtic.com), which are all handily clustered together.

The needs of late-arriving ferry passengers are catered for at a small array of **B&Bs**, notably along Newry Street and Walthew Avenue, off Beach Road. While *Orotavia*, 66 Walthew Ave (☎01407/760259, ⓦwww.orotavia.co.uk; ❷), is simple, cosy and perfectly serviceable, the best of the bunch is *Yr Hendre* (☎01407/762929, ⓦwww.yr-hendre.co.uk; ❸), in a charming ex-manse around the corner on Porth-y-Felin Road. Alternatively, *Sea Breezes*, 95 Newry St (☎01407/765682, ⓦwww.sea-breezes.com; ❷) is one of several budget places on this street.

Though fast **food** rules, you can still eat well in Holyhead. The *Castle Bakery*, 83 Market St, is one of the better cafés, and *Raja's*, 8 Newry St (☎01407/760333),

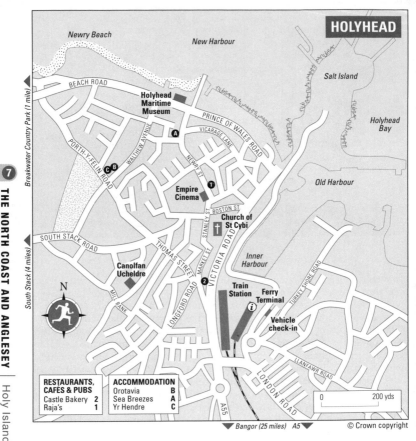

HOLYHEAD

Newry Beach

New Harbour

Salt Island

Holyhead Bay

BEACH ROAD

Breakwater Country Park (1 mile)

Holyhead Maritime Museum

PRINCE OF WALES ROAD

VICARAGE LANE

A

PORTH-Y-FELIN ROAD

WALTHEW AVENUE

NEWRY ST.

C B

Old Harbour

Empire Cinema

1

BOSTON ST.

STANLEY ST.

Church of St Cybi

South (4 miles)

SOUTH STACK ROAD

THOMAS STREET

MARKET ST.

VICTORIA ROAD

Inner Harbour

Canolfan Ucheldre

2

Train Station

Ferry Terminal

i

TURKEY SHORE ROAD

N

LONGFORD ROAD

MILL BANK

Vehicle check-in

LLANFAWR ROAD

LONDON ROAD

RESTAURANTS, CAFÉS & PUBS		ACCOMMODATION	
Castle Bakery	**2**	Orotavia	**B**
Raja's	**1**	Sea Breezes	**A**
		Yr Hendre	**C**

0 200 yds

▼ Bangor (25 miles) A5 ▼

© Crown copyright

serves the tastiest Bengal curries for miles around. The multipurpose Canolfan Ucheldre (☎01407/763361), a former convent chapel above the town centre, is Anglesey's premier centre for the **performing arts** and often has exhibitions too. For **films** check out the Empire Cinema (☎01407/761128) at the corner of Newry and Stanley streets.

Holyhead Mountain and South Stack

The northern half of Holy Island is ranged around the skirts of **Holyhead Mountain** (Mynydd Twr), rising 700ft to the west of Holyhead. Its summit is ringed by the remains of the seventeen-acre Iron Age **Caer y Twr** (unrestricted access; CADW), one of the largest sites in north Wales. Seemingly, it was only used during times of war, as no signs of permanent occupation have been unearthed, just a six-foot-high dry-stone wall enclosure around the ruins of a Roman beacon. Although you can pick your way up rough tracks from the Holyhead side in an hour or so, the best approach is by bus #22 or your own transport to the car park at **South Stack** (Ynys Lawd), two miles west of Holyhead. A path (45min) leads from the car park to the top of Holyhead Mountain, though you'll find most people walking the few yards to the clifftop,

RSPB-run **Ellin's Tower Seabird Centre** (Easter–Sept daily 10am–5.30pm; free). From April until the end of July, binoculars and closed-circuit TV give an unrivalled opportunity to watch up to 3000 birds – razorbills, guillemots and the odd puffin – nesting on the nearby sea cliffs while ravens and peregrines wheel outside the tower's windows.

A twisting path, with over four hundred steps, leads down from the South Stack car park to a suspension bridge over the surging waves, once the keeper's only access to the now fully automated pepper-pot **lighthouse** (Easter–Sept daily 10.30am–5.30pm; £3), built in 1809. Views on to the cliffs are stupendous as you climb down to the island and, once there, you'll find exhibitions on local wildlife and can take a tour of the lighthouse itself. Tickets are issued at the *South Stack Kitchen*, a café-cum-interpretive centre a hundred yards back down the lane.

William Stanley, who named Ellin's Tower (Tŵr Elin) after his wife, did most of the excavation work on the **Cytiau'r Gwyddelod** hut circles (CADW), across the road from the Seabird Centre car park. The name translates as the "huts of the Irish" – a common name for any ancient settlement – but evidence from excavations reveals little more than that the builders were late Neolithic or early Bronze Age people. The visible remains comprise nineteen low stone circles – some up to ten yards across – though there seem to have originally been fifty buildings, formed into eight distinct farmsteads separated by ploughed fields.

Trearddur Bay and Rhoscolyn

At the pinch of Holy Island's hourglass shape, a couple of miles south of Holyhead, the scattered settlement of **TREARDDUR BAY** (Bae Trearddur) shambles across low grassy hills, around a deeply indented bay punctuated by rocky coves. There's no centre to speak of, but it's a much nicer base than Holyhead with a good, clean swimming beach.

If you can afford it, the best **place to stay** is the venerable, creaky *Trearddur Bay Hotel* (℡01407/860301, www.trearddurbayhotel.co.uk; ❼), overlooking the main bay. It has a heated indoor pool, a good traditional restaurant and decent bar meals for those whose pockets aren't quite so deep. There's also the *Tyn Rhos Campsite* (℡01407/860369; £8 per tent), though it is often packed with caravans. Apart from the *Trearddur Bay Hotel* and a couple of chippies, **eating** is restricted to the *Waterfront Restaurant*, Lôn Isallt (℡01407/860006) which cooks some of the best fish dishes around for £13–18.

Crossing over to Ireland

You can sail to Dublin or Dun Laoghaire (6 miles south) on **ferries** that take three and a quarter hours, or high-speed **catamarans** taking around an hour and three-quarters. Stena Line (℡08705/707070, www.stenaline.com) runs ferries (2.30am & 2.30pm) to Dublin Port and huge, car-carrying catamarans to Dun Laoghaire (8.55am, 1.45pm & 6.30pm); Irish Ferries (℡08705/171717, www.irishferries.com) operates both ferries (2.50am & 3pm), and catamarans (2.30am, 9.20am, 2.50pm & 8.15pm) to Dublin. Schedules change, so call ahead. Check-in is generally thirty minutes before departure.

Passenger fares are very competitive with diverse deals and special offers, but Irish Ferries usually has the edge by a few pounds. Typically, the catamarans cost £30 each way for adults in high summer, and the ferries £5 less. Some **day-return deals** are priced as low as £14 but subject to so many restrictions that it's more realistic to expect to pay £30 for up to five days in Dublin.

At the southern tip of the island, a mile or so south of Trearddur Bay, a lane runs down to **RHOSCOLYN**, another scattered seaside settlement, even smaller and more appealing. With a couple of exquisite sandy beaches, lots of rocky outcrops and some delightful coastal walking, this is the ideal place to spend a few days chilling out. There's a small range of water-sports gear for rent at *The Outdoor Alternative* (℡01407/860469, Ⓦwww.outdooralternative.org), a relaxed, simple **campsite** (£4 per person) a few yards from the beach which also runs a **self-catering hostel** with made-up bunks (£14) during school holidays (essentially Easter & Aug); phone for directions. Meals are available on request and staff can point you to some of the best walks, or the nearby White Eagle **pub** with a beer garden. Just short of the beach car park, the pleasant *Glan Towyn* (℡01407/860380; ❸) offers comfortable **B&B**.

Northern and inland Anglesey

The **northern and eastern sides of Anglesey** are quieter than the south and west; its settlements cluster behind sheltered coves that, with the odd rocky headland, form an appealing (if seldom dramatic) coastline. This is primarily family holiday country, though its thinner spread of caravan sites makes it much less oppressive than the north Welsh coast. None of the resorts is especially notable but all are well spaced, making cycling between them, or walking the coastal path, an ideal way to get around. Relying on **buses** is possible, though less rewarding.

Accommodation is detailed under the appropriate town account, but if you're exploring the coast with your own transport you may wish to head inland to stay at one of two farmhouses near Llanerchymedd, both of which serve wholesome, hearty dinners and are highly recommended. *Drws-Y-Coed* (℡01248/470473, Ⓔdrwsycoed2@hotmail.com; ❹) is a comfy, non-smoking B&B on a working farm a mile and a half east, while *Llwydiarth Fawr* (℡01248/470321, Ⓦwww.angleseyfarms.com; ❹), is a spacious, agreeable Georgian mansion amid rolling hills half a mile north on the B5111.

The northwest coast to Cemaes

The main A5025 leaves Holyhead to follow the island's perimeter clockwise. There are plenty of nice sandy beaches around the village of **LLANFWROG** where there's the lovely farmhouse B&B of *Penrhyn Farm* (℡01407/730134, Ⓦwww.angleseyfarms.com; ❸). A few miles inland, you might be tempted to swing off the main road for **LLANDDEUSANT**, where a signpost points to **Melin Llynnon** (Easter–Sept daily 11am–5pm; £2.50), Anglesey's sole remaining working windmill. At one time, fifty-odd mills all over Anglesey ground away to feed all of north Wales; today, over thirty can still be seen, their sail-less stumps either rotting away in field corners or converted (some imaginatively) into barns and houses. Only Melin Llynnon survives in anything like its original form. Restored from dereliction under the guidance of Lincolnshire millwrights, it is now white-painted, canvas-sailed and once again producing flour. Everything in the mill is wind-powered, even the hoists that lift the grain through trapdoors, and almost extinct milling skills have had to be re-learnt by modern millers who now demonstrate the process and sell the result – in bag and cake form – from a good café.

Back along the coastal drag, the highlight of the northwest coast is gently understated **PORTH SWTAN** (Church Bay), a diffuse settlement gathered loosely around a picturesque sweep of sand backed by yellow rocks dating from the pre-Cambrian era, some 570 million years ago. Just back from the beach, the **last thatched cottage on Anglesey** (Fri–Sun noon–4.30pm; £2) has been restored and fitted with a small folk museum. Across the road, the wonderful *Lobster Pot* restaurant (℡01407/730241; closed Sun & Mon except in Aug, and often closed in winter) has live lobsters in tanks that end up as delicious dishes (from £25). Nearby are a couple of low-key **campsites**, the church that gives the area its English name, and the friendly *Church Bay Inn*.

From here, the coast dives and ripples northwards to the harbourside village of **CEMAES**, wedged between the brooding bulk of the ageing **Wylfa Nuclear Power Station** and the 24-tower Rhyd-y-Groes **windfarm**. It is a charming spot with one of the most attractive harbours on the north coast, occupied by the odd trawler and boatloads of yachties. Tiny **Llanbadrig Church** (May–Sept daily 10am–noon & 2–4pm), on the headland at the eastern side of the bay, is one of only two Welsh churches dedicated to St Patrick. The present structure is mainly fourteenth century, but the church's origins go back to the fifth century, when Ireland's patron saint is supposed to have been shipwrecked on the small island offshore, and made his way to a cave below the site of the present church. The building was restored in the nineteenth century by Lord Stanley of Alderley, Bertrand Russell's grandfather, a Muslim who used Islamic imagery in the stained glass.

Another point of pilgrimage is the *Stag* on High Street, the most northerly pub in Wales, which serves up some of the best pub **food** around. If you want to **stay** around these parts, make for the non-smoking *Treddolphin Guesthouse* (℡01407/710388; ❸) 200 yards down Beach Road from the *Stag*.

Amlwch and Parys Mountain

AMLWCH, five miles east of Cemaes, would be just another tiny fishing village but for **Parys Mountain** (Mynydd Parys) a mile or so inland, once the world's largest source of **copper**. The Ordovices, a great Celtic tribe who occupied north Wales in the Neolithic era, probably began to extract the ore, and the Romans certainly did so, but it wasn't until the eighteenth century that production reached industrial levels. Amlwch boomed in Wild West style, its population ballooning to six thousand by the late 1700s, making it Wales' second largest town. Pollution had become a problem, but people noticed that the iron hulls of ships didn't corrode in the copper-laced harbour waters, fuelling a demand for protective copper sheathing that boosted the market for Parys copper. International competition in the early nineteenth century saw the town sink back into its role of a fishing port, although copper has been mined on Parys ever since. You can reach the ruined pumping mill on top of Parys Mountain by a path from the car park on the B5111, a mile south of town, just next to the premises of the one company still trying to squeeze a profit from the exhausted mountain. The waymarked Industrial Heritage Trail (25p leaflet available) leads around Parys' ravaged moonscape, made all the more bizarre by the derelict remains, multicoloured rocks, coppery pools of water and patches of scrubby heather and gorse.

Back in town, in the Watch House by the spruced-up Amlwch Port, locals have set up the **Amlwch Industrial Heritage Centre** (Easter–Oct daily 11am–5pm; free), full of material on Amlwch's remarkable past, and with a café on the intentionally sloping floor of a former sail loft. The centre distributes a free "Porth Amlwch Heritage Trail" leaflet, but to explore the subterranean workings you'll have to join the Parys Underground Group on its weekly **underground tours** (Wed 6.30pm; £10; ℡01407/832255): you'll be supplied with helmet and lamp but should bring gumboots.

After visiting so many ancient churches in Wales, **Our Lady Star of the Sea**, a couple of hundred yards along the A5025, to the west of Main Street, comes as something of a novelty. Built in the 1930s of reinforced concrete, the great parabolic ribs of what could be a giant toast rack are supposed to represent an upturned boat, complete with portholes.

From Moelfre to Red Wharf Bay

MOELFRE has a reputation for shipwrecks, though wandering around the peaceful grey-pebbled cove on a sunny day it seems unlikely. An anchor behind the beach was salvaged from the *Hindlea*, which went down in October 1959, exactly a century after the 2700-ton *Royal Charter* foundered, with the loss of 450 lives and nearly £400,000-worth of gold. The dead are remembered by a memorial stone thirty minutes' walk north along the coastal path that starts at the end of the cove, past a small offshore cormorant colony.

Moelfre's only other point of interest lies a mile west off the A5025, where the late Neolithic **Din Lligwy Hut Group** (unrestricted access; CADW) forms the centrepiece of a site spanning three thousand years of human occupation. A five-sided walled enclosure contains the foundations of several circular and rectangular buildings dated to the second and fourth centuries which, along with the hut group on Holy Island, give the best indication of how these people actually lived, rather than how they buried their dead. To the northeast of the main enclosure stands **Capel Lligwy**, a forlorn-looking twelfth-century church, and a short distance to the south is the **Lligwy Burial Chamber** with its 28-ton capstone. All are just a short stroll from the road. Overlooking wide sands a few miles south of Moelfre is the east coast's principal resort, **BENLLECH**, mainly a retirement centre for elderly English and thus lacking in appreciable stimulus. Better on all counts is **RED WHARF BAY** (Traeth Coch), a mile southeast, a broad, enticing sweep of golden sand that never gets too crowded. The most popular end is at Red Wharf Bay village: for more solitude and bigger views, go to the other end, reached down narrow hairpin lanes from the village of **LLANDDONA**.

Red Wharf Bay is backed by the atmospheric, wooden-beamed ♣ *Ship Inn* where, on sunny days, the tables outside by the water are invariably packed with people supping real ales and tucking into the excellent meals (£8–13 mains). At such times you might want to wander down the road to *The Old Boathouse Café & Restaurant* which does comparably tasty meals for a pound or two less.

If you want to **stay** hereabouts, try the welcoming *Hafod*, Amlwch Road, Benllech (✆01248/853092; ❸), in a large, comfortable Edwardian house.

Llangefni

About the only reason to venture inland is to visit **LLANGEFNI**, Anglesey's low-key county town, and the **Oriel Ynys Môn** gallery (Tues–Sun 10.30am–5pm; 50p), half a mile along the B5111 from the town centre. Examining various aspects of Anglesey life, from pre-Christian sites and the dynastic lines of the Princes of Gwynedd to exhibits about conservation and the Welsh language, Oriel Ynys Môn provides an excellent overview of the sheer variety of factors in the island's turbulent history. A corner of the gallery is devoted to a mock-up of Charles Tunnicliffe's Malltraeth studio (see p.489), from where he made many of his wildlife paintings. Llangefni is five miles west of Llanfairpwll, and on the #4 bus route between Holyhead and Bangor.

Travel details

Unless otherwise stated frequencies for trains and buses are for Monday to Saturday services; Sunday averages 1–3 services, though the main routes are more frequent and some routes have no Sunday service at all.

Trains

Bangor to: Chester (25 daily; 1hr); Colwyn Bay (21 daily; 25min); Conwy (11 daily; 20min); Holyhead (20 daily; 30–40min); Llandudno Junction (27 daily; 20min); Rhosneigr (7 daily; 25min); Rhyl (21 daily; 35min).

Colwyn Bay to: Llandudno Junction (32 daily; 6min); Rhyl (36 daily; 15min).

Conwy to: Bangor (11 daily; 20min); Holyhead (6 daily; 1hr); Llandudno Junction (10 daily; 3min).

Holyhead to: Bangor (20 daily; 30–40min); Chester (20 daily; 1hr 30min–1hr 50min); Conwy (6 daily; 1hr) ; Llandudno Junction (20 daily; 50min); Llanfairpwll (7 daily; 30min).

Llandudno to: Betws-y-Coed (6 daily; 40min); Blaenau Ffestiniog (6 daily; 1hr 10min); Llandudno Junction (6 daily; 10min).

Llandudno Junction to: Bangor (27 daily; 20min); Betws-y-Coed (6 daily; 30min); Conwy (10 daily; 3min); Holyhead (20 daily; 50min–1hr); Llandudno (6 daily; 10min); Rhyl (36 daily; 20min).

Llanfairpwll to: Bangor (7 daily; 10min); Holyhead (7 daily; 30min).

Rhosneigr to: Holyhead (7 daily; 10min); Llanfairpwll (7 daily; 15min).

Rhyl to: Bangor (21 daily; 35min); Holyhead (16 daily; 1hr 10min–1hr 40min); Llandudno Junction (36 daily; 20min).

Buses

Bangor to: Beaumaris (every 30min; 30min); Bethesda (hourly; 30min); Betws-y-Coed (3 daily; 1hr 15min); Caernarfon (every 20min; 30min); Conwy (every 30min; 45min); Holyhead (every 30min; 1hr 15min); Llanberis (hourly; 30–50min); Llandudno (every 30min; 1hr); Llangefni (every 30min; 35min); Menai Bridge (every 30min; 12min).

Beaumaris to: Bangor (every 30min; 30min); Menai Bridge (every 30min; 15min); Penmon (11 daily; 15min).

Conwy to: Bangor (every 30min; 45min); Llandudno (every 30min; 20min); Llanrwst (every 30min; 30min).

Holyhead to: Amlwch (6 daily; 50min); Bangor (every 30min; 1hr 15min); Cemaes (6 daily; 40min); Llanfairpwll (every 30min; 1hr); Llangefni (every 30min; 45min); Menai Bridge (every 30min; 1hr 5min); Rhoscolyn (5 daily; 15min); Trearddur Bay (8 daily; 10min).

Llandudno to: Bangor (every 30min; 1hr); Conwy (every 30min; 20min); Llanrwst (every 30min; 1hr); Rhyl (every 15min; 1hr).

Llanfairpwll to: Bangor (every 30min; 15min); Holyhead (every 30min; 1hr); Llangefni (every 30min; 15min); Newborough (11 daily; 20min).

Prestatyn to: Flint every (30min; 50min); Rhyl (every 30min; 20min).

Rhyl to: Denbigh (every 30min; 45min); Llandudno (every 15min; 1hr); Prestatyn (every 30min; 20min); St Asaph (every 20min; 25min).

St Asaph to: Denbigh (every 30min; 20min); Rhuddlan (every 20min; 15min); Rhyl (every 20min; 25min).

Ferries

Holyhead to: Dublin (4 ferries daily; 3hr 15min; 4 catamarans daily; 1hr 45min); Dun Laoghaire (2–4 catamarans daily; 1hr 40min).

Contexts

Contexts

History

The beginnings

Before the end of the last Ice Age around ten thousand years ago, Wales and the rest of Britain formed part of the greater European whole and the early migrant inhabitants eked out a meagre living on the tundra or a better one amongst the oak, beech and hazel forests in the warmer periods. Most lived in the southeast of Britain, but small groups foraged north and west, leaving 250,000-year-old evidence in the form of a human tooth in a cave near Denbigh in north Wales and a hand axe unearthed near Cardiff.

It wasn't until the early part of the **Upper Paleolithic age** that significant communities settled in Wales, those of the Gower peninsula interring the "Red Lady of Paviland" around 24,000 BC (see p.160). This civilization was far behind those of central France or northern Spain, and remained on Europe's cultural fringe as the melting ice cut Britain off from mainland Europe around 5000 BC. Migrating Mesolithic peoples had already moved north from Central Europe and were followed by **Neolithic colonists**, whose mastery of stone and flint working found its expression in over a hundred and fifty cromlechs (turf-covered chambered tombs) dotted around Wales, primarily Pentre Ifan in Mynydd Preseli (see p.224), Bryn Celli Ddu (see p.487) and Barclodiad y Gawres on Anglesey (see p.489). Skilled in agriculture and animal husbandry, the Neolithic people also began to clear the lush forests covering Wales below 2000 feet, enclosing fields, constructing defensive ditches around their villages and mining for flint.

The earliest stone circles – more extensive meeting places than cromlechs – were built at this time and continued to spread over the country as the Neolithic period drifted into the **Bronze Age** around 2000 BC. Through their extensive trade networks, the inhabitants of Wales and the rest of Britain gradually adopted new techniques, changing to more sophisticated use of metals and developing a well-organized social structure. The established aristocracy engaged in much tribal warfare, as suggested by large numbers of earthwork forts built in this and the immediately succeeding period – the chief examples being at Holyhead Mountain on Anglesey and the Bulwarks at Chepstow.

The Celts

Celtic invaders spreading from their central European homeland settled in Wales in around 600 BC, imparting a great cultural influence. Familiar with Mediterranean civilization through trading routes, they introduced superior methods of metalworking that favoured iron rather than bronze, from which they forged not just weapons but also coins. Gold was used for ornamental works – the first recognizable Welsh art – heavily influenced by the symbolic, patterned **La Tène** style still thought of as quintessentially Celtic.

The Celts are credited with introducing the basis of modern Welsh. The original Celtic tongue was spoken over a wide area, gradually dividing into Goidelic (or

Q-Celtic) now spoken in the Isle of Man, Ireland and Scotland, and **Brythonic** (P-Celtic) spoken in Wales and Cornwall, and later exported to Brittany in France. This highly developed language was emblematic of a sophisticated social hierarchy headed by **druids**, a ritual priesthood with attendant poets, seers and warriors. Through a deep knowledge of ritual, legend and the mechanics of the heavens, the druids maintained their position between the people and a pantheon of over four thousand gods. Most of these were variations of a handful of chief gods worshipped by the great British tribes: the Silures and Demetae in the south of Wales, the Cornovii in mid-Wales and the Ordovices and Deceangli in the north. Great though the Celtic technological and artistic achievements were, the people and their pan-European cousins were unable to maintain an organized civic society to match that of their successors, the Romans.

The Romans in Wales

Life in Wales, unlike that in most of England, was never fully Romanized, the region remaining under legionary control throughout its three-hundred-year occupation. **Julius Caesar** made small cross-Channel incursions in 55 and 54 BC, kicking off a lengthy but low-level infusion of Roman ideas which filtered across to Wales. This flow swelled a century later when the emperor **Claudius** took the death of the British king Cunobelin (Cynfelyn) as a signal to launch a full-scale invasion in 43 AD which in four years swept across southern England to the frontier of south Wales. Expansionism fomented anti-Roman feeling along the frontier between the Lowland Zone (southern and central England) and the Highland Zone (northern England, Scotland and Wales). Traditionally insular Welsh hill tribes united with their Brythonic cousins in northern England to oppose the Romans, who proceeded to force a wedge between them. The Roman historian **Tacitus** recorded the submission of the Deceangli near Chester, giving us the oldest written mention of a Welsh land. The Romans, held back by troubles at home and with the East Anglian revolt of **Boudicca** (Boadicea), were limited to tentative dabbling in Welsh affairs, sending expeditionary forces against the Silures and the toughest nut, the druid stronghold of Anglesey. The obdurate nature of the Welsh on their back foot kept the Romans at bay until around 75 AD, when legionary forts were built at Deva (Chester, England) and Isca Silurium (Caerleon) to act as platforms for incursions west along specially built military roads.

By 78 AD, Wales was under Roman control, its chief fortresses at Deva, Isca Silurium and Segontium (Caernarfon) boasting all the trappings of imperial Roman life: bath houses, temples, mosaics and underfloor heating. Through three centuries of occupation, the Celtic people sustained an independent existence while drawing material comfort from the proximity of Roman cities and auxiliary forts. Elements of Roman life filtered into the Celtic culture: agrarian practices improved, a new religion was partly adopted from the newly Christianized Romans, the language adopted Latin words (pont for "bridge", ffenestr for "window") and the prevailing La Tène artistic style took on classical Roman elements.

The Roman Empire was already in decline when **Magnus Maximus** (Macsen Wledig) led a campaign to wrest control of the western empire from Emperor Gratian in 383 AD. Maximus' rule was short lived but Wales was effectively free of direct Roman control by 390.

The age of the saints

Historical orthodoxy views the departure of literate Latin historians, skilled stonemasons and an all-powerful army, as heralding the **Dark Ages**. In fact, a civic society probably flourished until a century later, when the collapse of trade routes was hastened by the dramatic spread of Islam around the Mediterranean, and Romanized society gave way to a non-classical but no less structured form of **Celtic society**.

For the next few centuries, **Teutonic barbarian tribes** were struggling for supremacy in the post-Roman power vacuum in southern and eastern England, having little influence in Wales, where the main dynastic kingdoms set to steer Wales' next seven hundred years were taking root. The confusion that surrounds the early years of these dynasties was further muddied in 1136, when Geoffrey of Monmouth published his *History of the Kings of Britain*, portraying **King Arthur** as a feudal king with his court at Caerleon. Victorian Romantics embellished subsequent histories, making it practically impossible to extract much truth from this period.

In the fifth century, the **Irish** (Gwyddyl), who had a long tradition of migrating to the Llŷn and parts of mid-Wales, attacked the coast and formed distinct colonies, but were soon expelled from the north by **Cunedda Wledig**, the leader of a Brythonic tribe from near Edinburgh, who went on to found the royal house of Gwynedd, consolidating the Brythonic language and ostensibly naming regions of his kingdom – the modern Ceredigion and Meirionydd – after his sons. In the southwest, the Irish influence was sustained; the kingdom of Dyfed shows clear Irish origins.

These changes took place against a background of increasing religious energy. Between the fifth and the sixth centuries the **Celtic Saints**, ascetic evangelical missionaries, spread the gospel around Ireland and western Britain, promoting the middle-Eastern eremitical tradition of living a reclusive life. Where their message took root, they founded simple churches within a consecrated enclosure, or llan, which often took the saint's name, hence Llanberis (Saint Peris), Llandeilo (Saint Teilo) and very many others. In south Wales, **Saint David** (Dewi Sant) was the most popular (and subsequently Wales' patron saint), dying around 589 after a miracle-filled life, during which he made a pilgrimage to Jerusalem and established the religious community at St David's, which had become a place of pilgrimage by the twelfth century.

The Welsh kingdoms

Towards the end of the sixth century the **Angles** and **Saxons** in eastern Britain began to entertain designs on the western lands. The inability of the independent western peoples to unify against this threat left the most powerful kingdom, Gwynedd, as the centre of cultural and political resistance, a position it has retained to this day. The weaker groups were unable to hold the invaders, and after the battle at Dyrham, near Gloucester in 577, the Britons in Cornwall were separated from those in Wales, who became similarly cut off from their northern kin in Cumbria after the battle of Chester in 616.

Though still geographically in a state of change, Wales could by now be said to exist. At this point the racial mix in Wales was probably little different from that to the east where Saxon numbers were small, but Wales was held together by the people's resistance to the Saxons. The Welsh started to refer to themselves as **Cymry** (fellow-countrymen), rather than the Saxon term "Welsh", used by English-speakers today and which is generally thought to mean either foreigners or Romanized people. The construction of **Offa's Dyke** (Clawdd Offa) – a linear earthwork built in the middle of the eighth century to mark rather than defend the boundary between Wales and the kingdom of Mercia – gave the Welsh a firm eastern border and allowed them to concentrate on a gradual unification of the patchwork of kingdoms as their coasts were being harried by **Norse and Viking invaders**.

Rhodri Mawr (Rhodri the Great) killed the Viking leader off Anglesey, earning himself the formal thanks of the Frankish king Charles the Bald (Charlemagne), and helped the country's rise towards statehood through his unification of most of Wales. By this stage, England had developed into a single powerful kingdom for the first time since the departure of the Romans, and though the various branches of Rhodri's line went on to rule most of Wales down to the late thirteenth century, the princedoms were frequently forced to swear fealty to the English kings. Defensive problems were exacerbated by internecine struggles borne of the practice of partible inheritance that left each of Rhodri's sons with an equal part of Wales to control.

Rhodri Mawr's grandson **Hywel Dda** (Hywel the Good) largely reunified the country from Deheubarth, his power base in southwest Wales. He added Powys and Gwynedd to his domain, but his most valuable legacy is his codification and promulgation of the medieval **Law of Wales** (Cyfraith Hywel Dda) in around 930 at modern-day Whitland (see p.185), called Hendy Gwyn ar Daf, "the White House on the Taf". Regional customs were fashioned into a single legal system that was forcibly abandoned under the 1536 Act of Union with England, though many elements of it survived in common-law practice. Eleven hundred years on, the laws are still breathtaking in their modernity and compassion: women were allowed to initiate divorce proceedings, could inherit and own property (something not introduced into English law until 1883) and had the right to compensation if beaten by their husbands; children born out of wedlock had full parity with legitimate offspring; medical treatment was legally available (and mostly free) to all; and theft of food went unpunished if it was to keep people alive. This last law is in painful contrast to the English policy, legal into the nineteenth century, of executing people for stealing so much as a loaf of bread.

After Hywel's death in 950, anarchy and internal turmoil reigned until his great-great-grandson, **Gruffydd ap Llywelyn**, seized power in Gwynedd in 1039. He unified all of Wales, taking the coronation of the weak English king, Edward the Confessor, as an opportunity to annex some of the Marches in Mercia. Edward's successor, Harold, wasn't having any of this and killed Gruffydd, heralding a new phase of political fragmentation.

The arrival of the Normans

In 1066, the **Normans** swept across the English Channel, killed Harold, the English king, and stormed England. Though Wales was unable to present a unified opposition to the invaders, the Norman king, William, didn't attempt to conquer Wales. The **Domesday Book** – his masterwork of subjugation commissioned in 1085 to record land ownership as a framework for taxation – indicates that he only nibbled at parts of Powys and Gwynedd. Instead, he installed a huge retinue of barons, the **Lords Marcher**, along the border to bring as much Welsh territory under their own jurisdiction as possible. Despite generations of squabbling, the barons managed to hold onto their privileges until Henry VIII's Act of Union over four hundred years later.

The payment of homage by **Rhys ap Tewdwr** (the king of Deheubarth), and **Gruffydd ap Cynan** (the king of Gwynedd) kept the Welsh borders safe until the death of William I in 1087. His son William Rufus made three unsuccessful invasions of Wales but finally left it to his Marcher lords (now numbering over 140) to advance from their castles into south Wales, leaving only Powys and Gwynedd independent. A lack of English commitment or resources allowed the Welsh to claw back their territory through years when distinctions between English, Normans and Welsh were beginning to blur. One product of this was the quarter-Welsh **Giraldus Cambrensis** (see p.428), who left a valuable record of twelfth-century life in Wales and his opinions on Welsh character. "They are quicker witted and more shrewd than any other Western people", he informs us, a quality which helped them form three stable political entities: Powys, Deheubarth and Gwynedd. The latter, led by **Owain Gwynedd** from his capital at Aberffraw on Anglesey, now extended beyond Offa's Dyke and progressively gained hegemony over the other two. Owain Gwynedd's grandson, **Llywelyn ap Iorwerth** (the Great), who earned his laurels through shrewd campaigning, progressively incorporated the weaker territories to the south into his kingdom and captured several Norman castles to reach the peak of the Welsh feudal pyramid. Manipulating the favours of the English king John, Llywelyn managed to extend his control over southern Powys before a fearful John led two devastating campaigns into north Wales. Llywelyn was humiliated and forced into recognizing John as his heir should Llywelyn's union with John's illegitimate daughter Joan not produce a son. Channelling a now united Welsh opposition against John, Llywelyn struck back and won some degree of Welsh autonomy. Worried that his unified Wales would disintegrate on his death, Llywelyn engineered the smooth succession by commanding his princes to assemble at Strata Florida (see p.307) and pay homage not just to him (as was now his by right) but also to his son, Dafydd. This plan succeeded until after his death, when Wales began to disintegrate to the point where at Dafydd's death in 1246 the country had only nominal unity.

Most of the work of regrouping Wales around one standard fell to Llywelyn the Great's grandson and Dafydd's nephew, Llywelyn ap Gruffydd (Llewellyn the Last).

Edward I's conquest

By 1255, Llywelyn ap Iorwerth's grandson, **Llywelyn ap Gruffydd** (the Last), had won control of Gwynedd. During the next three years he pushed the English out of Gwynedd, then out of most of Wales. The English king Henry III was forced to respect Llywelyn's influence and ratified the **Treaty of Montgomery** in 1267, thereby recognizing Llywelyn as "Prince of Wales" in return for his homage. The English monarchy's war with the barons allowed Llywelyn time to politically consolidate his lands, which now stretched over all of modern Wales excepting Pembrokeshire and parts of the Marches. The tables turned when Edward I succeeded Henry III and began a crusade to unify Britain. Llywelyn had failed to attend Edward's coronation and refused to pay him homage – at the same time, Llywelyn's determination to marry the daughter of Simon de Montfort lost him the support of the south Welsh princes and some Marcher lords. Edward was a skilful tactician and with effective use of sea power had little trouble forcing the already weakened Llywelyn back into Snowdonia. Peace was restored with the **Treaty of Aberconwy**, which deprived Llywelyn of almost all his land and stripped him of his financial tributes from the other Welsh princes, but left him with the hollow title of "Prince of Wales".

Edward now set about surrounding Llywelyn's land with castles at Aberystwyth, Builth Wells, Flint and Rhuddlan (see p.468). After a relatively cordial four-year period, Llywelyn's brother Dafydd rose against Edward, inevitably dragging Llywelyn along with him. Edward didn't hesitate and swept through Gwynedd, crushing the revolt and laying the foundations for the remaining castles in his **Iron Ring**, those at Conwy, Caernarfon, Harlech and Beaumaris. Llywelyn, already battered by Edward's force, was captured and executed at Cilmeri (see p.263), after fleeing from the abortive Battle of Builth in December 1282. The **Statute of Rhuddlan** in 1284 set down the terms by which the English monarch was to rule Wales: much of it was given to the Marcher lords who had helped Edward, the rest was divided into administrative and legal districts similar to those in England. Though the treaty is often seen as a symbol of English subjugation, it respected much of Welsh law and provided a basis for civil rights and privileges. Many Welsh were content to accept and exploit Edward's rule for their own benefit, but in 1294, a rebellion led by **Madog ap Llywelyn** gripped Wales and was only halted by Edward's swift and devastating response. Most of the privileges enshrined in the Statute of Rhuddlan were now rescinded and the Welsh seemed crushed for a century.

Owain Glyndŵr

Throughout the fourteenth century, famine and the Black Death plagued Wales. The Marcher lords appropriated the lands of defaulting debtors and squeezed the last pennies out of their tenants, while royal officials clawed in all the income they could from the towns around the castles. These factors and the pent-up resentment of the English sowed seeds of a rebellion led by the tyrannical but charismatic Welsh hero **Owain Glyndŵr**. Citing his descent from the princes of both Powys and Deheubarth, he declared himself "Prince of Wales" in 1400, and with a crew of local supporters attacked the lands of nearby barons, slaughtering the English. Henry IV misjudged the political climate and imposed restrictions on Welsh land ownership, swelling the general support Glyndŵr needed to take Conwy Castle the following year. By 1404, Glyndŵr, who already had control over most of western Wales and sections of the Marches, took the castles at Harlech and Aberystwyth, summoned a parliament in Machynlleth, and had himself crowned Prince of Wales, with envoys of France, Scotland and Castile in attendance. He then demanded independence for the Welsh Church from Canterbury and set about securing alliances with English noblemen who had grievances with Henry IV. This last ambitious move heralded Glyndŵr's downfall. A succession of defeats saw his allies desert him, and by 1408, when the castles at Harlech and Aberystwyth were retaken for the Crown, this last protest against

Edward I's English conquest had lost its momentum. Little is known of Glyndŵr's final years, though it is thought he died in 1416, possibly in Herefordshire, leaving Wales territorially unchanged but the country's national pride at an all-time high.

The Tudors and union with England

During the latter half of the fifteenth century, the succession to the English throne was contested in the **Wars of the Roses** between the houses of York (white rose) and Lancaster (red rose). Welsh allegiance lay broadly with the Lancastrians, who had the support of the ascendant north Welsh Tewdwr (or Tudor) family. Through the early part of the wars, one Henry Tudor lived with his widowed Welsh mother, Margaret Beaufort, at the besieged Harlech Castle, escaping to Brittany when Yorkist Richard III took the English throne in 1471. Fourteen years later, Henry returned to Wales, landing at Milford Haven, and defeated Richard at the Battle of Bosworth Field, so becoming **Henry VII** and sealing the Lancastrian ascendancy.

Welsh expectations of the new monarch were high. Henry lived up to some of them, removing many of the restrictions on land ownership imposed at the start of Glyndŵr's uprising, and promoting many Welshmen to high office, but administration remained piecemeal. Control was still shared between the Crown and largely independent Marcher lords until a uniform administrative structure was achieved under Henry VIII.

Wales had been largely controlled by the English monarch since the Statute of Rhuddlan in 1284, but sovereignty was finally fixed in Henry VIII's 1536 **Act of Union** (and a subsequent act of 1543). It's a misleading title, and one that was not used to describe the act until the twentieth century, for it implies a level of equality between the two nations that did not in fact exist. Unlike the Acts of 1707 and 1800 that brought Scotland and Ireland into the Union – and were the decisions of independent parliaments in Edinburgh, Dublin and London to merge their identities – the 1536 Act was a unilateral decision by Westminster, a parliament that, at the time, had no Welsh representation in it at all. It decreed that English was to be the only language of the courts and other official bodies, effectively creating a two-tier Wales of English-speaking lords and masters and a Welsh-speaking proletariat. At the same time the Marches were replaced by shires (the equivalent of modern counties), the Welsh laws codified by Hywel Dda were made void, and partible inheritance (equal amongst all offspring) gave way to primogeniture, the eldest son becoming the sole heir. In many ways, this period set in stone the struggles and the injustices that are still playing out nearly five hundred years later.

Just as Henry VIII's decision to convert his kingdom from Catholicism to Protestantism was borne more from his desire to divorce his first wife, Catherine of Aragon, than from any religious conviction, it was his need for money, not recognition, which brought about the **Dissolution of the Monasteries** in 1536. Monastic lands were divided amongst the local gentry, but since Christianity had always been a ritual way of life rather than a philosophical code in Wales, Catholicism was easily replaced by Protestantism. What the Reformation did promote was a more studied approach to religion and learning in general. Under the reign of Elizabeth I, Jesus College was founded in Oxford for Welsh scholars, and the Bible was translated into Welsh for the first time by a team led by Bishop **William Morgan** (see p.457).

With new land ownership laws enshrined in the Acts of Union, the stimulus provided by the Dissolution hastened the emergence of the Anglo-Welsh gentry, a group eager to claim a Welsh pedigree while promoting the English language and the legal system, helping to perpetuate their grasp. Meanwhile, landless peasants continued in poverty, only gaining slightly from the increase in cattle trade with England and the slow development of mining and ore smelting.

The Civil War and the rise of Nonconformism

A direct descendant of the Tudors, **James I** came to the throne in 1603 to general popular approval in Wales. Many privileges granted to the Welsh during the Tudor reign came to an end, but the idea of common citizenship was retained, the Council of Wales remaining as a focus for Welsh nationalism. James, fearful of both Catholicism and the new threat of Puritanism – an extreme form of Protestantism – courted a staunchly Anglican Wales and curried the favour of Welsh ministers in the increasingly powerful Parliament. Though weak in Wales, Puritanism was gaining a foothold, especially in the Welsh borders, where William Wroth and Walter Cradock set up Wales' first dissenting church at Llanfaches in Monmouthshire in 1639.

The monarchy's relations with the Welsh were strained by **Charles I**, who was forced to levy heavy taxes and recruit troops, but the gentry were mostly loyal to the king at the outbreak of the **Civil War**, which saw the Parliamentary forces installing **Oliver Cromwell** as the leader of the **Commonwealth**. The Puritan support for Parliament didn't go unnoticed, and after Charles' execution, they were rewarded with the livings of numerous parishes and the roots of Puritan Nonconformism spread in Wales. As Cromwell's regime became more oppressive, the Anglican majority became disaffected and welcomed the successful return of the exiled **Charles II**, and the monarchy was restored. Charles replaced many of the clergy in their parishes and passed the Act of Uniformity, requiring adherence to the rites of the Established Church, and so suppressing Nonconformity. The Baptists, Independents and Quakers who made up the bulk of Nonconformists continued to worship in secret, until **James II** passed the **Toleration Act** in 1689, finally allowing open worship, but still banning the employment of dissenters in municipal government; a limitation which remained in force until 1828.

The rise of Methodism

The propagation of the Nonconformist seed in this fertile soil was less a conscious effort to convert the populace from Anglicanism than to better educate the masses. The late seventeenth century saw a welter of new religious books in Welsh, but with most people still illiterate, religious observance remained an oral tradition. In 1699, the **Society for Promoting Christian Knowledge**, set about establishing schools where the Bible, along with reading, writing and arithmetic, were taught in Welsh as well as English. This met with considerable success amongst the middle classes in anglicized towns, but failed to reach rural areas where children couldn't be spared from farm duties. The next big reformist push came in 1731, when **Griffith Jones** helped organize itinerant teachers to hold reading classes in the evenings and in the quieter winter season, so farmers and their families could attend. Within thirty years, half the Welsh population could read. After Jones' death, **Thomas Charles** of Bala (see p.417) continued his work, establishing Sunday schools and editing the first Welsh Bible to be distributed by the **British and Foreign Bible Society**.

By the middle of the eighteenth century, a receptive and literate populace was ready for three eloquent figures of the **Methodist Revival**, all driven by a strong belief in a resurgent Welsh nation. In contrast to the staid Anglican services, the Methodists held evangelical meetings: **Howel Harris** took his preaching outside or into people's homes, **Daniel Rowlands** converted thousands with his powerful sermons, and **William Williams** became the most important hymn writer in Welsh history. Meanwhile, improved schooling brought about a literary revolution, and Wales re-established itself as the language for a vast body of literature.

Until now, Methodism had worked within the framework of Anglicanism, but in 1811, the Calvinist Methodists broke away. As the gentry remained with the Established Church, Methodism associated itself with the spiritual and social needs of the masses, becoming a rallying point for the growing sense of disaffection with the traditional rule of the parson and squire. The chapel became the focus of social life, discouraging folk traditions as incompatible with the Puritan virtues of thrift and temperance. Political radicalism was also discouraged, perpetuating the stranglehold on parliamentary power exercised by the powerful landed elite, the Williams-Wynn, Morgan and Vaughan families in particular. Only property owners were eligible to vote and few were prepared to challenge established dynasties, even when the rare elections took place.

Human rights became an issue in 1776 with the publication of the American Declaration of Independence and a piece by the radical Welsh philosopher, **Richard Price**: *Observations on the Nature of Civil Liberty*. The subsequent calls for a greater degree of democracy – universal suffrage and annual parliaments – increased during the early days of the French Revolution, but little was actually achieved until the next century, when radical Nonconformists were able to exploit the increasing political consciousness of the working class.

Wales and the Industrial Revolution

Small-scale mining and smelting had taken place in Wales since the Bronze Age, but agriculture remained the mainstay of an economy with a dangerously limited diversity: meat, wool and butter being about the only exports. With the enormous rise in grain prices in the early nineteenth century, Welsh farmers began to diversify and adopted the more advanced English farming practices of crop rotation, fertilizing and stock breeding. Around the same time, acts of Parliament allowed previously common land to be "enclosed", the grazing rights often being assigned to the largest landowner in the district, which left the previous occupant with few or no rights to its use. Inevitably, this forced smallholders to migrate to the towns where ever more workers were required to mine the seams and stoke the furnaces, fuelling the **Industrial Revolution**. In the north, **John Wilkinson** started his ironworks at Bersham (see p.352) and developed a new method of boring cylinders for steam engines; while in the south, foundries sprang up in the valleys around Merthyr Tydfil, where methods of purifying iron and producing high-quality construction steel were perfected under the eye of English ironmasters. Gradually the undereducated, impoverished chapel-going Welsh began to be governed by rich, church-going, English industrial barons.

Improved materials and working methods enabled the exploitation of deeper coal seams, most notably in the south Wales valleys, not just to supply the iron smelters but for domestic fuel and to power locomotives and steamships. South Wales was transformed: rural valleys were ripped apart and quiet hamlets turned into long unplanned rows of back-to-back houses stretching up the valley sides, all roofed in north Wales slate from quarries dug by the Pennant and Assheton-Smith families.

Transportation of huge quantities of coal and steel was crucial for continued economic expansion, and the roads and canals built in the early nineteenth century were displaced around 1850 as the rail boom took hold. Great engineers made their names in Wales: **Thomas Telford** built canal aqueducts and successfully spanned the Menai Strait with one of Britain's earliest suspension bridges; **Isambard Kingdom Brunel** surveyed the Merthyr–Cardiff train line, then pushed his Great Western network almost to Fishguard; and **Robert Stephenson** speeded the passage of trains between London and Holyhead on Anglesey for the Irish ferry connection.

In mining towns, working conditions were atrocious, with men toiling incredibly long hours in dangerous conditions; women and children as young as six worked alongside them, until this was outlawed by the Mines Act in 1842. Pay was low and often in a currency redeemable only at the poorly stocked, expensive company (Truck) shop. The **Anti-Truck Act** of 1831 improved matters, but a combination of rising population, fluctuating prices and growing awareness of the need for political change brought calls for reform. When it came in 1832, the **Reform Bill** fell far short of the demands for universal suffrage by ballot and the removal of property requirement for voters. This swelled the ranks of the Reformist Chartist movement, and when a petition with over a million signatures was rejected by Parliament, the **Chartist Riots** (see p.93) broke out in northern England and south Wales. The Newport demonstration was disastrous, the marchers walking straight into a trap laid by troops, who killed over twenty men and captured their leader, **John Frost**. Chartism continued in a weakened form for twenty years, buoyed by the **Rebecca Riots** in 1839–43, when guerrilla tactics put an end to tollgates on south Welsh turnpikes.

1850 to World War I

During the latter half of the nineteenth century the radical reformist movement and religion slowly became entwined, despite Nonconformist denial of political intentions. Recognizing that their flock didn't share the same rights as Anglicans, the Nonconformists petitioned for **disestablishment** of the Church in Wales and began to politicize their message. In the 1859 election, tenants on large farms (the only ones permitted to vote) were justifiably afraid of voting against their landowners or even abstaining from voting, and the conservative landowning hegemony held. But as a consequence of the 1867 Reform Act, industrial workers and small tenant farmers got the vote, finally giving a strong working-class element to the electorate and seeing **Henry Richard** elected as Liberal MP for Merthyr Tydfil the following year, the first Welsh member of what soon became the dominant political force. Bringing the ideas of Nonconformity to Parliament for the first time, he spoke eloquently on land reform, disestablishment and the preservation of the Welsh language.

The 1872 Secret Ballot Act and 1884 Reform Act, enfranchising farm labourers, further freed up the electoral system and gave working people the chance to air their resentment of tithes extracted by a Church that didn't represent their religious views. Although several bills were tabled in Parliament in the 1890s, the Anglican church was only disestablished in 1920. The Nonconformist Sunday Schools were meanwhile offering the best primary education for the masses, supplemented, after **Hugh Owen** pushed through the Welsh Intermediate Education Act in 1885, by a number of secondary schools. Owen was also a prime mover in getting Wales' first major tertiary establishment started in Aberystwyth in 1872 (the tiny St David's University College in Lampeter was already fifty years old by then), soon to be followed by colleges at Cardiff (1883) and Bangor (1884). Until they were federated into the University of Wales in 1893, voluntary contributions garnered by Nonconformist chapels supported the colleges. The apotheosis of "Chapel power" came in 1881 with the passing of the Welsh Sunday Closing Act, enshrining Nonconformism's three basic tenets: observance of the Sabbath, sobriety and Welshness.

The rise in Welsh consciousness

During the nineteenth century, Welsh language and culture became weakened, largely through immigration to the coal fields from England. English became the language of commerce and the route to advancement; Welsh being reserved for the home and chapel life of seventy percent of the population. But Welsh was still being spoken in Nonconformist schools when, in 1846, they were inspected by three English barristers and seven Anglican assistants. The inspectors' report – known as **The Treason of the Blue Books** – declared the standards deplorable, largely due to the use of the Welsh tongue, "the language of slavery". This unfair report did some good in fostering free, elementary education at "Board Schools" after 1870, though the public defence of Welsh that ensued failed to prevent the introduction of the notorious "Welsh Not", effectively a ban on speaking Welsh in school.

As the nineteenth-century Romantic movement took hold throughout Britain, the London Welsh looked to their heritage. The ancient tales of The Mabinogion were translated into English, the **Welsh Language Society** was started in 1885, eisteddfodau were reintroduced as part of rural life, and the ancient bardic order, the **Gorsedd**, was reinvented. But disestablishment remained the cause célèbre of Welsh nationalism which, despite the formation of the **Cymru Fydd** ("The Wales To Be") movement in 1886, with its demands for home rule along the lines of Ireland, wasn't generally separatist. Perhaps the greatest advocate of both separatism and Welsh nationalism was **Michael D. Jones**, who helped establish a Welsh homeland in Patagonia and campaigned vociferously against "the English cause" (see p.417).

By 1907 Wales had a national library at Aberystwyth, and a national museum was planned for Cardiff, by now the largest city in Wales and laying claim to being its capital – only officially recognized as such in 1955.

Industry and the rise of trade unionism

The rise in Welsh consciousness paralleled the rise in importance of the **trade unions**. The 1850s were a prosperous time in the Welsh coal fields, but by the end of the 1860s the Amalgamated Union of Miners was forced to call a strike (1869–71), which resulted in higher wages. A second strike in 1875 failed and the miners' agent, **William Abraham (Mabon)**, ushered in the notorious "sliding scale" which fixed wage levels according to the selling price of coal. This brought considerable hardship to the Valleys, which became insular worlds with strictly ordered social codes and a rich vibrancy borne from the essential dichotomy of the chapel and the pub. Meanwhile, annual coal production doubled in twenty years to 57 million tons by 1913, when a quarter of a million people were employed. Similarly punitive pay schemes were implemented in the north Wales slate quarries where membership of **Undeb Chwarelwyr Gogledd Cymru** (The North Wales Quarrymen's Union) was all but outlawed by the slate barons. This came to a head in 1900 when the workers at Lord Penrhyn's quarry at Bethesda started one of Britain's longest-ever industrial disputes, lasting three years.

From 1885, the vast majority of Welsh MPs were Liberals who helped end the sliding scale in 1902 and brought in an eight-hour day by 1908. The start of the twentieth century heralded the birth of a new political force when **Keir Hardie** became Britain's first Labour MP, for Merthyr Tydfil.

The two World Wars

World War I (1914–18) was a watershed for Welsh society. Seeing parallels with their own nation, the Welsh sympathized with the plight of defenceless European nations and rallied to fight alongside the English and Scots. At home, the state intervened in people's lives more than ever before: agriculture was controlled by the state while food was rationed, and industries, mines and railways were under public control. The need for Welsh food and coal boosted the economy and living standards rose dramatically. Many were proud to be led through the war by Welsh lawyer **David Lloyd George** (see p.429), who rose to the post of Minister of Munitions, then of War, becoming Prime Minister by 1916; but by the time conscription was introduced, patriotic fervour had waned. Many miners, reluctant to be slaughtered in the trenches and resentful of massive wartime profits, welcomed the 1917 Bolshevik Revolution, and though Communism never really took hold, the socialist Labour Party was there to catch the postwar fallout.

Similar dramatic changes were taking place in rural areas, where Welsh farming was embracing new machinery and coming out of nearly a century of neglect. High wartime inflation of land prices and the fall in rents forced some landowners to sell off portions of major estates to their tenants in the so-called "green revolution", breaking the dominance of a rural landed gentry.

The boom time of World War I continued for a couple of years after 1918, but soon the Depression came. All of Wales' mining and primary production industries suffered, and unemployment reached 27 percent, worse than in England and Scotland, which both weathered the Depression better. The **Labour movement** ascended in step with the rise in unemployment, making south Wales its stronghold in Britain. Their stranglehold was challenged by Lloyd George's newly resurgent Liberal Party, but his Westminster-centred politics were no longer trusted in Wales and Labour held firm, seeking to improve workers' conditions: the state of housing was still desperate, and health care and welfare services needed boosting. The Labour Party effectively became the hope that had previously been entrusted to the chapels and later the Liberals.

A new sense of nationalism was emerging and, in 1925, champions of Welsh national autonomy formed **Plaid Genedlaethol Cymru** (the National Party of Wales) under **Saunders Lewis**, its president for ten years. In one of the first modern separatist protests, he joined two other Plaid members and set fire to building materials at an RAF station on the Llŷn, was imprisoned, dismissed from his post and spent the rest of his life immersed in the world of literary criticism, becoming one of Wales' greatest modern writers. Similar public displays and powerful nationalist rhetoric won over an intellectual majority, but the voting majority continued to fuel the Labour ascendancy in both local and national politics.

Some relief from the Depression came with re-armament in the lead-up to **World War II**, but by this stage vast numbers had migrated from south Wales to England, leaving the already insular communities banding together in self-reliant groups centred on local co-ops and welfare halls.

When war became inevitable, the Labour Party was committed to halting the Fascist threat along with most of Wales. As a result of the demands of the war, unemployment all but disappeared and the Welsh economy was gradually restructured, more people switching from extractive industries to light manufacturing, a process which continues today.

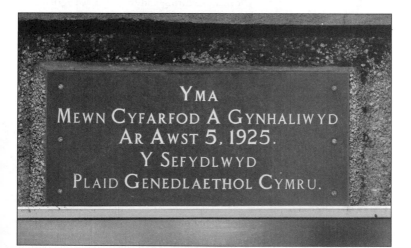

△ Plaid Genedlaethol Cymro plaque

Plaid Cymru were less enthusiastic about the war, remaining neutral and expressing unease at the large number of English evacuees potentially weakening the fabric of Welsh communities. Their fears were largely ungrounded and the war saw the formation of a Welsh elementary school in Aberystwyth and Undeb Cymru Fydd, a committee designed to defend the welfare of Wales.

The postwar period

Any hopes for a greater national identity were dashed by the Attlee Labour government from 1945 to 1951, which nationalized transport and utilities with no regard for national boundaries, except for the Wales Gas Board. However, under the direction of Ebbw Vale MP, **Aneurin Bevan**, the postwar Labour government instituted the National Health Service, dramatically improving health care in Wales and the rest of Britain, and providing much-improved council housing.

The nationalized coal industry, now employing less than half the number of twenty years before, was still the most important employer at nationalization, but a gradual process of closing inefficient mines saw the number of pits drop from 212 in 1945 to 11 in 1989, and just one in 2005. Sadly, the same commitment wasn't directed at cleaning up the scars of over a century of mining until after 1966, when one of south Wales' most tragic accidents left a school and 116 children buried under a slag heap at **Aberfan** (see p.107).

In the rural areas, the price stabilization that followed the 1947 Agriculture Act brought some relief to financially precarious hill farmers, who were given further protection with the formation of the Farmers' Union of Wales in 1955. A more controversial fillip came from the siting of an aluminium smelter and two nuclear power stations in north Wales, dubious benefits soon eroded by the closure of much of the rural rail system following the Beeching Report in 1963. Despite the switch to light manufacturing and the improved agricultural methods, unemployment in Wales rose to twice the UK average, and women continued to be greatly under-represented.

After its postwar successes, the Labour Party remained in overwhelming control during the 1960s and 1970s, though Plaid Cymru became a serious opposition for the first time, partly due to Labour's reluctance to address nationalist issues. Attlee had thrown out the suggestion of a Welsh Secretary of State in 1946, and not until Plaid Cymru was fielding twenty nationalist candidates in the 1959 election did the Labour manifesto promise a cabinet position for Wales. The position of **Secretary of State for Wales** was finally created in 1964 by the Labour government, led by Harold Wilson, who also created the **Welsh Development Agency** and moved the Royal Mint to Llantrisant in south Wales. With Plaid Cymru's appeal considered to be restricted to rural areas, Labour was shocked by the 1966 Carmarthen by-election, when **Gwynfor Evans** became the first Plaid MP. It wasn't until 1974 that Plaid also won in the constituencies of Caernarfon and Meirionydd, and suddenly the Party was a threat, forcing Labour to address the question of devolution. By 1978 Labour had tabled the **Wales Act**, promising the country an elected assembly to act as a voice for Wales, but with no power to legislate or raise revenue. In the subsequent **referendum** in 1979, eighty percent of voters opposed the proposition, with even the nationalist stronghold of Gwynedd voting against.

Modern Wales

In 1979, the Conservative (or Tory) government of **Margaret Thatcher** came to power, achieving an unprecedented 31 percent of Welsh votes. The 1979 referendum effectively sidelined the home-rule issue and Thatcher was able to implement her free-market policies with an unstinting commitment to privatizing nationalized industries. With 43 percent of the Welsh workforce as government employees, privatization had a dramatic impact. The number of jobs in the steel industry, manufacturing and construction all plummeted, doubling unemployment in five years. Despite this, the Tories held their share of the vote and, because of changes to constituency boundaries, increased their tally of MPs at the 1983 election, while Labour saw their lowest percentage since 1918.

Vast changes in employment patterns signalled the breakdown of traditional Valley communities and the labour movement was weakened by successive anti-union measures. None of this broke the solidarity of south Welsh workers during the year-long **Miners' Strike** (1984–85), after which women took a much greater proportion of the work now transferring out of the Valleys onto the south coastal plain. Living standards were still rising and the Welsh were now better off than ever before, but high unemployment and a large rural population meant that average income still lagged behind most areas of England, and despite free medical care, the Welsh remained in poorer health. As elsewhere in Britain in the second half of the twentieth century, the Welsh have turned their backs on the established religions. The chapel has ceased to be the focal point of community life, and something like two-thirds of the country's 6000 chapels have closed.

During the 1980s, support for Plaid Cymru shifted back to the rural areas, the party holding three out of four Gwynedd constituencies after the 1987 election. At the same time, general enthusiasm for the Welsh language increased and a steady decline in numbers of Welsh-speakers was reversed: the number continues to climb. New Welsh-only schools opened even in predominantly English-speaking areas, learners' classes sprouted everywhere and in 1982, S4C, the first **Welsh-language television channel**, started broadcasting.

Until their overwhelming defeat in the general election of 1997 (when Wales – and Scotland – elected no Tory MPs at all), the Tories landed the country with a succession of variously disinterested, and usually English, Secretaries of State who did little to further the Welsh cause. When Tony Blair and "New" Labour won a huge majority in May 1997, one of the central policy proposals was the **devolution** of some power from London to a parliament in Scotland and a **National Assembly for Wales** – the first all-Wales tier of government for six hundred years. The proposal was endorsed by the Welsh people only by the most slender of margins in a referendum. First elections to the Assembly took place in May 1999, when a huge swing to Plaid Cymru denied the Labour party its assumed overall majority. The second round of elections in 2003 saw Plaid slip back, but the Labour party still failed to get an overall majority. Although Labour still run the government in Cardiff Bay, with **Rhodri Morgan** as a fairly popular (and instinctively populist) First Minister, the opposition parties are more frequently working together to defeat them in a number of key areas. Whether this tactic will remain informal and infrequent, or develop into more formal pacts between the other parties (most notably Plaid Cymru, the Liberal Democrats and the Conservatives) remains to be seen, although such a route is perhaps the only possible way, in the short term, to see a non-Labour government in Cardiff.

To a large extent, the Assembly has seemingly failed to capture the public imagination – though the same could currently be said of all Western parliamentary institutions. Increasing powers are slowly drifting down from London, and the institution's snazzy new chamber building (see p.129) on the waterfront of Cardiff Bay, should give it a much-needed fillip. Perhaps the quietest vote of confidence in devolution is the increasing rarity with which the "abolish it" brigade surfaces these days. The institution is slowly bedding itself down into the fabric of Welsh life.

But it is not just in the political arena that the country has grown up: there has been a significant surge of national confidence and self-expression, particularly in the cultural and sporting arenas. That is not to say that everything is rosy: the property market is at snapping point in many areas, farming lurches along in a state of semi-paralysis, poverty and ill health still dog many old working-class communities. But these are interesting times in Wales: there is the undeniable feeling that this small country is slowly groping its way towards a brighter future than many would have dared predict even one generation ago.

Chronology of Welsh history

250,000 BC ▸ Earliest evidence of human existence in Wales.

4000 BC ▸ Agriculturalism becomes widespread in Wales.

2000 BC ▸ Arrival of **Bronze Age** settlers from the Iberian peninsula.

600 BC ▸ **Celts** reach the British Isles.

43 AD ▸ **Romans** begin conquest of Britain.

78 ▸ Roman conquest of Wales completed as Agricola kills druids of Anglesey.

80–100 ▸ Caerleon amphitheatre built.

early 4thC ▸ Roman departure from Wales.

5th–6thC ▸ **Age of Saints**.

c. 589 ▸ Saint David (Dewi Sant) dies.

616 ▸ Battle of Chester – Wales isolated from rest of Britain.

c. 784 ▸ Offa's Dyke (Clawdd Offa) constructed.

c. 900–50 ▸ Hywel Dda rules most of Wales.

1066 ▸ **Normans** invade Wales.

1067 ▸ Chepstow Castle started.

1180–93 ▸ St David's Cathedral built.

1188 ▸ Archbishop Baldwin (accompanied by Giraldus Cambrensis) recruits for the Third Crusade.

1196–1240 ▸ **Llywelyn ap Iorwerth** (the Great) rules as Prince of Gwynedd and later most of Wales.

1246–82 ▸ **Llywelyn ap Gruffydd** (the Last) intermittently rules large parts of Wales.

1270–1320 ▸ Tintern Abbey built.

1276–77 ▸ **First War of Welsh Independence**.

1277 ▸ Llywelyn humiliated by signing **Treaty of Aberconwy**. Edward I begins Aberystwyth, Flint and Rhuddlan castles.

1282–83 ▸ **Second War of Welsh Independence**. Llywelyn's brother Dafydd rises up against Edward I.

1283 ▸ Caernarfon, Conwy and Harlech castles started.

1284 ▸ **Statute of Rhuddlan** signed by Edward I.

1301 ▸ Edward I revives title of "Prince of Wales" and bestows it on his son, Edward II.

1400–12 ▸ Third War of Welsh Independence. **Owain Glyndŵr**'s revolt.

c.1416 ▸ **Owain Glyndŵr** dies in hiding.

1485 ▸ Accession of **Henry VII** to throne after landing from exile at Pembroke and beating Richard III at Bosworth.

1536–38 ▸ Henry VIII suppresses monasteries.

1536–43 ▸ **Acts of Union**: legislation forming the union of Wales and England. Equal rights but with a separate legal and administrative system conducted wholly in English.

1546 ▸ First book printed in Welsh: *Yn y Lhyvyr Hwnn*.

1571 ▸ Jesus College, Oxford (the Welsh college) founded.

1588 ▸ Translation of complete Bible into Welsh, chiefly by **William Morgan**.

1639 ▸ First Puritan congregation in Wales convened at Llanfaches, Gwent.

1646 ▸ Harlech and Raglan besieged during the **Civil War**. Harlech, the last Royalist castle, falls in 1647.

1660 ▸ Restoration of the monarchy.

1689 ▸ Toleration Act passed, allowing open, Nonconformist worship.

1743 ▸ Establishment of Welsh Calvinistic Methodist Church.

1759 ▸ Dowlais Ironworks started, followed by Merthyr Tydfil iron industry.

1782 ▸ Beginning of north Wales slate industry with the opening of Pennant's Penrhyn slate quarry at Bethesda.

1789 ▸ First **eisteddfod** for 200 years held at Corwen.

1793–94 ▸ Cardiff to Merthyr canal built.

1801 ▸ First census. Welsh population 587,000.

1839 ▸ **Chartist** march on Newport fails.

1839–43 ▸ **Rebecca Riots** close tollbooths on turnpikes.

1841 ▸ Taff Vale Railway built.

1845–50 ▸ Britannia Tubular Bridge built.

1865 ▸ Michael D. Jones founds Welsh colony in Patagonia.

1872 ▸ **University College of Wales** opens in Aberystwyth, followed by Cardiff (1883) and Bangor (1884).

1881 ▸ Passing of Welsh Sunday Closing Act.

1884 ▸ **Reform Act**. Farm labourers and small tenant farmers get the vote for the first time.

1900 ▸ Britain's first Labour MP, Kier Hardie, elected for Merthyr Tydfil.

1907 ▸ Founding of National Museum, Cardiff, and National Library, Aberystwyth.

1914–18 ▸ World War I.

1916 ▸ **David Lloyd George** becomes Prime Minister.

1920 ▸ Disestablishment of Church of England in Wales.

1925 ▸ Plaid Genedlaethol Cymru (Welsh National Party) formed.

1926 ▸ **Miners' strike** and General Strike.

1929–34 ▸ Great Depression.

1936 ▸ Saunders Lewis and colleagues burn building materials on the Llŷn.

1939–45 ▸ World War II.

1951 ▸ Minister for Welsh Affairs appointed.

1955 ▸ Cardiff declared capital of Wales.

1963 ▸ Cymdeithas yr Iaith Gymraeg (Welsh Language Society) formed.

1964 ▸ James Griffith, first cabinet-level Secretary of State for Wales, appointed.

1966 ▸ **Gwynfor Evans**, first Plaid Cymru MP, elected for Carmarthen.

Aberfan disaster.

1967 ▸ **Welsh Language Act** passed. Limited recognition of Welsh as a formal, legal language.

1979 ▸ Referendum on Welsh Assembly. Eighty percent of voters come out against a separate parliament.

1982 ▸ Welsh-language TV channel S4C begins broadcasting.

1984–85 ▸ **Miners' strike**.

1992 ▸ Welsh Language Bill gives Welsh equal status with English in public bodies.

1994 ▸ First Welsh film, *Hedd Wyn*, nominated for an Oscar.

1996 ▸ Another local government reorganization divides Wales into 22 unitary authorities.

1997 ▶ Referendum on Welsh Assembly. Only half the country vote, of whom 50.3 percent say yes, a majority of just 6000 nationwide.

1999 ▶ First **Welsh Assembly** elections. Assembly starts sitting.

The Rugby World Cup takes place with Wales as the host nation.

2005 Wales win the rugby Grand Slam.

Modern Welsh nationalism

Although Plaid Cymru – the Welsh nationalist political party – was formed in 1925, the political impetus that gave birth to the new movement had been bubbling for decades, if not centuries.

The Welsh identity had always been culturally rich, but was politically expressed only as part of the great Liberal tradition: in the dying years of the nineteenth century, Welsh Liberal MPs organized themselves into a loose caucus roughly modelled on Parnell's Irish parliamentarians and, although the Welsh group was without the clout or number of the Irish MPs, 25 or 30 MPs voting en bloc was serious enough to be noticed. **David Lloyd George** (1863–1945; Prime Minister 1916–22), fiery Welsh patriot and Liberal premier of Great Britain, had embodied many people's nationalist beliefs, although his espousal of greater independence for Wales came unstuck when, ever the expedient politician, he realized the potential difficulty of translating this ideal into hard votes in the industrialized, anglicized south of Wales. During Lloyd George's premiership, the Irish Free State was established, drawing inevitable comparisons with the Home Rule demands being less stridently articulated in Scotland and Wales. But the Liberal Party was in sharp decline, nowhere more markedly than in the industrialized Valleys, which had deserted them in favour of new socialist parties. With the urban slide of Liberalism, Welsh nationalism was gradually honed into the embryonic Plaid Cymru.

Initially, the party acted more as a pressure group, focused inevitably on the issue of the waning of the Welsh language and inextricably suffused with a romantic cultural air. As war loomed over Europe in the latter half of the 1930s, Plaid maintained a controversially pacifist stance, winning few new converts. Most sensationally, in September 1936, Saunders Lewis and two other Plaid luminaries, the Rev Lewis Valentine and D.J. Williams, set fire to the construction hut of a new aerodrome being built on the Llŷn as part of Britain's build-up to the war. They immediately reported themselves to the nearest police station, attracting huge publicity in the process. Interest in the ensuing trial electrified Wales, causing howls of outrage when the government decided to divert it from sympathetic Caernarfon to the Old Bailey in London. Even recalcitrant nationalist Lloyd George was outspokenly critical of the English decision. The three men were duly imprisoned for nine months, becoming Plaid Cymru's first heroes.

Postwar Wales

Despite having dwindled throughout the rest of Britain, the prewar Liberal tradition was still strong with the rural majority of Wales, though by the 1951 election this had become just three parliamentary seats out of 36. The **Labour party** was now the establishment in Wales, winning an average of around sixty percent of votes in elections from 1945 to 1966.

National feelings of loss and powerlessness began to take a hold in postwar Wales as the Welsh language haemorrhaged from the country. Although Wales consistently voted Labour, the Conservatives, the most fervently unionist of British political parties, were in power for thirteen years from 1951. Labour's 1945–51 administration had tinkered with a few institutions to give them a deliberately Welsh stance, but the Conservatives – winning only six out of 36 Welsh seats in 1951 – had little time for specifically Welsh demands. Two Welsh Labour MPs, Megan Lloyd George, daughter of the great Liberal premier, and S.O. Davies, spearheaded new parliamentary demands for greater Welsh independence, presenting a 1956 petition to Parliament demanding a Welsh assembly that was signed by a quarter of a million people. Massive popular protests against the continued flooding of Welsh valleys and villages to provide water for England shook the establishment. The 1963 formation of the boisterous *Cymdeithas yr Iaith Gymraeg* (the **Welsh Language Society**) created many headlines and attracted a new youthful breed of cultural and linguistic nationalists to the fold. The ruling Conservatives offered token measures in an attempt to lance the rising boil of nationalism: a part-time Welsh Minister was appointed, Cardiff was confirmed as capital and the Welsh flag authorized as official. The Labour party, meanwhile, was becoming more distinctively nationalistic, having formed a Welsh Council within the party, from where MPs, trade unionists and ordinary party members began to articulate the need for greater independence. In the **general election of 1964**, the party stood on a more nationalistic platform than ever before. As usual, they swept the board in Wales, and finally won throughout the UK as a whole. As promised in their manifesto, the post of **Secretary of State for Wales**, backed by a separate Welsh Office, was created, although with fewer powers than the Scottish equivalent which had existed since just after the war.

Wales and Scotland

Wales presents a very different proposition from Scotland where early nationalist movements are concerned. Scotland is a far more recent arrival (1707) in the British Union than Wales and still maintains identifiably different education, judicial and legal systems, whereas Wales' are totally subsumed into the English framework. Scotland is also relatively isolated, 400 miles from London, but Wales lies immediately west of large English conurbations: Birmingham, Liverpool and Manchester. Nor is Scottish nationalism so wrapped in linguistic pride: Gaelic is so thinly scattered that, unlike in Wales, nationalism has far transcended the language issue. Scottish nationalism has gained acceptance in both urban and rural settings, appealing to fiery socialists in Glasgow as much as well-heeled Tories of Grampian. By contrast, Plaid Cymru's support, with a few occasional exceptions, has usually been drawn from the rural, Welsh-language strongholds of the west and north.

Plaid Cymru starts to win

Despite these inherent drawbacks, it was Plaid who scored the first, and most dramatic, strike into Westminster, when Plaid President Gwynfor Evans won a by-election in Carmarthen in July 1966. Plaid Cymru and the Scottish National Party both soared in popularity in the wake of the Carmarthen result. Winnie Ewing, for the SNP, captured Hamilton from Labour in a 1967 by-election. Most dramatically, in the heart of socialist south Wales, Plaid ran the Labour government astonishingly close in two by-elections: in Rhondda West (1967) and Caerphilly (1968), the party saw swings of over 25 percent to cut Labour majorities of over twenty thousand to just a couple of thousand. From humble beginnings, it seemed that Plaid's time had come. Its traditional vote in the north and west was soaring, but, more importantly, Plaid was the only party threatening the dominance of Labour in the English-speaking industrial south. It appeared that the party had finally overcome its single-issue status around the Welsh language, and membership ballooned to forty thousand. Welsh nationalism reached new heights at the time of the Prince of Wales' theatrical 1969 investiture at Caernarfon, a gesture resented by many. The cause also gained its first martyrs, when two extremist nationalists blew themselves up at Abergele in Clwyd whilst attempting to lay a bomb on the rail line where Prince Charles was due to travel. In many ways, such acts had a detrimental effect on Plaid's cause, wrongly linking extremism with the more moderate and constitutional methods of the party.

Despite this, the **1970 general election** saw Plaid in more robust mood than had ever previously been justified. The astonishing results of the previous few years led them to believe that they could pick up a clutch of Westminster seats. Yet despite trebling their 1966 tally to 176,000 votes (11 percent of the poll in Wales), they failed to take any new seats and even lost their place in Carmarthen. Despite that, Plaid polled well in local elections, even taking control of Merthyr borough council. The second 1974 election returned Gwynfor Evans in Carmarthen to join two other Plaid Cymru MPs elected in the February election. Plaid's parliamentary band of three was dwarfed by the enormous success of the SNP in Scotland, who had succeeded in getting eleven MPs to Westminster. Furthermore, Plaid's earlier success in the industrialized south had evaporated, and they lost their deposits in 26 of the 36 Welsh seats. Once again, they were a party geographically concentrated in the rural outposts of Wales.

The combined strength of the nationalist parties at Westminster, added to the wafer-thin and dwindling parliamentary Labour majority, meant that the political demands of devolution were high on the government's agenda, as they could ill afford to lose the support of the SNP and Plaid Cymru MPs. The ruling Labour government set up the **Wales Development Agency**, supported the new Wales TUC (Trades Union Congress) and devolved the huge responsibilities of the Department of Trade and Industry in Wales to the Welsh Office in Cardiff. As their parliamentary majority became ever thinner, through the government losing a cache of by-elections, the nationalists' demands became more strident. Eventually, the Labour party put forward bills for Scottish and Welsh assemblies, subject to the result of referenda.

The 1979 referendum and beyond

In Wales, a massive four to one majority rejected the devolution proposal, and for many reasons. A large number of the eighty percent of the country who did not speak Welsh feared that a Welsh assembly would be the preserve of a new "Taffia", a *Cymraeg* elite. Both north and south Walians worried about potential domination by the other. People feared greater bureaucracy, particularly in the wake of the 1974 local government reorganization when a two-tier system of county and district councils had been imposed on Wales. A third tier, with few apparent powers, was not a terribly attractive proposition. On St David's Day 1979, the Welsh people made their feelings known.

The shock waves were great. Weeks later, the Labour government fell and **Margaret Thatcher**'s first Conservative administration was ushered in. Political nationalism seemed to have gone off the boil, and Plaid Cymru were back to just two MPs representing the northwestern constituencies of Meirionydd and Caernarfon. The early 1980s were dominated by swiftly rising unemployment and a collapse in Britain's manufacturing base. Nowhere was this more evident than in south Wales, where mines and foundries closed and the jobless total soared. Welsh nationalism was suffering an identity crisis, typified by Plaid Cymru's controversial 1981 rewriting of its own constitution to fight for an avowedly "Welsh socialist state", causing some of its more conservative members to quit the party. Basing itself as a republican, left-wing party would, it was believed, bring greater fruit in the populated south. The nationalists suffered by implication from the activities of Meibion Glyndŵr (**Sons of Glyndŵr**), a shadowy organization dedicated to firebombing English holiday homes in Wales. Plaid continued to plough a firmly constitutional and peaceful route to national self-determination, but many people assumed that the bombers received covert support amongst the party's ranks.

Gwynfor Evans might well have lost his Carmarthen seat in 1979, but he was singlehandedly responsible for the most high-profile activity of Welsh nationalism in the early 1980s. The Conservative party had fought the general election of 1979 on a manifesto that included a commitment to a Welsh-language TV channel. When plans for the new UK Channel 4 were drawn up, this promise had been dropped. The Plaid Cymru president decided to fast until death, if necessary, as a peaceful protest. It did not take long before this action, gaining enormous publicity in the media, forced the Thatcher government to make its first U-turn, and **Sianel Pedwar Cymru** (S4C) was born in 1982. Perhaps the Tories realized the political advantage of bringing Welsh nationalism into the legitimate fold, for the Welsh media industry, long accused of a nationalistic bent, dissipated many angry and impassioned arguments for national self-determination. Many of the most heartfelt radicals ended up in prominent positions within Wales' media.

Like so many other political affiliations and ideals in the 1980s, Welsh nationalism underwent something of a sea change during the decade. As the Labour party was routed in the 1983 election, precipitating a rightward slide for the rest of the decade and beyond, Plaid Cymru began to broaden its base as a radical and mature political force with a firmly socialist, internationalist outlook. The party developed serious policies on all aspects of Welsh life, from traditional rallying calls of language and media to sophisticated analyses of economic policy, the Welsh legal framework and the country's role in the European Union and the wider world. But Welsh devolution – if not outright nationalism – ceased to be the preserve of Plaid Cymru alone. Two of the three UK-wide parties, Labour and, in particular, the Liberal Democrats, inheritors of the great Liberal tradition, evolved devolutionary strategies for Wales and Scotland. Each party created a semi-autonomous Welsh branch, with its own party conference, election broadcasts and manifesto. Even the Conservatives reluctantly followed suit and, in government, continued to devolve more governmental decision-making out to the Welsh Office in Cardiff. This, ironically, strengthened the nationalist hand. Plaid and the other parties pointed out that a huge swath of government existed in Wales, overseen by no all-Wales authority, but run instead by unelected bodies, known as quangoes. The call for a Welsh assembly to oversee this vast array of public expenditure was consistently supported by huge majorities in opinion polls, and formed the basis of the Labour Party's manifesto for Wales throughout the 1990s.

Labour government and a new referendum

The **1997 general election** changed everything. The Conservatives, tired and tetchy after eighteen years in government, were spectacularly swept from power, failing to keep any seats whatsoever in Wales. Labour – or "New" Labour as the party was styled under Tony Blair – won hugely, denting any further Plaid progress and keeping the nationalists firm in their northern and western strongholds and on little more than one-tenth of the vote. However, as always, Plaid has been better placed to do well under a Labour government than a Conservative one.

Within six months of Blair's election, referenda took place in Wales and Scotland on the devolution proposals. Scotland voted wholeheartedly for its parliament; in Wales, the proposals barely scraped through. Although this was potentially the first piece of self-government for Wales in 600 years, many nationalists felt that it fell far short of expectations and was not worth supporting. Plaid Cymru's own stance mirrored this ambivalence: initially unenthusiastic and only coming out for the Assembly in the latter stages of the campaign. Wales itself was firmly, and almost exactly, split by the devolution vote. The border areas and Pembrokeshire, true to their historical anglicization, voted no, while Plaid's west coast strongholds and the "Old" Labour bastions of the industrial Valleys were enthusiastic enough – just – to swing the ballot.

The National Assembly for Wales

The strength of the "yes" vote in the industrial south of Wales was something of a harbinger to the campaign proper for the Assembly's sixty seats. Here, more than anywhere, Plaid Cymru achieved spectacular gains, taking Labour strongholds like Rhondda, Islwyn and Llanelli. The Plaid share of the vote was their highest ever, at nearly 30 percent, and it was enough to deny Labour – once the absolute party in Wales – an overall majority.

So far, this has proven to be Plaid's high-water mark. The 2003 Assembly elections saw the party lose all of its Valleys seats and only just cling on to the status of largest opposition group. UK-wide general elections in 2001 and 2005 have shown the party's support treading water somewhat. All three main opposition parties have reason to claim that they are the first amongst equals: the Conservatives in the popular vote, Plaid in the number of Assembly Members (AMs) and the LibDems in the number of Welsh MPs. With a minority Labour government operating in Cardiff Bay, these three parties are tentatively working together to see whether anything more formal, such as an electoral pact, is possible, but alliance with the Conservatives, in particular, could prove to be a way too bitter pill to swallow for many Plaid members, let alone the voters at large.

△ Welsh Assembly advertisement

With Plaid Cymru having to play it as a sober democratic party, much of the more interesting aspects of Welsh nationalism are to be found away from party politics. Regular dust-ups over patronizing English attitudes still periodically ignite the media, while debates rage on about English in-migration and the purchase of second homes in the heartlands of the Welsh language and culture. In a journalistic atmosphere that has at times been decidedly febrile and ill-tempered, the first casualty has been proper debate, with everything reduced to hysterical soundbites. Out of this environment has come new pressure group **Cymuned** ("Community"; ⊛www.cymuned.org), whose slogan "Dal dy dir!" ("Hold your ground!") is seen daubed all around Wales. Cymuned is slick, modern and thoughtful, and could well prove to be the intellectual driving force for modern Welsh nationalism, especially as Plaid Cymru continues to struggle with its wings clipped for electoral expediency. One of Plaid's main drawbacks has been confusion, and disillusion, over its leadership, particularly in the Assembly under the lacklustre Anglesey AM Ieuan Wyn Jones. There is, however, an impressive new generation emerging in Plaid, who, if given half the chance, should be able to restore some status to the party.

Since the arrival of the Assembly, it's hard for even the most ardent of nationalists to argue that Wales' system of government is the most pressing issue facing the nation. With farming in utter crisis, one of the poorest standards of living in the UK, and job opportunities limited to the low-wage old industrial sectors of the south, there are plenty of meatier matters to chew on. If the Assembly can be seen to make a difference to these issues, its reputation will soar, and this in itself is surely the best argument for according it greater power.

However, in the early years of the twenty-first century, it's safe to say that the majority of Welsh people are fairly happy with things as they are. Although percentages of Welsh speakers have fallen slightly in the language's heartlands according to the 2001 census results, huge rises in the anglicized southeast mean that the number of Welsh speakers in Wales is at its highest level for forty years, and rising. Language aside, the general sense of Welshness has been much augmented in recent years, as much by sporting achievements and rock music as by any politician. Wales is more and more happily, and very easily, calling itself a nation. The question that still hangs in the air is simply this: to be a nation, does Wales really need to be a state?

Natural history of Wales

A comprehensive account of Wales' landscapes, land use, flora and fauna would take several books to cover. What follows is a general overview of the effects of geology, human activity and climate on the country's flora, fauna and land management.

Wales is covered with a wide array of sites deemed to be of national or international importance, all seemingly with different designations. The three **National Parks** – Snowdonia, the Brecon Beacons and the Pembrokeshire Coast – comprise almost twenty percent of the country, with another couple of percent incorporated into the five **Areas of Outstanding Natural Beauty** (AONB): the Anglesey coast, the Llŷn coast, the Clwydian Range, the Gower peninsula and the Wye Valley. Smaller areas (from a few acres to large chunks of the Cambrian Mountains) with specific habitats such as lowland bogs or ancient woodlands are managed as **National Nature Reserves** (NNRs). Most are widely promoted, usually posted with information boards and threaded with easy, well-signed walking trails. All NNRs contain **Sites of Special Scientific Interest** (SSSIs; aka triple-SIs), a category including around another 700 locations in Wales singled out for special protection. Most are on private land with no right of access.

It must be remembered that nowhere in Wales is untouched, almost every patch of "wilderness" being partially the product of human intervention, thoroughly mapped, mined and farmed. Nor is anywhere free from pollution: the conurbations of England are too close, power stations and factories dot the countryside and some of the seas are in a poor state. That said, several clean-air-loving lichen species – found in few other places in Britain – abound in Wales.

Geology

Geologists puzzled over the forces that shaped the Welsh landscape for centuries before early nineteenth-century geologist **Adam Sedgwick** and his collaborator (and later rival) **Roderick Murchison** began to unravel the secrets. They were able to explain the shattered, contorted and eroded rocks that form the ancient peaks of Snowdonia, but fought bitterly over rock classification. By naming the **Silurian** rock system (400–440 million years ago) after one of Wales' ancient tribes, Murchison started a trend that continued with the naming of the earlier **Ordovician** system (440–500 million years ago) and the **Cambrian** system (500–600 million years ago), given the Roman name for Wales. Anglesey, the Llŷn and Pembrokeshire all have older **pre-Cambrian** rocks; those around St David's are some of the most ancient in the world.

Wales is packed with mountains, and several areas deserve brief coverage. Between 600 and 400 million years ago, **Snowdonia** was twice submerged for long periods in some primordial ocean where molten rock from undersea volcanoes cooled to form igneous intrusions in the sedimentary ocean-floor layers. Snowdon, Cadair Idris and the Aran and Arenig mountains are the product of these volcanoes, with fossils close to the summit of Snowdon, supporting the theory of its formation on the sea floor. After Silurian rocks had been laid down, immense lateral pressures forced the layers into concertina-like parallel folds with the sedimentary particles being rearranged at right angles to the pressure, giving today's vertically splitting sheets of **slate**, the classic metamorphosed product of these forces. It is known that the folded strata that rose above the sea bore no resemblance to today's mountains, the cliff face of Lliwedd on Snowdon showing that the summit was at the bottom of one of these great folds between two much higher mountains. One of these is now known as the **Harlech Dome**, a vast rock hump where the softer Silurian rocks on the surface all wore away and the Ordovician layers below were only saved by the volcanic intrusions, principally Snowdon and Cadair Idris. In between, the Ordovician rocks wore away, exposing the harder Cambrian sand and gritstones of the **Rhinog** range. In the very recent geological past from 10,000–80,000 years ago, these mountains were worked on by the latest series of **Ice Ages**, with glaciers scouring out hemispherical cirques divided by angular ridges, then scraping down the valleys, gouging them into U-shapes with waterfalls plunging down their sides.

Snowdonia is linked by the long chain of the **Cambrian Mountains** to the dramatic north-facing scarp slope of the **Brecon Beacons**, south Wales' distinctive east–west range at the head of the south Wales coal field. Erosion of the ancient Cambrian, Ordovician and Silurian rocks which once covered what is now northern Britain and much of the North Sea washed down great river systems, depositing beds of old red sandstone from 350–400 million years ago. These **Devonian** rocks lay in a shallow sea where the molluscs and corals decayed to form carboniferous limestone, which in turn was overlaid by more sediment forming millstone grit. Subsequent layers of shale and sandstone were interleaved with decayed vegetable matter, forming a band known as **coal measures**, from which the mines once extracted their wealth. The whole lot has since been tilted up in the north, giving a north to south sequence which runs over a steep sandstone ridge (the Brecon Beacons), then down a gentle sandstone dip-slope arriving at the pearl-grey limestone band where any rivers tend to dive underground into **swallow holes**. They reappear as you reach the gritstone, often tumbling over waterfalls into the coal valleys.

Erosion still continues today, slowly reshaping the landscape, hastened by the Welsh climate.

Land settlement and usage

After the last ice sheet drew back from Wales, the few plant species which had survived on the ice-free peaks (known as nunataks) were in a strong position to colonize, producing an open grassland community more than 10,000 years ago. Birch and juniper were amongst the first trees, followed by hazel. Several thousand years later this had developed into a mixed deciduous woodland including oak, elm and some pine, and in wetter areas damp-loving alder and birch. The Neolithic tribes began to settle on the upland areas, using their flint axes to clear the mountain slopes of their forests. The discovery of bronze and later iron hastened the process, especially since wood charcoal was required for smelting iron ore, and so began the spiralling devastation of Wales' native woodlands. As the domestication of the sheep and goats put paid to any natural regeneration of saplings, more land became available for arable farming. Thin, acidic mountain soils and a damp climate made **oats** – fodder for cattle and horses – about the only viable cereal crop, except in Anglesey which, by the time the Romans arrived in the first century AD, was already recognized as Wales' most important wheat-growing land. Cattle rearing was increasingly important on the lusher pastures, and even as late as the twelfth century, Giraldus Cambrensis tells us that "the whole population lives almost entirely on oats and the produce of their herds, milk, cheese and butter".

Giraldus lived at a time when the Normans were pushing into lowland Wales and acting as patrons of the monasteries. Until they were appropriated by Henry VIII in 1536, the seventeen Cistercian houses all kept extensive lands, cleared woods and developed sheep walks and cattle farms. With the Dissolution of the Monasteries, their lands became part of the great estates which still take up large tracts of Wales.

By contrast, the less privileged were still smallholders living simple lives. In the 1770s the travel writer Thomas Pennant noted in his *Tours in Wales* that the ordinary people's houses on the Llŷn were "very mean, made with clay, thatched and destitute of chimneys". The poor state of housing had much to do with the practice of *Tŷunnos* (literally "one-night house"), supposedly a right decreed by Hywel Dda, in which building a house of common materials close at hand within 24 hours staked your claim on a plot of common land. The practice hadn't completely died out in the 1850s when George Borrow's guide observed, "That is a house, sir, built yn yr hen dull in the old fashion, of earth, flags, and wattles and in one night – the custom is not quite dead."

In the eighteenth century, **droving** reached its peak. Welsh black cattle, fattened on Anglesey or the Cambrian coast, were driven to market in England, avoiding the valley-floor toll roads by taking highland routes that can still be traced. Nights were spent with the cattle corralled in a halfpenny field (so called because this was the nightly rate per animal) next to a lonely homestead heralded by three Scots pines, which operated as an inn. It was a tough journey for men and cattle, but easier than for geese, whose webbed feet were toughened for the long walk with tar and sand.

At home, women ground the wheat, aided by mills driven by the same fast-flowing mountain streams that later provided power for textile mills springing up all over the country. The Cistercians had laid the foundations of the **textile industry** for both wool and flannel, but it had generally remained in the cottages, with nearly every smallholding keeping a spinning wheel next to their harp. The same sort of damp climate that made Lancashire the centre of the world's cotton industry encouraged the establishment of a textile industry in Ruthin, Denbigh, Newtown, Llandeilo and along the Teifi Valley, but a lack of efficient transport made them uncompetitive.

The next major shift in land use came with a wave of **enclosure acts** from 1760 to 1820, which effectively removed smallholders from upland common pasture and granted the land to holders of already large estates. With the fashion for grouse shooting taking hold in the middle of the nineteenth century, large tracts of hill country began to be managed as heather moor, with frequent controlled fires to encourage the new growth that the grouse fed on. The people were deprived of their livelihood, and access to open country was denied to future generations of walkers, a situation only recently reversed.

The mountain building processes discussed above have left a broad spectrum of minerals under Wales. **Copper** had been mined with considerable success since the Bronze Age, and was further exploited by the Romans, who dabbled in **gold** extraction. But it wasn't until the latter half of the eighteenth century that mining became big business, with a rapid expansion in both north and south Wales. **Slate** (see p.412) was hewn from deeper mines and higher mountainsides, while the northern ends of the south Wales valleys echoed to the sounds of the ironworks. The fortuitous discovery of iron ore, limestone for smelting and coal for fuelling the furnaces made the valleys the crucible of the iron industry, and iron stayed at the forefront here long after richer ore finds elsewhere.

Originally a service industry, **coal mining** soon took over and shaped the development of south Wales for over a century. Further west, the processing of Cornish **copper** financed the development of Swansea, while Llanelli devoted itself to **tin**.

Flora

Wales supports 1100 of Britain's 1600 native plants, with ferns and other moisture-loving species particularly well represented.

Until five thousand years ago, birch, juniper, hazel, oak and elm covered the mountainsides, but devastating forest clearances and a wetter climate have left only a few pockets of native woodland in the valleys, their regeneration threatened by sheep grazing on fresh seedlings. **Pengelli Forest** in Pembrokeshire represents one of Wales' largest blocks of ancient woodland, comprising **midland hawthorn** and **sessile oak**, the dominant tree in ancient Welsh forests. Parts of the Severn and lower Wye valleys are well wooded, as is the Teifi Valley, where oak, ash and sycamore predominate. You can still occasionally see evidence of **coppicing** – an important and ancient practice common a century ago – where trees are cut close to the base to produce numerous shoots harvested later as small-diameter timbers. Under the canopy, **bluebells** and **wood sorrel** are common, and in the autumn look out for the dozens of species of

mushroom, especially the delicious but elusive **chantrelle**, found mainly under beech trees.

A far greater area of Wales is smothered in gloomy ranks of **conifers** (predominantly sitka spruce), a product of the twentieth-century monoculture ethic. Forbidding to most birds and too shaded and acidic for wildflowers, they are the object of widespread criticism directed towards the Forestry Commission.

Perhaps the most celebrated of all Wales' plants are the **arctic alpines** that grow away from grazing sheep and goats amongst the high, lime-yielding crags and gullies of Snowdonia and the Brecon Beacons, their southernmost limit in Britain. Ever since the ice sheets retreated ten thousand years ago, the warmer weather has forced arctic alpines towards higher ground, where they cling to small pockets of soil behind rocks. Some get unceremoniously cleaned out by thoughtless climbers trying to push up novel routes, but in the main, their spread hasn't changed since they were discovered by seventeenth-century botanists such as Thomas Johnson and Welshman Edward Lhuyd, who found *Lloydia serotina*, a glacial relic more popularly known as the **Snowdon Lily** (though actually a spiderwort), that looks not unlike a small off-white tulip. In Britain, it is found only around Snowdon and then only rarely seen between late May and early June, when it blooms.

The exemplary habitat for arctic alpines is widely regarded to be **Cwm Idwal** in the Ogwen Valley, where you may get to see some of the more common species, in particular the handsome **purple saxifrage**, whose tightly clustered flowers often push through the late winter snows, later followed by the starry and mossy saxifrages and spongy pink pads of **moss campion**. The star-shaped yellow flowers of **tormentil** are typical of high grassy slopes, and you may also find **mountain avens**, distinguished by its glossy oak-like leaves, and, when it blooms in June, by its eight white petals. From June to October, purple heads of **wild thyme** cover the ground, providing food for a small beetle unique to Snowdonia.

Sheep prefer the succulent **sheep's fescue**, but competition for the juicier shoots leads to overgrazing and the growth of tough mat-grass which chokes out the **woolly-hair moss**, the **reindeer moss** and the **dwarf willow**, which can otherwise be seen in yellow bloom during June and July. Just below the wind-battered mountaintops are the early colonizing species; **alpine meadow grass**, **glacier buttercup**, **mountain sorrel** and **alpine hair grass** among them.

Poor acid soils on the igneous uplands foster the growth of lime-shy bracken, bilberry and purple **heather** – bell, ling, cross-leaved and Scottish are all found – which combine with decayed **sphagnum moss** in wetter areas to form peat bogs. Though generally less extensive than in upland bogs elsewhere in Britain, the Welsh wetlands still support the **bog asphodel** which produces its brilliant yellow spikes in late summer, often in company with the **spotted orchid** and less frequently the tiny **bog orchid**. Insectivorous plants are also found, such as the **butterwort** (both pale and common varieties) and the **sundew** (long-leaved and round-leaved), which both gain nutrients that their poor surroundings cannot provide by digesting insects trapped on the sticky hairs of their leaves.

Limestone uplands such as the Clwydian ridges and parts of the Brecon Beacons are more likely to host less rugged plants, like the **harebell** and the **rock rose**. Streams running off these uplands tumble down narrow valleys hung with ferns and mosses and sometimes scattered with the yellow-flowered **Welsh poppy**.

At sea level, the rivers spawn estuarine "meadows", which in summer are carpeted with bright violet **sea lavender**, followed by a mauve wash of **sea aster** after August. An unusual coastal feature is the dam-formed string of **Bosherston Lakes**, south of Pembroke, where the fresh water supports rafts of **white-water lilies**. Further west, the Pembrokeshire coast is a blaze of colour in early summer, with white-flowered **scurvy grass** and **sea campion**, yellow **kidney vetch** and **celandine**, and blue **spring squill**. **Water crowfoot** is found in fresh water near the coastal footpath, where you can also find the hemispherical lilac heads of **devil's bit scabious**. **Bluebells** and **red campion** cloak Pembrokeshire's islands, while the majority of species mentioned can be found in abundance in Newborough on Anglesey. Here, some of Wales' finest sand dunes are bound by **marram grass**, interspersed with **sea holly**, **sea bindweed** and the odd **marsh helleborine**.

Birds

With its long coastline, Wales, as you might expect, abounds in sea birds, and the profusion of islands and its position on the main north–south migratory route make several sites particularly noteworthy. This remains the case despite the massive *Sea Empress* oil spill that contaminated the waters around Milford Haven in early 1996. Wind and tides distributed the oil around the fragile breeding grounds of Pembrokeshire, and some 5000 common scoter were lost, but it could have been a lot worse. Most breeding birds hadn't yet arrived and the worst of the mess was cleaned up before they did.

The Royal Society for the Protection of Birds (RSPB), Sutherland House, Castlebridge, Cowbridge Road East, Cardiff CF11 9AB (☎029/2035 3000, ⍟www.rspb.org.uk), operates twelve sites throughout Wales, half of them on the coast. The islands off the Pembrokeshire coast are incomparable for sea-bird colonies, the granite pinnacle of **Grassholm** (RSPB), 12 miles offshore, hosting the world's third-largest gannet colony with 30,000 pairs. Grassholm can only be visited by prior arrangement after mid-June, but the islands closer to the coast are more accessible, **Skokholm** and **Skomer** between them supporting 6000 pairs of **storm petrels** and an internationally significant population of 140,000 pairs of the mainly nocturnal **Manx shearwater**, which spend their winter off the coast of South America. Burrows vacated by rabbits on the islands also provide nests for puffins, while **razorbills**, **guillemots** (known as *elegug* in Pembrokeshire) and **kittiwakes** nest on the cliffs. Since the eradication of the rats that previously deterred burrow-nesting birds (the chough, a rare, red-billed, red-legged member of the crow family, was the only species to remain), Manx shearwaters are also now colonizing **Ramsey Island**, a few miles north. A few pairs of choughs are also found on the important migration stopover, **Bardsey Island** off the Llŷn coast, and at the wonderful **South Stack Cliffs** (RSPB) on Anglesey which, especially from May to July, are alive with breeding guillemots, razorbills and puffins. Like much of the coast, **fulmars** and **peregrine falcons** are also present in respectable numbers, as are **cormorants** – though these birds usually nest only by the sea, Craig yr Aderyn, a cliff four miles inland from Tywyn, hosts a small population that is in decline.

The mudflats and saltings of Wales' estuaries provide rich pickings for wintering waders. The **Dee estuary** (RSPB), on the northern border with England, plays host to Europe's largest concentration of **pintail** as well as **oystercatchers**, **knot**, **dunlin**, **redshank** and many others. Numerous terns replace them in the summer months.

Central Wales represents one of Britain's last hopes for reviving the population of **red kites** which, like many other raptors, were traditionally persecuted by gamekeepers and suffered from the use of pesticides, which caused thinning of egg shells. The banning of DDT in the 1960s allowed numbers to increase, but there are still only 500 of these fork-tailed birds left, predominantly in the Elan Valley. However, as with the other persecuted species, the hen harrier, the peregrine falcon and the sparrowhawk, numbers are increasing. Perhaps one day the heights of Snowdonia may again resound to the cry of the eagle which gives the mountains their Welsh name, *Eryri*.

The high country supports larger populations of **kestrels**, usually seen hovering motionless before plummeting onto an unsuspecting mouse or vole, and golden-brown **buzzards** gently wheeling on the thermals on the lookout for prey which can be as big as a rabbit. Buzzards and peregrine falcons are as happy picking at carrion, but have to compete with sinister black **ravens**, that inhabit the highest ridges and display their crazy acrobatics, often banding together to mob the bigger birds.

Acidic heather uplands between one and two thousand feet provide habitats for the black and red **grouse**, whose laboured flight is in complete contrast to the darting zigzag of its neighbour, the **snipe**. On softer grassland, expect to find the **ring ouzel**, a blackbird with a white cravat, and the **golden plover**, a bird still common but being threatened, like many others, by the spread of conifer forests, which welcome little except wood pigeons and blackbirds.

After the gloomy pines, it is a delight to wander in relict stands of the ancient oak woodlands, and along the streams where the **dipper** and **kingfishers** flourish. On sheltered water you might also find shelduck, Canada geese and three species of swan.

Mammals

During the last interglacial period, Wales was warm enough to support hippos and lions, but humans, pressed for space by the expanding ice sheets, killed them off, leaving bears and boars which in turn were dispatched by human persecution. Some of the last beaver lodges in Britain dammed the Teifi in the twelfth century, while half a millennium later, wolves disappeared from the land. What remains is a restricted range of wild mammals topped up with semi-wild and feral beasts: shy herds of **ponies** on the Carneddau in Snowdonia and on the Brecon Beacons are rounded up annually, deer occasionally stray from captive herds, and the **goats** in Snowdonia (on the Glyder and the Rhinog ranges especially) and on the Great Orme at Llandudno are descendants of domesticated escapees. Generally welcomed by farmers, they forage on the precipitous ledges, thereby discouraging sheep from grazing ventures beyond their capabilities. About the only other large land mammals are the soft-fleeced **Soay sheep** at Newborough Warren on Anglesey.

Though widely acknowledged as the scourge of wildlife, the spread of conifer plantations has seen a surge in the population of the elusive, stoat-like **pine marten**, which thrives in sitka spruce where its diet of squirrels is readily available. Both pine martens and the more common **polecats** are found in Snowdonia, in the ancient woodlands of Pengelli Forest on the slopes of Mynydd Preseli, in the relict beechwoods of the Brecon Beacons and the coastal dunes where they prey on rabbits. Trapped almost into oblivion in the nineteenth century, polecats have recolonized almost all of Wales and parts of western England over the last fifty years. **Foxes** are widespread, along with the **brown hare**, **stoat** and **weasel**, though the **badger** is rarer and still the subject of persecution through the cruel sport of badger baiting. **Rabbits** seem to be everywhere, and the North American **grey squirrel** has all but dislodged the native red squirrel from its habitat, though it still hangs on around Lake Vyrnwy and at Newborough on Anglesey. Of the smaller beasts, **shrews** and **wood mice** abound, and the island of Skomer has a unique subspecies of **vole**.

Otters almost became extinct in Wales some years back, but a concerted effort on the part of the Otter Haven Project has seen their numbers climbing in the Teifi and some of the rivers in Montgomeryshire. They remain an endangered species, and perhaps fortunately are seldom seen, but indicate their presence by their droppings.

The waters off the Pembrokeshire Coast around the Marloes peninsula and Skomer Island have been designated a **marine reserve**, though this doesn't cover the **grey seal** breeding colony on the west coast of Ramsey Island, where each year a couple of hundred white-furred pups are born. Sadly, marine pollution is being increasingly detected in the seals' blubber, a worrying sign too for the **dolphins** and **porpoises** inhabiting the coastline.

Fish, reptiles and insects

Wales' clean, fast-flowing rivers make ideal conditions for the **brown trout**, a fish managed for sport throughout the country. In Wales, the damming of rivers has seldom cut off spawning grounds, but the fishable limit of the Conwy in particular has been extended by the introduction of a fish ladder around the Conwy Falls. **Salmon** are less common, found mainly in the Usk and the Wye, the latter being the only river where it is important as game fish. Along with **roach**, **perch** and other coarse fish, the depths of Bala Lake (Llyn Tegid) claim the unique silver-white **gwyniad**, an Ice Age relic not dissimilar to a small herring, said never to take a lure. Llyn Padarn in Llanberis also notches up a rarity with the freshwater **char**. Conditions for successful fish farming do not exist in Wales, but commercially viable beds of **cockles** still exist on the north coast of the Gower and families still own rights to musselling the sands of the Conwy estuary.

With Welsh red dragons dying out along with King Arthur, much smaller lizards and two species of snake are all that remain of Wales' reptiles. The poisonous, triangular-headed **adder** is sometimes spotted sunning itself on dry south-facing rocks, but, except in early spring when it is roused from hibernation, it frequently slithers away unnoticed. The harmless **grass snake** prefers a wetter environment and is equally shy. Easily mistaken for a snake, the **slowworm** is actually a legless lizard and is common throughout Wales, as are **toads** and **frogs** – though the rare **natterjack toad** is only found in a few locations.

As for **butterflies**, southern British species – the common blue and red admiral – are abundant in sheltered spots, but aim for the woodland reserves, found dotted all over the country, to find the **dark green fritillary** and its pearl-bordered and silver-washed kin. South Wales is particularly good for insect life, with Pengelli Forest home to the rare **white-letter hairstreak** as well as one of Britain's rarest dragonflies, the bright blue **southern damselfly**, while the Gower peninsula harbours populations of **marbled white butterfly** and the **great green bush cricket**, uncommon anywhere else in Wales. Lastly, Snowdonia has the unique and aptly named **rainbow leaf beetle**.

Ecology and the future

With the smokestack industries now largely absent from Wales and the Valleys mostly devoid of working coal mines, nature (sometimes with the help of schemes to level and replant spoil heaps) is struggling to claw its way back. A verdure inconceivable forty years ago now cloaks the hillsides, and already, the industrial remains are being cherished as cultural heritage; as much a valid part of the "natural" landscape as the mountain backdrops. If you need convincing, climb up to the disused slate workings behind Blaenau Ffestiniog or walk the old ironworks tramways around Blaenafon.

In other areas, much remains to be done to restore the ecological balance. The increasing commercialization of farming has led not just to the damaging application of pesticides and excessive use of nitrogen-rich fertilizers, but to the wholesale removal of **hedgerows** and **drystone walls**, ideal habitats for numerous species of flora and fauna. Conservation groups promote the skills needed to lay hedges and build dry-stone walls, but for every success, another chunk of farmland is paved over with a new by-pass or a meadow is turned over to **conifers**.

The tax incentives which formerly encouraged vast expanses of spruce no longer apply, but economics still favour clear-felling a single species every thirty years or so. The largest forest owner, the Forestry Commission, is keen to shake off its monoculture image and aims to border its forests with a mix of broad-leaved trees and conifers of different ages. As an extended public relations exercise they also welcome mountain bikers in some forests.

Far from being areas where nature is allowed to take its course, the **national parks** can be their own worst enemies, attracting thousands of people a day. Some attempt is being made to control the effects of tourism through path management and the limited promotion of public transport, but this is more than outweighed by the increasingly aggressive promotion of these regions. Paradoxically, and for all the wrong reasons, **military zones** – Mynydd Eppynt and most of the Castlemartin peninsula, for example – have become wildlife havens away from the worst effects of human intervention.

Windfarms (see box on p.453) have become a contentious issue in recent years. Initial enthusiasm for this clean energy has waned as local people complain about the constant drone of the generators, and conservationists battle it out over the relative merits of a nuclear power station that will take 130 years to decommission (as well as several millennia for the fissile material to become safe) and several forests of elegant windmills on top of hills. Friends of the Earth: Cymru, 26–28 Underwood St, London, N1 7JQ (℡020/7490 1555, ❀www.foe .org.uk) stand firmly in favour of wind power, but have come up against the Campaign for the Protection of Rural Wales (CPRW), Tŷ Gwyn, 31 High St, Welshpool, Powys SY21 7YD (℡01938/552525, ❀www.cprw.org.uk), one of Wales' main independent environmental groups, which favours promotion of more efficient power usage.

Environmental groups are also keeping a weather eye on offshore **oil** and **gas** exploration, currently much under way off the Welsh coast, particularly in Cardigan Bay. Meanwhile in south Wales, reaction to the *Sea Empress* disaster hardened citizens' resolve to successfully resist the import of dirty but cheap Venezuelan orimulsion to fuel power stations.

One success in recent years has been the decision not to press ahead with the **Usk Barrage**, which was planned to create a freshwater lake on the outskirts of Newport by damming the estuary, forcing otters and other protected species to abandon the river. Things aren't as rosy on the shores of the Severn estuary nearby, where the construction of the second Severn crossing has engendered a new stretch of motorway across the environmentally rich Caldicot Levels, destroying several SSSIs.

The Snowdonia National Park Authority has recognized that sustainable management of farmland is not only ecologically beneficial, but that the landscape, with its character largely defined by past farming practices, is worth maintaining in its own right. In response it has set up the **Tir Cymen** (which loosely translates as "well-crafted landscape") scheme, a ten-year government initiative which pays participating farmers to maintain stone walls, slate fences, earth banks, traditional stone buildings and archeological features. Trial schemes are in place in the southern Snowdonian region of Meirionydd, Dinefwr in Carmarthenshire, and around Swansea and the Gower peninsula.

Music in Wales

U
ntil very recently, mention of Welsh music conjured up images of miners in their Sunday best collectively raising the roof of their local chapel, and, despite the near-obliteration of the mining industry, male voice choirs remain a feature of Welsh life, with many choirs opening their practice sessions to the public. But Welsh music extends far beyond the dwindling chapels, into the country's village halls, clubs, festival sites and pubs, where Dylan Thomas' observation that "we are a musical nation" is often seen, and heard, to be true. In quieter venues, harp players repay their musical debt to ancestors who accompanied the ancient bards (traditional poets and storytellers), while modern folk draws directly from the broader Celtic musical tradition. Exponents of Welsh-language rock have traded in their dreams of commercial success for unabashed nationalism expressed through a multiplicity of styles from punk to hip-hop. Some bands sing in both English and Welsh, and there is a fast-growing scene in English-language Welsh rock, which was one of the most dominant, and successful, musical genres in Britain in the late 1990s, thanks to the antics of bands like the Manic Street Preachers, the Stereophonics and Catatonia. Although the "Cool Cymru" hype has faded, Wales is still churning out a huge amount of good music for a country of just three million people.

What follows is a general overview of the main styles and a run through the stars, both past and present.

Folk

The word "folk" translates into Welsh as *gwerin*, but the Welsh word has a much wider meaning than its English counterpart, taking in popular culture as well as folklore. In a Welsh *gŵyl werin* (folk festival), you're just as likely to encounter

---

Where to get information

Cymdeithas Ddawns Werin Cymru (Welsh Folk Dance Society) is a useful source of events information, with an annual magazine and a twice-yearly newsletter, both bilingual. There's lots of information, details of events and further contacts on its comprehensive website ⓦ www.welshfolkdance.org.uk.

Taplas, the English-language bimonthly magazine of the folk scene in Wales, is a great source for current events. It's based at 182 Broadway, Roath, Cardiff CF24 1QJ (☎029/2049 9759, ⓦ www.taplas.co.uk).

The **South Wales Echo** newspaper carries comprehensive daily listings of events in Gwent and mid- and South Glamorgan.

The **St Fagans National History Museum**, near Cardiff (see p.137), is a vibrant museum and a vital centre for research and collecting work (☎029/2056 9441).

Watch out on **posters** for the word *twmpath* – it's the equivalent of a barn dance or ceilidh and is used when Welsh dances are the theme of the night. Calling (dance instructions) could be in Welsh or English, depending on where you are in the country. A *Noson Lawen*, literally "a happy night", is most likely to be found in tourist hotels and usually offers a harpist, perhaps some dancers and a repertoire of Welsh standards.

For eisteddfodau, see main text.

Cwlwm Celtaidd Porthcawl, near Bridgend ✆www.cwlwmceltaidd.com. Long weekend at Trecco Bay caravan park of Celtic music and partying. Early March.

Tredegar House Festival Newport, Gwent ✆www.tredegarhousefolk.ik.com. A laid-back and enjoyable weekend at the eighteenth-century country house, good for session players and dancers. Mid-May.

Fishguard Folk Festival Pembrokeshire ✆www.pembrokeshire-folk-music.co.uk. Up-and-coming event with a good spread of international performers. Late May.

Gower Folk Festival ✆www.halfpennyfolkclub.com. Varied line-up in beautiful surroundings. Mid-June.

Gŵyl Ifan Cardiff ✆www.gwylifan.org. Wales' biggest and most spectacular dance festival, with hundreds of dancers giving displays in Cardiff city centre, the Bay, the Castle and **St Fagans National History Museum**. Late June.

Cân ar Dân Dinas Mawddwy, Gwynedd. A weekend of classes and performances from Wales, Britanny and Euskadi (the Basque Country), based at the excellent village pub. Early July.

Small Nations Festival near Llandovery, Carmarthenshire ✆www.smallnations.com. Lovely camping event on a farm, with global beats from Africa to home. Early July.

Sesiwn Fawr Dolgellau, Gwynedd. Events indoors and in the streets. Mid-July.

Swansea Shanty Festival West Glamorgan ✆www.sesiwnfawr.com. Growing every year, the sea songs and music take place on and around a tall ship in the marina. July.

Pontardawe International Festival West Glamorgan ✆www.pontardawefestival. com. One of Britain's flagship folk events, with an ambitious line-up of international performers heading for the Swansea Valley town each year. Third weekend of August.

Pencader Pipe Festival Pencader, Carmarthenshire ✆www.pibaupencader.info. Weekend gathering of bag- and horn-pipers, including exponents of the traditional Welsh *pibgorn*. September.

A number of smaller dance festivals also take place around Wales, including the **Cadi Ha** in Holywell in early May and **Gwyl Werin** in Caernarfon on the first weekend of October. See the Welsh Folk Dance website (opposite) for up-to-date details.

the local rock band as the local dance team, and the whole community will be there – not just committed specialists.

It's often said that the Welsh love singing but ignore their native instrumental music. Welsh folk song has always remained close to the heart of popular culture, with modern folk songwriting acting as the common carrier of political messages and social protest, but traditional Welsh music and dance have had the difficult task of fighting back from near-extinction following centuries of political and religious suppression. Unlike their Celtic cousins in Ireland, Scotland and Brittany, many folk musicians in Wales have learnt their tunes from books and manuscripts rather than from older generations of players, and unlike the Celtic music boom of the 1970s, bands concentrating on Welsh tunes remained virtually unknown, a situation that has improved markedly in recent decades.

History

The bardic and **eisteddfod** traditions have always played a key role in Welsh culture. Often the **bard**, who held an elevated position in Welsh society, was

In the Dyfed and Gwynedd heartland of the Welsh language, folk music can be heard in many of the same venues that stage rock events. The language is considered more important than musical categories, and the folk club concept is alien to Welsh-speakers, who never saw the need to segregate music that was a natural part of their cultural life. Folk clubs are found in the anglicized areas and only a few of them feature Welsh music. In the south, check for folk in the general programme at the Welsh cultural clubs in the area: Clwb Ifor Bach in Womanby Street, Cardiff (☎029/2023 2199); Clwb y Bont in Taff Street, Pontypridd (☎01443/491424) and Clwb Brynmenyn near Bridgend (☎01656/725323).

There are scores of weekly, fortnightly and monthly sessions, gigs and jams around Wales: for the latest round-up, check out ⓦwww.folkwales.org.uk/Regulars.html. Below are a few of the best venues. All sessions are weekly on the specified day, unless otherwise stated.

South & West Wales

Barry Folk Club *Castle Hotel*, Jewel St, Barry, Vale of Glamorgan. Informal session; all are welcome to perform. Tues.

Folk in the Oak *Royal Oak*, Fishguard, Pembs. Informal session; all welcome. Tues.

Halfpenny Folk Club *The Greyhound*, Llanrhidian, Gower ☎01792/850803. Smart clientele rub shoulders with the chunky jumper brigade. Sun.

Llantrisant Folk Club *The Windsor Hotel*, Pontyclun, Vale of Glamorgan (Club Secretary ☎01443/226892). International guest list mixed with local sessions centred on Welsh tunes. Wed.

Newport Folk Club *Lyceum Tavern*, Malpas Rd, Newport, Gwent. Weekly jams and monthly guests. Thurs.

Pontardawe Acoustic Club *Pontardawe Inn (Y Gwachel)*, 123 Herbert St, Pontardawe (details ☎01792/865171). Mainstay of the Welsh folk scene, good for anything from very traditional stuff to modern folk-rock. Monthly, third Fri.

Y Mochyn Du Sophia Gardens, Cardiff. Music sessions and occasional gigs, usually traditional or folk. Mon.

Mid-Wales

Black Lion Pontrhydfendigaid, Ceredigion. Monthly all-comers sessions alternated with Celtic and Welsh bands. Sat.

Gwerin Aber *Y Cŵps (Coopers Arms)*, Llanbadarn Rd, Aberystwyth. Folk session, all instrumentalists welcome. Tues.

Royal Head Shortbridge St, Llanidloes. Jam session; all welcome. Wed.

North Wales

See also ⓦwww.tony-franks.co.uk/northwalesfolk.htm.

Clwb Gwerin Conwy Folk Club The Malt Loaf, Rosehill St, Conwy. Session open to all. Mon.

Llangollen Folk Club *Sun Inn*, Regent St, Llangollen. Cheerful session. Wed.

Theatr Clwyd Cymru Mold, Flintshire ☎01352/755114. Monthly, first Tues.

The Nelson Beach Rd, Bangor. Great pub by the pier with often packed, mainly Irish sessions. Fri.

Y Mount Dinas Llanwnda, Gwynedd. Jam and session. Thurs.

the non-performing composer, employing a harper and a *datgeiniad*, whose role was to declaim the bard's words. The first eisteddfod appears to have been held in Cardigan in 1176, with contests between bards and poets and between harpers, *crwth*-players (see p.540) and pipers. Henry Vlll's **Act of Union** in 1536 was designed to anglicize the country by stamping out Welsh culture and language, and the eisteddfod tradition degenerated over the next two centuries.

The rise of **Nonconformist religion** in the eighteenth and nineteenth centuries (see "History", p.508), with its abhorrence of music, merry-making and dancing, almost sounded the death knell for Welsh traditions already battered by Henry VIII's assault. **Edward Jones**, *Bardd y Brenin* (Bard to the King), observed sorrowfully in the 1780s that Wales, which used to be one of the happiest of countries, "has now become one of the dullest". Folk music only gained some sort of respectability when London-based Welsh people, swept along in a romantic enthusiasm for all things Celtic, revived it at the end of the eighteenth century. As late as the twentieth century, old ladies who knew dance steps would pull the curtains before demonstrating them, in case the neighbours should see.

The **National Eisteddfod Society** was formed in the 1860s, and today, three major week-long events are held every year – the International Eisteddfod at Llangollen in July, the Royal National Eisteddfod in the first week of August and the Urdd Eisteddfod, Europe's largest youth festival, at the end of May. The National and the Urdd alternate between north and south Wales.

Because competitions need rules, eisteddfodau have always tended to formalize Welsh culture, and such parameter-defining is naturally alien to the free evolution of traditional song and music. When Nicholas Bennett was compiling his 1896 book *Alawon Fy Nghwlad*, still one of the most important collections of Welsh tunes, he rejected a great deal of good Welsh dance music because it did not conform to the contemporary high-art notion of what Welsh music ought to sound like. Despite this frequently heard criticism, eisteddfodau have played a major role in keeping traditional music, song and dance at the heart of national culture.

The harp

Historically the most important instrument in the folk repertoire, the **harp** has been played in Wales since at least the eleventh century, although no instruments survive from the period before the 1700s, and little is really known about the intervening years. The only surviving music is the famous manuscript of **Robert ap Huw**, written about 1614 in a strange tablature that has

Recordings

Bob Delyn a'r Ebillion *Dore* (Sain). Hazy, Eastern smoke over Celtic folk-rock melodies. Inspired. *Sgwarnod bach Bob* is livelier, touching anthemic at times.

Carreg Lafar *Hyn* (Sain). 1998 blast from this Cardiff-based Celtic folk outfit that was nominated for a US Grammy award.

Crasdant *Crasdant* (Sain). Harp, horn and other traditional instruments combine in this exuberant collection.

Dafydd Iwan ac Ar Log *Yma O Hyd* (Sain). Compilation CD of two great mid-1980s albums which celebrated legendary joint tours around Wales by these performers.

Elinor Bennett *Telynau a chân* (*Harps and song*) (Sain). Wales' master harpist proves she can sing folk too.

Sian James *Distaw*, *Gweini Tymor* and *Di-Gwsg* (Sain). Original, modern and traditional songs on harp and keyboard with spine-tingling vocals.

Julie Murphy and Dylan Fowler *Ffawd* (Fflach). Superb vocals and soaring melodies on this firmly contemporary take on Welsh folk.

Pigyn Clust *Otitis Media* (Sain) and *Perllan* (Fflach). Haunting vocals from new exponents of stomping Welsh quickstep folk.

Tudur Morgan *Branwen* (Sain). Project of songs and music based on the Mabinogion legend.

KilBride *KilBride* and *Sidan* (Fflach). Silky sounds from the increasingly popular and respected south Wales group.

Llio Rhydderch *Enlli* (Fflach). Gorgeous harp collection inspired by Ynys Enlli (Bardsey Island). Other albums include the haunting *Melangell*.

Meic Stevens *Er Cof am Blant y Cwm and Mihangel* (Crai). The "Welsh Bob Dylan"'s most recent albums (1993 & 1998). *Y Baledi* (1992), a collection of his ballads, is perhaps the best way into this absolute one-off of a performer.

Robin Huw Bowen *Telyn Berseiniol fy Nghwlad* (Teires). Self-produced CD of dance music and airs for the triple harp.

Various *Rough Guide to the Music of Wales* (World Music Network). Perfect introduction to traditional Welsh music, from the strange, almost Eastern European, musical rendition of the Bible, to raunchy folk classics by the likes of Fernhill, Rag Foundation, Julie Murphy and Llio Rhydderch.

Various *Tradd-Matic* (Rasp). A real roll call of Welsh folk royalty, re-twiddled for the dance music generation.

intrigued music scholars: five scales were used, but no one has yet defined satisfactorily how they should sound. In recent years craftsmen have re-created the *crwth* (a stringed instrument which may have been either plucked or bowed), the *pibgorn* (a reed instrument with a cow's horn for a bell) and the *pibacwd* (a primitive Welsh bagpipe). Some groups have adopted these instruments, but their primitive design and performance means they rarely blend happily with modern instruments.

The simple early harps were ousted in the seventeenth century by the arrival of the **triple harp**, with its complicated string arrangement (two parallel rows sounding the same note, with a row of accidentals between them), giving it a unique, rich sound. The nineteenth-century swing towards classical concert music saw the invasion of the large **chromatic pedal harps** that still dominate today, but the triple, always regarded as the traditional Welsh harp, was kept alive by gypsy musicians who preferred to play something portable. A notable, and unique, Welsh harp performance that's well worth catching is the **Cerdd Dant**, where the harpist leads with one tune, accompanying soloists and groups take a counter-tune, and they all end up together on the final note.

Musicians

Undoubtedly the most influential player of recent years is the triple harpist **Robin Huw Bowen**, who has revived interest in the instrument with appearances throughout Europe and North America, and has done tremendous work making unpublished manuscripts of Welsh dance music widely available through his own publishing company. In north Wales, the current pacemaker is **Llio Rhydderch**, whose lineage in playing the triple harp stretches back centuries. For a more contemporary take on the instrument, **Twm Morys**, with his band **Bob Delyn a'r Ebillion**, blends modern Welsh and Breton influences and has won admiration from *Folk Roots* magazine in England. One of Wales' most well-known harpists, **Elinor Bennett** (coincidentally the wife of Plaid Cymru's former leader Dafydd Wigley), has been much in the ascendant of late, even accompanying some of Wales' biggest rock acts.

The father of Welsh folk, politician/songwriter **Dafydd Iwan**, remains as hugely popular and prolific as ever with his charismatic performances, and songwriter **Meic Stevens** is still producing good work on the borderlines of folk and acoustic rock: if you get the chance to see him live, grab it. Singer/harpist **Sian James**, from mid-Wales, is gaining recognition both at home and way beyond for her spine-tingling voice and exquisite tunes. Other pacesetters among the women include **Julie Murphy**, born in Essex but now a fluent Welsh speaker, and the veteran singer **Heather Jones**, who still sounds as pure as ever.

The Hennessys, led by broadcaster, TV personality and songwriter Frank Hennessy, still have a huge and well-deserved middle-of-the-road following in the Cardiff area, twenty-odd years after joining the procession of Irish-influenced trios on the folk circuit. **Huw and Tony Williams**, from Brynmawr in the Gwent Valleys, are popular names on the British folk-club circuit whose following, like other English-language performers, is greater away from home than it is inside Wales. Huw's songwriting – notably songs like *Rosemary's Baby* – has been embraced by Fairport Convention and a string of other big-name performers, but he's best known in Wales for his Eisteddfod-winning clog dancing.

Dance

After a long period of religious suppression, **traditional dance** in Wales has been revived over the past fifty years. It plays a big part in the folk culture of Wales, and the top teams are exciting and professional in their approach. Dances written in recent years, often for eisteddfod competitions, have been quickly absorbed into the repertoire. **Cwmni Dawns Werin Caerdydd**, Cardiff's official dance team, have taken their spectacular displays abroad – Texas and Japan are among the many trips they've made in their first 25 years. Their musicians are recommended as well. **Dawnswyr Nantgarw**, from the Taff Vale village that was the source of the country's romantic and raunchy fair dances, have turned Welsh dance into a theatrical art form: concise, perfectly drilled and very showy. **Dawnswyr Pen-y-Fai**, from Bridgend, have an adventurous band full of good session players, while Anglesey-based **Ffidl Ffadl** also boast an excellent musician in fiddler **Huw Roberts**, formerly with the early 1980s bands **Cilmeri** and **Pedwar Yn Y Bar**. **Dawnswyr Brynmawr** also have a capable band who play for *twmpath* dances as **Taro Tant**. In the northeast, **Dawnswyr Delyn** are a competent and enjoyable troupe.

Pop music in Wales

The historic lack of international pop artists to emerge from Wales – long blamed on the music-industry dominance of London-based labels and media – has changed utterly in the last fifteen years, at least for groups working in the English language. It started with the **Manic Street Preachers** in the early 1990s, who spawned a long-overdue interest in contemporary Welsh rock, as London A&R men descended on Cardiff and Newport in search of the next big thing. Bands like the **Super Furry Animals**, **Catatonia** and the **Stereophonics** were the main beneficiaries of what became rather ironically known as the "Cool Cymru" phenomenon. Although the hype has long fizzled out, no more do bands from Wales feel hampered by their provenance, and there is plenty of fine new talent coming through.

Many of the surging Welsh rockers hail from the country's anglicized southeast and speak little or none of the native language. Some profess support for Welsh and there is a relatively thriving scene in Welsh-language rock throughout the country. With rare exceptions, however, this does not generally make it into the mainstream and, consequently, many Welsh-language bands have turned their backs on commercial success, launching Welsh record labels and helping to stoke a less obvious, but perhaps just as exciting, buzz.

English-language Welsh pop

The biggest, most enduring name in English-language Welsh pop is undoubtedly 1960s sex symbol **Tom Jones**, still pulling crowds around the world and at home. Hailing from Treforest in south Wales, Jones' slick presentation and booming voice has seen him turn his love of black American soul music into an enduring career. Similarly, Cardiff-born singer **Shirley Bassey**, the daughter of a West Indian seaman, has carved out a hugely successful career since the mid-1950s. In 1964 she sang the theme song to the James Bond movie *Goldfinger*, and in 1972 scored a major American hit with *Diamonds Are Forever*. Although these days records are rare, she still performs.

Cardiff musician-turned-record producer **Dave Edmunds**, whose first band Love Sculpture scored a UK hit in 1968, has had his hands on many a hit record since – both as a producer and a solo performer – during the 1970s and 1980s. Classically trained pianist **John Cale**, born in Garnant near Ammanford, went to America in 1963 and found fame with the **Velvet Underground**, one of the most influential avant-garde rock bands of the 1960s. He has since recorded solo (including in collaborative projects with other Welsh artistes) and, more recently, has worked with the reformed Velvet Underground.

In the 1980s, Welsh rock music was personified by Rhyl's rabble-rousing rock fundamentalists **The Alarm**, fronted by Mike Peters, who relaunched his solo career early in 1994, digging deeper into his Welsh roots as he did so. Swansea's husky-toned rocker **Bonnie Tyler** achieved huge commercial success from the late 1970s onwards, and still tours. Possibly the most surprising – some would say ludicrous – Welsh success story of the 1980s was Fifties rock'n'roll impersonator **Shakin' Stevens**, who had a string of massive, nostalgia-driven hits.

It all changed in the 1990s. South Wales rock nihilists the **Manic Street Preachers**, hailing from the small town of Blackwood in the Sirhowy Valley, have become the most successful Welsh band ever. Few would have predicted this from their early career of sneering bedsit-punk-meets-rock, topped with inflammatory statements such as "I laughed when John Lennon got shot", from the single *Motown Junk*. It was the mysterious 1995 disappearance, and presumed suicide, of fractured, anorexic guitarist Richey James, that changed everything for the Manics. They returned as a three-piece, storming the charts worldwide with their anthemic album, *Everything Must Go* (1996), which spawned huge hit singles, including the title track. Their follow-up album, *This Is My Truth, Tell Me Yours* (1998) only continued the progress to megastardom, and included their first UK number one single, *If You Tolerate This, Then Your Children Will Be Next*.

△ Shirley Bassey

These weighty, faintly pompous, titles (*The Masses Against the Classes* was their next chart-topper) show how seriously they take their role as Wales' answer to Ireland's self-important stadium-rockers, U2.

By the time the Manics' star was firmly in the ascendant, the hunt was on for new Welsh talent. The now legendary Welsh bands compilation album, *Dial M for Merthyr* (1995), showcased the Manics alongside many who subsequently became huge: most obviously the Super Furry Animals, Catatonia and the Stereophonics. If there's anything that links these and other Welsh bands, apart from their country of origin, it is a tendency towards clever, zeitgeist lyrics, an assuredly Welsh loquaciousness and delight in the possibilities of language. Most exciting are the **Super Furry Animals**, whose fusion of Seventies psychedelia with Noughties clubland quirkiness and techno-geekery has created a niche all of their own: their seven albums to date, mixing both Welsh and English, are extraordinary. From poignant ballads to thumping, raw rock, they have proved to be masters of many genres and true innovators. Their all-Welsh language album, *Mwng* (2000), became the best-selling work ever in Welsh, reaching number eleven in the UK album charts.

Another three-word name to note is **Gorky's Zygotic Mynci**, Carmarthen's biggest contributor to music. A well-established band, they've been hotly tipped for stardom for years, and recent albums, particularly *Spanish Dance Troupe*, have made their brand of whimsical ponderings much better known in the wider world.

Cerys Matthews' talent for producing intelligent lyrics also had much to do with the success of **Catatonia**, the band that she fronted, and utterly dominated. Hitting contemporary observations with unerring sweet perfection threw out some fine pop moments: most notably their massive hits *Road Rage* and *Mulder and Scully*. They called it a day in 2001, shortly after releasing their final album, *Paper Scissors Stone*, the follow-up to the decidedly bittersweet *Equally Cursed and Blessed* (1999). Their pinnacle, however, was one of the finest albums of the 1990s in the shape of *International Velvet* (1998), whose title track, with its verses in Welsh and its roustabout English chorus of "every day, when I wake up, I thank the Lord I'm Welsh" became something of an unofficial national anthem. Since the split, Cerys has married, had children and moved to Tennessee, releasing a country album *Cock-a-hoop* in 2003.

More lyrical dexterity, combined with clean-cut guitar chords, are the hallmarks of the **Stereophonics**, from Cwmaman in the Cynon Valley. Their rise has been meteoric – from highly competent pub-rockers to one of the country's favourite bands in less than a year. Their sound is utterly distinctive, thanks largely to singer Kelly Jones' rasping voice, and it has spawned massively successful albums and singles. Although not as identifiably Welsh as these acts, mega-group **Feeder** have more and more happily taken on the national label, particularly since the suicide of drummer Jon Lee from Newport. Their style is hugely diverse, encompassing haunting tunes of aching melancholy right through to bombastic rock blow-outs, best seen in their last two albums, *Comfort in Sound* (2002) and *Pushing the Senses* (2005).

Selected releases by Welsh bands

The Alarm
Standards (IRS). Compilation LP from 1990.
Raw (IRS). Last LP, released in 1991, with a Welsh-language version released on Crai Records. The sound of a band ready to split.

Catatonia/Cerys Matthews
International Velvet (WEA). Their finest hour? Certainly, the biggest hits.
Equally Cursed and Blessed (WEA). More whimsical collection, with Cerys' lyrics getting intensely personal.
Paper Scissors Stone (WEA). Catatonia's swansong: bittersweet, with the emphasis firmly on bitter.
Cock-a-hoop (Blanco y Negro). Cerys goes country; includes a luscious twang-a-long version of old Welsh hymn *Arglwydd Dyma Fi*.

Feeder
Echo Park (Echo). Perhaps the band's poppiest collection, including the novelty hit *Buck Rogers*.
Comfort in Sound (Echo). Sometimes melancholy collection, hardly surprising as this was recorded in the wake of drummer Jon Lee's death.
Pushing the Senses (Echo). The grief continues: but with an edge that captivates.

Goldie Lookin' Chain
Greatest Hits and *Safe as Fuck* (Atlantic). Fast, furious and very funny offerings from Newport's bling-meisters.

Gorky's Zygotic Mynci
Spanish Dance Troupe (Mantra). Whimsical collection that became their most commercially successful, including a couple of minor hit singles.

Llwybr Llaethog
Hip Dub Reggae Hop (Ankst). A "best of" Ll Ll's first fifteen years, showcasing their groundbreaking methods with a host of guest Welsh stars.
Stwff (Neud Nid Deud). Superb recent album of well-crafted samples fused with coruscating dub rhythms.
Anomie Ville (Neud nid Deud). Beguilingly mid-European cruise through strange beats and techno wizardry.

Manic Street Preachers
Generation Terrorists (Sony). Debut double LP. Rock ballads meet punk ferocity and anti-establishment politics.
Gold Against the Soul (Sony). Second, more mature and darker LP. Straight-up rock with some rousing choruses. *From Despair to Where* – also released as a single – is a classic.
Everything Must Go (Sony). The most mainstream offering so far, spawning massive hits in the shape of its

Making far fewer concessions to the hype of Cool Cymru have been a new generation of bands whose influence has come more from the thrashier elements of post-millennial American rock. South Wales has been a particularly fertile breeding ground for this angst-ridden wall of noise, producing some of the genre's most celebrated protagonists in the shape of Swansea/Bridgend rockers **Funeral for a Friend**, Rhondda nu-metal screamers **The Lostprophets** and Bridgend counterparts **Bullet For My Valentine**.

But Welsh music isn't all guitars or misty, acid-fuelled weirdness. The thriving **dance music** scene, in all its fragmented glory, has a number of notable exponents. Most successful have been the awesome tongue-in-cheek rappers **Goldie Lookin' Chain** from Newport. Rap and hip-hop have captured Wales as surely as everywhere else, with **Llwybr Llaethog**, Wales' most respected crew, having forged the way for later protagonists such as **MC Mabon** and **Pep Le Pew**, all of whom principally record in Welsh. Rural west Wales is the base for dub gurus **Zion Train**, whose spliffed-up remakes of classic new wave tracks have

CONTEXTS | Music in Wales

title song, *A Design for Life and Kevin Carter*.

This Is My Truth, Tell Me Yours (Sony). More gutsy anthems and a slightly more wistful tone than the previous album.

Know Your Enemy (Epic). As the band get bigger, their socialist credentials are worn ever more on their sleeve.

Forever Delayed (Epic). The inevitable greatest hits collection, including their finest single – *The Masses Against the Classes*, previously unavailable on any album.

Lifeblood (Sony). Decidedly mixed latest addition to the stable: big production, big tunes but often rather small ideas.

Melys

Kamikaze (Sylem). Gutsy tunes, some startling observation and always the gorgeous crooning of lead singer Andrea Parker.

Suikerspin (Transformed Dreams). Wonderful collection, including the superb singles *Chinese Whispers* and *Un Darllenwr Lwcus*.

Stereophonics

Word Gets Around (Banana). Stunning debut of powerful three-minute, three-chord classics.

Just Enough Education to Perform (V2). Slower pace, but still with the hallmark of Kelly Jones' rasping voice, heard to best effect on the gorgeous Rod Stewart

cover *Handbags and Gladrags*.

Language. Sex. Violence. Other? (V2). Clumsy title for a faintly clumsy album that doesn't quite hang together.

Super Furry Animals/Gruff Rhys

Fuzzy Logic (Creation). Highly acclaimed debut album containing the new wave charge of *God! Show Me Magic* and *Something for the Weekend*.

Radiator (Creation). Rockier, harder follow-up album that didn't go down quite so well.

Guerilla (Creation). Altogether brighter and more accessible album, includes the stirring hit *Fire in my Heart*.

Mwng (Creation). SFA's finest hour, think many, in this all-Welsh language power trip through funky rhythms and spine-tingling vocals.

Rings Around The World (Creation). The Furries crank up the pace in this fast, feelgood piece of post-millennial musing.

Phantom Power (Creation). Lush aural landscape that couldn't help but warm you up.

Love Kraft (Creation). The summer factor ups another ante: warm, witty and wise.

Yr Atal Genhedlaeth (Placid Casual). Frontman Gruff's solo effort, stripped down from SFA sophistication and all in Welsh.

won many friends. Big beatz'n'breaks come from Cardiff's **Phantom Beats**, lead exponents for the capital's **Plastic Raygun** breakbeat label.

Welsh-language rock

Whilst English-language Welsh bands have usually enjoyed success by making their nationality an irrelevance, Welsh-language bands have purposely expounded their strong national identity. As a consequence, a unique, self-propagating Welsh-language rock scene has developed, albeit with a widespread lack of major commercial success. However, boundaries are becoming increasingly blurred: many bands choose to sing in both Welsh and English, and not for expedient purposes, but simply because that is the way most of their members use both languages.

The roots of this thriving, youthful and innovative scene owe much to a musical revolution whose shock waves emanated not from Cardiff or Newport, but from London. The **punk** explosion of 1976 kicked over many of rock's statues, partly thanks to the anarchic fervour of London bands like the The Clash and the Sex Pistols (who made it to the south Wales town of Caerphilly on the ill-fated Anarchy Tour in 1976), but also by virtue of its strong DIY ethic.

It was in the 1980s, though, that the home-grown Welsh-language pop scene really began to consolidate itself. In 1983, Caernarfon punk band **Anhrefn** (Disorder) set up **Recordiau Anhrefn**, churning out what it called "dodgy compilations of up-and-coming left-field weirdo Welsh bands". This enthusiasm is a trademark of the Welsh-language rock scene. In fact, throughout the Eighties, any band that couldn't get some sort of record deal would simply press their own vinyl and sell their records at gigs. The market for the music was small, but the bands made up for it with their have-a-go attitude. From this era, perhaps the most enduring legacy is from the band **Datblygu**, most often described as a Welsh version of spectacularly misanthropic The Fall.

The scene was developing nicely, and in the early 1980s, the late Radio One DJ **John Peel** – to many, the standard-bearer for underground pop in the UK – became aware of the growing number of Welsh-language bands and began playing their records on air and inviting them in for sessions. This introduced Welsh music to a Europe-wide audience and proved an important catalyst to new Welsh bands. By the 1990s, Welsh-language pop music had established a solid infrastructure of bands, labels and venues. One of the most prolific, eclectic and innovative of these labels is **Ankst**. Started as a part-time venture in 1988, the label is now a full-time concern releasing Welsh-language pop of varied styles, best seen in some wonderful compilation albums, including *S4C Makes Me Want To Smoke Crack*, which contained tracks by Catatonia and professional Welsh weirdos **Rheinallt H. Rowlands** and **Ectogram**. Ankst is also the home of the awesome multilingual dub-meets-punk twosome **Llwybr Llaethog**, and wild Welsh-language rappers, **Y Tystion**, whose album *Shrug Off Your Complex* is full of hilarious observation. Former Tystion rapper Gruff Meredith has metamorphosed to great acclaim into **MC Mabon**, also on Ankst.

Another major promoter of Welsh-language pop is the Caernarfon-based **Crai Records**, a subsidiary of the more folk-oriented **Sain Records**. The label began life in 1989, and its current roster includes the back catalogues of original Welsh punks Anhrefn, folk-roots band Bob Delyn (see "Musicians", p.541), ex-Alarm vocalist **Mike Peters**, Celt rockers **Fernhill** and the Welsh outpourings of **Big Leaves**. Other home-grown labels promoting Welsh-language bands include the **Cwmni Fflach** label in Aberteifi (Cardigan), Dyfed, and their subsidiary **Rasp** for dancier artistes and projects. The grassroots Welsh **gig circuit** is also healthy, with a lively local pub and club scene. The student unions

Most major towns in Wales have a Welsh Shop (*Siop Gymraeg*), which will often stock an extensive Welsh-language music selection. Cob Records in Porthmadog (see p.539) is also worth checking out, and has a good online catalogue. Even better is *Cerdd Ystwyth* of 7 Portland St, Aberystwyth (℡01970/623382, ⓦwww.cerddystwyth .co.uk), whose online shop is comprehensive and efficient. For those in the USA, ⓦwww.hiraethcelticgoods has a fair selection of Welsh music.

Some of the major bands that record wholly or partly in Welsh are distributed through major UK and international record companies. Less mainstream fare, though, comes in the shape of the following independent Welsh labels, together with some of their releases. As more bands are recording in both English and Welsh these days, there is inevitably some cross-over with the entries in the box for English-language bands, pp.544–545.

Ankst The Old Police Station, The Square, Pentraeth, Anglesey LL75 8AZ ℡01248/450155, ⓦwww.ankst.co.uk.

Crai Records Canolfan Sain, Llandwrog, Llandwrog, Gwynedd ℡01286/831111, ⓦwww.sain.wales.com.

Cwmni Fflach/Rasp Records Llys-y-Coed, Heol Dinbych y Pysgod, Aberteifi, Ceredigion SA43 3AH ℡01239/614691, ⓦwww.fflach.co.uk.

Slacyr Records 18 Parc Sychnant Conwy LL32 8SB ⓦwww.slacyr.co.uk. New largely Welsh-language label with some impressive performers.

Recordings

Big Leaves: *Pwy sy'n Galw?* (Crai). The Waunfawr whimsy technicians show their style and humour on their first album.

Datblygu: *Datblygu 85-95* (Ankst). Retrospective intro to one of the most influential Welsh bands of all time, dubbed by the *NME* as "Kraftwerk with a hangover". Genius singer-songwriter David R. Edwards' melancholy presence permeates through everything.

MC Mabon *Nia Non* (Ankst). Ex-Tystion goes solo and produces mind-exploding chaos.

Various artists: *Da! Da!* (Ankst). 1999 compilation, featuring the full range of Welsh music, including the punchy dub of Llwybr Llaethog.

Various artists: *Egnileniwm* (R-Bennig). The full range of this distinctly esoteric label, from cutesy to just plain crazy, on this 1999 compilation.

Various artists: *Radio Crymi Playlist Vol 1 1988-1998* (Ankst). A double album of Ankst's early successes, a roll call of Welsh rock royalty including early SFA, their legendary predecessors Ffa Coffi Bawb (literally "everyone's coffee beans" but pronounced "fuck off i bawb" or "fuck off everyone"), Catatonia, Gorky's, Melys and Datblygu.

Various artists: *Welsh Rare Beats* (Crai). Wonderful compilation of ground-breaking Welsh stuff from the 1960s and 70s.

Y Tystion: *Shrug off your Complex* (Ankst). Clever, often bile-drenched, lyrical effort by the Welsh-language rappers.

Zabrinski: *Yeti*, *Koala Ko-ordination* and *Ill-gotten Game* (Ankst). New psychedelia and warped melodies from the inheritors of Gorky's and SFA's crowns.

C

of Lampeter, Bangor, Cardiff, Swansea and Glamorgan at Treforest universities also regularly put on Welsh bands. Welsh-language pop bands can also be found at the **National Eisteddfod**, especially in the "Maes B" fringe field and local bars and clubs.

Books

S ome of the books listed here are published by small local presses, and you're unlikely to find them in bookshops outside Wales, though all can be ordered via Internet sites. The Welsh Books Council website (ⓦwww.gwales.com) is a good place to find a huge selection to buy, and you'll often be able to pick up rarer titles, and many of those listed here as out of print (o/p), by scouring the many independent or second-hand bookshops in Wales – Hay-on-Wye (see p.256) is particularly good for the latter. Books with this symbol 🐾 are particularly recommended.

Travel and impressions

George Borrow *Wild Wales*. Highly entertaining, easy-to-read account of the author's walking tour of Wales in 1854 which says as much about Borrow and his ego as it does about Wales and the Welsh, who he treats with benign condescension.

Giraldus Cambrensis *The Journey Through Wales* and *The Description of Wales*. Two witty and frank books in one volume, written in Latin by the quarter-Welsh clergyman after his 1188 tour around Wales recruiting for the Third Crusade with Archbishop Baldwin of Canterbury. Both superb vehicles for Gerald of Wales' learned ruminations and unreserved opinions, *The Journey* breaks up the seven-week tour "through our rough, remote and inaccessible countryside" with anecdotes and ecclesiastical point-scoring, while *The Description* covers rural life and the finer and less praiseworthy aspects of the Welsh character, summing up with "you may never find anyone worse than a bad Welshman, but you will certainly never find anyone better than a good one".

Tony Curtis (ed) *Wales: The Imagined Nation* (o/p). A wonderfully varied selection of essays and wry poetry on a great diversity of topics, including writers such as R.S. Thomas and Dylan Thomas, together with the representation of Plaid Cymru in Welsh and British media, Wales in the movies, images of Welsh women and the country's indigenous theatre. Learned, often funny, and extremely rich.

Daniel Defoe *A Tour Through the Whole Island of Great Britain*. Classic travelogue opening a window onto Britain in the 1720s, with twenty pages on Wales.

🐾 **Gwynfor Evans** *Eternal Wales* (published as *Cymru o Hud* in Welsh). With magnificently moody photography by Marian Delyth, this was Evans' last book before his death in 2005. A passionate and erudite tour de force through some of Wales' lesser-known corners.

🐾 **Peter Finch** *Real Cardiff* and *Real Cardiff Two*. Utterly compelling ambles around the Welsh capital, full of oddball nuggets and with a terrific sense of context and place. Fellow poet Nigel Jenkins is due to produce a companion volume to *Real Swansea*.

Ralph Maud *Guide to Welsh Wales*. Day tours around the country, highlighting places of historical significance for the Welsh patriot.

Jeremy Moore and Nigel Jenkins *Wales, The Lie of the Land*. A gorgeous, glossy tome that combines the luscious photography of Jeremy Moore (often seen in the Wild Wales postcard series) and the musings of poet Nigel Jenkins. Spirited, passionate and a fine souvenir of contemporary Wales.

Jan Morris *Wales: Epic Views of a Small Country* (a rewrite of her earlier *The Matter of Wales*). Prolific half-Welsh travel writer Jan Morris immerses herself in the country that she evidently loves. Highly partisan and fiercely nationalistic, the book combs over the origins of the Welsh character and describes the people and places of Wales with precision and affection. A magnificent introduction to a diverse, and occasionally perverse, nation.

H.V. Morton *In Search of Wales*. Learned, lively and typically enthusiastic snapshots of Welsh life in the 1930s. A companion volume to his *In Search of England*.

Chris Musson *Wales from the Air*. Fascinating tour of the country via aerial photography and accompanying text, focusing on its historical development from pre-history to post-industry.

Thomas Pennant *A Tour in Wales*. First published in 1773, the stories from Pennant's horseback tour

helped foster the Romantic enthusiasm for Wales' rugged landscapes.

Pamela Petro *Travels in an Old Tongue*. An American woman comes to Wales to study, is bewitched by the place, attempts to learn Welsh and then sets off on a wild global pursuit of Welsh enclaves and speakers from Japan to Norway, Germany and Patagonia. Funny, informative and extremely perceptive about the language and its wider cultural significance.

Peter Sager *Wales*. Not so much a travel guide as a 400-page celebratory essay on Wales, and especially its people, by a German convert to the cause of all things Welsh. A passionate and fabulously detailed book.

Meic Stephens *A Most Peculiar People: Quotations About Wales and the Welsh*. Fascinating and varied volume of quotations going back to the century before Christ and up to 2000. As a portrait of the nation, with all of its frustrating idiosyncrasies and endearing foibles, it is a superb example. Most tellingly, it is easy to see how the typical English attitude of sneering at the Welsh is rooted way back in history.

History, society and culture

Jane Aaron et al (ed) *Our Sisters' Land: The Changing Identities of Women in Wales*. A series of challenging and well-written essays that delve deep into male-dominated Welsh society, from the home to the political system. Includes personal testimonies and some startling facts about just how entrenched bigotry still is within much of the Welsh establishment.

John Aitchison and Harold Carter *Spreading the Word: the Welsh Language 2001*. A thorough analysis of the state of the language according to the 2001 census.

David Berry *Wales and Cinema: The First Hundred Years*. Thorough examination of this small country's contribution to the big screen, both in terms of stars, directors and writers and its frequent role as subject and setting. From the sublime – some of the superb recent young movies kick-started by S4C – to the ridiculous – Hollywood's take on Wales for blockbusters like *How Green Was My Valley*.

Richard Booth *My Kingdom of Books*. Typically bullish autobiography by the man who made Hay-on-Wye the world's biggest second-hand bookshop. Amidst the self-regard is some interesting stuff on his tussles with authority and his semi-serious declaration of Hay as an independent country.

Janet Davies *The Welsh Language*. The most up-to-date history and assessment of one of Europe's oldest living languages. Packed full of readable information, together with plans and maps showing the demographic and geographic spread of Welsh over the ages.

John Davies *A History of Wales*. Exhaustive run through Welsh history and culture from the earliest inhabitants to the late 1980s, reassessing numerous oft-quoted "facts" along the way. Translated from the original 1990 Welsh-language edition, this is clearly written and very readable, but, at 700 pages, it's hardly concise.

Alice Thomas Ellis *A Welsh Childhood*. Wonderfully whimsical reminiscences of growing up in north Wales. Welsh legends and folk tales form a large part of the backdrop, fermenting excitedly in the young imagination of the popular novelist.

Gwynfor Evans *Land of My Fathers* and *For the Sake of Wales*. Plaid Cymru's late elder statesman first produced the former tome in Welsh, translating it into English for publication thirty years ago. It's a thorough and polemical history of the country. The latter work is his autobiography, covering Welsh political and social life from the war to the National Assembly. Hugely readable and inspirational.

Geoffrey of Monmouth *History of the Kings of Britain*. First published in 1136, this is the basis of almost all Arthurian legend. Writers throughout Europe and beyond used Geoffrey's unreliable history as the basis of a complex corpus of myth.

David Greenslade *Welsh Fever: Welsh Activities in the United States and Canada Today*. Essential companion for anyone searching out Welsh and Celtic roots in North America. Commentary on regions from Quebec to San Diego, along with accounts of a hundred individual sites of Welsh or Celtic interest.

Alan Llwyd *Cymru Ddu/Black Wales: a History*. A fabulous book that takes a long look at the history of multi-racial Wales in both Welsh and English.

John Matthews *A Celtic Reader*. Selections of original texts, scholarly articles and stories on Celtic legend and scholarship. Sections on the druids, Celtic Britain and The Mabinogion. Assumes a deep interest on the part of the reader.

Elizabeth Mavor *The Ladies of Llangollen*. The best of the books on Wales' most notorious and celebrated lesbian couple. This volume traces the ladies' inauspicious beginnings in Ireland, their spectacular elopement and the way that their Llangollen home, Plas Newydd, became a place of pilgrimage for dozens of influential eighteenth-century visitors. A fascinating story, lovingly told.

Jan Morris and Twm Morys *A Machynlleth Triad/Triawd Machynlleth*. Three-part saga in Welsh and English about Machynlleth, Glyndŵr's capital. Jan Morris evokes the town at the time of Glyndŵr, looks at the place in the mid-1990s and imagines it "sometime in the 21st century" as the charmingly self-assured capital of an independent Wales. The book says much about Wales as a whole, is beautifully written and often very funny.

Trefor M. Owen *The Customs and Traditions of Wales*. Pocket guide to everything from outdoor prayer meetings to the curious Mari Lwyd, when men dress as grey mares and snap at all the young girls. Easy to read and fun to dip into.

Mike Parker *Neighbours From Hell?* A light-hearted study of a thousand years of English attitudes – from lofty condescension to outright hostility – to Wales and the Welsh, written by the co-author of this book.

Ned Thomas *The Welsh Extremist.* A good introduction to the political landscape that spawned the anti-English bombing campaigns of the 1970s. An evocative argument around the issues of oppression and emancipation.

Patrick Thomas *Candle in the Darkness: Celtic Spirituality from Wales.* Tales from the "Age of Saints" in Wales, with particular focus given to the numerous Celtic saints who originated here.

Wynford Vaughan-Thomas *Wales – A History* (o/p). One of the country's most missed broadcasters and writers, Vaughan-Thomas' masterpiece is this warm and spirited history of Wales. Working chronologically through the pre-Celtic dawn to the aftermath of the 1979 devolution vote, the book offers perhaps the clearest explanation of the evolution of Welsh culture, with the author's patriotic slant evident throughout.

Art, architecture and archeology

Chris Barber and John Godfrey Williams *The Ancient Stones of Wales.* Comprehensive directory of standing stones and monoliths throughout Wales, together with some of the most potent legends and stories associated with them. Exhaustively researched, if a little user-unfriendly.

CADW *Wales: Castles and Historic Places.* General chat and rich colour photos of the major CADW sites around the country.

Peter Lord *The Visual Culture of Wales.* Lavishly produced and beautifully illustrated three-volume overview of the art and architecture of Wales, from the early industrial society to the present day.

John Meirion Morris *The Celtic Vision.* Masterful examination by

the superb Welsh sculptor of La Tène Celtic art and its religious meaning.

Pevsner et al *The Buildings of Glamorgan; Clwyd; Powys; Pembrokeshire; Gwent (Monmouthshire); Carmarthenshire & Ceredigion.* Magisterial series covering just about every inhabitable structure. This project was initially a one-man show, but later authors have revised Pevsner's text, inserting newer buildings but generally respecting the founder's personal tone. Further volumes in the pipeline.

T.W. Potter and Catherine Johns *Roman Britain.* Generously illustrated account of Roman occupation, written by the British Museum's own curators.

Literature

Leonora Brito *Dat's Love.* Best of the new black voices emanating from the UK's oldest ethnic minority community in Cardiff Bay. A spicy tale of love and life in a very Welsh cultural melting pot.

Michael Carson *Stripping Penguins Bare.* Hilarious and poignant semi-autobiographical account of a young gay man arriving at university in Aberystwyth in the pre-liberation 1960s.

Bruce Chatwin *On the Black Hill*. This entertaining and finely wrought novel follows the Jones twins' eighty-year tenure of a farm on the Radnorshire border with England. Chatwin casts his sharp eye for detail over both the minutiae of nature and the universal human condition, providing a wonderfully gentle angle on Welsh–English antipathy.

Alexander Cordell *Rape of the Fair Country; Hosts of Rebecca; Song of the Earth*. Dramatic historical trilogy in the best-seller tradition, partly set in the cottages on the site of the Blaenafon ironworks during the lead-up to the Chartist Riots. *This Sweet and Bitter Earth* immortalizes Blaenau Ffestiniog in a lusty slate epic.

Lewis Davies *Work, Sex and Rugby*. Perennially popular novel that tells you all you need to know (and much you don't) about Valleys men.

Richard John Evans *Entertainment*. Scabrous rollercoaster ride through Rhondda living and loving, guaranteed to offend and cause maximum hilarity.

Thomas Firbank *I Bought a Mountain*. One of the few popular books set in north Wales in which Anglo-Canadian Firbank spins an autobiographical yarn of his purchase of most of the Glyder range and subsequent life as a Snowdonian sheep farmer during the 1930s. Generous but patronizing observations about his neighbours and his wife mar an otherwise enjoyable, easy read.

Iris Gower *Copper Kingdom; Proud Mary; Spinners' Wharf; Black Gold; Fiddler's Ferry; The Oyster Catchers* – the list goes on. Romantic novels by Wales' most popular author.

Niall Griffiths *Grits; Sheepshagger; Kelly + Victor; Stump; Wreckage*. Arguably the best dissector of darkness, drugs, comradeship and hopelessness in modern Britain, Griffiths' panoply of books set between Aberystwyth and Liverpool are huge achievements and suffused with a metaphysical sense of culture and landscape.

James Hawes *White Powder, Green Light*. Dazzling send-up of the incestuous Welsh media industry, coked-up Soho movie moguls and modern life, together with ruminations on just where – or what – is home.

Emyr Humphreys *The Gift of a Daughter*. Latest in a long line of mystical, well-placed novels by perhaps the greatest extant Welsh novelist. In this one, the mood and landscape of Anglesey is beautifully evoked.

Siân James *Not Singing Exactly*. Dazzling and diverse short-story collection from one of Wales' premier romantic novelists.

Glyn Jones *The Island of Apples*. Set in south Wales and Carmarthen in the early years of the twentieth century, this is an artful portrayal of a sensitive Valley youth's enthralment in the glamour of the district's new arrival.

Gwyn and Thomas Jones (trans) *The Mabinogion*. Welsh mythology's classic, these eleven orally developed heroic tales were finally transcribed into the *Book of Rhydderch* (around 1300–25) and the *Red Book of Hergest* (1375–1425). Originally translated by Lady Charlotte Guest between 1838 and 1849 at the beginning of the Celtic revival.

Lewis Jones *Cwmardy*. Longtime favourite socialist novel, written in 1937 and portraying life in a Rhondda Valley mining community in the early years of the twentieth century. Followed by its sequel, *We Live*.

Richard Llewellyn *How Green Was My Valley; Up into the Singing Mountain; Down Where the Moon is Small; Green, Green My Valley Now*.

Vital tetralogy in eloquent and passionate prose, following the life of Huw Morgan from his youth in a south Wales mining valley through emigration to the Welsh community in Patagonia and back to 1970s Wales. A bestseller during World War II and still the best introduction to the vast canon of "valleys novels", *How Green Was My Valley* captured a longing for a simple, if tough, life, steering clear of cloying sentimentality.

Caradoc Pritchard *One Moonlit Night*. Dense, swirling tale of a young boy's emotional and sexual awakenings in an isolated north Wales village. Full-blooded Welsh prose at its most charged.

Malcolm Pryce *Aberystwyth Mon Amour*. Surprise bestseller in the shape of this furious, funny black comedy set in an Aberystwyth overlaid with film noir surrealism and dastardly twists of plot. The joke begins to wear rather thin in the sequels *Last Tango in Aberystwyth* and *The Unbearable Lightness of Being in Aberystwyth*.

Kate Roberts *The Living Sleep* and *Feet in Chains*, amongst others. Penned by one of the best-selling contemporary Welsh-language writers, these two novels, available in English translation, tell the tales of life in a north Wales slate village.

Ruth Janette Ruck *Hill Farm Story* and *Along Came a Llama*. Evocative stories about a farming area around Beddgelert.

Dylan Thomas *Collected Stories* and *Under Milk Wood*. Far better than buying any of the single editions, the *Collected Stories* contains all of Thomas' classic prose pieces: *Quite Early One Morning*, which metamorphosed into *Under Milk Wood*, the magical *A Child's Christmas in Wales* and the compulsive, crackling autobiography of *Portrait of the Artist as a Young Dog*. In all of Thomas' works, the language still burns bright in a uniquely robust way. *Under Milk Wood* is his most popular play, telling the story of a microcosmic Welsh seaside town over a 24-hour period. Reading it does little justice – far better, instead, to get a tape or record version of the play, and luxuriate in its rich poetry or, as Thomas himself described it, "prose with blood pressure".

Gwyn Thomas *A Welsh Eye* (o/p). A partly autobiographical, partly anecdotal view of how it feels to grow up in a small Rhondda town; full of arcane and idiosyncratic wit and much more.

Alice Thomas Ellis (ed) *Wales – An Anthology* (o/p). A beautiful book, combining poetry, folklore and prose stories rooted in places throughout Wales. All subjects, from rugby and mountain climbing to contemporary descriptions of major events, are included in an enjoyably eclectic mixture of styles. Possibly the best introduction to Welsh writing.

Charlotte Williams *Sugar and Slate*. Beautifully written memoir of mixed identity: the author is the daughter of a black Guyanese father who grew up in a Welsh-speaking community. Questions of home and hearth, elegantly picked over with unstinting humour and honesty.

John Williams *Five Pubs, Two Bars And A Nightclub; Cardiff Dead; Temperance Town*. The first a very funny short story collection, something of an inspiration for the E-culture hit film *Human Traffic*, the second a full-length novel that packs in the Welsh cultural references effortlessly and to great effect, the third a novella in the same vein.

Raymond Williams *Border Country*. Recently re-issued 1960 novel that perfectly captures the sense of change overwhelming rural Welsh life in that era. A timeless classic.

Poetry

Dannie Abse *Welsh Retrospective* and *Arcadia, One Mile*. Two recent collections from one of Wales' most prolific modern poets, showing his huge range of intellectual interests and warm, beguiling style of writing.

John Barnie *The City* and *The Confirmation*. One of Wales' best contemporary writers, notable mainly for his combination of poetry and prose styles, narration and description. Evocative tales of wartime childhood and stifling parenting, leading to a poignant search for love.

Ruth Bidgood *Lighting Candles*. Light, elegiac verse inspired by the Welsh landscape. Bidgood's interweaving of climate, scenery and emotion is delicately done, producing fine and deceptively robust pieces that stand up as physical description, spiritual discussion or both.

Gillian Clarke *Collected Poems*. A good introduction to the nature-inspired and homely poetry of one of Wales' leading contemporary writers, now in her sixties.

Gerard Manley Hopkins *Collected Works*. The religious poetry of this late nineteenth-century Anglo-Catholic still bears scrutiny today. Much of his best work was inspired by Wales – "the loveable west" – and the metre and rhythm of the Welsh language that he strove to learn. Heartfelt and often profoundly sad, with an exquisite ability to marry the grandeur of the landscape with the intensity of his feelings.

Dafydd Johnston *Iolo Goch: poems*. All of the surviving poems of Owain Glyndŵr's court bard are shown in translation and context. A fascinating insight into courtly medieval Wales at a time of great national resurgence.

Gwyneth Lewis *Keeping Mum*. Wales' new National Poet shows her verbal power and dexterity with this recent collection, most thrilling when it combs over the irregularities of bilingual existence.

Robert Minhinnick *Selected Poems*. Overview of the recent career of one of Wales' brightest young writers: best when picking over his English-speaking south Walian youth in rich, impassioned imagery.

Owen Sheers *The Blue Book*. Gently uplifting and wry collection from the young Welsh wunderkind. A biographical account of his family in Africa – *The Dust Diaries* – is superb.

Meic Stephens (ed) *New Companion to the Literature of Wales*. A customarily thorough volume of Welsh prose, spanning the centuries from the folk tales of The Mabinogion to modern-day writings. A succinct and entertaining collection.

Dylan Thomas *Collected Poems*. Thomas' poetry has always proved less populist than his prose- and play-writing, largely due to its density and difficulty. Many of his lighter poems resound with perfect metre and precise structure, including classics such as *Do Not Go Gentle Into That Good Night*, a passionate yet calm elegy to his dying father.

R.S. Thomas *Selected Poems 1946–1968*. The much-missed recluse, Thomas, wrote poetry that tugs at issues such as God (he was an Anglican priest), Wales ("brittle with relics") and the family. His passion shines throughout this book, probably the best overview available of his prolific work.

Harri Webb (ed. Meic Stephens) *Collected Poems*. Fine collection of 350 works by a modern-day patriot and poet of biting satire and eloquent expression.

Wildlife and the environment

Douglas Botting *Wild Britain: A Traveller's Guide*. Not much use for species identification but plenty of information on access to the best sites and what to expect when you get there. Excellent photos.

Collins Field Guides Series of thorough, pocket-sized identification guides. Topics include insects, butterflies, wildflowers, mushrooms and toadstools, birds, mammals, reptiles and fossils.

William Condry and Jeremy Moore *Heart of the Country*. Jeremy Moore's gorgeous photography is the perfect accompaniment to the late William Condry's Country Diary entries from *The Guardian*.

Michael Leach *The Secret Life of Snowdonia* (o/p). Beautifully photographed coffee-table delvings into the least visible natural sights of Snowdonia, from feral goats to the Snowdon lily and a close-up of a raven in its nest.

David Saunders *Where to Watch Birds in Wales*. Enthusiasts' guide to Wales' prime birding locations, along with a bird spotting calendar and a list of English–Welsh–Scientific bird names. Not an identification guide.

Outdoor pursuits

Bob Allen *On Foot in Snowdonia*. Inspirational and superbly photographed guide to the hundred best walks, from easy strolls to hard scrambles, in and around the Snowdonia National Park. Well-drawn maps, faultless instructions and a star rating for each walk help you to select your route. An essential guide, perfect but for its weight.

Cicerone Guides *The Mountains of England and Wales; Wales, The Ridges of Snowdonia; Hill Walking in Snowdonia; Ascent of Snowdon; Welsh Winter Climbs; Scrambles in Snowdonia* and others, various authors. Clearly written pocket guides to the best aspects of Welsh mountain activities.

A.J. Drake *Cambrian Way: A Mountain Connoisseur's Walk* (o/p). Thorough and detailed lightweight guide to Wales' most demanding long-distance path by one of the original proposers of this three-week-long, 274-mile Conwy–Cardiff route along Wales' backbone.

Lawrence Main *The Dyfi Valley Way* (o/p) and *The Spirit Paths of Wales*.

The first is a comprehensive guide to this long-distance path by one of its creators; the second is a wonderful guide to twenty Welsh walks, each along ley lines and other spiritually significant routes.

Terry Marsh *The Mountains of Wales*. A walker's guide to all 183 of the 600-metre peaks in Wales, giving step-by-step descriptions of one or more routes up them all with additional historical references and local knowledge.

Ordnance Survey National Trail Guides Large, paperback editions full of instructive step-by-step descriptions and additional side-walks from *Offa's Dyke North*, *Offa's Dyke South* and *Pembrokeshire Coastal Path*.

W.A. Poucher *The Welsh Peaks*. The classic book on Welsh hill-walking, but fairly dated now; initially, it's also a little awkward to find your way around the 56 routes.

Stillwell's National Trail Companion Excellent big-pocket directory of reasonably priced accommodation close to some of the more popular UK long-distance paths. Welsh routes include the Cambrian Way, Glyndŵr's Way, the Offa's Dyke Path, the Pembrokeshire Coast Path and the Wye Valley Walk.

Shirley Toulson *The Drovers' Roads of Wales with Fay Godwin* and *The Drovers' Roads of Wales II: Pembrokeshire and the South with Caroline Forbes*. A pair of complementary books giving background material along with instructions on how to trace the routes along which Wales' characteristic black cattle were driven to market in England in the eighteenth and nineteenth centuries. The first book covers the northern two-thirds of Wales with superb shots in black-and-white by photography star Fay Godwin, the much more recent second book covers south Wales with more high-quality photos.

Film

Wales has formed the backdrop to many a movie, from low-budget local efforts to Hollywood (and even Bollywood) blockbusters, and we give a selection below. Few of the big films, however, have Welsh themes: more often than not, the country is either masquerading as somewhere else or just providing generic scenery. A huge new film studio near Bridgend (inevitably christened "Valleywood" by the press) is due to begin the first phase of its operation in 2006, though it's impossible to say what effects that will have quite yet. Meanwhile, Wales' biggest current splash on screen – albeit the smaller one – is the revamp of *Dr Who*, made to startling effect by BBC Wales and with many local landmarks prominent.

Movies with specifically Welsh stories tend to be at the lower budget end of the spectrum, and in recent years, have usually played on a slightly whimsical view of Wales. Despite the huge success of Welsh film stars like Richard Burton, and today's crop like Rhys Ifans and Ioan Gruffudd, there is little big-budget interest in Wales: *Glyndŵr: the Movie*, a Welsh *Braveheart*, is still just a pipe dream.

An American Werewolf in London (1981). Classic shlock horror movie; the moor sequences at the beginning are the Brecon Beacons.

The Englishman Who Went Up a Hill and Came Down a Mountain (1995). Bumbling comedy full of cod Welsh stereotypes and Hugh Grant as a similarly one-dimensional Englishman; filmed around Llanrhaeadr-ym-Mochnant and near Cardiff.

First Knight (1995). Sean Connery stars as King Arthur, with Richard Gere as Sir Lancelot, in this patchy action movie filmed largely in Snowdonia.

Happy Now (2001). Distinctly oddball thriller, filmed in and around Barmouth, which becomes mysterious Welsh seaside town Pen-y-Wig. Worth seeing alone for Alison Steadman's towering performance as a tyrannical landlady trapped in an iron lung.

Hedd Wyn (1994). Lovely Welsh-language film about the north Wales poet who went off to fight in World War I and never returned. Garnered the first Oscar nomination for a Welsh movie.

House of America (1997). Dark and depressing tale of secrets and yearning in one family stuck on a mouldering farm in west Wales.

How Green was my Valley (1941). None of it was filmed in Wales, but this Oscar-winning version of the classic Welsh book came to define the world image of Wales for a very long time.

Human Traffic (1999). Feelgood E-culture movie, with a star cameo by Welsh drug-trafficking guru Howard Marks. Filmed in Cardiff.

Inn of the Sixth Happiness (1958). Ingrid Bergman leads in this classic tale of self-discovery, where Snowdonia doubles up as China.

King Arthur (2004). Big-screen epic, with huge battles and a rather less sensational account of the "real" king of the Britons than had gone before. Ioan Gruffudd sparkles as Sir Lancelot.

Kyun! Ho Gaya Na Pyaar (2004). Translating as "It has happened – love", this is a big-budget Bollywood production, with former Miss World, Aishwarya Rai, as the love interest. Large sections were filmed in mid-Wales and Snowdonia.

On the Black Hill (1987). Hauntingly beautiful adaptation of the downbeat Bruce Chatwin novel about twin brothers growing up in the Black Mountains.

Lawrence of Arabia (1962). The south Wales sand dunes of Merthyr Mawr doubled up as Arabia for Peter O'Toole, Omar Sharif and company.

The Prisoner (1971). Big-screen version of the enigmatic cult TV series, also filmed largely at the fantasy village of Portmeirion.

Solomon a Gaenor (1998). Filmed in both Welsh and English versions, this Oscar-nominated weepie is a *Romeo and Juliet* tale set in the Edwardian Valleys.

Twin Town (1997). The best modern Welsh movie of all: a hilarious drug-fuelled romp set in Swansea that introduced Rhys Ifans to the world.

Under Milk Wood (1971). Phantasmagoric take on the classic Dylan Thomas "play for voices", with an all-star cast that included Richard Burton and Elizabeth Taylor.

Very Annie Mary (2001). Wonderfully offbeat tale of love and singing in the Valleys, with Ioan Gruffudd and Matthew Rhys camping it up to the nines as the only gays in the village.

Glossary of architectural terms

Aisle Clear space parallel to the nave, usually with lower ceiling than the nave.

Altar Table at which the Eucharist is celebrated, at the east end of the church. When the church is not aligned to the geographical east, the altar end is still referred to as the "east" end.

Ambulatory Passage behind the chancel.

Apse The curved or polygonal east end of a church.

Arcade Row of arches on top of columns or piers, supporting a wall.

Bailey Area enclosed by castle walls.

Barbican Defensive structure built in front of main gate.

Barrel vault Continuous rounded vault, like a semi-cylinder.

Boss A decorative carving at the meeting point of the lines of a vault.

Box pew Form of church seating in which each row is enclosed by high, thin wooden panels.

Buttress Stone support for a wall; some buttresses are wholly attached to the wall, others take the form of a tower with a connecting arch, known as a "flying buttress".

Capital Upper section of a column, usually carved.

Chancel Section of the church where the altar is located.

Choir Area in which the church service is conducted; next to or same as chancel.

Clerestory Upper storey of nave, containing a line of windows.

Corbel Jutting stone support, often carved.

Crenellations Battlements with square indentations.

Crossing The intersection of the nave and the transepts.

Decorated Middle Gothic style, about 1280–1380.

Fan vault Late Gothic form of vaulting, in which the area between walls and ceiling is covered with stone ribs in the shape of an open fan.

Finial Any decorated tip of an architectural feature.

Gallery A raised passageway.

Gargoyle Grotesque exterior carving, usually a decorative form of water spout.

Hammerbeam Type of ceiling in which horizontal beams support vertical pieces that connect to the roof timbers.

Jesse window Stained-glass window depicting the descendants from Jesse (the father of David) down to Jesus.

Keep Main structure of a castle.

Lancet Tall, narrow and plain window.

Misericord Carved ledge below a tip-up seat, usually in choir stalls.

Motte Mound on which a castle keep stands.

Mullion Vertical strip between the panes of a window.

Nave The main part of the church to the west of the crossing.

Ogee Double curve; distinctive feature of Decorated style.

Oriel Projecting window.

Palladian Eighteenth-century classical style, adhering to the principles of Andrea Palladio.

Pediment Triangular space above a window or doorway.

Perpendicular Late Gothic style, about 1380–1550.

Pier Massive column, often consisting of several fused smaller columns.

Portico Colonnade, usually supporting a porch to the building.

Rood screen Wooden screen supporting a Crucifix (or rood), separating the choir from the nave; few survived the Reformation.

Rose window Large circular window, divided into vaguely petal-shaped sections.

Stalls Seating for clergy in the choir area of a church.

Tracery Pattern formed by narrow bands of stone in a window or on a wall surface.

Transept Sections of the main body of the church at right angles to the choir and nave.

Vault Arched ceiling.

Language

Language

Language

W elsh – or *Cymraeg* as it calls itself – is spoken widely throughout
the country and as a first language in many parts of the west and
north. Indeed, one of the most startling findings of the 2001 British census was a significant increase in Welsh speakers throughout
Wales, and the headline figure (around 600,000 in a population of
3 million) is now higher than it's been for forty years. From the sharp decline
of the mid-twentieth century, it's a remarkable turnabout and testament to
bold policies, particularly in education and mass media. National TV and radio
stations broadcast in Welsh, road signs are written in both Welsh and English,
Welsh-medium schools are everywhere, books in Welsh are published at a
growing rate of around 400 every year and magazines, newspapers and websites
in the old language are mushrooming. The language's survival, and modest
resurgence, is a remarkable story, especially considering the fact that the heart
of English culture and its language – the most expansionist the world has ever
seen – lies right next door.

In the families of Celtic languages, Welsh bears most similarity to largely
defunct Cornish and defiant Breton, the language of the northwestern corner
of France. Scots and Irish Gaelic, together with defunct Manx, belong to a
different branch of Celtic languages, and, although there are occasional similarities, they have little in common.

Some history

The Welsh language can be traced back to the sixth century. Through Celtic
inscriptions on stones, a section of written Welsh in the eighth-century

△ Welsh–English dictionary

Lichfield Gospels, the tenth-century codified laws of Hywel Dda in neat Welsh prose and the twelfth- and thirteenth-century **Mabinogion** folk tales (believed to have been collated from earlier Welsh writings), it can be seen that Welsh was a thriving language in the centuries up to the Norman invasion of 1066. Moreover, the early language is still identifiable and easily comprehensible for any modern-day Welsh-speaker.

English domination since the Norman era has been mirrored in the fate of the Welsh tongue. The Norman lords were implanted in castles throughout Wales to subjugate the natives, with official business conducted in their native French. **Edward I** (1272–1307), who conquered Wales in 1284, was politically sensitive to the power of the language to define a nation, and is said to have promised the Welsh a prince, born in their own country who was unable to speak English. This promise was delivered when Edward made his pregnant wife take up residence in Caernarfon Castle, enabling the king to hold the newborn infant up as a non-English-speaking, Welsh-born prince.

Real linguistic warfare came with the 1536 **Act of Union** under Henry VIII. This stated that "from henceforth no Person or Persons that use the Welsh Speech or Language shall have or enjoy any Manner, Office or Fees within this Realm of England, Wales or other of the King's Dominion, upon pain of forfeiting the same Office or Fees, unless he or they use and exercise the English Speech or Language". This only legitimized the growing practice of imposing English lords and churchmen on the restless, but effectively cowed, Welsh. Had it not been for **William Morgan**'s 1588 translation of the Bible into Welsh, it is likely that the language would have died. As it was, bringing written Welsh into the ordinary, everyday arena of the public ultimately ensured its survival.

The fate of the language became inextricably linked with its religious use. Right up until the early part of the twentieth century, Welsh was actively, even forcefully, discouraged in educational and governmental establishments, but new and Nonconformist religious movements from the seventeenth century onwards embraced the language. The **Industrial Revolution** brought mine owners and capitalists from England into the rapidly urbanizing southeastern corner of Wales, further diluting the language which was, nonetheless, upheld as the lingua franca in the growing numbers of chapels. In the first half of the nineteenth century, it is estimated that over ninety percent of the country's population spoke Welsh, with the remaining ten percent comprising those around the English border, in the small pocket of Pembrokeshire long known as "Little England Beyond Wales" and the wealthier classes throughout Wales, for whom English was part of their badge of status.

In 1854, **George Borrow** undertook his marathon tour of Wales and noted the state of the native tongue throughout. As a natural linguist, he had mastered Welsh and fired questions at people he encountered as to their proficiency in both Welsh and English. The picture he paints is of poorer people tending to be monoglot Welsh, wealthier people and those near the border bilingual. Discouragement of Welsh continued in many guises, most notably in it being forbidden in schools in the latter half of the nineteenth and early twentieth centuries. Anyone caught speaking in Welsh had to wear a "Welsh Not", a piece of wood on a leather strap, that would only be passed on if someone else was heard using the language. At the end of the school day, the child still wearing the Welsh Not was soundly beaten. There are still older people in Wales who can remember this barbaric practice, and it is hardly surprising that use and proficiency of the language plummeted. Figures are borne out by the official British census, the first of which was undertaken in 1851, when 90 percent of the country are recorded as speaking the language. Every decade, the figures

dipped quite spectacularly – 49.9 percen..
percent in 1951 and 18.9 percent in 1981. The..,
and again in 2001, the percentage of Welsh speakers .
fifth mark but showing the most marked increase amongst ..
those most able to ensure its future.

Where Welsh is spoken

The figure of twenty percent (ie around 600,000 people), usually quoted as the current number of fluent Welsh-speakers in Wales is best seen in its geographical context. Considering the fact that nearly half of the nation's population lives in the anglicized regions of Gwent and around Cardiff, the spread of the language becomes clearer. Although it is unusual to hear it regularly in the border counties, it is commonly understood throughout most of West Glamorgan, Carmarthenshire, the northern half of Pembrokeshire, right around Cardigan Bay up to Caernarfon, the Llŷn peninsula and Anglesey and in parts of inland Denbighshire and Montgomeryshire. The northwestern corner, centred on Snowdonia, Anglesey and the Llŷn, is the real stronghold of Welsh, reflected in these areas' steadfast political affiliation to Welsh nationalism.

The politics of the language

If Welsh ended the twentieth century on a more upbeat note than could ever have been predicted thirty or so years ago (when it was believed to be dying out), it is largely due to those who campaigned to save it. The campaign dates back to the eisteddfod revivalists of the eighteenth century, although movements with a more political aim are a product solely of the twentieth century. The formation of **Plaid Cymru**, the Welsh National Party, in 1925 was largely around the issue of language, as indeed its politics have been ever since. In the early 1960s, concerns about the language reached a zenith in the 1962 radio broadcast entitled *Tynged yr iaith* (The Fate of the Language) by the Plaid founder member, Saunders Lewis. This became a rallying cry that resulted in the formation of *Cymdeithas yr Iaith Gymraeg* (the **Welsh Language Society**) the following year. One of the most high-profile early campaigns was the daubing of monoglot English road signs with their Welsh translations, including any town sign written solely in the anglicized format. As any visitor to Wales sees, nearly all signs are now in both languages. A 1967 Welsh Language Act allowed many forms of hitherto English officialdom to be conducted in either language, stating that Welsh, for the first time in over 400 years, had "equal validity" with English.

Bilingual road signs and tax forms are all well and good, but they could do nothing to stem the linguistic haemorrhage that Wales was threatened with. In the multinational, cross-media world of the late twentieth century, the keys to maintaining and promoting a language were in education and media, particularly television. Following the 1967 Act, **Welsh-medium education** blossomed, with bilingual teaching in all primary schools and for at least a year in all secondary schools. Many secondary schools, particularly in areas traditionally associated with the language, had Welsh as a compulsory subject for five years. Increasing numbers of schools all over the land educate their students in all subjects through the Welsh language. These trends have brought little but sneers from the English establishment, profiling loud complaints from numbers of parents, often English in-migrants, who object to their children being "forced" to learn a "dead" language. Although there are still periodic rumbles of discontent, most have come round to the well-founded view that a

...ercent of the world's children

...g aptitude for other languages.

...m, Welsh-language courses in the

...ularity and status, meaning that, for

...y, it is possible to be educated in Welsh

...n has been the other modern cornerstone for

...n **broadcast media**. The BBC Welsh-language

...e 1970s, to be joined – after a considerable battle

...ar Cymru (S4C) TV station in 1982. Together, they

...mmed popular Welsh learners' programmes and given

...space than it has ever enjoyed before.

Th...n today

Critics ... ...ke to believe that this is a false dawn, but this can easily be dismissed ju... by touring Wales and seeing the sheer number of Welsh-language classes on offer right across the country, including in some of the most anglicized of border towns. Welsh classes can invariably be found out of Wales too, in language centres across Britain, and universities in Europe and North America.

The Welsh language is both one of Wales' key strengths and its key drawbacks in the quest for some sort of national emancipation. There is still suspicion, occasionally bordering on hostility, towards the Welsh-speaking "elite" who are seen to control the media and local government in the country. Welsh nationalism is so defined by the language that Plaid Cymru has nearly always had great difficulty in appealing to those who speak only English, particularly in the urban southeast. Nonetheless, the Welsh language seems to be facing the future in greater heart than could ever have been expected only a few decades ago. The **Welsh Language Board** was formed in 1994, and with the arrival of the **National Assembly** in 1999, with around half of its members proficient in Welsh, the language has gained a number of firm footholds in official life. It is nonsensical to believe that Wales can ever become a monoglot Welsh-speaking nation, but it does seem to be developing well as a model bilingual entity, in which there is room for both languages to thrive together.

Alphabet

Although Welsh words, place names in particular, can appear bewilderingly incomprehensible, the rules of the language are far more strictly adhered to than in English. Thus, mastering the basic constructions and breaking words down into their constituent parts means that pronunciation need not be anywhere near as difficult as first imagined.

The Welsh **alphabet** is similar to the English, although with seven vowels instead of five, and a different collection of consonants. As well as the same five vowels (a, e, i, o, u), Welsh also has y and w. Most vowels have two sounds, long and short: a is long as in c**a**r, short as in f**a**t; e long as in br**e**r, short as in p**e**t; i long as in s**ea**, short as an t**i**n; o long as in m**o**re, short as in d**o**g; u roughly like a Welsh i; w long as in s**oo**n, short as in l**oo**k; y long as in s**ea** and short as in b**u**n or p**i**n. A circumflex over any vowel lengthens its sound.

Adjoining vowels are common in Welsh. Ae, ai, aw, ew, iw, oe, oi, ou, wy and yw are the usual forms and are pronounced as the two separate sounds, with, generally, the stress on the first.

There are no letters j, k, v, x and z in Welsh, except in occasional words appropriated and Cymrified from other languages. Additional Welsh consonants are ch, pronounced as in German or as in lo**ch**, dd, pronounced as a hard th as in **th**ose, ff and ph as a soft f as in **f**ive and si as in **sh**oe. The typically Welsh consonant that causes the most problem is the ll, featured in many place names such as **Ll**ango**ll**en. This has no direct parallel in English, although the tl sound in Bent-**l**ey comes close. The proper way to pronounce it is to place the tongue firmly behind the top row of teeth and breathe through it without consciously making a voiced sound. Single Welsh consonants are, for the most part, pronounced in similar ways to English. The exceptions are c and g, always hard as in **c**at and **g**ut (never soft as in ni**c**e or ra**g**e) and f, always pronounced as v as in **v**ine.

A further difficulty for those trying to recognize words is the Welsh system of word **mutation**, where a previous word can affect the beginning of a following one, principally to ease pronunciation. Prepositions commonly mutate the following word, turning an initial B into F or M, an initial C into G or Ngh, a D into Dd or N, F into B or M, G into Ngh or the initial letter being dropped altogether, Ll into L, M into F, P into B, Mh or Ph, T into Th, D or Nh. Thus, "in Cardiff (Caerdydd)" is "y**ng Ngh**aerdydd" (note that the "yn" also mutates to ease pronunciation) and "from Bangor" is "o **F**angor". Mutated words are extremely common in the component parts of place names.

Welsh vocabulary

Alban	Scotland
Amgeuddfa	museum
Ap (ab)	son of
Ar Agor	open
Ar Gau	closed
Ar Werth	for sale
Araf	slow
Arafwch	slow down (instruction)
Bara	bread
Bore	morning
Bore da	good morning
Brecwast	breakfast
Bwrdd	table
Bws	bus
Cân	song
Cenedlaethol	national
Crefft	craft
Croeso	welcome
Croglen	rood screen
Cromlech	literally "curved stone", generally used to refer to megalithic burial chambers
Cwm	glacially formed, cliff-backed and often lake-filled bowl in mountains. Also called cirque or corrie
Cyhoeddus	public
Cymdeithas	society
Cymraeg	Welsh
Cymraes	a Welshwoman
Cymreictod	Welshness
Cymro	Welshman
Cymru	Wales
Cymry	the Welsh people
Cynulliad	Assembly
Da	good
Dewi Sant	Saint David
Dim	no (as an instruction), nothing
Diolch	thank you
Diwedd	end
Dŵr	water
Dydd	day
Dyn (-ion)	man (men)
Eglwys	church
Eisteddfod	festival
Faint?	how much?
Gorsaf	station
Gweddol	fair
Gwely	bed
Gwesty	hotel

Hafod	temporary summer house	Noswaith dda	good evening
Hanner	half	Olaf	last
Heddiw	today	Os gwelwch chi'n dda	please
Heddlu	police	Pêl-droed	football
Heno	tonight	Pentre(f)	village
Heol	road	Plaid Cymru	The Party of Wales
Hiraeth	longing, yearning	P'nhawn da	good afternoon
Hwyl	spirit	Rhiniog	buttress
Laith	language	Saesneg	English language
Lawn	fine, very	Sais	Englishman
Llech	slate	Sant	saint
Llety	lodging place, B&B	Sarn	causeway
Llew	lion (often found in pub names)	Senedd	Parliament
		Shwmae	hello
Lloegr	England	Siop	shop
Llwybr	path	Sir	county, shire
Llyfr	book	Stryd	street
Marchnad	market	Sut ydych chi? (formal) or Sut ywt ti? (informal)	how are you?
Menyw	woman		
Mihangel	Michael, as in Llanfihangel		
		Swyddfa	office
Milltir	mile	Swyddfa'r Post	post office
Neuadd	hall	Tafarn	pub
Neuadd Y Dref	town hall	Tocyn	ticket
Nofio	to swim	Y, Yr or 'r	the
Nos da	good night	Yma	here
Noson/noswaith	evening	Ysbyty	hospital
		Ysgol	school

Welsh place names

The following list is of the most common words that you will see in town and village names. For a brief guide to pronunciation, see "Alphabet", p.566.

Aber	mouth of a river; confluence of two rivers	Carreg	stone
		Cartref	home
		Castell	castle
Afon	river	Clun	meadow
Bach	small, lesser	Clwyd	gate, perch
Bro	neighbourhood	Coch	red
Bron	slope of a hill	Coed	forest, woodland
Bryn	hill	Craig	rock
Bwlch	mountain pass	Crannog	artificial island on a lake
Cadair	stronghold, chair		
Caer	fort	Cwm	valley
Canol	centre	Cyntaf	first
Cant	hundred	De	south
Capel	chapel	Din or dinas	fort

Dôl	meadow		Melyn	yellow
Dros	over		Merthyr	burial place of saint
Du	black		Moel	bare or rounded mountain
Dwyrain	east			
Dyffryn	vale		Môr	sea
Esgair	ridge		Morfa	coastal marsh
Fach	small, lesser		Mynydd	mountain
Fawr	big, greater		Nant	valley, stream
Fferm	farm		Newydd	new
Ffordd	road		Nos	night
Fforest	forest		Pant	vale
Gardd	garden		Parc	park
Glas	blue		Pen	head, top (as of a valley)
Glyn	valley			
Gogledd	north		Pentre(f)	village
Gorllewin	west		Plas	hall, mansion
Gwyn	white		Pont	bridge
Gwyrdd	green		Porth	port, gateway
Hen	old		Rhiw	hill
Isaf	lower		Rhyd	ford
Llan	sacred enclosure, early church		Tomen	mound
			Traeth	beach
Lle	place		Tref	town
Llwyd	grey		Tŵr	tower
Llyn	lake		Tŷ	house
Llys	place, court		Uchaf	uppermost, highest
Maen	stone		Uwch	higher
Maes	field		Wrth	near, by
Mawr	big, greater		Ynys	island
Melin	mill			

Welsh numbers

un	1		dau-ddeg-un	21
dau (fem. dwy)	2		dau-ddeg-dau	22
tri (fem. tair)	3		tri-deg	30
pedwar (fem. pedair)	4		pedwar-deg	40
pump	5		pum-deg	50
chwech	6		chwe-deg	60
saith	7		saith-deg	70
wyth	8		wyth-deg	80
naw	9		naw-deg	90
deg	10		cant	100
un-deg-un	11		dau gant	200
un-deg-dau	12		tri chant	300
un-deg-tri	13		pedwar cant	400
dau-ddeg	20		pum cant	500

chwe cant	600		naw cant	900
saith cant	700		mil	1000
wyth cant	800		miliwn	1,000,000

Resources for Welsh learners

Welsh-language classes are held throughout Wales – a list can be obtained from the Welsh for Adults Officer at the Welsh Language Board (see below). Otherwise, there are rafts of publications, on paper and electronically, as well as TV and radio programmes and support groups for the Welsh learner. The list below is by no means exhaustive.

Acen Tŷ Ifor, Bridge St, Cardiff CF10 2EE ☎029/2030 0800, ⓦwww.acen .co.uk. S4C-originated company, now providing a multimedia Welsh course, together with a regular magazine and copious numbers of useful contacts.

Canolfan Iaith Nant Gwrtheyrn Llithfaen, Pwllheli, Gwynedd LL53 6PA ☎01758/750334, ⓦwww.nantgwrtheyrn.org. Residential national language centre on the coast of the Llŷn.

Cymdeithas Madog (North American Welsh Studies Institute) Cymdeithas Madog, 1540 S St, Gering, NE 69341, USA ⓦwww.madog.org. Annual residential language courses, plus a directory of resources.

Cymdeithas yr Iaith (Welsh Language Society) Pen Roc, Rhodfa'r Môr, Aberystwyth SY23 2AZ ☎01970/624501, ⓦwww.cymdeithas.com. Campaigning and political organization dedicated to improving the status of the Welsh language.

National Language Unit of Wales Welsh for Adults Officer, Welsh Joint Education Committee, 245 Western Ave, Cardiff CF5 2YX ☎029/2026 5000, ⓦwww.wjec.co.uk/nlu. Provides a comprehensive guide to Welsh teaching provision.

Welsh Language Board/Bwrdd yr Iaith Gymraeg 5–7 St Mary St, Cardiff CF10 1AT ☎029/2087 8000, ⓦwww.bwrdd-yr-iaith.org.uk.

Travel store

TRAVEL

& MORE

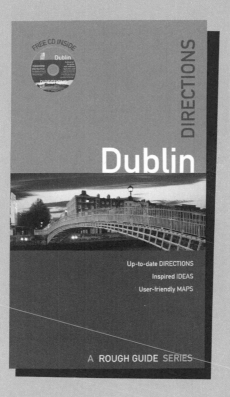

Visit us online

www.roughguides.con

Information on over 25,000 destinations around the wo

- **Read** Rough Guides' trusted travel info

- **Share** journals, photos and travel advice with other readers

- Get exclusive Rough Guide **discounts** and travel deals

- Earn membership points every time you contribute to the

  Rough Guide community and get free books, flights and trips

- Browse thousands of **CD reviews** and artists in our music area

ONLINE

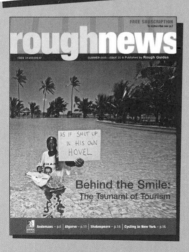

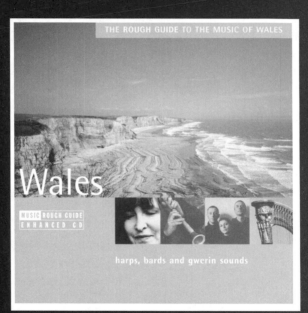

NOTES

NOTES

NOTES

NOTES

NOTES

NOTES

Small print and

Index

Acknowledgements

Mike: Glenda Davies and all at Bwrdd Croeso Cymru, co-author Paul and editor Annie, Carys Hedd, Penny Andrews, Paul Woodland and the poker sharks of Swansea, Lou Hart, Griff Rowland Williams, Dewi Fluffylovebubble, Emyr and Diane Jenkins, Helen Williams-Ellis, Jan and Elizabeth Morris, John Barnie, Gwilym Morus, Francesca Rhydderch, Damien Walford-Davies, Tammy Jones, Meic ac Angela Llewelyn, Alun Evans, Nia Dryhurst, Cathryn Scott, Mair Tomos, Meg Thomas, Meri Wells, Llinos Jones-Williams, pawb yn Nh Maengwyn ac yn Esgairgeiliog. Biggest thanks of all to Patsy the hound and to Preds, who bore my deadline-induced grumpiness with amazing poise. Diolch, cariad.

Paul: Glenda Lloyd Davies at the Wales Tourist Board and all those who shared thoughts, experiences and Welsh mountain paths including Jo Farrington, Neil Woods, Brett McGill and Carl Pulley. Also to Liz Porter for guiding me around the Wind Street nightlife, and to Irene for putting up with half-done DIY projects abandoned during lengthy bouts of research and writing.

Thanks also go to Maxine Repath and Ed Wright for cartography, Sarah Smithies for tireless picture research, Ankur Guha for typesetting, Karen Parker for proofreading, and Claire Saunders for superb project management.

Readers' letters

Thanks to all the readers who took the trouble to write in with their comments and suggestions (and apologies to anyone whose name we've misspelt or omitted):

Geoff Bridgman, J. Burkitt, Richard Chandler, Helen Clough, Alina Congreve, Tamzin Costello, Tony Davies, Caroline Duckworth, Lucia Floridi, Liz Fraser, Christian Ganzeboer, Janette Gibson, Nicole Glaser, M. Habberley, Sharon Harris, Danny Heijl, Marc Hopkins, Peter Hopkins, P. Hughes, Stephen Hughes, Neil Humphreys, Rhiannon Humphreys, Samir Hussain, David James and Dawn Gameson, Peter Johnson, Lowri Elen Jones, Jens Kronborg, Yonnie Kwok-Pickles, Nathan Kuppermann, Ian Langmead, Pauline Lawrence, Tom Lewis, Benjamin Levy, Eric Lien, Tim Lloyd, Richard Lysons, Stephanie McCarthy, Lynden Mack, Pam Martin, Dave Palmer, Dewi Rhys-Jones, Peter Roberts, Claudia Senecal, Stella Shaw, Gareth Simpson, Mark Tami, Imogen Taylor, Eddie Thomas, Jeffrey Walter, Barbara Wescombe, Andrew Young.

ROUGH GUIDES

SMALL PRINT

Photo credits

All photos © Rough Guides except the following:

Colour Introduction
Snowdon from Capel Curig © Chris Ballentine/
Paul Thompson Images/Alamy
Welsh rugby fans © Jeff Morgan/Alamy
Katherine Jenkins singing National Anthem,
Millennium Stadium, Cardiff © The Photolibrary
Wales/Alamy

Things not to miss
04 National Waterfront Museum, Swansea © Jeff
Morgan/Alamy
06 Portmeirion © Skyscan Photolibrary/Alamy
09 Misty oak woodland, Ceredigion © The
Photolibrary Wales/Alamy
10 Cockle, shellfish and laverbread stall, Swansea
market © The Photolibrary Wales/Alamy
11 Wales v England rugby © David Williams/
Alamy
15 Jumping between the Adam and Eve stones
on the summit of Tryfan © Doug Blane/Alamy
23 Llechwedd Slate Caverns © Michael Booth/
Alamy
29 Street market, Machynlleth © The Photolibrary
Wales/Alamy

Colour insert: Festivals and events
Outdoor stage, Bryn Terfel's Gwyl y Faenol © The
Photolibrary Wales
Eisteddfod © Jeff Morgan/Alamy
Royal Welsh Show, Builth Wells, Powys
© Graham Lawrence/Alamy
The Guardian Hay Festival 2005, Hay-on-Wye
© Jeff Morgan/Alamy
Sesiwn Fawr © The Photolibrary Wales

Bryn Terfel, Gwyl y Faenol © The Photolibrary
Wales
Wakeboarding, Pembrokeshire © The
Photolibrary Wales
Performance artists entertaining visitors to
the annual Abergavenny Food Festival
Monmouthshire © Jeff Morgan/Alamy
Competitor in the annual World Bog Snorkelling
Championships at Llanwrtyd Wells, Powys
© Jeff Morgan/Alamy

Colour insert: The great Welsh outdoors
Mountain bikers at Cwm Carn © Seb Rogers/
Alamy
Cliff, rockface climbing, Carreg y Barrcud © The
Photolibrary Wales
Glyndŵr's Way © The Photolibrary Wales
A kite surfer at Pembrey Sands © Graham
Lawrence/Alamy

Black and whites
p.78 Tintern Abbey, Wye Valley © J. Schwanke/
Alamy
p.209 Manx Shearwater taking off © Ronald Weir/
Albaimages/Alamy
p.226 Foeldrygarn © Royal Commission on the
Ancient and Historical Monuments of Wales
p.324 Owain Glyndŵr statue, City Hall, Cardiff
Civic Centre, Cardiff © The Photolibrary Wales/
Alamy
p.353 Parterre garden at Erddig House, Wrexham
© Eric Crichton/Corbis
p.435 R.S. Thomas © The Photolibrary Wales
p.543 Shirley Bassey © The Photolibrary Wales

SMALL PRINT

Index

Map entries are in colour.

INDEX

Map symbols

maps are listed in the full index using coloured text

▬ ▬ ▬ ▬	Welsh border	ᵼ	Church (regional maps)
— — — ·	Chapter division boundary	ⵣ	Gardens
▬▬▬▬	Motorway	⅍	Viewpoint
═══════	Major road	⊙	Statue
═══════	Minor road	⼑	Wind farm
- - - - - -	Footpath	△	Youth hostel
━━━━━━	Railway	⋏	Campsite
—————	River	◉	Accommodation
— —	Ferry route	⚐	Golf course
————————	Wall	⊞	Hospital
✕	Airport	🏊	Swimming pool
♦	Place of interest	ⓘ	Tourist office
▲	Mountain peak	⊠	Post office
⌒	Cave	@	Internet access
∿∿∿∿∿	Cliff	ℙ	Parking
ⴡ	Marshland	★	Bus stop
∴	Ruins	⊠—⊠	Gate
�🏛	Archeological site	▬	Building
⚱	Waterfall	╬	Church/cathedral
⛾	Lighthouse	⬭	Stadium
♛	Castle	▒	Park
🏛	Stately home	░	Forest
❀	Country park	░	Beach
🏛	Monument	▓	Mud flat
⚱	Museum	⊞	Cemetery
⌂	Abbey